EXIT

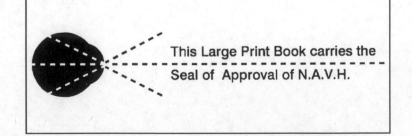
This Large Print Book carries the
Seal of Approval of N.A.V.H.

EXIT

THE ENDINGS THAT SET US FREE

SARA LAWRENCE-LIGHTFOOT

THORNDIKE PRESS
A part of Gale, Cengage Learning

GALE
CENGAGE Learning·

Detroit • New York • San Francisco • New Haven, Conn • Waterville, Maine • London

GALE
CENGAGE Learning·

ALL RIGHTS RESERVED
Thorndike Press® Large Print Nonfiction.
The text of this Large Print edition is unabridged.
Other aspects of the book may vary from the original edition.
Set in 16 pt. Plantin.

LIBRARY OF CONGRESS CATALOGING-IN-PUBLICATION DATA

Lawrence-Lightfoot, Sara, 1944–
 Exit : the endings that set us free / by Sara Lawrence-Lightfoot.
  p. cm.
 Originally published: New York : Sarah Crichton Books, 2012.
 ISBN-13: 978-1-4104-5049-4 (hardcover)
 ISBN-10: 1-4104-5049-X (hardcover)
 1. Farewells. 2. Separation (Psychology) 3. Manners and customs.
 I. Title.
 GT3050.L397 2012b
 394—dc23   2012017042

Published in 2012 by arrangement with Sarah Crichton Books, an imprint of Farrar, Straus and Giroux, LLC.

Printed in the United States of America
1 2 3 4 5 6 7 16 15 14 13 12

CONTENTS

INTRODUCTION: EXITS:
VISIBLE AND INVISIBLE 9

1. Home. 31
2. Voice 91
3. Freedom 154
4. Wounds 202
5. Yearning 263
6. Grace 332

CONCLUSION: RITES AND
RITUALS 380
NOTES. 411
SELECTED SOURCES 421
ACKNOWLEDGMENTS 439

INTRODUCTION:

EXITS: VISIBLE AND INVISIBLE

I have always been fascinated by exits, endings, leave-takings — by the ways in which we say goodbye to one another, to the lives we've led, to the families we've been part of, to the children we've nurtured, to the organizations we've worked for, to the communities where we've belonged, to the identities that have defined us, to the roles that have given us purpose and status. My curiosity includes exits big and small, those goodbyes that are embroidered into the habits of our everyday encounters as well as those that are forever memorable and rock our worlds. Those that go unnoticed and underappreciated and those that are accompanied by elaborate rituals and splendid ceremony. I have been just as intrigued by the ordinary exits that punctuate our days — goodbyes at the door as our children leave for school each morning (I would always stand at the window, secretly watch-

9

ing the backs of my young children to see if they were determined and tall, if their postures tilted forward, if in their exits I could see the strength they would need to take on the world), hugs at the airport as we leave to go on a trip, farewells to our students at the end of the school term — as I am about the leave-takings that become the major markers of our lives: the rupture of a long friendship; the dissolution of a marriage; the death of a parent; the departure of our children for college; the decision to leave a lifelong career; the abrupt firing of a veteran employee; the exits from the "closet," the priesthood, our countries of origin.

I think there must be some relationship between our developing the habit of small goodbyes and our ability to master and mark the larger farewells, a connection between the micro and the macro that somehow makes the latter smoother and more bearable because one has successfully accomplished the former. I certainly believe that the art of attending to, practicing, ritualizing, and developing a language for leave-taking in the most ordinary moments and settings augers well for taking on the more extraordinary exits that life is sure to serve up.

This book explores the large and small stories of exit, the coexistence and layering of the micro-encounters of everyday experience and the long arc of macro-dramas that take shape across our lifetimes and within a larger cultural narrative. I am interested in the ways in which people leave one thing and move on to the next; the ways in which they anticipate, define, and reflect on their departure; the factors and feelings that motivate their leave-taking; the ways in which the exit both opens up and closes paths forward, offers new opportunities and unanticipated casualties, and feels like victory or defeat, or both. I am particularly curious about how people revisit and reconstruct their moments of decision making, the setting in which they make the decision to move on or have the epiphany that something is over and done. What actually happens — in the noise and the silences — that provokes the moment? What are the events that anticipate the climax and precipitate the exit? How is the decision communicated and to whom? What is the tone and texture of the encounter? Is there anger, sadness, relief, or resolution in the aftermath; ambivalence or closure; feelings of loss or liberation? Whom do people turn to for support, reassurance, and validation?

I believe that people's memories of these exit moments are unusually vivid, colorful, and detailed; that their recollections are full of feeling and emotion, imagery, symbolism, and metaphor; and that the specificity, authenticity, and power of these moments speak to their significance in shaping life journeys, in taking new paths, in reconstructing one's sense of self. I also believe that these moments are pregnant with paradox — the counterpoint and convergence of vulnerability and toughness, inertia and movement, urgency and patience, chaos and control. I always imagine these moments in bold relief, standing out in Technicolor, refracted images reconstructed with complexity, subtlety, and nuance.

I am sure that one of the reasons that the topic fascinates me is because I have known such moments, and they stand as signposts of courage and treachery in my life, those moments when I said to myself — after months of deliberation, indecision, and ambivalence — "I'm out of here." The moment when confusion turned to certainty, doubt to clarity, hemming and hawing to tough resolve; when complexity and opaqueness seemed to become transparently simple; when I stopped making lists of the pros and cons, the opportunities and liabilities, and decided instead to take the leap of faith.

I recall the details of such exit moments — what I was wearing, what my breathing felt like, how my stomach cramped, what I said, the tears I shed, whom I rushed to for support, the place I went to calm down — when I pulled my son out of a fancy private school to which he was fiercely loyal but where he was unappreciated and marginalized . . . or when I decided to exit the traditional scholarly track and embark on a research project, imaginative and controversial in its methodology and design, that all my senior colleagues felt might threaten my becoming tenured at the university . . . or when I declared that a long and close friendship was finally over after years of tolerating my friend's chronic inattention, her unwillingness to share the responsibilities and burdens of sustaining our relationship . . . or when I decided to initiate divorce proceedings, after years of quiet suffering, earnest stints in couples therapy, and deepening fractures impossible to heal.

I recall feeling in all these instances that I had somehow failed — in my own eyes and certainly in the sights of others. Even as I recognized the rightness of the decision and the courage required to make it, there was

13

some part of me that felt weak in giving up and moving on, something in me that questioned whether I might have stuck it out longer. I remember, in each case, searching for cultural rituals and social scripts, a set of protocols, ceremonies, or practices that might offer me support and guidance or bring me into community with others who were charting similar exits. And I remember the disappointment of finding myself without a compass or reference group. I am struck, as well, by how these big exit markers — those that are most vivid in my memory — are tinged with sadness, poignancy, a sense of defeat, even though they all, in the end, led to something better and brighter.

I find this idea of exit intriguing and worthy of deep exploration because I think there are few lessons — in our culture, in our schooling, in our socialization — in how to do it well, even gracefully. Our culture seems to applaud the spirit, gumption, and promise of beginnings. We admire the entry, the moment when people launch themselves into something new, plan and execute a new project, take on important work, get married, embark on an adventure. These are likely to be moments of hope, optimism, and expectation as we compose the next chapter for ourselves. We give kudos to someone who is entrepreneurial, who paves a path for himself, who has a plan for what's next and can plot the strategy to move from here to there. By contrast, our exits are often ignored or invisible. They seem to represent the negative spaces of our life narratives. There is little appreciation or applause when we decide (or it is decided for us) that it is time to move on. We often slink away in the night, hoping that no one will notice, that the darkness will make the departure disappear. If the entry recalls a straight and erect posture, a person who is strong and determined, then we imagine a person stooped, weakened, and despairing as he makes his exit.

This cultural regard of exit is particularly troublesome in a society where leave-takings are the norm, where, for example, more than half of the marriages end in divorce,[1] forcing tortured exits, publicly exposed and privately endured; where tens of thousands of immigrants flood into our country each day,[2] exiting the place where their lives and families have been rooted, leaving the continuity and familiarity of their pasts, rupturing their cultural traditions and practices; where demographers predict that our young adults, now in their twenties, will

15

likely have ten careers[3] — not just ten jobs — and it will be crucial that they learn not just the art of beginning anew but also the grit and grace of good exits; where, in these tough economic times,[4] the agony of exits seems to be the dominant narrative, as everyone knows someone in her family or among her close friends who has lost her job or is experiencing the painful assault of forced unemployment; and where the depleted job market forces young college graduates to move back home under their parents' roofs,[5] postponing the exits that were long planned and producing a developmental condition that psychologists have begun to describe — pejoratively — as a "failure to launch." And, of course, there is the inevitable and ultimate exit of death that, from my point of view, begs for more clear-eyed and respectful attention, more beautiful rituals, and more cultural honoring.

Our societal neglect of the rituals and purposes of exits is not only a puzzling contemporary phenomenon; it is also strange when we consider the history of our country — a history that has been primarily defined by leave-takings, departures, and journeys away from home. Except for Native Americans, who were our country's first

16

inhabitants, or enslaved Africans, who were brought here against their will,[6] the history of the United States has been defined by exits. Albert Hirschman, whose book *Exit, Voice, and Loyalty* (1970) remains the classic theoretical text on the subject, underscores its centrality in the American tradition and psyche even as he offers an economic framework and analysis.[7] After citing the seventeenth-century settlers fleeing European life, the American Revolution, and the westward expansion, Hirschman even paints the American idea of success — upward social mobility — as a sort of exit. He claims that the ideology of exit has been dominant and powerful in America:

> With the country having been founded on exit and having thrived on it, the belief in exit as a fundamental and beneficial social mechanism has been unquestioning . . . To most of its citizens — with the important exception of those whose forefathers came as slaves — exit from the country has long been peculiarly unthinkable.[8]

Not only has the American geographic and sociological map been defined by exits — chosen and forced — it is also true that

17

exiting is a central marker and lever in our individual developmental journeys. I learned about the power and poignancy of exits most vividly as I became immersed in the research for my last book,[9] *The Third Chapter.* Witnessing and documenting the new learning of people between the ages of fifty and seventy-five — a time in life when demographers tell us that we are "neither young nor old" — I became keenly aware of the fragility and bravery associated with exits. It is difficult, sometimes excruciating and painful, to leave the places that are familiar, the roles that have shaped our identities and self-images, the work in which we have become skilled, knowledgeable, and authoritative, to do something that — at least initially — feels awkward and uncertain. More than half a century ago, when Erik Erikson, the developmental psychologist, charted the stages of lifelong development,[10] he envisioned each stage as a conflict between progression and regression — an inevitable tension between staying put and moving on, between sticking with the familiar and moving toward the strange. At the center of the contrary weights moving us forward and pulling us back is, of course, the leave-taking, the exit.

In an earlier book of mine,[11] *Respect,* I

also wrote about the ways in which exits — gracefully communicated, negotiated, and ritualized — were interpreted as signs and symbols of deep respect. The trust and rapport of respectful relationships were built on knowing that in the end, someone would not just disappear and walk away, but would find a way of recognizing the importance and visibility of good departures. Likewise, the symmetry and authenticity at the center of respectful encounters require that we navigate the boundaries of restraint and connection, balancing coming together and moving away from one another. One of the protagonists in *Respect* is a hospice worker, psychotherapist, and Episcopal priest who speaks about "attention" — gentle, generous, and undiluted — as the most important dimension of respect. As he sits and talks with dying patients, he waits for them to take the lead and let him know what they need and want; he asks them questions others are too afraid to ask, about things they are dying to talk about. He is openhearted and unafraid, seeing the opportunities for growth and reconciliation in these final moments. He helps the dying person exit with dignity and grace.

Visual reminders of exit surround us each day of our lives, guiding our moves, anticipating our turns, flashing directions to us. We follow the exit arrows to find our way out of the parking garage; we notice the neon signs in the dark movie theater showing us where to go in case of an emergency; the flight attendant points out the exit doors in her instructions to us before we take off. It is one of the first words kindergartners learn as their teachers line them up single file before heading out to recess or as they practice their efficient formations during fire drills. The exits become signifiers of efficiency, safety, orderliness, and protection. Bloodred exit signs, like beacons in the hallway.

We drive along the highway tracing our fingers over the map or listening to the fake voice coming out of our GPS, and we count the exits, moving to the right lane in preparation for the turn that will get us to our destination. Or we travel the familiar highway to work and back and hardly need to attend to the exits that we know by heart; our mind is in automatic pilot mode. The exits — glowing white letters on green metal — mark distance, time, effort, belonging . . . how many exits until we get there, how many until a rest stop, how many until we merge onto a new road, how many until we can breathe more freely. We are pissed off when we miss them. Exits also hold memories. Exit 2, just before the Tappan Zee Bridge, takes you to our second cousin's house, where we used to go for their big July Fourth bash . . . the smell of barbecue, cold beers, dips in the pool, lazy days, and laughter. Exit 13 off the Palisades Parkway is coming back home to the place where I haven't lived for fifty years, where my ninety-seven-year-old mother still waits for me.

We also hear the language and metaphors of exit all around us. Exit visas must be applied for weeks before our departure, giving us legal permission to leave the country. In preparing for a theater performance, a director blocks out scenes with his actors onstage, noting the place where the playwright indicates they should exit, stage left. Accepting the fate of a lousy hand, a poker player "folds," walking away from the table, exiting on his own terms. Television newscasters, quoting police reports, give an account of a lurid crime and describe the survivor's "exit wounds." How did the bullet pass through the body? How did the knife slice through the flesh? What organs were nicked, impaired, destroyed? What arteries gushed blood? The emergency-room doctors must act quickly to close up the hole, sew back the edges, fuse the muscle fibers back together — to regenerate despite the injury. Exit wounds are for survivors; the ones who took the bullet or the knife, barely escaped death, and now feel the pain of living. The pain is a beautiful reminder of their survival, their proof of being alive.

Exits, therefore, are ubiquitous, marking the physical landscapes we inhabit, embedded in our language and metaphors, embroidered into the historical narrative of our country, braided into the sequence and arc of our individual development, shaped by the contemporary scene of our economic crises and global mobility, and laced into the intergenerational tensions and discourses in our families and communities. Perhaps it is the very ordinariness, familiarity, and ubiquity of our experiences of exit that make them invisible to us. And perhaps it is our overvaluing of the launch, the promise of entry, and the hopefulness of beginning, that render our exits ignoble by contrast.

Another interesting twist to the paradoxical ubiquity and invisibility of exits — big and small — is the way in which technology has reshaped our sense of connectedness and community,[12] our very identity; the ways in which our global access to one another through cyberspace channels has changed the pace and texture of our discourses and redrawn the boundaries between our public and private lives, remapped the edges of intimacy, even redefined the very meaning of friendship. In this fast-emerging context of technological advancement, beginnings and endings take on a different pace and meaning, exits are less clearly drawn, and entanglements seem easier to undo but harder to escape. Freshmen experiencing their first year of college text their parents several times a day, seeking and resisting advice on the courses they should enroll in, their dating life, and the pounds they've put on since eating cafeteria food. Moms and dads of summer campers receive daily videos recording their children's swim meets, canoeing trips, and group sings around the campfire at night. Young adults heading for the Peace Corps in Samoa or Namibia stay in close touch with their family and friends back home even as they try to build new relationships with the exotic strangers they are seeking to serve. The boundaries of exit become attenuated and eroded, yet another sign of their invisibility.

■ ■ ■ ■

For two years I sought out and listened to people tell their big and memorable stories of leaving. As we talked together, some were in the midst of composing their exits, anticipating and planning their departures, anxious and excited about moving on. Others had exited long ago and used our dialogues as an opportunity for reflection — revisiting the ancient narratives that had changed the course of their lives, discovering new ways of interpreting and making sense of their journeys. Some interviewees told tales of forced exits; others spoke about designing and executing their planned departures. Still others found it hard to determine whether the impetus for their exits came from within — a decision motivated by them, within their jurisdiction and control — or whether their leave-takings were a response to subtle pressuring from friends and families, covert warnings from bosses, or influenced by the social prescriptions, norms, and rhythms deemed appropriate by our institutional cultures.

In all our conversations I followed the lead of my interviewees as they decided where to begin their stories, chose the central arc of their exit narratives, and rehearsed the major transformational moments of their departures. I listened carefully to the talk and the silences, the text and the subtexts of their narrations. I was attentive to those revelations that surprised them, to those discoveries that disoriented them, to the places where they feared to tread. I pushed for the details of long-buried memories. I stopped my probing when I felt myself crossing the boundaries of resistance and vulnerability. We took breaks, went for walks, and drank lots of water to hydrate us through what one storyteller called "the desert of my despair." For many — in fact, most — these were emotional encounters, filled with weeping and laughter, break-throughs and breakdowns, curiosity and discovery.

There were some who at first found it hard to compose stories focused on "endings," after a lifetime of being taught — as one of my interviewees put it — "that stories have a beginning, a middle, and an end . . . and you begin at the beginning." For a few of my interviewees, I was fortunate enough to observe the public ceremonies and occasions marking their departures, listen to their impassioned and teary farewell speeches, and hear the gush of adulation and applause that honored their leaving and legacies. For others, we combed through personal diaries and journals, tracing the meanderings of their interior dialogues as they relived the maze of decisions and choices that preceded their exits. Some people showed me photographs that spurred detailed reflections of their leave-taking.

Although all the insights from my dozens of interviewees resonate in the themes, analysis, and arc of this book, I have chosen to write the narratives collected here because of their richness and variety, their subtlety and complexity. Like all good ethnographic inquiries, these stories help us see the strange in the familiar, the exotic in the ordinary, the visible in the invisible. Individually and collectively — in their similarities and differences, their harmony and dissonance — these tales offer a counterpoint to our usual exit narratives, challenging our cultural views and presumptions, helping us see the exits in our lives differently, and offering us intriguing metaphors and language for interpreting their meaning. And, like all stories, they allow us to glimpse the universal in the particular.

They tell of a gay man finding home and wholeness after exiting the closet; of a sixteen-year-old boy forced to leave Iran in the midst of the violent civil war; of a young boy who, after years of enduring terrifying bullying in school, finally discovered the exit that would set him free; of a woman who, after twenty-five years of building and nurturing a small nonprofit, decided it was time to leave, only to discover the loss, disorientation, and emptiness that followed; of a Catholic priest who — after prolonged deliberation and painful ambivalence — leaves the church he has always been devoted to, the life he has loved, and the work that has been deeply fulfilling; of a psychotherapist who helps her patients shed the painful haunts of ancient traumas and exit the abusive relationships that have left deep scars, at the same time as she prepares them for their successful "termination" from therapy; of an anthropologist who carefully stages her departure from the "field" after four years of research and understands, for the first time, the respect, trust, and truth telling that are critical to exiting well; of a woman who fulfilled her promise to her dying husband that his final months would be filled with abundant and luminous living.

In these stories, exit is not only the central subject and focus, the phenomenon under study and scrutiny; it also becomes the light, the lens, that allows us to understand other things — like home, like a parent's love, like the price of freedom, like the meaning of grace, like the living in dying — more deeply. The structure of this book, in fact, follows the light, illuminating those dimensions of our life stories that we are able to see — newly and differently — through the lens of exit.

Ultimately, it is my hope that the wisdom, insights, and perspectives found in this book will help create a new conversation, a bold counter-narrative illuminating the power and possibilities of exits. They will help us discover how we might accomplish our exit journeys with purposefulness and dignity, how we might see the movement away from the old as the productive prelude to entering the new, even when it may feel like failure or retreat. How might we find ways of reframing our exits, giving them the attention and significance they are due? Are there steps to take, routines to be practiced, discerning questions to be posed to make our departures more bearable, revelatory, and generative? Are there rituals we might invent to light a clearer path toward the exit? Are there institutional arrangements and norms, ceremonial events, a new language and way of seeing that would encourage a different approach and attitude toward leave-takings?

This book, then, examines the cultural, developmental, relational, and organizational dimensions of these exit moments in all their emotional, intellectual, and spiritual manifestations, in all their colorful and textured detail — seeking to capture their importance in the productive propulsion of next chapters and new journeys; hoping to discover the lessons they hold for guiding and helping folks to muster the energy, master the steps, and weather the chaos of their departures; and searching for ways to challenge and reframe our cultural expectations and priorities that have for too long exalted the hope of beginnings and diminished the power and value of exits.

ONE:
HOME

When most of us think about *home,* we
picture a physical place: the house where
we grew up, the address we learned by heart
in case we got lost, the room we painted
hot pink when we turned eight and our
parents allowed us to choose the color, the
crack in the third flagstone step leading to
the front door, the way no one used the
front door anyway, since everyone came in
through the back door right off the kitchen.
Or our vision of home might be of the house
where we now live with our children, where
we make the mortgage payments each
month and pay the electricity and oil bills,
where we have set up a basketball hoop in
the driveway for the kids to practice for the
big games on Friday night up at the school,
where we have barbeques for the neighbors
on hot summer evenings, where the traffic
and chaos of kids and dogs and busy schedules and homework are both comforting

and exhausting. Our vision of home, whether it is the home of our childhood or the home we are creating as adults, has a location, an address, a mark on the map. It is a physical, tangible place. We have photo albums that chronicle our growing family over the years, everyone lined up on the front steps in the same pyramid arrangement — parents on top, kids on the bottom — with smiles that stay the same even as the bodies get bigger and bulkier.

Home is also the place where life is most familiar, where we fall into old patterns, where our roles become scripted and predictable, where there is a fine line between the bonds that bind and constrain. It is also a place where we live by secret codes and allusions that outsiders — even intimate outsiders — don't understand or appreciate. In her beautiful essay "On Going Home" (1961), Joan Didion speaks about the power and pull of home.

I am home for my daughter's first birthday. By "home" I do not mean the house in Los Angeles where my husband and I and the baby live, but the place where my family is, in the Central Valley of California. It is a vital though troublesome distinction. My husband likes my family but is uneasy in their house, because once there I fall into their ways which are difficult, oblique, deliberately inarticulate, not my husband's ways. We live in dusty houses ("D-U-S-T," he once wrote with his finger on the surfaces all over the house, but no one noticed it) filled with mementos quite without value to him (what could the Canton dessert plates mean to him? How could he have known about the assay scales, why should he care if he did know?) . . .[1]

Home, here, is defined as much by those who are outsiders — who have no real clue of what is going on, where signals seem opaque and oblique — as by those who have the inside track, who know the secrets and shadows, the habits and artifacts, the history of the family that lives in this house. Home is made more vivid by the contrasts that get drawn between the outsider's discomfort and cluelessness and the insider's ancient and intuitive understandings.

In his biography of the poet Wallace Stevens (1968), Robert Pack echoes Didion's portrayal of going home, drawing the connection between the intimacy and belonging that home represents and the intimacy with his readers that Stevens achieves through his poetry. Stevens translates the language, rhythm, and cadence from his childhood home into his verse, capturing the themes of family and the feelings of familiarity with which we can all identify. Writes Pack:

Home is the place where one understands the routine, knows the secret rhythms of family activity and communication, and feels the fullness of the presence of the familiar objects. It is this sense of intimacy that Stevens seeks with the world, and it is this sense of order a poet achieves that makes this intimacy possible.[2]

Here we get a sense of home as the place where we learn to interpret the noises and the silences, the texts and the subtexts of our lives, where the layers and subtleties of our communication are inscribed in our hearts and minds, our bones and bodies, eventually turning up — at least in Stevens's and Didion's case — in the form and texture of their art.

The novelist Paule Marshall takes us a step further into the auditory dimensions and cadences of home. In her autobiographical novel, *Brown Girl, Brownstones,* she offers an evocative and searing portrait of an immigrant family transplanted from Barbados to Brooklyn, and she speaks about home as the sound of the language of the Bajan women as they sit talking in the kitchen.[3] It is a language that Marshall herself heard as a child as she sat on the edges of the women's circle soaking up the gossip, the stories, savoring the rhythms and poetry of their words. In "From the Poets in the Kitchen," a short essay published in *The New York Times,* Marshall speaks about the language of home — particularly the talk among the women in the kitchen — that carried with it beauty, wisdom, poetry, and culture, that survived the transplantation from the blue-green sea and open horizons of Barbados to the city streets and brownstones of Brooklyn.

I grew up among poets — whatever that breed is supposed to look like. Nothing about them suggested that poetry was their calling. They were just a group of ordinary housewives and mothers, my mother included, who dressed in a way (shapeless housedresses, dowdy felt hats, dark, solemn coats) that made it impossible for me to imagine they had ever been young.[4]

So whether we envision home as a place, a physical location on the map that we can now google for directions; whether we feel it in the familiarity, obliqueness, and intimacy of family; or whether we hear it in the language and poetry of our mothers, home is the place we return to. It is the place that forms us, that embraces and inhibits us, that shapes our identity. It is a place where our arrival is awaited.

The tales of exit found in this chapter reframe and transfigure the meaning of home. The two stories — of a teenage Iranian boy escaping the political strife and violence in his war-torn country to come to America, and of a middle-aged gay man reflecting on his long and brave exit from the closet — shape a view of home that is earned and discovered after the protagonists have traveled far away, literally and figuratively, from their family's place of origin, far away from the cultures and communities that nourished and raised them. The lens of exit in both narratives points to the emotional and spiritual construction of home as a hardwon place of comfort, safety, belonging, and love. Finding home requires leaving and searching, trials and tribulations, and many exits along the way.

HUNGRY FOR HOME

"I'll go."

It did not hit him that he was actually leaving — his family, his country, his life — until he arrived at the airport in Tehran, surrounded by his parents and siblings and a huge crowd of aunts and uncles, some of whom had traveled hundreds of miles to say goodbye. He was carrying one small cardboard suitcase, and his mother had sewn a zippered pouch into his underwear to hide the $3,000 he was taking with him. His father had had to sell a plot of land, use all of the family's savings, and borrow from his uncles in order to come up with the money that Bijan Jalili needed to travel to the United States.

Suddenly the fear swept over him, and he froze. How could he have said — in a moment of weakness — that he would go to school in America? How could he have committed to something that now seemed so scary and wrong? How could he leave all those he loved and the life he knew? This was unbearable. "Just then it hit me . . .

What have I done! But it was too late to back out," says Bijan, his whole body shivering as he must have done on that fateful day. "I couldn't stomach it . . . my belly was burning. I was scared out of my gourd . . . I was like a child afraid of the dark . . . I felt like I was lost in the jungle, being swallowed up by dangerous creatures."

Bijan looked over at his father, whose head was bowed in prayer, his face washed in tears, a picture of agony and faith. His mother couldn't stop crying — huge, sobbing wails that echoed through the airport lounge — as she clung to him for dear life. Finally his plane was announced and the waiting was over. Bijan hugged everyone hard and kissed them each on both cheeks before beginning the long march down the ramp to the plane. "Leaving my parents behind was unbearable. My feet were like Jell-O. I could hardly move them. I thought that I would just collapse." Bijan had never even seen an airport before, never been on a plane. He stowed his suitcase and climbed into the window seat. "The fear was overwhelming as I looked down after takeoff and saw Tehran disappear behind me." I look across the table and see the sixteen-year-old scared boy. It is thirty years later, and Bijan's face is contorted in a grimace. He looks down to wipe away the tears with the back of his hand.

The plane touched down at Kennedy Airport at 8:00 p.m. As he heard the screech of the landing gear, Bijan's fear took over his body and he started to shake. He looked out the window and saw the city stretched out below, "an ocean of light." "I was new to electricity," says Bijan as he remembers the strange sensation of seeing a whole city of twinkling lights that seemed to form the shape of "a fiery dragon." His only thought was that he wanted desperately for the plane to turn around so he could go home. "I wanted to go back to my mom, to bury my head in her bosom . . . to have her hold me again."

Once he was off of the plane, the scene was shocking. "I thought to myself, Everything in New York looks so big! I had never seen people over six feet tall . . . and there were all kinds of people, all sizes, shapes, and colors. They hardly looked human to me." Not only did the people look strange, but New York did not look like the America Bijan had seen on television back in Iran. It was not pretty or spacious or orderly; it was a confusing blur of smells and sensations. "It was as if I had landed on a different planet," Bijan says as he admits to being at a "loss to find the adjectives to describe how foreign the place felt." Even the air seemed unbreathable as he made his way from the international to the domestic terminal where he would board a plane to Washington, D.C. And the water, when he stopped on the way to get a drink at the fountain, tasted terrible, "undrinkable," so different from the fresh well water he was used to having at home.

Bijan Jalili, a handsome and lean light-brown-skinned man, is now the CEO of Purple Rain, a technology company that makes digitally based software for large firms all over the world. The engineers and designers for the company are based in Tehran; Bijan and the design and marketing team have offices in the United States. But the virtual world is really where they all spend most of their time. Storytelling is Bijan's medium, imprinted in his family and his culture, embedded in his passionate personality. He spins his yarns with drama and subtlety, picturing the scene, capturing the sights and sounds, relishing the details, enjoying the rhythm of the words, and loving the surprising punch line. His vivid descriptions help me imagine remote parts of Iran, places I've never even seen in photographs.

He begins with the geography of his childhood. "I grew up in Razan, a small town in the mountainous region in northwest Iran. You don't have that type of smallness in the U.S. . . . There were fewer than a thousand people, and there was no electricity, no running water (we used manual pumps), no utilities. My mother cooked on a small stove top that used kerosene, like the ones you take camping . . . We took a shower in the local bathhouse once a week." Bijan, the second to the oldest, had two brothers and one sister, and they had the special privilege of going to the bathhouse once a week because his father enjoyed a large measure of local status. He was the "equivalent of the school superintendent" for Razan and several of the surrounding tiny villages.

By the time Bijan was seven, the family moved briefly to the ancient city of Hamadān, the site of the old Persian capital, founded twenty-five hundred years ago. When they found that they could not afford to live there on his father's modest salary, they moved again, this time to Shavarin, and they lived in the house where his father had grown up. By the time Bijan was eleven, his father had saved up enough money to move back to Hamadān, where he took out a bank loan and they were able to build a house. "Now we had electricity," says Bijan with excitement. "Gas and oil were hand delivered to the house . . . there was a well for drinking water and an outhouse that was unbearably cold in the winter." Hamadān was located in the shadow of a very high mountain, and the winters were fierce. For several freezing months each year, the town was literally buried in snow. Bijan remembers the snow tunnels he used to walk through in order to get to school, when the drifts would pile higher than the roofs of the houses. And he recalls the *koursi* heater — something resembling a hibachi, fueled by coal — that would be put under the table and then covered with blankets. All winter long, while the rest of the house stayed freezing, everyone would huddle together under the blankets with their feet close to the stove.

"It was a fanatical religious environment," says Bijan about his family's deep and unquestioned devotion to Islam. The Muslim rituals and restrictions were embroidered into their days. Five times a day they knelt and turned toward Mecca to pray; there was no alcohol and no hanging around with "the opposite sex." The family fasted for the entire month of Ramadan, and Bijan's father and brothers went to the

42

mosque for religious gatherings "all the time." By the time he was fourteen or fifteen, Bijan and his older brother, Sohrab, had begun to mix religion with radical politics, joining the political revolution that was beginning to catch fire all over Iran. "We were teenagers, and there was not much to do in our town . . . the revolution captured our hearts and our minds. We were great recruits, revolutionary religious kids, young and impassioned and devout," he recalls.

The brothers joined the Mojahedin, a political party, working underground in support of Khomeini, where they became part of the stealth "distribution channel," delivering newsletters and tapes undercover and hiding them in secret places in the brick walls that snaked their way through the town. Before they would go off to school in the morning, Bijan and Sohrab served as the party's "runners," picking up and distributing political propaganda. In the evenings they would join the noisy street demonstrations, chanting and cheering radical rants, then gathering to listen to the fiery, provocative speeches from their party leaders. Their father never wanted his sons to attend the political rallies and demonstrations. He did not agree with their "radical ideologies," and every moment that they were gone, he feared for their lives. "He did not want us to get killed," says Bijan simply.

One night when a prominent and important radical clergyman was coming to speak at the mosque, Bijan's father knew that there was likely to be violence, and he forbade his sons from going. Not heeding their father's threats, Bijan and Sohrab slipped out of the house under cover of night, climbed over the stone walls of the courtyard, and went to the mosque, where a crowd of more than a thousand men — no women — had gathered. As the clergyman delivered his fierce oratory, the guards and police surrounded the mosque, ready to arrest him as soon as it was over, but as he spoke his last words, all the lights went out. In the darkness and chaos that followed, the clergyman escaped and the police opened fire. In the mayhem, bullets were blasting, men were screaming and running; some lay bloodied on the ground.

Bijan managed to dodge the bullets, but he got separated from his brother. "I thought they had got him," says Bijan, trembling. When he arrived home, his clothes torn and spattered with blood, Bijan found his father standing in the courtyard. "He was white as a ghost . . . completely frightened . . . he held his Koran in his hands." Bijan stood silently with his father, hearing the gunshots and screaming in the distance, terrified that his brother would never come home. It was hours before Sohrab appeared, worn, weary, and very scared, but not wounded. No one said a word; their father could not find the energy to punish them. "Having his sons at home was good enough for him," recalls Bijan about the strange, haunting silence that filled the house for several days after. It was on that night, Bijan believes, that his father promised himself that his sons would have to leave the country. There was no way to protect them from the danger and the violence, and no way to blunt their revolutionary fervor.

And then the unthinkable happened. A few months later, Bijan's younger brother, Pedram, was taken from them in a horrible accident in the backyard. Before he can begin the story of his brother's death, Bijan is already weeping.

"Electricity was a new thing in the town, and so there was no regulation, no codes or standards. Our home had electricity, but it was all made up of dangerous, makeshift wiring. It was a steamy day in the summer . . . In the yard of our house we had a wading pool, and my little brother Pedram — he was fourteen years old at the time — decided to cool himself off in the water. The little pool was right next to an electrical pole with a short. As he came out of the pool, he touched the pole . . . and he was fried . . . That afternoon I was at home studying for my exams, and all of a sudden I heard Pedram screaming my father's name. At first I thought he was screaming because my father was punishing him for something. Then I heard my mother's wails . . . so I went outside and saw my father kneeling down with Pedram's head on his lap . . . He was gone."

Soon after the terrible tragedy Bijan's father asked his two older sons to leave the country. "He was afraid of losing another son. He just couldn't stomach it," says Bijan about his father's anguish that his older sons would be taken too, swept away by the revolution. No amount of pleading could convince Sohrab to leave. "He was too deep in the revolution . . . so devoted, committed, passionate. He refused to go," says Bijan. But in the next moment, when his father turned to him, Bijan surprised himself by saying, without so much as a moment of thought, "I'll go." And it was done.

Within a few weeks the papers, documents, passport, and tickets had been arranged, and Bijan had been admitted to a prep school in Washington, D.C., that had to agree to sponsor him before the Iranian government would give him a visa. It was August 1978, and political demonstrations were happening everywhere; violence was erupting in the street and "the shah's regime was falling apart." Fortunately, Bijan's uncle, an official high up in the shah's party, was able to pull strings at the American embassy so that he was able to secure all the documents he needed to travel. "Irony of all ironies" — Bijan smiles — "there I was, having been a young radical with the Mojahedin, the revolutionary party . . . riding with my uncle in the shah's police car through the gates of the American embassy to get permission to leave the country."

When I ask Bijan why he said yes to his father, he looks at me, puzzled, as if he has never bothered — or dared — to ask himself that question. "I had a love affair with English . . . and the English we learned in school was all about grammar, basic and primitive," he says at first. "And I liked the American shows I watched on our neighbor's tiny black-and-white TV . . . *Ironside, Streets of San Francisco, Charlie's Angels . . .*

alluring images of America." But Bijan chuckles at the incompleteness of his reasoning, at the way he gave such a huge decision so little thought as a teenager, and at the way, as a mature adult, he seems to have protected himself from having to relive that moment. "Maybe it was my childishness or my stupidity," he concludes, his voice drifting off.

But there is one thing of which he was, and is, certain. As soon as he said that he would go, he began having doubts, fears, and nightmares — all of which he kept to himself as he got swept up in the planning and preparations; as he saw his father selling his land, going to the bank, and counting the dollars Bijan would need to make the journey. And just the announcement of his trip to America changed the way he was treated by everyone in the town. He became Hamadān's newest hero. "As soon as I said I'd go, I became a celebrity. I went from being a child to being a man in their eyes . . . I felt foreign to myself."

It turned out that the prep school in Washington, D.C. — advertised as an elite academy for international students — was a "scam," "a moneymaking machine, where in exchange for getting visas for foreign kids, the American embassy would take kickbacks." The whole school was in a run-down office building, and all the students were rich Iranian and Arab trust fund kids. "There was probably something comforting about finding other Iranian students at the school, but they were rich and I was poor, so there was a large distance between us. They were spending big wads of cash on luxury stuff. Whenever I wanted to buy something, I needed to excuse myself to go to the bathroom so I could unzip the money from my underwear." He shared a shabby dormitory room with another Iranian student, and in order to save money, he ate only breakfast and dinner — no lunch — in the school cafeteria.

By the time Bijan had been there "three months and twelve days" and paid for his dormitory room and fall tuition, his $3,000 was gone. He knew he could not ask his father for any more money, but every few weeks he would call and beg to come home. The phone calls were expensive (three minutes for ten dollars), so Bijan would wait until he could no longer bear not hearing his father's voice, and he would have to put an entire roll of quarters into the pay phone. "I would try to explain to him my condition . . . I feel sick, depressed, and miserable . . . I'm horribly thin and weak . . .

everything tastes terrible and smells awful." And although he never told his father, Bijan truly thought that he might even die from loneliness and heartbreak. He could hear the sadness in his father's voice on the other end of the phone; he just could not stand to hear his son suffer. But his father tried hard to be reassuring, comforting him and then staving off his requests by offering him a "deal." If Bijan would stay just three more months and successfully complete the English courses, he would let him come home. At least then he would return to Iran fluent in the language he loved. Never did Bijan have the heart to break it to his father, the top educator in his town, that the school he was attending was just a "moneymaking scam," that even the English training was substandard, that the teachers were not well trained, that grades could be bought.

By the time three months had rolled around, the Iranian revolution was in full swing. Khomeini was in power, the war had broken out with Iraq, the airports were closed, and it was impossible for Bijan to go home. He had run out of all his money and couldn't pay the room and board at school. He managed to rent a small apartment with three of his fellow students in a run-down neighborhood close to the school, and he

50

found a job as a dishwasher in a restaurant, where he worked for $2.75 an hour and was paid under the table because his student visa did not permit him to work. "The apartment was three hundred dollars a month, but there were four of us, so my share was seventy-five. I ate one meal at the restaurant, which had to last me the whole day," he says, remembering every detail of every dollar earned and spent.

After six months, having successfully completed the courses he had promised to his father, Bijan once again begged to return home. But by that time the war with Iraq had escalated, the borders were closed, and military service was mandatory for all young men. This time his father didn't even try to be reassuring. He had no more deals up his sleeve. He told his son, "You will be drafted and sent off to war as soon as you touch down at the airport. You come back, and you will die, for sure . . . I'd rather have you be sick over there than dead over here." Bijan knew his father was right. Even though he was still lonely and miserable and longed to be in the embrace of his family, he couldn't go back. At that moment it hit him that he was in the United States for good, and something in him shifted. Rather than focusing his fantasies on escape from a life that felt unbearable, and rather than hoping his father would somehow save him from it all, Bijan decided to take hold of himself, stay in school, and get a good education. He would somehow find a way to make it on his own.

He spent the next few years finishing school and doing any job — however unsavory or menial — to earn his keep. He throws back his head and laughs. "I've done everything but prostitution and pushing drugs . . . hard labor, working for a moving company, a gas station, a cleaning service, painting houses, dipping ice cream." By the time he was admitted to American University as an engineering student, he was working at a gas station from 7:00 p.m. to 7:00 a.m. and going to his first class of the day at 8:00. He was eating sandwiches of Wonder Bread — which he bought in bulk — smeared with ketchup and mustard, which he took from the condiments counter at Burger King. And he was sharing one small room with two other Iranian guys who were not in school, so they slept in shifts in the one bed that they had on the floor. He shakes his head at how hard his life was then, but he was filled with a fierce determination that seemed to make it all possible.

Despite being chronically tired and hungry

during his three years at the university, Bijan made straight A's and graduated with honors. He even made a little money on the side, tutoring other undergraduate students. "But all the time, I'm wanting to go back," he says about the deep yearning to return to Iran that never abated. Sometimes he would call his father to beg anyway; there was some comfort in just hearing his voice, and the exchange between them had by now become a well-rehearsed script. "I knew he would just keep playing with my brain . . . making the old deals which we both knew would never happen."

After college, Bijan got "a big break" when he landed an engineering/technology position at Dell Labs, where he stayed for a year and a half, until they learned that his visa had expired and they fired him. Now he had a visa problem and had to worry about getting deported. Just as he was leaving Dell, the "hostage crisis hit" in Iran, and "overnight, we were the enemy." Bijan remembers the huge painted sign hanging at the entrance to American University — ALL IRANIANS GO HOME — and how his good friends from college suddenly deserted him. He remembers the jeers and racial slurs people hurled at him as he got on the bus or walked by them on the street. For their protection, Iranians closed ranks, hung together, watched each other's backs, and tried to live under the radar.

After several months of looking for work in Washington, Bijan reunited with an old childhood friend he knew from Hamadān, who was now living in Philadelphia. They schemed together, made a business plan, used up all their savings, sold their cars, and opened a restaurant in West Philadelphia. The ingredients for success seemed promising. The food was yummy — they cooked exotic and savory recipes from home — the decor was funky and welcoming, and they worked all the time serving breakfast, lunch, and dinner. They hoped to attract the college crowd and ethnic food lovers from Drexel and the University of Pennsylvania, which were within walking distance. But the restaurant was off the beaten path, so they were never able to attract the necessary foot traffic to make it work and pay the bills. A year after opening, they had to close it down, but the disappointing entrepreneurial venture turned out to have a silver lining. Bijan got $7,000 back on his tax returns that year, and he decided to use it to bring everyone together for a family reunion in Turkey.

It took months of planning and scheming

to make it happen, but in the end everybody came. It was the peak of the war in Iran, and their journeys across the borders were taxing and treacherous. Bijan's parents flew from Tehran to Istanbul; his brother and sister and their spouses and children took the long bus ride. There were eleven of them, all "happily stuffed" into a studio apartment Bijan had rented. It was the first time he had seen his family in more than ten years, and he was beside himself with joy. His face lights up as he remembers the scene. "It was an amazing reunion . . . wonderful, passionate, a one-of-a-kind experience. I had such a hunger for them. I coveted every minute of being with them. There was so much to talk about . . . I wanted it to last forever. They listened to all of my stories, and they were overwhelmingly proud of me . . . for surviving, for sticking it out, for doing so well." He laughs. "Of course, they had no idea that I was going home to nothing. I had paid for everyone's trip, and they didn't have a clue that I was completely broke."

There was something about the reunion in Turkey, the loving embrace of the family, the endless conversations, their adoration of him, how safe and secure he felt in their midst that allowed Bijan to finally exit Iran.

Nourished by his family's soulful companionship, lifted up by their laughter, he knew then that he would never, ever leave them. He might build a life very far away, he might have friends they would never meet and experiences they could barely imagine, but he knew they would always be inextricably, forever joined.

And as it has turned out, after all those years of painful struggle, decades of dissonance and dislocation, periods of unemployment, and the distaste of absorbing and resisting ethnic slurs and racial profiling, Bijan is now living a life of abundance, doing work that is creative and satisfying, raising two children who are smart and sweet, and running a business that has feet in both his homes, Iran and America. He recognizes the bitterness and cynicism that still rise up in him; he can still sometimes "taste the deprivation" and loneliness of having had to leave his family too early. But all that is mixed with the sweet pleasures and many good memories of his life, an imperfect and exotic brew he has grown to appreciate.

I ask Bijan what in his character or temperament might have contributed to his resilience, his courage and stamina after leaving Iran, and his determination to stay the course. He immediately says, "Loyalty . . . loyalty to my dad. I couldn't dishonor him, and I trusted him to guide me and be there with me even if we were thousands of miles away, living on different planets." He pauses and says quietly, "I knew how much education was valued by my father. And I knew how he suffered after my brother's death . . . My father and mother would never laugh again after we lost him, and I wanted to somehow make up for that loss and live a life of meaning and commitment."

Bijan now brings this same deep loyalty and devotion to his own family, his wife and his two children, and their close friends. He always wants to be there for them. He knows, however, that he would never ask his son — now a teenager — to leave his family and his country behind, to go and make his way in a strange, foreign place. His final question floats in the air as we both fall silent. "Were my parents stupid or naïve . . . or did they know something about me that I didn't know about myself?"

We hear the myriad meanings of home echoing through Bijan's story. Home as place — the twenty-five-hundred-year-old city, Hamadān, at the base of the towering mountain, where his family huddled together under blankets in the freezing winters, warmed by the tiny coal heater; where Bijan and his brother became young radicals, hiding secret political messages in the ancient brick walls that wound through the city; where the snow got so deep that children carved tunnels underneath to walk to school; where Bijan's little brother came out of the wading pool, touched the electric pole, and "fried" to death.

Home is also the place where we are in touch with the familiar, oblique rhythms of our family; where our communication with one another is often gestural; where words unspoken can carry enormous meaning. As Joan Didion reminds us, home is in the "troublesome" and "oblique" nuances of family intimacies.[5] After telling his sons that they are forbidden to go to the mosque to hear the radical cleric, Bijan's father waits alone in the courtyard, his face creased with fear, the Koran in the tight grip of his hands, praying for his sons' safe return. The gunshots from the mosque ring out in the night air; he can hear the screams of desperate men trying to escape the bloodshed and the mayhem. Bijan comes home first, bloodied but safe, and waits with his father. He knows not to say anything; he knows his father is more frightened than angry. He knows that his father has already made a deal with Allah that he will do anything — including not punish his sons — if he brings them home safely. When hours later Bijan's big brother climbs over the wall, they all go silently to bed. No reprimands, no punishments, no apologies. This is the familiar way they deal with danger and fear and terror in this family; this is the silence and sound of home.

These familiar rhythms and resonances from home stretch across the globe — from Washington, D.C., to Tehran — and across the years, as Bijan pleads with his father over the phone, begging to come back to Iran. He is desperate and miserable, sick, hungry, and lonely. Over and over, father and son cut a deal that they both know will never see the light of day. Over and over, they play the "brain game," knowing the dueling exchanges by heart, shielding each other from the truth. As they rehearse the familiar script, Bijan listens for what Paule Marshall calls the "language and poetry" of home.[6]

The deals and exits last for years and years until Bijan — flush with a new resolve and the surprise bounty from his tax returns — decides to stage his own "homecoming." His parents, sister and brother, their spouses and children — eleven of them in all — crowd into a tiny studio apartment in Turkey, a place that none of them call home. For seven delicious days they experience the thrill and familiarity of one another's company, an orgy of eating, drinking, and most of all talking and telling stories. As Bijan says his farewells and his precious family returns to the country where he was born and raised, the place to which he has been dying to return, the idea of home and belonging are transfigured. He has an epiphany. Home is where the love is, a place that is impossible to leave.

In many ways, Bijan's exit — from the parental home — seems archetypal. It reminds us of the stories played out in fairy tales, myths, legends, and memoirs. The son leaves in due course to start his own family, or he runs away, or he is cast out. All three leave-takings are emotionally searing; all three have their share of turmoil. Even if the exit in the first scenario is anticipated and planned, even if it fits with what is deemed developmentally and culturally appropriate, it may still be a departure filled with ambivalence, conflict, relief, and liberation. But the drama seems heightened in the exits that deviate from the conventional mold. Those who run away from the parental home and those who are kicked out are exiting an untenable situation. Running away may be a desperate act, but it is an act of will. It is an exit of one's own choosing. Being kicked out is a forced exit, a circumstance that wasn't chosen, but one that must be endured and survived, where the connections to home are harder to repair or brutally severed forever.

Bijan's departure weaves together all three archetypal narratives. He chooses to leave; he surprises himself by saying, "I'll go." But the choice comes on the heels of his older brother's staunch refusal and his younger brother's tragic death. As soon as the words escape his mouth, it does not feel like free choice. It is a choice made out of loyalty, the son protecting his parents from additional, unbearable grief. As soon as he arrives in New York, he wants to run back to his mother's waiting arms and feel the softness and warmth of her bosom. But his leave-taking is also a story of running away — from the seductions of radical politics, from the war, the violence, the bloodshed — and a story of being cast out by a father who does it out of love, not punishment or anger. The father's insistence that he go and stay away are indicative of the tremendous protection and life-giving care he feels for Bijan. Exiting home is a family love story.

DANCING ALL THE WAY HOME

**"It always begins with
a declaration to yourself."**

This next exit narrative — of homecoming — does not have the geographic sweep of Bijan's story; it is not about traveling many time zones away from a parental home or about the clashes in language, politics, and culture that mark the separation between a son and his family of origin. Rather it is a story played out on a smaller scale, where the movements and exits reflect an interior journey, where the borders and barriers are partly defined by public presumptions and societal prejudices, but also by the deeply embedded definitions of manhood and morality that were shaped by growing up in a working-class Irish Catholic family and neighborhood. Andrew Connolly, a fifty-eight-year-old gay man, tells the brave and hopeful story of coming home to himself after a long series of exits from the "closet."

It is impossible for him to talk about exiting from the "closet" without returning to his roots — the home where he was raised;

the neighborhood where he played and made friends; the school where he learned, competed, and secured his place in the pecking order; the church he attended; the gods he worshipped. Andrew Connolly begins at the beginning with these pieces of his background. "I grew up in a very Catholic, working-class, ethnically identified Irish family," he says plainly. Andrew's father was a firefighter, his mother a stay-at-home mom until her three children, all sons, finished high school, when she went back to school and became an elementary school teacher. They lived modestly on his father's income in a triple-decker house that they saved for and eventually owned in a neighborhood in Worcester, Massachusetts. Family life — which Andrew remembers as "nurturing and loving" — largely centered on the church. Andrew was a devoted altar boy, donning vestments and participating in services every Sunday morning and a few times a week. Their parish priests and the professors from the nearby College of Holy Cross were frequently honored guests at their dinner table, and Andrew's maternal uncle — a family favorite — was a Jesuit priest, a highly educated, well-traveled, worldly man who was seen as a worthy role model for his three nephews.

Although the family was solidly working class in terms of income, Andrew remembers home as a "pretty middle-class intellectual environment," with "ideas and politics thrown around at the dinner table," a huge emphasis on education, and the visiting professors offering them a larger vision of the world. As a matter of fact, all three Connolly sons grew up to be highly educated achievers who earned advanced degrees and enjoyed successful careers. The oldest is a physician, the youngest a clinical psychologist, and Andrew — in the middle — is an educator and university professor.

Andrew smiles at the way in which his parents divided up the world. "They were fighting the Reformation," he says. "It was the Protestants versus the Catholics . . . the Democrats versus the Republicans." As a matter of fact, all these things were seamlessly combined into a collective identity. "My parents were Roosevelt, liberal Democrats . . . Irish/Catholic/Democrats . . . It was all one word, melded together." It wasn't until Andrew went to college, when he discovered that there was a tiny but vocal Republican Club actively trying to recruit student members, that he even knew there was such a thing as a "Republican Catholic." The "us against them mentality" extended beyond politics and religion to class divisions. Andrew recalls, "My dad was a labor leader. He always saw the struggle between the workingman and the *man.* I never heard racist remarks, because blacks were considered allies, part of the working class . . . on our side.

"The assumption going in was that I would be a priest," says Andrew about the way in which early on he was identified as the one who would honor his family in that way. In most of the families he knew, parents hoped and prayed that at least one of their boys would become a priest. I ask Andrew why he was the one "chosen" in his family, and the question seems to surprise him a bit, as if his "being the one" felt so natural and inevitable to everyone. "Well," he says tentatively, "I was deeply religious . . . I liked church, the liturgy, and all the rituals, and I probably wasn't chasing after girls the way my brothers were." He smiles. "I must have lacked the same kind of enthusiasm for the opposite sex that my brothers exhibited," he says with understatement.

Andrew's relative "lack of enthusiasm for girls" reaches back to early adolescence, a time when he seemed to be sitting on top of the world. "I was athletic, popular. I loved sports and fishing . . . I liked to do boy things." He contrasts his popularity and his devotion to sports with the characteristics of many gay boys who grow up feeling "alienated from the guys," who are so often marginalized or even bullied by the straight boys who won't let them join the masculine cliques. "You know," says Andrew, underscoring his very different experience, "the story of the last kid chosen for the team . . . I was the one choosing the team. I was the exemplar . . . I very much belonged." The feeling of being one of the boys "with muscles" — one of the very masculine boys — seems to be an important theme in Andrew's exit narrative. In eventually declaring himself gay, he was not leaving a community in which he had been diminished or excluded; he was not responding to being an outcast, derided for being effeminate, a "fag." He was leaving a group of his peers where he was admired and included, where he was considered strong and powerful, a leader. And he was finding his way into a community where he wanted to connect with gays, like him, who had muscles and were winners, whose experience had not been overwhelmed by the feeling of being "other" or "less." Andrew's adolescent experience of being a popular, admired leader in the straight boys' world seems to have provided him with a level of self-confidence that made his exit out of the closet less fraught, less painful. "You see, I was feeling good about myself, comfortable in my skin . . . exiting from a place of strength." he says.

Andrew was thirteen years old when he had his first sexual encounter with a boy who was one of his best friends. At the time — and all through high school — he was openly and "pleasantly" dating girls, but this encounter with his good friend seemed "special and sweet." Andrew chuckles at the memory. "I enjoyed it. There was nothing negative about it . . . except that it was sinful." It only happened once, and neither of them ever spoke about it after that. After high school Andrew decided to attend college at Holy Cross, where he entered as a day student because his family did not have the money to pay for room and board. He continued to date girls, but he remembers "a growing attraction for men at an emotional and physical level."

Again Andrew recalls one encounter with a straight guy, during his freshman year, where he "acted on his attraction a bit." But it was more of a flirtation, not the real thing; nothing was acknowledged by either of

them. This was 1968, a time when no one
— "not a single guy" — at the all-male
Catholic college "would have called himself
gay." From time to time Andrew reminds
me of how "different things were back
then," how "gays were invisible and everything was underground," and "how much
guilt, shame, and secret pleasure were part
of the hidden life." Even though no one at
Holy Cross admitted to being gay, there was
definitely "gay sex going on." There were
the real effeminate "glee club guys" who
everyone believed were having sex with one
another. "But that was not me," says Andrew about how he never found "those
types" attractive. And there was also gay sex
going on between a few well-known professors who were "actively cruising their
students." In fact, Andrew remembers being hit on by two faculty members. "They
came on to me, but I never acted on it," he
says casually.

Although Andrew did not identify with
the glee club guys, he did begin to frame a
political outlook that redrew the map between gays and straights. "I was beginning
to develop an identity as a progressive
thinker," he says about opening his mind
and heart to the gay world. One evening he
went with a bunch of his friends to see *The*

Boys in the Band, a play about gay men at a party. Andrew explains, "The playwright had a preliberation perspective . . . you know, the view that these gay guys are pathetic and we need to have sympathy for them . . . a view that would today make most people cringe." Andrew missed all the political and social subtexts. All he remembers is sitting in the audience lusting after the sexy-looking actors on the stage. He is grinning at the memory of his big, surprising response. "I sat there thinking, These are some hot guys who are gay . . . they are not like the guys in the glee club."

After college, Andrew went on to graduate school in Rochester, New York, his first time away from home. But even there — even without "the inhibiting influence of home" — he really didn't do "gay stuff." He shakes his head, remembering a single encounter. "There was sexual stuff with one guy, but we didn't really go far." Occasionally Andrew dated women, but by now it had become "more of a cover." There was some pleasure, but no sexual attraction. His heart was definitely not in it. He remembers one woman that he very much enjoyed being with, so they dated off and on for several months and it "got pretty serious." When she began to talk about the future and hint at marriage, Andrew — for the first time — confronted himself. "I thought to myself, It is wrong to be doing this . . . I'm lying to her and lying to myself. This is not honest, not authentic." And although he didn't yet have the nerve to tell her that he was gay, he broke off the relationship, felt guilty and sad for how he had misled her, and never dated a woman again.

After his year in Rochester, in 1973, Andrew moved to Boston, a city he had known growing up, a city that had a lively gay community and an emerging gay political movement. There was also a tempting nightlife that beckoned to him. He began frequenting a gay bar — the Cabaret — first joined by his friend and roommate, a straight male, and a couple of straight girls who were his "good buddies," then finding his way to the club on his own. "It felt open and cool, and I would go there and dance the night away," he says about his beginning dance steps into gay life. But when he stopped dancing, he realized that the Cabaret was not a place where he really felt comfortable. A lot of the guys there reminded him of the glee club boys from college. "Back then," Andrew recalls, shrugging his shoulders, "it was fashionable to be thin and very effeminate. These were gay guys who called each other by girls' names, and I wasn't comfortable with that . . . I was looking for guys with muscles."

Several months later Andrew heard about another bar — Rizzo — that "catered to guys like" him. "The first time I walked in there," he says dramatically, "I thought I was in heaven . . . and I was!" He reminds me that discovering and finding his way to Rizzo was not easy. This was 1976, and there was, of course, "no Internet and no gay news channel that kept folks in touch with one another or helped direct you to the right gay resources." Finding Rizzo and mixing with the musclemen felt to Andrew as if he had come "home." It was also the moment when he definitively came out to himself, when he said, "I'm not going to fake it anymore. I'm going to pursue relationships with men, and I'm going to call myself gay."

Although he can identify the moment when he declared himself gay — first to himself — he wants me to know that the process of coming out is "long and layered." "It is not binary," he says, "like one day you're in the closet and the next day you're out. It's like peeling an onion . . . slowly removing the layers that cover and mask." And "it always begins with a declaration to yourself" that you are gay, and then announcements along the way to family, friends, acquaintances, and colleagues. It is "tedious and difficult" to carefully spread the news, to not fall back into the old habits of obfuscation, to ride out the ambivalence that sometimes reemerges even if you feel sure of what you are doing.

As he relives those early days, Andrew says that for him the process of coming out may have gone a little more quickly for two reasons. First, by then, he was loving his work as a special education teacher and had become deeply involved in the "disability movement." His advocacy for the fair treatment of disabled students made him think, "If I can do this for them, I can also stand up for myself and other gays." And second, his "progressive political orientation" easily mixed and merged into the gay rights movement, which was in its early stages. "All at once, I was having sex with men, going to Provincetown as a gay person, and joining the gay rights struggle in the streets. I no longer wanted to live a separate, private life, hiding my gayness, muting my voice."

Even though he was clear that he no longer wanted to be closeted, Andrew did worry about losing his job. At the time, he was teaching at a vocational high school in a suburb of Boston, where he definitely would have been fired had they discovered that he was gay. "There was no job security. We were always having to watch our backs," he recalls. "This was the terrifying era of Anita Bryant's 'holy war on homosexuals,' and folks were doing witch hunts against gays. It was a dangerous time." As a matter of fact, Bryant's religious crusade — when she unleashed her infamous slogan, "Gays can't reproduce so they have to recruit" — was initially focused on prohibiting gays from becoming teachers. Andrew felt somewhat safer when he found an administrative job in the Boston public schools; he immediately joined a newly formed activist coalition called Gay and Lesbian School Workers. "The fact that the teachers called themselves workers gave a sense of where they were coming from." He smiles. At first they were suspicious of Andrew's wish to join; as an administrator, he was seen as "the enemy." All the other members were lefty teachers — "workers" — who were suspicious of his "establishment credentials." But it didn't take long before they realized that his heart was in the right place and that he was a valuable political ally. "Even though Boston was more open, and even though there were clear signs of political change, these were still very frightening times," explains Andrew. "We wanted to make schools safe places for gay teachers. At the time, we were not even focused on the vulnerability of gay students." Within a couple of years they had secured job protection for gays in the Boston school contract.

One of the leaders of the movement — Earl Haywood — became a close friend and an important and valued mentor. Several years older than Andrew, he was an experienced and savvy activist, an outspoken teacher at a local progressive independent school, and someone who seemed both fearless and strategic. It was at his urging that Andrew and he collaborated in starting the Gay and Lesbian Political Caucus. When Andrew thinks back on his gay identity and his political activism, he often points to the critical role of mentors in his life, Earl being at the top of the list. "I was fortunate to meet guys who really pushed me and guided me." He underscores the ways in which his mentors combined the personal and the political, blending passion and discipline, strategy and courage. As Andrew paved his own path, their influence on him was big and exciting. "Coming out sexually and politically was exhilarating . . . I loved being part of the gay rights movement." He beams. The exhilaration, of course, had its dark and scary side. In the summer of 1979 at Boston's first gay rights parade, many of the marchers wore bags over their heads to hide their identity, and people watching along the parade route threw bottles and rotten tomatoes and shouted ugly homophobic slurs.

The first person Andrew came out to was Greg, his best straight friend and roommate, with whom he "shared political views" and whom he "trusted implicitly." He knew this would be the easiest, least stressful of his coming-out conversations. "Greg was not at all surprised," recalls Andrew. "Within a few weeks we were double-dating." By contrast, another good friend, a working-class Italian kid he had known from his childhood, acted as if Andrew's news were a death sentence. "He said, 'I feel terrible for you. I can't believe what pain you must be experiencing' . . . He was patronizing and sympathetic," says Andrew, shaking his head. "My response was, 'Time out, man . . . being gay is not a tragedy. I see it as a gift.' " He tried to draw an analogy. What if his friend could take a pill that would render him non-Italian, would he do it? Of course not! He was proud of his Italian roots, his heritage, and his culture; he would never do anything to alter that. So neither would Andrew take a pill to become straight; he loved being gay.

Coming out to his brothers was a "piece of cake; they were completely cool with it." They were right there with him, cheering him on, embroidering him into their straight lives, going out dancing with him at gay clubs. It was mostly the same with the rest of his family, many of whom had not thought of him as gay and expressed some surprise, but then accepted him fully. One Sunday he even hosted a big brunch at his place in the South End for all his cousins, nieces, nephews, and gay friends — bringing his two worlds together — and everyone had a great time.

It was only his mother and father who never fully accepted his being gay. They never wanted to talk about it, and Andrew did not "force the issue." Even though he tried to "have the conversation" several times, they always came back with the same brief, dismissive response. "We love you . . . It's your business. We don't want to talk about it." Andrew's face is resigned but sad. I ask him how he has made sense of his parents' refusal to talk, and he says gently, "They came from a different generation, and sex wasn't anything my parents ever talked about . . . I knew my mother was opposed to birth control because of the church, but nothing else was ever said." He describes the "huge family tragedy" when his older brother got his girlfriend pregnant in college and they had to get married by a justice of the peace because the church refused to allow them to have a wedding. "They were thought to be living in sin," says Andrew as he recalls "where his parents were coming from" and the prohibitions and guilt piled on by the church.

Andrew can somehow manage to understand the generational and religious reasons that his parents could never accept his being gay. What he can't bear, and what still makes him angry and bitter, is the fact that they never recognized his long-term partner, Matthew, "as my spouse." And when he died of AIDS after a decade-long union, they refused to attend his funeral. "It was devastating," says Andrew, his eyes filling with tears. "My uncle, the Jesuit priest — my mother's brother — was completely accepting. He gave Matthew his last rites and did the funeral service, but my parents never came around." Looking back on what now feels like "the ultimate betrayal," Andrew wishes he had at least "forced the issue" with his parents when his spouse was buried. But even now he doesn't seem to have a clue about how he might have confronted them in a way that would have changed their disrespectful behavior.

Andrew had to peel another layer of the onion back at work, in his professional life. Because of his very public role in the gay rights movement around town, most people at work knew and accepted the fact that he was gay. Fairly quickly he rose in the administrative ranks in the school system, and he remembers an incident around his gayness that backfired in unexpected ways. Andrew, the youngest in his department, was about to be promoted to the top position, director of special education for the whole school system. At that time, there were two warring factions in the department — the old guard and the young Turks who had very different philosophical and political takes on the field of special education. Andrew was clearly in the latter camp.

When he was about to be appointed, the old guard decided to voice their opposition directly to the five members of the school board, complaining that a gay person should not be allowed to get the top job. "You see, they used the gay thing because they couldn't get me on my competence," says Andrew about their "pathetic attempts" to be obstructionists. But in each meeting they had with individual board members, their requests were denied, and they were turned away. In fact, in a couple of cases, members of the board actually threw the petitioners out of their offices. The old guard hadn't counted on the fact that Andrew had either exchanged political favors or developed a personal relationship with each and every member of the board, and he already knew the votes were there. And it turned out that the most conservative woman on the board, a middle-aged single mother from Dorchester, was the most sympathetic. She had a son and an administrative assistant who were both gay. The victory was sweet, but the bitterness still lingers. "It was a five–zero vote . . . but for me it was very hurtful."

The evening after the vote, Andrew went to a community gathering, where the man sitting next to him offered congratulations on his new job and asked him for the "backstory." Andrew was forthcoming, telling him about the opposition's efforts to stop his appointment, how they had used his gayness as their rallying cry. The next day, the whole story appeared in the Metro section of *The Boston Globe*. The stranger sitting next to him had never identified himself as a newspaper reporter. Although it was shocking and unsettling to see the article in the paper, after a while Andrew saw the whole thing as positive, even liberating. "As it turned out, being in the newspaper was wonderful. I didn't have to do any more of this coming out . . . it had all been made very public."

From Boston, Andrew moved to Chicago to become associate superintendent of schools, and once again he was forced "to figure out how to be out." Some of his friends said that the Midwest would be a much less friendly place for gays, that he needed to be more cautious. And Andrew didn't want his sexuality to take center stage; he didn't want it to become "the issue" in Chicago. "I was always wanting to be careful that my gay identity wouldn't distort or compromise the work I was doing in the disability movement," he says about a calculation that always seems particularly pointed when he enters a new political environment and must decide whether to peel back another layer of the onion. Before arriving in Chicago, he decided to dismiss his friends' warnings and come out to his boss, who was "cool with it." And soon after he arrived in the Midwest, he met and befriended the mayor and his wife, who had a disabled son, and they became staunch allies in his work on behalf of disabled students and then big supporters of gay rights. Andrew had arrived just in time to lead the AIDS prevention work in the Chicago schools, developing a sex education curriculum, setting up health clinics, and distributing condoms to students who were sexually active. The culminating event was the walk for AIDS down Michigan Avenue. "That was my very public way of coming out," Andrew recalls of the moment when his political and personal worlds converged and he marched at the front of the line with the mayor.

Andrew's time in Chicago was cut short by the deteriorating health of Matthew, who had stayed behind in Boston. "I gave up my position in Chicago to go take care of my spouse," says Andrew sadly, reliving the traumatic moments when Matthew was hospitalized for six weeks with AIDS and finally died in his arms at home. While he sat nursing Matthew in the hospital, he received a call from President Clinton's people at the White House, offering him the job of director of special education for the United States. He said yes to the new job, told them he would not be able to come immediately, and then notified his new staff

81

that his partner was very ill and on the edge of death. "I came in as a gay widow." He recalls about the openheartedness and positive reception he received from his staff and the huge welcome he got from his new boss, who loved the fact that he was gay. She "saw it as an asset."

It turned out that twenty-four of Clinton's appointees were "out" gays, a record number for the federal bureaucracy. In fact, in order for Clinton to make the openly gay appointments, he had had to rescind a "don't ask, don't tell" order still on the books from the Eisenhower days. The *Washington Blade,* D.C.'s gay newspaper, did a full-page spread listing all the appointees along with their government positions. A big press conference followed, with all of them lined up for the whole country to see. "It was the ultimate coming out!" Andrew shakes his head as he traces the progress. "It had only been twenty years since I was in Boston — so afraid that I would lose my teaching job because I was gay — to that moment when the president of the United States was standing behind us, saying he was really with us and he valued our contribution to the nation . . . and it felt good to feel as if I had been a small part of that change."

Now, at fifty-eight, Andrew sits before me, slender and fit, his muscles bulging under his T-shirt. He is still an athlete, at home in his body. His posture is strong and relaxed; his gaze is intense. His mostly gray hair is cut short and thinning. As he relives his story, his eyes mist over with the emotional shedding of each layer of the onion — "joyful tears" he admits, wiping his eyes. His days as an altar boy in Worcester feel like long ago and far away, even though he has no need to dismiss or disparage his roots or the values he was raised with. "Self-loathing has never been a part of me," he says quietly. "There are no other peels of the onion to make. At this time in my life I don't have to worry . . . I haven't had to worry for a long time."

Andrew's voice rises in a triumphant crescendo. "I love gay people . . . I like being with my people. It is a gift to be part of a counterculture." He bangs his fist on the table, his eyes now filled with mischief. "I live in the South End, and I cruise for men . . . it is spiritual to be around my brothers and sisters. We are different in so many wonderful ways." He is at his most expansive when he stumbles upon another metaphor ("besides peeling the onion") to describe the feeling of being fully out. "It is like being at the dance . . . it is a revelry . . . you're completely free. It is the antithesis of being in the closet. You're on the dance floor, and everyone is smiling and acting foolish." He lifts both arms, spreads them wide, snaps his fingers, and moves his torso to the beat of the dance music that echoes through him.

We are coming to the end of our time together, ending on a high note, an exultant bravado celebrating the long journey. I ask Andrew whether "coming out of the closet" is a good example of an exit story, and he assures me that it is. Not one open-and-shut exit, rather a series of exits that allow you over time to "be fully evolved . . . to be completely yourself." "The closet is damaging," he says pensively. "If you don't get out of it, then you never can be healthy or whole." He flashes to the profiles he sees when he surfs the Internet. "When gay guys use the word 'discreet' online, that is a sign that they are not out." He talks about the pain for those who feel they have to "de-gay" their apartment before their parents arrive for a visit from out of town. He remembers the time, a couple of decades ago, when he was having dinner with some principals in Boston after spending a couple of weeks with his lover in Provincetown, and when they asked him where he had been on his vacation, he told them he had rented a house in Truro. Provincetown would have signaled that he was gay. "The masking and hiding take a toll. We only have one life to live . . . and it goes by very quickly."

There are two more thoughts — about time and place — that Andrew wants to leave me with. He wants me to know that he is aware of the ways in which his coming out of the closet, his gay identity, and his activism were very much shaped by "historical context." He points to a "huge historical marker" that separates generations of gay men. "I am young enough to have experienced the Stonewall riot — Greenwich Village, 1969 — that sparked the gay revolution." He muses, "If I were ten years older, I might have been a priest or an alcoholic, or both, not a free gay man . . . I know very few men older than I am who have fully exited."

He also recognizes the "power place has had" in shaping his identity, his sense of belonging and community. Now his voice is almost prayerful. "San Francisco is our spiritual home . . . our Vatican, the place where we can be completely gay." He looks off into the distance, imagining the scene, his arms carving curves in the air. "I remember last year going out there to bury one of my best friends who I had found dead in his place in Provincetown. I was high up on one of the hills, looking down on the Castro Theatre. The fog was lifting, and the sunlight was hitting the fog . . . there were sprays of sparkling light . . . I sat there and just cried. I was home."

For Andrew, exit is homecoming — not just into the home of self but also into the home of community. His exit makes possible the realization that you can be yourself, and be with people, just the way you are. His homecoming was a hard-won, lengthy process; there were a series of exits. Even though Andrew is able to capture the exact moment when he declared to himself that he was gay — where he was, what he was wearing, how a weight suddenly seemed to lift from his shoulders — he reminds me that being in or out of the closet is not a "binary" experience. Rather, it is ongoing and iterative. It is like slowly, strategically "peeling the onion" as you shed the masks that lie and the personas that deceive, as you begin to reveal who you really are, your "authentic self." For Andrew, there were public exits — the ones that got written about in the paper, celebrated in gay pride

86

parades, and announced at press conferences — and private ones where he revealed himself to friends and family. The coming-out conversation with his parents was by far the most painful, and he still blames himself for not pushing them harder, for "not forcing the issue" with them. Until their death, they "silenced the conversation," deflecting his many attempts to tell them the truth, refusing to come to his spouse's funeral.

Their refusal, of course, reflected their roots and their generation — their Irish immigrant origins, their working-class values, and their unerring devotion to the Catholic Church, all of which saw homosexuality as sinful. As a matter of fact, in order for Andrew to begin his exit story, he tells me he must begin at the "hardest place," where the pulls of gravity and belonging were the strongest — with his "working-class Irish Catholic" family who lived in a triple-decker on a street in Worcester, where everyone believed the same thing, belonged to the same parish, wanted their sons to be priests, and looked to the Vatican as the almighty authority. It is against these powerful forces of home — the close-knit neighborhood where Andrew was raised, where he was loved by his parents, and where he spent a "happy childhood" — that he must begin his exit moves, challenge the deeply ingrained cultural imprints, and calculate his successful advances.

As I listened, I was struck by the ways in which Andrew's exits out of the closet seemed consistently strong and hopeful, filled with self-confidence and clarity. Yes, there were real dangers and fears, ambivalence and retreat along the way, but mostly he seemed to move — even dance — from strength to strength, a self-confidence in part born out of his happy and abundant childhood. Even though his parents would not allow him to tell them the truth, Andrew always knew they loved him, believed in him, and had his back. The self-esteem that allowed him to navigate the gay/straight borders came, I believe, from the security and support that his mother and father provided; from the close-knit Catholic neighborhood where he felt like the "chosen one"; from the embrace of friends and teammates who admired his muscles, his skills, and his leadership; from the professors and priests who sat around the family dinner table and included him in smart, worldly conversations. Ironically, all those early familial, cultural, and religious forces that disapproved of homosexuality and found it sinful were the very same as those that nourished the self-confidence in him that ultimately allowed him to emerge from the closet whole and happy. In the end, Andrew's exit story does not feel unlike the long journey many of us — gay or straight — must take toward self-understanding as we try to make peace with how we differ from the expectations and projections of our parents. In fully accepting ourselves, we pave the way for others to accept us; we both embrace and resist the gravitational pulls of home.

Beyond the shaping influences of family and church, it is important to see Andrew's coming out as part of a larger political and social narrative and to recognize how much "times have changed." Tracing his journey, we see him in the late 1960s at Holy Cross, a Catholic men's college where no one dared admit he was gay, where the glee club boys were rumored to be having sex, and where everyone knew the names of the male professors who cruised their students. Ten years later we see Andrew trying to avoid being fired from his teaching job and growing into his activism while Anita Bryant waged her national crusade against gays, became the national spokesman for orange growers, and was named *Good Housekeeping*'s "most admired woman" of the year.

And we hear about Andrew joining the brave marchers in Boston who put paper bags over their heads as they walked in the first gay pride parade and had rotten tomatoes and homophobic slurs hurled at them as they passed by.

Andrew guides us to the most important marker of change — the generational divide, the fault line that put the gay rights movement on the map. The timing of the Stonewall riot was fortuitous, giving inspiration and impetus to Andrew's generation of activists, providing fuel for the movement, and forcing the battle out into the open. Andrew looks at his gay elders, most of whom remain closeted, and recognizes how his exit — his homecoming — might not have happened had he been born a few years earlier. He is a "free gay man," he is "home," he is able to join the jubilation "dance" — not only because he gained strength from his family's enduring love and from being in the struggle with the activist community, not only because he was willing to go the distance and courageous enough to brave the dangers, but also because he was lucky enough to have come of age when he could catch the winds of change.

Two:
Voice

Voice is sound. It is auditory. We listen for its timbre, tone, and texture. We enjoy the suppleness, virtuosity, and range of the mezzo-soprano singing *Carmen*. We immediately recognize the gravelly, deep voice of our son calling long-distance on Sunday afternoon. We recoil from the angry, cynical voice of our teacher catching us — again — in some rule violation. We catch our voice as we talk to ourselves in a moment of frustration or as we scream out when we slip and fall down the stairs. We respond to the timbre and phrasing of the voice as much as — and sometimes more than — the content of the message. We've heard people say "God damn" as if they were sending up a prayer, or "yes, sir" as if they were swearing. In the tonal variations of voice we hear respect, anger, resignation, sadness, confusion, curiosity. We hear the opening and closing of conversations. We sense that it is time to leave.

Social scientists often use "voice" metaphorically to refer to the social, emotional, and political meanings conveyed when people speak up or speak out, claim their space, challenge authority, and become empowered. Political scientists and policy analysts, for example, describing the responsibilities of citizens in a democratic society, see the vote as a way for people to give voice to their views, to make themselves heard, to register approval or complaint. Voice in this context speaks about the individual's responsibility and accountability to the whole community. A democracy cannot function without people lifting up their individual and collective voices. In authoritarian regimes, voices are silenced and dismissed. People are not allowed to stand up for what they believe or give voice to their views.

The feminist psychologist Carol Gilligan stretched the metaphor even further when she wrote *In a Different Voice* (1982), her now classic account contrasting the ways in which women and men define the boundaries of their identities.[1] Men, she argued, tend to see themselves as separate, their identity defined by the lone pursuit, the edges of their autonomy clearly drawn. Women, on the other hand, see themselves in relationships, knowing themselves through their connectedness to each other. It is through relationships that women's development and self-definition is shaped. Here Gilligan uses the notion of the "different voice" of women to challenge the male-centric focus of the developmental studies that not only used men as their primary "subjects" but also viewed male developmental and moral trajectories as normative, even optimal. In lifting up the voices of women, whose life journeys and identities took a different path, Gilligan was not only offering a corrective to the literature — claiming that feminist patterns were different, not deviant — she was also using her own voice, the voice of challenge and critique, to speak to her male academic colleagues. The layering of voices, those of her subjects in duet with her own, offered a powerful counterpoint to the prevailing frameworks that had, until that time, dominated academic studies and discourse.

Economist Albert Hirschman was the first to draw the theoretical links between "voice" and "exit."[2] In 1970 he published a slim volume titled *Exit, Voice, and Loyalty: Responses to Decline in Firms, Organizations, and States,* which forty years later continues to have a huge influence on social scientists' conceptions of why people choose to leave or stay in organizations, communities, or even relationships that are no longer serving their needs. In a book crammed with references to the economic staples of supply and demand, the pricing of products, outcomes, influences, and quality, Hirschman surprises us by quoting some lines from a 1966 satirical play about Adlai Stevenson's inability to resign from government — a bow to how hard it is to leave the familiar, break the bonds of attachment, and become an outsider:

To quit the club! Be outside looking in!
This outsideness, this unfamiliar land,
From which few travelers ever get back
   in . . .
I fear to break . . .[3]

The beginning of Hirschman's theory is grounded in the inevitable decline or deterioration of organizations. In fact, he holds a deeply pessimistic stance:

Firms and other organizations are conceived to be permanently and randomly subject to decline and decay, that is to a gradual loss of rationality, efficiency, and surplus-producing energy, no matter

94

how well the institutional framework within which they function is designed.[4]

The situation is this: the firm is not doing what it is supposed to be doing — in terms of product quality, service, or price — for its customers. Management finds out about the firm's failings via two alternative routes or two discrete actions that the customers exercise: exit and voice. When customers stop buying the firm's products or services, or some members leave the firm, they are exercising the exit option. This compels the management to search for ways to correct the firm's faults that have led to the exodus. In the voice option, customers and firm members express their dissatisfaction directly to the management, or to anyone who will listen; this too compels the management to search for ways to cure the firm's failings. As such, exit and voice are generated out of decline and perpetuate the organizational life cycle. Though Hirschman calls his view "radical pessimism," one can discern a more positive outlook within his theory, one that considers decay as the birthplace of new possibilities.

Hirschman paints exit as a neat, terminal, impersonal, discernible, and quantifiable action that is highly efficient. It is the most direct and purest way to express dissatisfaction. Voice, on the other hand, belongs to the realm of politics. Voice is "messy," spanning everything from faint grumbling to violent protest. Moreover, in the political realm, exit has been branded as criminal, labeled as desertion, defection, even treason. Although Hirschman speaks of exit — its clarity and edge — as "uniquely powerful," he claims that "the precise modus operandi of the exit option has not received much attention." A customer resorts to exit rather than voice when he or she no longer attempts to change an objectionable state of affairs, whether through individual or collective petition, appeal to a higher authority, or protest. In situations where there is a lack of opportunity for exit — where there is a pure monopoly, for example — the potential for voice increases. Voice, if effective, can postpone or prevent exit. Voice is both complement and substitute for exit. It is hard to read Hirschman without sensing some bias: "While exit requires nothing but a clear-cut either/or decision, voice is essentially an art constantly evolving in new directions . . . the presence of the exit alternative can therefore tend to atrophy the development of the art of voice."[5]

The seesawing, complementary, yet unequal options of exit and voice are further complicated by Hirschman's addition of "loyalty" to the theoretical mix. Loyalty, the third leg of his conceptual triangle, refers to a special or deep attachment to an organization that helps group members resort to voice when exit is a possible alternative. As a rule, loyalty holds exit at bay and activates voice.[6]

THE ART OF VOICE

"I wanted to become more of a solo voice."

The first narrative in this chapter both echoes and challenges Hirschman's theory, pointing to the complicated tensions, balances, and entanglements between exit and voice. In Theresa Russo's story of leaving the leadership role of a nonprofit that she founded twenty-five years ago, exit is neither clear-cut nor efficient, neither easily discernible nor quantifiable. The "outsideness" that she experiences is messy, ambivalent, and disorienting. Also, in contrast to Hirschman's model, it is in the performance and layers of exit — the public rituals and the private agony — that Theresa begins to discover and to lift up her voice.

Theresa Russo has postponed our interview a few times before she finally arrives on a sunny morning in April. Over the months, we have had numerous e-mails — heartfelt, anxious missives from her about anticipating the interview (will she be able to be coherent and articulate about something that still causes her so much confusion and pain), about her concerns over my methodology (how many interviews, how deeply will I go, will I ask to review any of the documents that she has on file), and about her worry that our time together might add another layer of emotional processing that will further block her movement forward. In my communications back to her, I have tried to be reassuring about the interview process, about my confidence in her ability to express her thinking and feelings with clarity and authenticity, and about my responsibility to create a safe space for us to talk together. I say that others have found the interviews "educative," "illuminating," even "honoring, helpful, and healing." But I am also very careful to offer her — each time — the opportunity to retreat without guilt or embarrassment. It is fine, I say, over and over again, if she chooses not to move forward with the interview.

In retrospect, this dance of approach and avoidance seems right for this time in Theresa's life, when she is so ready to move forward to the next chapter while she still desperately clings to the past; when she has publicly exited the organization with grace, purposefulness, and certainty while she privately feels her decision to leave it was precipitate and ill-timed; when she is mourning a life that used to be incredibly busy, joyful, and productive and — at the same time — trying to forge a positive path forward when the terrain feels barren.

The pain is written all over her face as she sits down across from me, her arms tightly wrapped around her, and begins her soliloquy, which — it turns out — is both coherent and articulate. She has thought deeply about the casualties and opportunities of leave-taking. She has worked hard to find the language for the layers of emotion she navigates every day. And she is openhearted and generous about expressing her anger, her fears, her ambivalence, and her yearnings. Her interview is not in the past tense; it is not a retrospective. She is speaking about the present, about the mixture and mélange of emotions she is currently experiencing that shape her outlook of the future.

Three years ago Theresa began thinking

about leaving Red River Expeditions, a nonprofit organization in rural Wisconsin that she founded and directed for twenty-five years. For much of that time, she had combined her work at RRE with teaching in a counseling program at the university, where she also earned her doctorate. The two part-time jobs were really both full-time commitments, filling her days with strenuous, exciting work that she loved, adding up to a very busy life with intellectual and emotional benefits and a "reasonably good paycheck." Theresa enjoyed the balance and counterpoint of teaching and supervising graduate students and designing and directing outdoor environmental programs for adolescents. Her double commitments required that she commute in her trusty old Saab three hours each way from the country to the city, spending half the week in each place.

When Theresa began to think about leaving RRE, she was still very much involved with and enjoying her teaching duties at the university, and she was anticipating continuing her work there. But she began to feel that two "full-time jobs" were too much for her. She recalls, "I was getting exhausted, realizing that I did not have the stamina for working twelve-hour days, seven days a week." But it was more than the weariness of burning the candle at both ends; although she was confident about fulfilling her duties and responsibilities at the university, she felt less secure in her capacity to be at full strength as executive director of a hands-on educational program for adolescents. Her physical stamina was clearly not what it used to be. The trips she used to organize and lead — strenuous mountain climbing, weeklong hikes through the backwoods, camping in the wild, canoe trips, white-water rafting, and fishing expeditions, all of which she used to relish — now, at fifty-five, were impossible for her. "Even five one-day trips a year felt hard," she admits. "Although I was the administrator, I still wanted some level of contact with the teens, and I hated losing the immediacy and close-ness with them."

Theresa was also struggling with significant hearing loss that made it hard for her to decipher what the teens were saying. "They talk so quietly. There is so much mumbling . . . so much nuance and code when they speak, and I began missing what was going on." She had always prided herself on being an attentive, compassionate listener, listening for what was said and not said by the teenagers, finding the right question to ask that would unleash their stuck emotions or support a moment of discovery for them. Now this kind of close connection was being compromised, even lost.

At the same time as Theresa was feeling the need to — slowly but surely — leave RRE, she was becoming more engaged at the university and experiencing a new vitality and authority in her work there. When she founded RRE, she primarily thought of her work as "political activism." She saw her role as "making sure the voices of the rural families were heard, and helping youth advocate for themselves." At the university she began to see the possibility of developing her own voice through influencing the work of graduate students, but also through writing her own books and articles. She could begin to reach broader, more diverse audiences. "RRE was always a choir," she says about the collective approach she encouraged. "I realized that at the university I could have this solo voice. I began to feel that in my mid-fifties, if I'm going to have another chapter, I'd better get on with it."

Theresa makes a distinction between the "personal" reasons that motivated her exit from RRE and the "organizational" ones. The tone of her voice shifts — becoming more distant and analytic — as she speaks in general about organizational leadership and change. She begins, "If founding directors stay for more than twenty or twenty-five years, it can become a personality-driven organization." Before starting RRE, Theresa had been a public school teacher who found herself always worrying about the ways in which schools tended to "silence and pacify students," the ways in which the children seemed to lose their curiosity, their authority, and their voices in the process of conforming to the institutional culture. "I always wanted my kids to be assertive . . . to grab hold of themselves," she says passionately. So she invented an organization — outside the walls of school — where she hoped to offer kids a safe place to be themselves, a challenging and supportive educational environment that might help release them from the bondage of caution and inhibition. She wanted to build an adolescent empowerment zone.

Leaving her teaching job, Theresa had a great plan, but no money. She looks back on those heady and hopeful days. "It was a force of will building this organization. I had no salary, moved in with my sister and her son because I couldn't pay the rent, and worked out of the back of my car." She was driven by passion, by a progressive political agenda, by her determination to "give voice" to young people and their families. And over the years — actually a quarter century — although the organization has grown and matured, the early imprint of her principles and values has survived intact. She reminds me again what happens when founders stay around a long time, maybe too long. "The personality, style, and legacy of the founder get woven into the organization. The habits of work get deeply imprinted on the organization."

Theresa sees an "essential irony" in the way she has developed and led RRE. On the one hand she has always emphasized the collaborative, communitarian nature of her leadership, and on the other hand she is able to recognize her individual mark, her singular imprint. "You know," she says reflectively, "it was always a choir. My manner was one of relationship building . . . but undeniably there was the force of my personality as well that permeated everything." In part it was her recognition of this "essential irony" that helped Theresa know it was time to leave; if she had actually managed to build a sturdy institution, it should be able to go on — even thrive — without her at the helm.

Again Theresa's voice takes on an analytic

edge. "For founders who do a credible job, the organization they've loved and nurtured inevitably gets bigger than them. They need to leave so the organization can move from being personality driven to being theory based. It is, after all, a sign of strength and maturity if the organization can survive the founder's leaving." Her voice — so clear and concise about leadership succession and organizational health — barely masks the thunderous emotions that she admits to feeling. Theresa offers an important caveat about the shift from a personality- to a theory-driven organization — a caveat that captures her "principal concern" about the casualties of progress. "Organizations going through this kind of change have to find a way of not living in the past, but they also must not ignore the past!"

Relationship building is the signature of Theresa's leadership style. It also, not surprisingly, reflects her personality and her political stance. She is most comfortable sharing the power, reaching out to diverse constituencies, and being consultative and inclusive. "I gather up as many voices as possible," she says about a process that always hopes to be democratic and distributive but is often slow and inefficient. After twenty-five years leading RRE, she is keenly aware that her collaborative style is deeply rooted in her unwillingness — or inability — to be assertive, in her resistance to being the "solo voice and spokesperson." Her more natural inclination and attitude is one of working behind the scenes, reaching out to others, listening and supporting, leading through developing a consensus. She is gentle, respectful, and gracious by nature, not edgy and aggressive, never personally ambitious.

Yet in the last several years — particularly since she finished her doctoral work in organizational development — she has wanted to become more assertive. Both as a person and as a leader, she has found that it is almost impossible to change in an organization where your "habits of interacting" are so deeply imbedded. "After twenty-five years there is so much in place, so much assumed about who you are and how you operate, that change is hard. Even though I wanted to become more of a solo voice in my last years there, I found that people were resistant to my attempts to be more assertive." The organizational expectations created a kind of inertia that compromised her purposeful efforts to modify her leadership style, and this made Theresa realize that "the personality-based habits needed to change so the organization could be taken into its maturity."

When she reflects on her anguished exit from RRE, she says it feels as if she has been "living two lives" — the public face of transition that has been "cool, calm, and collected" and the private experience that has been "the darkest time" of her life. As she anticipated her leave-taking, she designed and gracefully implemented a rational process of transition, announcing her plans to her board of directors and working through their various concerns about institutional stability — identifying, welcoming, and mentoring the next director; writing an upbeat and heartfelt farewell letter to the various constituencies she has worked with over the years; even enthusiastically participating in a glorious farewell party that featured not only family, community, and friends but also generations of the teens she had worked with over the decades. She was determined, she remembers, not to have RRE go through the kind of "public drama" that ruins so many transitioning institutions — particularly small nonprofits — and leaves bad scars that deface the place for generations to come.

But underneath all her grace and maturity, all her optimism and bright outlook, Theresa was feeling great ambivalence and a growing sense of dread. She was claiming publicly that her departure was the right thing for the organization, perfectly timed to fit the changing institutional narrative, and all the while she was feeling "but this is not the right time for me!" And she has continued to worry daily about the "practicality and rationality" of her decision as she finds herself facing an unreceptive world and an economy in steep decline.

Since officially leaving RRE two years ago (she has continued to serve as mentor, consultant, and senior adviser on various projects, but has relinquished her office space, stayed out of the decision making, and retreated from being the public face of the organization), Theresa has struggled to find work. Part of her original decision to resign three years ago was predicated on the fact that leaving would allow her to focus more time and energy on her university responsibilities. But as fate would have it, her contract at the university was not renewed (her department was being merged with another, and faculty were being let go), and she was given one year to finish up and move on. Even though she understood the "structural" reasons for her dismissal, it felt like a real slap in the face, a painful kick in her gut, an injury to her ego that stung even more than her exit from RRE because it was not something she had chosen. At RRE she was able to publicly write the story of her departure, stage her exit, and plan the ritual events. At least that much was in her control. But at the university she was simply dismissed after doing what she thought was a more than creditable job, and after discovering how much she loved developing her "solo voice."

So when Theresa stepped out into the world in search of new work and a reinvented professional identity, she took in the empty terrain. It felt like a blank slate with few options — options that kept on unraveling right before her eyes. It was a frustrating, difficult, often humiliating time. Her voice is tearful as she recounts the seemingly endless rejections she faced and the doors that closed in front of her. "This is not a world that is receiving me . . . everything was conspiring against me — my gender, my social class, my age, my disability." At first she says that — at fifty-eight — she feels the sting of ageism most deeply. A lean, lithe white woman who dresses in elegant suits of colorful textured wools whose handsome, lined face is framed by thick, curly red hair that is fast turning silver, she is well aware that when people first meet her, they may see her as "old." She is also well aware that in this job market, universities and colleges would rather hire a faculty member in his/ her early thirties, with a newly minted Ph.D., than spend their money on an older person with deep experience and a long résumé. Theresa is able to recount dozens of jobs where she has been one of a few finalists, only to discover that the job — sometimes paying as low as $32,000 — was given to a person twenty-five or thirty years her junior.

Her age combines with her "disability," a hearing loss that affects both ears and often makes it hard for her to follow discussions or hear the questions being asked of her at interviews. But worse still is the way she starts to grow anxious weeks before the meetings, worrying that she will not be able to hear the questions, that she will respond to what she thinks they might have said and make a fool of herself. She also worries that people will link her hearing difficulties with their perception of her as an old woman who is out of it, who won't be able to function in her job.

Even though Theresa begins with her age as the primary source of discrimination she is facing in her job hunt, she ends up talking about another, more deeply felt discriminatory lens that she believes distorts people's perception of her and undermines her self-confidence. It is her working-class Italian background that catches up to her every time and makes her feel awkward and insecure when she is out there presenting herself to the world. It is her roots that haunt her progress forward and make her feel marginalized.

I see Theresa's face grow gray and mournful. She looks like a wounded child — the young girl she used to be who grew up on the other side of the tracks and struggled mightily, who finally succeeded in gaining access to fancy schools only to be blindsided — four decades later — by the haunts of exclusion and insecurity that marked her childhood. "These are old traces from my family," she says sadly. "I certainly have become savvy about how to posture as a middle-class person who belongs, but I stand up there thinking, Am I using the correct language here? . . . I worry about how I am speaking. Am I being too Pollyannaish, too idealistic, too excited about other people? Am I trying too hard? And then this other voice rises up inside of me that says, You know too much . . . you don't have to temper your voice . . . you don't have to support this male ego who is judging you . . . that's ridiculous!" This conversation — of insecurity and shame pitted against challenge and confidence — rises up in her as she faces her audiences and introduces her work. It is a source of humiliation and insight, insecurity and skepticism. She feels the shame come on at the same time as she feels the righteousness of her journey, the satisfaction of her growing sense of authority and voice.

The formal transition of leadership took place at the annual meeting of the RRE board of directors. Theresa thought hard about how to make the public ceremonial moment "symbolic, meaningful, and ritualized." She was handing off the baton to Michael, a thirty-seven-year-old man whom she knew well, admired, and respected, "a wonderful person with a terrific wife and two beautiful kids," a colleague who had several years earlier done a stint at RRE. Theresa began the meeting telling the board about the smooth process she and Michael had been through, transferring information, wisdom, experience, and files. After saying — "briefly, cheerfully, and coolly" — how she felt about leaving the organization in the capable and creative hands of the new leader (actually, her stomach was churning,

112

her head was hurting, her mind was spinning . . . the last thing she wanted to do at that moment was to hand over the organization to Michael), she gave him three symbolic gifts: a Flair pen, since he would now be in charge of signing all the documents, a box of business cards with EXECUTIVE DIRECTOR written under his name, and a bag of food to eat at his desk, as he would be too busy to leave the office for lunch. Having offered the gifts, Theresa left the meeting, went back to her office, cleared out all her stuff, and loaded it into boxes. "My whole desk area was naked," she says, as if this felt as if she were stripping the clothes off of her body.

The whole time she was packing and hauling the boxes — denuding the space she had inhabited for twenty-five years — she was trying to gird her loins and find a way to be brave in the face of so much sadness and loss. Her eyes fill with tears as she recalls the still-haunting moment. "There I am, all alone, thinking to myself, This is the right thing. You know it, Theresa. You have to be brave and move through it. I was crying and grieving." Then she made the mistake of stopping to look through some of the files, so full of history, so saturated with the blood, sweat, and tears of hard labor. "I couldn't stand it, thinking this is only important to me, no one else cares . . . all that was in those boxes, nobody would know or care about." (Actually Michael has, in the last several months, consulted the files from time to time to see what he can glean from the letters and documents that might help in guiding the organization forward.)

Although the formal transfer of leadership was accomplished at the board meeting, followed by a gracious farewell letter that Theresa wrote to all the folks — parents, kids, teachers, community leaders, and staff — who had worked with her from the beginning, she still did not completely separate herself from RRE. The board hired her on as a consultant, to supervise and train some of the new staff and to work with Michael once a month as he got used to the reins. They even asked her to launch and lead one final major event — her "swan song" — the following summer, a demanding three-month-long project that she completely immersed herself in and then felt a big letdown when it was over. After the dust had settled, she moved to the margins, to her ambiguous status as the former executive who is still around, who still has so much to give but feels in many ways invisible and without voice. "I still have an official role," she says sadly, "but I don't know where I belong or what I can ask for.

"It is Michael's work to lead RRE — my work is to leave," she says, as if she is rehearsing a line she repeats to herself daily. "It was Michael's turn. I knew that intellectually, but I struggled with the level of my emotional need to know. I hated my lack of identity." When she was in the office, she felt invisible. People would walk right by her. A new staff member didn't even know who she was when she arrived to do supervision. "That's pathetic. Somebody should have told her. She knew nothing about the history of the organization or my role in it," she says with hurt in her eyes. "I felt expendable. The door had closed behind me so quickly."

Theresa feels the hurtful sting of being unrecognized and ignored. But what makes her even angrier is the way she has given in to the hurt, the way she can't seem to let go of her sadness and neediness. "I'm actually angry with myself for feeling this level of need. I hate how much I am letting this hurt me," she says, making a fist. "I'm really angry at not having enough of a life outside of RRE . . . the feeling of lost identity — no schedule, no purpose . . . the loss of community . . . all the families, kids, town officials, colleagues who were part of my life." The accumulated losses have been humiliating. She hasn't even wanted to be seen, for fear she will look into the face of someone and recognize their pity. Or worse still, people would stop her on the street and say something like, "Oh, congratulations. You must feel so relieved," when all she was feeling was grief and emptiness. "I longed for the kind of big, fat, juicy problems that I used to solve every day that were now Michael's problems. I wanted to say, Give them to me, send them my way . . . and I felt starved for information about what was going on, completely out of the loop."

One day, she even made a date to have lunch with a few women friends she had known since high school and hadn't seen for a long time. Maybe a small reunion with childhood friends would help her remember herself. Maybe she would feel the warmth and companionship of their shared history and be comforted by the old memories and stories. But the lunch was anything but comforting. Even with these old friends, Theresa felt strange and estranged. "All they talked about were their children and grandchildren and their work. I found I had nothing to talk about . . . it was a real mistake for me to have gone. It left me feeling un-tethered."

Theresa's tears and passion about the excruciating losses and her reference to the pain of hearing about "other people's children" make me ask whether leaving RRE felt to her as if she had lost her baby. She has clearly asked herself this very question many times. Her voice is strong as she reflects on her complex feelings. "I have always resisted that analogy, but more and more, part of it is resonating with me. RRE was certainly not my baby in the suckling at my breast sense, but I do recognize the part where parents have to let their children go. In order for children to thrive, you have to let them be on their own, but it is also true that parents are desperate for children to call . . . and I'm feeling all of those things." Theresa is trying to convey to me the depth of her grief and her sense of dislocation, how the anguish and pain have been writ-ten on her body, causing her to actually become physically ill. In the midst of the leave-taking, she developed Graves' disease, a hyperthyroid condition that was "the physical representation" of her emotions. She says wearily, "Physically, I was out of control. Even the name of the disease — Graves' — is right on for how the pain inhabited my body and my mind . . . my soul."

I ask Theresa what metaphor comes to mind when she thinks about how she was feeling during this time, and she first mentions William Bridges's book — *Transitions* — where he writes about the difference between a "ghost town" and a "cemetery." In a cemetery, Theresa reports, "everyone is dead and buried, and people come to pay homage and lay flowers at their graves, but ghost towns are places that used to be vibrant communities that suddenly become vacant. You see signs of life, indications that people were living and working and loving there . . . but nothing remains . . . it is all gone." Exiting the place she founded, sustained, and protected, the place where there was so much good work and life and pleasure, feels like she has entered a ghost town. There is nothing left for her except the signs that the place was once alive with people and activities. Theresa muses, "There is lots of imagery about death and dying . . . I'm sick of feeling this way. I want it to be about life, not death. I don't want the exit to be about closed doors. Where is the open door? Where is the new life?" Her voice trails off in a question.

Quickly she names a second metaphor. "I

feel like I've been on a merry-go-round. My work at RRE was playful and joyful. It was meaningful, always hectic and busy, maybe too busy . . . Now I've stepped off the carousel and I'm on the ground, still feeling dazed, dizzy, and totally disoriented. I want to be able to focus on something, to gain some sense of perspective, but the world keeps spinning around — and inside of — me." As she sits across from me, Theresa is twirling her arms in circles, literally looking as if she is struggling to find some balance, some stability. After ghost towns and carousels, she moves on to her third and last metaphor for the life she is now experiencing as dizzy and deathlike. "I see myself leaving the shore, setting out to sea . . . but I'm not sure what I'm taking with me. I find myself out in the water, and I can no longer see the shore. I've lost all sense of direction, no reference points. There is no sense of place in my work, my relationships, or my family."

Hearing her talk about being unmoored from her family and friends, I ask Theresa to whom she goes to for support, for nourishment, for counsel. She immediately mentions her closest sister (she is the eldest of five children). "Rosa is my anchor," she says gratefully. "I tell her everything. She is my sole consistent source of support." Rosa was the sibling Theresa moved in with when she left her teaching job to start — on a wing and a prayer — RRE twenty-five years ago, and she is the one Theresa has depended on during these hard days, weeks, and months of farewell. Sometimes she feels as if Rosa knows her better than she knows herself. She is definitely less judgmental and more forgiving than Theresa is likely to be of herself.

Theresa admits, however, that she has not gone to her friends for support and counsel. Part of her reluctance comes from the dense web of relationships between her friends and her colleagues. They are almost inter-changeable, and she does not want her disil-lusionment or her insecurities to become part of the unruly grapevine that includes both professional and personal relation-ships. But a bigger part of her reticence in approaching friends is that they are used to coming to *her* for help and reassurance; they have always brought their worries to her, and she has always been the listener, the counselor. As we talk, she seems to discover a new insight. "It could be," she says tenta-tively, "that I need to find new friends who know me in a different way. When I'm sit-ting at the table with my old friends these days, I always end up feeling excluded. My friends know me as a listener, not a speaker. All of this is about needing to change habits."

In fact, changing habits is at the core of moving forward. She knows she will have to shift the way she enters relationships. "I'm entering a part of my life that will require that I let go of the old baggage, the old inhibitions and constraints," she says. And one of the biggest pieces of "letting go" is "worrying less about someone else's ego and concentrating more on developing the authenticity and authority of my own voice."

She offers a small example, one "tiny step" in that direction. Recently she was working with a group of high school teachers — mostly male and middle-aged — in a public school where she is currently serving as a consultant. Several of the men were resisting the idea of teachers being required to lead student advisory groups, an innovation Theresa had suggested as a way to build a stronger educational culture and more caring relationships in school and as a way to give students a more welcoming home base. In the past — actually the recent past — Theresa might have let the men's voices dominate. Or she might have tried to carefully, gently nudge them toward her point of view. She might even have retreated from what she knew was the right thing to do. Instead, this time, she said forcefully to them — as she spoke, she could even hear the strength in her own voice — that "if they were not prepared to develop real relationships with their students, they would be missing the boat." Surprisingly, the teachers did not balk; they did not dismiss her. Rather, Theresa "experienced respect" from them. They seemed to like the fact that she was "claiming her authority position." "I am," she says hopefully, "testing the waters of being assertive and discovering that when I am, the sky does not fall."

In Theresa's arduous and poignant story of exit she uses the metaphor of voice to try to capture her quest for autonomy and authority, to describe her journey toward strength and self-definition. All her professional life, she has counseled, supported, and listened to others. In fact, she founded her nonprofit because she wanted to empower teens who had been caught up in a school bureaucracy that rendered them passive and "voiceless." She wanted to help them discover what they believed and express what they needed; she wanted them to take responsibility and stand up for themselves. "I wanted to help them discover the power of their voices," she says over and over again. In taking on the leadership role of RRE, Theresa was also seeking to nourish the expression of voices in her staff. She worked to develop an organizational structure that would be collaborative and inclusive, a place where everyone would have a say and be able to participate in decision making. Over time and with intentionality, she created a "choir" by casting a wide net, "gathering up all the voices." Her singular and dominant voice — as distinguished from or more important than theirs — was rarely heard. The choir sang out the institutional culture and mission, creating a sound at once harmonious and dissonant.

After a quarter of a century at the helm of RRE, Theresa recognized the organization's need for new leadership. The place had become "personality driven," too enmeshed with her style and character. There were many voices in the choir, but they had all gotten stuck in the same groove — a groove that echoed Theresa's. This "essential irony" helped her see the path toward the exit. But she also felt the need to leave RRE for her own reasons. In her other job, at the university, she had — through her teaching and writings — gotten a taste of speaking in her own "solo voice," and she had begun to like the sound of what she heard. Besides, she was feeling the developmental imperative. At fifty-eight, she wasn't getting any younger. If there was to be a new and bold chapter, she had better get on with it.

It was one thing, however, to be convinced that it was time to leave RRE — for personal and institutional reasons — and quite another thing to do it. The public departure was nowhere near as difficult as her private journey. With grace and gratitude, with parties and accolades, Theresa was "cool, calm, and collected" as she invented goodbye rituals. But privately she was bereft, tormented, rudderless. The losses seemed overwhelming — the loss of community and relationships, of a structure and purpose, of being at the center of the mix, of being needed as the go-to person. In the midst of the chaos and suffering, grieving and weeping as she packed up the boxes in her office that contained her life's work, Theresa began to glimpse the light at the end of her "dark tunnel of despair." She began to recognize that the "authority and authenticity" of her "solo voice" would require that she exit RRE. The separation would mark the beginning of liberating her voice. As long as she remained tethered to the choir, she would never be able to see her full reflection in the mirror, never be able to even know herself fully.

When Theresa finally takes that small leap of faith and expresses her views at the meeting with high school teachers, she can actually hear the literal change in her voice. It sounds more confident to her, more clear and powerful; and it seems to strike her listeners in a way she never expected. They stop their whining and listen to her respectfully.

Theresa's path to exit is different from the one suggested by Hirschman's theoretical triangle. His framework argues that when organizations are in decline, members must choose between exit ("a clear-cut either/or decision") or voice (a "messy" engagement, more like an "art form").[7] Those who choose the latter work hard from within to support the institutional changes that will help the organization become more efficient, more rational, and more forward-looking. However, for Theresa her exit is not at all clear-cut (in fact, she is still in the midst of it); neither does it stand in contrast to the expression of her voice. Voice and exit are not divergent paths. Rather, she discovers their necessary convergence. In order to "discover and nurture" her "solo voice," she finds that she must exit the organization. And unlike Gilligan's notion of women knowing themselves through their relationships and connections with others, Theresa discovers that she can develop her authoritative, critical, singular perspective only if she draws boundaries around herself. The emergence of her voice requires that she begin to practice the messy and creative, hard and imperfect "art" of separation, exiting from her former way of being in the world.

VOICES IN CONVERSATION

"I was entrusted with people's most intimate stories."

When I think about the roots of my interest in examining the motives and meanings of *exit,* I am often drawn back to my fumbling experiences as a young researcher, making it up as I went along, trying to figure out how to comfortably and gracefully leave the "field" after I had spent months or even years living among the people I was studying. The methodology texts I read as a graduate student offered me little guidance, no road map, no useful protocols, no suggested rituals for exiting. Instead, they focused on beginnings, suggested strategies for the best ways to *enter* the field — in the trade we call this "gaining access" — which included recommendations for mapping the research terrain, identifying good informants, and developing trust and rapport with them.[8] Novice researchers were instructed in developing the casual and attentive stance of "hanging out"; trained to wait, witness, and listen before questioning; and warned about navigating the balance between being a participant and an observer. The textbook guidance that I read and heeded attended to both empirical and moral considerations, focusing on good science and ethical behavior. Of course, success in gaining access allows the researcher to begin her work, collect the data, and get the goods. Being turned away and prohibited entry can cancel out months, even years of anticipation and planning.

If the folks we hope to study do not trust our motives, if our presence feels too intrusive, if our asking seems disrespectful and our tone entitled, then people are likely to deny us entry into their lives. We will be turned away. The research will not proceed; the whole thing will unravel. No wonder researchers — mostly out of self-interest — have traditionally focused on the treacherous and nervous moments when we do not have the upper hand, when we are suddenly thrown into the role of supplicant asking for something we desperately need: the consent and participation of those people we want to study. And if researchers are not careful, their supplications can turn into begging, overpromising, pushing too hard — and everyone's dignity will be at stake. Not surprisingly, then, we have invented and codified a set of strategies for gaining entry, methodological protocols that will help us open doors, mask our nervousness, and let us get on with our work.

Once we have gained the consent of our subjects, developed trusting relationships with them, shared their stories, mined their insights, observed their lives, gathered our data, and gotten the goods, we leave. We exit. Sometimes we just disappear, avoiding the farewells that may feel awkward or too painful. We may even convince ourselves that it is kinder for "them" if we just slip away unnoticed, better if we don't make such a big deal about it. For the most part, researchers make it up as we go along. As we exit, we are given very little guidance or direction, no rules or rituals, no clear codes of ethical conduct for saying our farewells. Anyway, this lack of clear methodological direction and moral vagaries are what I experienced as a new researcher, searching for guidance and wanting to say a responsible goodbye to those whose life narratives I had harvested. I wanted to exit in such a way that people would not feel abandoned or ripped off. I wanted to thank them, let them know how much I cared and how much they meant to me. I wanted to rebalance the scales of give-and-take.[9]

Over the last three decades I have come to understand that researchers' exits from the field are at least as important as our entries and even harder to accomplish with dignity and grace. We must never just disappear. I feel strongly that we must anticipate our departures, announce our plans, express our heartfelt gratitude, and always leave the door open for reconnection. But it is still true — three decades later — that methodology texts and those of us teaching research methods courses to our students tend to focus on the empirical, ethical, and social dilemmas of "gaining access," and we continue to neglect the equally complex and treacherous processes of leave-taking.

The exit stories of social scientists engaged in doing fieldwork also raise the question of voice. How is the informant's voice being heard, interpreted, and represented by the researcher? Whose story is this anyway? Who is the creator? Who gets the credit? In exiting the field, are we stealing people's stories, rifling through their drawers and making off with their valuables, their precious life experiences? Anthropologist Shin Wang wrestles with these ethical and empirical conundrums of voice and discovers the complex relationship between exiting and good storytelling.

From the time she was very young, Shin Wang wanted to be a teacher, like her father. She always loved school and excelled in it; she loved reading and writing and thinking; she loved the competition and public praise. When school let out in the afternoon, she even loved playing pretend school with her friends. So after she graduated from college, becoming a teacher seemed the only natural path forward, a career choice that she knew would fit her like a glove. She chose to teach in the inner city, at a charter school for brown, black, and poor kids, because she felt most at home working with the kids who needed her the most. And because she had always believed in the inextricable link between education and opportunity in our society, she saw schools as the engines of equality and social justice. Shin Wang had come to this country with her parents from South Korea when she was two years old, and she knew firsthand how important schools were as sites of access, assimilation, and achievement for newcomers.

In the five years that she taught at the charter school, Shin began to recognize the ways in which her students' learning outside the classroom — in their families and communities, on the streets and among their peers, through music and digital media — were often seen as in conflict with or as a distraction from their in-school instruction. And she began to see the ways in which their families were systematically excluded from or at least not welcomed into their children's classrooms. The parents had no idea of what their children were being taught or how to navigate the school bureaucracy; they felt marginalized and powerless in making the school work better for their children. In her efforts to connect with her students and make their education seem real and relevant, Shin became interested in figuring out how to build more productive relationships with their parents, not in a superficial or symbolic way, but in a way that showed her respect for what they knew and might bring to the education of their children. But soon she began to realize her limits as a teacher trying to chart this new ground with families, limits that she believed were both conceptual and pragmatic. She realized that she needed to know more about the broader ecology of education, more about institutional change and relationship building, more about the power dynamics and politics of educational reform.

Shin decided to return to graduate school and enter a doctoral program in the anthropology of education, focusing on the ways in which urban schools in poor neighborhoods can partner with families and communities in an effort to better support the development and achievement of students. Her doctoral dissertation and subsequent research as an assistant professor have given theoretical heft and empirical definition to her study of the ways in which community organizers working with parents — particularly first- and second-generation immigrant parents — can begin to participate in school improvement efforts, the ways in which parents can become engaged and informed actors who can help make schools better places for their children. For the past four years Shin Wang has taken her anthropological research to Via Victoria, a densely populated, mostly poor and working-class

Mexican American neighborhood in Denver. She has recently made her "exit from the field," a process of farewells and retreats that has raised many relational and ethical challenges for her.

When I ask Shin how she navigated her exit from Via Victoria, she considers my question for a long time and says tentatively, "You know, I was consciously concerned about entry . . . about whether they would like me, about learning Spanish well enough to communicate with them, about gaining their trust, but I did not put a whole lot of thought into how I would leave." She remembers being nervous about the part of her personality that is "introverted," shy about connecting with lots of people, and the part of her that is "extroverted" and enjoys knowing a few folks deeply and well. In gaining access, she realized that she would have to pass the first difficult hurdle of greeting many — circulating, networking, glad-handing — before she could get to the second, the place of knowing, trust, and intimacy with a few people. Shin's preference — and her gift — she realizes, is building and sustaining relationships, getting to know a few people deeply, learning what is most important and precious to them, all the while doing it "carefully, appreciatively, and respectfully."

I listen to Shin drawing the contrasts between her extroverted and introverted sides, and I feel surprised by the two-sidedness she sees in herself. One of the first — and lasting — impressions I have of her is her wholeness, her completeness, the way she always seems balanced and centered. Part of her balance definitely resides in her body. In her mid-thirties, she has a lean, strong, and graceful body, revealing her three decades of dance training. But her balance also seems to reflect an essential quality of all good researchers. She is a listener — attentive, receptive, nonjudgmental. I look into her face, lovely in its unadorned beauty, and imagine that the quality of her listening and the earnestness of her curiosity must make people feel that they can trust her, that she will keep their stories safe, that she will not leave them without saying goodbye.

From the moment she set foot in Via Victoria, there was some "heaviness" tugging at Shin. "I felt the ominous presence of leaving from my very first trip. As I entered, I struggled with my worries about leaving." Shin never felt the burden of worry with the folks she interviewed just once or twice, the people with whom she never established a deep emotional connection. But she felt very differently about those who shared their "anxieties, fears, frustrations, and stories" with her, who often told her things they had never revealed to anyone else. It was these "close people" whom she worried about leaving from the moment she met them. "A lot of people, the closer I got to them, the more I felt that I did not want to lead them on." Shin can't think of any other way to say it, even though she recognizes that "leading them on" feels like language that belongs with romantic entanglements. "I was entrusted with people's most intimate stories. They were baring their souls to me, and I felt a huge responsibility."

Shin wants to make sure that I recognize that this "heaviness" she carried around right from the beginning was "not guilt." "I was not fooling them. Everyone knew I was not moving to Denver, that I lived in New York, and that my family was there." As a matter of fact, over the four years that she moved in and out of Denver, her exit was designed to be slow, staged, and anticipated. For the first two years, she spent a week of every month at Via Victoria, hanging out in the schools, interviewing and observing the mothers — mostly Mexican immigrants who were being trained as teachers' aides and community liaisons — as well as documenting the work of the community organizers, the leaders and trainers from the local nonprofit. By the third year, Shin was visiting less frequently, narrowing her focus to deeper conversations with fewer people, and by the fourth year everyone knew that she was beginning her retreat.

Shin remembers trying to do "something different and special" in her last conversations with the Via Victoria mothers. She saw their final encounters as "conversations," not interviews, much more informal. The tape recorder was not running; she did not take notes. "I planned them as special events," she recalls, her voice tinged with the sadness she must have felt then. She took them out for coffee or lunch and brought with her an excerpt from one of the hundreds of memos she had written about her observations of them. "I wanted them to know that they had been seen and documented. After all, they had no idea how their individual stories would figure into the narrative that I wrote." I imagine, too, that the experience of being "documented" must have held special meaning for these new arrivals from Mexico — a marker of their presence, their visibility, their significance in this still-foreign place that was becoming their home.

As well as wanting this moment of farewell to mark their documented identity as community workers and advocates for their children, Shin saw it as a moment to "shift the balance a bit." She did not want to leave without sharing more about herself. So for the first time in four years she talked more than they did. "I not only wanted to acknowledge and appreciate them . . . I also wanted to tell them how much I learned from them about being a good person, about becoming a good mother, about becoming a better researcher."

In retrospect, Shin is very glad that she made "such a special deal in these last ritualized, appreciative conversations." Something in her must have suspected that it would be hard to track them down once she left, hard to stay in touch. Her voice is tinged with regret. "I wonder if I had some sense that it might be difficult to stay connected with the mothers after I left. Maybe I realized that they would probably not be there when I returned." These were families in transition, she explains, vulnerable and fragile, who struggle mightily to hold it all together. As it turned out, Shin's premonitions held true. When she said goodbye to them, for most it was a final separation.

They did disappear. Some moved out of the neighborhood; their phones were disconnected; there were no forwarding addresses that she could find to track them down. Not being able to "follow up with them" felt like a huge loss; it made her feel as if she'd let them down in some way. Her mind lingers over the question: Should she have looked harder for them?

The same was not true, however, for the staff of community organizers and trainers who remained in place and continued to be in touch with Shin after she left — often telephoning, e-mailing, and texting her several times a week; catching her up on what was happening in the "hood"; alerting her about the important events, the births, deaths, and arrests; and occasionally seeking her counsel and guidance on matters personal and professional. When she finished writing up her research, she remembers feeling both thrilled and deeply anxious as she shared the first draft with Blanca, the lead organizer, and waited for her response. "Opening up my manuscript to her was like offering her the chance to look inside of me," says Shin about the surprisingly intimate feeling of "really being known" and the lovely sensation of trusting that Blanca would never take advantage of "this shift in roles from observer to being observed." But even more striking than the new closeness Shin felt for Blanca was the recognition that the work was not hers alone. She may have been the chronicler, she may have written the manuscript, but the recorded lives and voices represented a collective, communal effort. Shin almost whispers this discovery. "In that moment, I realized that this was not purely my project; this was her story too. I really grew to understand that she cared as much about this work as I did . . . and I understood this only after I had exited the scene."

As Shin recalls the final conversations with the Mexican mothers and the continuing relationships with the community organizers, she realizes that the exits in each case were navigated very differently. "I now recognize that there were two treatments of exit. With the families whose lives were so full of transition and upheaval, they were lost to me and I to them after I left," she says, still seeming to struggle with the "forever loss." "With the organizers, there is no sense of wrapping it all up. When I go to Denver the next time, I know exactly where to find Patricia or Maria or Sophia, and I know I will walk in the door and they will greet me with huge hugs!" With both "exit treatments," however, Shin sees the strength and intimacy of the bond defining the exit. It surprises her that the exits — in both cases — "felt so personal, so wrapped up in connection." "I now," she muses out loud, "think of exit as relationship."

When Shin anticipated making her entry into Via Victoria, she worried not only about the part of her that feels "introverted" and finds it difficult to meet and greet scores of people, but also about the distance between her life and theirs. "Here I am," she says, "a middle-class Asian American academic and researcher, flying in from New York, very worried about my proficiency in Spanish . . . and there they are, poor Mexican mothers, new to this country, many speaking only Spanish, skeptical, I'm sure, about what researchers do, and having no real reason to trust me." As it turned out, they did share something very important; she and they were mothers. But they did wonder about her. If Shin was such a good mother, why in the world would she leave her one-and-a-half-year-old daughter behind in New York and come to Denver to be with them? It seemed a curious choice.

Even though "on the face of it," Shin was "very different from them in so many ways," she probably worried most about her

"cobbled-together Spanish" — a literal barrier to communication and the perfect
metaphor for all the potential problems they
might have bridging the cultural chasm and
understanding each other. As it turned out,
Shin's stumbling Spanish seemed to invite
empathy from the mothers, who were very
patient and solicitous, reaching out to help
her with her fractured sentences. "By virtue
of me trying so hard, my effort and vulnerability provided a point of connection with
them."

And although Shin left her young daughter
at home, she was able to tell them that her
baby was being very well cared for by her
husband and her mother, who traveled to
New York from her home in Pittsburgh and
moved into their apartment every time Shin
traveled to Denver. In fact, the grandmother's "taking over the child raising"
seemed familiar and comfortable to the
Mexican mothers; they experienced the
same kind of closeness and devotion with
their own mothers. As a mother and as a
daughter of her child's grandmother, Shin
soon forged deep bonds with them; they
began sharing their stories and confidences
with her, revealing their failures and successes, and, each time she traveled back to
New York, sending kisses home to plant on

her baby's cheek.

But the place where the connections seemed the deepest and most natural was in their shared history as immigrants. Shin recalls how hard it was for her family — she was two, and her brother was born soon after they arrived — when they immigrated to the United States. Her memories of her first days in kindergarten are the most vivid. "I remember my first painful experiences of public school in Pittsburgh," Shin says, drawing the connections with the Denver mothers. "I remember my parents struggling to speak English, and the ways in which my teachers did not understand, appreciate, or respect them. My parents also had a hard time making ends meet. They struggled to put food on our table. My father had been a politician in South Korea, and when he came here, he had to sweep the floors at restaurants and clean the pots in the kitchen to make a living." Her eyes are moist with the memory of how hard it was and how painful it was to see her parents — well educated and dignified — reduced by the disrespect of the people who were so unwelcoming. "The Mexicans in Via Victoria tell similar stories . . . of being teachers and professionals in Mexico and having to work in some plastic factory in Denver."

But with all the connections Shin had with the Mexican mothers, and all the ways Via Victoria began to feel welcoming and familiar, for the four years that Shin was there, she always felt that she "was leaving somebody." "Even though I was a mother and an immigrant," says Shin, "I came there to go to work, and then I would leave. All along, my identity was shaped by the expectation that I'd be going back to my home, to my city, to my family. I think my anxiety about exiting was much more pronounced in me than it was in them . . . and of course, leaving my family behind was very hard for me." She sums up the chronic heaviness about which she was rarely aware until we began talking about it together. "Most of my research journey turned into leaving relationships, and it all had a very personal and emotional dimension about it."

The "feeling undercurrent" reminds her of the ways in which we "as a culture don't tend to acknowledge the deep connections we have, nor do we honor the difficulties of leaving." She shakes her head, thinking about the rushed tempo of her life, her friends in their thirties and forties whom she rarely gets to see because they are all so programmed and busy — young, ambitious professionals still very much on the make, "wrapped up in the logistical details that keep us running." From her point of view, the ambition, the busyness, the striving keep them from offering support to one another, developing nourishing relationships, and building a sense of community. "We are people," she says passionately, "who need and thrive on connection." Even in a culture that does not appreciate "deep connections," and even living among friends and colleagues who rush through their over-scheduled lives, Shin has tried to hold fast to her belief in the power of human connection. "I am," she says softly, "careful and intentional about the relationships in my life."

The "intentionality of connection" reminds Shin of her husband, Willard, an oncologist, who studies and treats patients with cancers (including sarcoma and chordoma) that originate from bone and connective tissues in the body and helps his very sick patients plan for how they will live out their final weeks. Many of them, says Shin, have an eerie sense of the end. "They've aggressively tried to treat the disease, it has gone into remission for a while, and they have a last chance at life. Then the disease slips back . . . and there is a quiet acceptance that the end is near."

Tears well up in Shin's eyes as she talks about witnessing the "beauty and passion" in Willard's connections to his patients and how he helps them prepare for their final exit. "I live with a husband who deals with death regularly. As a physician, he has a healthy, honest view of dying. For a lot of oncologists, death is not something they want to deal with. At the end, they focus on giving the most aggressive treatments, hanging on, engaged in a frenzy to prolong life. Willard believes that there should be a certain intentionality and care about how you leave this life. He helps patients grapple with the closing chapter. They've got to do it on their own terms."

Now Shin is weeping, letting the tears roll down her face. Her husband's ability to travel the final road with his patients, always following their lead, is rooted in his "deep connection" to his patients. When he first started treating cancer patients seven years ago, Shin assumed that he would be able to sustain himself and serve his patients only if he kept some "professional distance" from them, some clearly drawn boundaries, a practiced objectivity. But now she realizes that she was wrong. In fact, Willard is able to do the work because he "is emotionally connected to his patients." His close connection to them nourishes him. And he is not afraid to stick with them and stand by their side until the very end. "He considers the end full of meaning and choice and willfulness . . . respect and dignity, and he is in there with his patients, watching their backs, listening to their yearnings, advocating for them."

Just last week Shin heard Willard screaming into the kitchen telephone late into the night ("The only time he gets furious is when he feels a patient is not getting good care. Then he's a man on fire!"), trying to convince Delta Air Lines to let one of his patients fly home to Puerto Rico so she could die in the arms of her family. This was where she wanted to spend the last moments of her life. "During her long, painful treatment in New York, she had lost a couple of limbs, her body was badly disfigured . . . and Willard is on the phone with the airlines, spending a ridiculous amount of time, first reasoning with them, then begging them, then screaming as if his life depended on it. Please let her fly . . . we will send a doctor and nurse with her." He finally was successful in convincing them, a small victory in a long day packed with sadness and grief. The woman died the day after she arrived home, surrounded by her family.

The intentionality of Willard's helping his patients design the closing chapter of their lives contrasts sharply with Shin's memory of her father's death a year ago, when "one fine day, he suddenly collapsed" while he was teaching, and he was pronounced dead after being rushed by ambulance to the hospital. He had left home that morning looking fit and healthy. Shin and Willard just happened to be visiting their folks in Pittsburgh because her grandmother was very sick and in the hospital, and they had driven down to say their last goodbyes. Shin had even packed a black dress just in case she had to attend her grandmother's funeral. When the call came from Shin's aunt — saying that her father had fallen down at work — they rushed over to the hospital. Her tears return as Shin relives the terrifying moment. "This is the kind of exit you can't prepare for. It is so sudden. The day before, he was healthy and doing well."

But even in the case of a sudden and unexpected death, says Shin, "the moment of exit is profoundly shaped by what happens before it." She is able to tolerate the loss — although she misses him every day — because theirs was a relationship that was loving and deeply satisfying. "My father leaving this earth is very much about my relationship to him. If I had lost him and our relationship had been unresolved, difficult, and painful, I would still be consumed by regrets and anguish. But as my life has unfolded, it is very much the life my father wanted for me. Perhaps he wasn't thrilled when I decided to become a teacher, because he worried about the low status of teachers in this country. But then he saw me teaching, saw how good I was at it, and his mind was completely changed. He admired, adored, and approved of me."

Even though the goodness and completeness of Shin's relationship with her father has allowed her to mourn and move on, still feeling the support of his uncomplicated adoration, she rails at the idea of exits ever being clear and simple. Whether we are talking about leaving "the field" after finishing the data collection on a research project; whether we are witnessing the compassionate and intentional work of an oncologist helping his patients choose how they will live their last hours; or whether we are faced with the loss of a loved one who has suddenly dropped dead — from Shin's point of view the exits are "messy" and complex. Her voice is as passionate as I have heard it as she challenges the "black-and-white" version of exits. "I have trouble with the traditional ways we characterize *exit* in this culture. It makes it seem so concrete, so tangible, so open-and-shut. But exits are actually very messy. There is no instruction manual. It is not like an exit sign on the highway, where it assumes that you have a clear idea of where you are going, are looking at a map, have a route you are following, and can see the right exit and get off the road. And it is not like an exit above the door of a building, where you neatly file out under the neon sign. It is so much more complicated in reality, so much more messy because it involves people's life stories. In this culture we are always so tempted to see things simply . . . but they are not simple." Shin seems surprised by the passion that has risen in her voice. She sums up her feelings in a joyful flourish. "I'm mesmerized by the complexity."

Exits on highways and exit signs above the doors of buildings are not useful ways of describing a process that is often fumbling and awkward, uncertain and ambiguous. Shin muses about a metaphor that might more accurately reflect her views and her temperament, and she says finally, wistfully, "I think of exit as a new beginning."

"Instead of the idea that you are closing a chapter . . . instead of the idea that you live life facing backward, looking behind you to see what you are leaving — I do not think of exits as the end. As human beings, we are creatures of the moment and tomorrow. Our life is always changing and evolving. We are moving forward, focused on the future." She admits to being a "planner," someone whose style is not to be preoccupied with the past, but rather to gain energy and momentum by anticipating and designing a future.

Yet it is more than her temperamental inclination to face toward the future that makes her see exits as new beginnings. Since exits are "about relationships," and since relationships can live on in you even if someone departs or dies, then exits can certainly usher in new beginnings. Shin seems to be surrounded by the good ghosts of her father as she offers a closing reminiscence — a final prayer — about how he lives on in her. "Today, I see my father in my son. I see him when I look in the mirror and see him in the way I am growing older, the lines and contours on my face . . . There are so many ways he is still alive in me. He stays with me always and helps me chart the new beginnings."

Shin Wang, like Theresa Russo, sees exits as "messy." The metaphor of exit signs on highways — where you follow the map and know where you are going — does not adequately reflect "human exits," which are so much more complicated because they "involve people's life stories." But unlike Theresa, Shin does not find the messiness of exits painful or unmooring. Rather, she embraces, even relishes the surprises, the ambiguities, the fuzzy boundaries. The messiness, she believes, reflects the embeddedness of exits in every relationship. At one point she says sharply, "Exit is relationship." And she vividly remembers the "heaviness" she felt when she first met the Mexican mothers in Via Victoria, the "ominous presence of leaving" that consumed her from the moment she arrived there. From the very beginning she felt the responsibility of exiting in a way that was honoring and respectful of the people whose stories she was gathering. More than anything, she did not want to "lead them on."

As she reflects on the best way of navigating through the messy terrain of exit in her work as an anthropologist, Shin sees inspiration and guidance in the way her husband, Willard, cares for his patients in their dying days. He believes that "there should be a certain intentionality and care about how you leave this life." As his patients make their final exits, he lets them lead; he finds out what they need and want; he begs the airlines to let them fly home to die surrounded by their families. It is this "intentionality and care" Shin wants to mimic as she designs special occasions and rituals in her farewell conversations with the mothers in Via Victoria. She also notices that Willard seems to draw clarity and strength from the deep bonds he develops with his patients, who he knows, from the moment he meets them, will likely die in his care. He is able to sustain his energy and devotion as a doctor not by erecting professional barriers between himself and his patients, not by objectifying and distancing them, but by entering into "authentic relationships" with them. He too welcomes the messiness of intimacy. For him, "doing no harm" means exiting with care.

Finally, there is another part of leaving honorably that Shin discovers as she tells me about the rituals that shaped her exit from Via Victoria. The special occasions she designed at the end gave her the chance to let folks know how much she admired and respected them and how much she valued their contribution to the work. But even more important was her realization that she needed to shift the balance of give-and-take between herself and her "subjects." In her final conversations with them, she was not just the listener, hiding behind the mask of receptivity, soaking up their stories. This became the moment to let them hear her voice. She became the storyteller, revealing more about her own life, letting them know how much living in the midst of them had changed so much in her.

Months later, when she let one of her key informants review what she had written, she was amazed at how "opening up the manuscript to her was like offering her the chance to look inside of me." She had — for the first time — the surprising and welcome feeling of really being known. At the moment of exit, the tables were turned; the observer became the observed. But even more striking was Shin Wang's realization that the manuscript was not hers alone. It belonged to both of them. This was their shared story, a duet of voices and care.

THREE:
FREEDOM

Jean-Paul Sartre's *No Exit*[1] was first performed in a theater in Paris in 1944. It is a one-act play with four characters and is forty-seven pages in length. It presents a version of hell — a place from which it is impossible to exit, a place that is surprisingly banal, and a place of interminable suffering through the torture of self-reflection and the toxic relations among human beings.

When I first read *No Exit* in a college philosophy course forty years ago, I found it beautiful and terrifying, searing, haunting. I couldn't stop imagining the agony of people forever imprisoned, ravaged by their dark histories, their malevolent deeds, their guilt and shame, their inaction. In my most recent reading of the play, I see even more clearly how Sartre captures the hellish opposite of freedom. We are free when we are able to exit from those forces and circumstances — the people, relationships, institutions, countries, ideologies, religions, ourselves — that hold us down or back, that hurt and oppress us, that limit and lie to us. Sartre helps us understand the powerful and productive forces that propel leave-taking — the lifesaving and life-giving meanings of exit.

For those of you who have not read — or recently reread — this short and towering play, let me draw the scene and briefly summarize the plot, a prelude to this chapter's narrative of a young boy who was mercilessly bullied and tortured by his peers in school. After years of numbing abuse, humiliation, and heartbreak, he found the door out of the hellish place where he and his family had been held as prisoners. He discovered the exit that would set him free.

The three condemned souls in Sartre's play are a man named Garcin and two women, Inez and Estelle. The fourth character, the valet, appears at the beginning of the play. The action takes place in a room furnished in the Second Empire style. The valet ushers in three characters, Garcin first. Through Garcin's questions to the valet, we learn several interesting features of this hell. The room contains no mirrors, no reflective surfaces at all. There are no instruments of torture. There is no sleep, no dreams, and no blinking. Garcin comes to understand the horror:

> Your eyelids. We move ours up and down. Blinking, we call it. It's like a small shutter that clicks down and makes a break. Everything goes black; one's eyes are moistened. You can't imagine how restful, how refreshing it is. Four thousand little rests per hour. So that's the idea. I'm to live without eyelids. No eyelids, no sleep; it follows, doesn't it? I shall never sleep again. But then — how shall I endure my own company?[2]

Also, you cannot turn off the lights in the room, there are no windows, and there is a bell that rings but is not guaranteed to bring the valet. A penknife, a heavy bronze ornament, and three couches complete the description of the room.

Inez and Estelle are next to be brought into the room/hell, and the play's momentum and action are carried by the conversation among the three characters. They first share their manner of death — Estelle by pneumonia, Inez by a gas stove, and Garcin by twelve bullets in his chest. As they begin to wonder why they were placed in this room together, it is Inez who puts forth the idea that they themselves will carry out the torture that is their punishment:

> We'll stay in this room together, the three of us, for ever and ever . . . and no one else will come here. In short, there's someone absent here, the official torturer. It is obvious what they are after — an economy of man-power, or devil power, if you prefer. The same idea as in the cafeteria, where customers serve themselves. Each of us will act as the torturer of the other two.[3]

They make a pact to "look into themselves, to never raise their heads"[4] and thereby avoid harming one another. However, it is not long before they are drawn back to each other. Estelle wants to apply her lipstick and needs a mirror. Inez offers to be her mirror and expresses her attraction to Estelle. When Estelle rebuffs her, Inez points to an ugly spot on her face. Estelle seeks refuge from Inez with Garcin, who is busily ignoring the two of them, seeing their drama and incessant bickering as part of his punishment. In despair, he acknowledges that the three of them were less than honest, that they did not disclose the reasons they were deserving of hell.

By turns, we learn of the sins of their lives. Garcin was a deserter, refusing to fight with the army by claiming to be a pacifist. When he tried to escape to Mexico, he was captured and executed. Estelle, married to a rich and much older man, had an affair that produced a child. She drowned her baby and returned to her wealthy husband; her lover shot himself in the face. Inez drove her husband to despair by having an affair with his female cousin.

Garcin then proposes that they help each other. But that fails too. He asks Inez for pity and sympathy, which she refuses to give him. Estelle asks Garcin for attention and affection; he in turn rebuffs her. With the voices of the living clamoring in his head, proclaiming him a coward, he asks Estelle for her trust in exchange for his love. Estelle is not capable of faith and trust; neither is she capable of receiving Inez's attention without disgust. Garcin exclaims, "There's no need for red-hot pokers. Hell is other people."

As the reality of their situation becomes more and more horrible, Garcin flings himself upon a locked door, which suddenly flies open. As they peer into the dark hallway and argue about who should go, none of the three leave the room. They shut the door themselves. Rage mixes with sorrow as Garcin says that he died too soon, that he wasn't allowed time to finish his life's deeds. Inez cuts that line of thinking short: "One always dies too soon — or too late. And yet, one's whole life is complete at that moment, with a line drawn neatly under it, ready for the summing up. You are — your life, and nothing else."[5]

Spare, ironic, and thought provoking, Sartre's play presents hell as a place or condition from which exit is impossible. It pointedly suggests that just as we take living for granted, we take the ability to exit for granted. We live knowing full well that we could leave, change, be different, do something else, start anew. But having this potential does not mean that we use it; in fact, many of us do not. Like Garcin, who cries that he died too soon, we live in the comfort of being able to change without making the change. Exit, in this scenario, symbolizes potentiality, possibility, movement, freedom, life itself.

For Ehsan Kermanian, going to school and facing his tormentors every day is like being sent to Sartre's room without mirrors or dreams. For several years, there seems to be no exit from the hell of abuse and humiliation he is subjected to, no light in the scary darkness, no path to freedom. The assaults from his bully classmates begin to define him; he becomes imprisoned in their view of him; he blames himself for his own victimization; he absorbs their blows to his body and spirit. The story of Ehsan's entrapment and his fight for freedom are told by his mother, Neda, who, in her fierce protectiveness and advocacy for her son, struggles — courageously and desperately — to do the right thing, the loving thing.

A FRAGILE FREEDOM

**"I've used up all I've got.
There is no more."**

It started right away, the bullying and harassment. Neda begins the story by asking the question that has haunted her for the last seven years, the question that always causes her so much pain and guilt. "Why didn't I see the signs?" she asks, her eyes misting over. "Why did we hang in for as long as we did?" Actually, Neda can't remember a time when school was safe for Ehsan, not one day that was peaceful and joyful. She remembers him coming home with a sad face the day he started kindergarten. She remembers his stories about how the kids were teasing him and making him do things he didn't want to do. He told her that the scary kids would make him be "a soldier" and order him to hit or kick another child. At first Neda asked him in disbelief why he would do such things. This was not the sweet and reticent boy she knew; she had never seen him do anything the slightest bit hurtful or cruel to anyone. He was not a fighter; he didn't have it in him. But he told her that the kids threatened him if he didn't do what they ordered him to do, that he was afraid.

The Kermanians had moved to Waverly when Neda was pregnant with Ehsan. For months they had looked for a house they could afford in a suburban community with a reputation for good schools and high-achieving students. In fact, they had almost closed on a house they loved in Brookhaven when the Realtor — seeing their brown skin and suspecting that they were Iranian — refused to accept their larger-than-usual down payment. He claimed that the certified check must have come from suspicious origins. How could people who looked like they did have that kind of money? And if they did, the Kermanians certainly could not have gotten it lawfully. Neda explains that Iranians often save up for large down payments on their homes — it's "a cultural thing" — wanting to be assured that they will be able to afford the mortgage payments later on.

Neda and her husband, Toraj, knew that the Brookhaven Realtor's response to them was racist and that they might well have been able to sue him for housing discrimination. But frankly, they did not want to spend the time or money to bring him down (even though he had been stupid enough to record his "suspicions" in a letter to them), and besides, they did not want to live in a lily-white neighborhood where they were unwelcome. So Waverly was actually their second choice, another largely white, well-educated, middle- to upper-middle-class Connecticut community also known for its fine schools and its record of getting students into elite colleges and universities. Five years later, when Ehsan was entering kindergarten — in the place they had chosen because they wanted their children to have an excellent education, where they hoped to live out the American Dream — everything seemed to turn sour. Their son, Ehsan, who could barely wait to be old enough to go to "real school" — so enamored was he with books and learning — was returning home each day with terror in his eyes, afraid to speak of his torture.

A few weeks after the opening of school, when Neda could no longer bear to hear Ehsan's scary stories or see his bruised spirits, she made her first trip to the school and spoke to the principal about what was happening to her son. She told him that the five- and six-year-old bullies in his class called themselves "a team" (she always thought of them as "gangs"; they were horrible "little punks"), and they had leaders and soldiers, special handshakes, rules and routines, and tactics of torture and exclusion. The "team" seemed highly organized and very scary. The principal, dubious that these young children were even capable of such mean offenses, nevertheless gave her a hearing, asked a few guarded questions, and, before she departed, came up with what he saw as a "solution."

The next morning, he made a big announcement at an all-school assembly that there would — henceforth — be no more "teams." Neda, of course, knew immediately that the principal's facile prohibition wouldn't solve anything. The "problem was not the word 'team' "; the problem was that there were some violent little kids in her son's class who picked on the weaker ones.

163

The problem was that the adults in the school were not adequately supervising the children; they were not intervening to protect the vulnerable ones; they were doing nothing to stop the threats and the bullying. The worst place, of course, was the playground, where there was no teacher supervision. The teacher aides were supposed to be in charge, but they stood up against the wall, talking to one another, ignoring the kids. No one was watching or taking any responsibility. And when Neda inquired about who was in charge during recess, "everyone just passed the buck."

As everyone at the school kept dismissing their concerns and complaints, at home, Neda and Toraj had long conversations with their son, trying to offer him support and reassurance. They would cheer him on. "We are your team. We are with you, Ehsan." Almost every morning before he marched off to school, Neda would whisper in his ear, "Just look behind you, and I'll always be there." To which he began to respond, more desperately each day, "I look back, but you're not there." Their counsel and love were not nearly enough to protect him; there was no shielding him from the "bad kids."

Neda shakes her head, as if she is trying

to chase away the memories of the ways her precious son was selected as the victim, "partly because of his personality and partly because he is brown and Iranian." It is harder for her to name the individual qualities of Ehsan that might have "brought on the bullying" than it is for her to identify the currents of racism and xenophobia that surely had a part in his victimization. Her voice is sad and tentative. She is searching for a way to give an honest appraisal of "how Ehsan might appear to his peers," but she does not want to be disloyal to him. "Ehsan is a follower, very fragile and not assertive. Anyone who would see him would guess that he is studious, bookish, very earnest. He's not a boy's boy who is strong and athletic, not tough and aggressive. Maybe there is something in the way he moves through the world that announces his openness, his vulnerability . . . He broke his leg in the first grade, and he still walks with a bit of a limp. After he broke his leg, I didn't take him to physical therapy, so he never walked quite right again. That's a source of huge guilt for me." Her face is stained with tears as she looks back on a moment when she might have helped him make a stronger comeback — a mother's guilt and self-incrimination seared into her memory.

But even though she is able to admit Ehsan's fragility and the ways he might have made himself an easy target for the bullies, Neda is confident that "a big piece" of the abuse was rooted in racism, prejudices passed down from parents to their children, and the harsh echoes from the post-9/11 fears that swept through the community. Neda's voice is hard and angry as she recalls the "virulent brand of racism" they have suffered as a family living in "lily-white Waverly" and the ways in which Ehsan has absorbed the worst blows. "Some of the racism here comes out of sheer ignorance and lack of sophistication. When we moved into Waverly, the woman across the street said to me 'Oh, it's so exciting you are here . . . we love ethnic food, so long as it's clean.' Mr. Howard, a few doors down, came up to my husband as he was watering the lawn and said, 'What are you, Indian or Pakistani?' Toraj told him we were Iranian, and he actually jumped back with a kind of panicked look on his face, as if terrorists might have moved onto the block. Things have settled down some, and some of these folks have become good neighbors, but there are still undercurrents of fear. At school, Ehsan got the brunt of it. You know, I think that if there were black kids who were getting treated like this at school, no one would have put up with it, but there is tolerance for assuming Iranians might be terrorists — a tolerance for their making my son into a violent soldier so that he will fit their stereotype of him. It's horrible!"

Neda's whole body is shaking and her fists are clenched as she recalls "the awful coming together" of Ehsan's personal qualities — "how he moves through the world" — and the "virulent racism" in the town. She hates that those same qualities she loves so much in him — his studiousness, his earnestness, his empathy, even his softness — are the very ones that seem to invite the bullies' torture. And she hates the fact that it is so hard to identify the roots of abuse, so hard to actually figure out why a child — any child — might become the chosen target. It is complicated and painful to unravel the sources of victimization.

She thinks, for example, of a boy in Ehsan's class who is from Sri Lanka, whose skin is much darker than Ehsan's, and who turns out to be "one of the top bullies." "He knew," says Neda bitterly, "that in this all-white class (actually there is one Asian girl), if he didn't join in the bullying, he would be next." And closer to home, Neda notices the contrasting experiences of her two children, both brown and Iranian. Sadaf, Ehsan's younger sister, has always "fit in and thrived" in school; the "world is her oyster." In fact, ever since she entered school, Sadaf has enjoyed popularity among her peers, who seem to respond to "her exuberance, her fairness, and her strength." Whatever the complex causes of abuse are, whoever initiates it, however it happens and gets sustained, Neda knows one thing: it is bad and wrong, and no one deserves to be bullied.

By the time Ehsan reached the second grade, he had learned that "you don't snitch." The awful stories of being terrorized seemed to disappear, and "everything went subterranean." Although in retrospect it is clear that his sullen silence was hiding the ongoing abuse, Neda and Toraj hoped desperately that things had changed at school. They greeted his silence as good news, or at least as evidence of his toughening up, his developing survival skills. Without the everyday evidence of torture, second grade seemed relatively uneventful — except for some troublesome reports from his teacher, who complained that Ehsan was "getting stuck on stuff," that he was unable to complete his assignments in class and move on to the next thing. He would "analyze things to death." But even the teacher's worries did not upset Neda that much; she admits she also is a bit "obsessive," also someone who "analyzes things to death." Maybe these were qualities in Ehsan that he simply inherited from her.

But by the third grade, Ehsan's teacher was suggesting that he was not merely getting "stuck"; she claimed that he was "falling further and further behind cognitively." This description of Ehsan — as cognitively impaired — did not at all square with his parents' view of him. "How could that be?" they asked his teacher. "At home he speaks and reads Farsi as well as English fluently. He devours his science books, asks great questions. He plays the piano and practices diligently . . . He seems to have a really good mind." But the teacher persisted, offering enough "evidence" to prove her point and raise doubts in the minds of Neda and Toraj. She insisted on signing him up for a battery of special education assessments before sending him on to fourth grade.

When Neda consulted with family, friends, and colleagues who had known Ehsan over the years, they all — each and every one of them — expressed suspicion at the way he was being seen, labeled, and pigeonholed by his teacher. They urged Neda to resist and refuse to follow the teacher's wrong-headed prescriptions. They begged her not to let her child endure what they were sure were racist insinuations. But her desire to prove the teacher wrong got tangled up with her own real worries about her son's struggles and caused Neda to agree to the teacher's plan for an evaluation.

Fortunately, the results of the special education assessment, scheduled for the beginning of the next school year, arrived at the same time as Ehsan's scores on the fourth-grade Connecticut state exams, on which he received a "remarkably high score" that put him well beyond most of his peers in academic preparedness. And when Neda and Toraj met with the school counselor, social worker, psychologist, and neurologist — the diagnostic team that had tested Ehsan as part of the special education assessment — each of them talked about his intelligence and thoughtfulness, his eagerness to please, and his capacity to engage in relational conversations. They could see no evidence of a cognitive deficit.

They did report, however, that he was being compromised by a hostile educational environment, by his fears for his own safety, by his isolation and ostracism in school. Ehsan's fourth-grade teacher, who liked and admired Ehsan from the start and could see that he was both very bright and very vulnerable, designated herself as his "big protector," an assignment that she took seriously. Neda remembers her fondly. "Mrs. Rhodes was a large, plump woman, a protective figure who took him under her wing," she says appreciatively. When the other children went out for recess, Mrs. Rhodes would have Ehsan stay inside with her to help with classroom chores. She was careful not to assign him a seat close to one of the known bullies. She had eyes in the back of her head, always alert to the subtle, covert signs of threat and harassment in her classroom.

As Neda tells the long, painful saga, there are moments that stand out as pointed and powerful, moments when she felt as if someone were kicking her in the stomach. One such moment happened right before returning to the United States after spending the summer in Iran, just before Ehsan's fourth-grade year. Every summer, the Kermanians visited Iran, the place where Ehsan always seemed happiest, where he loved hanging out with his cousins, who treated him like some kind of "rock star" because he lived in America, the country they thought of as the promised land. As they were packing their bags to come home, Neda remembers Ehsan saying out of the blue, "I don't have any friends." His face — which had been animated and smiling the whole time they were in Iran — turned sad and sullen. She asked, "Who do you play with at recess?" "No one," he responded. "How about lunchtime?" "Ricky won't let anyone sit with me at lunch." Ricky was the ringleader who had bullied Ehsan since kindergarten, a big, scary figure who ruled all the other kids, whose threats had for four years defined and limited Ehsan's life at school.

Ricky was the boss of everyone, even Jessica, a popular Chinese American girl who often did his bidding and was the first to confront Ehsan when he returned from Iran. One day at recess she got up in his face and said provocatively, "China is the best country in the world." To which Ehsan responded with as much strength as he could muster, "No, Iran is the best country in the world." "Iran," said Jessica, "is where all the terrorists come from!" Ehsan slunk back from her, but when he got home, he told Neda that he wanted her to "take action." This felt like such a deep insult to him, so stupid and mean and untrue.

The next day, Neda took herself to school and found Jessica and her mother standing just outside the front door. Seeing Neda striding toward them, Jessica's mother (one of the "in moms" in town) urged her daughter to go inside. "Go along, my darling," she said gently, pushing her daughter toward the door. But Neda insisted that Jessica stay; she wanted to talk to both of them. She made the little girl repeat what she had said to Ehsan about Iran being the place where all the terrorists lived. And when Jessica's mother asked her daughter why in the world she would say such a thing, the girl responded immediately, "Because that's what you tell us at home." There was nothing her mother could say; she had been "outed" by her daughter.

After hearing the story, Mrs. Rhodes sat down and talked with both children and afterward made Jessica write an essay on Iran, a seven-page paper on the country's rich and long history. "For Ehsan," remembers Neda, "it didn't take away the hurt, but it felt like some small redemption." But the exchange caused Mrs. Rhodes to worry. Maybe the bullying might be avoided if Ehsan would stop wearing his cultural identity on his sleeve; maybe he was being the provocateur. If he would just stop boasting about Iran to his classmates, they might stop teasing him. "She was trying to be helpful," says Neda. "But in this post-9/11 environment, where everyone saw us as the dangerous enemy, there was no way Ehsan could avoid their prejudice . . . and besides, he is very proud of his country!"

Soon after the Jessica incident — just when Neda was beginning to hope that things were settling down at school — she was drying Ehsan's head with a towel after he had taken his evening shower, and she discovered several bumps and lesions. "Ricky pushed me on the playground," he responded when she pressed him about what had happened. "But I don't want any trouble. He's done it many times before," Ehsan mumbled. Neda stayed quiet, but she was shaking, and her stomach was in knots. "That was the biggest mistake I've ever made," she confesses about her silence and inaction at that moment. Because the brutality didn't stop as Ricky and his "team" continued to beat up on her son.

One day, when she couldn't hold her tongue any longer, Neda approached Ricky at school and tried to find a tone that was both casual and threatening. "Hey, Ricky, cool it on the playground. Ehsan's coming home with bruises." That night, just as they were sitting down for dinner, the phone rang, and when she answered it, Neda heard Ricky's mother raging at her. "Don't you ever speak to my child like that again!" she screamed. Ricky's mother, a big-time lawyer, refused to believe that her son was bullying; and she wanted Neda to back off and leave him alone. There was no apology, no effort to understand or empathize. No remorse. "After that," says Neda, weeping, "the thing began to crescendo, and I began to realize the huge role that the mothers were playing in this harassment. It was the mothers who were promoting this at home." Just as their children were ostracizing her son, so too were those mothers beating up on Neda. Her voice is almost shrieking at the double injustice. "I am not one of those kiss-ass moms. They resented me. When I would approach them, they would stop talking and just stare at me, as if they were hiding something."

I look across the table at Neda — a beautiful, graceful woman, with ringlets of cascading black hair framing her face and fine features that reveal every emotion — and wonder why the "kiss-ass" mothers hate her so much. Is it her brown skin, her mother country, her steely strength, or even her effortless grace that gets stuck in their craw?

Or is it their fierce protection of their children, who have inherited their parents' prejudices, whose guilt they are determined to hide? Whatever their motivations, Neda has the clear sense that the bullying begins — and is condoned — at home. And these mothers are power brokers in Waverly, not only in the way they band together and protect their children but also in the way they influence and control the teachers and principal at school, who do not want to get on their wrong side.

By the time Ehsan reached fifth grade, it was obvious to everyone that he was suffering; the abuse had turned inward. In class he would often be seen staring vacantly into the distance, rocking back and forth in his chair, or holding his pencil in his tight fist until it splintered under the pressure. He was anxious all the time and developed lots of nervous tics that became the focus of further teasing. At home he engaged in obsessive rituals around food and eating, washing up, and cleaning his room. Neda and Toraj found a child psychiatrist for him to see, and Ehsan had regular appointments with the school counselor. They went into crisis mode, seeking support, searching for answers, plotting interventions. Their efforts to help sometimes brought out conflicts among them as they tried to figure out the most protective strategies of defense for Ehsan. The psychiatrist, school counselor, and to some extent Toraj thought that Ehsan needed to develop a thicker skin, a tougher stance; he needed to learn how to fight back. They suggested karate lessons; they used role-playing to help him learn quick, automatic responses to the attacks. Neda, on the other hand, hated the thought of violence, even if it was for the purpose of scaring the bullies away. And she believed that training Ehsan to be more aggressive would certainly backfire. He didn't have a fighting bone in his body, and his abusers would surely see through his brittle armor.

As they all searched for some way to "fix" the situation and watched Ehsan spiral into despair, Neda felt more and more helpless — a helplessness that soon turned into rage, which finally got unleashed. She speaks in the present tense, as if she is still in the midst of the pitched battle. "Now I am really angry. In America, if you show passion, they call you a crazy woman. All along, I had been trying to hold it in, appear calm and collected, stay focused . . . but now I was ranting and screaming." When Ehsan's class was preparing to take a weekend nature expedition at a camping site a couple of hours away from Waverly, Neda put "everyone on alert." She insisted that the teachers and parents, who were accompanying the children, let her know what their plan was for constant and vigilant supervision. Her voice was threatening. Her "teeth were bared" in her fierce lioness protection of her boy. The whole time they were away, she worried, tossed and turned in her sleep, and woke up screaming from her horrible nightmares.

Another unforgettable moment sticks in Neda's mind as a "turning point." Soon after the class returned from the camping trip, she went up to the school to pick up both of her children. The kids were outside in the back field, and as she turned the corner around the school, she could see far across the field — Ehsan in the center of a circle of taunting children, swinging his backpack, trying to protect himself from their threatening advances. She could hear the nasty singsong in their voices: "Ehsan where's your gun? Don't you terrorists have guns? Shoot us if you want to . . . Kill, kill, kill." Then she saw her daughter running toward the school, screaming as she tried to get some teachers to come out and help. Neda tore across the field, yelling at the top of her lungs. The bullies scattered when they saw her coming.

But this time she could clearly see the "escalation of things"; this time she knew it was "the beginning of the end." "I saw this as the beginning of physical violence against both of my kids," she says, her voice hard and angry. "This time Sadaf was being pulled in as she tried to protect her brother. It was as if the whole thing was rotting away, with worms coming out of it." Returning to the car, with both of her children sobbing, Neda decided that school had become much too dangerous and that life — for all of them — had grown toxic and "rotten." There were only a couple of weeks left to the school year, but she was determined that her son would not enroll in the sixth grade in September. He would not advance to one of the two middle schools in Waverly.

It turned out that Ehsan was not ready to give up. After all, he had been raised by his parents to believe that "giving up meant failure." If he threw in the towel, he would always be seen as weak and unworthy. For as long as he could remember, his mother and father had told him what their parents had always told them: "The Kermanians never give up." It had been the family litany, their immigrant survival chant, passed down through generations, spoken with bravado

and pride. Those four determined words —
"Kermanians never give up" — had covered
over their fears, stoked their courage, and
made them feel as if they had the upper
hand even when they were being threatened
and ostracized.

Besides, Ehsan thought that he had a
chance in middle school, where there would
be some new kids from two of the other
elementary schools in town; maybe this
would offer him a new opportunity to
change the way other kids treated him. He
knew that William, one of his neighborhood
buddies who lived right down the street and
had always been nice to him, would never
turn against him. A year older than Ehsan
and well liked in school, he might even
become a kind of protector. Ehsan pleaded
with his parents. "William will watch out
for me . . . I'll be okay . . . let me try it."
Reluctantly Neda and Toraj gave in to their
son's pleadings. They worried a lot, but they
admired his courage, his determination to
stick it out. And once they gave him their
consent, they stopped their doubting and
offered words of encouragement and support. "We're with you . . . always with you."

Neda and her children had just come in
from buying school supplies at Staples when
they discovered the bullying messages on

Ehsan's computer. "You are a disgusting creep." "You fucking ass-hole." "There we were, the night before school opened," recalls Neda sadly, "with all of these new, shiny things — backpacks, notebooks, pencils — allowing ourselves to feel so hopeful, and then this crap comes over cyberspace. We were feeling so violated." She searched to find the address of the offenders and discovered that the messages came from a housing project across town — Atrium Homes — one of a handful of places in Waverly built for low-income residents. Toraj was out of town on business. Neda's mother rage could not be contained. She told her children to lock the door behind her, and she jumped into her car and raced across town, determined to track down her prey. Even though she found the apartment complex, she had no idea where the cyberbullies actually lived. She stalked around in the darkness for a while, checked the mailboxes downstairs in the entry, watched a few residents come and go, and finally realized that "this was crazy." Her rage had taken her to a dangerous place. "If I had been able to figure out where they lived," she says without bravado, "I would be in jail now."

It turned out not to be the bright opening

day they had all hoped for, filled with new energy and resolve. Neda headed up to the middle school without her son and announced to the principal that she was pulling him out. The principal heard her story of the night before, promised to follow up immediately and punish the offenders. Then he begged Neda to let Ehsan return to school, claiming that he would take "personal responsibility" for seeing that the boy was safe. Neda was wary of the parade of promises, weary of hearing all the principals (by now she had dealt with four of them) express concern and offer solutions that never worked, but there was still something in her, some shred of hope, some shadow of belief in her son's ability to survive. Maybe this time the principal's words would be followed by protective actions that would keep Ehsan out of harm's way. So she gave in. And Ehsan — with fear and hope in his heart — arrived at middle school the following morning.

"The principal did try to provide him with a safe space," Neda recalls with resignation and rage creasing her face. "He talked to the teachers and asked them to keep a special eye out for Ehsan. He had him come to 'quiet lunch,' a small room set aside for the children who felt intimidated in the big cafeteria. He allowed him to stay in from recess whenever he chose to." But it was only days before Ehsan was coming home with bruises from being thrown up against the lockers by the bullies from his old school, with stories of their dumping his science notebooks in the garbage, with tales of being cornered and roughed up in the boys' bathroom. If anything, the bullying was more brutal and treacherous than what he had suffered in elementary school.

When Neda — once again — begged the principal to contact the parents of the children she knew to be the culprits, he was reluctant, then dismissive. "You should have seen how fast he retreated when he realized how thick all of this was . . . and which parents were involved. They were the blue bloods, and he was not going to approach them." Her voice oozes cynicism. "Very quickly that principal made the political choice not to confront them.

"It was a Thursday afternoon, on a very cold, blustering day in January," Neda begins, shuddering with memories of the frigid weather and the horror that was on the horizon. "I drove up to the middle school to pick up Ehsan and waited for a long time out front, after all the buses and cars had left. When he didn't come out, I decided to drive quickly over to get Sadaf at her school and then circle back. Sadaf and I drove back to the school. It was now more than an hour after dismissal. Finally I went into the school and found only the janitors sweeping up the floors. Everyone had gone home. We looked around outside. He was nowhere. I decided to call the police to tell them he was missing. Everything in me was trembling with fear. As we're driving back toward home, I spot a figure moving through the woods along the side of the road. It's Ehsan. He's all scratched up, looking terrified. At the end of the day, those punk kids had ambushed him inside the school building. They wouldn't let him leave. He laid low, and finally, after they had grown tired of taunting him and left the building, he escaped and made his way through the woods so they wouldn't spot him."

A couple of weeks later, as he was getting his books out of his locker between classes, Ricky and his guys pushed Ehsan so hard against the locker that he came home with blood running down his face. Neda remembers the scene as if it were yesterday. "When I picked him up from school, he was wearing his big winter boots, and he kicked the side of the car so hard . . . I can remember the sound of his boots hitting the car, and I remember thinking, This is the sound of a wake-up call." Ehsan was angrier than Neda had ever seen him, dark with fury. He walked into the house, shoved his sister out of the way, stomped up the stairs, crawled into bed, pulled the covers up over his head, and refused to move or talk to anyone. It was at that "dark and miserable moment" that Neda knew they were at the end. "I can't take this anymore," she recalls saying out loud to herself. "This is tearing my family apart. I'm done. We're not going back!"

Neda and Toraj had no idea what they would do after pulling their son out of school. They had no Plan B. They were propelled completely by their "sense of desperation, exhaustion, helplessness, and hopelessness" and their determination that they would no longer allow Ehsan to be brutalized. For several days they flirted with the idea of sending him to live with Toraj's brother in Iran. On their annual summer visits there, he had developed a close relationship with his uncle, and Iran was the place where Ehsan always felt strong and safe, embraced and adored by his extended family. But the thought of sending him so far away, even to trusted relatives, felt unbearable to his parents. Private schools were well beyond their means, and they reasoned that those elite places might also be sites of abuse for Ehsan. They "thrashed around," hoping to find a viable option. Every day, it seemed, Neda spent "hours and hours" making calls and sending e-mails; reaching out for guidance and advice from friends, colleagues, and associates.

In one such conversation, with a former professor and trusted mentor, she wept her way through the long and terrifying saga of the bullying, and she received a surprising response. "Why," said her mentor, "don't you homeschool him?" A wave of relief washed over Neda as she listened to the "sage advice" of someone whose judgment she trusted. At that moment a door seemed to open for them, an option they had never considered, and Neda and Toraj grabbed on to it for dear life. "It was as if something very heavy and ominous lifted from around us . . . we could finally let go and breathe!"

Monday, February 23, 2009 — the date is etched in Neda's mind — was Ehsan's first day of homeschooling, and at the end of that week they marked the occasion with a family celebration. Toraj made special Iranian treats for dinner; they decorated the table with their fanciest silverware and dinner plates, warmed themselves around the woodstove in the kitchen, and raised their crystal glasses to make toasts. It was a beautiful moment. Neda looked over at her son and for the first time in years saw the sparkle in his eyes and heard the magical sound of laughter come out of his mouth. "In five days," she recalls, "he was giggling . . . he had returned to us. From that moment on, we never looked back."

Now Neda is smiling, a radiant mother-lion smile. But almost immediately her tone turns somber again as she asks herself the question that began our interview. "Why, oh why, did I wait so long to rescue my boy?" This time she turns toward the past, revisiting images and feelings from her own childhood. When she thinks about the abuse of Ehsan and the way in which the terror almost destroyed their family, she sees herself as a young girl of eight watching the sadness that was eating away at her father when he moved his family from Brooklyn to Matunuck, Rhode Island, hoping to escape the dangers and dirtiness of the city, hoping to find some measure of safety and peace. Instead they found themselves in a place where they were even more isolated and ostracized, a place that felt foreign and strange and inhospitable to them. Her father had moved his family to this small fishing village — "we are from the desert," says Neda with exasperation — where everyone in the town was white except for one African American family.

"My father was so depressed," Neda recalls tearfully. "I would go into that tiny room where he was sitting all alone, all bent over, the air thick with his anguish." But even in the midst of his deep sadness and disappointment, her father "loved America and everything American," and he believed that the hardships and prejudice they faced had to be endured, that they could not give up; they needed to push on. When Neda and Toraj were "self-destructing as a family," when they were enduring "battle after battle, trying to push Ehsan when he was in so much danger," she must have been hearing the echoes of her father's admonitions. Never, ever give up. Be grateful that you have the opportunity to become a part of this great country. Count your blessings. "As a matter of fact," Neda muses, as if she is discovering this for the first time, "I'm now realizing that Toraj and I probably bought this house in this neighborhood so that my father would approve of us . . . approve of our very American choice."

When Neda's family arrived in America

and moved to a tenement in Brooklyn, it was the middle of the school year, and she spoke not a word of English. Her older brother, who knew some English, walked to school with her on the first day and registered her in the first grade. The second day, he also accompanied her on the mile-and-a-half trek to school. But on the third day she was on her own, with a note pinned to her that said, "My name is Neda. I am lost. This is my phone number." "It was very scary, and I was desperately lonely," she says, reliving the moment and connecting it to her own deep survival instincts, her own capacity to endure the pain and keep going, and her own reluctance, as her son's mother, to give up on his behalf forty years later.

When her family moved to Matunuck a few years later, she, like Ehsan, had no friends. She, like Ehsan, endured lots of teasing, although no physical bullying. And she was torn apart by her desire to fit in, her pride in being Iranian, and her devotion to the place her family still called "home." Now she is able to see and name what was going on. "These are the struggles of an immigrant," she says evenly, "the contradictions and tensions of assimilation and acculturation . . . the casualties and choices we are faced with." But being able to offer an analysis of the "contradictions" is not the same as witnessing your son being beaten up and feeling — in your stomach — the burn and fury of a very personal unfairness. She feels the mother rage in her body. "When I think back to that day in January when Ehsan was so furious and out of control that he kicked our car, I still can feel it in my gut. It is still in my body . . . the fear, the rage, the anger . . . and the feeling that I've used up all I've got. There is no more." Now she is raising her fist and beating the air at the memory of the moment when the decision to exit was made. "This is not quitting. We're done."

When Neda says "in my body," she starts to weep. Several months ago she was diagnosed with breast cancer, and she is certain — beyond a shadow of a doubt — that the malignancy is a result of the stress and grief that consumed her life and settled in her organs. "My cancer is a response to all the toxic nights of no sleep, all the pain and anguish running through my body," she says definitively. Lean and strong, Neda has been a marathon runner and vegetarian for most of her adult life; she has never been seriously ill or hospitalized for even a day. The evening that the oncologist called with the diagnosis, Neda knew the bad news before he even said the words.

She had been standing outside on the deck of their new country house, looking out across the lake. The house had been in foreclosure, and they had "bought it for a steal." After all the stress over the last several years, they had wanted a place to go on weekends for peace and healing, where they could go with friends to "create laughter in the house," where the family "could compose a new set of memories." "After so much suffering," says Neda softly, "we wanted a place to change the energy, to detox as a family." Their first night there, with hope shining through the moon's rays, listening for the laughter of her children, Neda heard the news of her illness, and all she could say — softly to herself — was "of course." "I knew something like this was going to happen . . . it was inevitable. The cancer was the embodiment of all of those years of anguish."

It turned out that not having to return to school not only brought laughter back into the house, it also meant that Ehsan was able to pursue learning in a way that was more in keeping with the way his mind — and heart — works. Without the regimen of schedules and classes and tests, without the constraints of teacher-directed learning, without having to worry about what his classmates might think of his earnestness, his seriousness, and his probing questions, Ehsan was free to follow his curiosities, learn at his own pace, pursue subjects and fields deeply, and work late into the evening. His path could be self-directed and organic, completely individualized to his appetites and ambitions. Very early on, Neda and Toraj knew that they would not become his teachers. They each had full-time work — Toraj is a financial analyst, Neda a graphic designer — and they knew the costs and casualties of trying to combine teaching and parenting. They saw themselves as "resources" for Ehsan — perusing Listservs for homeschoolers, collecting names of people, curricula, and programs, and networking with a new community of parents and children who were also making it up as they went along. And they were able to find a fairly well-developed set of resources — a myriad of classes, experiences, and settings that could be quilted together to create a rich and rigorous curriculum for Ehsan.

The town of Waverly required them to submit a plan that spelled out the principles and pieces of his educational program — an "odyssey of the mind" workshop at the Museum of Science, a research apprenticeship in a university chemistry lab, a comparative religion class for children and their parents in the next town, tutoring in math, karate, piano lessons, and of course self-study on topics of his choice at home. "I'm not doing any of the teaching," Neda reminds me "I check out the resources, and I do have to drive him from place to place." She and Toraj also decided that there would be no testing, no assessment of his work. "Let the town ask whenever they want to have him tested," she says dismissively. "Let them knock themselves out!" Then, more gently, she reflects on their philosophy of "constructivist learning" that "fits Ehsan like a glove." "There is no homework. Ehsan just keeps on working until he stops . . . sometimes until nine-thirty or ten at night. He moves forward at his own pace and in his own way. I've stopped worrying whether he will learn specific content . . . I've begun to think that now that he has a clearer and freer mind, he will absorb it all."

Neda offers me an example of how Ehsan follows his own learning path, how his fascinations lead to questions, study, data gathering, and projects. A few months ago he went to the bat mitzvah of one of his friends who lives across the street, and he became fascinated with Judaism. His curiosity led to questioning and reading. They got the DVD of *Fiddler on the Roof,* which they watched on one of their ritual family pizza nights, which led to a "unit" that Ehsan designed for himself on World War II . . . which led to his reading *Maus: A Survivor's Tale* and *Anne Frank: The Diary of a Young Girl.* Then Ehsan became interested in knowing more about the Japanese side of the war, so they watched Clint Eastwood's movie *Letters from Iwo Jima.* Soon after, when Toraj had to go to Hawaii on a business trip, he took Ehsan along so that they could visit Pearl Harbor. When Ehsan returned from Hawaii, Neda tracked down the class in comparative religion for home-schooled children and their parents, extending and expanding his original interest in the Jewish ritual of bar mitzvah — a learning journey that had taken some amazing twists and turns.

Ehsan is focused and disciplined about finishing the work that he sets out for himself. Occasionally he will take a break and go to Home Depot with his mother to buy plants for the garden, or he will play some computer games, or he will practice the piano or get on his bike and take a ride around the neighborhood. But the self-directedness and autonomy he relishes come with a haunting loneliness, a lingering sense of failure, shadows of self-doubt. He still wishes he could have survived the bullying and found a way to feel comfortable — even make some friends — in school. Although he feels himself learning so much more at home than he ever did in school, he still longs to be a "regular kid like the other kids" who hang out and have fun together. And Ehsan is still afraid. He will not ride his bike into the town center after three in the afternoon, because he is still panicked that he might run into the bullies when they are getting out of school and heading home. He can still hear their harassing threats; he can still feel the pain of being hit hard and physically hassled. Neda encourages him to take small steps out into the scary territories, but Ehsan's movements continue to be circumscribed by fear — a fear, however, counterbalanced by a freedom he has never known, the freedom to learn, to be himself, to push the limits of his intelligence.

The other day, when Neda was buying vegetables at the Orchards, she spotted the mother of the big bully Ricky standing by the tomatoes, and she offered her a broad smile. Ricky's mother looked back quizzically and then forced a stiff smile in her direction, trying to figure out why Neda seemed to be greeting her so kindly. "I smiled at her in thanks," says Neda genuinely. "I wanted to say to her, You pushed us over the edge until we could not bear it any longer . . . and now we are free!"

In Sartre's play, the condition of no exit — hell — is one that has no mirrors, no sleep, and no dreams. This represents total entrapment. Without a mirror, you cannot see yourself with your own eyes; you must rely on other people to tell you what they see. This inability to regard yourself is compounded by the fact that others will never see you the way you see yourself. Without sleep, there is no rest, no respite, no suspension of reality. And without dreams, you cannot conceive of nor make a different reality. The ability to exit, then, is the ability to see yourself, to give yourself a break, to make yourself a new life.

Ehsan faces the horrors and evils of hell each day as he walks into school. He is bullied and beaten, taunted and terrorized by the gang of kids who — on the first day of kindergarten — decide that he will be their victim. The bullies force this gentle, reticent boy, this lover of books, to become a street fighter, always watching his back, raising his fists to his face to deflect their blows. They call him their "soldier" and force him to do their dirty deeds. They egg him on: "Kill! Kill! Kill!" They enjoy watching him try to turn into someone that he isn't. He gets so beaten up that he becomes unrecognizable to himself. Like Sartre's hell, there are no "mirrors" for Ehsan to see his own reflection; there is no chance to "sleep," to rest up for the next onslaught; there is no safe place "to dream" of a different reality. Like the three protagonists in *No Exit,* he turns the torture back on himself; he absorbs the abuse; it becomes who he is and how he feels about himself. Over time, the way out becomes less and less clear. Even when he is given the chance to leave, to escape from the hell in which he is entrapped, he resists. As we listen to his mother tell this tale of torture, the suffering of this child becomes unbearable, even for us. We want to scream, "Get out! Get out!"

Through it all, Ehsan's mother is by his side, fighting for his protection, bolstering his spirits, cheering him on, weeping as she cleans his wounds, suffering with him every day. She suffers as well, not knowing what advice to give her son. Should she — as the child psychiatrist suggests — prod him to learn the moves of a fighter, help him learn to fake his fierceness? Or should she — as his fourth-grade teacher, Mrs. Rhodes, warns — tell him to stop wearing his Iranian heritage on his sleeve? Or should she try to help Ehsan find within himself a sturdy self-confidence, a nonviolent self-defense that might eventually erode the motivations of the thrill-seeking torturers?

The daily grind of humiliation and abuse are punctuated by unforgettable moments that rock their world. Neda discovers the lacerations on her child's head as she dries him after his shower; she tries to track down the cyberspace bullies when they sully Ehsan's e-mail with dirty name-calling; she chases away a crowd of kids who are circling him in the field behind the school, hurling racist jeers at him. Each time Ehsan gets hit, Neda feels it in her gut; his scars are seared into her body. With each mounting transgression she struggles with herself; she weighs the toll of suffering, the costs of staying. And she looks for the exit sign.

Finally the day arrives; it is crystal clear in her memory. That day, when she goes to pick him up after school, Neda can hear the sound of Ehsan's deep pain, his desperation, his big winter boot kicking the side of her car — "the sound of the wake-up call." At that moment she knows in her bones it is over, all over. There is no turning back. Unlike Sartre's three prisoners who are so far gone, so damaged and ruined that they refuse to leave hell even when they are given the chance, Neda and Ehsan see the exit sign over the door, and they walk through.

We listen to this tortured tale and wonder why they stayed so long, why they remained so stuck in their misery, why they were willing to absorb so much abuse. As she tells the story of her son, Neda discovers echoes from her own childhood. She remembers the lonely, scary walk on her first day of school after her family arrived in Brooklyn, and the sign her parents pinned to her jacket just in case she got lost, since she did not speak a word of English. Rehearsing Ehsan's story has made her recall the ways in which she too was bullied and ostracized by the white kids in Matunuck who hated her because she was brown and foreign. (Wasn't it punishment enough that this desert girl was forced to live by the sea?) She suffered and survived. She absorbed the blows (although hers were not physical) and kept moving. Perhaps it took Neda so long to save her son because the terrain — of terror — felt so recognizable; it was ugly, but painfully familiar. She has the scars to prove it.

But beyond her childhood memories of

abuse at the hands of her schoolmates, Neda can still hear her father's voice singing his love for America, claiming it as the land of opportunity, urging his children to be grateful for their blessings, admonishing them to face and endure any hardships, any barriers that might stand in their path. "Kermanians never give up" was the family chant that Neda absorbed and then passed on to her son. It is an immigrant story — a story of sacrifice and endurance, of punishment and survival, of selling your soul if that is the price of admission, the bargain you make for reluctant acceptance. The "American choice" sliced in with grief. When Ehsan faces the bullies in school and suffers their humiliations, he is carrying on the proud and painful generational legacy. He is not just trying to stand up for himself; he is suffering in the name of those who came before him. His battle scars are signs of his gratefulness. Over and over, he battles and suffers and is grateful, until he can do it no longer. When the torture finally becomes too excruciating for this noble and beaten "soldier" to bear, he wins by walking away.

But the freedom is fragile and the wounds are deep. It is a costly win. For the first time in years, Ehsan's parents see the light return to his eyes; they hear his giggles of laughter. He is set free to learn, to be curious, to be as smart as he dares. But the wounds are still raw; he is wary and afraid; he is still watching his back and staying under the radar just in case the bullies might ambush him in town when he passes by on his bike. His mother protector also suffers the "exit wounds" from their fight for freedom. They are seared into her body; they have taken over her organs and given her cancer, an "embodiment of all those years of anguish." But even their wounds and their grieving do not stop her from feeling gratitude toward those who "pushed them over the edge," because if it weren't for them, Neda and her son would never have seen the exit.

FOUR:
WOUNDS

The costs and casualties of Ehsan's and Neda's escape to freedom remind us of the
wounds we may carry with us long after we
have walked through the exit to freedom.
The wounds are physical and emotional,
visible and invisible, conscious and unconscious, layers of injury that cause damage
and leave scars. Ehsan's bloody face after
he is thrown against the locker, the lesions
on his head after Ricky has pounded him
on the playground are the physical signs of
battle, but they may not be as brutalizing as
the injuries he suffered to his soul and spirit.
Likewise, Neda's cancer appears to be a
physical expression of all the years of grief
and anguish she absorbed trying to protect
her child.

Their years of suffering at the hands of
the bullies (and their "kiss-ass" mothers)
also remind us that wounds are both in-
flicted by others and self-inflicted. The

entrapment of Sartre's protagonists is a result of the unspeakable deeds that landed them in hell but also a result of their own self-hatred and shame, the tortured ways they caused themselves misery. Likewise, after years of abuse at the hands of his schoolmates, Ehsan begins to punish himself, banging his head against the wall, obsessing over his food, cutting himself on the shards of pencils he has gripped too tightly. His self-destructive acts are as toxic and deeply felt as the bullies' taunts.[1]

The wounding also travels across generations. The loneliness and pain from Neda's childhood echoes in her heart, messes with her mind, and distorts her judgment as she struggles to protect her son. She can visualize her own father bent over in a dark room after he has moved his family to the town by the sea, his face creased in despair even as he chants the blessings of his American life. This sadness gets passed down from generation to generation,[2] coursing through the bloodstream, making the grandson more susceptible to melancholy, more accepting of the loneliness that his parents and grandparents endured. Freedom is the opposite of entrapment. It is also the balm for the physical, emotional, and spiritual wounds passed down through the generations.

Sometimes the visible and invisible scars left over from our injuries are disabling; they hold us back, distort our self-image, compromise our strength, and make us feel ugly. We try to hide them, repress them, camouflage the pain that they represent. But scars can also signify the opposite. They can be badges of courage, signs of survival and resilience, beautiful adornments of our hard-won victory. They can remind us of our strength and our fight, and the wisdom we have earned from having endured.

The stories in this chapter are of those who seek to heal the invisible and visible wounds. Linda Gould, a psychologist and clinical psychotherapist, and Anthony Brown, an intensive care unit attending physician, minister to patients who have been deeply scarred by emotional and physical trauma. And both of them keep their eyes focused on the exits. Much of Linda's therapeutic work, in fact, is designed to help her patients exit from the histories, relationships, and self-perceptions that have made them anxious and depressed, compromised their happiness and productivity, and prevented them from realizing their full potential. She listens to their anguished stories of addiction — to alcohol, drugs, food, pornography — their tales of infidelity and abuse, their everyday neuroses, and she tries to help them discover the roots of their pain and a way out of their misery. She helps them trace the wounds that echo across the generations, from their grandparents to their parents to them. Many patients come to her in their determined effort to stop the emotional toxins that seem to flow across the generations. They do not want to pass the psychic wounds on to their children. As she helps her patients identify the path out of their misery, she also prepares them for their exit from the therapeutic relationship that they have forged together — for the day when she and they decide it is time to move on, even though their work is rarely done.

HONORING THE WORK
AND THE WOUNDS

"Farewells are often bittersweet . . . fruitful and sad . . . just as life is."

We meet in her home office, a simple, sun-filled space containing a large oak desk and swivel chair where the therapist sits, a cozy couch where her patients perch, lots of books lining the walls, and fresh flowers in a hand-blown glass vase. Linda Gould, a clinically trained psychotherapist, has for thirty years had a private practice working with adolescents and adults in individual, couples, and family therapy. At seventy, she swims half a mile every morning, takes vigorous daily walks, and happily loses track of long hours as she tills and trims her "wild" city garden. Her short and chic silver hair frames a lined face, a cragginess she has begun to appreciate and call "handsome." She moves her strong and lean body with a sexy swagger, wears lovely amber and turquoise jewelry, and decorates herself in designer clothes, most of them carefully chosen from thrift shops. She loves a good bargain. As she talks, she digs deep for emotional insights, and she punctuates her intensity and seriousness with raucous laughter.

As she talks to me, Linda avoids the therapist's chair and sits with me on the couch — a signal that she is prepared to change roles from listener to talker, from guiding to receiving the questions. Piled around her on the couch are patient folders filled with the notes she writes after every session, documenting their time together. In anticipation of our interview and wanting to protect the privacy of her patients, she has temporarily taped over their names and written pseudonyms that she refers to from time to time as she tells their stories, masking, as well, some of the details of their histories and backgrounds. Occasionally Linda glazes over the specific data that might be identifying, or she deftly refuses my inquiries for more information, all in the name of shielding her patients and doing no harm.

I have come to talk to Linda about how she guides her patients through their exits — the word therapists use is "termination." I want to hear her stories of farewell — what principles she applies, rituals she designs, protocols she practices — and I want to know how she feels saying goodbye, how she herself is affected by their leave-takings, whether she experiences relief, abandonment, or sadness. Before our meeting, she has done her "homework," gathering documents, letters, and articles from professional journals and displaying the "genograms" — her specialty — multicolored drawings on a poster-size pad that visually record the "intergenerational maps" of her patients, their family, medical, and psychological histories. From her very first meeting with her patients Linda uses the huge pad to chart the roots and branches of their stories, filling in the information as it unfolds over the months and years, and ultimately producing a summary document of intimate discoveries, often painful revelations, and surprising epiphanies.

"I start by asking new clients if they have any questions for me, before I begin to ask them my many questions," she explains. "Then I tell them how I work, which is by taking notes on this pad so that they may see the patterns. I quickly flip through the genograms of former clients and point to colors that represent major life events and experiences . . . saying, 'The black lines and circles represent alcoholism; blue is drug abuse; red refers to sexual issues; green is for prison.' I want to make certain that as the sheets flip by, they see that this is a safe place to talk about these often hidden and humiliating issues. This is a place where we can speak about anguish, shame, and guilt. I draw a horizontal line on the page, indicating whether they are only children or whether they have siblings . . . and we begin. It is often sputtering and halting at first; it takes a while to get going, but soon the information begins to flow, and they can begin to see themselves on the page." This beginning drawing, filled in over time, is the very first step on the path leading to the exit.

Linda's "generic" comments about termination quickly move to specific stories. In fact, it turns out that all the farewell rituals are highly specific, shaped by the individual and idiosyncratic relationships she forges with each of her patients. Painting with a broad brush, she begins, "Generally, in my mind, I make sure that the endings are formal. It is very important to honor the client, honor our relationship, and most of all honor the work. It is also important to help them know what work still needs to be done. We are all works of art . . . there is always more to do." Optimally, it takes two or three sessions to say goodbye productively and meaningfully, to feel that there is closure or to make a successful transition to the next therapist.

Even though Linda says that primarily she is talking about the endings of long-term therapeutic relationships, often lasting several years, she starts with her most recent example, fresh in her mind, of a patient who terminated after only two very intense months of therapy. At age twenty-four, Allison had come to Linda in early April, just before graduating from law school and just before her anticipated move to her first job in a fancy Washington law firm in late May. They knew going in that this would be a short-term therapy. From an affluent white Protestant family in Dallas, Allison had gone to an elite prep school, done her undergraduate work at Mount Holyoke College, and graduated near the top of her law school class at Georgetown University. Beautiful and graceful, she carried herself with a smoothness and dignity that belied the turmoil and terror she was feeling.

The "crisis" that brought her to therapy had to do with sexual addiction. Linda recalls, "I named it in our first session together, surprising myself by asking her whether she looked at porn . . . and that opened the door for her to talk about the trauma and shame of contracting herpes with Andrew, the man she had been seeing for three months. She came in saying that she wanted to maintain the relationship because she had herpes, even though she knew their relationship was destructive — that Andrew was emotionally distant and dismissive of her — and she lamented the fact that her herpes would keep her from having the one-night stands that had become routine for her." During their sessions Allison did a lot of crying, and "she remained addicted." Sex with Andrew, she reported, was extraordinary, "like a drug," "a monkey on her back" that would not let her go even though the pain of his disrespect and deceit was a constant and she did not trust him. The therapeutic work was primarily focused on doing what she had to do to end the relationship. They role-played together how Allison would break up with him, a termination that — ironically — paralleled the anticipated termination of their therapeutic relationship. "This was crisis management," says Linda, reflecting on the focus and rapidity of their work and the need to get it done in the two months they had together before Allison's move to Washington. Allison did manage to end her relationship with Andrew, although not in the way she and Linda had planned. The first — and easiest — place she was able to let him go was on Facebook, where she deleted his name. But she refused to change her telephone number and found it almost impossible not to respond to his text messages.

Linda was able to refer Allison to a therapist in Washington, hoping she would be able to do the "deep work" that was impossible for them to accomplish. Even though their time together was brief, Linda felt as if they had done some "good work" together; it was a start, and it was promising. At their penultimate session, Linda asked the two questions that usually frame the termination ritual with her patients. First, "What was useful in this therapy?" And second, "What do you wish that we might have covered — but didn't get a chance to — in our time together?" Allison's answers came with tears of sadness and appreciation: "This was a validation," she reflected bravely, "that I am not crazy . . . that I am not deluded. I was able to explain myself in an ordered way to someone who is not bending in my direction, someone who is wise and impartial, someone who has seen it all before."

Allison paused, looking down into her lap, trying to regain her composure, and Linda let the silence linger. Even though Allison had named the progress she had made in therapy, she knew she was far from "cured." "I could not have done what I did without therapy. But I know I need more fortification, more strengthening so I can move on and get better." Allison's awareness of the value and edification of her short-term therapy and her cognizance of those things left undone were instructive to her therapist. "I learned a lot from her," says Linda gratefully. "When someone is really focused, is as smart as hell and as motivated as she is — and has a good support system like she has with her mother and her best friend — then you can make some progress, even if they are the first baby steps, in a very little time."

The endings seem clearer and more definitive when the therapy is intentionally short-lived, when both therapist and patient are anticipating termination from the very first meeting. Exits from long-term therapies of several years are more layered and complex, with fits and starts, ambivalence and uncertainties. "In these cases," says Linda, "termination is a flow, not an end point . . . or perhaps there are a series of end points." She thinks of Mandy, now forty-two, in therapy for seven years, who came to Linda when she was twenty and a first-year law student. Linda pulls out a bright yellow folder and shows me the more than twenty years of correspondence between them, mostly holiday cards and greetings (always signed "Be well, Love, Mandy and family") and short responses by Linda, that she has xeroxed before mailing, offering appreciation and support, cheering her on (always signed "Warm wishes, Linda").

Mandy was one of seven siblings from a "dysfunctional family" where she "got very little parenting." Her mother, who suffered from psychosis, was verbally and physically abusive, unleashing most of her rage on

Mandy, who, as the oldest child, was primarily responsible for parenting her younger siblings. Over their seven years together, Linda saw Mandy through several suicidal episodes, through the discovery that she was not gay, through her studying for, failing, and then passing the bar exam, through the struggles of her love relationship with John and their marriage, through the birth of her first child, through discovering that she could manage to continue being a lawyer if she took a relatively undemanding job where she would not be working to make partner in the firm. When she moved with her family to Cleveland, Linda found her another therapist but continued to be in touch from time to time. Now that Mandy is the age of Linda's own daughters, Linda reflects on the "comfortable and easy" relationship that has survived their years of separation. "For those patients who are about the age of my children, I always feel as if I'm raising them . . . in a detached parental way." Now Linda is laughing. "Maybe I'm raising my patients in the way that I would like to be with my own kids as a parent, somewhat less involved and intrusive, somewhat less judgmental."

The kind of detached raising of Mandy, where distance and time have shaped a caring but remote relationship, is in sharp contrast with Linda's "almost boundaryless" connection to Nadine. "Nadine is in my life," Linda says unapologetically. Now thirty-one, Nadine started treatment with Linda when she was twelve, and there "has been no formal termination." Very bright, but suffering from a mild form of autism, Nadine has showed slow and steady improvement in her ability to connect with the social world around her; she has successfully completed high school and college, become certified in information technology, and is now volunteering at a hospital and working to find gainful employment. Over the years, Linda and Nadine's mother, Rachel, have seen themselves as "co-parents," "working as a team." (Nadine's father, who is divorced from her mother, lives on the other side of the country, a distant but benign presence.) The collaboration does not confuse their different roles. Linda is quick to say, "I tell Rachel that she is the mother. I'm in Nadine's life a few hours a week, but the work has to continue when I am not there." And she points out that Rachel is a very "competent, sensitive, and artistic" woman whose vulnerabilities and challenges mothering Nadine are related to her own abuse suffered at the hands of an alcoholic mother.

When Nadine enrolled at the University of Miami, it was Linda — who happened to be vacationing in southern Florida — who helped her through registration and settled her into her dormitory room. Even though it has been ten years since they have met for formal therapy sessions in Linda's office, they will sometimes meet for conversation at a local coffee shop ("At least I've stopped paying for her lattes." Linda smiles. "Now I tell her, 'When you can afford it, you can have it.' "); or they will sit outside on a bench and strategize about how Nadine might more successfully deal with the "horrible bureaucratic maze of state mental health rehab," where she is seeking additional resources and support. "I take notes as we talk," says Linda, "and then give her the notes so that she can follow up. Our work together is very focused and practical."

As the longest of Linda's ongoing clients, Nadine is special, in a category of her own. Their connection to each other is deep and heartfelt; there is no end in sight to their long relationship, even though its tone and texture have changed over the years. Linda is parent and therapist, cheerleader and strategist, mentor and guide; and she combines these roles with alacrity, without hesitation. When I ask her how she thinks about the traditionally drawn "boundaries" that mark most therapists' relationships with their patients, Linda claims, again, that the boundary drawing is "very individualistic," defined by the nature, depth, and duration of the connection. As an experienced clinician whose work has become almost intuitive and whose moves are not constrained by orthodoxy — the traditional rules or protocols of therapy — she claims that she doesn't "worry or obsess" about boundaries. But that does not mean she doesn't "think about being more restrained and contained" or occasionally feel that she has transgressed in territories where she does not belong. Occasionally there are missteps and mistakes in judgment that haunt Linda for days afterward. During these moments of confusion and disorientation she will often consult with a trusted colleague for feedback and guidance.

When I ask her about the boundaries she draws with Nadine, she searches for some defining markers and comes up with only two. "Nadine has never met my husband. Steven is trained to wander away when my patients approach me. And Nadine has never been in any other room in my house, only in my office." And there are the other boundaries that all her patients, including Nadine, experience — the white noise machine outside her office door that creates a sound barrier, the message on her telephone that directs patients to emergency services when she is out of town or unavailable, and of course the HIPAA forms she tells patients about when they first arrive, alerting them to the fact that she is legally bound to report evidence of child abuse and inform the authorities when she believes her patients might hurt themselves or others. As we talk, I hear the connections between boundaries and endings, between defining the contours of the therapeutic relationship and being able to leave it, move beyond it. It somehow doesn't surprise me that with the minimal boundaries that have been in place for twenty years between Nadine and Linda, termination would be neither desired nor necessary for either of them.

With almost every termination — however formal and ritualized — Linda offers a last salvo. "The door is always open," she says to those who are departing, whose faces are often creased with sadness and wet with tears. The emotional weight of these goodbyes reminds Linda of another reason that "good terminations" are so valuable. "They serve as a corrective emotional experience," she muses. "They help people understand that farewells are often bittersweet . . . fruitful and sad . . . just as life is." The bittersweetness reminds her of saying goodbye to Cecelia, a Czechoslovakian doctor who had been in treatment for two and a half years. When Cecelia arrived, she was having a "major depressive episode," and her life was unraveling around her. Because of her depression, her professional life had deteriorated and she had recently been relieved of her clinical duties at the hospital. Linda's voice is angry and protective as she describes a major reason for Cecelia's cycling down. "There is only one word I can think of for her mother — a word I don't think I've ever used before in my practice. She was *evil.* I was trying to help Cecelia end the endless attempt to get anything from her mother . . . her ceaseless attempts to get kindness, empathy, attention, even civility from her mother. She was spending all her emotional energy in pursuit of something she would never get." At one point Cecelia's father, an engineer who was still living in Czechoslovakia and spoke no English, came with her to her therapy session. Even with Cecelia's expert translation, the emotional connections were hard and brittle, so distant was he from his daughter's life, so out of touch with her emotional needs.

At one point in her therapy Cecelia decided to "take a break." Without any fanfare she announced that she was leaving and would return when she was ready. But she offered her therapist no explanation, no opportunity for conversation or negotiation about her decision. Linda recalls how hard this was for her, how bad she felt. "I immediately thought I had made a mistake, maybe a mistake in the billing that might have upset her . . . then I was feeling very sad, as if I might have done something that violated her trust." Within three months Cecelia had returned, resuming the relationship "as if nothing had happened . . . as if nothing was wrong." Perhaps she just needed the space, thought Linda, because she returned ready to work harder and go deeper. The next months were very productive. "She did such great work," recalls Linda admiringly.

As they approached the end of her therapy and together anticipated its termination, things began to fall into place in Cecelia's life. "She presented her research at a professional conference and this time took full credit for it (in the past she had always taken a backseat and been overly deferential to her colleagues); she managed to get the job she really wanted; she learned to express her thoughts and feelings more forcefully and feel less marginalized at work." Her answers to Linda's two ritual questions at termination were fulsome and self-reflective. She recognized how far she had traveled, how hard she had worked, and how much she had done. She saw the connections between the insights and courage she had gathered in her therapy and the progress she was making in "real life." And she understood that there was so much more to do and conquer, so many ways she still retreated into herself, so many times she still cycled into sadness and despair, so many ways she was still involved in trying to gain her mother's love.

On the day of their last session together Cecelia arrived dressed in pink from head to toe. She was wearing a plaid pink jacket, pink high heels, and a pink band in her hair, and she was carrying a pink patent leather pocketbook. "She looked like a bowl of strawberry sherbet," says Linda with tears in her eyes. This was a moment that needed memorializing. Linda asked her whether she wanted to have her picture taken, and with an enthusiasm that seemed to indicate that this had been her plan all along, Cecelia said she would. She helped Linda figure out how to work the lens on her digital camera, and Linda took six pictures, both of them checking after each one to admire the pretty shot. As Cecelia walked out the door that afternoon, Linda said gently, "I hope to hear from you." To which Cecelia responded without hesitation, "You are family." "I teared up in that moment," says Linda, remembering how surprised she was by her own deep emotions. "I was so profoundly moved." As she relives the satisfaction of work well done by her patient, the staged ending, the emotional leave-taking, and the symbolism of the pink photos recording Cecelia's sense of herself as put together and pretty, Linda discovers the value of the termination ritual for the therapist. She discovers how she needs to review the work and say goodbye perhaps as much as her patients do.

I am interested in how Linda works with patients who come to her wanting help with an exit in their own lives. How, for example, does she guide a couple through a separation, a divorce? She immediately thinks of Riko, a thirty-seven-year-old Japanese woman who recently returned to therapy after a hiatus of seven years because of trouble in her marital relationship. She and her husband, a white American with a very high-paying job, had not had sexual intimacy for four years, although Riko claimed he was the love of her life, the man of her dreams. And although he claimed that he loved her deeply and she was his best friend, he said he had no interest in having sex with her except for when they both decided that they wanted to make another baby. Linda saw them each separately a few times and then several times together, uncovering the story of Riko's nightly practice of sleeping with her three-year-old child, not with her husband, and his nightly viewing of porn on the Internet. Their sessions together gave them a forum for learning how to communicate in a way that eluded them in their daily lives and offered them a place to unleash the disappointment and rage they each felt. Within the first few weeks of therapy Riko decided that she and her husband were too far apart in what they each wanted from the marriage, and she said she had no interest in trying to salvage it. Her voice shrieked as she spoke her horrible feelings. "I'm not going to be married to a turkey baster . . . and let him insert his penis into me only when I'm fertile." Riko wanted to file for divorce and be done with it.

Linda's response was purposefully "instructive, almost didactic," urging her to give the process some time — at least six months. "Riko tends to be very moody and erratic, with large swings of emotion from one extreme to the other," says Linda, enumerating one of the reasons she cautioned Riko about being too hasty. But Linda admits that in general, her attitude is one of wanting to help her patients try as hard as they might to save their marriages. "I definitely have a point of view," she admits. "In fact, I used to be far more opinionated and rigid about it." Now she at least tries to get couples to slow down. She suggests a longer time frame before a final decision is made, or she might recommend a trial separation, where they agree not to have sexual intimacies with other partners while they continue their couples therapy. And she hopes that if they ultimately decide to split, they will choose to use a mediator rather than lawyers, that they will find a way to preserve the dignity of both parties, and that they will work out a way to peacefully co-parent their children. If all these goals are met, Linda believes that they have done the groundwork for a successful exit.

Some of Linda's wish to preserve the marriages of her patients, or at least to insist that they "try their best and work their hardest" before declaring them over, may be related to the suffering she experienced when her own parents decided — after almost forty years of marriage — to divorce. Even though her parents' marriage had been troubled by extramarital affairs for as long as Linda can remember, and even though she was a grown woman with children of her own when they divorced, she was surprised by their decision and consumed by a sadness that lingered for years. I ask Linda whether she believes that her own painful history of her parents' divorce frames the way she approaches her patients' experiences, whether she offers her patients the counsel and guidance that she wishes her parents might have followed. My question seems "obvious" to her, but she gives a "counterintuitive" response. "One of the things I believe about myself as a clinician," she says with great certainty, "is that after all these decades, I continue to be riveted on the content of what my patients are saying. I'm focused on what they need. I feel myself being fully present with them. I do not think of myself except to the extent that I'm obviously formed by my own history. My story does not override theirs."

The question of her own emotional history distorting or interfering with the way she is able to "hear the content" of her patients' narratives brings up for Linda the ways in which her work as a therapist allows her to be her best, offering her the chance to use her plentiful gifts and insights. For a moment the tables turn, and I feel myself drawn into the role of therapist, listening to Linda's ancient haunts. She tells me of a dream she had the night before our interview. She was preparing to take an exam for a graduate course in which she was enrolled, and she couldn't focus on the material or remember any of the facts that were sure to be on the test the next day. She woke up in a panic, disoriented and drenched in sweat, and realized almost immediately that her dream was about the "huge anxiety and dread" she was feeling in anticipation of our interview. "I was so fraught and so worried," she says, reliving the moment and recalling the way she used to throw up every day before going to elementary school because she was so "school phobic." "I was never enough in school. I went to a private high school on the Upper East Side of New York, and I never felt as if I was enough intellectually or financially," she recalls sadly before snapping her fingers and bursting into laughter. "In high school I developed the persona of Sexy Linda to avoid feeling that I wasn't enough . . . a creative and provocative teenage solution to escape feeling all that pain."

As Linda prepared for our interview — gathering folders, journal articles, and correspondence, trying to anticipate the questions I might ask, role-playing with herself the smart and impressive answers she might give — she realized that she was rehearsing the awful experience of preparing for an exam that would reveal, once again, that she was "not enough." Now there are tears in her eyes as she says to me, "This is so unbelievably sad that — at seventy — I still struggle with these old feelings."

But when Linda sits listening to her patients, her mind "riveted," her "heart open," she knows she's good. She's more than enough. Now she's smiling broadly. "I feel plentiful and abundant as a therapist. I do not doubt my competence." As she practices therapy, attentive to her patients' journeys, living fully in the present with them and honoring their work, she is released from the old school phobias that made her feel incompetent and anxious. She finds freedom and plenty in her work, a freedom that allows her to engage fully with her patients and, when it is time, to let them leave . . . an exit that is dignified, a "termination" that admits there is still much work to be done.

I am struck by how much of Linda's work is focused on helping her patients figure out a way to leave those relationships, marriages, families, institutions, and communities that are compromising their lives, undermining their self-confidence, and making them feel anxious and depressed. Whether she is helping Cecelia, the Czechoslovakian doctor, relinquish her desperate quest for her mother's attention and love, even when she knows that her mother does not have the interest or the capacity, or whether she is supporting Allison, the young lawyer, in breaking up with her boyfriend, who is dismissive of her, whose attraction to him seems to be tangled up with his abuse of her, the path to healing is defined by exits. Exits are the markers of recovery and development, of becoming.

Linda's long years of experience free her from the conventions and orthodoxies practiced by therapists who rigidly mark the boundaries of their professionalism. As she helps her patients navigate their exits, she plays many roles. She is their critic and advocate, their guide and mentor, their companion and confidante. She listens for the sound and the silences in her patients' revelations, their masking of pain, and their detours away from the truth. She is attentive to the places where they fear to tread, the spaces where they continue to get stuck. She is nonjudgmental and fearless — she has heard it all before — but clear about what she believes, confident about her knowledge of the human psyche, its capacities and frailties. Several times, in fact, Linda calls her approach to therapy "didactic." She sees herself as a teacher — attentive, probing, challenging, and directive. She wants to teach her patients a new way of seeing, an alternative view, the "art of reframing" their experiences so that they might be released from the unproductive perspectives that have haunted their progress. Looking through a different lens, they might be able to identify the blind spots that have inhibited their progress; they might be able to rewrite the ancient narratives and see the path toward healing.

But Linda is also a pragmatist; her work is not purely retrospective — delving into the dark history of her patients and helping them see the light. It is prospective; it searches for what they might actually do today and tomorrow to make themselves feel better and happier. She gives them "homework," exercises they must do between sessions that will help move their work from talk to action, from the asylum of the therapist's office to the rough-and-tumble of the real world. In addition to the reframing and the pragmatism that are part of her pedagogy, Linda hopes to teach her patients courage — the courage to speak the truth about what they are feeling. Exiting the wounding afflictions of their lives, then, requires that they refocus their lenses, learn and practice new habits of interaction, and find the courage to tell the truth.

When the therapist and her patients have gone as far as they can go — the work is always unfinished, always imperfect — they make plans to "terminate," a ritual exit that "honors the patient, honors their relationship, and honors the work" they have done together, a ritual that is both generic and idiosyncratic, anticipatable and improvisational, formal and spontaneous. Optimally, all of Linda's patients use their last three sessions to wrap up, review their time together, and say their farewells. As they stand poised at the threshold of their therapeutic exit, Linda asks everyone the same two questions: "What was useful in this therapy? And what do you wish we might have covered — but didn't get a chance to — in our time together?" But even though the ritual is framed by these "generic" practices,[3] each goodbye is different, individually shaped by the doctor and her patient, by the depth and length of their relationship, the chemistry of their personalities, and the complex excavation of the emotional layers they have uncovered together.

The Czechoslovakian doctor comes to her last session all dressed in pink, looking like a bowl of strawberry sherbet, her bright prettiness and femininity an expression of her hard-won self-confidence and a sign of her emerging visibility and voice at work. She stands tall, clutching her pink patent leather purse, and her therapist takes a series of photos, capturing her courage, documenting her healing, marking the exit. By contrast, Nadine — who is now thirty-one and has been in a therapeutic relationship with Linda since she was twelve — never fully exits. There is no formal end point with pictures and declarations to mark the occasion. Rather, the relationship evolves and changes over time as she grows from a child to an adolescent to a young adult, as the mother and therapist become "co-parents." The boundaries between Linda and Nadine shift; the therapy moves from the office to the coffee shop. Says Linda unapologetically, "In these cases, termination is a flow, not an end point . . . or perhaps there are a series of end points."

As I listen to Linda rehearse the exit stories of her patients, I am fascinated by the language — of "termination" — that she and her colleagues use to describe these moments. It is a word that sounds both inadequate and misleading to me, seeming to connote a finite moment in time when things are over and done and people move on. For me, the word even seems to have a dismissive quality, as when an employer speaks about having to terminate his employee. Similar to the leave-takings described in the previous chapters, the exits from therapy are, in fact, not open-and-shut, not black or white; they are not "binary." Rather they are layered, messy, and iterative, and they are embedded in relationships. The boundaries and bonds that get forged in therapy shape and light the path to the exit.

In addition, the finality carried in the language of "termination" does not reflect the fact that when people emerge from therapy, they are never "done"; they are never "finished" with their work. The ritual of exit, in fact, is in part about "honoring the work that is still to be done." "We are all works of art," says Linda, pointing out the ways in which we must — after the intervention of therapy — continue to revise the shapes and designs that we paint on our life canvases. Armed with the skills, insights, perspectives, and courage that have been forged in therapy, Linda hopes that her patients' paths toward healing will be more productive and rewarding, but she knows that their wounds will not disappear.

As a matter of fact, Linda Gould's last story, which concludes our interview, speaks to the subterranean presence and the surprising reappearance of our wounds when we least expect them — even when we have not felt the injuries for many years, even when we have developed successful strategies to compensate for them, even when we, like Linda, have been through therapy, more than once. As Linda prepares for our interview, she grows more and more anxious. She has a horrifying nightmare whose interpretation is so transparent that we don't even need the help of Dr. Freud.[4] She dreams that she is in graduate school studying for a big exam, that she is sure to fail no matter how hard she tries, no matter how much she cares, because school was always the place where she was "never enough."

Now, fifty years later, Linda worries that she will not be enough for me. She will not know enough, not be smart enough, not be articulate or wise enough, and I will be disappointed. And she worries about these things even though she knows that she is very good at her work, even though she "feels plentiful and abundant" as a therapist, even though she doesn't "doubt her competence" for a moment.

The frustration and sadness gather like a storm on Linda's face. She does not welcome the dark undertow of grief that has momentarily overtaken her. But she does recognize how the unmasking of her own primal wounds is a perfect coda for our conversation. The therapist — who, despite her worries about not being enough, has spoken most eloquently and wisely about the healing power of ex-its — is able to confirm that in revisiting our haunts, in analyzing our hurts, in discovering the way forward, in terminating from therapy, we will never fully escape our wounds. Rather, the exit will take us to that imperfect place where — if we are lucky — our scars will turn into badges of courage.

"What is the core problem here?"

Dr. Anthony Brown's patients have wounds that are physical, multiple, and critical; their diseases require dramatic and lifesaving interventions. As the director and chief attending physician in the intensive care unit (ICU) of University Hospital, he works with his residents to care for the sickest patients, those who are plagued by serious illnesses, who require the most extreme measures to keep them alive. He teaches the young doctors in his charge how to read the daily cataloging of scientific data, how to synthesize the various consultations from the myriad medical specialists, how to talk with the patients' families about life-and-death decisions, how to read the clinical signs that may trump the scientific evidence, how to act swiftly and with courage. As he guides his team of nurses, technicians, and physicians, they are all pointed toward the two exits out of the ICU. The patients who get better in their care are wheeled through the exit that takes them to the "floor" of the hospital, where they will stay for a while before heading home. For those whose lives cannot be saved, there is the final exit of death.

Dr. Brown meets me in the downstairs lobby of University Hospital, and after a warm greeting he guides me through a labyrinth of back corridors and elevators up to the ICU. Along the way, he gives me a snapshot description of Mr. Arthur, the patient his team is now visiting on their morning rounds, an eighty-five-year-old man who is "so sick in so many directions" and will probably die before leaving the ICU. When we arrive, the team — three residents, three interns, and the nurse taking care of Mr. Arthur — are emerging from behind the curtains covering the entrance to his hospital room. They automatically head toward the sanitizer dispenser outside the patient's room to clean their hands, take off their yellow plastic protective smocks, and then crowd around the computers and desks at the center of the unit. I know it is my age, but the young doctors look to me like adolescents dressed up in blue hospital gear. Silvia, an intern, sports a nose ring and orange hair, and Paula, a first-year resident, has old-fashioned black Converse All Star sneakers on her feet with Day-Glo socks peeking out. A few are chewing gum; all have stethoscopes dangling around their necks. But as soon as they open their mouths, to report on the patients' current status, they are all business, very focused, and completely adult in their demeanor.

They talk quickly, spitting out lots of numbers and acronyms and speaking the foreign language of procedures, therapies, consults, and medicines that sounds like gibberish to my ears. Dr. Brown — whom everyone calls Tony — takes a central place standing behind a large computer, consulting the charts, graphs, medicines, and data on each of the patients; listening intently to the residents' reports; occasionally asking a question, providing a clarification, or offering a historical perspective; and sometimes giving a brief monologue on some facet of their diagnosis, a rare didactic moment. The residents listen to his every word, look into his eyes for confirmation, or respond to his nod of affirmation and approval. Although he is doing many things at once — listening, searching the data, asking and answering questions, offering alternative perspectives, keeping track of the dynamics among his team — Anthony seems to be the still center of the storm surrounding him: soft-spoken, calm, unflappable. When his beeper goes off, he looks at it briefly, returns it to his pocket, or hands it off to his chief resident, never stopping the flow of conversation. When the respiratory therapist — a large, dark-skinned black man — steps behind him to whisper something about a patient's ventilator, he takes it in without skipping a beat.

Dr. Brown is the opposite of my caricature of the autocratic attending physician who screams at his residents, barking orders and bullying them into submission. If I did not know that he is forty years old, it would be difficult to guess his age. He is about six feet tall, with handsome features and a medium build; his head is balding and shaved close; his face is ageless, with the unlined, open, and somewhat innocent look of a very young man and the calm, wise, knowing gaze of someone much older. He wears brown khakis, suede loafers, and a light blue shirt with a burgundy-patterned tie. The stethoscope dangling around his neck offers the only signal that he is a doctor. Three white doctor coats hang on the back of his office door, looking barely worn. He moves quickly but with an economy and grace that doesn't ruffle the environment around him.

Anthony's authority is unquestioned, but he never seems to use or flaunt his position or status. He models curiosity, expertise, rigor, and professionalism — showing, not telling; questioning, not demanding. As I watch him in action, I suspect that his quiet, absolute authority reflects his gentle personality and empathic style as well as his intentional philosophy of education. He seems to believe that people learn best in an environment of openness and fairness, where everyone feels free to ask questions and no one spends time worrying about getting clobbered for mistakes. Later on, he tells me that "yelling and screaming just produces in learners a conditioned response, but it doesn't help the residents learn to think through a question or reason toward a diagnosis."

When he prods one of his interns about what medicine she would suggest for the diagnosis she has made, she blushes for a moment, then says, "I don't know, one of those weird endocrine things." In the midst of the laughter that follows, the chief resident helps her out with the exact name of the medicine. "I did not know that," she says gratefully, but without apparent embarrassment. There is an atmosphere of collegiality and support, a culture of teamwork. Anthony is a rigorous, focused taskmaster, intent on getting the work done — the pace is breathtakingly fast — but always aware of creating space for the questions and uncertainties that are part of the science and the art of clinical medicine.

There is a rhythm, pace, and routine to rounds. The intern begins the presentation of data: the patient's blood pressure, heart rate, respiratory rate, significant lab results, medicines, therapies; the consults with neurologists, radiologists, surgeons, orthopedics, etc. I am fascinated by the length and complexity of these reports, signaling the multiple, layered, interactive illnesses of their very sick and fragile patients. Then the nurse responsible for the patient reads from her chart — a close-up descriptive view of what she has experienced on the ward, a detailed clinical appraisal that sometimes raises questions about or challenges the course of action presented by the resident. Anthony is the disciplined arbiter, naming the disparities, seeking to understand and resolve the contradictions, searching for patterns, themes, and meanings in the data presented. He asks one of the residents to consider alternative perspectives or strategies. "Any other things you worry about with this kind of guy? It's a little like a fishing expedition." He asks the nurse for her clinical view of the patient's mental state during the night. "What are your observa-

240

tions, Sue?" "Well," she says, looking frustrated and exhausted, "he is awake and agitated, or he's asleep . . . nothing in between. It is one extreme or the other . . . very difficult."

When they have gathered all the pieces of information together, they put on the yellow plastic coats, sterilize their hands, and visit the patient. Anthony raises his voice as he enters the room, the only time he ever speaks loudly. "Hello, Mr. Shulman. This is Dr. Brown and the ICU team. Can you open your eyes, sir? I'm just going to listen to your heart." He spends a couple of minutes at the bedside, checks the monitors and ventilators, asks the nurse about the patient's comfort and stability, and makes a quick exit back to the computers. His movements are swift and practiced as he braids his observations of the patient in with the data they have before them. "I'm concerned that he is not moving his arms more," he says simply, the one sentence whose language I understand completely. "Last night he had a wildly elevated PTT," offers a second-year resident. "Not sure what to make of that."

At the end of the reports and bedside visits, Paula, the first-year resident, is in charge of summarizing each case and articulating the plan of action moving forward. She makes sure they have covered all the essential areas — an automatic inventory that one of the interns on this rotation has named "the Big Six" (more traditionally called the "core clinical measures"). Anthony smiles as he explains to me later what the Big Six stands for: nutrition, pain control, vascular devices, code status, prophylactic care, and referrals.

Occasionally during rounds, someone mentions the patients' families who come to visit, who are frustrated and fearful, who hope for a miracle, who have a voice and point of view about how far the doctors should go in extending the life of their loved ones. The last patient they review, Mrs. Washington, has been in the ICU for forty-eight days, longer than any other patient. At fifty-two, she is mildly retarded and has multiple serious illnesses, including renal failure, anemia, heightened fever induced by the drugs she is taking, and gastrointestinal bleeding. She has had several blood transfusions, is attached to ventilators and multiple monitors, cannot speak, and is in great discomfort. "If anything," says Anthony, emerging from her room, "in the last two weeks she has looked worse." As they reconvene at the computers, the resident says that she has had an ongoing discussion with the family about a possible tracheotomy, but they seem unsure. "They keep waffling." Anthony's voice signals a crucial fork in the road, marking a moment when they all need to "step back" and take stock. "This is the time," he says in summary, "when we have to have a big-picture discussion with the family." The nurse nods in agreement and says that the family — the patient's sister, brother, and daughter — are coming in at 5:30 to meet with them, to have the "big-picture" conversation, to consider whether they have all gone far enough in trying to keep Mrs. Washington alive.

Later, as we talk in his small, unadorned office, Anthony tells me that of the eight patients they have seen in morning rounds, two will die. "Death," he says evenly, "is inevitable for many of our patients." On average, about 20 percent of the patients in the ICU die there, and Mrs. Washington will be one of them. There are two kinds of deaths, explains Anthony. The first he calls "letting go." "Mrs. Washington and Mr. Arthur would die very quickly — within minutes — if they were not in the ICU. With this kind of patient, you have to start by setting limits, being clear about how far we will go. In these two cases, and in consultation with the families, for example, we won't use chest compressions, shocks, or do further surgery. Every day they will get weaker . . . there is an inevitable decline where we de-escalate care and choose the therapies around comfort." The "letting go" Anthony refers to obviously includes the doctors and nurses as well as the patients and their families. It is always a hard and painful call; and a big part of Anthony's job is distinguishing between "fixable versus non-fixable" problems.

When he speaks to Mrs. Washington's family this afternoon — one of a series of ongoing conversations with them — Anthony will review all the things they have done to try to save her life and all the things that have not worked. "I will begin by sharing with them my sense of where she is clinically — what I see as the options now — and present the information in as objective a way as possible," he says solemnly. Together they will talk about some of the more "invasive procedures" that might allow them to sustain her for a little while longer. Anthony will ask whether this is what the family wants. At some point they will consider whether it is time to take the breathing tube out. These conversations are never perfunctory or brief. The doctor proceeds with caution and empathy, careful about his tone and pace, committed to hearing the voices of everyone, respectful of the complex, often tangled relationships within families.

This afternoon he will probably repeat a line he often uses when he is consulting with families about the end. "We can do a lot to her, but we cannot do a lot for her" — a line that usually follows the family's request that Anthony finally "say what he really thinks." When there is nothing more to be done, when everyone agrees it is time to let go, the efforts shift, away from "aggressive interventions" toward therapies that offer comfort and reduce pain. "Most patients facing death," says Anthony, "want to be comfortable. They don't want to suffer. They don't want to have pain. In the end, most people do not say they don't want to die."

Anthony estimates that 90 percent of the deaths in the ICU are of the "letting go" kind. The other 10 percent are the rapidly progressive extreme illnesses that you "can't keep up with because they are moving too quickly." Those are the ones that look like scenes from the television program *ER*, where someone is in cardiac arrest and everyone is in the room fighting to save the patient's life, using chest compression, inserting breathing tubes, using electricity to start the heart, offering acute life supports. Even though this scene — of disaster and heroism — is the one we imagine, Anthony says that these kinds of deaths are actually very rare in the ICU. "My job," he reports, "is actually to anticipate these problems so that we can avoid these crises."

Death in the ICU is the final exit that the team must anticipate, prepare for, and navigate, always considering the objective evidence, calculating the limitations of medicine, listening for the voices and views of the patient and his family, and occasionally consulting with other medical professionals who have treated the patient before he entered the ICU. The "letting go" is an "iterative process" — with conversations started, stopped, and returned to; weariness and frustration mounting; relief and sadness coming together with the final realization that it must be over. The other — more dramatic and much rarer — kind of death hits all of a sudden, requires immediate action, and offers no time for deliberation or conversation. It is a no-holds-barred fight for life. The ICU team is left defeated and exhausted, having done everything they could, but not able to do enough. These ways of dying in the ICU — one slow and iterative, the other fast and dramatic — are both anticipatable, though not welcome, exits from the ICU.

The other kind of exit that everyone refers to is the one that crosses the boundary between the ICU and the rest of the hospital — "the floor." For at least 80 percent of the patients, the single goal is to get them well enough to send them on to a bed in the regular hospital; very few patients leave the ICU and head home. As a matter of fact, Anthony underscores the boundary lines and amplifies the exit when he frequently tells his residents, "There are two kinds of people in the world: ICU patients and everyone else." As he draws the clear distinction for his residents, he encourages them to focus on those "fixable" illnesses that have brought their patients to "the most controlled environment" in the hospital. Why are they ICU patients? What makes them different from everyone else in the world? Anthony wants his residents to "identify the problem" that must be fixed so the patients will be "okay enough to go to the other part of the hospital."

As I listened to the morning rounds, this exit — to the floor — seemed to be the primary focus, the one that required deliberation by the team and preparation of the patient, the one that brought out the us-versus-them dichotomy between the ICU team and the regular hospital staff. As attending physician, Anthony keeps this boundary line and goal of exit in mind. He is aware of the myriad roles he plays and balances, and the ways in which they overlap and occasionally conflict with one another.

First, he is the doctor who, above all, seeks to "offer rational, safe, and reasonable care" for his patients. Being a good doctor, engaged in excellent patient care, is always his first priority. Second, he is mentor and teacher, guiding his interns and residents to a deeper understanding of clinical practice in the ICU; helping them identify the problems, offer diagnoses, and develop an organized way of presenting the relevant information; modeling for them a calm professionalism, "a gravitas," an approach to the work. "These are complex and confusing patients with an unusual and difficult array of diseases," he says, "and there is a lot to learn to decipher, a disciplined approach to moving forward, and a daily review of the data followed by a plan of action." Anthony tries to help his residents see the patterns that can be traced through the data. The young doctors tend to be sharp at identifying the discrete pieces, but they are less likely to see the shape of the whole, the inconsistencies and surprises or the disruptions to the patterns in the data.

Anthony admits that the teaching part of his role is not the most straightforward way of getting the work done. "There are much more efficient ways to do the rounds," he says. "If I did them alone, I could do them much more quickly and productively. I would not always be thinking about what the skills are that will help the interns and residents do my job. I would just be — based on my long experience, knowledge, and clinical judgment — doing it myself." But this is not a private practice where he works on his own; it is a large teaching hospital connected to one of the country's top medical schools. And Anthony believes that despite the obvious inefficiencies, he always learns from the residents' observations and questions. When he teaches, he becomes more articulate about what he knows, and how he knows it.

The third role that Anthony plays as he keeps his eye on the exit door to the hospital "floor" is as team leader, communicator, and coordinator. He is very conscious of building a "team" with a "horizontal" authority structure, where everyone has an important role, a legitimate perspective, and a valued voice; where he is always being intentionally inclusive. The culture he is creating in this professional community is purposefully different from the traditional hierarchies in most hospitals, with the attending physician at the top and the nurses close to the bottom. Anthony turns the traditional structure on its head, recognizing, for example, that the nurses have the best clinical intelligence on the team. They are the ones closest to the action, the ones creating relationships and establishing rapport with the patients, the ones with the most subtle and complex "granular view." The nurses' voices and views are particularly important in the ICU, where the patients are so sick, where the interaction of medicines and therapies can so easily go wrong, where data need to be fed back to the team in a timely, immediate way. "The nurses," says Anthony, "are the experts in this environment. They know so much more than the residents do about the patients, the illnesses, the therapies . . . and their impact on individual patients. We listen to them very carefully. We respect their point of view."

As a matter of fact, as a convener of the

team, Anthony believes that his authority as an attending comes not from some show of dominance or power, or even from his knowing the answers to all the questions. Although I suspect this is one of the many places where Anthony is being overly modest (several doctors and nurses tell me, without my soliciting their views, that Anthony is the best doctor they have ever worked with, the most brilliant and the most compassionate), he sees his authority and reputation growing out of the way he "deals with an average busy day." It is the small, everyday stuff that deserves vigilant attention. It is his ability to remain "unflappable" in the face of all the chaos and complexity that comes at him every day — that is what gives him his authority (he does not use the word "power") as a teacher, mentor, and doctor.

A critical part of handling the "everyday stuff" rests on his getting to know the individual qualities of his interns and residents, their strengths and weaknesses, their ambivalence and fears, their learning styles, their personalities and character. Luke, the chief resident, does not have the social skills or the "gravitas" you would expect from someone in his position. In fact, Anthony admits with a smile that he is "a bit weird" and turns people off with what strikes many as immaturity and a lack of professionalism. But, says Anthony, "he is very bright and has trained himself to do other things very well. He is interested in organizational issues — how to create safer, more efficient medicine in the ICU — and has developed operating systems that increase the cohesion and communication among the team." By contrast, Roger, a second-year resident, is "thoughtful, conscientious, capable, and very smart . . . a natural leader, a talented clinician whom everyone likes." During the morning rounds I observe Roger's ease and geniality as he mixes with the nurses, technicians, and interns, his blend of confidence and humility, his curiosity and attentiveness in listening to his colleagues. Even though he has been there all night, his attention does not flag. And there is Paula, the first-year resident, who just a couple of weeks ago made the transition from being an intern and has found the move to her new status — and the responsibilities that go with it — unsettling. Anthony tells me that she is bright and learns quickly, but she expresses a lot of "fear and uncertainty."

The mention of Paula's fears reminds Anthony of one of the things he stresses and talks about openly with his residents. "Even if you have fears," he tells them, "you must act courageously. Courage is not the absence of fear. Courage is what you can do in spite of your fears. And courage is something you have to practice." In the ICU, the stakes are high and the fears mount — fear of patients dying, fear of making a mistake, fear of missing a crucial diagnosis. Anthony tells me about a former resident who was so uncertain and afraid that he was reluctant to "own the care of his patients." His fear not only put his patients at risk, it also alienated and angered the nurses. When the resident came to Anthony wondering why the nurses seemed to "hate" him so much, Anthony explained that they did not hate him; they just "smelled the fear" on him. They wanted him, above all, to do his job, and his job was to make a decision. They wanted — and needed — more from him.

Sometimes the fear and stress of doing this high stakes work is relieved by humor. As I watch the rounds, there are some moments of quiet laughter, when everyone seems to ease up a little bit, a brief rest from the speedy staccato of voices reporting measures and diagnoses. I ask Anthony about those rare moments of reprieve, and he tells me that humor in the ICU is a "double-edged sword." In such a high-anxiety environment, it is important to be able to laugh, to lighten up from time to time. But it is critical that the laughter never degenerate into "adopting a gallows humor, which tends to be a pretty typical defense mechanism for doctors," and it is critical that it never devolve into making fun of patients. As I observe the rounds, there are, in fact, a couple of times when I hear laughter erupting in response to an intern's slightly off-color remark about a patient, a response that I suspect is mostly a reflection of his own frustrations and uncertainty. At these moments Anthony's face, I notice, remains impassive, clearly but quietly projecting his sense that such remarks are inappropriate. One way to avoid the "dehumanizing" echoes of gallows humor is to be slightly self-deprecatory. "Self-effacing humor helps." Anthony smiles. "I'll often tell my residents about silly mistakes I've made that have led to unlikely outcomes. But even those kinds of remarks I do in moderation."

Our time together is drawing to a close, so I ask Anthony a question that has been on my mind since I entered the strange and extreme environment of the ICU several hours ago and noticed immediately how much at home he was — and is — there. I ask him what draws him to this work that he so clearly relishes, and he receives the question as if he has been given a gift. This is not the first time he has considered these sources of commitment and attraction to his work, and his answers are immediate and revealing. He comes up with a list of seven dimensions that still — after ten years of directing the ICU — continue to excite and engage him, continue to turn him on.

First, he points to the spreadsheet of numbers and graphs on his big-screen computer and says, not surprisingly, "I like the data. I like to make sense of the data." As I see him in action in the ICU, it is impossible not to notice his command of and appreciation of the numbers, his curiosity and skepticism about what the numbers and patterns seem to be saying, and his experienced understanding of the ways in which the numbers blend with, and sometimes contradict, his clinical insights. Second, he likes the fact that in the ICU "the stakes are so high," allowing him to feel "viscerally connected to the work." Third, he mentions how much the work gives him a chance to build relationships with patients and their families, the kinds of deep and trusting bonds that are forged especially when life and death are in the balance. Fourth, he talks about how much he likes the "procedural aspects" of clinical practice, the experience of actually placing the tubes in the patient's arm, hooking up the ventilators, doing the emergency heart compressions. Fifth, he loves the pace: fast, focused, and efficient. Things change very quickly, and you have to be prepared to stay out ahead of crises. Sixth on the list, he says tentatively, is "control . . . something about control." I wonder whether he means his own need to be in control. His explanation, however, offers a somewhat different perspective. "The ICU is the most highly controlled environment in the hospital, and in that way it is the safest. On a very small scale, for example, I can look on the screen here and see how much urine Ms. Johnson made between eight p.m. and nine p.m."

And finally, Dr. Brown mentions his love of teaching — all the ways he hopes to convey knowledge and compassion; standards, rigor, and courage; and clinical insight to the young doctors in his charge. "When I was a new attending, I used to be much more didactic, telling them all about the most recent randomized trials. I used to cite the newest journal articles. Although I still know all that stuff and stay current with it, when I teach my residents now, I'm likely to ask, Is this patient sick or not sick? What is the core problem here?" These questions — simple and stark — require that his residents do something very complex and difficult. In order to respond, they must synthesize the data, trace the patterns of disease and therapies across time, use their clinical judgment, think on their feet, actually see the whole person who is their patient, take "ownership" of their diagnosis, and finally draw on their practiced courage to make a decision. These are the hard-core questions that — when answered thoughtfully and rigorously and acted upon quickly and gracefully — lead the way to the exit.

Exits are absolutely necessary for the existence of some places. In fact, they may define a place. The boundary between there and here is marked by the exits. The ICU is such a place, set apart from the rest of the hospital, the rest of the world. In fact, Anthony Brown frequently marks the clear boundaries, and the unique space within, when he claims that the ICU is the "the most controlled environment in the hospital" and when he tells his residents that "there are two kinds of people in the world: ICU patients and everyone else." With patients who are "sick in so many directions," with extreme wounds that are hard to diagnose and fix, Anthony urges the young doctors to see the ICU as a place unlike any other — a protective, respectful, safe place; a dangerous, daunting, high-risk place — where exit is the goal.

This controlled — brilliantly lit, highly sanitized, densely staffed, intensely monitored — environment is the opposite of Sartre's dark and banal hell. People are not left alone to prey on one another, to indulge in self-mutilation, to remain in the inferno even when the exit door beckons them toward freedom. Rather they are carefully watched and fiercely protected. They are allowed to sleep and dream, ask for help, and decide when the pain has become unbearable. In this benign, extreme environment, Anthony urges the young doctors to focus on the "fixable" illnesses, the "core problem" that will — when solved — lead to the exit. He is the guide, master of "the way to the exit," modeling what it takes to accomplish exit — courage and authority; rigor, precision, and decisiveness; attentiveness and respect.

As he leads the way, Anthony wants his residents to embrace the contradictions and appreciate the art and science of clinical practice.[5] He urges them to pay attention to the details as well as the whole, to work fast as well as deliberately, to dig into the data and transcend the numbers, to identify the many layers and pieces as well as synthesize the whole and notice the patterns, to consider a multitude of options and possibilities as well as make a clear diagnosis, a definitive decision. This balancing act, this mix of paradoxes is what is needed to bring the ICU patient to the other side — "the floor" or death — successfully.

The exits can be classified into specific types based on the answers to simple — yet immensely complex and subtle — questions. Exit can be a letting go, inevitable but deeply considered and decided upon, an "iterative" process that depends on a series of difficult conversations with the patient's family. Exit can be unstoppable, too fast to catch, running ahead of the dramatic interventions, out of control. Exit can be a move out of the extreme environment of the ICU to a more stable condition on the floor, executed with calculated interventions and treatments. Exit can be shepherded by a master and teacher. The art and science of leading the way to the exit can be taught.

Just like Linda Gould, who sees teaching as a critical dimension of her therapeutic work with patients, Anthony Brown thinks about himself primarily as a teacher. He is teaching his residents how to blend the clinical and empirical aspects, the relational, aesthetic, and moral dimensions of their practice. He is aware of modeling calm, seriousness, and "gravitas," respect and empathy for patients. He recognizes the "inefficiencies" that would not be there if he did the work by himself, but he is also aware of the ways in which his students raise questions, search for explanations, and challenge presumptions that bring insight to his own learning. His teaching has changed over time. In the beginning it felt more like performance — citing the newest findings and insights from journal articles, displaying his deep and vast knowledge to his young charges. Now he teaches through inquiry, asking the fundamental questions that get to the "core problem."

He is guided by a well-developed "philosophy of education" that includes building a nonauthoritarian, inclusive culture where there is space for everyone to reason and question, to try alternative interpretations, to fail and recover; where the traditional hierarchies of medicine are upturned.[6] The nurses — who are close to the action, have a "granular view," and spend the most face-to-face time with the patients — have the most comprehensive and pragmatic take on things. The young doctors begin to appreciate the nurses' perspectives, learning to be especially attentive to those aspects of the work that cannot be reduced to quantitative measurement or scientific data, those understandings and actions that grow out of long experience, those insights that come from closely connecting with patients.

In the extreme environment of the ICU, courage is essential, and Anthony — like Linda Gould — believes that it can be taught, practiced, and learned. Courage, he says, is not the absence of fear; it is "what you do in spite of your fears." The fears and terrors are always hovering in the ICU, and there are lots of opportunities to do the wrong thing, with life-threatening consequences. The stakes are very high. Anthony keeps a steady hand, anticipating crises, distinguishing between what is "fixable" and what is not, guiding his residents toward the "big-picture" conversation with families whose loved ones are facing the final exit. But even as he holds it all together — the calm in the middle of the storm — he insists that his residents begin to "practice courage," reduce their awkwardness and uncertainty, and start to "own the care" of their patients. He wants the residents to develop a fearlessness and courage that will help them know when to keep fighting for survival, for life, and when it is time to let people let go.

FIVE:
YEARNING

As I listened to people tell stories about the events, experiences, and motivations that precipitated their exits, I often heard a quality in their voices — a sound of longing, struggle, and desire — that I began to call "yearning." As they described their fears and ambivalence, their reluctance and caution, even their anticipation and excitement about leaving the old and entering the new, their reflections resonated with melancholy and tenderness, as if in facing the challenges of change and new choices, they felt a certain sympathy for themselves, a recognized vulnerability for wanting something so much, a hunger for what remained out of reach. Sometimes the yearning was for something concrete; they could visualize the place, the lifestyle, the new identity they wanted to get to, and the exit that would take them there. They could see the path forward, and they yearned for the courage, the energy, the resources, and the imagination that would allow them to get moving. Other times the yearning was for something inchoate and ephemeral, something unclear and elusive, something they could not name — perhaps an earnest and heartfelt thirst for experiencing something more meaningful and worthy. I am intrigued by both kinds of yearning — for the known and unknown, the named and unnamed — and by the ways in which exiting, at least voluntary exiting, always seems to begin with a disappointment and melancholy about what is and a burning desire, a yearning, to make a change.

In a language far more theoretical than the exit stories I listened to, the sociologist Helen Rose Fuchs Ebaugh begins to uncover some of the texture and dynamic of the yearnings I heard in the voices of my interviewees. In her book *Becoming an Ex* (1988),[1] Ebaugh offers a dense and comprehensive analysis of the processes of leave-taking experienced by people exiting from roles that they defined as central to their lives. Her huge and diverse sample included more than one hundred people who had experienced career changes (ex-cops, ex-doctors, ex-teachers, ex-athletes, ex-military, ex-professors), people who underwent major changes in familial roles (divorced people, widows, parents who lost custody of their children), and people who exited highly stigmatized roles (ex-convicts, ex-prostitutes, ex-alcoholics). Her interviewees even included ten transsexuals who were going through sex change surgery. Even though a quarter of a century has passed since the publication of her book, her study remains the only serious inquiry into the reasons that people, as Ebaugh puts it, "learn and unlearn, engage and disengage from the social roles that define who we are, especially in this rapidly changing world in which role exit is becoming commonplace."[2]

In reading Ebaugh, I was particularly intrigued by the confluence of autobiography and theory, by the blend of self-reflection and sociological analysis running through her text. As a doctoral student in the late 1970s, Ebaugh — a Roman Catholic nun — had focused her dissertation research on the growing number of nuns leaving religious orders. She wanted to know what precipitated their exits, how they negotiated their departures, and what their life experiences were as ex-nuns. In my language, she wanted to trace the yearnings in their hearts, the paths they traveled, and the ways these yearnings got translated into choices and actions. In the process of doing the research, Ebaugh became one of her "own statistics,"[3] left the order, and, shortly after leaving, married a divorcé. She was struck by the similarities of their exits — hers from the convent and his from his first marriage. Several years later, in *Becoming an Ex,* she explored the ways in which a "stage theory of role exit" might apply more generally to a variety of exits: from careers, from political and sectarian groups, from families, relationships, and organizations.

Ebaugh defines "role exit" as the process of disengagement from a role that is central to your identity and the reestablishment of an identity in a new role that takes into account your ex-role. She also notes that some exits are so common and frequent in society that they have become institutionalized; there are terms for these exiters — retiree, divorcé, recovered alcoholic, widow, alumnus. These institutionalized exits carry certain expectations, privileges, and status. Other, noninstitutionalized exits are also numerous in our society and simply carry the prefix "ex." Ebaugh frames role exit as a basic social process in which, regardless of the role being departed, there are underlying similarities. Every exit, for example, begins with "disengagement" (withdrawing from the role and the expectations associated with it), accompanied by a process she calls "disidentification" (ceasing to think of yourself in the former role), and concludes with resocialization (forming a new identity that includes adapting to the new role and hanging on to the vestigial residue of the previous role).

According to Ebaugh, the role-exit process proceeds forward through four distinct stages. The first stage is that of "first doubts," in which individuals begin to question the role commitment they had previously taken for granted. They start to reimagine, reinterpret, and redefine the qualities and responsibilities they have always seen as central to their identity. Usually, the doubting stage is gradual, often fraught; at other times it may occur surprisingly rapidly. The next stage is the seeking and weighing of "role alternatives." Here the quest for viable paths and attractive possibilities grows from a vague general awareness to a conscious step in the exiting process. Ebaugh calls the third stage the "turning point," when the individual actually leaves the role, often going public with his decision, making it more difficult for him to change his mind or turn back. The last stage of the exit process is "creating an ex-role," where one's previous role identification (a "hangover identity") is incorporated into a future identity. On the other side of the exit, people often struggle with establishing themselves in their new role while they continue to disentangle themselves from the self-perceptions and social expectations of their previous role. The tensions and incongruities between the new self-definitions and the old identity and patterns of behavior ("role residual") can become a big struggle for people during this time.

In many ways, Ebaugh's stage theory offers a useful framework for interpreting many of the narratives I heard, particularly those tales people told of exiting from their careers, from the organizational anchors and professional roles that had defined their work identities. Her analysis helpfully traces the sequence and order of exiting, the difficulties of letting go and leaving, the moment when we decide to take the leap of faith, and the tensions and ambivalence we experience defining ourselves in the new role when we still feel the vestigial residue from the old. I particularly like the way she helps us see that we never fully exit; we never fully escape our former selves. Those qualities and experiences "hang over" and become embedded in the reconstructed new role.

But as in most stage theories, there is a lot missing, a lot that gets masked by the discrete stages and categories that Ebaugh lays out. The progression of stages she presents as a unidirectional, relatively straight road misses the twists and turns and the retreats and regressions of our exits. Likewise, the sociological concept of "role" (a person's place in the normative structure of a group or organization) distorts our view of the individual characteristics and agency of the exiting person. We do not see the various and idiosyncratic ways in which people take leave; neither do we get to glimpse the universal patterns that are found in their unique stories. And although Ebaugh recognizes the ambivalences and apprehensions that make exiting hazardous, her framework does not resonate with the haunting sound of yearning, the melancholy of desire, the undertow of regrets that echoed through the stories I heard.

The two narratives in this chapter pulsate with yearning. Joe Rosario, an ex-priest, tells a long and arduous story of his exit from the Roman Catholic Church — a journey away from work that he loved, the parishioners to whom he was devoted, and the church in which he had grown up, a leave-taking full of ambivalence, procrastination, and caution, desire and yearning. After weighing the alternatives and balancing the pros and cons, after consulting with mentors and rationalizing the risks, Joe finally takes the plunge into medicine — a field he had been drawn to when he was an adolescent, a field that appeals to many of the same values and strivings that shaped his priesthood. But even though he ultimately finds deep satisfaction and reward in being a physician, the yearning continues to burn in him, a wistful yearning for what he has left behind.

By contrast, Josh Arons's decision to leave his job as the CEO of a major philanthropy is sudden and impulsive, arriving like an epiphany, surprising even him. But in the midst of his quick exit he discovers the yearning that has been in him for a long time, a deep desire — after twenty-five years at the helm — to find something different, meaningful, and creative; a yearning to have the inspiration for his next chapter come from within, "organically," and not feel compelled to rush into something that would feel like "more of the same in a different guise."

THE BURN OF YEARNING

"The ache became consuming."

His title is big — chief of internal medicine (at one of the top teaching hospitals in the country) — but his manner is modest and his office is tiny and spare. Except for two photographs of his wife and children on the wall beside his desk, the physical space is unadorned. A computer sits on his desk, and its organized surface contains a telephone, a small pad for jotting notes, and three neat piles of folders. A bulletin board is full of colorless medical charts, scientific graphs, and hospital announcements; and two simple blue chairs are available for patients and visitors. A large window looking out over the city lets the bright sun come in and makes the small space feel less claustrophobic. My eyes land on three pairs of shoes — all brown (much like the ones he has on) — lined up by the door, and I immediately wonder why they are there. Knowing he is a former Catholic priest, I imagine — in their modesty, sameness, and neatness — that they are left over from his monastic life. Maybe they would have been his entire collection of footwear when he lived a more spartan existence; or maybe they reflect the relative bounty of his life now that he does not have to limit his worldly possessions. Throughout our interview, my mind and fantasies return to the look-alike brown shoes.

Joe Rosario is forty-eight years old, but he looks much younger. He is about five feet seven inches tall, lean, and compact, and he moves with the ease and confidence of an athlete. His shiny black hair frames an open face, attentive brown eyes, and a radiant smile that is infectious and disarming. Everything about him — his dress, his gestures, his stories — feels a bit understated and modest. He does not seem to be aware of his handsomeness; he does not flaunt it. He seems to be most comfortable as the listener — responding to others' requests and needs, empathizing with others' struggles and pain — not the talker. There is a shyness and reticence about focusing on himself, and a style that is always slightly — and charmingly — self-deprecatory.

After I give a brief introduction regarding my project, there is an awkward silence. It is hard for Joe to know where to begin his story of exit — his "transition from being a priest" — so he jumps to the end. "I might as well cut to the chase," he says tentatively.

"Leaving the priesthood was not complicated. It was celibacy . . . and I knew it
would be an issue for me even before I
became a priest." I was warned by one of
his former patients — now his friend, who
described Joe as "the world's best, most
empathic doctor" — that I should not "let
him get away with the celibacy story." It is
not that his friend doubts that celibacy was
"a big deal" in Joe's decision to leave the
priesthood; it is that she has been curious
about the "struggle and ambivalence" that
she imagines must have been part of his
journey to the exit. But as I listen to Joe's
opening words, I do not feel worried by his
spare, truncated explanation. I suspect that
the single-word motivation for his exit —
"celibacy" — is part of a well-worn script
that masks years of history and layers of
emotion. It feels like a warm-up, so I listen
as he pushes on with the script.

"I actually loved the work of being a
priest. I was teaching at a Catholic school
in rural Virginia, working with teachers and
kids, involved in a campus ministry, doing
social service, and saying Mass on Sundays
at a nearby parish. I was idealistic and stub-
born . . . You see, I agree with celibacy in
principle . . . and my work was great, but I
knew deep inside of me that I was unhappy.

I had a yearning —" Joe's eyes look to me for help. He has finished cutting to the chase; now where to begin. So I ask a grounding question: "Where did you grow up?" And he throws me an appreciative smile.

Joe Rosario was the youngest of five and the only boy in an Italian Catholic family who lived in a small town in Virginia. "We were routinely religious, laid-back Catholics," he confesses, as a way of describing how religion was naturally embedded in the routines and rituals of their lives and as a way of emphasizing how nondogmatic his parents were in conveying the principles and practices of Catholicism. "We were not overtly religious . . . we never had God or Jesus conversations. Our life was not rigid or rule-bound." He offers an example. Joe had a gay nephew, just eight years his junior, who was very close to and admired by his parents. When he "came out" in college — the family had really known all along — Joe's parents accepted the announcement without flinching or pulling back. "The Catholic Church is clear about the sinfulness of being gay, but my parents never skipped a beat. They loved him the way they always had loved him," Joe remembers.

Even though he describes his family's

laissez-faire approach to Catholicism as laid-back, he also admits that religion was everything. It defined him; it surrounded him. He sums it up. "Catholic was who I was." And Catholicism was deeply linked with his Italian roots. Everyone he knew growing up was both Catholic and Italian. "Forty percent of the town was Catholic, but the circles that I ran in were one hundred percent Catholic," he says. Although both his parents were born in America, their parents were immigrants who settled in small, rural towns about ten miles apart. Joe's father, one of twelve children, grew up speaking Italian at home and only went to school through the eighth grade. His mother, who spoke mostly English as a child, went to college, a rare event for a first-generation Italian American woman during the 1930s and '40s. She dropped out after her sophomore year to marry Joe's dad and "fell into the traditional woman's role," cooking three meals a day, spending her days cleaning the house and taking care of children, and never driving a car.

All five of the Rosario children went to parochial schools, and three went on to Catholic colleges and universities. When Joe traces his early fascination with the priesthood, he actually goes back to his memories of high school, where he admired many of the priests who taught him. "Their good influence sort of opened up that door for me," he recalls wistfully. He liked what they did, the way they combined the spiritual and the practical, and their devotion to service in the community. And he liked the way they responded to their students with a winning combination of friendship and discipline. "The priests were very kid oriented," he recalls. "They did a lot to empower the students, helping us develop our leadership skills, guiding us in service and volunteer work." To Joe, the priests seemed to be living models of goodness, kindness, and grace generously given, and they knew how to really connect with the children in their charge.

Always a disciplined and high-achieving student, Joe was admitted to Villanova, where he immediately declared himself as a premed major, but he had an "interior life that gravitated" toward the priesthood. He remembers, in fact, "living two lives" — one in which he did "all the things kids do in college" and the other devoted to fantasizing about becoming a priest. For the most part, living these dual lives did not make him feel anxious or stressed out. As a matter of fact, he recalls feeling "comfortable and easy" balancing both realities. The two paths reached a point of divergence and some "unease," however, during Joe's junior year, when he studied very hard for the MCAT (medical college admissions test) but then decided at the last minute not to take it.

Even then, he recognized that an "internal decision" to enter the priesthood had taken place, one that he was not fully ready to recognize or talk about with anyone. When I ask him whether there was anyone who knew about his "deep yearnings," he mentions his college roommate, with whom he may have had a brief conversation, and he tells me about one of the priests who taught him in high school and became a "sort of mentor," to whom he sometimes turned for advice and guidance when he was home on vacation. But even after he told folks he had decided not to go to medical school, he did not mention the priesthood. Instead, he talked about going to graduate school in psychology (his minor in college).

Senior year forced his hand. He could no longer sit uncomfortably on the fence, between his two lives. He felt this most powerfully when he was with his girlfriend of two years, a Catholic girl with whom he had developed a sweet and loving relationship. He cared deeply for her; she was his best friend, a person with whom he shared his confidences. But their intimacy was always compromised by "the big secret" that remained hidden from her — his growing interest in the priesthood. Parting was hard, full of sadness and guilt. Even today Joe occasionally fantasizes about the road not taken and feels some remorse for the anguish he might have caused her. Even today he wants to protect her by not telling me the details of their relationship and separation.

The phone rings, startling both of us back into the present, and Joe excuses himself as he turns away from me and the past and answers it. One of his patients, a man in his mid-fifties, whom he saw a couple of weeks ago at the obesity clinic he directs, has suddenly died at home, his final exit. The caller is asking Joe for any information he has on the patient's condition when he was last seen at the hospital, and Joe punches his chart up on the computer. This is surprising, upsetting news, completely unexpected. Joe looks stunned; his voice grows quiet and intense. He tries to piece together the meager information he sees on the chart — obesity, high blood pressure, unemployment, living alone, etc. — and ends the call quickly with a promise to follow up. He shakes his head; there is sadness written all over his face as he tries to bring back the memories of the last time he saw the patient. Were there any signs he might have missed? I listen as his sentences trail off and he finds his way back to the spring of his senior year in college, when finally — "after endless procrastination and processing" — he contacted the Catholic Diocese of Virginia to inquire about training for the priesthood.

"I was completely naïve . . . I had absolutely no idea of what becoming a priest might involve. I did not even know that the priests at Villanova were different from the priests who taught me in high school." Joe's voice is incredulous as he laughs at his ignorance. I ask for clarification of the differences and distinctions. It turns out that the priests at Villanova are part of the Order of Augustine. They are not tied to a particular geographic region. Joe's high school mentors, on the other hand, were called secular priests, who are defined by geography and community, not by a particular order. Even though Joe did not know the various priestly classifications when he first contacted the diocese, he did know that he wanted to be like the priests who taught him in high school. "What I saw in high school is what I wanted to be," he says definitively.

"It was a coming out of sorts," he recalls about the moment when he finally, definitely stopped deliberating and took action. Everyone did not welcome his news. His girlfriend, whom he dated right up to the end of senior year, was hurt and crushed, even though she admitted to seeing the writing on the wall much before and even though she bowed out as gracefully as she could, her quiet retreat a cover for the anguish she must have been feeling. Joe's parents were surprised at his decision and definitely not enthusiastic when their son announced his plans. "They thought I was not making a mature decision," says Joe wanly. And his sisters — all four — were deeply skeptical. As a matter of fact, they did everything they could to dissuade him. Joe grins at the memory. "My sisters are all pretty Catholic, but they all sort of ganged up on me. They kept asking me why I wanted to do this, what my motivations were, and how I could possibly have come to this decision." Joe's oldest sister, a Hollywood costume designer, offered what she considered to be the ultimate seduction. She invited him to come out to Los Angeles for the summer, with the hope of introducing him to some gorgeous girl who would steal his heart. "She wanted to hook me up with someone; then I would be persuaded not to become a priest." Joe, in fact, did go to L.A. for the summer. He even dated a couple of girls while he was there. But when September rolled around, he was on his way back east to begin his "transitional year" of priesthood training.

Joe is quick to tell me that when his parents and sisters finally realized that he was fully committed to the idea of becoming a priest, they were completely behind him, offering him encouragement and support. And on the day he was ordained, they all turned out and cheered him on. "They were extremely proud. They stood there, completely amazed, very gaga. My family is terrific, incredibly supportive," he says about the ways in which his folks have always been there for him, always believed in his capacity to do whatever he sets out to do, always supported his decisions. And he reminds me that being from the community he comes from, becoming a priest is, after all, a big deal, "pretty, pretty cool."

The "transitional year" before actually entering the seminary is a time for asking the hard questions, for raising doubts and testing one's resolve. Through all the teaching, learning, and reading during that year, one question prevails: Are you sure that you want to do this? The theological curriculum at Saint Joseph's Seminary, where Joe was enrolled, had two parts — the first "academic" and the second "formative," dealing with the life of the spirit, community building, and the discipline of celibacy. For Joe, the year went by quickly and relatively smoothly. His answer to the big question about whether the priesthood was the right vocation seemed to be a resounding yes as he made his plans to enter Saint Vincent's in Philadelphia for the four-year march to ordination.

Joe remembers his early training in seminary as a time of spiritual devotion and probing questioning. "I was a practical skeptic," he says, comparing himself with those of his classmates who were unabashed believers. "I would say that I was a non-mystic in my beliefs. Many of my classmates were certain of the existence of God. They believed that miracles were real . . . that God's will was woven throughout their lives in very tangible ways. That was not me. I believed what I believed because I chose to, and I believed that there were legitimate alternative viewpoints that might be acceptable. Mine was not the one and only truth."

Not only was he a skeptic and a doubter, he also believed in the pragmatic, real-life implications of religious belief. He wanted to witness — and participate in — making God's imprint on the world around him. "I believed that religion must be applied in a pragmatic way. We must make a difference in the world."

He offers a recent example. This past Easter, for the first time in years, Joe decided to go to church. "I've made several exits from the church," he says sourly. At Easter Mass, he found himself doing what any priest might do while listening to another priest's homily. He made up his own, to himself. "You can't help doing your own homily in your head, and mine was about resurrection giving me hope . . . asking myself the question about how hope over-flows in my life . . . searching for a specific story, a real, lived experience, not a theoreti-cal abstraction." Just in case I have not yet understood the contrast he is drawing between his own practical, real-world bent and other believers who turn inward in their devotion to God and the church, he says, "If I was making the distinction between applied and theoretical math, my approach would always be the former."

Luckily, Saint Vincent's was a fairly liberal

seminary that offered the space for critical thinking and the questioning of church dogma. "In our discussions, there was always room for skepticism, openness, and discourse, which allowed me to become more comfortable talking about spirituality and my approach to religion," Joe recalls. As a matter of fact, he believes that in general, seminaries have become more rigid and closed-minded in their interpretation of church doctrine than they were when he was a student, and he feels fortunate that he matriculated at a time when progressive thinking and alternative views were welcome.

As we talk, Joe remembers a long-forgotten conversation he had during his third year of seminary, an exchange that presaged a struggle that would haunt his priesthood. He recalls saying to a friend one day, " 'If I leave [the priesthood], it will be because of celibacy.' I knew even then this was a big yearning." And by celibacy he meant "the whole thing," not just the sex. He was yearning for the "connection, the intimacy, the closeness" of a relationship as well. And he recalls one evening that same year going to a party with a bunch of old college friends, having a few too many drinks, and going home with a girl. Nothing happened between them; she knew he was a seminarian. But the lingering memory is of feeling the yearning and the guilt, the attraction and the repulsion, and the wish that he had not put himself in such an awkward position.

After seminary, Joe was assigned to a small parish, close to a college campus in a rural town in Virginia, near where he had grown up. "They ask you what sort of work you want to do, but really they assign you . . . plug you in to a place where they think you are needed." The fact that Joe had no real choice in selecting the place for his first ministry did not bother him. "It was the perfect place for me," he recalls with pleasure. "But then I'm the kind of person who feels whatever place I end up is perfect for me." He loved the work — the variety and the meaningfulness of it, the chance to build close relationships and help people, the feeling of appreciation and adulation from his parishioners. He speaks about a paradox of priesthood that most people do not recognize. "The work is great because there are lots of ways of working, and you can do lots of things. Even though the church is a rule-bound and seemingly rigid institution, priests have a lot of autonomy and flexibility." Joe enjoyed the hidden degrees of freedom that were there to be seized and the way he was able to make choices about how he would do his work.

He also began to recognize the value of celibacy in a priest's life, the advantages and benefits that came with not being married, that came with sexual abstinence. "I never really bought into the religious notion of celibacy, the part about giving yourself to God . . . the part about Jesus not being married," he admits. "But there is something about not being married, not being committed to a family life with a wife and children that leaves room for developing close and intimate relationships with the people you are serving. If you are a social kind of person, you can become part of people's families, get connected to lots of people in really deep ways." His voice is wistful. It is clear that now that he is not a priest, he misses the kind of closeness and trust that comes with being free of the responsibilities and expectations of family life. He admits sadly, "I've never found that kind of intimacy since I left the priesthood."

But it is not only that there are opportunities for connecting with people deeply through priestly work; there are also the benefits of being known and appreciated by an entire community, particularly in a rural

Catholic town. Joe is still amazed — and slightly embarrassed — by the status and adulation he enjoyed as a young priest. "You were put up on a pedestal. Everybody knew you." He tells me the story of a community fund-raiser for a health center in the small town where he worked, where the big prize they offered was the chance to have the priest over to your house for dinner. The raffles sold out immediately. Folks clamored for the privilege.

The intimacy and the reverence that came with the access and trust afforded priests now makes Joe shake his head in anger and disgust. With the worldwide exposure of abuse and pedophilia by priests and bishops of the Catholic Church, he is outraged by the ways in which people's trust has been betrayed, the ways in which the clergy have taken advantage of their cherished place and high station to do violence to innocent children. The heightened visibility of the rampant pedophilia not only enrages and disgusts him, it also has made him recall and question the motivations and behaviors of some of the priests he admired and revered in high school whose closeness to the students — his classmates and friends — now seems suspect, "even creepy." It makes him wonder, and feel suspicious, about moments of physical closeness and gestures of intimacy he experienced with his high school teachers that he, in his innocence, interpreted as benign and salutary. Recently he heard that a couple of those priests he knew in high school had, without admitting their guilt, quietly resigned under a cloud of suspicion. Again he closes his eyes and shakes his head, glad not to be a part of such a tarnished fraternity, furious at a church that would cover up and protect the abusers.

Even though Joe loved his ministry, loved serving the small community, loved the intimacy and flexibility of his work, and loved the priestly status and adoration from his parishioners, the yearning for a love relationship was always there. It was as if he were living two lives. "On the surface I was the same functioning and happy priest, but inside I was unhappy, and no one knew. Ultimately I couldn't reconcile these parts of me." Finally, when "the ache became consuming," Joe decided to talk about it with his spiritual director, and then he sought help outside of the church. "In the midst of this woefulness I recognized that I was truly depressed, that I needed the emotional support of a clinical psychologist."

The psychologist he saw was, in fact, a practicing Catholic who listened to him with patience and sympathy. During his therapy sessions Joe found himself drawn back time and again to the memories of his girlfriend in college, the one he had left when he decided to become a priest. "In some ways, I felt I had never gotten over her," he recalls. "It is not as if I wanted to erase all the years in between — they had been good — but I wanted to just go back to that time when we were together. She symbolized all that I was missing and yearning for."

Just as he had done before entering the seminary, when he was struggling with his family's worries about his chosen vocation, Joe traveled out to visit his sister in Los Angeles, the place that has over the years come to represent escape and freedom for him. His sister has always been loving and fiercely protective, but she has also offered him the space to express his ambivalence and uncertainty. "She is very unconventional, very different from me," says Joe with appreciation. Her home has always felt far away from the rules and routines of his priest life, far away from the watchful scrutiny of the church.

On this particular visit, his sister introduced him to one of her girlfriends, actually someone who was about Joe's age. They ended up spending all their time together. "We had a great time . . . nothing intimate or sexual. It was just fun and flirtatious . . . sitting close, next to each other. It was sixth-grade kind of stuff," says Joe about a time he still remembers as wonderfully "liberating and carefree." However innocent it was, he left L.A. knowing something for sure. He returned to the East Coast with a new clarity. He was going to leave the priesthood; he could no longer live the celibate life.

Joe returned to face the resistance of his spiritual director, who remained skeptical about his decision and tried to dissuade him, coaching him to "hang in." He even went to see his old mentor from high school, who surprised him with his straightforward, no-nonsense advice. "If leaving the priesthood is what you want to do, then do it." Something about the clarity and brevity of this response was "pivotal" for Joe. It helped to release him, propel him into action. For the first time, he remembers, a whole "new life opened up" for him. Leaving no longer tugged so hard at his heart. Now it was just a matter of jumping the church's hurdles and navigating the exit procedures. The psychologist who had counseled him wrote a letter of support to his bishop. Then Joe met with the bishop and told him "the whole story" behind his decision. Still hedging his bets, he did not ask for a complete separation, but for a leave of absence from the church. The bishop listened attentively and responded supportively. "Take all the time you need," he said gently. "We are here for you."

The bishop made the departure relatively easy, leaving the door wide open for Joe's return. It was harder — much harder — for Joe to say goodbye to his parishioners and the teachers and students he worked with at the local school. He had, by then, become "very good friends" with so many of the people, and he felt that they needed to hear the truth from him. But the bishop had insisted that when he said his farewells at his final Mass, he should "not go into the reasons why." So he stood up in front of the congregation — full of many people he had grown to love — and spoke ambiguously. He "left it enigmatic," giving a stilted presentation that satisfied neither him nor his listeners. It was also a talk that left people wondering and skeptical, perhaps fantasizing that he was trying to cover up something, that he had been "part of a scandal." But mostly Joe hated that he had to lie to the folks who had been so "incredibly supportive and generous." He was not giving them what they deserved — the "real story" of why he needed to leave them. "That was what made me feel the most guilty," he whispers.

With the reassurance of the bishop, Joe explored every option he could think of, from doctoral programs in psychology and education, to M.B.A. programs, to law school and medicine. He visited the campuses, went on tours, had interviews, studied brochures, and filled out applications. There is no one, he claims, who is more methodical and comprehensive — perhaps to the point of being "obsessive-compulsive" — than he is. "I process everything to death," he says about the way he always weighs his alternatives and is never impulsive or rash in making decisions. Finally, after more than a year of casting about, Joe applied — at thirty-six — to a post-baccalaureate premed program at a college near L.A. that was known for its personalized mentoring of students and for getting them admitted to prestigious medical schools. It had been so long since he graduated with an undergraduate premed major from Villanova that there were whole new fields and courses — such as molecular biology — that he had to study.

During the two years there, Joe lived with his sister and worked at a series of odd jobs to earn spending money. Even though he was a full-time student, he was still "officially" a priest, an identity that remained mostly hidden from view. He had saved about $25,000, a "huge sum" that disappeared amazingly quickly. With the savings, he was able to spend the first seven months just going to school. But then he needed to hustle and make a living. Having spent the last decade and a half in religious life, Joe felt frustrated by a job market where his experiences and skills held little value. After applying to — and being rejected by — several low-level service jobs, he finally found work as a courier, driving 150 miles a day on the L.A. freeways, delivering movie scripts and legal documents. One memory — of the humiliation of his new low status — stands out. He recalls delivering a document to a Hollywood agent's office and being treated dismissively by "some eighteen-year-old kid" receptionist. Motioning to the empty chair, he told Joe, "Sit right there. I'll deal with you when I'm ready." In that moment Joe came face-to-face with his fall from grace. "Doesn't feel very good," he says, smiling wanly, "to go from being a big shot to being a thirty-six-year-old delivery boy."

Every night as he left the college library, Joe would call his sister to say that he was heading home. "I come from a family of worriers," he tells me, "and my sister was taking on my mother's role, wanting to know my every move." Not only was his sister committed to keeping him safe; she also was always looking to introduce him to women. She wanted him to relish his new freedom. She wanted him to celebrate his release from the "claws of celibacy." One day she spoke to a former neighbor whose daughter was looking for a job as a costume designer, and she happened to mention that Joe had left the priesthood and was living with her. The neighbor, who recalled having met Joe years earlier, thought he might be an excellent match for one of her coworkers, and she gave Joe's sister the woman's number.

It took weeks for him to get around to calling Angelina, a real estate agent and divorcée who was a single mom of a five-year-old daughter. They met for lunch and "really hit it off." It was several months — of dinners, dates, and adventures together — before Joe met her daughter at a family gathering. For some reason, that moment of meeting her child stands out. The little girl was wearing a red hat, tilted to the side of her head. Joe recalls, laughing, "She was a real charmer . . . she worked the room. It was easy to fall for her in a superficial sort of way." But Joe was aware of some resistance inside of him, some need to not fully succumb to the little girl's wiles. "I sort of stood back and watched, thinking that there was more to this story than I knew or could see . . . feeling that I was not quite ready to take this on."

Over the months, Joe's reluctance slowly melted as he continued to date and enjoy Angelina and as he grew closer to her daughter. But he still did not feel completely sure about his path to medical school; nor was he 100 percent certain about leaving the priesthood forever. "This was still somewhat of an experiment," he says about his romance and his newly chosen vocation. "I was ninety-nine percent sure of pursuing my medical degree, but there was still that one percent possibility that I would return to the priesthood. I'm one of those people who holds on to the possibilities until I finally make a decision. Then I let them go." Since he was still not 100 percent certain of his path, he decided to tell the medical schools to which he was applying that there was a dim possibility that he might return to being a priest. He also dangled his indecision in front of Angelina, believing that it was only fair that she know the truth as well, know about his lingering ambivalence.

As he applied to medical schools, he felt the double edge of excitement and dread. "It was thrilling to be thinking about starting my new life, but I was also worried about not getting into medical school and having nothing that was marketable." Keeping as many options open as possible, Joe applied to scores of schools, had lots of interviews, and "daydreamed often about what it might feel like to receive an acceptance letter." At first he did not put fancy schools on his list, thinking they would be out of his reach, but his professors insisted that with his record, he could get in anywhere. It turned out that he was accepted at almost every place he applied. The letters from Columbia and Yale arrived on the same day. I am surprised when Joe tells me that his sister opened the letters before he arrived home; and as he walked in the door, she handed him the open envelope from Columbia. Rejection. Then, feigning thirst, she walked to the refrigerator and pulled out a bottle of champagne to which she had attached the letter from Yale.

Acceptance! Joe was surprised and over-joyed. "It was a no-brainer. Yale has a great program, and I always knew I wanted to come back east," he says, victory still in his voice.

He headed east the following fall, leaving Angelina and her daughter behind — still feeling "on the fence" about their relation-ship, vowing to "see what happened" once he "got going in school." They kept in touch through the fall and visited back and forth at Thanksgiving, Christmas, and during his spring break. He did not date any other women. "Then," he admits quietly, "I started worrying about her." He furrows his brow, admitting again, "I come from a fam-ily of worriers . . . it is a sort of strange way to show love, but that is the way we do it." During the first three years of medical school, there were longer visits between them. He even took a Spanish immersion course so he could do a rotation at a com-munity clinic in L.A. that served Latino patients. And while he was there, he lived with Angelina and her daughter.

After living together, even Joe, the big "processor," the "huge worrier," knew that decision time was near. How long could he string this out? It was his mother who finally said to her son, in a fit of frustration, "Shit or get off the pot! If you're going to marry her, do it now." The next day, Joe and his sister went out to find the ring, and that evening Joe proposed to Angelina. "I'm the least spontaneous person I know," he says with understatement. But once Angelina said yes, life flew by with the speed of lightning. She gave two weeks' notice at her agency, they packed up the rental truck, and the three of them — Joe, Angelina, and her daughter — drove across the country and into the future. They had no jobs, no plan, and no place to live. Something had turned the worry into an adventure.

In many ways, Joe Rosario's long leave-taking from the church resembles the stages of role exit identified by Ebaugh. He goes through a protracted period of "first doubts," keeping his "longings" secret, his "woefulness" under the radar; enjoying — and feeling guilty about — hanging out and flirting with a girl in a "sixth-grade kind of way"; feeling a huge nostalgia for the serious girlfriend he abandoned in college when he decided to enter the priesthood. His mounting doubts make him feel that he is leading a "double life" — on the outside he is the jovial, compassionate priest; on the inside he is aching with anguish. When the dualities and masks get to be unbearable, he consults with mentors, former teachers, a psychologist, and his bishop, explicitly asking for their guidance, implicitly begging them for their permission and blessings. A second summer in L.A. — under the protective and liberating tutelage of his sister — finally convinces him that exit is the only option. But even then Joe hedges his bets and decides to take a leave of absence rather than resign from the priesthood.

Joe plays out the second stage of Ebaugh's theory — weighing "role alternatives" — with his signature caution and meticulousness: casting a wide net, investigating numerous options, holding on to his allegiance to the church even when he submits his applications to medical school, even when he is 99 percent sure that he wants to leave the priesthood and become a doctor. The "turning point" — Ebaugh's third stage — actually comes several years later, when his mother forces his hand ("shit or get off the pot") and his older sister goes with him to buy the engagement ring for Angelina. All of a sudden, after years of "processing and procrastination," a decision that has been waiting to happen propels life forward, a mighty wind that sweeps the family of three across the country in their U-Haul.

As Joe rehearses all these stages of exit, there is an undertow of regret and "yearning," a word he uses more than any other to describe the "ache" that never leaves him, that gets rationalized in his caution and deliberation, in his meticulous listing of the pros and cons, the opportunities and liabilities at every fork in the road. His exit is marked by huge "what-ifs," endless deliberation, and processing, an internal decision that lives for years inside of him, not ready to be revealed, more a response to circumstance than an exercise in agency. His tale shows us how much not being able to exit can hurt, and how we can begin to accept that hurt as part of our lives for a very long time. Some of the hurt seems to be inherited. Joe comes from a "family of worriers"; worrying is the way they show their love. Worrying is embedded in the family's approach to life decisions and in the ways they relate to one another. Being raised in the bosom of the Catholic Church must have added another layer of yearning and hurting, fueling his aching guilt for having abandoned his sacred duties and promises and deepening his wistful longings for the people he left behind.

The path toward exit, Joe claims, "begins and ends" with his unwillingness to live a celibate life forever. He knew that the vow of celibacy would be a problem even before he signed up for the priesthood. But when he yearns to be with a woman, he realizes he is speaking about something more than sex. He wants the intimacy, commitment, and companionship of a "fully realized relationship." He wants a partnership with a woman that is "liberating and carefree." He wants the pleasure of flirting and playing, feeling the comfort and warmth of her body next to his. But when he meets Angelina's five-year-old daughter — charming in her fetching red outfit and precocious femininity — he is not at all sure he wants to take her on. He wonders whether he is ready for the responsibilities, the compromises, and the risks of embracing family life. He wonders whether he is ready to leave the safe harbor of celibacy.

As Joe tells me about the dark, aching side of celibacy and recounts his years of yearning to break its hold on him, he discovers its silver lining. He has a sudden, surprising epiphany. He doesn't believe that the reason priests should take a vow of celibacy is so that they can give themselves fully to God, or because Jesus never married. But he does believe that the celibate life offers priests the emotional space to be present with the people they are serving, to enter fully into their lives. "I have never known an intimacy like that since I left the priesthood," he admits. There is an irony in Joe's exit search. After long years of yearning for the intimacy and devotion of marriage, he exits the priesthood and discovers what he has lost and left behind, some of the deepest human connections he has ever known.

There is wistfulness in Joe's voice, a sadness that seems to run deep when he tells the story of his saying goodbye to the small parish in Virginia. It was hard enough to leave those people who depended on him, whom he had grown to love, who had loved him back with a purity and adoration he would never experience again. But even harder than leaving was the way he had to muzzle his message, telling his parishioners vague half-truths that left them feeling uneasy and suspicious. By far, the biggest injury was his having to lie to them, leaving a hurt that continues to haunt him today.

Joe's unsettling departure — compromised by lies of omission — helps us understand the importance of truth telling and authenticity and the critical role of ritual in paving the path to successful exits. His last lame sermon, full of ambiguity, did not give Joe the chance to offer his appreciation to and affection for his congregation, nor did it give him the vehicle to express his loss and grief at leaving. And it did not give his parishioners the opportunity to record the sadness in their hearts or their rage at his going. There was no ceremony to hold their overflowing emotions, no way to channel their beautiful/ugly mix of feelings, no way for Joe to bow out with grace.

Rituals that are intentionally and artistically designed, that allow us the chance to revel in our emotions — of appreciation and love, of regret and despair — give us the chance to mark the separation, say our goodbyes, and move on. Otherwise the exit feels incomplete, nourishing a yearning that burns on forever.

YEARNING TO MAKE SENSE

"Stepping out, looking back, measuring myself."

I am witness to the elaborate farewell ritual that marks the departure of Josh Arons from the Beacon Fund, the largest philanthropic organization in New Hampshire, which he has masterfully led for a quarter of a century. Almost a thousand people have come to celebrate Josh's leadership and to mark the growth of the fund that under his stewardship has more than quadrupled its endowment — serving as a safety net for the poorest citizens, offering major grants to community service organizations, lobbying the state legislature for public funds that will contribute to sustainable economic change, and pushing through some of the most controversial and progressive public policy initiatives in the state. Colleagues and friends, politicians and community organizers, and leaders of corporations, colleges, and nonprofits are gathered in the Hyatt Hotel in the state's capital to honor Josh and say their goodbyes. Eight hundred fifty chairs fill the ballroom (with 150 more in an anteroom with a video feed), a glittering space with ornate chandeliers, heavily draped windows, and deep burgundy carpeting. The stage has two huge screens on either side of a giant photograph of a New Hampshire scene, with mountains in the background and in the foreground a bridge over a gushing river. "Bridge" is the symbol and metaphor of the evening. An abstract graphic of a bridge appears on the invitation, the program, and the 2009 annual report, marking Josh's bridging of the past and the future, underscoring his transition and journey.

A planning committee — of board members, staff, donors, and grantees — has worked for almost a year to find a way to honor their leader, hoping to strike a balance between their wish to lavishly celebrate him and his wish to "keep it simple." Finding within him the discipline to "stay out of it," and knowing how important it is for folks to "make a big deal," Josh has made only three requests. He does not want any big speeches, he wants everyone at some point to join in singing "Stand By Me," and he wants everyone to be given a piece of dark chocolate (in this case shaped like the state of New Hampshire). The first request is the hardest to honor, admits the master of ceremonies, but they do manage to finesse it by asking about ten people — longtime friends and colleagues — to speak for two minutes or less on an essential quality they have admired in Josh. And surprisingly, everyone sticks to the time frame, even the governor, who leads the parade of tributes.

While people are taking their seats and greeting one another, a Ghanaian music and dance troop, dressed in the traditional kente cloth, are onstage beating their drums. The sound is loud and thrashing, reverberating through the hall, causing some people to grimace, cover their ears, and shout to hear one another in conversation. For me the juxtaposition is jarring: the dark black musicians — smiling, gesticulating, bodies gyrating, barefoot — and the very white, traditionally garbed audience sitting primly in their seats. It is a black/white contrast that continues to be underscored throughout the evening, signifying Josh's rebel activist days in the civil rights movement in Mississippi and his long tenure as executive director of the Beacon Fund, working with white communities — many of them poor and rural — across the state. I sit there feeling troubled, even sad, as I imagine how the dissonance and distance between these black and white worlds must have required more than bridging, more than compromise and negotiation. I think there must have been some suffering as well, some ways in which Josh has had to dampen his progressive, activist impulses and mask his rebellious spirit in order to be successful at his work in New Hampshire.

The tributes and numbers speak to his amazing success and commitment — the huge growth in resources, endowment, and grants; the initiation and development of new government programs and policies; the outreach to marginalized, impoverished

306

communities; the building of social capital in neighborhoods around the state. The statistics of expansion and growth under Josh's leadership appear on the screens and make people gasp and applaud. But the tributes are a much more poignant reflection of his contributions and the respect, even reverence, in which he is held. Each speaker chooses a word or two to describe him — energetic, imaginative, productive, attentive, creative, hardworking, empathic, visionary, masterful, extraordinary, politically savvy — and several of them choke up as they tell stories of his deep listening, his steady support, his love of ideas, his large and nimble mind, his big embrace.

When Josh rises to make his comments, the audience stands in lengthy applause, and he is clearly moved. His voice is soft and hoarse; he speaks slowly and carefully, from the heart. He speaks mainly about his growing appreciation for the meaning and power of "place" — the way he has come to love this place called New Hampshire, the special qualities of the people and the ways they have worked together, powerfully connected in their collective mission, bridging the differences, nourishing the bonds. At one point he brings up the work of his rebel youth, reminiscing about the ways in which the black folks from rural Mississippi talked about their responsibility to place. "I does where I am," he says, sounding black and southern. But he quickly returns to the Beacon Fund story, the last twenty-five years of labor he has loved in a place he loves, back to his testimony that there is no place he would rather have spent this part of his life. Oddly, there are no comments from his family — children and grand-children — who are all sitting in their black, white, and biracial splendor in the front row, and no appreciations from old and dear friends who have known him for forty years and have traveled from Rome, Chicago, and Seattle to be here. The celebrants are all closely linked to "place," New Hampshire and the Beacon Fund. The ceremony is intentionally focused on his work com-munity, not his family; it is designed to focus on his public, not his private, life.

The gathering concludes with the song Josh requested. On three huge screens flashes the face of an old black street musi-cian strumming his guitar. With a bag in front of him open for tips, he sings a soul-ful, raunchy version of "Stand By Me." His eyes are shut; his head sways back and forth to the blues rhythm. Then the video pans to other places where brown and black people are singing "Stand By Me," voices from around the globe joined in a universal anthem. The audience is surprised and delighted when the video turns back to their "place," to groups of folks they recognize, white people from across their state singing "Stand By Me," awkwardly smiling, tentatively swaying, trying to loosen up and catch the rhythm in their bodies. For minutes we take in the contrast — the sensuous, soulful bodies; the raw, husky voices and plaintive calls of the blacks from the United States, Africa, the Middle East; even a Native American group dressed in their tribal costumes . . . and the white folks from the office, community groups, and local churches around New Hampshire giving it their best shot, trying their hardest to find the melody and move to the beat, enjoying themselves. I sit there wondering what Josh feels about all this. How is he taking in this celebration of his good works? Whom does he want to stand by him once he crosses the bridge? Where does he want to stand next?

Josh Arons remembers the exact moment when he decided to cross the bridge. It was December 2008, and he was attending a conference in San Francisco sponsored by Civic Ventures, a nonprofit on whose board of directors he sits. Each year Civic Ventures awards a Purpose Prize to a dozen people over sixty who have embarked on "Encore Careers" — visionaries whose ingenious and generous vocational shifts are making a big difference in the world, locally and globally. Even though Josh has attended this annual awards ceremony since it was initiated a decade ago, and even though his own work for the past twenty-five years has focused on public service, this was the first time he felt the powerful impact of the stories he heard in a "deeply personal way."

He was inspired by the sixty-five-year-old perfume baron who left his lucrative spot as the CEO of a major international company to work with men leaving prison, helping them find work and dignity on the outside. He loved hearing from the former cameraman whose Hollywood career had dried up long ago, who had suffered through years of poverty and unemployment but finally, at the urging of an old friend, traveled to West Africa to work with indigenous folks to invent a technically simple and elegant machine that shelled peanuts, increasing the productivity of the rural region tenfold. There were other amazing stories from "ordinary people making extraordinary contributions" — discovering new life paths, taking big risks, learning new skills and disciplines, awakening new passions — and Josh drank it all in.

He recalls the "enormous impact" of those "amazing stories" and the excitement, the provocation, and the urgency that rose up in him. Right then he knew that something had shifted in him; he felt it in his gut. He knew — with a clarity and poignancy that surprised him — that it was time for him to "move on"; it was time to "embark on his next chapter." Josh returned to his hotel room that night and called his partner, Joyce, to tell her the exciting news. And two days later, when he landed back in New Hampshire, he sat down with his board chair to tell him that he would, within the year, be ending his tenure as CEO of the Beacon Fund. Even though Josh suspects that his decision to exit must have been stirring in him for many years, his "moment of epiphany" came like a bolt out of the blue. It arrived without warning and required no rational listing of pros and cons, no calculated deliberation.

Josh welcomes the opportunity to reflect on his exit from the Beacon Fund. His decision to leave sneaked up on him all of a sudden, but he knows that moving forward — with "purposefulness and grace" — will require that he revisit his journey and rehearse the mixture of feelings that have converged in him during this moment of transition. He leans back in his chair and strokes his chin in thoughtful meditation. He furrows his brow; his voice is almost a whisper. "What has interested me in leaving . . . is how much I have loved the work as much as I've ever loved anything. I'm struggling to make sense of it all, wanting to learn as much as I can from it." He asks me whether I've ever read *Stranger in a Strange Land,*[4] a science-fiction book that he loves, where the characters invent a new verb — "grok" — that means to "be at one with some truth." Josh smiles. "That's what I want to do now . . . grok what it means to be leaving."

In his effort at meaning making, he begins at the beginning, sketching out his early biographical route. Adopted at birth, Josh grew up in New Jersey and attended public schools all the way through high school, then attended Williams College. After college he earned a master's in foreign policy at Columbia before heading off to do relief work in West Africa. Within a year he had returned to the United States, intent on becoming part of the civil rights movement. "I kept reading about the struggle in Mississippi and Alabama," he recalls, "and I thought, I need to be there." He was right. His work in the South was deeply engaging and formative for him; even now it seems to serve as a touchstone, a reference point against which much of the rest of his life is measured. The stories from Mississippi — his work with sharecroppers, doing voter registration, sitting in at lunch counters, joining the bus boycotts — remain a "huge part" of his identity, giving early definition to his lifelong commitment to social justice. The Selma march stands out as an unforgettable marker: blacks and whites, Christians and Jews, southerners and northerners coming together in collective action, marching side by side, singing freedom songs. These are the songs that still echo through him as he gathers with friends around the dinner table or takes his activist work to the rural regions of New Hampshire; these are the songs he hoped to hear at his goodbye gala.

John Lindsay's campaign for mayor of New York pulled him away from his work in the South, and when Lindsay won the election, Josh, at twenty-five, stayed on in a major policy position, overseeing the antipoverty, welfare, and educational initiatives — a lefty Democrat working for a progressive Republican mayor. It was a heady, even glamorous time. Josh points to the teachers' strike he helped organize, which closed down the public schools from September through November. A recently completed documentary about the Lindsay years stars him as one of the chief protagonists, giving him the opportunity to relive those amazing days of his youth and reflect on the way he shaped and was shaped by the political and cultural landscape. After eight years with the Lindsay administration he moved to New Hampshire to work as a university provost, and twelve years later he was hired as the CEO of the Beacon Fund.

And Josh says that, like the John Lindsay days and his time in Mississippi, his twenty-five years at Beacon have "never felt like a job." Life has been "seamless and deeply rooted in the community"; colleagues have become close friends; public has blended into private; professional relationships have been sustaining and familial. He talks about the "seamless" blending of life's pieces as a way of emphasizing that his exit from Beacon is "not like leaving a job . . . it's like leaving a life." One of the ways in which he has begun to get a "purchase" on his feelings of exiting has been to speak about them in a public forum. "There is a discipline of having to say it publicly . . . having to actually say it, not just write it." In a speech that became his final published piece for the fund's newsletter, Josh examined the long sweep of his work, focusing on the ways he let himself and his constituents down, the ways he felt compromised, the places where "the institutional ways and the individual values were in conflict" and the former won out over the latter. Here are some of his poignant and brave reflections:

As I leave this job that I love beyond description, my greatest feelings of personal failure, of not rising to the challenge, were where I surrendered to the institutional inertia rather than challenging it. Where I deferred taking actions that may have offended the norms of the institution.

Where my individual sense of what was right would have required me to choose the unconventional: to ask the Fund to weigh in more publicly and directly on behalf of those who wanted change and to go against the broader and accepted norms of our community.

I didn't push hard enough on issues of race. Even on symbolic issues such as honoring Dr. King's birthday, where New Hampshire was among the last states in the country to do so. Nor on immigration reform, though virtually all of us, somewhere in our own family past, came as immigrants to this country. We have not done enough to franchise the disenfranchised.

Although the speech is a self-critical meditation — he quotes Atticus Finch in *To Kill a Mockingbird* when he says, "The one thing that doesn't abide by majority rule is a person's conscience" — Josh's analysis seems neither morose nor self-flagellating. Rather his words offer a gentle, courageous summing-up of a quarter of a century of work that has been at once exciting and unnerving, productive and imperfect, sweet and bitter. Josh avoids the platitudes, the facile conclusions. He resists the congratulatory voices of all those around him who say that — on the contrary — he took a lot of risks at the fund and showed uncommon courage and brave leadership while he was there. "But I am not lulled by their claims," says Josh quietly. "My efforts were often engaged in trying not to offend. My actions were too often premised on caution and cordiality."

Even though the institutional inertia and norms forced a kind of caution, Josh has always worked hard to move the fund toward the arena of public policy. Now his voice is almost strident. "I believed — and I still do — that you can't make substantial change with grant moneys. You must wade into the political process. In the beginning there was a lot of discomfort about that . . . I had early political battles with conservative governors who pushed back against my efforts to challenge and engage the political system . . . who called me a pushy New Yorker, a code word for my being Jewish." Now, at almost sixty-eight, Josh indulges this kind of "stocktaking," weighing the wins and losses, holding up the balances and tensions between the individual and institutional forces, admitting the compromises and the things left undone. He believes that he would not have been capable of this stocktaking — this "groking" — any earlier in his life. This moment of maturity, slowing down, and leave-taking has forced a new capacity for reflection — "stepping out, looking back, measuring myself." It doesn't matter what others say, claims Josh. "It's what is in me."

Interestingly, this taking stock of his work at the fund came at the same time as a large gathering in New York City celebrating the Lindsay retrospective. All the folks who had

worked in major roles in Lindsay's administration — and were still alive — came
together to view the documentary, to share
memories, to reminisce at a big celebratory
event. "It was an amazing convergence,"
says Josh about how the New Hampshire
and New York events made him realize that
in the busyness and zest of his life, he had
rarely made time or space for self-reflection.
"I realized while making the documentary
that I had never reflected on those Lindsay
years. The journalist interviewed me for
hours, and I remember being shocked by
the questions he asked, shocked at the fact
that I never stepped out of it. I was able to
do storytelling — lots of stories — but no
analysis, no reflection."

In fact, by the time he got home from the
interview, Josh felt depressed and embarrassed by his inability to speak critically and
analytically, his sense that he had been
caught with his pants down, sounding facile
and quixotic. "I was sufficiently un-
nerved . . . enough to call the reporter back
and ask if we could do the interview again.
I said I thought his questions were unfair,
even hostile." The reporter, who thought
the interview had gone well, was surprised
by Josh's defensiveness and anxiety and
tried to assure him that he had not only

made a lot of sense, but he had a prominent place in the film. His words had provided the moving ending of the documentary; his reflections were the perfect coda. Now Josh is shaking his head at his surprising feelings of vulnerability. "I guess I must have been worried about how my peers would see me. I thought, God, I'm going to be exposed . . . and maybe what I said will betray others."

Josh thinks that his inability to "step out of himself" and look at his work may be related to the fact that he does not live his life in parts, separating the personal from the professional, family from work. "I am more and more aware of how much my professional life is embedded everywhere. I am one person. This place is family and life . . . seamless," he muses, spreading his arms to embrace the office space around us. Although he sees the great benefits in living life holistically ("You hope that your children will also find work that they love . . . putting all the pieces together"), Josh also recognizes the possible liabilities. "There could also be solace unlinking these various parts," he says as he thinks about the freedom that might result from drawing boundaries and creating separations.

When Josh returned home from San Francisco — after his "great epiphany" —

he was consumed by two warring emotions. "It all felt very exciting and very clear, but I was also hugely sad about leaving this place, and I still have not reconciled these feelings." Since he made the decision to exit, each day has felt like a "countdown." Each meeting, each conference, each speech feels like "the last this or that." But he does not necessarily view these final steps as a path to freedom. "There is no sense of liberation on the horizon," he says. "I don't feel, Oh boy, I will finally be free." As he spends his last year counting down and taking stock, Josh is determined to "keep both feet planted" in the present. "I didn't want to use this last year with one foot in and one foot out of this place," he says. "I did not think that would be honorable or fair to others." So when calls have come in — and many have — from folks who want to feel him out about his next career move or even offer him a job, Josh has told them he will not talk with them until after he leaves Beacon. And even then, he feels as if he does not want to rush on to the next thing. Rather he wants the space and time to "stop and breathe and see what swims up inside" of him.

A big smile covers his face as he remembers the one call he could not resist taking.

One of his friends, a big banker and a great guy, who owns the minor-league baseball team in town, called several weeks ago to see if Josh might be interested in joining his organization in some capacity. Immediately Josh's heart began pumping, his mind began racing, so much so that he didn't listen to a word his friend was saying. Now he's laughing at the memory. "I'm thinking to myself, He sees I've still got it. I could play third base. I could do it . . . or maybe I could be the designated hitter." It took a while for Josh to realize that he had gotten swept up in his own fantasies, a while before his friend's voice finally brought him back to reality. And then he was embarrassed. "Dummy, he means are you interested in being the manager." Now he can laugh about it all, but at that moment it felt confusing and humiliating, out of time and space. He didn't even tell Joyce — with whom he usually shares his wildest fantasies — until weeks later, when he made it into a big joke.

Now Josh sees the baseball fantasy as "illustrative" of the energy and imagination he hopes to find in his next work. He is determined not to do the same old things. He does not want to join any more boards or manage any more institutions. He wants to go through a process of discovery, wants the ideas to flow from within. "I want to find inside myself what I want to do. I do not have a bucket list. I don't have hobbies I want to expand on . . . But there is something in me that is confident that I will find something meaningful and creative to do."

He is reminded of the three-month sabbatical he took in San Francisco ten years ago. A friend of his had suggested that he go to one place and plant himself there, not spend his time traveling from place to place. Josh not only took his friend's advice about "staying still"; he also decided to separate himself from all things familiar. He recalls, "I stopped reading *The New York Times* . . . I let all my friends out there know that I would not be seeing them . . . I found myself involved in all sorts of things I had never tried." His San Francisco days were completely different from his New Hampshire ones. Every day, he went to the gym and did karate; he took drawing and painting lessons; he learned to cook Chinese food. After three months he came back not only renewed but also feeling that "there was so much more in life." The San Francisco experience seems like a good way to anticipate entering his next chapter — with an open mind and heart, with curiosity and eagerness, with the determination not to fall back into old, comfortable patterns.

Despite Josh's optimism about finding something new and meaningful after the Beacon Fund, he admits to feeling a chronic, low-grade worry about his capacity to live a life without work being at the center of it. His face is pensive, his voice plaintive as he muses about his feelings of unease and vulnerability. "I've never not worked. I don't know whether work actually gives me my sense of wholeness and identity. The traffic in my life has always been tied to work . . . that's been the commerce of my life." Josh's decision to not jump into the next thing immediately — even though he believes he has "one more big piece of work" still in him — adds to his eagerness and his nervousness. "Because I'm doing it this way, counting on sitting still, it all feels unsettled, and I'm scared about waiting for something to come up inside of me." He seems to be talking to himself, or maybe he's trying to convince himself. His voice is soft and searching. "There is, I believe, a new discipline in doing it this way, leaving myself totally vulnerable . . . not interested in being defined by institutional anchors, not measuring my life in comparison to others . . . just wanting to bare myself."

Even though the decision to "sit still" feels scary, Josh is clear that when he leaves Beacon, he will not for a moment regret the decision to exit. He will walk away and never look back. "As soon as I leave," he says without ambivalence, "this will be behind me. It will be done. It will look very distant, and I say this without wanting to betray all the people I will leave behind."

Knowing that he wants to leave space in his life to let the next phase emerge naturally and organically, I ask him what other roles and responsibilities might begin to fill the spaces left empty. Will his fathering and his grandfathering assume a bigger place and pleasure in his life? Josh has three children and four grandchildren, and he has spent a good deal of time telling me about them. But my question seems to come as a surprise, and Josh takes a long time to form his answer. "I don't necessarily see these roles becoming larger or more prominent. There is no doubt about how important they all are to me, but as much as I love these kids, I still see myself as a player in the game. I want to be a part of making change in the world . . . I still want to be a part of the larger struggle." Not only does Josh still want to use his energies to "continue the justice work in some form"; he also believes that his job as a father has changed a lot as his children have become responsible adults. He is not — and should not be — at the center of their realities. "My job as father has been to enable, empower, and love them. Then it is up to them to make their own lives. It is like teaching a child to ride a bike. You hold on for a while; then you let go. They fall and get up . . . and finally ride away from you."

Even though he anticipates that his children — and their children — will not fill a bigger space in his life after he leaves Beacon, he is keenly aware of the "aging part of it." He knows that at any time, his life, or those of his loved ones and friends, might be shattered by illness or death. "We are not free agents," he says, in reference to how much more vulnerable he feels, even though his health is good and his mortgage is paid. He remembers how many funerals he has attended and how many good friends he has eulogized in the past year. He thinks of the folks he has known for forty years who are now in their eighties and growing frailer, of his old mentor whom he visited just last week in Florida who is suffering from Parkinson's, and the one he still visits weekly who no longer recognizes him because of her dementia. More than ever, he is aware of the finiteness of his own life and the urgency of getting on with it.

As he talks of illness and death, his musings shift to the subject of religion and his claim that he "has nothing to say on the spiritual side." His statement surprises me as he "continues taking an inventory, a checklist, of the various domains" of his life. But then he draws a distinction that settles my puzzlement, claiming that he is actually "very Jewish" but his "Judaism" is more about his connection to a community of people, his embeddedness in the culture. The sacred rituals matter a lot. Every Friday evening he and Joyce celebrate Shabbat with candles and prayers, and when his children were still at home, Josh used to bake the challah bread that would grace the table. And for the past fifty years, eighty to ninety members of Josh's extended family have gathered at a restaurant in New York City for the Passover seder, coming from all over the country to be together. In all this time, he has missed only one Passover (when he was in his early twenties working in West Africa), and this year, for the first time, he got to preside at the seder, and he loved it. The uncles have now grown too old to carry on, and he has accepted the mantle enthusiastically. "It is all about affirming and nestling," Josh says with great feeling. "These are my people, and this is who I am." Now he is weeping. "There is a huge sense of peace and connectedness."

As we sit quietly together, the inventory taken, the interview over, I think that despite Josh's claims to the contrary, it is this anchoring and connectedness, this sense of peace that will scaffold and nourish him as he tries on the new discipline of "sitting still and letting the next thing come from within." It is this spiritual source that will help him navigate his exit.

Although I still have not read *Stranger in a Strange Land* (science fiction is not my thing), I do love the verb — "to grok" — that Josh has borrowed from the book's probing protagonists. "To be at one with some truth" is Josh's form of yearning. The "bridge" he is building from the old to the new, from the familiar to the strange, is filled with earnest moments of self-interrogation. He goes public with his self-examination of the last twenty-five years. It is one thing to write down what you believe, another thing to give your views public voice, to hold yourself audibly accountable, to stand up and be counted. His public self-appraisal is followed by some deeply private reflections, strange feelings of uncertainty and vulnerability, and determined efforts to "sit still," feel the spirit, and listen for the "organic" unfolding of the next chapter.

Unlike Joe Rosario's exit from the priesthood — which roughly mimics the four stages laid out in Ebaugh's theory — Josh's departure from his CEO position follows a very different trajectory. One night in San Francisco he listens to the extraordinary stories of brave and generous "social pioneers" who are changing the world, and he has an epiphany — a sudden and surprising surge of inspiration that propels him forward immediately and decisively. And unlike Joe, who spends years in protracted deliberations, seeking out mentors for advice and counsel, weighing the costs and the benefits, hedging his bets until he can no longer, Josh makes the firm decision to exit, announces it to his board chair, and decides to spend the next year fully immersed at the Beacon Fund — "with two feet planted" — turning away inquires from bidders who want to offer him a job or tempt him with predictable opportunities. Purposefully, he does not seek advice or guidance from friends and colleagues; he wants to heed the call from within. His intention is not to make a rational list of pros and cons; he wants to be moved by the spirit.

Even though Josh knows that he wants his next chapter to be different, that he does not want to repeat the patterns and rhythms that have shaped his life at the Beacon Fund, he is clear that he has one more "big" piece of work in him. And he knows that he wants that work to allow him to be more deeply and directly engaged in social change, in the struggle for justice. He does not know what form it will all take, but he is excited by the freedom that comes with not knowing, the liberation that comes with the chance to imagine. The freedom allows for some wild fantasies. His brief moment of thinking that he might play third base for the local minor-league team speaks to his yearning to do something big and energetic, something fun and youthful, something that will recapture the kid in him. As a matter of fact, his wish to bring back the old days, when he might have picked off the runner at first with his perfect throw from third, speaks about the largeness and boldness of his imagination, the strange sensation of looking backward into the future.

Josh's yearning for a new adventure, for risking the unknown and charting a new path, does not surprise me. It marks a critical stage in his developmental journey. I listen to him and hear echoes of the voices of folks who told me their stories for *The Third Chapter*,[5] my most recent book, which focuses on the creative and purposeful learning that goes on for women and men between the ages of fifty and seventy-five. It turns out that for many of us, this is a chapter in life when the traditional norms, rules, and rituals of our careers seem less encompassing and restrictive, when the status and station we've earned no longer seem so important, when we are ready to embrace new challenges and search for greater meaning in our lives. Demographers in fact tell us that in the twenty-first century, the Third Chapter is becoming a distinct developmental stage — mapped into our identities, relationships, and institutions; imprinted on our culture — when those of us who are "neither young nor old" are prepared to exit the old and enter the new, choose change over constancy, and compose a new reality for ourselves. Like Josh, we yearn for adventure and inspiration. For the first time, we see the arc and finiteness of our lives, and that produces urgency in us. If not now, when?

At the huge goodbye gathering, tears spring to Josh's eyes as he speaks about the power of "place." By place, he means the physical setting, the ecology and geography, the towns and cities, the rural countryside, the mountains and lakes of New Hampshire, where he has labored for the last quarter century. He means the people, the relationships he has built, the political networks he has established, the "social capital" he has worked to forge in poor and struggling communities. But place also speaks about his devotion, his attachment, his passion and love — the sense of "wholeness and identity" that he gains through the work. "What has interested me in leaving," he tells me later, "is how much I love the work as much as I've ever loved anything." Place is home, with all the complex layers that bind and constrain, and it is hard for him to leave, even when his friends and colleagues build the bridge for him to walk across. "I does where I am," says Josh, quoting the rural black folks in Mississippi who said it best as they stood on their land — their "place" — looking out over the cotton fields, as they marked their sense of belonging and commitment and traced the boundaries of home. Now, as Josh says goodbye to the place he loves, as he "groks" what it means to sever his "institutional anchors," he leaves himself "totally vulnerable" to the yearning.

SIX:
GRACE

In a haunting essay, "Of Beauty and Death," from his collection *Darkwater: Voices from Within the Veil* (1920)[1] W.E.B Du Bois philosophizes about the beauty in nature and the relationship of beauty to the finite, of ugliness to the infinite, and of both beauty and ugliness to death. He reminisces about the beauty of Bar Harbor, Montego Bay, and the Grand Canyon and then lets his mind wander over the contrasting terrains of Paris and Harlem as he seeks among the myriad experiences of his recent life for a clue to a mystery he sees as essential to life:

There is something in the nature of Beauty that demands an end. Ugliness may be indefinite. It may trail off into gray endlessness. But Beauty must be complete . . . whether it be a field of poppies or a great life, it must end and the End is part and triumph of the Beauty. I know there are those who envisage a beauty eternal. But I cannot. I can dream of great and never ending processions of beautiful things and visions and acts. But each must be complete or it cannot for me exist.

On the other hand, ugliness to me is eternal, not in the essence but in its incompleteness; but its eternity does not daunt me, for its eternal unfulfillment is a cause of joy. There is in it nothing new or unexpected; it is the old evil stretching out and ever seeking the end it cannot find; it may coil and writhe and recur in endless battle to days without end, but it is the same human ill and bitter hurt.

But Beauty is fulfillment. It satisfies. It is always new and strange. It is the reasonable thing. Its end is Death — the sweet silence of perfection, the calm and balance of utter music. Therein is the triumph of Beauty.[2]

With language both searching and defiant, Du Bois claims that beauty — whether it is a field of poppies or a great life — must have an end; it must be a complete experience; it is defined by its finiteness. I hear in his words, as well, a bow to the importance of endings well done, exits — as Josh Arons says in the previous chapter — accomplished with "purposefulness and grace." It is not only that ending is "part of the triumph of beauty"; it is also that how we end — with intentionality and care, with music, metaphors, and rituals, with elegance and form, with "calm and balance" — shapes our experience of fulfillment.

In this chapter we hear the stories of two women — Carla Anderson and Gwen Taylor — who care deeply about beautiful endings, exits gracefully done, and the rituals designed to mark and honor our farewells. In her mid-fifties, Carla Anderson has navigated many vocational exits — enjoying the changes, transitions, and movements; relishing the "hunt," the seductions, the new opportunities, and the feeling of being sought after, always poised for the next challenge. Looking back, she now recognizes that her exits — largely defined by the opportunities, expectations, and needs of others, by her own wish to be needed and her desire to be at the center of the action — have not been particularly uplifting or fulfilling. She has left without ritual or ceremony, without experiencing the completeness of her work, without letting people chant their praises or sing their sorrowful songs of goodbye. This time, Carla — like Josh Arons — wants to exit differently; she wants to listen to her own muse and music; she wants to "sit still" and let it all unfold "organically." And she is determined to move through the exit slowly and gently, with intentionality and with "grace."

Gwen Taylor promises her dying husband that the ending will be beautiful and triumphant. They will move his bed into their large, sun-filled living room with the spectacular view of the city. They will welcome a steady parade of family and close friends, celebrate with flowers, fresh vegetables, and music; and every day he will be nourished by "fabulous conversations," rich recollections, and wonderful storytelling. Gwen wants there to be — as Du Bois puts it — "a never-ending procession of beautiful acts"[3] before the final exit. She wants "grace to prevail" every day, in every way, all around them. Her husband's last days will be filled with the best living he — and they — have ever known.

GRACE AND STONES

"Exits matter completely."

The setting is beautiful. The view from the ninth floor looks out in one direction over the tall, stately buildings of downtown, and in the other direction over the neat rows of brownstones with their tiny, pretty backyards. When the sun begins to set, there is a rose glow to the sky until the night suddenly appears and the vista is full of magical lights gracing the city landscape. The apartment is large and elegant, filled with art, with textured spaces designed for cozy comfort and lots of company. Burgundy, magenta, and deep orange are the dominant colors in the living room and the dining room, which has a large square table that can easily seat twenty people. I am not surprised when Carla Anderson tells me later that she loves "convening" people, bringing folks together for fun and conversation, nourishment and intellectual engagement. In fact, Carla spent years searching for this apartment and then years more making it beautiful, wanting a space that would give her pleasure and asylum after her long and busy days, that would also be inviting and enveloping for the collections of people she brings together.

336

Carla is as elegant as her surrounds. At fifty-six she has her own signature style. She drapes large textured scarves in luscious colors around her shoulders; a wide Afghani silver belt stretches around her middle, emphasizing her lovely curves; and she is bejeweled in silver and stones from North Africa, big bracelets with turquoise and coral and three intertwined necklaces that create a dramatic choker. She sits across from me at the kitchen table, looking out the window for inspiration, choosing her words with care, wanting to convey — with honesty and candor — her feelings, her confusions, her hopes, her "hungers," and her "fantasies." When I ask if I can tape our interview and take notes as she talks, she surprises me by saying, "As my grandmother used to say, I have no secrets . . . I really don't." And she lives up to her claim. She is thoughtful and unscripted, using the opportunity to be self-reflective, to push beyond her earlier thinking, to make connections. By the end of our three hours together, she says, with gratitude, that our session has been "therapeutic" and "provocative." "It has been a deeply honoring time," she says softly.

Carla begins right at the center of her current preoccupations and ruminations, with a succinct description of her essence. "I am a person who is endlessly curious and enthusiastic. I have always jumped into the middle of things with both feet. I've never been planful, envisioning a five-year goal, for example. And things have always come to me unbidden. I haven't had to search them out or chase after them." But recently her life has felt very different. It has not had the same energy or inspiration; it has not been fulfilling or life-giving. Rather than feeling fulfilled, she has felt "overfull" — stuffed with "too many things around, too many e-mails, too many phone calls, too many friends, too much going on." She is no longer feeling energized by her busy, complex days, and her "life has become a check-off list of to-dos" that has begun to make her very uncomfortable. Carla wants me to understand her feeling of being "overfull" — distinguishing the good kind of nourishment and pleasure from the nausea that results from gorging yourself on overly fatty foods or too many sweets. "Sometimes fullness is a very positive thing, a robust way to live," she explains, "but the kind of fullness I feel now makes me hungry . . . hungry to meditate, yearning to go on a silent retreat and make a new space."

In the past when Carla occasionally faced

this feeling of over-fullness, she would try to "solve" it, find a way to simplify the complexity of her life, try to unravel the knots of stress and confusion that were tangling her up. But this time — for the first time — she is feeling different. She does not want to "solve" it, make it right so she can keep moving forward in her familiar and comfortable patterns. This time she wants to change directions and create a different reality for herself. She wants to get rid of the tedium of routines that no longer challenge or inspire her, get rid of the to-do list, with all of its compulsions, distractions, and responsibilities.

In deciding that she needs a change, however, she is realizing — again for the first time — that she does not simply want to "shut the door" on her old life and move on. This time she wants to "navigate her way" through the uncertainties and choices consciously and thoughtfully. This requires a "reframing" for her. Rather than just thinking about "how to go on to the next phase," Carla finds herself considering how to leave with "grace and dignity," "without regrets." She is thinking about "saying good-bye" in a way that will liberate her, that will give her the energy and creativity to compose the next chapter. "I want my soul to be free," she says with deep feeling.

Carla believes that the grace she seeks must be accompanied by ceremony and ritual, that we in our culture tend to under-estimate the value of ritual, particularly the rituals connected to leaving. But she admits that, aside from the general cultural neglect of rituals, her family of origin was "com-pletely not ceremonial." "We did not mark the moment, either the celebrations or the downsides . . . we did not pay attention to closings and endings." With this "absence of meaningful ritual" in her family, Carla — who has always loved the "art and shape of things" — has had to make it up as she goes along. "Having children has helped me," she recalls as she thinks back on all the ways she tried to embroider rituals into her homelife with her own children, and how these occasions were important "markers" for them, providing moments of anticipa-tion, recognition, celebration, and apprecia-tion.

Carla was trained as a botanist. Her first job after college was in the laboratory at the Botanical Gardens, a job she loved for its scientific exactness and its beautiful sur-roundings. Although she loved science, even as a young woman fresh out of college she knew that she would not be able to live her life in a laboratory. The lab life was too contained and insular, too removed from the action. More than anything, she wanted to be involved in the world; she was an activist at heart. In an exit that did not require much calculation or deliberation, she left the lab and enrolled in law school, training that she thought would prepare her to participate — with skills, analysis, and argument — in changing the world, fighting for justice, protecting powerless people. Her first job after law school was working as a public defender in the district attorney's office.

After a couple of years on the front lines, she moved on to private practice, where she specialized in trial law. "I loved trying cases," she says with enthusiasm as she recalls the energy and the high, the homework and intense preparation that came with being in court. But it was not just passion that fueled her love for trial law. She also loved the way it "felt"; the way she had to get to know her "audience" and "what would fly" with them; the way she had to figure out how to tell a "story" in order to inspire, inform, and convince the jury. It was the kind of hard work and high-wire act Carla relished — the risks, the calculations, the ways you needed to seize opportunities and run with them. But trial practice also absorbed an enormous amount of energy and time, a work life that was hard to combine with her family responsibilities. With children who were by then five and seven and a husband who was a hard-driving venture capitalist who traveled all over the globe, Carla decided to leave her job and leave the practice of law.

For years, she had been on the board of the Global Environmental Research Institute, founded by her father, a scientist and entrepreneur, and she decided to commit her time to fund-raising for the institute. "I adored my father," she says wistfully about her decision to become more fully involved in the family business. Not only did she — in record time — raise twelve million dollars for the institute; she also found that she "fell in love with institutions" and "discovered the world of nonprofits." Soon she was heading the board of a new start-up company, chairing the local board of Planned Parenthood, becoming a trustee of a major university, chairing the board of the city's largest homeless shelter for women, and continuing to maintain her leadership role on the board of the institute. The variety of organizational agendas — focused on science and social service, spanning the theoretical and the practical — appealed to Carla. It was a professional life that offered her great responsibility and amazing freedom, accountability, and autonomy. She was able to craft each day in her own way while still playing a crucial role in institution building and advocacy. She relished the busy and eclectic life she had spawned — the rich array of activities, the wonderful opportunities, the creative challenges, the development of ideas, the convening of people and communities, the networking to build coalitions and raise money. For the last fifteen years, this way of living and learning has given her "a robust feeling of fullness."

Part of the reason that Carla is now exploring other career options and fantasizing about new work ("I have another body of work in me," she says, looking toward the future) is because the "robust feeling of fullness" has slowly turned into an "interior hunger." "The stories are fairly negative," she says when I ask her for an example of how she experiences the hunger. "I find that I can't produce even when I know I am responsible and must be accountable for doing something . . . I feel stuck." She points to her role as chair of the board for the homeless shelters, an organization that she believes in and has generously supported, with colleagues whom she loves and admires. "These are people who are deeply embedded in my life," she explains. "I care about the work, but I find I cannot rally the enthusiasm. It's just not in me anymore . . . and I think it is fundamentally wrong to continue to do it just because I've signed up for it. That is what I am dying not to do." Her voice is determined, urgent.

"Here are some of my fantasies," she says as she considers the possible choices in front of her. She points to a beautiful photograph on the wall next to her, an image she chose for her Christmas card. It shows Carla — unrecognizable from a distance — sitting on top of a huge sand dune with a clear, cloudless blue sky behind her. It is a photograph from a recent trip she took to the Gobi Desert, and she thinks of the picture as a metaphor for the way she hopes to exit this chapter of her life and enter the next. "I am looking forward, feeling the promise and the possibility . . . It is simple, clear, unencumbered." Having shared the image, she spins out three of her fantasies.

"I could run a not-for-profit . . . but the idea feels overwhelming to me, the work too long and hard and demanding. I think I've had too much freedom in my life for the last fifteen years to choose something that requires that kind of daily, unrelenting dedication and devotion.

"It would be great to work overseas and make a significant difference in the world. I fantasize, for example, about finding an Indian entrepreneur who has made a fortune in the U.S. . . . and wants to return to India . . . working together with him or her on a model for social philanthropy there.

"I could become a diplomat. I love to convene people . . . I love entertaining. I enjoy moving a project forward. I like to bring people together to share ideas . . . I want to create salons."

Her eyes get misty as she recalls a loving and admiring comment made by her son, a young journalist working in London. He was pitching a job with *The Washington Post* and telling them about his personal qualities. "I am," he wrote, "one of the most curious people I know and a great listener, both attributes that I have inherited directly from my mother."

One of the qualities Carla likes most about herself is her "fearlessness in bringing people together." A lot of people are afraid of the unease, the combustion, the conflict that can erupt when people come together from different geographies, cultures, and ideologies, when they are likely to disagree with or mistrust one another. But Carla enjoys the whole process — the edgy discourse that engages and incites, the spirited and fiery conversations that lead to arguments and sometimes reconciliation. "It is freeing for everybody when it works, and at least interesting and provocative when it doesn't," she muses. Carla admires President Obama for just that reason; he is a daring and creative convener, an attentive listener, a brilliant synthesizer. He is not afraid of discord. She offers an example. When Obama was recently trying to decide whether to send more troops into Afghanistan, he brought experts — policy makers and politicians, military men, Middle East scholars — to the table who had very different points of view and perspectives. "It was a phenomenal process," says Carla, "whether you agreed with his solution or not. He listened to everybody; he asked great questions; it was a thoughtful and probing deliberation . . . He is an incredible convener."

Ironically, Carla believes that her experience as a trial lawyer turned out to be great preparation for being a convener of people. Not the adversarial part that yields winners and losers, but the part that requires careful listening and the development of a narrative, a story line. Yes, she now yearns for something less black-and-white, more complicated and nuanced than trial law, but she also sees the imprint of her early training in her fantasies of new work.

There is mischief and glee in her eyes as she reveals her most recent fantasy. Her voice unwraps the "secret" as if it is a precious gift. "I love stones," she whispers. "I love the less-refined materials, the colors, the textures, the coolness to the touch." I look around us and notice that her couches are covered in soft velvet, with pillows decorated in ancient hand-embroidered fabrics from North Africa. Her bathroom wall is even covered in a subtle brocade textile that is both soft and rough to the touch. "I'm a completely tactile person," she says with understatement. "The other day a friend of mine said to me, 'You always glow when you talk about this stuff . . . you need to find a way to follow that passion.' " Carla points to the large amber ring on my hand. "I'm deeply drawn to that kind of stuff, big and smooth and luminous."

As recently as a few weeks ago, Carla admits, she would never have talked about her passion for stones, and she certainly would not have had the nerve to even think out loud about "doing something" with them. It would have sounded impossibly trivial, nowhere near as serious as others see her or as she imagines herself to be. But for the last few days she has found herself giving in to her fantasies and "playing" with ideas like getting her certification in gems or going on a fact-finding trip to a place in Denmark that has an incredible collection of stones, where you can be tutored by experts. A smile spreads across her face. "I'm completely wide open. I would have been embarrassed to say this a month ago . . . it might have felt frivolous, somehow ungrounded."

I ask how her love of stones translates to her body, which she drapes with dramatic jewels and gems, and her response is immediate and exuberant. "My body is all in it. To the extent that life can be luscious, then live it!" she crows, standing up and dancing around. But there is another reason Carla is drawn to stones. When she wears them, she senses something wonderful and mysterious. "Power isn't exactly the word I'm looking for," she says as she tries to give the feeling of "excitement and enhancement" a name. The stones decorating her body seem to have a "dynamic energy" that propels her forward and settles her down.

They are both peaceful and provocative, "centering and inspiring."

As Carla talks, her fantasies swell with hope and determination, imagination and energy. So I ask her whether there are any downsides, whether she has any worries, any apprehensions as she begins to make her exit. "Oh my God, yes," she responds without skipping a beat.

"Maybe people will think of me — or I'll begin to think of myself — as a dilettante. That would feel awful.

"Maybe there is no magic IT . . . that I will find that I am pursuing something false or ephemeral.

"Maybe I'm just old and tired and have run out of steam. I do believe you need to invigorate your life, or else, as you grow older, you grow stale. I've seen that in some of my friends.

"Maybe I'll fall off of everyone's screen . . . I'll never be invited to do anything again."

As she races through her list of fears and names the risks that are inevitably part of "doing the unthinkable," Carla admits that her apprehensions are amplified by a keen sense of "urgency." She asks herself, "If not now, when?" "For the first time in my life, people are dying around me — friends, associates, people my own age — and that creates a kind of compelling immediacy." She also recognizes that she has always been reluctant to reach out to people, to let them know what she needs, to tell them when she is feeling pain. She has been reticent to seek their guidance, support, and feedback as she tries to chart a new path. "I haven't turned to people enough," she says sadly. "I'm not afraid to talk to people about what I'm thinking, but it is difficult to examine what might be next on the horizon. It feels more vulnerable for me, but it is probably not as risky as I think." As Carla talks about how hard it is to reach out for help, she notices that she has never approached, nor sought help from, her grown children and that drawing them in might have the salutary effect of making them feel more needed and "empowered." She suddenly laughs, recognizing the similar places they are in their lives, the ways in which they are all facing some form of transition. "You know, the three of us (she and her young adult son and daughter) are in the same spot."

A few weeks earlier Carla had had an extraordinary "earth-shaking experience." She was spending the weekend in Canada with her man at his rustic cabin in the woods, sitting in front of the fire and soaking up the peacefulness and warmth of their rare times alone. She decided to do something she has never done before, listen to the audiotapes of a popular celebrity therapist — a favorite guest of Oprah's — whose books have sold millions of copies and captured the hearts and minds of a huge following. The author had, in her forties, suffered a severe mental breakdown, a disturbing prelude to a kind of spiritual awakening. In her tapes, workshops, seminars, and performances the therapist tells her own story of survival and liberation, narrates the tales of her patients' struggles and healing, and offers her wisdom to those seeking to break bad habits and change their lives. Carla still cannot believe that she brought the tapes up to the cabin and that she decided to listen to them that evening. "This didn't even feel like me!" she says, surprised at herself. She has always considered these kinds of pop psychology testimonials superficial and hokey. But that night, for four hours straight, she stared into the fire, let the tapes roll, and became completely absorbed, captivated by the message and the messenger.

I ask her what in the stories and lessons grabbed her, and her response is immediate. "It is the work of reframing things for people, seeing the world around you — and the relationships you are involved in — in a different way." She offers two examples of the stories of revelation and survival that the therapist told. The first was about a woman whose daughter was a drug addict, whose life had been controlled and consumed by trying to solve her daughter's problems and save her life. Carla was surprised by the therapist's "reframing" of maternal love and responsibility. The mother, said the therapist, should not try to be her daughter's savior or problem solver; she should not try to rescue her from her self-inflicted injuries and abuses. Trying to take control and make things right only weakens and infantilizes her daughter and makes her feel as if she is not strong enough to be in charge of her own life.

The second case focused on a woman now in her fifties who had been raped by her foster father from the time she was four to when she was fourteen. Years later, when she brought allegations against him, her family had cast her aside, refusing to believe her charges of abuse. Carla listened with special interest to the "re-framing" of this story, since years ago, as a public defender, she had had a good deal of experience prosecuting sex crimes, and she had an intimate understanding of the fear, guilt, rage, and victimization that tend to be part of the complex web of child molestation. Again, the therapist's words surprised her, disrupting her usual presumptions about the victim's role and responsibility. The therapist urged the rape victim to "forgive herself for letting this happen to her." But then she went on to say that the victim of the rape was the responsible party; she had to stand up and be accountable for her own healing, or she would forever be locked in a prison of guilt and remorse and forever see herself as helpless and hopeless. Carla remembers giving these stories her rapt attention, not missing a word, losing track of time and staying up until past midnight. "I heard it, felt it, took it in."

Almost as if it had been scripted, the next morning, Susannah, Carla's twenty-five-year-old daughter, called from Chicago to say that she had — once again — been kicked out of school; she was begging to be rescued. Her daughter's urgency and desperation and her pleas for help were not surprising; since early adolescence she'd had a history of stumbling, getting herself into trouble and asking to be saved, counting on her mother to make everything right. But this time Carla felt an unlikely impulse stir inside of her. Right then, with the morning sun rising in the sky, barely awake before her morning coffee, Carla responded in a way that felt unfamiliar. Her voice even sounded strange in its decisiveness. "I knew right then that this was Susannah's problem, not mine!" she exclaims, huge relief written all over her face. "I felt as if a gift had been handed to me."

She could look back and see that her "sympathy, handouts, and problem solving" were killing Susannah. "I was not letting her grow up and take responsibility . . . I need to be real and kind, but I can't solve it for her. Supporting her and giving her money suddenly seemed ridiculous to me." Carla is smiling at what feels like an amazing breakthrough for her. "This is huge for me . . . huge and exciting . . . because it leaves me feeling so much less constrained." She looks directly at me, another mother of grown children, still stuck in the problem-solving/rescue mode, still wavering in my efforts to both help them and support their autonomy and adulthood. Her voice rises with authority. It all feels very new and untested, but Carla feels convinced and oddly certain about this "reframing" of the responsibilities and boundaries of her motherhood, and she wants to convey to me the rightness and goodness of her changing views.

This "huge" shift in perspective — and actions — in relation to her daughter is becoming a part of Carla's exit narrative. She realizes that in order for her to move on to her next chapter, she must cast off some of the "primal and primary" obligations and self-imposed constraints that have limited her imagination and restricted her movements. She also recognizes that the relationship she has forged with her daughter — rescuing her whenever she screamed for help — is part of a larger pattern of family dynamics, forged in her early childhood and still present fifty years later. "I'm part of a huge family — two brothers, eight stepbrothers, twenty-five nieces and nephews — and I have always found myself being the source of advice, problem solving, and support. I'm the convener."

She offers a recent example. "For thirty years, at Christmas, the whole extended family has always gone skiing together, and I have always been the convener, planning all of it, making it happen, but this year it turned out that no one could do it. People were busy with travel or work . . . neither of my kids or the nieces and nephews could come. I was completely depressed by this. I was panicked about how I would navigate the season, stave off the loneliness." Forced to figure it out on her own, Carla created a much simpler Christmas. She decided not to travel out of town. Instead, she stayed put, bought a tiny tree that she could carry up to her apartment herself, spent almost no time decorating it, and then invited two couples over for a simple, intimate dinner. Everything was a "tiny portion of what might have been, smaller scale and spare, much quieter, more deliberate." And she found that she had a great time. "It felt fantastic!"

Susannah's call for help that morning in Canada and Carla's experience of the foiled Christmas plans have left her with a clearer path, a more open mind, and many more choices. She is beginning to feel less encumbered by the constraints and responsibilities of mothering and less burdened by her role as family convener. Recasting these relationships and retreating from the lifelong expectations will put her, she hopes, "on the path to liberation." As I listen to her fierce determination and her earnestness, I sense that the path forward will be bumpier and more treacherous than she now imagines. She is still experiencing the first blush of new discovery. I suspect that there will be minefields along the road, moments of regression to past patterns, even feelings of loss as she unpeels the old personas and tries on new ones. But for now, all she seems to feel is relief and freedom. "I am reclaiming my life," she whispers. "It has been a good life, but it has not all been mine . . . Here is the opportunity to make it mine."

Even though her new take on mothering seems to have washed over her all of a sudden, Carla mostly believes that exits should be done slowly, deliberately, thoughtfully, and generously; and she thinks that her view could well be seen as "countercultural." She muses, "This notion of exit is a very American concept, an abrupt leave-taking." It is also the way she was raised by her father, who would always say to her when she was ending something, "What's next? What's coming up?" He was always urging her to press on and not look back. But at fifty-six, this notion of a quick exit "no longer resonates" with her. She delivers her next lines very slowly, mirroring the sensation that she is discovering within her. "Exiting feels liberating, but only if it is well navigated . . . and that takes time."

Carla feels, for example, proud of the way she got divorced — slowly, carefully, not precipitately, trying to be careful of her husband's needs and feelings. "I love how I got divorced," she says adamantly. "It took us six years between separating and getting a divorce. Many of our friends and family did not approve of the way we did it. But our daughter was not well, and we both needed to offer her our ongoing, collective support. My ex-husband and I both gave each other the space to work it out." And now that they have been divorced several years, Carla feels completely comfortable with her ex-husband's new wife, wanting to keep her "intimately and directly informed" and seeking her counsel about decisions that need making with regard to the children.

She has one last thought about the value of exits "well negotiated." Carla believes that there is a "negative cultural narrative about exiting," that we tend to honor entrances and denigrate leave-takings, that we do not give enough attention to the rituals or ceremony of our goodbyes. Now she is beginning to recognize that "exits matter completely," that they must be "done with dignity and grace," and that it is important to leave feeling "responsible, good, and whole." In fact, it is crucial that those you are leaving behind have the opportunity to express their appreciation, honor your work, and throw a party. Carla is about to depart from a board she has been chairing for the last decade, an organization whose mission she loves, a place to which she has devoted a tremendous amount of her time. At first she imagined slipping away quietly into the night, doing a stealth action, going out under the radar. The thought of a big, ceremonial goodbye made her feel awkward and uncomfortable. Only recently has she begun to recognize how important it is to let those you have worked with, partnered with, and given to have the opportunity to celebrate you in a way that is meaningful to them. "You owe it to them to let them raise a glass and toast you."

But a "well-negotiated" exit includes not only letting people express their sadness about your leaving, their sense of loss and abandonment; it also means giving them the space to express their love and admiration. And Carla believes that you need to be prepared to listen to them, to really absorb their words and feel their meaning. Now she sounds like she is offering up a prayer. "Grace is carried in being open and receptive to the ritual." "Exits matter completely," she says once again as she lifts an imaginary champagne glass and looks into the future.

Carla feels the impetus for her exit in her

body, and she uses the metaphor of food to explain the oddly paradoxical sensations. She is feeling "overfull" from trying to manage too much and put together too many pieces in her life, yet she is feeling "hungry" for real emotional and intellectual nourishment. She hungers, as well, for quiet, for the time to meditate, for spiritual sustenance, for grace. She hates the feeling of being greedy, "overstuffed" with the wrong kinds of food, nauseated from gorging herself; and she is searching for the discipline that will allow her to know when to push back from the table, when she is just full enough — a "fullness that is robust."

As she moves toward the exit, she cares as much about how she leaves as she does about what she is leaving or where she is headed. She wants to "navigate" her way deliberately, slowly, paying careful attention to her own feelings and those of others. She wants to leave with "dignity and grace" and engage in "countercultural" rituals that will give form and substance to the endings. And she wants to leave "without regrets" because she believes that only then will she find the energy and imagination to compose her next chapter. Her exit quest is about setting her "soul free," releasing her from the inhibitions and busyness that have, by now, overtaken her life and limited her fantasies and choices. Like Du Bois, she sees beauty in endings and ugliness in the infinite — the "trailing off into gray endlessness."

In order to exit — and set herself free — Carla must "reframe" many of the presumptions, perspectives, and values that have defined her essence and identity, her place in her family, and her mothering. Refusing to rescue her daughter Susannah and insisting on her independence liberates her from a mother-daughter relationship that has grown exhausting and consuming; it allows her to feel less constrained and inhibited in her choices and helps pave her path to the exit. Likewise, removing herself from her longtime role as family convener releases her from the tangled web of habits and expectations that have by now become presumed and unspoken. Forced to do Christmas without all the holiday artifacts and hoopla, Carla discovers something more satisfying, simple, and salutary; she can begin to see a new reflection of herself in the life she is now free to compose.

Recalibrating her relationships to family and friends helps Carla carve out the space to imagine, and then welcome, her most far-out fantasies. She is able to "play" with new options and ideas, turn them over in her mind, and project them into the future. But this is not a straightforward or easy process. She is occasionally weighed down by her doubts; she worries about the risks to her professional and personal relationships, her anchoring in the community. Will she be exposed as a dilettante? Is she searching for something elusive and ephemeral, something she will never find? Will her name disappear from people's BlackBerries? Will her cell phone stop ringing? There is an ongoing calculation — of risks and benefits, costs and liabilities — that she needs to hold in check if she is going to set herself free.

Her good friend sees the glow in her eyes when she begins to talk about her love of stones, and their conversation gives Carla the permission she needs to reveal the depth of her passion for them. She loves the varieties and textures of stones, their beauty and resonance, their luxuriousness. She uses them to adorn her body and feels their "dynamic energy" when she wraps them three times around her neck to make a choker. The stones do not weigh her down; they lift her up. She senses the way they help her to "sit still" and propel her forward, the way they make her feel "wide open" to new possibilities. Gems and stones — in all their unadorned natural beauty — become her inspiration and talisman, symbols of her slow and intentional, grounded and graceful journey to the exit.

AMAZING GRACE

"As glorious as possible."

For Gwen Taylor, it is the final exit that matters the most. She has one last shot to make the ending beautiful for her dying husband, one more opportunity to honor and celebrate his completed life. Her last fervent promise to him — a promise she is sure she can keep — is that his final weeks and days will be full of abundance and grace.

It is less than two months after Tom Taylor's death when Gwen welcomes me into their home. She stands tall at six feet, with a large frame and an erect posture. She moves slowly, with waltzing steps. Her bright red dress, hanging loosely, is covered with a hand-woven multicolored shawl that she wraps around herself for comfort and protection as she tells the hardest, most painful story of her life. We sit in her elegant, large living room that stretches across the top floor of one of the city's most stately, and pricey, buildings. The room has enough space to hold several couches,

363

sideboards, lamps, tables, and desks, all fine Victorian pieces.

Every surface is cluttered with piles of paper; the huge oval dining-room table is strewn with an array of photographs, newspaper clippings, books, magazines, and correspondence. Gwen casually apologizes for the mess and claims that she has always created this kind of chaos, but it has grown way out of hand since Tom died. "I always struggle with too much paper," she admits. "I'm interested in too many things, but this mess is even more terrible than usual." Toward the end of our interview she links the mess in her living room to her description of herself as "a complete emotional mess" since the death of her husband. "I almost can't find my life anymore," she says finally about the excruciating experience of feeling "unmoored and in so much pain."

We sit at a small table by the window that is, like every other surface, piled high with papers. Gwen cleans it off enough to make room for my tape recorder and notepad, and she fishes in the pile from time to time to show me a photograph or a letter that documents a story she is telling. Before I can ask her an opening question, she begins. "I am assuming that you want me to talk about Tom's dying — because there are also other exits in my life, ones I am going through myself that I could tell you about. But the one with the most emotional power, the richest and most complete experience, is the story of Tom." And it is a long story that begins in 1976, the year they were married. "Tom was fourteen years older than I . . . he had four adolescent children, and I worried a lot about the marriage for three reasons," she starts. First and foremost, she worried about becoming the stepmother of four adolescents. ("And I had good reason to worry." She smiles.) Second, she worried about the age difference between them. And third, she worried about the difference in their "financial circumstances." Gwen had come from a middle-class — "actually barely middle-class" — background, and Tom had grown up "with a lot of money." He was the heir of a huge family fortune, the grandson of the founder of an international cosmetic conglomerate.

Three years after they were married, Tom had his first encounter with a major illness. He was diagnosed with a cancerous melanoma. Thus began a series of medical consultations as they tried to figure out the best option for treatment. At that point, they — and the medical establishment — knew little about the disease, and Gwen recalls that she was "frozen by fear." "I was terrified," she says. "I knew nothing about cancer." In the end, at the recommendation of their primary care physician, they decided to do the surgery to excise the melanoma, but not to follow it up with either radiation or chemotherapy. After the surgery Tom returned to his normal energetic life — his international development work, his philanthropic activities, his travels to East Africa, and his active physical life of sailing, biking, and running. But one day five years later, when he experienced some pain and discomfort in his chest, he drove himself to the hospital and the doctors discovered that he was suffering from heart failure that required immediate surgery and a new regimen of medicines.

Gwen tells the story of Tom's long history of illness, being faithful to the chronology and to the changing, increasingly serious diagnoses. I am amazed by her level of recall, the way in which she remembers not only the month and year of the diagnosis, but often the exact day, the way she chronicles the many competing diagnoses delivered by the several specialists they consulted, the way she remembers pieces of the actual conversations with the doctors, the ways they delivered the bad news, the questions she asked to seek clarification or some measure of hope, the way she can still hear Tom's voice — brave and determined, then resolute and accepting — as they went through years of illness and decline together. During all these procedures and surgeries, comebacks and recoveries, one of their close friends remarked, "Tom actually had nine lives or more," a statement that stuck in everyone's mind as one of the best descriptions of the extraordinary resilience and fortitude he showed after each major assault on his body.

Toward the end of the interview, after hearing the long parade of serious and painful infirmities that stretched over their thirty years of marriage, I ask Gwen whether her experience of their time together was completely shaped by Tom's illnesses, whether doctors and hospitals and medicine and pain and fear and sleeplessness were most of what she remembers. Her response is immediate. No, those are not her primary recollections. Her memories are mostly filled with good and healthy times, with being engaged fully in their worlds, adventurous travel, beautiful times in their house in the country. Life was full, plentiful, and pleasurable for the most part. Yes, there were clearly moments of crisis and fear and trauma, there was panic and worry, and there were periods of profound weakness and excruciating pain. But they would always navigate through those tough times, emerge hopeful and determined, and move on with their lives.

It takes more than an hour for me to hear the details of Tom's nine lives. As Gwen releases the story, her eyes spill over with tears, her face becomes swollen and red, and she uses a whole box of tissues to absorb the tears that seem to come from every pore in her face. She does not try to stop the flow; she makes no apology. She also seems determined to continue despite the pain that accompanies the narration — almost as if there is something about the flow of tears that is cleansing and restorative.

I hear about the prostate cancer in 1997 that the oncologists treated with radiation (avoiding surgery because of Tom's age, his heart condition, and their wish to "protect sexual functioning"), his many episodes of pneumonia over the years, the terrible fall in 2006 that caused a blood clot on his brain that had to be surgically removed, the scarred bladder in 2008 that made it impossible for him to urinate, when he had to go by ambulance to the hospital to have his bladder emptied — the suggestion, finally, that Tom "self-catheterize" nine times a day. "He was such a trooper," Gwen moans. I hear about the tumor they found growing out of his prostate on June 12, 2009, which had protruded into his bladder and rectum, the endless trips to the hospital emergency room, the scary moments when the pain seemed too extreme to bear, the constant calibrations of medicine, the deliberations and choices following conflicting diagnoses and treatment plans ordered by doctors. And through it all, Gwen recalls never feeling as if Tom was dying. "We were still in our minds fighting to get him well."

But by the summer of 2009 there was too much evidence to avoid the reality of Tom's decline. The doctors could no longer figure out the source of the cancer, it was "so aggressive and undifferentiated." Gwen remembers the moment when one of Tom's trusted doctors suggested to her that she needed to "think about a do-not-resuscitate order." "That was a stark moment for me," she says, recalling it as a clear turning point, a dose of unwelcome reality. She immediately began to check into hospice care and make arrangements for Tom to "come home to die." He had made his wife promise that she would make sure he would die at home.

He remembered that both of his parents had died at home, a dignified, honoring death, surrounded by friends and loved ones, comforted by everything familiar in their surroundings. He wanted the same.

On his last trip home from the hospital Tom asked Gwen whether he was going to die. She responded that she did not know, because at that point she had not yet accepted the doctors' warnings that the end was near. But she was able to tell him — with clarity and certainty — that they would make this time "glorious"; they would have a nourishing, caring, beautiful, and loving time together; and they would do that for as long as he had, for the rest of his life. They would be surrounded by friends and family; the house would always be full of beautiful flowers; people would come from far and near to visit with him, to say things that had been left unsaid before this moment.

Gwen soon decided that his hospital bed would be placed in the most prominent place in their home, in the middle of the action, at one end of the huge living room, near the windows looking out over the city. "I couldn't bear for his bed to be set up in the guest room," she says, weeping again. They bought a large Chinese screen to put up around his bed for privacy when he wanted it and for those times when he was too weak to welcome guests. Every day, people flowed through the house to visit Tom, bringing food, memories, photographs, old videos, and yummy corn and fresh tomatoes from their gardens in the country. His older daughter made a magnificent quilt to cover him on his bed. His other daughter bought bright Marimekko fabric and made him long wraps to replace the ugly johnnies he had worn in the hospital, colorful garments that got bigger and bigger as his body withered away. His daughter-in-law wove him a cover for his pillow.

His children — now in their middle years at 52, 50, 48, and 47 — were vigilant, attentive visitors, often arriving together, sometimes with the grandchildren, and staying at the apartment in one of the three "big, puffy blow-up beds" Gwen had bought for company to sleep on. Their sibling time together tending to their dad seemed to draw them closer together, closer than they had ever been. One son, who lived nearby, came to fix Tom scrambled eggs every morning; another would read him the newspaper or essays from *The New Yorker*. The neighbor next door — whose name Gwen had barely even known before Tom's illness — several times brought dinner over, enough to feed twelve, and allowed them to keep their overflow food in her refrigerator. The outpouring of love and care was amazing, and as Gwen had promised, the time actually did turn out to be "glorious."

More sustaining than anything else were the "fabulous conversations" Tom was able to have with everyone who came by. This is what seemed to keep him alive — the intense, deep, rich exchanges he was able to have at his bedside. Gwen orchestrated the visits, the dinners, the readings, and the occasional quiet moments of being alone. But Tom got to choose who came, and they invited only people he loved and wanted there. His children used the time to have conversations that had seemed to elude them — perhaps out of conscious or unconscious conflict avoidance — earlier in their lives. They talked to their father about proud and painful moments from their childhood, times of feeling misunderstood or confused, times of feeling overshadowed by his goodness and generosity. They talked to him about how hard it was when their parents divorced. They told him about how his good parenting had helped them to be good parents. They argued with him about politics and art. They held his hand and caressed his brow when he was too weak to talk or when his sudden silence spelled the onset of acute, debilitating pain. Gwen admits that these conversations with his children were often not "easy," but she insists that they were "fabulous" and that Tom was fully and deeply engaged in them. The ten grandchildren provided a welcome lightness; their constant activity — running around, squealing, eating, playing games — brought everyone back to the ordinariness of the day. The cross-generational mix felt warm and somehow hopeful. And their love for their grandfather was so uncomplicated and pure.

Friends came too — friends who had worked with Tom in Africa, friends who sat on nonprofit boards with him, friends from Human Rights Watch and other causes he was devoted to, longtime friends from the country. Many came several times a week in a constant and devoted vigil. There was always a houseful of guests staying over, fixing food, and sharing stories. Creating this "glorious" occasion was not always easy for Gwen, however. She had never been someone who enjoys the chaos and complexity of a full house, with lots of people underfoot creating a whirlwind of activity. She says with amazement in her voice, "I would never have believed I could tolerate all this invasion of people, and none of my good friends would have believed it about me either, but somehow my wish for Tom to have these fabulous conversations overrode all my need to be in control of what was happening in my surroundings."

Gwen occasionally joined in on Tom's conversations with friends, but most of the time she retreated and let the conversations go on without her. She says, "I do believe that it is important to let people have private conversations, and also I was so exhausted that I would sometimes use these moments to escape and rest or to do the endless errands that needed to get done." She remembers their good friend Julia, a psychiatrist, who visited Tom daily, a woman they had known since she was very young, who had always been "sort of like a daughter" to them. Julia's conversations with Tom were almost always private, and Gwen suspects that he "sort of used Julia to relay messages" to his wife, to say those things that were hard for him to tell her directly. It was from Julia, for example, that Gwen learned that Tom did not want to be "force-fed." He did not like her constant encouragement that he should eat and drink more. He wanted to be left alone to eat as little as he wanted, or nothing at all if he chose to. It turns out that the hospice workers had also recommended that he not be force-fed. They told Gwen not to try to get Tom to eat or walk. "They felt that this was a dying man, and you must let him live out these last days exactly as he wanted," says Gwen with an edge to her voice. "The kids and I clearly violated that part. If that makes us inglorious, then so be it!" The second message Julia transmitted to Gwen was that Tom did not like it when she took so long saying goodbye to people as they were leaving. He wanted her to come to him, to be with him. "Tom was at the center of everything," says Gwen without an ounce of bitterness in her voice. "Everything revolved around him."

As Tom's health continued to decline and his death seemed imminent, another long-time friend, Deborah, a divinity school graduate (although not an ordained minister), helped them plan the burial and memorial services, a collective effort in which the children and grandchildren and Tom's brothers and sisters were all centrally involved. Tom was also a big part of the planning, offering up ideas, expressing his wishes, vetoing those things that did not feel right. "We wanted the services to be as glorious as possible," says Gwen, "as close as possible to what Tom wanted." As a matter of fact, at a certain point, after weeks of deliberation and consultation about the details of the funeral service, Tom said he had had enough. "I'm tired of it. I'm through," he declared. "I do not want to spend any more time on this." I ask Gwen what sorts of things required a lot of discussion, compromise, and resolution. "Tom and I wanted to sing 'America the Beautiful' — we love its simplicity and message — but his daughter, who lives in Paris and works for an international relief organization, thought it was too patriotic, too narcissistic, so we decided on 'For the Beauty of the Earth.' " A second example: "I love Rudyard Kipling and wanted to read one of his poems, but the children vetoed that idea, so we scratched that."

By far the hardest decision for Gwen was deciding on whether Tom would be cremated. Amazingly enough, until the last couple of months they had not discussed a burial plan, nor had they selected a burial site. Without much discussion they chose a plot at Green Hill Cemetery — they had always loved to walk there — and one of their friends took a picture of it and brought it back to Tom so he would know where his ashes would be laid. But when all the children announced that they wanted their father's body cremated, Gwen balked. "I come from Kentucky, where we have embalming and lay people's bodies out in the coffin," she explains. "My initial thought was that I cannot do this . . . I cannot burn him." She struggled mightily with the decision; the family discussions were exceedingly difficult, very painful for her.

But finally, one night, she had a conversation with one of Tom's daughters, who listened to her worries without judgment, let her express herself until she was completely done, exhausted from her purging. By the end of the conversation they decided together that Tom would be cremated. "What changed your mind?" I ask in amazement, having heard her powerful resistance and initial repulsion to the idea. "I decided finally that when I die, I will be cremated and our ashes will be combined. That seemed to soothe me . . . I could anticipate being with him again."

Gwen remembers the time exactly. It was 5:00 on Tuesday afternoon when Tom took his last breath. One of his daughters had come to visit that morning and had left at noon after saying what she knew would be her last goodbye. Both of his sons — Simon and David — were there with Gwen, as was Tom's favorite caretaker, a medical assistant named Kosi, a tall Ugandan man with whom he had developed a deep bond over the last several weeks. The four of them all held hands, circling his bed as they watched Tom take his final breath. "Actually," recalls Gwen, "we weren't sure whether he had stopped breathing. It was hard to tell. But Kosi told us that it was so." Gwen's tears turn to full-blown sobbing as she remembers the moment, the end. Simon began singing softly to his father, a final, sweet lullaby. And each of them took a turn offering a blessing, some words of send-off. They called Maria, the head nurse who had been in charge for the last several months, and she came over immediately to fill out the medical paperwork that is required when someone dies. "It took a long time," says Gwen about a task that threatened to distract them from the sacredness and immediacy of the moment. But Maria's respectful, loving presence seemed to override her procedural duties, and she became one of the small community of intimates bidding Tom farewell.

Then the most beautiful thing happened. Together Gwen and Simon washed Tom's body — slowly, carefully, lovingly. "I thought of the washing as part of what we thought was glorious," says Gwen when I ask where she got the idea — and the nerve — to do it. It was "glorious," but not all pleasant, recalls Gwen. "We had to turn him over to do his back, and when we did it, all kinds of brown guck came out of his mouth, and it kept coming . . . so we kept mopping it up until it finally stopped. Then we oiled him. Maria said he looked like marble."

CONCLUSION:
RITES AND RITUALS

INTO THE RELUCTANT ARMS
OF THE COMMUNITY

Fulfilling her promise to her dying husband, Gwen Taylor gives him a "glorious" send-off. In the intimacy of their home she creates a monumental exit — fabulous and warm, beautiful and sacred. Tom dies out in the open, in the epicenter of the action, surrounded by the most precious people in his life. He has conversations with his children that were never possible before: hard, revelatory, searching dialogues that fill the spaces between them that had, before now, been inhabited by silences, opaqueness, and fear. The new and raw truth telling summons breakthroughs of understanding and reconciliation between them. The siblings relinquish the traces of competition left over from adolescence and discover the mature bonds of collaborative care. Tom and his grown children trade places; his daughters

380

mother him with beautiful handmade garments to cover his withering body; his sons father him with nourishing breakfasts. They read him the morning newspapers the way he used to read them their favorite bedtime stories when they were children. Tom's friends circle around him, bringing memories and stories, food and flowers, music and musings. And Gwen orchestrates it all, relishing each day that Tom is alive, interpreting the hospice rules in her own way, tolerating the chaos and constant activity that usually drive her crazy, and finally participating in the sacred ritual of oiling her husband's body. The final death is not perfect or pleasant — but absolutely beautiful.

We see in this story of "amazing grace" a transfigured view of dying and death, rites and rituals of exit that help us reframe our views of other endings, both large and small, ordinary and extraordinary. The dying person does not suffer alone and isolated in the dark shadows of some back ward; he is in the light, at the center, prominent and visible, surrounded by family and friends. Only people he loves are allowed to come near; he calls the shots and makes his wishes known. It is the "fabulous conversations" that seem to sustain him the most — the rehearsal of old memories with Gwen, the declarations of love from his grandchildren, the vigorous political duels with old friends, the spiritual meanderings with the young divinity school graduate. He actively participates in composing his final ritual, seeing a picture of the plot where his ashes will be buried, voicing his choices of the readings and hymns for the memorial service, and telling his wife when he has had enough. In the weeks and days before his death, Tom Taylor lives large.

Ira Byock, the author of *Dying Well* (1997)[1] and a national leader and advocate for palliative care, speaks of his decades-long efforts — to reframe and reshape the medical practices and health-care policies focused on the final exit — as a "cultural agenda." He begins with his own "counter-cultural" practices and the "extraordinary rewards" of helping his patients discover the fullness of life as they are dying. "I get to care for people with advanced psychological, existential, and social concerns . . . people who have a chance to reestablish, reconcile, and complete relationships," he says with enthusiasm as he compares his work in palliative care to the other medical disciplines he formerly practiced in family and emergency medicine. "This," he crows, "is life affirming. This is the real stuff." But the "real stuff" is also painful, searing, and sorrowful, full of yearning, fear, and regrets. "A person with multiple infections, in the fourth stage of cancer, his gastrointestinal tract not working, his liver shut down — there are physical costs, pain, life-quality changes. Mortality will have its way with you." Ira's voice sounds harsh to my ears as he rehearses the inevitable decline. "I can't apologize for mortality any more than I can apologize for gravity.

"As a physician," he says with certainty, "my first goal is the well-being of my patients, to alleviate pain and the deep emotional hurts that contribute to their suffering. When their time is running out, the gentle revisiting of ruptured relationships may help with one area of unresolved suffering. I strive to teach that it is possible to expand the realm of what people consider possible — to imagine, to move beyond our own constraints." Over the years, he has found that even the worst atrocities — such as child abuse, neglect, and abandonment — can be overcome, leading to "a renewal in the relationship." Often these moments of reconciliation — a dying father who has been estranged from his son for twenty-five years and decides he wants to "seek resolution" — start with an apology. Two words, "I'm sorry." "That's pretty benign," says Byock about the courageous work he encourages in his patients.

Like the "fabulous conversations" that sustained Tom Taylor until the end, storytelling and listening are key to nourishing the imagination that paves the way to a gentle ending. "Storytelling expands the realm of what's possible," says Ira. "It offers some tangible example of something that might resonate with people who are dying. We are a death-defying culture, and we have few examples to draw from. Stories allow us to imagine what's possible . . . they become the key to creating the future." Stories, he adds, also help dying people to get to a deeper emotional level, allow them to explore the buried feelings they may have never been in touch with, allow them to feel growth in the midst of decline. "This is a time when you can become newly empowered, even as you know that you are losing so much."

In order to encourage imagining and storytelling, however, doctors and other caregivers have to learn how to listen. Ira laughs at something that sounds so obvious but is often hard to teach. "I tell my residents to breathe whenever possible, and I mean that literally and metaphorically." After all, he explains, in medical school, communication is equated with giving information, with telling, with advice, with offering guidance and direction; but little time and attention is given to learning how to listen, how to probe for stories. If you take time to breathe, then there is space for the patient's voice. "People can discover and hear their voices, and they can feel heard . . . the transaction can be complete."

Taking the breath that opens the space for listening to the stories is an act of intimacy and connection, one that is best when it is wrapped in the surround of a community. "People must die into the reluctant arms of the community," says Byock in one of his many "countercultural" statements. Our cultural tendency is to "silence and marginalize" people who are dying, to withdraw from them, to "pathologize" and fear them. In giving her husband a glorious send-off, Gwen Taylor re-creates community, reestablishing what Byock claims is the connective tissue that is latent in all human communities. He draws the contrast between the political and biological frames, and his voice rises to an urgent crescendo. "Whatever political paradigm emphasizes Jeffersonian independence, biologically, we are connected . . . we matter to one another." He uses an example from the other end of life. "When the baby cries, the lactating mother gets wet, and if the baby cries in the supermarket, three lactating mothers who hear him get wet. When a baby cries in a restaurant, no one can eat — not because it is too noisy (there may be trucks rolling on the highway outside making more noise than the baby), but because we are all connected."

Our sense of community is reinforced and expanded through rituals — rituals that create a structure, form, and medium for emotional and spiritual expression, rituals that mark and make visible our exits. Religious rites and liturgies often serve this purpose. Even though Ira Byock claims that he has a "nonromantic view" of religion, he admits that there is "wisdom embedded" in rituals and that religion is a "way of human beings reaching out to one another, in community, across generations" — that religion offers guidance in facing the "most existential experiences of human life: marriages, births, deaths, graduations, comings-of-age." He smiles at the memory of how he viewed religion — with suspicion and arrogance — as a young man coming of age in the 1960s, and he admits that "we were

386

wrong." Now, especially after working for years with hundreds of dying patients, he is able to see the healing and holding power of religious rituals and the way it has "morphed" over his lifetime and become more relevant to our generation. "We have found a way to rediscover, revise, and renew the ritual."

Byock's reflections on dying well and Tom Taylor's glorious journey to his final exit echo many of the voices and experiences of the protagonists in this book who were seeking and searching for meaningful exits in their lives — exits that would carry them home, heal their wounds, soothe their yearnings, open the door to freedom. Their exit narratives, for example, speak about the importance of rituals that mark and honor endings, that allow for the expression of the joy and grief and the loss and liberation that accompany our departures from the communities and relationships in which we were embedded. Years after leaving the small parish in Virginia where he was priest, Joe Rosario still grieves for the things left unsaid, the purposeful omissions to the story he told to his parishioners that masked the truth and muted his voice. It was a staged stealth exit, an empty form, a bogus platform that did not allow him to exit fully from his priesthood, a leave-taking never fully realized.

Josh Arons helps to design his huge New Hampshire farewell, owning up to his need for a ceremonial send-off and balancing his wish that it be a low-key affair with his colleagues' desire for big fanfare. His request that everyone — the thousand attendees in the gilded hotel ballroom — join in singing "Stand By Me" speaks to Josh's understanding of the power of community as witness to his exit. He exits the "place" he has inhabited — which has defined him, where he has left his large imprint — in "the reluctant arms of the community." And when Carla Anderson feels overstuffed by the multiple and layered demands of her too-busy daily existence, seeking a life with greater focus and simplicity, she understands, for the first time, that she must not steal away in the night. She must leave in the light; her exit must be visible, offering herself and those she is leaving a chance for ceremony and grace. She recognizes the challenge of naming and honoring exits through rituals — the "countercultural" events in a society that tends to devalue and mask endings. And she also reflects on the ways in which her own family rarely marked the moments of completion, always poised for the next move, always tilting toward the future before honoring the past.

This book, then, points to a radical re-framing of the meaning and worthiness of exits, moving exits from the shadows to the light, from the invisible to the visible, recognizing the ways in which exits are enhanced and expressed through ritual — the ceremonial moments that give us a chance to channel our conflicting emotions of joy and sorrow, a chance to stand up and be counted, an opportunity for bonding and community building — witnessing the ways in which exits can become moments for listening, storytelling, imagining, and creating choices that were unimaginable before. These productive dimensions of exit can be true whether we are talking about ordinary, everyday goodbyes or large public farewells. As a matter of fact, I think the micro and the macro are inextricably linked. Learning to name and navigate the daily leave-takings — a hug at the door, a lullaby at bedtime, a thank-you as you leave the office — helps us design and enact the grander public send-offs with intentionality and authenticity.

I want to borrow Ira Byock's notion of a "cultural agenda" (as opposed to an ideological or intellectual one) to underscore my wish — no, my strong proposal — that the practice of exiting with visibility and voice should not only be privately enacted in our relationships and within our families; it should also be braided into the policies and practices of our institutions, schools and colleges, hospitals and community organizations, corporate and political structures. I am, of course, not talking about the empty ritual of awarding gold watches to veteran employees at the end of twenty-five years of service, a sorry sign of their time having elapsed. I am referring to the ways in which organizations and communities might honor endings in a way that is substantive and inspirational, creative and collective, structured and improvisational, that speaks to the heart and the head and allows people to walk away with their heads held high rather than slink off in the night.

EXIT SIGNS: BOLD AND BLURRED

There is a central paradox in most people's recollections of their journeys to the exit. On the one hand, they can recall the exact moment — in bold relief, like the bloodred exit sign in a darkened movie theater — when they decided to leave, when they felt they no longer had any choice, when all the forces and sensations came together in a perfect storm and they said to themselves, "I'm out of here." On the other hand, their retrospective gazes allow them to see the long process of retreat that came well before the marked moment of announced leaving and the many aftershocks of exiting that followed. The protagonists in this book speak about the paradoxical sensation of exits — the moment frozen in time like an old Polaroid photograph, the long, arduous road to the exit, and the fallout and reverberations that inevitably follow — as "iterative" and "messy."

Andrew Connolly remembers every detail of the moment when he could no longer lie to the young woman he was "pleasantly" dating in graduate school as a "cover" for his real feelings of attraction for the "men with muscles" whom he longed to be with openly. He recalls her not-so-veiled hints about marriage as they sat across from each other at dinner that night; her earnest, blushing face as she stumbled awkwardly on her words; the knot in his belly when he realized how unfair he was being in hiding out from her; and how he was finally forced to confront his unkindness and cowardice. Although he did not announce to her that he was gay that evening, he knew in his heart that he could not mask his homosexuality any longer, that beginning the next day, he was going to live a life in which he was "out."

But even though that exit encounter — which Andrew remembers in vivid Technicolor — is clear, he is quick to point out that his coming out of the closet was not a "binary" experience. There were many exits, public and private, and it took several years to come out fully — years of determination, patience, and resolve; years that allowed for a deepening self-understanding. He uses the metaphor of "peeling the onion" to refer to the uncovering of each layer of his emerging identity; to reflect the exciting unmasking of his "authentic" self; and, I believe, to make sense of the tears of joy and relief that flowed when he stood high up in the San Francisco hills, looked down on the fog lifting, pierced by the glistening sunlight, and finally knew he was "home."

Although Andrew names the paradox of exit — of recalling "the moment" and living the "journey" — he also makes a distinction between those exits that were publicly announced and those that were privately experienced; and he tells me that the latter were generally more difficult and messier than the former. As a gay rights activist, he was surrounded by a community of comrades fighting together for a cause. They stood side by side and watched one another's backs, waging war on homophobia in all of its institutionalized and interpersonal guises, celebrating the occasional victories they won. The public exits — marching in gay rights parades, engaging in political campaigns, even being blindsided and "outed" in the newspaper after unknowingly sharing his story with a journalist — were all easier and less fraught than the private ones. Opening up to his parents, who "silenced the conversation" and refused to talk about his homosexuality, who would not even attend the funeral of his beloved spouse, was the hardest and most intimate exit of all. But he also understands how his parents' unconditional love, their unerring support, and the "happy childhood" he enjoyed were the bedrock of the self-confidence that allowed him to take the journey to the exit and emerge from the closet strong and whole.

Theresa Russo also draws the contrast between exit moments vividly and publicly expressed and the long years of private, "iterative" goodbyes. She recalls how relatively easy it was for her to decide — after twenty-five years of leading the nonprofit she founded — that it was time to leave, a decision that she believed would be good for the organization, which had become too "personality driven," and a decision that would ultimately support her individual growth, allow her to raise up her "solo voice" and establish her identity separate from the institution she had spawned. Even writing her letter of resignation to her board, her staff, and the community of kids and parents she had known for more than two decades did not seem terribly onerous. She found the words and sentiments and composed a letter that was both heartfelt and professional, expressive and restrained. And her speech at her farewell party seemed to flow with an elegance and alacrity she had never before experienced when presenting publicly to a large gathering. But the reality of leaving was much "messier," much more difficult and emotionally searing. She wept as she packed up her life in boxes; she felt marginalized and dismissed by the staff who no longer came to her for advice and counsel; and she hated the way she felt, needing them so much. Although she tried to resist the metaphor, it almost felt as if she had lost her baby, the one she had no time to have or care for during the time she was growing the organization. Her neediness and sadness left scars on her body. In the midst of it all, she contracted Graves' disease, an infirmity that lived up to its name.

Theresa's and Andrew's narratives and several of the other stories in this book trace the longitudinal and messy undercurrents of our leave-takings and challenge Albert Hirschman's theoretical framing of our exits. Hirschman speaks about exit — from institutions, and by extension from identities and relationships — as a clean, open-and-shut process whereby people decide that they can no longer be engaged in or tolerate the values, norms, and processes of the organization; neither do they see any way to change them. So they leave and never look back. "Voice," he claims, is messier; it is the "art" of staying put and making your views and criticisms known in an effort to improve the functioning and productivity of the organization. In his view, exit and voice are binary paths, divergent ways of responding to the inevitable decline in mature organizations.[2]

But the tales of exit told in this book point to the ways in which voice and exit may converge and the ways in which both processes are messy and artful. Theresa, in fact, needs to exit her nonprofit in order to begin to develop her voice; she needs to draw clearer boundaries between herself (the solo voice) and others (the choir) and establish the outlines of her singular identity in order for her to successfully end one chapter and begin the next. Her emerging voice gives fuel to the exit. Anthropologist Shin Wang relishes the messiness of exits, enjoying the refracted, layered interpretations of the folks who are leaving and those who are being left; finding intentional, caring ways of ritualizing her departures from the "field"; and joining her voice with those of her "subjects" to create a collective story, owned and authored by all of them.

Not only do the protagonists in this book talk about their exits as iterative and messy, a few of them are even intentional in slowing the exit process, not wanting to accelerate it, force it, or push it toward a decisive conclusion. Rather they want it to emerge "organically"; they want to witness its evolution, watch themselves facing the inevitable moments of ambivalence, fear, and emptiness that anticipate the leap of faith, the new opportunity or adventure. Carla Anderson, for example, tries to hone this "discipline" of slowing down and waiting for the muse, making a space for her imagination and fantasies to emerge, offering her options she would never consider if she rushed ahead in decision mode. She is proud of the way she and her ex-husband managed their divorce, slowly and respectfully, making sure they were not causing undue hurt to each other, wanting to be there, apart and together, to provide a safety net for their troubled child. Josh Arons also slows down his exit from his CEO position at the Beacon Fund. On purpose, he decides not to calculate the pros and cons or weigh the opportunities and liabilities of a rational plan. Rather he wants to listen to his internal "yearnings," which he will be able to hear only if he "sits still" for a moment. He wants to leave himself "vulnerable" and exposed to possibilities he might never have considered before in his life.

In her large-scale sociological study of "role exits," Helen Rose Fuchs Ebaugh identifies four distinct stages of disengagement from a role that is central to a person's identity and the reestablishment of an identity in a new role — a process that includes entertaining "first doubts," weighing "role alternatives," and coming to a "turning point" where the person makes the move, often announcing it publicly as a way of deterring retreat. Ebaugh's fourth stage — "creating an ex-role" — however, is a subtle recognition of the messiness that can protrude even into a neat and linear stage theory; one identity bleeds over into the next. During this fourth and final stage, people struggle with incorporating their "hangover identity" into their future identity; seeking to find a balance between who they were and who they are becoming; working to find the skills, experiences, and perspectives that are translatable from one identity to the next and the ones that must be discarded; and, most important, struggling to establish themselves in their new role while they continue to disentangle themselves from the social expectations of their previous one.[3] Here Ebaugh, like Andrew Connolly and Theresa Russo, underscores the nonbinary quality of exits — the ways in which the former identity gets merged, mingled, and balanced with the new one; and the difficult work of developing and shaping the new identity when the gravity of the vestigial continues to pull us back and weigh us down.

Coming from a very different disciplinary perspective that considers the person and psyche behind the "role," psychotherapist Linda Gould recasts our interpretation of the language of "termination" that marks, but does not end, the therapeutic relationship. When Linda and her patients say farewell, they go through the ritual steps of celebrating their progress, reflecting on the process, and anticipating the work that still lies ahead. The ceremonial exits of "honoring the work" are both structured and idiosyncratic, predetermined and highly individualized, but they are always unfinished and imperfect. It is not as if the therapy has vanquished the pain or erased the wounds; nor is the exit a sign that people are cured. Rather, Linda hopes that when they depart from the protective asylum of her office, her patients will have developed a deeper understanding of the roots of their addictions and neuroses, the courage to tell themselves the truth about their pain and the ways in which they are implicated in their own unhappiness, and a way of seeing and a set of skills that will put them on a path to a healthier daily existence. When she says goodbye to her patients, she knows that their way forward will be messy and uneasy, that there will still be minefields and rocky roads ahead, and that their wounds will reappear from time to time in new and ancient guises.

In recasting our views of exits — big and small, minute and momentous, public and private — it is, I believe, important to see the double image: one, of a moment in time sparkling with colorful details, of a clear decision, a sudden, edgy action; and the other of a messy, nonlinear journey, a process of forward and retreating moves, uncertainty and resolve, ambivalence and clarity. And it is important to recognize that at least for voluntary exits, we have it in our power to be intentional and reflective about our leave-takings, to see ourselves as the authors of the exit narratives we are composing, listening for the emergence and expression of our "voices," doing the "artful" work of defining a new identity that honors the losses and the liberation of crossing the exit line.

DEVELOPMENTAL AND GENERATIONAL MARKERS

Exits are also deeply embedded in our developmental journeys. Again I turn to the signature work of psychologist Erik Erikson, who charts eight developmental stages across the life cycle, from birth to death. At the very center of each life stage is the choice each of us must make — consciously or unconsciously — between change and constancy, progression and regression, counterbalancing forces pulling us in opposite directions, demanding our allegiance and attention. In order to grow, people must resolve the contrary, competing pulls by ultimately exiting, resisting and surmounting the gravitational pulls that would maintain stasis and keep us in the same place.[4] Exits, therefore, are part of our biological, emotional, and social trajectories, part of the fabric and shape of our life journeys, projecting us forward, helping us evolve as developing human beings. As a matter of fact, one way of mapping our developmental milestones might be by tracking the exits. Not seeing them as negative spaces in between positive launches forward, but by regarding them as the necessary, preparatory steps of progress. If we are able to successfully exit this stage, this place, this identity, we will be able to see and seize the shape and opportunities of the next chapter.

The stories in this book also reveal the exits that are part of the way our cultural scripts shape the developmental sequence. Bijan Jalili's tale of leaving Iran is at its core a narrative about an adolescent separating from his parents — his excruciating first steps away from their embraces at the airport and his yearning, as soon as he touches down at Kennedy Airport, to race home to the warmth and protection of his mother's bosom; his continuing telephone duels with his father, desperately pleading to come home, playing their "brain games," the approach/avoidance dance that is part of the cultural script of adolescent exits. The struggles of separation and self-definition are played out in bold relief in Bijan's story of flight from his family — a teenage tale made more dramatic because of the backdrop of warfare, social dislocation, and geographic distance. But the exit is embedded in and shaped by the unfolding of a developmental journey taking him from childhood to manhood.

We also see the developmental markers in Josh Arons's decision — at sixty-five — to leave the Beacon Fund. After a quarter century of guiding and growing the organization, after "loving" his work and the "place" he has established and imprinted on the philanthropic landscape of New Hampshire, he is inspired to change his life in one of those paradoxical experiences of exit that seems both "all of a sudden" and long anticipated. He wants his next chapter to emerge "organically"; he wants to "sit still" and listen to the stirrings from deep in his "soul"; and he wants to do the unexpected — all in search of something fulfilling and meaningful. As I listen to Josh's "yearnings," I hear the echoes of other Third Chapter folks[5] between the ages of

fifty and seventy-five, whom I have interviewed, who are ready to risk the uncertainties of the unknown, embark on bold adventures, and learn something new. This
developmental stage, whose contours have
been given new definition in our contemporary culture, is becoming a time when those
of us who are "neither young nor old" face
the finite years we have left with eagerness
and urgency, when we finally proclaim, "If
not now, when?" The exits we take from the
places we have worked, the relationships
that have sustained us, and the institutions
that have constrained us are departures
written into our developmental scripts.

These developmental exits are also shaped
by our families of origin and by the relationships forged across generations that have an
impact on how we navigate our leave-
takings. Carla Anderson, for example, not
only points to our "very American" cultural
neglect of ceremonial exits and the ways in
which our society tends to denigrate and
diminish the important rituals of exit; she
also recognizes the ways in which her family
never honored farewell moments, never
celebrated acts of completion, never recognized the beauty in endings. Her father's
first, and urgent, message to his offspring
was always focused on the future, what was

403

coming up on the horizon, what was next. When Carla became a mother, she found herself actively resisting the echoes of her father's voice urging her on to the next thing. She was intentional in trying to design family rituals for her own children that would mark both endings and beginnings, successes and failures, moments for coming together face-to-face in thanks and gratitude, in sadness and disappointment. When she is now faced with exiting from her too-busy life, overstuffed with meetings, commitments, travel, schedules, even friends, she understands — in a way she never did before — the meaningfulness of exits gracefully accomplished; and she sees beauty and wisdom in those "countercultural" events.

We also hear the generational echoes in Neda and Ehsan's fragile freedom from the assaults of the school bullies and the abuses of their "kiss-ass" mothers. From the very first day of kindergarten Ehsan is targeted by Ricky and his gang, who turn him into their "soldier" and insist that he carry out their violent orders. When Ehsan resists or tries to hide out, they threaten him and beat him up. Despite Neda's constant vigilance and her aggressive efforts to seek protection for her son, the teachers and principals are never able — or willing — to offer Ehsan a safe asylum. Even when Neda has had enough; even when she can no longer bear to see the lesions and bruises he is suffering at the bullies' hands and begs him to withdraw from school, Ehsan asks for one more chance to face his predators and prevail, one more chance to make it right. He has begun to see himself as his predators see him; he has begun to accept his unworthiness. His endurance, his courage and self-sacrifice, his willingness to withstand the abuse, even his gratitude for being an American have been passed down across the generations.

His mother before him was also bullied at school, singled out and emotionally tortured for being the only brown immigrant child in an all-white small town that felt threatened by her family of foreign interlopers. And as a child, she learned not to whine or complain; she learned that the abuse was the price she paid for the privilege of being in America. She listened to, and heeded, her father's litany — "the Kermanians never, ever give up" — and she passed the message on to her son, who whispered it to himself as he withstood the blows of the big bullies. The final straw, the photo finish that will always be imprinted in Neda's memory

— Ehsan kicking the side of their car with his big winter boot — was an act of desperation, rage, and resistance. In exiting from Sartre's hell,[6] Ehsan was resisting the generational imperatives; he was resisting the voice of his grandfather that had insisted that he hang in and endure the pain, that he trade his gratitude for their abuse of him. His exit, an act of bold defiance against the gang of bullies and against his immigrant inheritance, led him to freedom and saved his life.

THE BEGINNING LEADS TO THE END

There is something overwhelming and awe inspiring about finding an ending — a beautiful ending — for a book about exits. A self-consciousness overtakes me as I try to conclude with words that hold the wisdom and passion, the intentionality and care, the visibility and voice of the protagonists whose exit stories populate this book; and I find myself searching for the most primal and innocent expression of the power of exits. I think about myself at six years old being offered a chocolate almond ice-cream cone — my favorite flavor — and not wanting to yield to the pleasure of licking it, because once I started, I would already experience my disappointment when it would all be gone. Or I reflect on my grown-up version of going to Symphony Hall to hear Bach's Mass in B Minor — a rich and profound piece of music that always moves me — and feeling the melancholy of arriving at the last chord of the final chorale even as I listen to the opening phrases of the Mass.

In an evocative short story, "Getting Closer," published in *The New Yorker* (January 2011), Steven Millhauser[7] tells about a nine-year-old boy who goes with his family on a picnic by the side of the river, a treat he has been looking forward to all summer. He arrives at the riverbank; he is ready to begin.

But who's to say when anything begins really? You could say the day began when they passed the wooden sign with the words "INDIAN COVE" and the outline of a tomahawk, on a curve of road with a double yellow line down the middle and brown wooden posts with red reflectors. Or maybe it all started when the car backed up the slope of the driveway and the tires bumped over the sidewalk between the knee-high pricker hedges. Or what if it happened before that, when he woke up in the morning and saw the day stretching out before him like a whole summer of blue afternoons? But he's only playing, just fooling around, because he knows exactly when it all begins: it begins when he enters the water. That's the agreement he's made with himself, summer after summer. That's just how it is. The day begins in the river, and everything leads up to it.

Not that he's all that eager to rush into things. Now that he's here, now that the waiting's practically over, he enjoys prolonging the excitement of moving toward the moment he's been waiting for. It isn't the swimming itself he looks forward to. He doesn't even swim. He hangs on the inner tube and kicks his legs. He likes it, it's fine, he can take it or leave it. No, what he cares about, what thrills him every time is knowing that this is it, the beginning of the long-awaited day at the river, as agreed to by himself in advance. Everything's been leading up to it and, in the way of things that lead up to other things, there's an electric charge, a hum. He can feel it all over his body. The closer you get, the more it's there.[8]

We see the young boy's rapt anticipation,

his intentional stalling, putting off the beginning by playing a game with himself about how to measure the day's start. Tingling with excitement, he savors the waiting, the luscious lingering before heading into the water — for to begin the swim would be to face the end, the inevitable disappointment that is just waiting there once he commits his body to the river.

Exits hold that power, that inevitability. If we begin our journey toward home, our quest for freedom, our yearning for a meaningful life — if we choose to lift up our voices in celebration and protest, if we survive the exit wounds and walk forward with grace, we will move inexorably to the exit. In seeing our lives through the lens of the exit, we transfigure the journey, we feel the "electric charge" of anticipation, we learn to celebrate completion, and we witness the "triumph of beauty" that is the end — whether it is a refreshing dip in the water, the sweet taste of ice cream, or the radiance and resolution of the final chord in Bach's B-Minor Mass.

NOTES

Introduction: Exits: Visible and Invisible

1. For statistics on divorce rates, see National Center for Health Statistics, www.cdc.gov/nchs/fastats/divorce.htm and U.S. Census Bureau, www.census.gov/hhes/socdemo/marriage/.
2. For recent statistics on the numbers of legal permanent residents, naturalized citizens, and refugees, see U.S. Department of Homeland Security, www.dhs.gov/files/statistics/publications/yearbook.shtm and U.S. Census Bureau, www.census.gov/population/www/socdemo/immigration.html.
3. For statistics on employment and career changes over a lifetime, see Bureau of Labor Statistics, http://www.bls.gov/oco/ and *Wall Street Journal,* September 4, 2010, http://online.wsj.com/article/SB10001424052748704206804575468162805877990.html.

4. For recent unemployment statistics, see Bureau of Labor Statistics, www.bls.gov/bls/unemployment.htm.

5. For more on "boomerang kids" or the phenomenon of college graduates moving back home, see *CNN Money,* November 15, 2010, http://money.cnn.com/2010/10/14/pf/boomerang_kids_move_home/index.htm.

6. See Howard Zinn, *A People's History of the United States* (New York: Harper & Row, 1980).

7. Albert O. Hirschman, *Exit, Voice, and Loyalty: Responses to Decline in Firms, Organizations, and States* (Cambridge, MA: Harvard University Press, 1970).

8. Ibid., 112–13.

9. Sara Lawrence-Lightfoot, *The Third Chapter: Passion, Risk, and Adventure in the 25 Years After 50* (New York: Sarah Crichton Books/Farrar, Straus and Giroux, 2009).

10. Erik H. Erikson, *Identity and the Life Cycle* (New York: W. W. Norton, 1959).

11. Sara Lawrence-Lightfoot, *Respect: An Exploration* (Cambridge, MA: Perseus Books, 2000).

12. For more on the effects of technology on intimacy, relationships, and private/

public boundaries, see Max van Mannen, "The Pedagogy of Momus Technologies: Face-book, Privacy, and Online Intimacy," *Qualitative Health Research* 8, no. 20 (August 2010): 1023–32; Sonia Livingston and David R. Brake, "On the Rapid Rise of Social Networking Sites: New Findings and Policy Implications," *Children and Society* 24, no. 1 (January 2010): 75–83; Paul Benjamin Lowry, Jinwei Cao, and Andrea Everard, "Privacy Concerns Versus Desire for Interpersonal Awareness in Driving the Use of Self-Disclosure Technologies: The Case of Instant Messaging in Two Cultures," *Journal of Management Information Systems* 27, no. 4 (spring 2011): 163–200; and Marist Poll, December 18, 2009, http://maristpoll .marist.edu/1218-technologys-impact-on -relationships/.

1. Home

1. Joan Didion, "On Going Home," in *Slouching Towards Bethlehem* (New York: Farrar, Straus and Giroux, 1961).
2. Robert Pack, *Wallace Stevens: An Approach to His Poetry and Thought* (Piscataway, NJ: Rutgers University Press, 1958).
3. Paule Marshall, *Brown Girl, Brownstones*

(New York: Random House, 1959).

4. Paule Marshall, "From the Poets in the Kitchen," *New York Times,* January 9, 1983.

5. Didion, "On Going Home," 166.

6. Marshall, "From the Poets in the Kitchen," 3.

2. Voice

1. Carol Gilligan, *In a Different Voice: Psychological Theory and Women's Development* (Cambridge, MA: Harvard University Press, 1982).

2. Hirschman, *Exit, Voice, and Loyalty.*

3. Ibid., 115.

4. Ibid., 15.

5. Ibid., 43.

6. For more on Hirschman's theory of exit-voice-loyalty, empirically explored in the fields of psychology, management, and politics, see C. Rusbult, I. Zembrodt, and L. Gunn, "Exit, Voice, Loyalty, and Neglect: Responses to Dissatisfaction in Romantic Involvements," *Journal of Personality and Social Psychology* 43, no. 6 (1982): 123–24; D. Farrell, "Exit, Voice, Loyalty, and Neglect as Responses to Job Dissatisfaction: A Multidimensional Scaling Study," *Academy of Management Journal* 26, no. 4 (1983): 596–607; and W.

Lyons and D. Lowery, "The Organization of Political Space and Citizen Responses to Dissatisfaction in Urban Communities: An Integrative Model," *Journal of Politics* 48 (1986): 321–46.

7. Hirschman, *Exit, Voice, and Loyalty,* 15–16.

8. For more on the methodology of entering the field and gaining access as a qualitative researcher, see R. Bogdan, and S. K. Biklen, *Qualitative Research for Education: An Introduction to Theory and Methods* (Needham Heights, MA: Allyn & Bacon, 1992); C. Glesne and A. Peshkin, *Becoming Qualitative Researchers: An Introduction* (White Plains, NY: Longman, 1992); C. Marshall and G. Rossman, *Designing Qualitative Research* (Thousand Oaks, CA: Sage, 1989); J. A. Maxwell, *Qualitative Research Design: An Interactive Approach* (Thousand Oaks, CA: Sage, 1996); J. M. Nielsen, ed., *Feminist Research Methods: Exemplary Reading in the Social Sciences* (Boulder, CO: Westview Press, 1990); and I. E. Seidman, *Interviewing as Qualitative Research* (New York: Teachers College Press, 1991).

9. For more on rebalancing the scales of give-and-take between the researcher and

the researched and on reciprocity, see chapter 5: "On Relationships," in Sara Lawrence-Lightfoot and Jessica Hoffmann Davis, *The Art and Science of Portraiture* (San Francisco: Jossey-Bass Publishers, 1997), 153–55, 165.

3. Freedom

1. Jean-Paul Sartre, *No Exit and Three Other Plays* (New York: Vintage Books, 1943).
2. Ibid., 5–6.
3. Ibid., 17.
4. Ibid., 45.
5. Ibid., 43.

4. Wounds

1. For more on bullying, see Christine Barter and David Berrige, eds., *Children Behaving Badly? Peer Violence Between Children and Young People* (Malden, MA: Wiley-Blackwell, 2011); Monica J. Harris, ed., *Bullying, Rejection, and Peer Victimization: A Social Cognitive Neuroscience Perspective* (New York: Springer, 2009); and Dorothy Espelage and Susan Swearer, eds., *Bullying in American Schools: A Social-Ecological Perspective on Prevention and Intervention* (Mahwah, NJ: Erlbaum Associates, 2004).
2. For more on the intergenerational trans-

mission of trauma, see Carol Whatman et al., eds., *Formative Experiences: The Interaction of Caregiving, Culture, and Developmental Psychobiology* (New York: Cambridge University Press, 2010) and Yael Danieli, ed., *International Handbook of Multigenerational Legacies of Trauma* (New York: Plenum Press, 1998).

3. For more on termination practices in therapy, see William O'Donohue and Kyle Ferguson, *Handbook of Professional Ethics for Psychologists: Issues, Questions, and Controversies* (Thousand Oaks, CA: Sage Publications, 2003) and Jeffrey Barnett and Brad Johnson, *Ethics Desk Reference for Psychologists* (Washington, DC: American Psychological Association, 2008).

4. See Sigmund Freud, *The Interpretation of Dreams* (Oxford, UK: Oxford University Press, 1999).

5. For further reading about the art and science of clinical practice, see Atul Gawande, *Complications: A Surgeon's Notes on an Imperfect Science* (New York: Metropolitan Books, 2002); Atul Gawande, *Better: A Surgeon's Notes on Performance* (New York: Metropolitan, 2007); Oliver Sacks, *The Man Who Mistook His Wife for a Hat* (New York: Perennial

Library, 1987); Oliver Sacks, *An Anthropologist on Mars: Seven Paradoxical Tales* (New York: Knopf, 1995).

6. For more on the culture of medical training and medical education, see Robert Rogers, Amal Mattu, Michael Winters, and Joseph Martinez, eds., *Practical Teaching in Emergency Medicine* (Hoboken, NJ: Wiley-Blackwell, 2009); Commonwealth Fund Taskforce on Academic Health Centers, *Training Tomorrow's Doctors: The Medical Education Mission of Academic Health Centers* (New York, Commonwealth Fund, 2002); Stephen J. Miller, *The Medical Elite: Training for Leadership* (New Brunswick, NJ: Aldine Transaction, 2011); and Tim Swanwick, ed., *Understanding Medical Education: Evidence, Theory and Practice* (Chichester, West Sussex, UK: Wiley-Blackwell, 2010).

5. Yearning

1. Helen Rose Fuchs Ebaugh, *Becoming an Ex: The Process of Role Exit* (Chicago: University of Chicago Press, 1988).
2. Ibid., 206.
3. Ibid., xvi.
4. Robert Heinlein, *Stranger in a Strange Land* (New York: G. P. Putnam, 1961).

5. Lawrence-Lightfoot, *The Third Chapter.*

6. Grace

1. W.E.B. Du Bois, "Of Beauty and Death," in *Darkwater: Voices from Within the Veil* (New York: Harcourt, Brace, and Howe, 1920).
2. Ibid., 246–47.
3. Ibid., 247.

Conclusion: Rites and Rituals

1. Ira Byock, *Dying Well: The Prospect of Growth at the End of Life* (New York: Riverhead Books, 1997).
2. Hirschman, *Exit, Voice, and Loyalty.*
3. Ebaugh, *Becoming an Ex.*
4. Erikson, *Identity and the Life Cycle.*
5. Lawrence-Lightfoot, *The Third Chapter.*
6. Sartre, *No Exit and Three Other Plays.*
7. Steven Millhauser, "Getting Closer," *New Yorker,* January 3, 2011, 58–61.
8. Ibid., 59.

SELECTED SOURCES

Byock, Ira. *Dying Well: The Prospect of Growth at the End of Life.* New York: Riverhead Books, 1997.

In failing to deal with that ultimate of exits — death — Ira Byock, in *Dying Well,* argues that Americans have "paid dearly . . . and are culturally poorer for failing to explore the inherently human experience of dying" (p. xiii). In telling ten stories of death, including that of his own father, Byock enacts healing and connection, and builds a theory of death as a time of growth and potential for both internal understanding and interpersonal relationships. It was the experience of his father's death that led Byock to reexamine his experiences as a hospice doctor and to question his assumptions about dying and the care of those dying. Rather than conceptualizing death as a problem, and rather than classifying some deaths as "good," he coined the term "dying well" to evoke a sense of living, engagement, process, and action. This reframing is analogous to the reframing of exit as essentially a positive development rather than a mere ending, absence, or leaving. In addition to these developmental and interpersonal aspects, Byock addresses health-care policy, medical education, assisted suicide, financing strategies, and other large-scale issues, and offers advice for clinicians, families, and policy makers. He ends the book with a set of questions a family could use to begin a conversation about dying and how to treat it with the respect, reverence, and involvement it deserves.

Didion, Joan. "On Going Home," in *Slouching Towards Bethlehem.* New York: Farrar, Straus and Giroux, 1961.

"The question of whether or not you could go home again" (p. 167) raised by Joan Didion in this short essay evokes the archetypal exit from home upon reaching adulthood, and the way that such an exit redefines home. Recounting visiting her childhood home with her husband, Didion draws the distinction between being privy to the secret rituals and language that are open only to the people who grew up in her family, and the misunderstanding and non-understanding experienced by her husband, who is welcomed into the home, but not of it. Didion also defines home and belonging through a generational lens — growing up is an exit in itself. Looking at her sleeping daughter, Didion says she "would like to give her *home* for her birthday, but we live differently now and I can promise her nothing like that" (p. 169). As she comes back home, the separation between the past and present becomes evident, as well as the inevitable exit of the future generation.

Du Bois, W.E.B. "Of Beauty and Death," in *Darkwater: Voices from Within the Veil.* New York: Harcourt, Brace and Howe, 1920.

W.E.B. Du Bois argues that endings — because they are complete and finite — usher in beauty, which "lies implicit and is revealed in its end" (p. 120) and is the antithesis of eternal, incomplete, indefinite ugliness. To the extent that endings are embodied in exit, beauty becomes a component of exit. Juxtaposing the beauty of "sea and sky and city" with the least of the world's ugliness — the "little hatefulness and thoughtlessness of race prejudice" (p. 111) — Du Bois expresses the relationship between beauty, life, and death in this essay. The stories of ugliness include riding on the "Jim Crow" car on the train, the experience of buying a movie ticket in a segregated theater, and the degradation endured by black men volunteering for armed service. The rapturous images of beauty show the mountains of Maine, the Grand Canyon, and "the bugles of Harlem" heard by the town pump in a French village. Weaving among these moments of ugliness and beauty — indeed, entering and exiting each one — Du Bois's writing demonstrates the completeness, satisfaction, and fulfillment of experiencing beauty.

Ebaugh, Helen Rose Fuchs. *Becoming an Ex: The Process of Role Exit.* Chicago: University of Chicago Press, 1988.

Helen Ebaugh's interest in role exit began when she was a sociology student — and a Sister of Divine Providence — at Columbia University, studying with Robert Merton in the late 1960s and early 1970s. Her doctoral research project explored the relationship between changes in religious orders and exit rates and the reasons "why nuns left, the factors that precipitated the exit, what the exiting process was like, and the experience of life as an ex-nun." During the course of her research, she became fascinated with the personal accounts of role exiting that she was hearing, and she began to notice similar patterns and operating influences, which she later defined as stages or sequential events of role exit. Doing this work, Ebaugh herself made a transition and was struck by the similarities of her exit as an ex-nun and her fiancé's exit as a divorcé. She began to wonder how the process or stage model of role exit might apply to other kinds of voluntary exits, such as career changes, departures from ideological and sectarian groups, etc., and she assembled a research group to study the role-exit process across a variety of social roles, with the goal of discovering similarities and differences in the exiting process as experienced by people exiting roles they defined as central to their lives.

Ebaugh defines the term "role exit" as the process of disengagement from a role that is central to one's self-identity and the reestablishment of an identity in a new role that takes into account one's ex-role. She points to a lack of general theory that views role exit as a generic social process, and she frames her book as an attempt to explore and suggest basic issues involved in conceptualizing a theory of role exit. She ascertained a strong pattern in the sequencing of events in the role-exit process. The first stage is that of *first doubts,* in which individuals begin to question the role commitment they had previously taken for granted. The next stage is the seeking and weighing of *role alternatives.* The third stage is the *turning point,* when the individual actually leaves the role, followed by the last stage, which concerns the establishment of an *ex-role identity* during post-exit. Ebaugh also names eleven properties — or variables — that influence the nature and consequences of the role-exit process. These variables are voluntariness, centrality of the role, reversibility, duration, degree of control, individual versus group exit, single versus multiple exits, social desirability, degree of institutionalization, degree of awareness, and sequentiality. Her argument — that role exit be inserted into the broader landscape of sociological literature on role theory and become as central as the traditional concept of socialization into new roles — is an empirically based, unique contribution to the field.

There seems to be little that followed her 1988 book theorizing exit as a staged phenomenon, generalizable to most social roles.

Erikson, Erik H. *Identity and the Life Cycle.* New York: W. W. Norton, 1959.

Erik Erikson defines the stages of development of a healthy personality as the progression through critical psychological conflicts, from childhood to adulthood. Movement from one stage to the next is marked by a radical change in perspective, or an exit from seeing and accepting things one way to seeing and acknowledging another way of being. These developmental stages, in Erikson's terms are: (1) basic trust vs. basic mistrust (infancy); (2) autonomy vs. shame and doubt (early childhood); (3) initiative vs. guilt (play age); (4) industry vs. inferiority (school age); (5) identity vs. identity diffusion (adolescence); (6) intimacy vs. isolation (young adulthood); (7) generativity vs. self-absorption (adulthood); and (8) integrity vs. despair and disgust (mature age). These psychosocial crises occur within relationships with significant people and structures — such as family, school, peer groups, and partners — and therefore are locations of development influenced by both biology and society. Exit from one stage into the next, then, is growth into a healthy self.

Harper, Hill. "Quitting versus Changing Your Mind" in *Letters to a Young Brother: Manifest Your Destiny.* London, UK: Penguin Books, 2006.

In this series of letters influenced by Rilke's *Letters to a Young Poet,* Hill Harper delivers mentorship and advice to young men. Letter 6, "Quitting versus Changing Your Mind," is on the topic of quitting (a young man wants to quit the track team), and Harper develops a nuanced difference between "quitting" and "changing your mind/ doing something else/moving on." Quitting is performed out of fear, discomfort, and difficulty. Changing your mind, however, means stopping doing something that is holding you back from realizing your true potential. Harper recalls his own experience with changing his mind versus quitting when he graduated from Harvard Law School and was expected to start his career as a lawyer; instead of following this path, he decided to pursue his love of acting and moved to Los Angeles. In this exit, he enacts serious commitment to be an active architect of his life. Though he positions quitting as a negative response and changing your mind as a positive one, both seem to require justification; in this regard, he confirms the normative stance that exit is something that needs to be explained and rationalized rather than accepted and celebrated like entrances and beginnings. His counterpoint is that both quitting and changing one's mind can be purposeful, productive, powerful moments in the arc of a person's life, exits that beget success.

Hirschman, Albert O. *Exit, Voice, and Loyalty: Responses to Decline in Firms, Organizations, and States.* Cambridge, MA: Harvard University Press, 1970.

Albert Hirschman's seminal work of economic theory paints exit as a neat, terminal, impersonal, quantifiable, and discernible action that is highly efficient. It is the most direct way of expressing dissatisfaction. A customer resorts to exit, rather than voice, when he/she no longer attempts to change an objectionable state of affairs — whether through individual or collective petition, appeal to a higher authority, or various actions and protests

— although Hirschman admits the possibility of acquiescence or indifference as the space between voice (articulation) and exit. Though the exit option is widely held to be uniquely powerful, he states that the "precise modus operandi of the exit option has not received much attention." He attempts to explicate the phenomenon of exit by comparing it with voice, which is not only the opposite but also a complement to and a substitute for exit. The seesawing, complementary, yet unequal options of exit and voice are further complicated by Hirschman's addition of loyalty into the theoretical mix. Loyalty, or a special attachment to an organization, helps group members resort to voice when exit is possible; loyalty holds exit at bay and activates voice. In addition, loyalty calls into question the voice/exit dichotomy by posing a different dilemma: How does *voice from within* differ from *voice from without* (after exit)?

Hirschman supports the idea that exit is a ubiquitous cultural experience and indeed a hallmark of American society. He also positions exit as a regenerative force in the face of inevitable deterioration and decay, even as he warns of the high cost exit can bring to both the individual and the organization. Though he favors voice as a response to dissatisfaction, he nevertheless portrays exit as a powerful force and is respectful of exit as an entity necessary for the functioning of businesses, economies, and nations. For him, exit doesn't feel like a "problem," but rather a powerful and complex action. For example, he challenges the idea that full exit is ever possible and questions the balance of power between the one who exits and the one who stays. In portraying exit as a fluid, complex, and contradictory experience, Hirschman values this component of our culture and economy through his multidimensional theory.

Lawrence-Lightfoot, Sara. *Respect: An Exploration.* Cambridge, MA: Perseus Books, 2000.

This book illuminates the roots, development, and expressions of respect, a concept, idea, and practice that in its presence — or absence — marks the essence of public and private lives. It is an exploration that regards respect in ways contrary to the traditional perspectives: respect as empathetic and connective rather than submissive and boundary marking; respect as developing and growing over time rather than a static quantity; respect as commitment and desire rather than compliance and duty. The six portraits of respect in this book also highlight the ways in which respect is tied with exit, especially when considering boundaries, taking risks, relationships and connections, the symmetry of movement back and forth, the beauty of completion, and the way that exit — with and in respect — can be a generative force.

Lawrence-Lightfoot, Sara. *The Third Chapter: Passion, Risk, and Adventure in the 25 Years After 50.* New York: Sarah Crichton Books/Farrar, Straus and Giroux, 2009.

The Third Chapter redefines the period of life that has traditionally been limited to post-career aging and decline, and positions it as a developmental stage full of possibility, challenge, and transformation. It is perhaps not surprising that exit — from work, from established roles, from comfortable identities and relationships — is what grounds the contours and experiences of this stage of life. Exit — from the "old" life into the new — is the catalyst for learning, creativity, and risk taking undertaken by folks in their fifties, sixties, and seventies who yearn for challenge and meaning not yet experienced. In fact, exits can be regarded as a necessary condition of development at this stage of life, developmental in their very essence. Most profoundly, exit enables being and becoming at this stage of life; exit is the transition that propels people toward achieving their fullest self at an age long regarded as the time to retreat and disengage.

Lawrence-Lightfoot, Sara, and Jessica Hoffmann Davis. "Chapter Five: On Relationships," in *The Art and Science of Portraiture.* San Francisco: Jossey-Bass Publishers, 1997.

In this seminal methodological text, which breaks open the boundaries of aesthetics and empiricism, relationships are at the heart of developing understanding and knowledge. These relationships are marked by the challenges of reciprocity and responsibility; recognizing, sustaining, and negotiating boundaries; and, of course, exit. The importance of exit is especially vivid when considering reciprocity; in respecting the contribution of the research participants to the researcher's work, and in acknowledging that the relationship between the researcher and the research participants is delimited, exit becomes a vehicle by which to act responsibly, ethically, and with goodness. Seldom considered, the idea and practice of exit in research relationships is critical for social scientists.

Marshall, Paule. *Brown Girl, Brownstones.* New York: Random House, 1959.

The story of immigration is a classic exit story, the story of leaving the home of one's native land to make another home on foreign soil. Paule Marshall published this novel at the age of thirty, exploring her own childhood and adolescence growing up in the Barbadian immigrant community in 1930s Brooklyn. She captures the fullness and contradictions of home and community as well as the love and the hurts that define her family's experience after exiting their homeland. The rich language of the novel's characters transforms their particular experience into the universal themes of tradition, history, spirituality, and identity; for Marshall, the texture and sound of this language is what defines home, both before and after the exit of immigration.

Marshall, Paule. "From the Poets in the

Kitchen." *New York Times,* January 9, 1983.

In this widely cited *New York Times* article, Paule Marshall writes about the language of home — the legacy of language and culture — that she learned in "the word-shop of the kitchen." Writing about her mother and her mother's friends who, after their long days as housecleaners, gathered around a kitchen table to talk about life, politics, and home, Marshall acknowledges these women and their talk to be the literary giants who taught her narrative art, trained her ear, and set a standard of excellence. The poetry and beauty of this everyday language was found at the kitchen table and within the books, stories, and poems by West Indian and black Americans. For Marshall, this language was home — and her home was this language; within the embrace of the kitchen and her mother's talk, she began to think of someday being a writer herself.

O'Kill, Brian, ed. *Exit Lines: Famous (and Not So Famous) Last Words.* Essex, England: Longman Higher Education, 1986.

This is a collection of accounts of the various ways famous figures in history — from six continents, across two millennia, and including Beethoven, Julius Caesar, Chekhov, Descartes, Isadora Duncan, Goethe, Hobbes, John Lennon, Molière, Napoleon, Isaac Newton, Picasso, Socrates, Gertrude Stein, Thoreau, and Richard Wagner, to name a few — have died and the words they have spoken at their end. Brian O'Kill explains popular fascination with dying words through the commonly held belief that one's manner of dying mirrors one's manner of living. In this ultimate exit — death — O'Kill brings up the possibility that how one dies — expressed in the words one utters — matters. Related to this is also the idea that in the act of leaving life, a person can reveal some essential characteristic or give some meaning to the ones who are left living. Though death is an unplanned exit, it is an inevitable exit; that there is considerable cultural variation regarding rituals and understanding of death points to the possibility that human beings have long grappled with the mystery the exit of death represents.

Sartre, Jean-Paul. *No Exit and Three Other Plays*. New York: Vintage Books, 1956.

The play *Huis Clos* (No Exit) was first performed in a theater in Paris in 1944 and presents a version of hell — a place from which it is impossible to exit, a place that is surprisingly banal, and a place of interminable suffering through the torture of self-reflection and relations with other human beings. The three condemned souls — Garcin, Inez, and Estelle — learn what each of them did in life to deserve hell after death, and they attempt to tolerate one another's presence. They fail, provoking Garcin to exclaim that famous line, "Hell is other people." When given the opportunity to exit the room in which they are confined, they are unable to leave. Hell, therefore, is not only other people, but one's self too; symbolizing potentiality, possibility, movement, and life itself, exit is the ultimate freedom. It is through the ability to exit present circumstances into the abyss of the unknown — to imagine another way of existing that is reachable through leaving what one knows — that Sartre offers a vision for a full and meaningful life.

Weiss, Robert. *The Experience of Retirement.* New York: Cornell University Press, 2005. Robert Weiss offers a carefully researched sociological perspective on the experience of retirement, characterized as an exit from working or from an occupation, generally defined by age. Weiss's descriptive work supplements the mostly survey and policy analyses of retirement and attends to this social rite of passage through three perspectives — the economic, the sociological, and the psychological. Observing how people exit their professions, their working routines, and their job-related identities, Weiss finds this exit to be multifaceted, complex, and sometimes perplexing. He notes that in planning for retirement, people consider the financial realities of their exit much more than the social and psychological changes that accompany leaving the sphere of work and occupational engagement. He recommends preparing for this exit, especially regarding transitions, activities to replace work, and sustaining relationships. As with some of the folks in the present book, the rituals of retirement are both essential and incomplete.

ACKNOWLEDGMENTS

This project required that I ask folks to take a difficult, counterintuitive journey; to begin at the end, to reflect on, and to make visible the exits in their lives, to honor the departures that are so often shadowed by guilt or diminished by inattention. I want to express my appreciation to the nearly forty people whose insights and observations helped shape the arc and argument of this book, most especially the dozen women and men whose solo voices and life-giving narratives are braided through the text, allowing us to hear the resonant and dissonant soundings of their stories, offering us the chance to see the universal in the particular. The storytellers were heroic, openhearted, and authentic in expressing their mix of emotions of loss and liberation, pain and joy, laughter and tears. They were brave in reliving ancient tales, turning old scars into badges of courage, using our conversations as opportunities for discovery, celebration, and healing. I am awed by their trust, inspired by their witness, and forever grateful for their wisdom. Although their voices, experiences, and journeys have been faithfully documented and recorded, I have — by mutual agreement — altered all the names, a few of the narrative details, and most of the places to protect their privacy and that of their families.

Wendy Angus, my extraordinary assistant, was once again by my side, with steady encouragement, probing observations, sage counsel, and discerning attention to things big and small. Irene Liefshitz, my brilliant research assistant, brought her rigor and imagination, her lightness and laughter, her soulfulness and sophistication to our conversations. Her writings, reviewing the literature and musing on the metaphors, were lucid, her analyses penetrating. I am so grateful for Wendy's and Irene's generous contributions to this work.

My magnificent friends Susan Robbins Berger, Andrea Fleck Clardy, Jessica Hoffmann Davis, Mary Graham, Marita Rivero, and Marti Wilson were my confidants and coconspirators as we took our long walk/talks around the Jamaica Pond, along the Muddy River, on the beaches and through the marshes in Woods Hole, as we watched the sunrise over Gilmore Pond and the sunsets on Squam Lake . . . rich conversations inspired by the water. I am thankful for their deep listening and spirited talk, their intelligence and truth telling, their abiding love.

My family, bless every one of them, nourished me with food for my body and my soul. My mother, Margaret, who, at ninety-seven, has seen it all, offered me her spiritual countenance and amazing grace. My sister, Paula, a fearless sojourner, asked the gentle/hard questions that lead to new discoveries. My brother, Chuck, loved the conceit of this book, immediately challenging and stretching my nascent understandings. And my children, now young adults, stuck to the family script: Tolani seeing the art and imagery, the metaphors and poetry in exit journeys, and Martin offering his funky wit and heartfelt encouragement, rescuing me from computer disasters. Irving Hamer sustained me with his fierce love, his huge heart, and his unyielding belief in me.

As always, my agent, Ike Williams, shepherded this project forward with his signature blend of cool and passion. I am always grateful for his friendship, his strategic guidance, and his unerring support. Still rivers run deep with Hope Denekamp, who is always there, holding down the fort, graceful and tough in her advocacy on my behalf. I thank my smart, savvy, and sophisticated editor and publisher, Sarah Crichton, who pushed just enough, practicing her delicate mix of demand and restraint. She was ably assisted by the steadiness, intelligence, and welcome humor of Dan Piepenbring.

ABOUT THE AUTHOR

Sara Lawrence-Lightfoot, a MacArthur prize–winning sociologist, is the Emily Hargroves Fisher Professor of Education at Harvard University, where she has been on the faculty since 1972. An educator, researcher, author, and public intellectual, Lawrence-Lightfoot has written ten books, including *Worlds Apart: Relationships Between Families and Schools* (1978), *Beyond Bias: Perspectives on Classrooms* (1979; with Jean Carew), and *The Good High School: Portraits of Character and Culture* (1983), which received the 1984 Outstanding Book Award from the American Educational Research Association. Her book *Balm in Gilead: Journey of a Healer* (1988), which won the 1988 Christopher Award, given for "literary merit and humanitarian achievement," was followed by *I've Known Rivers: Lives of Loss and Liberation* (1994) and *The*

Art and Science of Portraiture (1997; with Jessica Hoffmann Davis), which documents her pioneering approach to social science methodology, one that bridges the realms of aesthetics and empiricism. In *Respect: An Exploration* (1999), Lawrence-Lightfoot reaches deep into human experience to find the essence of this powerful quality. *The Essential Conversation: What Parents and Teachers Can Learn from Each Other* (2003) captures the crucial exchange between parents and teachers, a dialogue that is both mirror and metaphor for the cultural forces that shape the socialization of our children, and *The Third Chapter: Passion, Risk, and Adventure in the 25 Years after 50* (2009) explores new learning during one of the most transformative and generative times in our lives.

Lawrence-Lightfoot has been the recipient of twenty-eight honorary degrees. In 1993, the Sara Lawrence-Lightfoot Chair, an endowed professorship, was established at Swarthmore College, and in 1998, she was the recipient of the Emily Hargroves Fisher Endowed Chair at Harvard University, which upon her retirement will become the Sara Lawrence-Lightfoot Endowed Chair, making her the first African American woman in Harvard's history to have an endowed professorship named in her honor.

Lawrence-Lightfoot did her undergraduate work in psychology at Swarthmore College and received her doctorate in the sociology of education at Harvard.

The employees of Thorndike Press hope you have enjoyed this Large Print book. All our Thorndike, Wheeler, and Kennebec Large Print titles are designed for easy reading, and all our books are made to last. Other Thorndike Press Large Print books are available at your library, through selected bookstores, or directly from us.

For information about titles, please call:
  (800) 223-1244

or visit our Web site at:
  http://gale.cengage.com/thorndike

To share your comments, please write:
  Publisher
  Thorndike Press
  10 Water St., Suite 310
  Waterville, ME 04901

Love Stories
of WORLD WAR II

Love Stories
of WORLD WAR II

Compiled by **LARRY KING**

 CROWN PUBLISHERS / New York

Published by Crown Publishers, New York, New York.
Member of the Crown Publishing Group.

Random House, Inc. New York, Toronto, London, Sydney, Auckland
www.randomhouse.com

CROWN is a trademark and the Crown colophon is a registered
trademark of Random House, Inc.

All illustrations reproduced by permission of those whose stories are
told, with grateful acknowledgment.

Printed in the United States of America

DESIGN BY BARBARA STURMAN

Library of Congress Cataloging-in-Publication Data
  Love stories of World War II / compiled by Larry King.—1st ed.
      p. cm.
    1. World War, 1939–1945—Biography.   2. Married people—
  United States—Biography.   3. United States—Biography.
  I. King, Larry, 1933–   .
  D736.L68   2001
  940.53′092′2—dc21   2001032518

ISBN 0-609-60723-5

10 9 8 7 6 5 4 3 2 1

First Edition

With grateful acknowledgment for the creative work of

John Malone and Tom Steele

in connection with the writing of this book.

ONTENTS

Introduction   ix

Miles and Betty TRIMPEY   3

William and Doris METZGER   15

Earl and Maxine BUTTERFIELD   27

Ed and Mary Jane RUSSELL   35

Joseph and Virginia STARNS   47

Edward and Patricia BURR   59

Paul and Frieda KINCADE   67

J. W. and Bea SUTHERLAND   77

Anne Hetrick KENNEDY   85

Lloyd and Miriam CLARK   99

Charles and Patricia LEE   107

Hank and Mary Jo SUERSTEDT   117

Mary Evelyn Porter BERRY   125

Lowell and Helen BAKER   129

Eli and Bernice FISHPAW   137

James and Virginia COWART   145

John and Angeline DARR   155

Louis and Judy FUNDERBURG   163

Hugh and Maudie OWENS   171

Harold and Adelle JENSEN   179

Jack and Marjorie VAIRA   187

Catherine M. ROBERTS-SWAUGER   195

Betty Law BACHMAN   211

Max and Ena McCLURE   227

Harold and Jeanne CONN   239

Anna Della Casa GONZALES   247

Erwin and Eleonora HAYES   259

Henry and Jane SCHLOSSER   267

Wharton and Miriam SCHNEIDER   277

Harry E. and Mary Lou HEFFELFINGER   285

Alfred and Shirley GOLDIS   297

Ron SMITH   307

Raymond and Kathleen WITHERS   321

$\mathscr{I}$NTRODUCTION

You are about to encounter some truly extraordinary couples, men and women who met by chance during the drama of World War II and, for the most part, stayed together for the rest of their lives. The men were going off to fight, many in legendary battles: Anzio, D-Day, the Battle of the Bulge, Guam, Iwo Jima. Some were bomber pilots or crew members flying treacherous missions over Europe and the far-flung islands of the Pacific. Others served at sea aboard destroyers, submarines, communications ships. Although many are willing to recall the battles and campaigns they lived through, altogether different stories remain more important to them. What they really like to talk about is how the war brought them together with the women who changed their lives, the women they met and loved and married in towns and cities across America, or in distant places all over the world.

Some of these couples were already in love, even married, when the United States entered World War II the day after December 7, 1941, when the Japanese bombed Pearl Harbor. But most found love in places they had never been before. Maybe a small town in the South near an army boot camp, where a girl in a red belt shone so brightly among the many pretty girls at a USO dance. Or maybe at the naval port of San Francisco, where a girl happened to emerge from a church and begin walking in the same direction as the soldier who would shortly decide he wanted to marry her. A marriage proposal might take place over the roar of air-raid sirens and pummel of anti-aircraft artillery in London. These men served in a harrowing war with diligence, courage, and distinction. But in the long run, a few intensely romantic moments changed their lives most completely—breathtaking moments when eyes met and hand brushed hand, resulting in memories to be cherished for a lifetime.

When we began gathering material for this book, we assumed that women would comprise the majority of people who wanted to tell their love stories. We were quickly disabused of that stereotypical notion. In the end, men accounted for at least half the respondents. Far from being uncomfortable with the subject of love, they relished the opportunity to tell the world about the romantic side of the World War II experience. As one man put it, "We've all got war stories. Some of us like to tell them and some don't. But the story of how we fell in love with our wives, well, that's still with us every day, and I know a lot of us can still get a little choked up over it. The war was a long time ago, one part of our lives. But we're still living the love stories. That's about now as well as then."

The wives have plenty of stories, too. You will meet a woman who decided she wasn't doing enough to help the cause by working in a defense factory, so she joined the Waves as an airplane mechanic. You will meet a spunky fifteen-year-old Neapolitan girl who was holding her sister's baby in her arms—the sister who had been killed in a bombing raid—when a GI approached to tell her that his friend was interested in her; she replied, "If he likes me so much, tell him to get some food for this baby." And you'll be introduced to women who stayed at home to care for infants whose first pictures had to be sent to a husband "somewhere" in Europe or the Pacific, a new father who might never see his child. The women's stories are as deeply felt and sometimes as dramatic as any experience their husbands might have had at the front.

Interestingly, very few of the men and women who told their stories for this book were specific about what first attracted them to the person they fell in love with. To some degree, that may be due to a generational sense of propriety. Obviously, a fervent sexual attraction between two young people must have played a large role in the initial stages of a soon-to-be-serious relationship. But nobody ever mentioned that directly. The men and women of the World War II generation still tend to believe that subtlety is worth something. Perhaps they're just true romantics in a way that is rapidly disappearing. If you ask what they think of today's movies, many of them will insist that the slightly hidden is a lot sexier than the flagrant. But perhaps it's not that they find such candor shocking; it's just that the partially veiled leaves so much, as one woman said, "to our own private dirty mind, which is much more fun."

Although these stories are told in the third person, every effort has been made to capture the voice of each teller. People were not pressed for information they did not want to give. These are *their* stories, and, in the fullest sense, this is their book. Each description of a romantic encounter contributes something special to the whole mosaic, illuminating and enlarging a broader picture of love in a time of war.

Because our cast of characters comes from such diverse backgrounds and they all had such a tremendous variety of experiences during the war, these pages enable us to see a unique period in our history from many different points of view. Though each of these stories is unique, both in circumstances and appeal, many of them reflect experiences that form common threads in the larger tapestry of World War II life. Again and again, we hear about the difficulty getting from here to there during the war years—not just overseas but right here at home. Those of us who fly a lot in this jet age, and complain endlessly about delayed flights, lousy food, and misplaced luggage, are likely to feel a little sheepish after reading these stories.

Buses, trains, planes—no matter what the mode of transportation, everyone knew there would be a problem, more likely lots of problems. Too busy making jeeps and trucks for the battlefields, Detroit had stopped making new cars. Gas was rationed, of course; you'll be hearing a lot about getting enough of it in the tank to make it through a single date, let alone connect with a loved one any distance away. Despite all the problems, luck sometimes broke the soldier's way.

Luck. A great many of the men and women whose stories appear here can still scarcely believe how lucky they were. More than one man was dismissed at the last minute from a mission on which the plane went down, killing everyone aboard. Some who did board planes that crashed ended up in the hospital for months, which would ordinarily be bad luck, except that while they were lying in bed, they first heard a nurse's voice that they would end up hearing for the rest of their lives.

Inevitably, there was horribly bad luck as well. Fifty million people died in the course of World War II, millions of civilians as well as soldiers; many survived with injuries that changed everything, including the outcome of their love stories. Not every story here has a happy ending, in the usual sense. Still, you'll see that some things are worth having even for a very short time. And sometimes what existed in the past remains so strong that years—even decades—later, it became necessary for those involved to seek out the love that was lost and try to make a new and different ending.

One of the more pleasant consequences of World War II is the fact that women from all over the world found soul mates in American men whom they might never have encountered had it not been for the war. Many international couples took enormous risks to remain together. Some parents of young women from other countries encouraged their daughters to follow their heart and embark on the highly uncertain adventure of moving to America and another way of life; other women had to overcome tremendous parental misgivings—or even sacrifice a parental relationship altogether.

The girls back home—and many of them were hardly more than that, even if they did have a newborn infant to care for—sent letters off into the unknown, to "somewhere in Europe" and "somewhere in the Pacific." They would receive letters back with blacked-out portions or even holes cut out to remove words that might threaten security. A great many of the women worried that their trivial day-to-day activities would bore their husbands and boyfriends in the midst of battle. Little did they realize they were a lifeline, helping to nourish the mind and soul of their loved ones.

Some women served away from home in the military themselves, as recruiters or nurses or airplane mechanics. Many of these women were officers, which, due to strict rules about officers of either sex fraternizing with enlisted personnel of the opposite sex, could complicate things. It took a great deal of ingenuity to get around the problem. In this book you will meet the only enlisted man actually arrested for having dinner with his wife.

Through the eyes of these men and women, you will catch sight of myriad small moments that help to convey the full panoply of a world at war: from President Franklin Delano Roosevelt's jaunty wave to a family on the streets of Hawaii as he was on his way to settle a major argument between the two most important commanders in the Pacific, to a Christmas service in the snow during the Battle of the Bulge; even the story of a German national married to an American woman who found himself incarcerated on Ellis Island with fellow "loyalty risk" Ezio Pinza, the great opera bass who was soon to become the toast of Broadway in *South Pacific*.

But above all, you'll hear the stories of "the man she was destined to marry" and "the woman across the crowded room." These love stories took place over half a century ago, but they become vivid realities once more of a time when every minute of life held a special intensity. Though this book contains many historical moments, it is not a history book. Although it demonstrates the courage of the men who fought around the world, it is not a book of war stories; it is a book of love stories. These men and women all believe that in the end, the most important facet of World War II wasn't the battles fought but the very simple fact that in the midst of war, they found each other.

Love Stories
of WORLD WAR II

THE BOMBING OF PEARL HARBOR on December 7, 1941, radically changed the plans of innumerable young couples across the United States practically overnight. War had been raging across Europe for over two years, ever since Adolf Hitler invaded Poland on September 1, 1939, but strong isolationist feelings dominated in the United States. President Franklin Delano Roosevelt had to muster all of his considerable cunning in order to convince Congress to institute the first peacetime draft in American history in September 1940. But with the ruthless attack on Pearl Harbor, America plunged into the war. Thousands of young couples got married over the next few months, in order to have some time together before the husband was inevitably called to duty.

Miles and Betty Trimpey in March 1945.

Miles and Betty
TRIMPEY

In 1998 Betty Trimpey gave her younger daughter, Linda K. Golby, a battered box of letters that had survived thirteen moves, still tied together with faded fifty-year-old hair ribbons. The letters included many that Linda's father, Miles Reid Trimpey, had written to his young wife during World War II, Betty's own letters back to him, as well as a number written to Miles by relatives and friends.

After she saw the Steven Spielberg movie *Saving Private Ryan*, Linda began wondering whether her father had been involved in the D-Day landings at Normandy. He never talked about the war before his death in 1990, and she had no idea where he served. She discovered from one letter that he indeed scrambled to the beach at Normandy that horrifying day, and spent his nineteenth birthday in a foxhole after the battle at Trévières on June 9, 1944, three days after D-Day One.

Increasingly intrigued, Linda read through all the letters and decided to type them up and assemble them in two loose-leaf volumes. She illustrated the volumes with photographs and reproductions of postcards and holiday greetings her father sent to her mother while he was in the army. She also included a number of documents pertaining to his service and annotated the top of each letter in her own elegant handwriting, explaining who had sent each letter and providing the postmark date and place. Over the following months, she also read all the letters aloud to her mother, whose eyesight had failed. The letters conjured up such vivid memories of fear and separation for Betty that the reading sessions often became extremely emotional. Linda, too, was deeply moved, as she was getting to know her father in ways she never had before.

Her father's letters were not very legible, written mostly in pencil on any paper he could get his hands on, including one on toilet tissue. Some gave the impression that a hard but not very flat surface—his helmet, his knee—was used as a writing desk. Betty maintained that she felt bad about writing her husband such boring letters, but Linda is certain that her small talk was exactly what her father needed and wanted to hear. Those letters served as his primary connection to the world he was fighting for and longed to come home to. Linda believes that the letters he sent and received actually kept him sane.

MILES TRIMPEY and Betty Romesberg both grew up near Rockwood, Pennsylvania. Betty lived with her parents on a small farm, and Miles worked in construction. They met one Saturday night when both were dining with friends at the same restaurant. Betty always told her two daughters, Nancy Lee and Linda, that it was love at first sight, and Miles would say that he had thought Betty was the most beautiful girl he'd ever seen in his life and that he knew instantly that he would marry her someday.

On their first date, Miles took Betty to the construction site where he was working, to show her that he was a hardworking, serious young man. In fact, he was only seventeen, and Betty eighteen. They soon married, on April 14, 1943. Because Miles expected to be drafted shortly after he turned eighteen, they moved in with Betty's parents instead of trying to find their own place. They also decided to have a baby right away. Miles wanted to have at least one child in case he didn't make it home from the war, and Betty agreed.

On June 9, 1943, Miles turned eighteen, and sure enough, the notice to report for induction (Order #12,472) was issued on September 13. He became an enlisted man on October 19 and was sent to Camp Wheeler, Georgia, for basic training. As soon as he got to camp, he started writing the letters that Betty prized so much.

In a letter from Camp Wheeler dated October 22, Miles told Betty that they had watched a movie show at the camp. "They were no good," he wrote, "but if I had you with me they would be better." On October

28, he noted, "I had to stop this letter just now. We were called out for a little training. We had to learn to salute an officer."

Training quickly got serious. In a November 4 letter, Miles told Betty that he had bought her a souvenir, a miniature replica of the automatic rifle he had been trained to use: "It shoots eight shells as fast as you can pull the trigger. Take notice of the knife on the end. They showed us how to kill a man with it today. You use the knife if you don't have any shells. The knife is 16" long. You run it through the neck or through the guts."

As if realizing that this description might upset Betty, he started a new paragraph: "To change the subject I want to thank you for the Bible you sent me. I will use it and often." Betty still has that small blue Bible, a bit tattered from its wartime service. On the flyleaf he inscribed his name, rank, and serial number, and listed Mrs. Miles Trimpey, Rockwood, Pa, R.D. #1, Box 6, as his nearest relative. On the opposite page was a printed note from the White House: "As Commander-in-Chief I take pleasure in commending the reading of the Bible to all who serve in the armed forces of the United States," it begins, and it is signed Franklin D. Roosevelt. It is clear from Miles's letters that he did use that Bible often and, like many others, learned to pray with considerably more urgency while serving in the war. As for the souvenir gun, Betty wrote to tell him that it was beautiful, and that she had placed it on her bureau as he had asked.

As the seventeen weeks of training continued, Miles wrote as often as possible, practically daily, but sometimes he was too exhausted to do anything but collapse at the end of the day. His letters are suffused with love for Betty and his concern about how she was feeling as her pregnancy advanced. (The word "pregnant" was not used by either of them; Betty spoke instead of "my condition," as proper young women were taught to do sixty years ago.)

There was discussion of Betty coming down to Georgia to see Miles, because he would not be able to come home for Thanksgiving or Christmas, but both finances and her "condition" prevented that. Miles did not get his first pay, which, after the allotment sent home to Betty was $15 for the month he had served, until November 30, and it was thanks only to dollar bills sent by relatives that he was able to buy much of anything. Betty and other family members and friends also sent him treats like candy and nuts. At one point he asked Betty to send him some "cigs," and more than once he wryly noted, "Another day, another 60 cents." When he did get paid, he went out and had his picture taken in uniform to send to Betty. It arrived with the frame and glass broken, despite his careful wrapping. In response, Betty offered some wifely advice about marking any other pictures "Glass, Handle with Care" or, even better, sending just the photo marked "Picture, Do Not Bend" and letting her buy a frame. But even with a broken frame, she loved the photo and wrote to him, "Boy are you ever good-looking."

When the couple exchanged Christmas letters, Betty wrote that it surely didn't feel like Christmas without him. After describing the family feast, she commented, "I wasn't very hungry for any food. All I was hungry for is your love." Miles described his meal, including turkey and pumpkin pie and "most everything we could think of," adding, "The only time you get a good meal in the Army is Thanksgiving or Christmas." He closed by telling her, "I hear 'White Christmas' playing. Does it ever bring back the good old days. I feel like crying. No fooling. Your True Husband, Miles."

Army realities soon returned to the foreground. In a letter written on the twenty-ninth, Miles complained, "We got a new sergeant yesterday and is he ever hell on earth." It was already clear that he would be "going over," using the phrase for European combat that was initiated during World War I. For a while, Miles had written about trying to join the paratroopers, but when he asked Betty what she thought, she firmly discouraged the idea, since his situation was likely to be dangerous enough without any leaping out of planes.

Like all soldiers, Miles was well aware that he could easily get killed. In his Christmas Day letter, he wrote, "So, Darling, never worry if anything happens to me and I never get back. Always think of these words, 'I will be in Heaven waiting for you, Darling.'" But however much he may have worried about what could happen to him, other letters make clear his pride in being a good soldier, and his delight that his unit had been singled out by an officer as the best around.

As his training drew to a grueling close, Miles had to spend two weeks living in a tent in the woods while his unit was put through combat exercises. Despite the cold and rain and lack of sleep, he was sustained by the hope that at the end of his training, he would get a week's leave to go north and be with Betty. The leave he prayed for came through at the end of February, and he was able to spend the first week of March with his wife, by then seven months "on the way." They shared an all too brief, bittersweet interlude, knowing every moment that Miles was about to be shipped overseas into battle.

On March 7, 1944, Miles was at Fort George G. Meade in Maryland, writing home "to my one I love most in all the world." The next day he was furnished with all new equipment for his overseas posting—where, exactly, he still didn't know.

On the thirteenth he received his shipping orders and wrote to Betty telling her not to worry if at any time she didn't hear from him for a couple of weeks. He sent her a cross and told her that while it might not cost much, "if you just think of it and the fellow who got it for you, I know it will help me get back much sooner and in good health." He promised to read his little blue Bible: "I know if I read it and live up to what it says, I will be back to you. And Darling you do the same. Darling, I wish I could hand you this letter . . . like a little baby with tears in my eyes I have to quit."

On the fourteenth, Miles wrote twice and must have tried to give her some hint about where he was being sent, since sections of the letter were blacked out by censors. There was one more letter from Maryland, and then two with no postmark. The next one came by V-Mail, written April 7 but postmarked April 18. Miles Trimpey was now overseas.

Miles added some new words to the flyleaf of his Bible during the transatlantic crossing: "April 2, 1944. As I lie here on this boat thinking how much I love you, I will give my life for you or the baby." He sent short notes by V-Mail for more than a month before he finally heard back that their baby daughter, Nancy Lee, had been born on April 30, 1944. "The best news I ever had in my whole life," Miles wrote in a letter dated May 12 but postmarked June 9—two days after D-Day, as he celebrated his nineteenth birthday in a cold, wet foxhole. Miles did not actually find out the baby's name until May 25, but from then on, his letters were usually addressed to both Betty and Nancy Lee. The letters Betty sent to him during this period were lost, but the first tangible evidence of his daughter survived: Betty sent him a piece of paper with Nancy Lee's inked footprints on it, and he put it in his Bible for safekeeping.

By the end of June, Miles was able to write "Somewhere in France" at the top of his letters. On July 4 he wrote about having gone to church the day before with other GIs and told Betty she should have seen how they all prayed and sang. "I believe this war made a lot of fellows look hard at their homes and wives and country and see how good they had it. I believe this war is to make people think a little more of God and to go to church a little more instead of going to a beer party. . . . Lots of people back home in the states still don't care, but I know for myself and the boys who've been on the battlefield and saw fighting do care. It made them all think . . . about living a different life." This was the letter written on toilet paper.

Over the following three months, the letters from Miles were short and intermittent. He seldom complained, and the roar of the war came through only once in a while, as when he reported seeing an American plane shot out of the sky but noticed figures parachuting from it and so assumed they were safe. He wrote about his respect for the Army Air Force, and about how much they had done to speed the way of American troops across France. He told of three soldiers praying in a foxhole and revealed that he was one of them. Always, he wrote longingly about his daughter and how he and Betty would raise her to be a good girl when he got home.

On October 1, 1944, he excitedly wrote: "Well, Darling, I am in Paris. I never thought a year ago I would be in Paris." He had finally received a picture of little Nancy Lee, and he declared her very cute, adding, "I never knew I was man enough. Ha, Ha."

Later in the month he referred to the Parisian postcards he had sent home, noting that now he had seen all those places. "Boy, this is too pretty of a country for a war," he added, echoing the thoughts of so many American soldiers who fought their way across historic lands they had never expected to see.

On November 15 he was somewhere in Belgium. Two days later he wrote, "You know a man never knows what a wife and a home means until he goes to the other side of the world. And, Darling, I am in Germany now."

On the twentieth, he forwarded home a poem, author unknown, that celebrated his regiment, "The Thirty Eighth (The Rock of the Marne)." The poem closes:

> In Conclusion, When Our Work Is Done
> Then Read of the Battles One By One
> For Our Part to You Folks at Home It Will Be
> "You're Welcome!"
> FROM THE 38TH INFANTRY.

There was one more brief letter, written on Thanksgiving Day, then Miles was separated from the Thirty-eighth, wounded in action.

A letter from the War Department, dated December 26, 1944, informed Betty Trimpey, "the latest report from the theater of operations states that on 9 December the recovery of your husband, Private Miles R. Trimpey, was not proceeding satisfactorily." The letter went on to tell her that some of America's finest doctors were assigned to overseas bases and that her husband was receiving the very best of medical care. At home in Pennsylvania, Betty could only wait helplessly for more news. It was not until January 11 that a two-week-old letter arrived to announce that Miles was "convalescing" and that further news would come as soon as possible.

Betty wrote to the War Department to beseech them for any information they could possibly give her and received a reply dated February 6: "Neither the original report showing that he was seriously wounded in action on 24 November, 1944, nor the progress reports reveal the nature and extent of his wounds. . . . With respect to your inquiry regarding the whereabouts of your husband, you will undoubtedly realize that in the interest of military security his present location cannot be disclosed."

Fortunately, a document bearing the previous day's date arrived, bringing far better news. It was from Thomas M. England General Hospital in Atlantic City, New Jersey, with Miles's name and serial number typed in, along with a description of his condition as "satisfactory." Best of all, the notice informed Betty that "You may visit him if you desire," and gave visiting hours.

There was also a letter from Miles, the first in two and a half months, dated February 7 and postmarked the same day in Atlantic City. "To the one I love most and will be seeing soon," it began, then continued: "Well,

Miles Trimpey in 1944.

THE WHITE HOUSE
WASHINGTON

As Commander-in-Chief I take pleasure in commending the reading of the Bible to all who serve in the armed forces of the United States. Throughout the centuries men of many faiths and diverse origins have found in the Sacred Book words of wisdom, counsel and inspiration. It is a fountain of strength and now, as always, an aid in attaining the highest aspirations of the human soul.

The Bible that Betty sent to Miles, with his note: "As I lie here on this boat thinking how much I love you, I will give my life for you or the baby."

Here is your daughters Nancy Lee's footprints.

Put this in your Bible and keep it with you with lots of love.

*The paper with baby
Nancy Lee's footprints.*

*Miles and Nancy Lee
Trimpey in June 1945.*

honey, I guess our prayers were answered. I had to get shot a few times to get back but I am here now."

Although Betty and Miles were able to see each other often, it was not until mid-July that his convalescence was completed and he received his discharge papers. Just before he returned home for good, he wrote a letter from the hospital on July 17 telling Betty that he had received two books from his old division the day before. "I will give you one and Mom one. They tell of every battle I have been in and every country and how many men were killed and wounded. We had 5,020 men killed and wounded. Quite a few. So I will close now. And write, Love Always, Your Old Man, Miles."

WHEN AMERICA ENTERED THE war, many young couples were already engaged, so they simply moved up their wedding date. But for many others, the war created more complicated circumstances. Some decided to delay marriage, usually because the man felt it was unfair to go off to war and leave behind a bride he might never see again. For still others, the advent of war gave a new relationship a sudden ardency. A wedding that might not have taken place for another year or longer now seemed a matter of urgency. Proposals were offered and quickly accepted. But even if both people wanted a hasty marriage, they usually faced obstacles. One way around such problems was to elope.

Doris and William Metzger in September 1943.

William and Doris
METZGER

William Metzger, Jr., was born in Philadelphia, Pennsylvania, but his family soon relocated to Atlantic City, New Jersey. He met his future wife, Doris, there—although, as they fondly recall, she was not much taken with him initially. Bill was, he admits, a bit rowdy and rough around the edges. He rode a motorcycle and was a daredevil driver. After his second accident, a prankster at the Atlantic City hotel where he worked secretly put a sticker that said "Wild Bill" on the windshield of his bike.

But Bill eventually won Doris over, and their relationship had grown quite serious by the time Pearl Harbor was bombed on December 7, 1941. He had a low number in the draft and knew he would soon be called up for duty. But he'd always wanted to learn to fly, so he persuaded his draft board to delay his date for a couple of months while he attended ground school.

While attending the school, he kept seeing a guy he didn't know, seeming to watch him from the sidelines. Bill finally asked an instructor who it was. The instructor told him that the man was from the draft board and was keeping an eye on Bill to make certain he was really learning to fly and not just dodging the draft.

Bill got into the air and began flying Piper Cubs. After his last night of classes, he dropped by Doris's house, and they discussed the likelihood of his being drafted any day. They were both Catholics, and in those days the Church didn't allow weddings during Lent, which had just begun.

Chances seemed all too likely that he would be gone by Easter, some forty days later. Doris agreed they should get married right away, and they decided to take a quick trip down to Maryland, where no waiting period was necessary. The weather was bad, and a trip on his motorcycle in the rain seemed out of the question. So on March 9, 1942, they borrowed Doris's parents' car and left a note saying simply, "We have gone to get married. Please don't worry. Wish us luck." Because Bill didn't have much money at the time, he bought Doris a $22 wedding band but didn't have any extra money for his own band. Instead, he took the signet right he was wearing and turned it so that just the band showed on the top of his finger and told her that would be his wedding ring. He's been wearing the ring that way ever since, for the fifty-nine years of their marriage.

When Doris and Bill returned home to "face the music," they were told that they needn't have eloped after all. Unbeknownst to them, the Church had made a special dispensation for weddings during Lent because so many young men were being drafted. So on April 6 they were married again in church, giving them two anniversaries to celebrate. As Bill recalls with humor, when he left work one day not long after he and Doris were married, he found a new message written on his motorcycle windshield: "Wild Bill Is Sweet William Now."

With his flying-school experience putting him in good stead, Bill was accepted into the army air corps. Although his pay was only $90 a month, Doris managed to stay with him throughout his training period, which involved several moves, starting out at Maxwell Field in Montgomery, Alabama, for preflight training, and then to several different fields in Georgia, Mississippi, and Arkansas, where he graduated and received his wings. He was then sent to El Paso, Texas, for postflight training on B-24s. There were only a few wives living off-base in El Paso, and while life was certainly not easy for them, sometimes Bill and his friends managed to smuggle out food to help them stretch their meager budgets. Bill was confined to base during the week but had a day pass on Saturdays. Doris got to know all the young men with whom he was in training, and a group of them tooled off one time to Juarez, Mexico, for some Saturday-night carousing.

After El Paso, Bill was sent to Harrington, Kansas, for his plane assignment. As soon as Bill saw the plane, he knew he was heading to the North African desert rather than the European campaign: The plane was pink, the camouflage color used in North Africa.

During World War II, it was common practice for a crew to give their plane a name, and they often painted a picture on the nose cone to further distinguish themselves. The pilot—in this case Bill—usually got to choose the name, but Doris said that wasn't fair, and she suggested that everyone put a name on a slip of paper to be drawn out of a hat. That meant there could be as many as ten different possible names, one for each member of the crew. But that wasn't how it worked out.

The crew members had gotten to know one another quite well by this time through off-hours socializing, and they all remembered a story Doris had told them about the tragic death of Bill's sister's young son Jackie, always called Jackie Boy. He had been quite a lively, unruly child, always getting into minor scrapes. On one occasion, he tried to hitch a ride on the back of a horse-drawn milk truck in his neighborhood and managed to pull a box of empty glass milk bottles onto his head. Bill's sister had stayed in Atlantic City near their family when she married. She lived on the bank of the inlet spilling into the bay, and the neighborhood kids regularly climbed the fence behind the houses—meant to keep them from the water—to go fishing. One day Jackie Boy fell from the fence and drowned. His own father discovered the body as he was walking home from work later that day. Everyone in Bill's crew had been touched by the story, and every single slip of paper selected from the hat said the same thing: "Jackie Boy."

A picture was painted on the plane's nose of a little boy with a dog at his feet and angel wings sprouting from his shoulders. Then the *Jackie Boy* flew off to combat in North Africa, separating Doris and Bill for the first time. She returned to Atlantic City to live with her parents for the duration of the war.

Bill and his crew flew missions to Europe out of Libya and then Tunisia, and were then dispatched up to Italy when the American invasion began in the fall of 1943. By early December they were flying missions out of Italy over Greece, which the Nazis had invaded and still largely controlled though by this time a civil war had also broken out.

Fortunately for the crew of the *Jackie Boy,* Greece was the home of an estimable British underground operation, as well as a growing Greek underground.

On December 6, Bill's plane was running a bombing mission over Athens when it was hit hard by German ground fire. The plane's windshield was shattered, and both Bill and his copilot were injured: Bill was shot and a piece of one of his ears was nicked off. When Bill surveyed the damage to the plane, he quickly realized they were in grave danger: the number-one engine was smoking and the number-two engine was fully ablaze. Bill feathered the number-three engine, meaning he turned its blades in such a way that it would create less drag on the airplane. Bill had little control over the plane, which was definitely going down. The only question was how far from German troops they could get. Bill fought hard to keep the plane aloft long enough to get away from Athens, which he says was "crawling with Germans," and headed out toward the surrounding hills. When he felt he could hold the plane no longer, he gave the call to bail out. The bombardier and navigator jumped out through the wheel hatch under the nose of the plane. The rest of the crew jumped out from the rear. Bill and his copilot were the last left. They could see German army trucks on a road below them.

The copilot had volunteered to substitute for the crew's regular copilot, who was sick. Not being assigned to a regular crew, he chose to fly with a flight crew he knew and trusted rather than being sent on a flight with "some hammerhead" pilot, as Bill says. He picked the right man to fly with that day.

As Bill prepared to bail out, he noticed the copilot struggling with his parachute, which was the bulky seat-pack style as opposed to the chest-pack style Bill wore. The seat-pack parachutes made maneuvering in the cockpit difficult, and the copilot was having a hard time getting himself free. Bill stopped to help him, and they both managed to eject and descend safely.

Once on the ground, Bill and the five crew members nearby faced the new danger of capture by German troops. They started running up the side of a mountain, looking to find cover, and saw a farm field up ahead. Then they spotted a young boy in the field waving his hands toward them, motioning to them to go back the way they'd come, or so they thought. They expected he was warning them away from German troops. Later, once they'd made their way to safety, they learned that in Greece that gesture means to come forward. They also discovered later that three of the crew had been less fortunate and were captured by the Germans. One of them was injured upon landing, and the others were slowed by stopping to help him.

Thanks to the British and Greek underground, Bill and five of his crew managed to get out of Greece by various routes. Bill and the copilot were smuggled out of the country by boat to Turkey. They were provided with false papers and civilian clothes, which were mysteriously pitched in through their hotel-room door by someone they never saw. First they had to make their way to Zelos in northern Greece, and from there they caught a boat that delivered them into Allied hands in Turkey. They made their escape on Christmas Day. On New Year's Day, they took a train south into Syria. From there, a British army officer arranged for them to fly to Cairo, where there was an Allied base. They arrived "looking like a bunch of bums," as Bill recalls. From Cairo, Bill sent Doris a cryptic telegram, selecting his message from a limited list of phrases approved by the military for use in telegrams: "All well. Children return home."

Back home in Atlantic City, Doris had received a telegram from the War Department on New Year's Day, informing her that Bill's plane had been shot down over enemy territory and that he was missing in action. She took the news calmly at first, but when she went over to her in-laws' house to tell them the news, she suddenly fainted and hit her head so hard on a radiator that she knocked herself out. The next day, Doris received a letter from a Lieutenant William Ashburn, who had been flying with Bill's squadron and had seen the plane go down. He reported that "it couldn't have happened in a better place," because many soldiers had been able to escape from that area; he had seen all of the crew "hit the silk," the colorful phrase used at the time for bailing out, and none of them had "hit the drink." Doris then wrote letters to the families of the other crew members to give them this good word.

After the ordeal he'd been through, Bill was reassigned to the States to train other fliers. He received the Purple Heart, and that wasn't the only medal he received for actions under fire, although he didn't know about the other until years later. Bill liked flying so much that he decided to stay in the army after the war, and one day in 1951, on a whim, he and a friend went to headquarters to look up their service records. There was the record of the Purple Heart and several other medals, as well as one he didn't recognize.

"What does 'SS' mean?" he asked the secretary in the office.

"Silver Star," she replied. "You got the Silver Star."

"First I've heard of it," Bill exclaimed.

The prestigious medal had been awarded to him in 1943, but he was never notified, which was not an uncommon occurrence in World War II. He had received it for keeping his plane in the air long enough to allow most of his crew to jump to safety.

During his postwar years in the army, Bill served as an instructor in a number of locations, including Nashville, Tennessee; Charleston, South Carolina; and locations around Texas and Florida. Although the moving around could be difficult at times, Doris insists it was nothing like the days when they were first married, when they had to move every nine weeks as Bill's training progressed, and they were often practically starving.

In 1953 Bill was "fired by Ike," as the soldiers of that period ironically referred to the downsizing of the military after Eisenhower became president and ended the Korean War. Bill was stationed at Westover, Massachusetts, at the time, and he and Doris had to decide whether to stay in that area and look for work, or return with their son and two daughters to their home grounds of Atlantic City. As it happened, the bombardier from the *Jackie Boy* had left the army right after the war and opened a successful clothing business in northwestern Massachusetts. He wanted to open a branch business in Northampton, the home of Smith College, and was looking for someone he completely trusted to run the branch. He offered the job to Bill.

The family was glad to stay. Not only is Northampton a beautiful part of the country, the daughters of residents could attend Smith for free—if they could do the academic work—which one of their daughters took advantage of.

Today, Bill and Doris Metzger still live in Northampton and have nine grandchildren and four great-grandchildren. At the age of eighty-four, Bill works out six days a week. When he tells the story of being shot down over Greece, Doris makes sure he adds that she knocked herself out on that radiator on New Year's Day in 1944, when she got the news that her husband was missing.

Doris with Bill after the 1943 ceremony during which he graduated and received his wings.

*A Valentine's Day card that Bill
sent Doris, on which he wrote,
"Roses are red, violets are blue,
the bees love honey, and I love you."
With a special note: "Junior is in the middle."*

*The note that Doris and Bill left for her parents before borrowing the car to go
and get married.*

M ANY YOUNG MEN AND WOMEN *already had sweethearts when America entered the war, but at least as many others were still looking for that special person to settle down with. Unattached young men left their hometowns for training bases all over the United States. Some young women did the same thing. They weren't looking for romance, they were fighting a war, but in their new surroundings, some of these young people met in chance encounters that led to a whole life together.*

Earl and Maxine Butterfield shortly after
they were married in 1947.

Earl and Maxine
BUTTERFIELD

In the summer of 1943, Second Lieutenant Earl Butterfield was busy assembling a B-24 bomber crew in Boise, Idaho, and training them for duty. One evening after going out in the town near the base, Earl boarded the bus back. "It was crowded with servicemen returning to base and civilians going to work on the graveyard shift," Earl recalls. "The driver made a very sudden stop, and all the people standing were thrown forward. I grabbed a girl in coveralls to keep her from hitting the windshield. She thanked me and told me she was working as an aircraft electrician. Before we could say much more, we arrived at the base. She intrigued me, and I boarded the same bus a couple of more times, hoping to see her, but I didn't."

Then one Saturday night not long after, when Earl was waiting to cross a street in Boise, two girls happened to drive by. One of them was the girl from the bus, and she and Earl recognized each other immediately. Moments later, the two girls walked up to Earl. They told him they were going bowling, and Earl asked if he could join them.

He discovered that the girls were roommates, and that they had worked for only a few days at the base in Boise en route from Everett, Washington, to a base near Boise in Mountain Home, Idaho. They hadn't been able to find a decent place to live at the new base, so they were commuting from Boise. The name of the girl Earl met on the bus was Maxine Cole.

After that night, Earl and Maxine went on a couple of dates, but suddenly he was transferred to another base, and after that to the Southwest Pacific. "I wrote to Maxine from the Pacific, as well as to several other girls," Earl explains, "including another one from Boise whom I had dated several times. Maxine wrote the most interesting letters, although they were quite . . . platonic."

When it appeared that he would make it back to the States in the spring of 1945, Earl wrote first to Margery, the other girl in Boise, asking her to meet him in Salt Lake City as he traveled by train across the country to his home in Syracuse, New York. After a few weeks, when he hadn't heard back from Margery, he wrote to Maxine and asked if *she* would meet him. When Maxine told her boss, who was a woman, about getting invited to Salt Lake by a guy she hardly knew, her boss asked what his rank was. "When Maxine said I was a captain," Earl recalls, "her boss said I would be loaded with money, and promptly wrote out leave papers so Maxine could go help me spend it."

When Earl arrived in San Francisco that April, he wired a hotel in Salt Lake City right away to make a reservation for two rooms. Getting no reply, he assumed they were set. "Wartime trains were notoriously late, and mine was no exception. Somewhere along the line, I wired Maxine that I would be late, but she never received the telegram. By the time I caught up with her, she was ready to turn around and go back to Boise. After a long-delayed dinner, we had to start searching for rooms, as my reservation was not honored. But we spent about three days in Salt Lake and got much better acquainted."

Earl and Maxine continued to correspond, with increasing ardor. He left the service and returned to his old job in Buffalo, New York, while she remained in Boise. Then, in the summer of 1946, Maxine and her girlfriend Lillian went east, Lillian to visit her fiancé in Oil City, Pennsylvania, and Maxine to see Earl. Earl took some time off to take Maxine to Syracuse to meet his parents. Then she went back to Boise, and many more letters were exchanged.

At the end of the year, Maxine invited Earl to Boise for a New Year's celebration, but she didn't think he'd come all that way, so she accepted another date. She was completely flabbergasted when Earl notified her that he'd be there, and she had to beg off the other date.

When Earl arrived, Maxine told him she'd just lost her job at the Idaho statehouse; the new Republican administration had replaced all the political appointees.

"Her brother Bob loaned us his Oldsmobile," Earl explained, "so we had wheels to explore the area. After seeing about everything we wanted to see, we began to explore our relationship. One fine sunny day, I facetiously said that if it weren't such a bureaucratic hassle, it would be a good day to get married. Maxine quickly replied that she could smooth the way because she knew everyone at the statehouse, and they'd process our application without delay."

They took blood tests that very day and picked up their license at the Idaho capital the day after. Earl and Maxine were married in the Methodist parsonage by Dr. Forrest Werts on January 9, 1947. Maxine's friend Lillian was her attendant, and a fellow pilot from Earl's home area, who happened to be living in Boise at the time, served as best man. After a small reception with Maxine's friends and relatives, the couple honeymooned in McCall, Idaho, thanks to her brother's Oldsmobile.

Earl and Maxine raised two children, and now they have two grandchildren. They're still together after fifty-four years, and it's all because a bus driver slammed on the brakes.

Earl Butterfield as a second lieutenant at Gowen Field in Boise, Idaho, in 1943.

Earl Butterfield's crew (Earl is in the center of the back row) in New Guinea in 1944.

Earl and Maxine on their fiftieth wedding anniversary.

WHEN HOMETOWN SWEETHEARTS *were separated by the war, communication became a serious issue. Mail was sluggish, even within the United States. Letters sent from North Africa or the European theater could take weeks to find their way home, and those dispatched from the South Pacific usually took even longer. Mail often arrived in bunches, both at the fronts and back home. The letters from home helped keep the fighting men sane, while those sent back assured that a loved one was still safe—at least as of a few weeks earlier. All letters were treasured, but some were particularly special: Some servicemen employed special talents to enliven their messages.*

Ed and Mary Jane Russell shortly after they were married.

Ed and Mary Jane
RUSSELL

During his last year of high school in Teaneck, New Jersey, Ed Russell drew a comic strip for the school paper. His main character was "Itchie," a skinny guy with big clown eyes and a prominent red nose. Ed recalls, "That same year"—1943—"I was introduced to the prettiest, smartest, and most popular young lady in school, if not in the entire United States of America. She said to me, 'I know you. You draw those wonderful cartoons.' I replied, 'For that I'm going to marry you.'" The name of the young lady who liked his cartoons was Mary Jane Walton. They went on just one date before he joined the navy. Ed remembers knowing that he would "have to work very hard" if he was going to realize his marital intentions.

In early May 1943, five weeks before graduation, Ed left for boot camp. The navy had not been his first choice. He and his friend Billy Roauer fervently wanted to join the marines, but they were underweight. As things turned out, Ed was assigned to duty with the marines after all.

After completing radio school at the University of Chicago, where he learned to send and receive Morse code, Ed was sent for training at the Marine Communications School, Amphibious Training, Pacific, at Port Hueneme, California. "We were issued marine combat gear and trained to set up and operate portable radios and portable generators," he says now. "Both pieces of equipment were very heavy. They were carried on our backs, which would make it very difficult to find a place to hide when in combat. Not to worry, we were told. The Japanese would probably mis-

35

take the radios for the dreaded flamethrowers"—weapons that shot streams of napalm, a jelly-like petroleum mixture that sticks to the skin and burns. They were used to devastating effect by the U.S. forces in the Pacific campaign.

While at Port Hueneme, Ed also took crash courses in amphibious landings and hand-to-hand combat, and he realized that the Morse code he had learned in Chicago wasn't going to count for much in the job he was now being prepared for. He underwent still further training at the marine base at Camp Pendleton, near Oceanside, California. Spending all that time as a navy man training alongside marines, Ed now notes wryly, "made it clear that sailors and marines didn't always get along."

Right from the beginning of training, Ed sent letters to Mary Jane in Teaneck, and these letters looked like no others sent to sweethearts back home. The envelopes were decorated with irresistibly charming cartoons featuring his character Itchie. An early one from Camp Pendleton displayed Itchie as the grinning pilot of a navy dive-bomber, with a sailor hat perched atop his virtually shaved head, trailing a "Via Air Mail" banner behind his plane. In one hand Itchie held a letter bearing Mary Jane's address, placed just perfectly so that the stamp on Ed's drawn letter was the real six-cent U.S. airmail stamp. On another envelope, Itchie morphed into a wryly smiling seaplane, with big eyes and nose serving as the plane's windshield and nose turret, a sailor hat perched between the wings. In the letter itself, Ed wrote, "Sometimes this love business can be regular hell. That's only when there's half the world between us, definitely not when we will be together. Yes, I love you Miss Walton."

These enchanting envelopes soon winged their way to Mary Jane from the South Pacific, where Ed was assigned to duty, reaching her at a summer vacation job, then at Sarah Lawrence College, as well as at her family home back in Teaneck. Ed also sent Itchie letters to his mother and—no fool he—to Mary Jane's mother.

Although Ed tried hard to be upbeat, using Itchie to raise his own spirits as well as those of Mary Jane and others back home, his service in the Pacific was often quite dangerous. He served aboard the U.S.S. *Hamlin* when she arrived at Iwo Jima less than twenty-four hours after the first wave of marines hit the shore on February 19, 1945. The ship was anchored near what the sailors and marines nicknamed "Hot Rock": Mount Suribachi, on which, as captured in one of the most celebrated photographs of World War II, the marines raised the American flag on February 23.

Ed recalls watching the battle of Iwo Jima from his ship: "We had front-row seats to the bloodiest battle of the war. Tank duels, aerial strafing attacks, and the two flag-raisings all took place within a few hundred yards of our ship. During one air raid, several of us went topside to watch. Anti-aircraft fire was so thick it had to be witnessed to be believed. Suddenly my buddy Pete Rooney yelled, 'I'm hit!' We ducked inside; his wound was a tiny piece of hot shrapnel in his palm. The next day we gave him a 'Purple Palm' as a thank-you for scaring us so. A few days later, the *Hamlin* was hit in the stack by a mortar shell while I was on radio watch just twenty feet away. Fortunately, the shell was a dud. Watching that battle made me glad I was not a marine."

But Ed's most harrowing experience of the war took place on the U.S.S. *Curtiss.* On June 21, 1945, the ship was the target of a savage kamikaze attack. "It started at twilight," he recalls. "Pete Rooney, Doc Savage, and I were on the fantail playing cards. An announcement had just come over the PA system telling us organized resistance on Okinawa had ended. The area was 'secure.' I noticed two fighters off in the distance doing loops. Unusual. I realized they were Japanese and let out a yell. No general quarters had been sounded. Also unusual." The Japanese planes were sending out a high-frequency radio signal that American planes transmitted to let Allied radar operators know they were friendly. The Japanese had cleverly transferred two of the signal devices from downed American planes to their own aircraft. "Their code signal was wrong," Ed says, "but radar did not report them as 'bogeys' because such an error was common."

One of the Japanese fighters, code-named Frank, "dove straight down, pulled out, and headed for my nose. Actually, he headed for my shoelaces; the deck I was on was thirty feet above the waterline, and he was below it. Those around me scattered. I stood and watched, amazed at what he was doing. He flew so low his propeller stirred up a wake in the water. I said, 'How can you do it?' and stayed with him all the way. I have no recollection of being frightened. When he got very close, he dipped one wingtip into the water, driving the plane amidship. He hit the photo lab and the sick bay, right above bomb storage. We had just taken aboard a batch of aerial torpedoes, and when they got the fire out fifteen and a half hours later, the torpedoes were just a mass of twisted metal. It was a miracle we weren't blown to kingdom come. We suffered sixty-one casualties, including thirty-seven killed."

After months of grueling service in these last battles of the Pacific campaign, the war was finally over. Ed received word that he would soon be heading home. He had been away from home, and from Mary Jane, for more than two years. Of course Mary Jane was alerted to his return by a special message from Itchie. In this letter, Itchie was perched on a graceful curve identified as "MJ's knee." The message below read:

"DEAR MARY JANE. This is Itchie talking, and we've got a serious problem. Eddie is coming home, and you have fallen in love with me.

What are we going to do about Eddie?

Beginning at the beginning, how are you going to greet him? Shake hands? Kiss? If so, will it be a kiss on the cheek? Or will it be an explosive release of suppressed passion you have held back for the last 28 months?

I suggest you go all out.

Ed had written to Mary Jane from the Pacific that he was ready to marry her; when she was ready, all she had to do was ask. Not long after he returned home in January 1946, she said she was ready, though her college schedule and a summer job precluded a wedding until the following December. Ed suggested December 21 because it is the longest night of the year, and Mary Jane agreed because it fell on a Saturday, which was a good day for a wedding.

Both Edward T. Russell and Mary Jane Walton Russell went on to make great use of their natural talents. Ed took a job in advertising and in seventeen years rose to become president of the legendary agency Doyle Dane Bernbach International. With her startling good looks, Mary Jane became a successful high-fashion model. One of her many magazine covers was the famous "Beauty Issue" of *Harper's Bazaar* for April 1953, during the glory days of high-fashion photography. Mary Jane appeared

Itchie as a pilot, delivering a letter to Mary Jane from the amphibious training school at Camp Pendleton, California.

Itchie, morphed into a plane.

Itchie sitting on Mary Jane's knee. Away for over two years, Ed realized Mary Jane might have another boyfriend. He wrote this letter when he was on his way home.

Iwo Jima's Mount Suribachi, photographed from the seaplane tender U.S.S. Hamlin on February 24, the day after the famous flag-raising. The flag can be seen (circled), near the top right crest. (Photo courtesy of Fred Munkner)

Above: Ed and Mary Jane Russell in black tie, posing for a photo shoot with famed photographer Louise Dahl-Wolfe during Mary Jane's modeling career. Right: Mary Jane on the cover of the April 1953 Harper's Bazaar.

in profile, wearing a large-brimmed chartreuse hat with a huge bow at the back, holding two black lacquered palm-shaped fans at right angles. She looked almost untouchably elegant. But of course the real Mary Jane fell in love with a scamp of a cartoon character named Itchie—not to mention his creator.

IF THE LOVE LETTERS THAT TRAVERSED *the world during the war kept hope alive for the soldiers and their loved ones back home, a package could provide a special, more tangible kind of solace. Not only did soldiers receive packages from home, many soldiers also sent home souvenirs from Italy, then France, and then at last Germany, as the European campaign progressed. Packages sent from home often took circuitous routes, chasing after a soldier from battle front to battle front, island to island. Amidst all the chaos of the war, the arrival of such a package could seem like a miracle, and the lucky soldier to receive it might well cherish whatever heartfelt gift it carried for the rest of his life.*

Virginia Racine Starns in 1942, shortly after she and Joe were married.
Joe Starns on September 24, 1942, the day he went overseas.

Joseph and Virginia

STARNS

When Joe Starns reflects on the war years, he likes to quote a favorite line of poetry from John Milton: "They also serve who only stand and wait." To Joe, the role his wife, Virginia (who goes by Gina)—and so many other wives and mothers and sisters—played back home, and the love they sent to their men overseas, were at least as important to the war effort as the work of the soldiers themselves. The admiration Joe feels for Virginia and the strength with which she bore his absence, as well as the hard work and sacrifices she committed herself to during the war, are palpable in his voice when he talks about her. "She was saving every cent to buy war bonds, giving blood. They gave you a pin when you gave blood, and Gina has enough pins to fill a pincushion. She's only five feet two inches tall; she gave all the blood they'd let her give." As so many other couples did, Virginia and Joe met by a long-shot chance during the war, but their relationship quickly grew serious and has lasted for a very happy fifty-nine years.

One of five sons, Joe was raised in the San Joaquin Valley in California, near Modesto. During the course of the war, four of the five Starns boys would be shipped overseas, and luckily, all of them came back. As Joe says, "Unlike the five Sullivan brothers, all of whom were assigned to the same ship and all of whom perished when that ship was sunk, none of us ever had more than the vaguest notion where any of the others were or what mischief they were up to. But again, unlike the Sullivans, we all survived."

In early 1941, Joe was serving as an army private at the Presidio in Monterey, California. In May he was temporarily assigned as a military policeman in San Francisco, stationed at the Ferry Building. His main duty was to greet incoming military personnel headed to the Presidio to line up their transportation; he often helped them find overnight accommodations and a meal. During the war, soldiers were sent on a moment's notice from one base to another, to cities and towns they had no knowledge of, and the military was trying to ease their confusion upon arrival.

One day in May, nineteen-year-old Gina Racine and her older sister, Mae, arrived in San Francisco by Greyhound bus from Manistee, Michigan, to stay with their older brother, who had moved there. They planned to stay for some time and perhaps to even find jobs there. Their brother lived in an apartment on Haight Street, which was much different in those days from the notorious hippie haven it would become in the 1960s. During their stay, Gina's brother often took her and Mae to the popular Avalon Ballroom. One night there, Mae met a soldier named Ray Paulson, who was a buddy of Joe's. When Ray asked Mae for a second date, she told him she'd go out with him again only if he brought a date for her sister.

When Ray later told Joe that he had met two sisters from Michigan who were visiting in San Francisco, and that he wanted Joe to escort the younger sister on a double date, Joe was dubious. As he forthrightly says, "Ray was a nice guy, but from what I knew of him, I figured the girls were probably dogs." Ray persisted, however, and Joe eventually allowed himself to be corralled.

To his surprise, the girls were quite attractive, and they all had a very good time. Gina was lively, petite, and very pretty, and Joe soon found himself spending as much time as possible with her, often at the Avalon. The last dance each night at the ballroom was danced to a song titled "Avalon," which became "their song."

In September, Joe was transferred back to Monterey and from then on was able to see Gina only when he could finagle a weekend pass. He decided to make the most of one of those precious weekends, and on October 31—Halloween and a night Gina remembers in jest as "fright night"—he proposed to her. Gina readily accepted, but they held off on a date because Joe was still a private, earning only $50 a month, and wanted to be able to support her in better style.

In November, Joe was promoted to corporal and received a nice raise. In addition, Gina took a job in the money-order department of Western Union's main office in downtown San Francisco. Their income was now sufficient that they felt comfortable going ahead and getting married, but Joe's new job required him to be away from San Francisco quite a bit. He was assigned to escort trainloads of recruits from Monterey to various training camps in the Midwest and South. Many tentative wedding dates had to be forsaken when he found out he'd be on another trip.

Then, on the first Sunday in December, the "date which will live in infamy," Joe managed to get away from Monterey and went to visit Gina at her brother's house. He arrived early in the morning to be shocked by the news about the bombing of Pearl Harbor. They spent the rest of the day listening to radio reports about the attack, and they decided that they "had not heard" the repeated announcements that all military personnel should return immediately to their bases. Joe dreaded what he knew would follow, and he wanted to spend as much time with Gina as he could before facing the inevitable. He returned to base the next day, as originally scheduled, and nobody asked any questions.

Several months later, in March 1942, Gina recalls that "My willingness and the army's understanding all met on common ground. Joe was promoted to sergeant on the eighteenth, and he and I were married on the twenty-first, in one of those quickie little marriages that never last."

As a sergeant, Joe was making the grand sum of $78 a month, $54 of which went for rent on the small apartment he and Gina found for themselves. After only three weeks of marriage, however, Joe was shipped off for three months of infantry officer candidate school at Fort Benning, Georgia. He had volunteered for the infantry school because he felt he should play a more important role in the war effort. Upon graduation, he joined the infantry as what he calls "a second lieutenant of idiocy" on July 23, 1942—as he says, "only an idiot would join the infantry," with the highest mortality rate during the war. The insignia of the infantry was crossed rifles, which people called "idiot sticks."

Meanwhile, back in San Francisco, Gina had undergone "her own basic training"—learning to live alone without Joe. They wrote to each other often, but Gina hated being apart. After Joe graduated, he had to wait an undefined time in Georgia to find out where he would be sent. They had talked about her possibly coming to Georgia, but then one day Gina just decided she wasn't going to be away from him any longer. She called her office to say she was leaving and set off across the country by Greyhound bus. Though she sent several telegrams from the road, none of them arrived before she did. Joe's first inkling of her trip was when a soldier came into his barracks at Fort Benning—which Joe refers to as "Benning School for Boys"—and announced, to Joe's delight, "Lieutenant Starns, your wife is waiting for you."

When Joe's orders were finally issued—he would be going to the Pacific—the army sent him and Gina back to San Francisco pending his shipment out. They enjoyed that summer together, and then on September 24, 1942, Joe departed for the Pacific. Gina returned to her job at Western Union to endure the wait until he returned. She wrote to Joe every day for that duration, which turned out to be over three years. Joe says, "In all that time, she didn't write one demoralizing word, no matter what problems she was going through at home."

Gina not only sent heartening words, she sent thoughtful packages, too. Joe was an avid pipe smoker, and she regularly went to the tobacco store he loved, Sutliffs Tobacco Shop on Market Street, to buy his favorite tobacco, as well as occasionally a new pipe. She also sent him weekly bundles of the articles by his favorite columnist, Herb Caen of the *San Francisco Chronicle*. One especially fine gift she sent was a Longines wristwatch, as congratulations for his graduation from officer candidate school. Joe has always regretted that he lost this watch during the chaos of an air raid while he was serving in the Solomon Islands. But one of Gina's packages in particular stands out in Joe's mind; he still finds it remarkable that she could find the extra money for these items, with all the war bonds she was buying and their moderate income. Most stunning of all was the present she sent him in honor of their second wedding anniversary in 1944: a fourteen-karat gold ring with a black onyx stone and one small diamond. He actually received the ring on the day of their anniversary, and even more remarkable to Joe is that it fit his finger perfectly. He was in the midst of training in New Caledonia before heading to the Philippines, which everyone knew would be a brutal battle. To receive that ring at such a time, and to have it slide onto his finger and miraculously fit just right, was a deeply emotional moment he has cherished all of his life. He has never taken the ring off since that day.

Gina's packages arrived erratically, often several at once: They had to follow Joe all over the Pacific, to Hawaii, Guadalcanal, New Georgia; back to Guadalcanal, on to New Zealand, up to New Caledonia, then to the Philippines. Joe's experience in the Pacific, like that of so many thousands of American soldiers, sailors, and marines, included a litany of famous island battles, but also like many veterans, he prefers not to discuss those experiences. What he does like to reflect on are two remarkable coincidences that have always stood out in his mind.

In 1942, Joe's seventeen-year-old younger brother was serving in the navy on the U.S.S. *Northampton,* which was taking part in the battle for Guadalcanal. One night the ship was torpedoed and sank. Joe's brother made it off the ship, then floated in the dark for nine hours in his life jacket before he was finally rescued and transported to a naval hospital in Noumea, New Caledonia, where he recuperated for three weeks before being sent back to the States. During the time Joe's brother lay in his hospital bed, looking out at the anchored ships, the troopship transporting Joe to Guadalcanal stopped over at Noumea. The troops were allowed off the ship one day, and Joe remembers aimlessly wandering around, having no idea that his little brother lay right there in the hospital.

Three years later, in early June 1945, Joe's even younger brother, then just sixteen years old, was serving in the merchant marine. His cargo ship docked in the harbor at Tacloban, on Leyte in the Philippines, where it laid over for about three weeks. The crew were free to leave the ship, and Joe's brother had received word that Joe's infantry unit was at that time in combat about 125 miles north of Manila on Luzon island.

Determined to try to find Joe, but with no means of transportation to Luzon, on June 8, he hitchhiked and actually managed to reach Joe's company's command post, arriving on June 8. But, to his great disappointment, he got there only to learn that just a few hours before, Joe suffered a serious leg wound and was evacuated to a hospital. Joe's brother sadly turned back toward his ship at Tacloban, but he did not return the way he had come. Instead, he worked his way to an airfield, Nichols Field, in Manila, where he finagled a ride on an Air Force transport to the airstrip at Tacloban, near the harbor where his ship was docked. Remarkably, Joe was making the very same journey: He was processed through a series of medical facilities until he arrived at, where else, Nichols Field, and was flown from there to none other than the field hospital at the Tacloban airstrip. For the next two weeks, while Joe lay in his hospital bed looking out at the ships in the harbor, his brother was on one of those ships not a half mile away. Joe and his brothers knew nothing of any of these coincidences until they were reunited in 1945 after the war and started sharing their war stories.

The coincidences don't stop there, however. Joe's leg wound was serious enough that the war was over for him, and a long period of recuperation lay ahead. He was sent back to the States, and on July 5 he arrived at the hospital at Hamilton Air Force Base just north of San Francisco. Gina had received no word as yet of Joe's injury, but that very morning before she left for work, she received a dreaded telegram from the War Department. Just as she was signing for the telegram, with the anxiety growing that it would carry horrible news, her telephone rang. In one hand she held the unopened telegram, and with the other she answered the phone—to find to her great joy that it was Joe calling from Hamilton Air Force Base. The first thing she did after she got off the phone was call her office at Western Union and quit her job. Then she tried desperately to find a cab to take her up to Hamilton, and when she couldn't, she rented a limousine for the then-princely sum of $35. As Joe says fondly, "It seemed to me like a pretty big car for such a little lady."

Joe Starns received a Silver Star for his service in the Pacific. Gina actually read about it in the *San Francisco Chronicle* before he'd been told. Joe remained in the army after his recuperation; he fought in Korea and was stationed for some time in Japan, where Gina and their four children joined him. He and Gina are proud to say that they now have five grand-children.

With great admiration, Joe points out that the house they have now lived in for 42 years was bought with the use of all those war bonds Gina saved up for while he was overseas.

Joe as an army private in 1941, while courting Gina. He was on duty at the Ferry Building at the foot of Market Street in San Francisco.

Gina and Sergeant Joe on their wedding day, March 21, 1942.

The telegram that made up Gina's mind not to wait for the army to make up its mind, and to join Joe in Georgia.

WESTERN UNION

FJ8 35 NT= COLUMBUS GA 25

MRS JOE E STARNS=

APT 3 1344 GEARY ST=

DARLING, GOT MY ORDERS TODAY, BUT DONT KNOW JUST WHEN
I LEAVE. COMING TO COAST SOON THOUGH. LOVE YOU AN AWFUL
LOT HONEY AND WILL BE SEEING YOU SOON. SO LONG FOR A
WHILE DARLING=

JOE.

Joe, now a lieu-
tenant, in 1944 in
New Caledonia
during training
for the invasion
of Luzon. A
photograph of
Gina sits on
his desk.

Lieutenant Colonel Joe
with Gina, at right, at
his retirement ceremony in
1958, seventeen years, two
wars, and four children
after they met.

Gina, Joe, and their oldest
daughter, Sharon, on Christmas
Day 2000. Gina was seventy-
eight and Joe eighty-two at
the time.

T HOUGH SO MANY GREAT ROMANCES *took off immediately during the war, others took longer to develop and were sometimes based almost entirely on letters. A young man might find himself seriously smitten by a woman who wasn't sure she wanted to commit to him or any one man right away. To make sure her correspondent understood this, the woman might make casual mention in her letters of various other boyfriends. That didn't necessarily mean that the man on the receiving end could stop hoping that one day there would be more between the two of them.*

Ned and Nikki Burr with Nikki's mother,
Lyra Nicholas, the day of their wedding,
December 21, 1947.

Edward and Patricia

BURR

At Christmastime in 1942, Ned Burr, a senior at West Point due to graduate in June, came home to Garden City, Long Island, to spend the holidays with his family. While there, he bumped into an old friend from grammar school days, Dud Whitney, who suggested they go into Manhattan on a double date. Dud Whitney's date was a girl named Nikki Nicholas (Patricia was called by this nickname) from Douglaston, Long Island. After Ned's graduation, Dud and Ned double-dated again, and again Dud brought Nikki Nicholas.

Before Ned left for training at Fort Sill, Oklahoma, his mother gave a small party to which Dud and Nikki were invited. Ned's mother was quite taken with Nikki, and in the tradition of "Mother knows best"—even though Nikki was there with another man—she told the young woman she should marry her son. Her reasoning? "Nikki and Ned" would look great written together on Christmas cards, she said, only half jokingly. Ned's mother encouraged Nikki to write to Ned while he was attending artillery school in Oklahoma, where he would be for the next three months. Nineteen-year-old Nikki did just that, later maintaining that at the time she was interested merely in adding a West Pointer to her rather long list of boyfriends.

That first letter was the start of a voluminous correspondence—over 140 letters in all—that lasted until March 1946 and which Ned refers to as his "wooing from a distance." Nikki and Ned saw each other face-to-face for only two more brief interludes before he was sent overseas. In October 1943, Ned briefly returned home to Long Island en route to joining the Eighty-third Division in Kentucky for training. He visited again in February of the following year. "We probably had no more than eight dates during those two visits," Ned recalls. But the letters that passed between them created a strong bond. Though Nikki's letters to Ned were lost—it was difficult for soldiers at the front to hang on to anything except their fighting equipment—when reading a sample of the letters Ned wrote to her, one doesn't question why she kept writing him back.

Just before Ned was shipped overseas on April 3, 1944, he wrote a beautiful letter to Nikki, an excerpt of which reads:

> NIKKI, when the going gets tough and the morale gets a little low, my thoughts are coming back to you like a homing pigeon. I'll try to write every day, even though they may not reach you each day. I can easily admit that not seeing you again has been a hard blow to swallow. (I try to figure ahead of time on what to write, but there doesn't seem to be much question as you are the letter). Do I bore you with this continuous topic? Don't answer that for it won't do you any good. . . . Again and again I can profess my love for you, but never will I be able to describe the loveliness and the pain I find in the moments when my thoughts are with you—never will I be able to make you know how much I will miss you while I'm gone.

The Eighty-third Division in which Ned was serving was one of the most battle-tested in Europe. Three days after the division relieved the 101st Airborne Division just south of Carentan in Normandy, Ned was ordered up to the front as a forward observer with the 331st Infantry Regiment. From there, on June 30, he wrote a letter that conveys vividly how much the letters he received from Nikki meant to him, as well as how much he was hoping that she would decide, before long, that he was the one for her:

> MY DEAREST NIKKI:
> I fell upon your letter today like a ton of bricks. The blue envelope has become well known and its arrival is heralded far and wide.

The biggest events in my life right now are the comings of your thoughts. With all this other stuff going on, I can truthfully say your letters mean more than all of it. Not just the fact of receiving word from you, but the idea of being closer to you . . . I search each and every letter for slightest indication that you have decided. Before, we may have had too little time to decide if what we felt was love, but I've thought of you far too often and yearned to be with you far too much for it to be anything else as far as I'm concerned.

However, I can afford to commit myself, while it's definitely not the best idea for you. It's a dangerous game we play and one's number can be up almost any time. Such unpleasant closeness to death and scenes of it around you don't increase your bravery or eating abilities. I'm satisfied though, now, that I can do my job in the face of it and that's the main thing. No matter what anyone thinks, you must be satisfied yourself of your nerve before you can feel content. You'd be surprised how much you help.

On the fourth of July, the Eighty-third Division began its attack on the entrenched Germans in the hedgerow country of Normandy. They were untested soldiers going up against veteran German troops, and the consequences were horrendous: the Eighty-third lost seventeen hundred men on the first day of the assault alone, and many more in the days that followed. Ned was seriously wounded that first day when a shell landed close to him and a fragment of it ripped into his back below his left shoulder, exiting just above his heart. He was transported to a hospital in England. When he recovered, he rejoined his division and stayed with it until it was deactivated in Austria in February 1946.

NIKKI WAS the only girl Ned wrote to during the war, but he knew that she dated a number of men during the two years he was fighting in Europe, and had even developed two serious relationships. The second of these was in full bloom when Ned was deactivated. "My last letter to Nikki in March of 1946, sent from Gmunden, Austria, sort of closed out our relationship, since I felt that too much of her life didn't involve me anymore. How wrong I was!"

When Ned returned to America in March 1946, he was sent to a pro-

Ned's West Point graduation photo.

Ned (kneeling third from left) with, left to right, Lieutenants Beard, Bradford, and Leonard in Normandy in late June 1944.

Christmas card with the "Nikki & Ned" signature Ned's mother thought would look so good, sent from Albuquerque in 1947.

Nikki and Ned in 1998.

cessing center at Fort Dix, New Jersey. Immediately upon his arrival there he gave Nikki a call at *The New York Times*, where she worked, just to say hello. She agreed to meet him at Grand Central Station. "We got into a cab, started kissing, and forty-five days later, when I had to return to Europe, we were engaged. We were married on December twenty-first, 1946, and will celebrate our fifty-fifth year together this December."

MILLIONS OF AMERICAN *servicemen carried pictures of their sweethearts and wives with them during the war. Some carried pictures of girls they barely knew, girls they'd maybe danced with a few times; anything to provide a distraction from the war. Girls were happy to supply these pictures, each of which soon found itself tucked in a soldier's pocket, some at the front in a foreign land. Pictures of movie stars adorned barracks and offices everywhere, even bulkheads above the bunks of ships at sea. Betty Grable and Rita Hayworth were the favorite pinups. Occasionally the boys would pin up a picture of a girl who was not a movie star nor even anyone's sweetheart: just a pretty girl whose smile suggested that home was a place you could return to, some happy day.*

*Paul and Frieda Kincade at dinner following their
wedding on December 23, 1945.*

Paul and Frieda
KINCADE

In February 1942, Paul Kincade was at navy boot camp in San Diego, California, sleeping in the top bunk adjacent to the table where other recruits sat to write letters home. Paul had grown up in San Diego and had no need to write letters to distant relatives, but he often sat on his bunk at night and kibitzed with those who did write. One night, a sailor writing home had his wallet open on the tabletop. Paul couldn't help noticing a picture of a gorgeous young woman. "I asked him if it was his wife," Paul remembers, "and he said, no, it wasn't. I asked if it was his girl-friend, and he said it was his cousin Frieda. Tongue in cheek, I told him, sure, every sailor carries his cousin's picture in his wallet. When he swore it was his cousin, I called his bluff and asked for her address." To Paul's surprise, the sailor wrote out the address and gave it to him.

"I put the address in my writing portfolio and proceeded to forget about it. After boot camp, I was assigned to signalman-quartermaster school for twelve weeks and was kept too busy to write letters. When we completed our training in early June, the entire class was issued orders to the naval armed guard—Atlantic, out of Brooklyn, to sail on armed merchant ships in convoy. We were ordered to empty our lockers and pack our seabags and hammocks to await the arrival of trucks to take us to the train station. As I opened the locker door, my writing portfolio tumbled out, and out of it fell that slip of paper with Frieda's address. Having some time to kill, I sat down and wrote her a letter, telling her about myself and asking if she would be interested in corresponding with me."

Paul and his fellow sailors took a cross-country train ride to New York, which became his home port. In July 1942 he was assigned to a newly commissioned Liberty Ship, the *Thomas Sumter*, out of Philadelphia. From there, he was assigned to a number of different ships and was never in one place long enough to have a mailing address, so when he finally returned to New York after several months, he picked up a huge pile of back mail. Among the letters he found a reply from Frieda, who had enclosed a photograph of herself. "She wrote such a warm letter that I rushed to respond, starting a long-distance correspondence that would go on for two and a half years before we ever met."

Paul was an artist and cartoonist, and he drew a pencil sketch of Frieda from the first photo she sent. He still has the photo, but he had to give up the sketch. When he was assigned to a British merchant ship, Paul taped the sketch to the bulkhead above his bunk so that he could lie there and gaze up at it. His two merchant marine roommates liked the sketch, too. "When I detached from the ship in Trinidad, the cadets wouldn't let me take the drawing," Paul remembers. "They, too, had fallen for Frieda's beauty. So I left it with them. Just three days later, the British ship MV *King James* left Trinidad and was torpedoed and sunk between Trinidad and Tobago, losing all hands except for the third mate and one of the British gun crew, and taking Frieda's picture to the bottom, where I presume it still rests."

In December 1944, Paul arrived in San Francisco, where he would wait for a new assignment that was highly classified. San Francisco was Frieda's hometown, and Paul took advantage of the opportunity to finally meet her face-to-face. Their first date was on the third anniversary of Pearl Harbor, December 7. They went to a movie, along with another sailor whom Frieda had asked Paul to bring along as a blind date for her girlfriend—he assumed she didn't want to be alone with him on their first meeting, despite all the letters they had exchanged. They went to see the John Wayne picture *They Were Expendable*. "It was," Paul says, "love at first sight, strengthened by two and a half years of an increasingly loving correspondence." In fact, as their letter writing progressed, Frieda had taken to marking her letters with her lipstick imprint, a gesture "popular among young women in those war years," according to Paul.

After just a couple of weeks, Paul had no doubts that Frieda was the woman for him; she felt the same way, and they became engaged. On Christmas Eve, they announced their engagement to friends and relatives. Just days later, Paul got word that he and the other troops waiting in San Francisco were being sent to Tanforan Racetrack in San Bruno, California, to train for their new assignment, which they still knew almost nothing about. In the interim they were sent to Treasure Island, off the coast of San Francisco, to a high-security compound with barbed wire and armed guards. They could neither make nor receive phone calls, receive or send mail. Paul was distressed because he had a movie date with Frieda that night, and he feared that when she showed up and he was gone, without word, she would think he had skipped out on her. Fortunately, a neighbor of Frieda's, whom Paul had met, was serving as a guard at Treasure Island. Paul managed to call him over and ask him to get word to Frieda that he still loved her and would contact her at the first opportunity.

Not for weeks, after he had been flown to Barber's Point Naval Air Station at Manus, in the Admiralty Islands, did Paul find out what his new assignment was. At a meeting in Quebec in late 1944, Winston Churchill had offered units of the Royal Navy to Roosevelt to aid in the decimating Pacific campaign. Paul and the others were being assigned to British ships, which were far below United States Navy standards. They were told the navy would be supplying special rations for them, as well as athletic equipment and American cigarettes, and also that each day they served would count double for rotation back to the States. None of these promises ever materialized. They were trained by war-wounded marines for first-wave landing, to set up panel markers on the beach, very dangerous work. But Paul managed to come back alive.

"I got back to San Francisco almost a year to the day after we first met, and we set our wedding date for December twenty-third, 1945. Because I wouldn't convert to her religion [Russian Orthodox—Frieda was of Albanian heritage], we couldn't get married in her church, and I became the bad guy with her family for not converting. Instead, we had a lovely wedding in a nearby Lutheran church, marred only by her mother's refusal to attend [her father had passed away in 1943]."

When they got engaged the year before, Paul had promised Frieda that they would spend their wedding night in one of the finest hotels in

San Francisco. But just before the wedding, the woman at the Military Hotel Reservation Bureau told Paul that even though the war was over, a hotel room in the city was impossible to get without booking two months in advance. "I told her about the promise I'd made and related my sad tale about being assigned to a ship of the Royal Navy, which came from the cold climes of the North Atlantic without being refitted for the heat and humidity of the central Pacific; how there'd been no food and I'd lost thirty pounds; and added in the daily kamikaze attacks. She said, 'You poor dear,' and picked up the phone to call the Mark Hopkins. I could hear the laughter at the other end, but the lady told my story of woe, and when she hung up, she said, 'Honey, grab a cab and get over to the hotel and make a deposit. She's holding a room for you.' I ran out, bought that nice lady a box of chocolates, and then raced to the Mark, as everyone called it. I was told the room rate was fifteen dollars and paid it in full." Paul notes that a double room these days is listed "in the AAA tour book at $380 to $475 a night!"

After the wedding, Paul's new brother-in-law drove the couple straight to the Mark, dropping them off after midnight. "When we walked into the lobby, we saw a huge Christmas tree surrounded by a host of drunks singing carols. A number of others were passed out around the lobby. There was no one at the registration desk, so I kept hitting the little bell for service. A man came to the desk and asked what I wanted. I told him I was registered, so he looked in the book and told me I didn't have a reservation. I showed him my receipt and told him we had just gotten married and weren't going to spend the night sleeping in the park. He said not to get excited; he wasn't the desk clerk but the house detective. There'd been a hotel party to celebrate the first postwar Christmas, and the clerk was passed out in his office. The house detective told me the only room available was a suite costing fifty dollars. When I balked at the price, he told me I had already paid, so we enjoyed a lovely suite overlooking the city by the bay."

Paul soon returned to his military duties. He got out of the navy in 1947 but stayed in the reserves and rejoined in 1952. He was commissioned as an officer in 1957 and retired in 1968 as a lieutenant commander. Despite the separations inevitable in a navy career—and the presentiment on the part of Frieda's family that the marriage wouldn't last—Paul is proud to say, "Our marriage persevered, and Frieda did an outstanding job of raising our two sons."

In 1990, on their forty-fifth wedding anniversary, Paul wrote to the general manager of the Mark Hopkins and told him the story of their wedding night there. Jokingly, Paul asked what the chances were of getting a $15 room so many years later. "To my utter surprise, he replied, 'What an interesting story. To think you were married forty-five years ago and spent your honeymoon in the Mark and are still married. It would be our pleasure to honor the fifteen-dollar-per-night rate for as long as you wish to stay with us. And, of course, you will be our guests in the dining room.' I hadn't told my wife I was writing that letter, and when I showed her the reply, she said, 'You didn't ask them to give you a room at the Mark for fifteen dollars a night, did you?' Unfortunately, we were unable to go at that time and had to skip the offer."

After his retirement from the service, Paul took classes in psychology and became a diplomate in psychology. He worked as a forensic hypnotist with the San Diego Police Department for twenty-two years, and currently he is a reserve detective with the Washoe County Sheriff's Office in Reno, Nevada. He was inducted into the International Hypnosis Hall of Fame for work with law-enforcement agencies all over the United States and also with Mexico.

He and Frieda had been married over forty-eight years when she died in 1994. Reflecting on the happy life they shared, Paul comments that "ours was indeed a love story that ended only when 'death did us part.'"

Paul Kincade in 1942 while waiting in Mobile, Alabama, to be assigned to a new merchant ship.

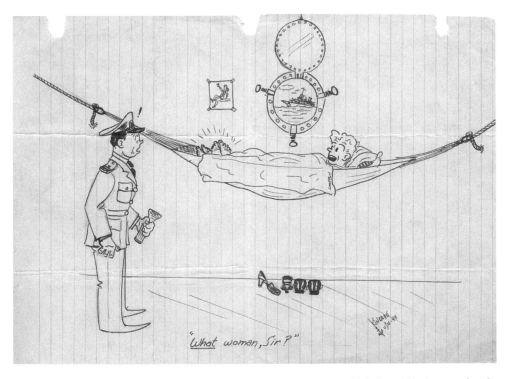

"What woman, Sir?"

One of many cartoons Paul enclosed with his letters to Frieda while he was in the NJROTC unit at Yale University in 1944 before, as he writes, "they realized their mistake and sent me back to the sea and the British Pacific Fleet!"

A painting Paul had made while he was stationed in Japan in 1959, from the photograph of Frieda that her cousin gave him.

Paul carrying the U.S. flag at the head of the "Pass By," or parade, in Portsmouth, England, at the fiftieth reunion of the British Pacific Fleet. Paul was the only "Yank," as he says, out of the over fifteen thousand veterans, and he wore his Stetson and boots so that everyone would know he was American.

M ILITARY BASES WERE LOCATED all over the country, especially along the coastlines, but the greatest concentration of training camps was in the South, where the warmer weather made year-round training more manageable. Hundreds of thousands of young men who had seldom traveled outside their own states suddenly found themselves in an entirely different part of the country. Many couples met at USO dances organized in the towns and cities near these bases. Often the girl who stood out from the crowd was a local resident, but sometimes she, too, was from another part of the country, uprooted by the war.

*Bea and John Sutherland while he was stationed
at Turner Field in Albany, Georgia, in 1944.*

J. W. and Bea

SUTHERLAND

John Wesley Sutherland was a private in the army air force in 1942, stationed at Seymour Johnson Field in Goldsboro, North Carolina. He went by the name of Johnny back then. Like most GIs, he couldn't wait for the USO dances held in town every weekend. On one of those Saturday nights, he became transfixed by a junior hostess he'd never seen before. "My eyes nearly popped out of my head," Johnny recalls. "She was the prettiest girl on earth. I even remember what she had on that night: a white blouse, a black skirt, and a wide red belt. There were always more soldiers than girls at the dances, so I had to keep cutting in. She thought that was funny. I was kind of a shy boy, but I just couldn't help myself."

The name of the stunning girl was Beatrice Victoria Kalayjian. She was originally from South Dakota but was working in Goldsboro as an X-ray technician for two local doctors. After cutting in several times, Johnny finally summoned the courage to ask Bea for a date—for the very next day. She taught Sunday school and invited him to join her for church services, which he did with pleasure. They had lunch after church and spent the rest of the afternoon together.

During November and December of that year, Johnny and Bea went on about six dates, culminating in a Christmas Day dinner at the house where Bea lived; her landlady, Mrs. Harrell, had invited Johnny to join them. After dinner, when Bea went into the kitchen to help with the preparations, wise Mrs. Harrell told her to get right back out to the living room. She was sure Johnny was going to propose to Bea. "How she knew that, I'll never know," Johnny says, chuckling. But that was indeed his intention, since he had orders to report to Boca Raton, Florida, for officer's training school on January 1, 1943, only a week away. "Bea wanted time to think it over," he recalls, "as well she should have. She was as smart then as she is now."

During his nine weeks of training in Florida, John wrote to Bea every day, plus a special delivery on Sunday, and she finally agreed to marry him. "The best letter I ever received," he says. When Bea told her father she was engaged, and that her fiancé's name was John Wesley Sutherland, her father replied that he must be a fine fellow, to have such a good Methodist name. (John Wesley, of course, founded Methodism with his brother Charles at Oxford, England, in 1729.) It still amuses John that in fact, he was named after his father, who was Baptist.

In March, shortly after they became engaged, John was transferred to New Haven, Connecticut, where the army air force had taken over part of Yale University. He was being trained as a maintenance officer. Bea and John set their wedding date for July 3, 1943, with the ceremony to be held in the Yale Chapel. Until the wedding, Bea stayed with her sister Marian in New York City, because she could travel easily from there to see John in New Haven.

Given the often helter-skelter circumstances of weddings in those strenuous days, when many ceremonies were quickie registry-office affairs, Bea and John felt lucky to be getting married by an air force chaplain in the beautiful Yale Chapel. "You couldn't ask for a lovelier place to get married," Bea remembers wistfully. In those days, families were often unable to travel to the ceremony, but Bea's father, a doctor in South Dakota, managed to get there, as did one of her brothers, her sister Marian, and other friends and family. None of John's family, however, could attend. John did at least have a good friend there, a fellow cadet from Arkansas named Fred Venable, to serve as his best man.

Though John and Bea had only a one-night honeymoon, their surroundings weren't too shabby for that, either: the Waldorf-Astoria in New York, then as now one of the most famous hotels in the world. "When John told me where we were going for our honeymoon, I almost fainted," Bea says with a laugh.

About two weeks after the wedding, John graduated as a second lieutenant, and he and Bea left by train for Maxwell Field in Montgomery, Alabama. He was then posted to Turner Field in Albany, Georgia, where they spent almost two years. Their daughter, Sue Fann, was born in Alice, Texas, after the war. "The light of our lives," John proclaims.

John and Bea Sutherland celebrated their fifty-seventh anniversary in July 2000. Their rich life together includes four grandchildren and three great-grandchildren. They've traveled abroad and visited all fifty states over the years, and have a network of friends and family across the continent. They are both great music fans and attend performances all over the country. They are particularly fond of opera and have enjoyed productions at all the major American opera houses and festivals, from New York's Metropolitan Opera to the San Francisco Opera House. When John retired from business nearly twenty years ago, they were free to travel at all times of the year. They're the kind of people who will make a trip several hundred miles out of their way to catch a Pennsylvania performance by the son of a second cousin starring in a production of Neil Simon's *The Odd Couple*.

The chance encounter in North Carolina of a young private from Texas and an X-ray technician from South Dakota never would have occurred if it hadn't been for World War II. "This may sound corny," declares John, "but to have found Bea at a USO dance—of all places— was the best thing that ever happened to me.

"I've read that the secret of a good marriage is one double bed and two bathrooms," John notes with amusement, but his and Bea's shared fondness for bridge games, travel, and fine music have had a lot to do with it as well.

All things considered, it was good that Bea was wearing that very noticeable wide red belt one Saturday night nearly sixty years ago in Goldsboro, North Carolina.

Private John Sutherland in 1942 at Seymour Johnson Field in Goldsboro, North Carolina.

Bea and John cutting their wedding cake at their reception in New York City on July 3, 1943.

Bea and John on their fiftieth wedding anniversary, July 3, 1993.

T HE LOVE AFFAIRS KINDLED AT SO *many USO dances came to many different ends. Some of these whirlwind romances intensified during the war through deeply felt letters, and many culminated in marriage. But even if marriage wasn't the ultimate outcome, sometimes those relationships, and those wonderful letters, were cherished for years and years.*

Anne Hetrick in her senior prom gown, with Lieutenant Harry Greissman in his uniform from the Seventy-eighth ("Lightning") Division in May 1943.

Anne Hetrick KENNEDY

Though Anne Hetrick was only eighteen in the summer of 1942, she was about to begin her senior year at Winthrop College in Rock Hill, South Carolina, not far from her hometown of Walhalla. As was fairly common in her generation, Anne had skipped a grade in elementary school, and at that time in South Carolina, there were only eleven grades. So Anne had entered college when she was just fifteen. She was spending this summer away from home in Raleigh, North Carolina, with her mother, who was there taking care of Anne's uncle, her mother's brother, who was ill. Though Anne's parents were still married, her father had moved back to his native Pennsylvania several years earlier because the hosiery mills his family owned in various towns in the South had failed during the Depression. Anne's mother, Ida, "couldn't abide" the North, and she stayed behind in Walhalla with Anne when he moved.

Anne was a poised and very pretty young lady with soft brown hair. While in Raleigh, she answered the call of the USO, whose slogan was "Morale is *your* job," and regularly attended the dances held that summer at the Memorial Auditorium. On one August evening, Anne met two different soldiers named Harry, who were friends. At first Anne was more attracted to Harry Claeyssens, because, as she recalls, he was such a "dashing dancer." But she dated both, and as time went on, Anne gradually realized that the other Harry appealed to her more. He might not have been as great a dancer as Harry Claeyssens, but Harry Greissman, who hailed from Brooklyn, could "make words sing." Whether talking or putting words on paper, he had a poet's instinct for the evocative phrase and the telling detail that illuminated a place or a feeling.

First Lieutenant Harry Greissman was twenty-four and a graduate of City College of New York. He spoke fluent German—his parents were immigrants—and he taught the language to other young officers at Camp Butner, North Carolina, where he was stationed during 1942 and '43. He was a member of the Seventy-eighth Division, famous as the "Lightning Division" during World War I and reconstituted as a World War II training unit.

Camp Butner was only thirty miles from Raleigh, and when Anne returned to college in South Carolina, Harry wrote letters and visited her at Rock Hill when he had weekend leave. She also saw him back in Raleigh when she visited her mother, who had decided to stay after the summer. Anne would almost always go to a dance there, with her mother as chaperone. Because her mother enjoyed entertaining—she had been a home economics major in college, graduating in 1918—she started to invite the soldiers Anne met at the dances and some of their friends back to her house to stay overnight and have a home-cooked Sunday dinner. Her mother's house had six bedrooms, and the soldiers loved the opportunity to spend time in a comfortable home, as well as the luxury of staying in Raleigh instead of crowding into the cramped buses that returned to the bases. Harry stayed over at Anne's mother's house several times when Anne was visiting, and he sometimes accompanied Anne back to college on the train.

In Rock Hill, Harry and Anne would sometimes spend time with Anne's aunt Kate, who was a music teacher at the college and lived a few blocks from the campus. Her aunt once asked Anne if, when she and Harry sat on the porch swing at her house, she allowed any "liberties." Anne explains with amusement that in those astonishingly innocent times, what her aunt meant by liberties was holding hands, which she and Harry most certainly did not do. But as time went on, Harry did begin calling Anne "darling" in the many letters he wrote to her, letters that Anne cherishes to this day.

His letters during this period say little about his army experience and instead talk about life apart from the war. Harry aspired to become a journalist, a dream that generated considerable enthusiasm for a James Cagney movie he managed to catch one weekend, *Johnny Come Lately.* "You and I shall see this picture together many times over, darlin'," he wrote to Anne. "It is the simple picture of every newspaperman's credo—with nary an ounce of sentimentality, it drives home the place of an honest newspaper in a small town, its place as a pleader of causes, some lost some won, but all bravely fought. The picture is racy as h—— and had moments of hilarity that nearly tore my ribs out—I don't remember laughing so long and loudly since the time I put the ketchup into my coffee instead of [on] the ham sandwich."

Though Anne loved Harry's writing, and she had come to love him, he was not the only soldier she corresponded with during the war. She was an avid letter writer and kept up extensive correspondences with several young men. Anne absolutely loved to dance, and with so many dances going on during the war, she danced with more soldiers than she could count. Many a soldier must have fallen a little in love with her, a standout in her favorite ball gown, and many of them wrote to her after meeting her. If they wrote, she wrote back as long as the letters kept coming.

One air force lieutenant she corresponded with, Alfred M. Kelly, traveled all the way from Florida, where he had been stationed, to attend her college graduation. His next base assignment was to a Pacific island, the name of which had to be withheld in his letters. Letters kept arriving for a time after he had shipped to the Pacific, but then they stopped, and Anne has never known for sure whether he met some other girl or, as she feared, was killed.

Through 1942 and '43, Anne also maintained a correspondence with her old hometown boyfriend, Jim Hughes, who was cocaptain of the football team at Newberry College in South Carolina. He even came up to Rock Hill and later, to Raleigh, to visit her. He entered the service, becoming an ensign in the navy, and she lost touch with him after he went overseas. For years she had no word of him but has since learned that he survived the war, went on to marry and have two children, and moved back to South Carolina.

Once, knowing how much soldiers liked to receive gifts from home, Anne tried to knit a sweater for one of her correspondents, but she says, laughing, "It turned out to be a sleeping bag." So she settled for writing her "fingers to the shoulder blades" instead. Dear Dan, Dear Joe, Dear Bill, Dear Al, Dear Ashby, and on and on. As much as all of these young men meant to her, when it came to love, there was only Harry.

As the war dragged on, more soldiers were needed at the front lines, and the Seventy-eighth began the transition from a training to a fighting unit. In February 1944, Harry's division was sent to Nashville, Tennessee, for two months of exhausting war games in what seemed to Harry like endless rain, "infinitely worse than snow," he wrote, "a cold, clammy rain, turning the best of roads (and most of those are the worst) into slippery trails to treacherous cliffs."

But Harry had some wry stories to tell, too. "Notice the new point on my pen? Yesterday, I managed to steal time to take a haircut in a real civilian barber shop, and while he was clipping my hair, the barber recited the sad tale of a soldier trying to work his way home on a furlough, with a pen as his only asset. The kindly barber gave the GI $4 for his pen, and then recalled his own illiteracy. He tried to trade the pen in for a shovel and failing that, decided to sell it. So, in the process of being clipped about the scalp, I emerged with a new pen but the same old scrawl."

Then the Seventy-eighth made the trip up to Camp Pickett in Virginia, a four-day convoy trip filled with tension: Every soldier knew that from there, you were certain to be shipped overseas. Sure enough, most of the soldiers in the convoy were shipped out to Europe for D-Day preparations. Harry and some of the other officers remained at Fort Pickett through the spring and into the summer, but he knew he'd be going across the Atlantic before long.

In mid-October, Harry was on his way over, and he wrote a letter to Anne while aboard ship. He had been listening to someone play "As Time Goes By" on the piano. *Casablanca* had been thrown together in a hurry for its release in 1942, but it was already a classic, and its bittersweet song could be heard everywhere. Harry noted that the pianist wasn't very good, but the music cast its spell even so: "As time goes by," he wrote to Anne, "the tide carries all of us farther and farther from the things each of us loves best." Back home, Anne read his words with a little trepidation. She knew that Harry wanted her to commit to him, but she was only twenty and just wasn't ready yet.

Though Harry narrowly escaped the carnage of D-Day, he soon

found himself plunged into the Battle of the Bulge, the largest land battle of the war. This German offensive, fought in the forested area of Belgium and Luxembourg known as the Ardennes, caught the Allies by surprise— the idea had astonished Hitler's generals when he first brought it up in September 1944. The German military command knew they faced plenty of challenge just trying to prevent invasion by the Allied forces, let alone trying to launch an attack. They pleaded with Hitler to abandon the plan, but he refused. At five-thirty A.M. on December 16, 1944, eight German armored divisions and thirteen infantry divisions launched an all-out attack on five divisions of the United States First Army. The Americans' losses that first day were staggering, but they quickly regrouped to block the German advance. Though the official military name of the battle was the Battle of the Ardennes, the frontline Americans referred to it as the Battle of the Bulge, because of the way the German line bulged out toward them. Journalists began using that moniker in their reports, and the name stuck forever.

Harry was a forward observer during the battle. His job was to call in artillery where it was needed, and he was stationed very close to the front. Amid all of the hellish carnage, he hunkered down on Christmas Day and wrote a truly remarkable letter to Anne:

> MY DARLING, I have just seen and heard something that I shall never forget, and there is SO much to remember already: Christmas services in a winter woodland blanketed with snow and ice, shattered by cannon and small arms fire. Above the cannon's roar and the angry spitfire of machine guns and rifles, you can still hear the still, small voice of an organ piping hymns forever old and new. It was a congregation that continued to wear steel helmets and side arms, and hand grenades still dangled brazenly from many a shoulder harness—but the Lord surely saw no blasphemy here—a more devout company never came to worship! Many a face was dirty and bearded and eyes gleamed across the organ notes through slits narrowed by nights with little sleep and less rest. And in the gallant company none was more brave than this chaplain, whose name I do not even know, for they tell me that he is wherever the fighting is. . . .
>
> The last notes of the last hymn are dying into the distance now,

darling, and each of that strange company is now returning to his separate duty, and yet as I too turn away from the heavens to hell again, I can not help but think that we are all of us alike, the chaplain and the rest of us, each serving God and country according to the manner set forth by the destiny beyond us all. . . .

Some of Harry's other communications from the front were of a different nature. He sent a set of Christmas cards, one depicting Hitler as a snowman with GIs throwing snowballs at him. Another card poked some fun at the U.S. Army command, with Sergeant George Baker's famous "Sad Sack" character carrying a huge bag filled with Santa's toys, while the general behind him strolled along unencumbered.

As American troops moved forward into Germany during the next few months, Anne received a number of packages from Harry. He sent wads of German money from the days of the Weimar Republic, just before Hitler rose to power. These bills were worth little enough during the days of the republic, due to tremendous inflation, and were utterly devoid of value now. GIs were constantly finding caches of the bills in the walls of bombed-out houses, where they had been hidden in the hope that one day they would regain their original value. Other things Harry sent home were of more value and beauty, including lovely china cups rescued from ruins and a small tapestry depicting a view of the Rialto Bridge in Venice, which Anne had framed. It graces her living room wall to this day.

Families all over America received such packages from the front in 1945, as the Allies moved on to Berlin. Some might call them "spoils of war," but to the soldiers who gathered them up from destroyed houses, they were souvenirs, a way of telling loved ones back home, "Look, we've come through, we're winning, we've fought our way across Europe to victory." There were certainly moments, however, when the soldiers' darker sentiments became painfully clear. Harry wrote in one letter to Anne, "In their homes are splendid icons, paintings of Christ and divine spectacles, in their hearts the hatred that is the only plausible cause for these generations of Hell on Earth. For their hypocrisy, one can only hate them and wish them nothing but the worst, in this world and the next. But don't let me speak of things like that."

On May 7, 1945, Germany signed an unconditional surrender at General Dwight D. Eisenhower's headquarters in Reims, France. Victory in Europe Day was celebrated on May 8, even as the war continued to rage in the Pacific. Many months passed before Harry could return home, because his ability to speak fluent German made him a valuable man. Not until January 1946 was he able to ship home to Brooklyn.

Harry wanted Anne to marry him, and that summer she went north to meet his family, staying with his sister in Pennsylvania, who was warm and welcoming, as were his other family members. But Anne still harbored doubts about spending her life with Harry. She had loved his letters and would treasure them always. She also loved him, but with the war over, she felt she had to think about the future, and she didn't quite believe that she and Harry belonged together. Her hesitance was partially a matter of their religions: Harry was Jewish and she was Christian. But more important, Anne felt a deep instinct that she tries to clarify now: "Somehow, I just *knew* it wasn't right. I can't really explain it. But I just knew that for Harry to lead a long and happy life, and for me to lead a happy life, our paths should separate."

Harry took a job at a small newspaper in Brooklyn, pursuing his longtime ambition, but then entered the burgeoning business of advertising. After graduation, Anne became an inspiring and much loved history teacher at Wake Forest high school. She continued to date a number of young men, one of whom was Frank Kennedy, who had fought in North Africa and then Italy, receiving a Legion of Merit for inspiring leadership and ingenuity in building a road he had reconnoitered under fire at Castellonarato. He was a staff engineer at North Carolina State University, a kind man of unassuming strength whom she liked a good deal. Her affection for him grew steadily, and in the autumn of 1948 she accepted his proposal of marriage.

Anne had continued to correspond with Harry during those years, though less often, and she wrote to tell him of her engagement. His reply started with a bit of humor: "Sorry to disappoint, but Truman is STILL the big surprise of the year." He added that he had known she would marry Frank when he visited her in September. "It will, of course, be impossible for me to see 'the last of Miss Hetrick'—but where your good church bells chime out the glad tidings, listen for the whisper of a sigh from the

*Anne's mother's
house in Raleigh,
North Carolina,
where they hosted
so many Sunday
dinners.*

*A V-Mail letter
from Harry to
Anne's mother,
Ida B., addressed
with the First
Army APO from
New York, sent
March 25, 1945.*

A letter that Harry sent Anne from "somewhere in Germany" on February 12, 1945, which starts, "Dearest Adorable, How much longer can it last, darling—or me? It's impossible to write much any more—no place, no time, no lights, not even candles." He also mentions in this letter the "old German paper money" he is enclosing for her.

The "Sad Sack" cartoon Harry sent Anne for Christmas, 1944.

Christmas card sent by Harry to Anne from Holland that same season.

The Christmas card Harry sent to Anne depicting Hitler as a snowman, also from that same season.

Anne and the "other man" she chose to marry, Frank Kennedy, at a party in 1948.

The telegram of congratulations that Harry sent to Anne on her wedding day, December 18, 1948.

CONGRATULATIONS
by WESTERN UNION
RA424
R.NA467 CGN PD=BROOKLYN NY 18 226P=
MR AND MRS FRANK KENNEDY, CARE HETRICK=
525 EAST JONES ST RALEIGH NCAR=

LUCK=

HARRY GREISSMAN=

1948 DEC 18 PM 3 20

FROM THE CONTINENT OF EUROPE · 1944

big, bad city of the North—and with that whisper will come all the fond hopes and best wishes for the noblest lady I have known. Always in all ways, Harry."

A wedding telegram from Harry read simply, "Luck," and she did not hear from him again for several years. In 1950 he married Iris Resnick, also from New York, and he reestablished contact with Anne. Every year, the Kennedys and the Greissmans exchanged Christmas cards with news of their growing families. Anne and Frank had three children and forty-nine years of a very happy marriage. Frank died in September 1997, after a long battle with Parkinson's disease. That Christmas, Anne received a card from Harry and Iris as usual, but a few days later, Iris telephoned to tell her that Harry had passed away. She told Anne that, among his treasures, he had always kept a picture of Anne Hetrick from the days when he had first known her.

Later, Anne would learn that Harry's wife and children had memorialized Harry's way with words on his tombstone. The inscription read, "He could make words sing." Anne found a way to memorialize him, too: She gave his hundreds of letters to the North Carolina Museum of History in Raleigh, providing an eloquent archive of the World War II experiences of a young man from Brooklyn who fell in love with a beautiful young woman from North Carolina. They had not spent their lives together, as Harry had wanted them to, yet they remain forever linked in ways that Anne Kennedy is happy to celebrate even now.

T HE YOUNG MEN FROM THE NORTH *who trained at military bases in the South were usually treated exceptionally well. Southern hospitality welcomed them into the towns and homes of Georgia, the Carolinas, and the rest of the Deep South with all the warmth and friendship that could be mustered. But a few pockets of lingering tension, passed down from the Civil War, could flare up unexpectedly. Here they added an additional degree of tension to an already high-strung wedding day.*

Miriam Clark and Lloyd Clark during the war.
The photograph of Lloyd is one he had taken while stationed in Ireland,
at Miriam's request, because she did not have a picture of him when
he left to go overseas. She says she wanted to be sure to have a picture
so that his child would know what he looked like in case
he didn't come back.

Lloyd and Miriam

CLARK

When war broke out in Europe, Lloyd Clark was one of those Americans who knew that his country wouldn't be able to stay out of it in the long run, despite deep-seated isolationist sentiments throughout the country.

Lloyd grew up in Rockland, Maine, attended Phillips Academy at Andover, Massachusetts, and went on to MIT. For several years he worked at General Foods in Rochester, New York. But after Hitler occupied Denmark, Norway, and France, Lloyd volunteered for the army and in January 1941 was sent to Camp Stewart in Hinesville, Georgia, with the 209th Coast Artillery Regiment. He turned twenty-nine that month, and with war on the horizon, he was not actively looking for a wife, especially not one who was nearly ten years his junior. But when he met Macon native Miriam Elizabeth Bidez, just turning twenty, his feelings quickly changed.

By the fall of 1941, Lloyd, whom everyone called Larry, knew that he wanted to marry Mimi, as she was nicknamed. Given his old-school upbringing and their age difference, he first went to Mimi's father to ask for her hand. Mr. Bidez liked and admired Larry and gave his permission without hesitation. When he proposed to Mimi, Larry told her that she should carefully consider the fact that he was nearly ten years older, because it could make a difference in their lives at some point. But Mimi was very much in love, and she didn't hesitate to say yes. They planned to marry in the spring of 1942.

After a year in the army, Larry was far more aware than the general public of rumors about an early American entry into the war, and at the end of November 1941, he suggested that they move up the wedding date to December 13. Naturally, Mimi's mother was somewhat distraught at the short notice, but she and Mimi managed to pull everything together. Mimi says Larry often commented that had her mother been born a couple of generations later, she would have made a great CEO.

Sure enough, Larry's sense that war was imminent proved to be all too correct. Pearl Harbor was bombed on December 7. With America suddenly in the conflict, Larry's life became far more complicated, and it was difficult for him to get away from Camp Stewart. He and Mimi dreaded a dispatch to another base far away, or even overseas.

On their wedding day, Larry was due at the Bidez house at two o'clock, and the wedding was scheduled for three o'clock. But he didn't show up at the appointed time. By two-thirty Mimi's father and brother were out pacing the sidewalk in front of the house. A neighbor from across the street came over and actually said, "I told you not to let Mimi marry that Yankee!" Mimi says that Larry showed up a few minutes after the neighbor's remark, "and we were off on the most wonderful, romantic life I could imagine."

As the war raged on, and more and more soldiers showed up for training in the South, a great many more Yankee boys married southern girls, and those lingering tensions subsided as the country came together to meet the challenge of the day.

Attached to the Royal Artillery of the British North Africa Force, Larry served in the campaign in Tunisia against the formidable forces of General Erwin Rommel, the "Desert Fox," and subsequently in the southern Italian campaign. After his discharge from active duty, he served as an instructor in the U.S. Army reserve officer school, retiring in 1972 with the rank of lieutenant colonel.

His consecutive business careers as a plant and contract engineer with Maxwell House Coffee and Hunt-Wesson took Larry and Mimi and their two daughters around the country, from New York to Florida, Tennessee, California, and eventual retirement in Savannah, Georgia, a peripatetic life that Mimi thrived on, having inherited some of her mother's

Larry in front of his tent at Camp Stewart in 1941. Every time it rained, he recalled, his cot was flooded.

Mimi out shopping in June 1943.

INVASION JOURNAL
Third of a series of eyewitness stories from the battle front

Two American tanks and a Yank move down a tree-lined street in Bizerte. The Grants ignore snipers, but the soldier is wary.

A photograph from the October 5, 1943, issue of Look. *The "Yank" mentioned in the caption is Larry.*

Larry and Mimi, at the far left, out on the town with friends in 1945.

Larry and Mimi at their fifty-fifth anniversary party.

remarkable organizational capabilities. "We started out from two completely different worlds," Mimi recalls, "and went on to explore a great many others together."

Their age difference was something Mimi never really noticed until Larry's death in 1997. "Now I understand what he was talking about," she says. "I miss him so very much."

D URING WORLD WAR II, MANY young couples found their sense of time warped by the circumstances. When a young man was about to be shipped overseas, he might feel as though he'd known a girl for months when he'd really met her a week before; the girl might feel that they had met just yesterday. While the young man was overseas, time could seem accelerated, so that when he returned to the States on leave and they could finally enjoy each other's company again for a bit, they might consider marriage. Should they marry right away, or perhaps the next time he got home; how long would that be? If they did marry, how would they calculate the time they'd known each other: add up the days and weeks since they met, or account only for the time actually spent together? Was it two years they'd been in love, or only two weeks?

Charles and Patricia Lee in August 1945 after Charles returned from thirteen months overseas.

Charles and Patricia

LEE

Throughout their fifty-six years of marriage, Charles and Patricia Lee have been very much aware that if it hadn't been for World War II, they never would have met. Of course, the same could be said of many couples. But Patricia has developed a stronger feeling than most that "fate takes over your life." Indeed, there are elements of the Lees' story that suggest the hovering presence of fate more convincingly than usual.

At the high school Patricia Skinner attended while growing up in San Francisco, the year was broken into two semesters, one from September to January and the other from February to June, along with a summer-school term. Students were assigned to either a fall class or a spring class, and Patricia was in the fall class of 1941, scheduled to graduate in January 1942. At the graduation a month after the Pearl Harbor bombing, half the boys in her class were already in the armed services. The graduation was supposed to have been held at the beautiful San Francisco Opera House, but because of the citywide blackout ordered shortly after Pearl Harbor, the ceremony was held in the school auditorium instead.

Along with San Diego, San Francisco was the most important West Coast port of embarkation for ships heading out to fight the war in the Pacific. A sense of tumult and excitement permeated the city on the hills, and also a sense of danger. Early in the war, many feared that the Japanese would attack the West Coast of the United States, with San Francisco as a major target.

Many volunteer organizations in the city quickly established programs
to help with the war effort and to offer solace to the young men from all
across the country who were flooding the city, preparing to sail off to war.
Patricia joined the Young Lady's Institute, which organized USO dances.
At a Sunday-afternoon dance, a young man named Charles Lee walked
over and asked Patricia to dance. She really liked this fresh-faced boy
from West Rutland, Vermont, a seaman first class who was stationed at
Treasure Island just offshore. Patricia says there was a strong physical
attraction between them from the moment they saw each other. Not that
she was about to give in to her feelings in any serious way—she was a
properly raised young woman in a much more innocent time. She did
spend the rest of that day with Charles (known as Chuck), showing him
the sights. At the end of the evening, he asked to take her home. There
was a general understanding among young women in those days about
how to handle such an offer: You said that would be fine if the young man
also took your girlfriends home. Any guy willing to do that was probably
okay. Chuck said fine and excused himself briefly. Although Patricia didn't
know it, he didn't have a penny, and he had to borrow a dollar from a
fellow sailor in case he needed to pay for a streetcar or a jitney—cars that
seated up to seven passengers. Chuck was so new to the city that he didn't
even know what a ride cost—only a dime back then. He had to take three
of Patricia's friends home that night, and she was suitably impressed.

After a week of seeing Patricia almost daily, Chuck asked her to go
steady with him. But she didn't feel ready for that kind of commitment.
Like so many other young women at the time, she had mixed feelings
about getting seriously involved with a young man in the armed services;
they arrived in port cities every day. While the supply of future husbands
dwindled in small towns across America, parts of the country with major
bases and ports swarmed with possibilities. Back in the small towns,
young women tended to get married before their potential husbands
shipped off to unknown destinies, but in the military boomtowns, women
had good reason to wait and see who they might meet tomorrow—unless
someone *very* special tumbled into their life. There was an unspoken
sense that unless you were sure you had met the love of your life, you
didn't need to rush into serious commitment.

Many young women had another concern: "Will I ever see him

again?" By the autumn of 1942, it was already clear that the war was going to be a long one, and that there were going to be great numbers of casualties. For young couples who were madly in love, that recognition fueled the desire to get married, or at least engaged, as soon as possible. But if either party felt doubt, the possibility that the young man might be heading off to his death often put a brake on an inclination toward marriage.

Patricia felt she simply did not know Chuck well enough even to say she would go steady. She had noticed among her friends and acquaintances that there were girls who would *say* they'd go steady but would start dating other young men soon after their "steady" was off at war. She didn't approve of that kind of behavior, and she didn't want to tempt herself to indulge in it. Better just to tell Chuck up front that as much as she liked him, she wasn't ready.

At the time Patricia met Chuck, he was a belly gunner in a torpedo bomber. That was a "top gun" kind of position, and Chuck was proud to have achieved it. But it was also perhaps the most dangerous job in the navy. The chances of survival as a belly gunner during the early stages of the Pacific war were close to zero.

One day shortly after Chuck had asked Patricia to go steady, he saw a notice on the bulletin board at Treasure Island that a new destroyer in port had just gone into service and needed men. This was an opportunity for him to switch out of his position as a belly gunner, and he signed up right away and shipped out on the destroyer to the South Pacific that very night. That decision almost surely saved his life. Every other belly gunner Chuck trained with was killed during the war.

After Chuck shipped out, he seemed to be gone from Patricia's life for good. He didn't write, which surprised her a little, even though she had refused to go steady. She wondered about him from time to time, whether he was all right. Though she'd dated quite a few other young men since Chuck left, none of them had been really special to her, and she regretted that they hadn't kept in touch. She asked a friend who worked at the Treasure Island base to see if there was any word of him. But the friend couldn't find his records, and Patricia was afraid he had been killed.

In September 1943, almost exactly a year since she had last seen Chuck, Patricia was pleasantly surprised by a telephone call from him. He was in port and asked if he could take her out that evening. She agreed, and they went to a movie. Chuck asked her for another date the next night, but then he didn't show. Patricia knew that this didn't necessarily mean she'd been stood up. His orders might have changed, and he might not have been able to get word to her. That happened frequently.

Still, she was surprised by the contents of a letter she soon received. Sure enough, Chuck was back at sea. But what stunned her was that he asked her to marry him. From a missed date to a proposal in one step was quite a leap. She wrote him a letter saying they'd discuss it next time he was on leave.

That was not until seven months later. Chuck got back into port on April 30, 1944, and they met again the next day. He proposed in person this time, and by now Patricia knew she was going to say yes. She was attracted to him in ways that went far beyond anything she had felt for anyone else. But even so, she made him wait a day before she accepted.

After all, she still didn't know him very well. In fact, when people soon began asking how long she had known him, she would say, "Two years," which was one kind of truth, though in terms of time she'd actually spent with Chuck, she had known him for only two weeks.

Both Patricia and Chuck were Catholic, which made them compatible in one sense but caused a problem in another. They knew that no priest would even think about marrying them for at least thirty days, and Chuck would probably be at sea again by then, although he did expect to be in port for a couple of weeks for repairs on his ship. They considered their options and decided to get married immediately, which they could do at city hall. This turned out to be much more of a saga than they expected.

Their plan was to meet at city hall on the morning of May 4, with Chuck and Patricia each bringing along a friend to serve as best man and bridesmaid. Patricia told her mother about the plan but said nothing to her more conservative father. He was a city inspector, and by an amazing coincidence, he happened to be working at the corner of Van Ness and Market Streets on the morning of the ceremony, very near city hall. Sure enough, Patricia's father looked up and noticed Chuck, whom he had met a couple of times, walking toward him, carrying a suitcase. He greeted Chuck and asked him where he was going. Chuck managed to stammer out that he was taking the suitcase to a friend who'd suddenly gotten leave. Patricia's father, totally unsuspecting, sent the nice young man on his way—to marry his daughter.

But that was just the beginning of the day's difficulties. According to California law at the time, the groom had to be twenty-one and the bride eighteen to marry without parental consent. The clerk at the courthouse asked them for identification. Patricia was nineteen and had no trouble with her identification, but when the clerk looked at Chuck's, he detected that the birthdate had been altered. Not to be thwarted, Chuck said he'd go get verification and dashed off to his ship, while Patricia waited, wondering how old Chuck really was.

After what seemed an eternity, Chuck rushed back in with a freshly signed paper from one of the officers on his ship. But all that it actually said was that he was serving in the navy and had seen combat in the South Pacific. The clerk read this over, looked at the expectant couple, read it again, and then, after what seemed like *another* eternity, he said, "Well, I'll accept this."

So Patricia and Chuck became Mr. and Mrs. Charles H. Lee on May 4, 1944. Exactly how old was Chuck that day? Like his bride, he was nineteen, but Patricia didn't find that out until after the wedding. Nor did she very much care.

Getting a hotel room on short notice in San Francisco in 1944 wasn't easy, but they were lucky, and they spent their first night together in real comfort. But then Chuck got the disappointing word that instead of remaining in San Francisco for repairs, his ship had received orders to undergo them in Hawaii, and he would be in town for just five more days. One of those would be taken up with the job of getting married all over again.

When Chuck and Patricia told her parents about the marriage—news only to her father, of course—they were determined that a traditional marriage service should be performed. Though a church wedding was definitely out, Patricia's mother pleaded with the priest at their church to perform the service, and because the couple was already legally married (if you didn't count Chuck's real age), he decided to make an exception for the special circumstances of the war. Chuck and Patricia were married once again in a small service in the priest's home.

During the following year, Chuck's destroyer, the U.S.S. *Lang*, DD-399, engaged in almost every major battle in the South Pacific, from Guam to Saipan to Leyte Gulf. Chuck wrote when he could find time, but his letters often took weeks, even months, to reach Patricia. All this time, she seldom knew in any detail where he was. All she really knew for sure was that the war in the Pacific was fierce and that he was in grave danger. Whenever he could, Chuck gave enough money to fellow sailors heading back to the States to buy Patricia a dozen roses, but not one of those bouquets ever got to her.

On April 12, 1945, Patricia was feeling particularly low. This was her twentieth birthday, and she hadn't heard from Chuck in months. To make a dismal day even darker, word suddenly came over the radio at the office of the hospital she worked in that President Roosevelt had died. Like many others, Patricia burst into tears. As was the case with offices all over the country, her office closed immediately. Roosevelt's death was a crushing blow to the country, and the world seemed an even more dangerous place with his passing. Few people realized at the time what good hands the country was in with newly sworn-in President Harry S. Truman.

Half a world away that April 12, Chuck was off the coast of Okinawa on "picket" duty: His ship formed part of the line of defense protecting the troops advancing on the beachhead. "We were suffering some of the worst kamikaze attacks of the war," Chuck would write years later. "I had just heard the sad news that President Roosevelt had passed away. It was my wife's birthday, and I had been gone for nearly a year. Some time before I had sent money with a shipmate who had been transferred off the ship to buy her red roses for her birthday. I was wondering if she had received the flowers. Then, above me, I saw a kamikaze headed straight for our ship. Our guns had damaged his controls, but I could even see the pilot's face as he tried to aim his plane at us. He missed the ship by only a few yards and crashed into the sea. I said a little prayer of thanks and at the same time wept for our departed president. It was the darkest day of the entire war for me."

But back in San Francisco, something life-affirming was happening. Remarkably, after so many failed efforts, Chuck's roses reached Patricia this time. When she got home early from her office that day, she discovered a box of twelve long-stemmed red roses at her door.

*Chuck and
Patricia on their
first date in
September 1942 at
the Lake Merced
Rod and Gun
Club picnic.*

*The ship Chuck served on,
the U.S.S. Lang. His gun is
the third from the left.*

*Chuck and Patricia
on a cruise in 1996.*

Soon she began to receive letters from Chuck again. Okinawa had been taken, and Chuck promised to be home soon. She was expecting him to show up for his birthday, but he surprised her and arrived several days early, with no warning, on June 23. Even though Patricia says with a laugh that she was perturbed because she was having what is now called a "bad hair day," she couldn't remember ever being happier.

Charles and Patricia Lee have a son and a daughter who have done their parents proud. On May 4, 2000, the Lees celebrated the fifty-fifth anniversary of a very happy marriage between a sailor from rural Vermont and a big-city girl from San Francisco, who had known each other for two years that were really only two weeks when they wed in the spring of 1944.

FOR EVERY COUPLE WITH NO
hesitations about running off on a moment's
notice to get married, there was probably
another couple in which one of the two had doubts.
Sometimes those doubts didn't surface until the last
minute. The woman might wonder if this was really
the right man, or whether he would survive the war;
what kind of future might they have together, since
they really didn't know each other well at all. This
could be the plot of any number of Hollywood movies
made during the war. Such movies varied a great
deal in quality, but even the most sentimental of
them, now long forgotten, held audiences in those
days because they dramatized a pressing issue. Real
versions of these stories were happening all the time
during the war, and some of them ended even more
happily than any Hollywood script.

*Hank and Mary Jo Suerstedt in the summer of 1946 at the
New Orleans NAS Officers' Club.*

Hank and Mary Jo
SUERSTEDT

Mary Jo Bass grew up in Laredo, a small Texas town on the Mexican border. "My father was a dentist, and Mother was the typical housewife of that time. We weren't rich, but we were comfortable. New clothes for Easter, that kind of thing. But most important, looking back, was the fact that my sister, brother, myself, and Mom and Dad lived in a real house. Front yard, backyard, and neighbors stopping by all the time just to say hello. Being kids, we didn't know how lucky we were. And little did I know that I wouldn't live in a house of my own again for many years. 'Home' was destined to become a succession of navy quarters, rental houses, and even an apartment or two."

That destiny began to unfold at the end of 1942. Mary Jo, a young woman now, was dating a naval officer stationed in Corpus Christi. One day she received a phone call from another young officer, who delivered a farewell message from the officer she had been dating, who had to leave abruptly for duty in the South Pacific. "I thought it was very kind of the friend to take the trouble to call me. He was, after all, a total stranger. I asked him his name." His first name was ordinary enough—Hank. But the last name, Suerstedt, was unusual. "What kind of name was that, I wondered. It never entered my mind that I would end up carrying that name around for the rest of my life! The humorous part is that this young man was just pretending to pass along a message of farewell. He'd simply 'inherited' his friend's address book. We would laugh about that a lot over the years."

Mary Jo and Hank talked more, and she agreed to meet him, but they postponed the date when she came down with strep throat. They rescheduled for New Year's Eve, 1943. As things turned out, she got to meet him three days earlier, because he showed up at her home with a navy doctor to make sure she'd be well enough to celebrate. "Whatever that nice doctor did, it worked!"

But there was more to it than that. Mary Jo admits that on the basis of just a few phone calls and that one visit to her home, she was falling in love for the first time in her life. Pictures from that time reveal why they would be attracted to each other. Both Mary Jo Bass and Hank Suerstedt were physically dazzling enough to have been movie stars. Mary Jo had the classic beauty of a Loretta Young, while Hank had Gregory Peck's rugged appeal, except that he was blond.

New Year's Eve came, and Hank presented Mary Jo with a lei made of red carnations instead of the usual corsage. "Impressive, to say the least," Mary Jo recalls. "Our romance began at midnight with a kiss."

They saw each other every second Hank could be away from duty over the next eight months. Then the inevitable happened; Hank was called to the Pacific in September 1943. He asked Mary Jo to marry him, and she had gone so far as to pack her bags to accompany him to San Francisco, where she would wait for him as his wife.

Then the enormity of her decision settled in. "Was I brave enough? Did I love him enough? I went a little bit crazy." She faced the unspoken fear that she could be a wife for a very short time, then suddenly a war widow. At the very last minute, she changed her mind about accompanying him. They would wait and see what happened.

Hank Suerstedt reported for duty to a composite squadron made up of fighters and torpedo bombers. He was assigned to the latter group and, during the ensuing nine months, was involved in training exercises up and down the West Coast, from San Diego to Pasco, Washington. In July 1944 he was finally deployed on the U.S.S. *Marcus Island,* an escort carrier, and he fought in the Battle of Leyte Gulf that October.

"Somewhere along the line," Mary Jo remembers, "I think we both decided we had done the right thing in not marrying. We exchanged many letters, telegrams, even phone calls, but by the time he left for the South Pacific, it just seemed to be over between us. I don't have to tell you that wars do horrible things to people. I'm not apologizing for myself, but I was young and very confused."

Mary Jo's confusion did not last long, however. In March 1946, with the war well over, Hank had to make a trip to Corpus Christi on naval business, so he telegramed Mary Jo to suggest that they meet for coffee at the Driscoll Hotel. That meeting was all it took for both of them to realize all over again that they were made for each other. "'Soul mates' wasn't a term in use at the time," Mary Jo recalls, "but in retrospect, I believe our forty-four years together were proof that it was meant to be. At least I like to think so, for our true romance began with our marriage in April of 1946."

Mary Jo and Hank wasted no time in starting a family. Before long, their daughter Candace arrived, with Cynthia following three years later. Hank had been accepted into the regular navy shortly after the couple were married. He did two tours during the Korean War, three during the war in Vietnam, and five in Washington, rising to the rank of rear admiral and serving as deputy commander of naval operations in Southeast Asia during the latter years of the conflict in Vietnam.

"We moved twenty-three times in twenty-seven years," Mary Jo says with a grimace. "It wasn't easy, to say the least, to have a nomadic life, especially for the girls. I have to brag about our daughters. They just got used to being uprooted and transplanted time after time. Making new friends and then moving on. Both of our girls were pros from day one."

Mary Jo has held on to an anonymous article a friend sent her several years ago, which she feels accurately describes what a military wife must cope with. In the article, a conversation takes place between an angel and the Lord, after he had spent six overtime days working on his model for military wives. The angel wondered why the Lord was having so much trouble. Wouldn't the standard model do?

THE LORD REPLIED, "*Have you seen the specs on this order? She has to be completely independent, possess the qualities of both father and mother, be a perfect hostess to four or forty with an hour's notice, run on black coffee, handle every emergency imaginable without a manual, be able to carry on cheerfully, even if she is pregnant and has the flu, and she must be willing to move to a new location ten times in seventeen years.*

Lieutenant Hank Suerstedt while serving in the Korean War from 1953 to 1954.

Hank being promoted to rear admiral on April 25, 1961, with Mary Jo at his side.

*Hank and Mary Jo
in the mid-1970s.*

Mary Jo at home in the mid-1990s.

"And, oh yes, she must have six pairs of hands . . ."

After a considerable discussion of the problems involved, the angel noticed something strange on the cheek of the Lord's creation.

"There's a leak," the angel announced. "Something is wrong with the construction. I am not surprised that it has cracked. You are trying to put too much into this model."

The Lord appeared offended at the angel's lack of confidence. "What you see is not a leak," he said. "It is a tear."

"A tear? What is it there for?" asked the angel.

The Lord replied, "It's for joy, sadness, pain, disappointment, loneliness, pride, and a dedication to all the values that she and her husband hold dear."

"You are a genius!" exclaimed the angel.

The Lord looked puzzled and replied, "I didn't put it there."

But while Mary Jo finds a good deal of wry truth in this piece, she is not about to complain. "I have to say that we had a front-row seat for history in the making. We joined the celebration in Hawaii when it became a state. We were in D.C. when President Kennedy was killed, and stood in the cold for hours to watch the funeral procession."

There were many other notable occasions through the years, and many pleasures of a quieter kind. "I can look back on an interesting and fulfilling life enhanced by wonderful friends, and blessings too numerous to count, though I continue to count them daily with thanks to God and Hank."

M ILLIONS OF WOMEN WENT TO *work in factories during the war, taking the place of men on assembly lines and building planes, tanks, and guns. The first published photograph of Marilyn Monroe was taken in the California aircraft factory where she worked, by a photographer for the fabled GI newspaper* Stars and Stripes. *"Rosie the Riveter" became the national symbol for these women. Other adventurous women joined auxiliary branches of the armed services, the Waves, Wacs, and SPARS. The new sense of independence and of larger responsibility that these women found in their work spurred enormous social changes in postwar America.*

Mary Evelyn Porter
BERRY

Mary Porter grew up in Depression-era Arkansas. With the outbreak of World War II, she took a job in a defense plant that manufactured the pellets used to trigger the explosion of bombs. One day, she and a friend who traveled to the factory in the same carpool decided that they weren't really doing enough to help win the war, so they marched themselves down to a navy recruiting station to join up as Waves (Women Accepted for Volunteer Emergency Service) in May 1943.

Mary was sent to what she describes as a fairly "cushy" boot camp— Hunter College in New York City, where Waves from all over the country were given their basic naval training. Next she spent time in Norman, Oklahoma, training as an airplane mechanic, then was transferred to Millinton Air Force Base, in Tennessee, where she spent the rest of the war as an aviation machinist mate, third class.

Along with many of her coworkers, she was a bit disappointed not to be sent overseas, but her work refurbishing planes for operation on aircraft carriers did satisfy her desire to participate more directly in the war effort. She felt proud knowing that her work on aircraft engines was crucial to the safety of the American pilots.

In the spring of 1945, Mary got a new boss. His name was Gerald Grey Berry, machinist mate, first class. Previously he had served in the Pacific, stationed in Hawaii, and he had made a number of voyages to the South Pacific to work on planes damaged in the brutal battles to retake the Pacific islands. Gerry Berry transferred Mary from working on engines to patching wings. This new work involved a great deal of crawling around, but she liked it better because she didn't end each day covered in grease from head to toe.

Before long, Gerry and Mary started dating. The rules of courtship were quite different during World War II than they are today, when such a relationship would be prohibited in the military. Though she took plenty of ribbing from her coworkers—she was a hard worker and had formed many fast friendships with her fellow Waves long before Gerry arrived—she didn't run into any real animosity about her relationship with him.

Gerry and Mary dated for six months, and when they discovered they were due to be discharged simultaneously, they decided to get married on their last day in the navy. Dressed in their uniforms, with Mary wearing an orchid corsage, they went to downtown Memphis on December 15, 1945, to be wed by a minister in his office.

Both went to college on the GI Bill, and both also eventually took master's degrees. They had a son, whom they named Gary. Mary laughs about the family names. "Gerry Berry, Mary Berry, and Gary Berry—nobody who ever met us once ever quite forgot us."

Mary recalls with fondness the way Gerry would always tell the story of how they met. "I was washed over by a Wave," he would say. That good-natured joke hints at the profound social changes in relationships between men and women that the war put in motion. By joining the Waves, Mary became one of the pioneers in the evolution of the American armed forces as well as the creation of a vast range of new career opportunities for women.

In the years after the war, when Mary told people she had been in the navy, they always assumed she had been aboard a ship, and she always felt a little funny explaining that she spent the entire war in landlocked Tennessee. Though she had hoped and expected to be shipped overseas, she has never regretted in the slightest the work that she ended up doing. Not only did she play an important part in the war effort, she also met the man with whom she enjoyed fifty-four years of a wonderful marriage.

Lowell and Helen
BAKER

In May 1944, Lowell R. Baker was assigned to photo-mapping training with the army air force at Will Rogers Field near Oklahoma City. On the twenty-fourth, a cloudy, dreary day, he joined the regular crew of ten aboard a B-24, along with three ground personnel who needed to complete their flying hours for the month.

His plane was flying below cloud cover at an altitude of fifteen hundred to two thousand feet. Lowell was in the tail section, talking on the intercom with the pilot, when the plane made a simple regulation turn and suddenly the number-one engine, out of four, conked out. Moments later, to the crew's horror, both the number-two and number-three engines also died, and the pilot was left with very little control over the plane. He desperately tried to make it back to the base landing strip, but about a mile and a half short, the plane started diving down, heading toward a group of children picnicking in a schoolyard. The pilot banked sharply to the right to avoid them, then immediately banked sharply left to miss a barn across the street from the school. Now completely out of control, the plane took the top off of a huge mulberry tree as it crashed and catapulted across a field, wing over wing. The tail turret snapped off, and the five men in that section of the plane survived; the eight others were killed. An investigation showed that the plane had been filled with 91 octane instead of 100 octane fuel.

Helen Mondzak, a second lieutenant nurse assigned to the base hospital, heard sirens go off at around noon that day and knew there was trouble. Along with all the other off-duty nurses, she rushed to the hospital to lend a hand. Miraculously, two of the survivors were not badly injured, but the other three had suffered serious burns. Lowell was the one in the worst shape, with burns on his head, arms, and legs.

Helen was assigned to the ward in which all three men—Lowell, Roy Splawn, and George Connor—recuperated. Lowell was in critical condition in an oxygen tent, with his eyes bandaged. For days, he couldn't see the friendly woman who was caring for him. Later, during months of recuperation in the ward, where there was always lots of good-natured joking between the nurses and the men, he and Helen got to know each other well. Eventually, Lowell, Roy, and George were all released from the hospital, and they returned to training. "By that point in the war," Lowell recalls, "if you were breathing, they wanted you."

Not long after, Helen attended church with a friend one Sunday. Lowell and Roy were also attending that day, and they took seats right behind Helen and her friend. As part of the continual joking that went on in the hospital ward, Roy and George had regularly teased Lowell and Helen about getting married someday. As they all left church, Roy said to the two of them, "I didn't know it was going to be a church wedding." That evening, September 16, 1944, Helen and Lowell went on their first date. They remember the exact date because it happened to be Lowell's father's birthday.

They already knew each other so well that a serious relationship developed quickly. But because Helen was an officer and Lowell was a staff sergeant, they had to maneuver around the rules governing the behavior of officers and enlisted personnel. They couldn't be seen together in public places, so they met almost every weekend somewhere off the base, either at a friend's place in Oklahoma City, where they would have a meal and play cards, or at the home of Lowell's great-uncle Art and great-aunt Ina, who also lived in Oklahoma City.

Before long, they started talking about getting married, but in that "probably" and "eventually" way that was so common for many wartime couples. Then, in March 1945, Lowell got word that he would soon be sent to the western Pacific. One Saturday evening, Uncle Art asked Helen and Lowell what they were planning to do the following Saturday, and Lowell blurted out, "We're getting married."

Because Lowell was about to be sent overseas, the army air force looked the other way about the marriage, and also didn't inquire too closely into how the nurse and former patient had become prospective bride and groom.

Lowell and Helen were married by a Baptist preacher in Uncle Art and Aunt Ina's living room on March 24, 1945, and they spent a one-night honeymoon at a hotel in Oklahoma City. Three weeks later, Lowell left for the Pacific. That day he went to say good-bye to Helen at the ward, but then came back when his flight was delayed by fog. Before long the fog cleared, and just before his flight took off, he telephoned her to say one last good-bye. "It was hard enough saying good-bye," Helen remembers, "without saying it all day."

Lowell was assigned to the Fifty-fifth Weather Reconnaissance unit. They flew out of Guam, Iwo Jima, and Okinawa, and spent weeks flying reconnaissance for the B-29 bombers coming from the Mariana Islands on raids over Tokyo. As the U.S. forces planned a full-scale invasion of Japan to begin in November, President Truman approved the dropping of atomic bombs on Hiroshima and Nagasaki, on August 6 and 9, and the war came to an abrupt end.

Helen requested a discharge in October, which was granted, and she returned to her family home in New Jersey to await Lowell's return. They were reunited in Philadelphia on December 7, 1945. The nurse and patient who had once conspired to circumvent the rules could now fraternize in earnest: They had seven children who gave them eleven grandchildren and one great-grandchild. Helen says she feels they've been blessed to have fifty-six years of marriage. They now live happily in Austin, Minnesota.

Helen at her desk at
Will Rogers Field
Base Hospital in
November 1944.

The ruins of
Lowell's plane
after it crashed.

The tree that the plane
crashed through, with
the number–two propeller
lying on the ground
in front. The plane
catapulted another
hundred yards and
landed in an oat field.

Newspaper article reporting the crash.

Top: The exit hole at the back of the plane where the survivors exited. Bottom: The remains of the plane after the fire was put out.

Lowell and Helen on their fiftieth wedding anniversary, in June 1995, with their seven children (top to bottom row, left to right): Bryan, Bryce, Blaine, Bradley, L. Robert, Loann, and Linda.

EVEN IF A COUPLE SPENT SEVERAL *months getting to know each other, a decision to get married could be driven by sudden changes in circumstances. If both the man and the woman were in uniform, the possibility of reassignment any time made long-term planning difficult, and such orders sometimes led to spur-of-the-moment weddings that resembled the plots of those wildly popular prewar Hollywood screwball comedies.*

Eli and Bernice Fishpaw in 1944.

Eli and Bernice

FISHPAW

Bernice Newton joined the Army Nurse Corps in September 1942. "I had just finished a postgraduate course in operating-room procedure," Bernice recalls, "and was eager to get into action." But her first assignment at Fort Wayne in Detroit, Michigan, proved disappointing. The military garrison was a huge ordnance depot, but at the time it consisted of little more than a detachment. The hospital had only twenty beds and was more like an infirmary. Surgeries were "limited and boring." So, Bernice explains, "I had no sooner been issued my old-style blue uniforms and learned to salute than I requested a new assignment to go overseas."

In mid-March 1943, Bernice was assigned to the 222nd Station Hospital, which was training at Fort Jackson, South Carolina. It was there that Bernice was really turned into an army officer. "The first six weeks we were taught how to drill. When a group is in formation and doing close-order drill, it brings them together better than any other experience I have ever had." The nurses also learned military law, procedure, and survival. The latter training included gas drill, which Bernice hated. "The gas chamber was a squad tent in which tear gas was released. We had to enter before we were allowed to don the mask—so that we could experience the gas and the protection we received from the gas. Some people threw up, but I held my breath and that didn't happen to me." They were also issued field equipment and taught how to erect pup tents, make bedrolls, prepare meals, and clean mess gear in the field. "One little glitch was that our fatigue suits were one-piece coveralls and did not have any accommodation for people who sit down to relieve themselves. This presented an interesting problem when using a straddle trench. Fortunately it was summertime, and hot."

During this rigorous training, Bernice met Eli Fishpaw, who was a member of the 100th Infantry Division, newly activated and training just down the road. "One day word was spread that there was a second lieutenant artillery officer who needed a date, but since he had hurt his knee playing football, he couldn't dance. I had never learned to dance myself, so this seemed the perfect date for me. When we were introduced, I misunderstood his name. I heard Eli Fishball instead of Fishpaw. I really thought someone was putting me on."

The nurses' quarters stood directly across the street from the number-two station hospital, and the hospital officers' club was used for the dance. The club was air-conditioned, which was unusual, so it was a good place to spend an evening. "Since we were not dancing, and I really didn't care to drink very much, we spent most of the evening talking. What did we talk about? Eli talked about his howitzers. Being a farm girl who had tagged along with my father, and knowing a lot about machinery, I was actually interested. So before the evening was over, Eli had invited me to come to the gun park and see his howitzers. I don't think he actually expected me to do that, though. The next day, when I was walking down the road toward the 374th Field Artillery area where they were training, he saw me coming and quickly gave the order to close up the guns and knock off for the day. He hopped into a jeep and drove down the road to meet me. He asked me if I would like a ride in his jeep. Strangely enough, the ride took me straight back to the nurses' quarters."

Bernice and Eli continued to see each other all that summer. Eli even let Bernice borrow his car when he was out in the field. "I would tell the nurses that if they would get some gas ration coupons, we could go to one of the lakes on the post and have a swim." It wasn't difficult to collect coupons from the hospitalized soldiers, because the coupons usually expired before they were well. "So even though the car had twelve cylinders, we always had plenty of gas. This suited Eli, since the tank was often full when he returned to camp to reclaim his thirsty car."

Bernice continues, "By the end of the summer, Eli and I—or anyway,

I—had decided we should get married." The division was scheduled to go on maneuvers in December, and the 222nd had left for the Pacific without the nurses. Bernice felt in limbo. "One Saturday in November, Eli and I drove to Camden in the next county and purchased a marriage license. We could have been married there, but I thought it would be nice to get married by a chaplain, so we headed back to the post. But on the way we had to pass the University of South Carolina football stadium, and there was a game in progress, so we decided to wait until the next week to get married and went to the game instead."

While they waited out the week's postponement, they planned "to get a little fancy and invite the 374th officers and the 222nd nurses and leave the church under an arch of howitzers." Bernice even rented a small apartment off-post. "But the best of plans can go astray. On Tuesday, the 222nd nurses received orders. Were we going to join our hospital unit in the Pacific? No. We were to proceed to Camp Forrest, in Tennessee, to be the cadre for the 216th General Hospital unit. By our wedding day on Saturday, I was on the train to Tennessee."

But Bernice and Eli must have been destined to marry. Remarkably, shortly after Bernice left, Eli's 100th Division was assigned to Tennessee for maneuvers. "This made it possible for us to see each other on weekends. Eli has always insisted that he came to see me just to get a warm hotel room, but it might be pointed out that there were probably better rooms and more activities available for military men in Nashville than in Tullahoma."

Even if he had shown up only for the warm room, Eli and Bernice agreed once again to get married, in December. Because the courthouses were closed on weekends and Eli couldn't get away during the week, Bernice had to get the license. "Eli had the battalion surgeon give him a letter certifying that he was free of venereal disease, while I had the appropriate tests done on post and took the bus to Manchester, the county seat, to get the marriage license. However, the clerk would not issue this important document, because she could not accept Eli's letter." Fortunately, as was well known, the neighboring state of Georgia didn't require certificates of health to get a marriage license. And there was a small town—Rossville, Georgia—just over the state line that had a good reputation as a weekend marrying spot. Bernice and Eli decided to get married in Rossville on Saturday, January 1, 1944.

Surgery personnel who took calls on New Year's Eve could have the entire next day off, so Bernice volunteered. "It turned out to be an unusually busy night. The weather was at its worst, with a sleet storm in the mountains. We had five jeep accidents to worry about, most of them serious. This was very stressful for me, as I thought Eli was on the road traveling to Tullahoma. I had absolutely no sleep. The place was still jumping at seven in the morning, and I had not heard from Eli, so I continued to work until about ten, when I gave up and went to quarters and to bed thinking I had been stood up."

But at about noon, Bernice was wakened and told she had a phone call. "It was Eli. He had not been able to leave the battery the night before because all the other officers had departed and he was the only one left and had to stay. I caught the shuttle bus into town and met him at the King Hotel. He had had all the driving he wanted for that day, so we took a bus to Chattanooga. It was a very busy travel day, and the bus company had put on an extra bus that was old and tired. The driver was also the company mechanic, which I found somewhat reassuring. We left Tullahoma about three in the afternoon, heading into the storm and the mountains, where the roads got higher and narrower as we approached Chattanooga. The ancient bus would shift into low and, when I thought it was about to stall, would go into a still lower gear and chug on. It seemed to have an endless number of low gears. After getting to the top of each tortuous mountain, going down became much more exciting, as the bus preferred to do it sideways."

They finally arrived in Chattanooga about eight o'clock that night, with no idea of what to do next. "We found a taxi driver with an old-fashioned wooden leg who knew all about Rossville and 'Marrying Sam,' the character from the *Lil' Abner* comic strip. He drove us out to the Rossville city hall and accompanied us upstairs, where the mayor/justice of the peace was doing a thriving business. When it was our turn, our driver served as our witness. The ceremony, though short, was not totally meaningless as 'Hizzoner' read and we repeated the traditional vows. Eli tipped the driver twenty dollars."

The newlyweds decided to take the train back to Tullahoma. "We had a steak dinner—the steak was tough—with some wine in a restaurant at the train station. No cake. We caught the northbound train around midnight. It was packed. The coach we boarded was jammed with sailors returning to Great Lakes, near Chicago, from furloughs. There were sleeping sailors in the seats, sleeping sailors on the floor, even sleeping sailors in the overhead racks. The only place we could find to stand was on the platform between the cars. Even this was crowded. There must have been six or seven people who had just come aboard. One was an older lady, and she was given a duffel bag to sit on. While I was cold and tired after having worked twenty-seven hours, plus the stress of the day, I was too numb to care. Only when we went through a tunnel did we notice the inconvenience—we were showered with coal smoke."

Back in Tullahoma, Bernice and Eli made their way to the King Hotel, where he had rented a room on the fourth floor. "As we were climbing the stairs, I met an officer who was dating one of the nurses from the 222nd. I was embarrassed to be caught in a sleazy hotel at four in the morning and wasted no time announcing that we were married, even flashing our new certificate to prove it. But there were chores to be done before we could fall into bed. It was raining, and the ceiling was dripping water. This was solved when we found an old-fashioned chamber pot in the closet. There was a real bathroom, too. Eli decided he wanted to wash his underwear and fatigues, which we did in the bathtub, stomping them primitive-style with our feet and then spreading them on the radiator to dry. I didn't have to report for duty until noon, and Eli had to be back at the battery the following morning.

"And that," Bernice says, "is the story of how I met and married my husband of fifty-six years, Eli Fishpaw." She and Eli have recounted this and other adventures in a charming self-published book titled *The Shavetail and the Army Nurse: The Bride Wore Olive Drab.*

THE GREAT PORT CITIES OF
*America, from New York to San Francisco
and San Diego to Norfolk, were bustling
hubs of World War II activity, and no port was closer
to the war than Hawaii's Pearl Harbor. Due to its
strategic importance as the major staging point for
the Pacific war, there was a special intensity to life
there, and important visitors showed up regularly,
though not always with any warning.*

James and Virginia Cowart in 1944,
just before he left for sea duty.

James and Virginia
COWART

Virginia Melville grew up in Hawaii, where her father, who had fought in World War I, took a shipbuilding job after retiring from the navy in 1934. In the spring of 1942, Virginia temporarily dropped out of high school to participate in the war effort as a civilian employee in the Registered Publications Issuing Office. That November, several new young naval officers were assigned to her office. They were nicknamed "ninety-day wonders," referring to their accelerated three-month training courses. One of these young officers was Ensign James Cowart, and it didn't take long for Virginia to realize that "Mr. Cowart" had taken more than a casual interest in her.

"I ignored it," Virginia says. "I had never dated an officer. I assumed that they were staid and constrained. Was it because my father was a retired navy chief? I don't know, but I commented to a friend, 'I don't think they're as much fun as enlisted men.' It was unfair of me to form such a biased opinion, and I found out later that I was wrong."

One day, Ensign Cowart said to her, "I'd like to take you out, but I don't have a car. I wouldn't want to take a girl on a bus." Again, Virginia ignored the advance, and another day, when he repeated his comment about the bus, she decided he wasn't interested after all. What was so bad about taking the bus? He must just be using that as an excuse, she reasoned: "Huh, I have to ride the bus every day." In any case, Virginia was never at a loss for dates: In wartime Hawaii, women were far outnumbered by men.

A while later, Virginia returned to high school so she could graduate with the classmates she had known since the second grade. Like her, many had temporarily put their education aside to help in the war effort. Others had evacuated to the States, frightened of Hawaii's vulnerability. Many of the young men from her class were now in the military. In fact, Virginia's class size had decreased from 1,330 to 717 pupils. Still, she was glad to have the chance to finish high school with the promise of the job at Pearl Harbor after graduation. The job itself—correcting secret, confidential, and restricted coded publications sent out to the American and British Pacific fleet—made her feel she was doing something significant.

When she returned to her job at the Issuing Office after graduation, there was Ensign Cowart working in the front office along with several other young officers and enlisted men she had known from before. They gave her a hearty welcome, and Jim Cowart seemed especially glad to see her. Maybe he was interested after all?

For Virginia's nineteenth birthday in August 1943, a close friend collaborated with Virginia's parents to throw her a surprise party. Ensign Cowart was among the fifteen or so invited guests, and when it came time for Virginia to open her presents, he took her aside and told her that he would like to give her his present privately.

As they walked outside into the darkness of the standard regulation blackout, lit only by a partial moon, Virginia remembers thinking, "Uh-oh, what is he up to?" On the way out, they passed Virginia's parents and her sister in the kitchen, who gave them a puzzled look. When she opened the gift, she was overwhelmed to receive something so valuable from this young man whom she had never even dated. In the box was a beautiful cultured pearl necklace, which he promptly placed around her neck. She stammered an embarrassed thanks, and when they went back into the house, she felt the blood rush to her face as her family looked at her in wonderment. "I detected the 'hmmmm' in my mother's eyes," Virginia says, laughing.

About a month later, Ensign Cowart finally asked Virginia for a date. "He furnished some gas ration coupons so that he could borrow my father's car for a ride to Blow Hole and Waimanalo before having dinner at the Halekulani Hotel, where he presented me with a beautiful orchid corsage and intimated that he would love to be the first to take me to the

States. I had told him that I was only three when my family left Coronado, California, and that I didn't remember it at all. So he now told me about all the places he wanted me to see.

"After dinner we saw *Hello, Frisco, Hello,* with Alice Faye and John Payne, at the Waikiki Theater. We arrived home before dark and the start of curfew. Jim asked if he could kiss me. That 'old-fashioned girl' feeling came over me. I shudder now when I think of my reply. 'But I hardly know you, Mr. Cowart.' It sounded like a line from a movie!"

This was not a line Virginia would ever use again. "Those World War II navy officers worked fast," Virginia says with a chuckle. "We became engaged two dates later. I guess he had to live up to the title of 'ninety-day wonder.'"

Now that they were a couple, the mystery of the bus excuse was revealed. Jim finally resorted to taking Virginia on the bus for some of their dates, and he explained that he had been reluctant before because he'd worried that enlisted passengers would make remarks. Officers with dates on buses weren't exactly a common sight.

Though their courtship was very fast, they took their time planning the wedding, and Virginia Melville and Ensign James Cowart were married on July 19, 1944.

Virginia vividly remembers an incident about a week after their wedding that combined a patriotic thrill, high-stakes presidential diplomacy, and domestic comedy. At that time, General Douglas MacArthur and Admiral Chester Nimitz were locked in a dispute about how the war in the Pacific should proceed. MacArthur was in a strong position at the time, because he had directed the campaign to retake New Guinea—which was just coming to an end—with strategic brilliance. He favored retaking the Philippines, thereby making good on his famous promise, "I shall return." Admiral Nimitz, however, backed by the Joint Chiefs of Staff, wanted to bypass the Philippines and move on to capture Formosa. The dispute had become so tense that President Roosevelt flew to Hawaii to meet jointly with MacArthur and Nimitz. MacArthur disliked Roosevelt, both personally and politically, and the president well knew it, but this was an election year, and he agreed with MacArthur that Americans felt a moral obligation to the people of the Philippines. It took him a month to convince Nimitz and the Joint Chiefs to go along.

Virginia and Jim were having dinner with her parents during Roosevelt's visit to Hawaii when they heard sirens. "It was unlike the usual police siren," Virginia recalls. "It sounded more like a parade motorcade. That was it! I had heard that the president was in Hawaii to confer with top military officers. 'It's President Roosevelt!' I shouted excitedly. 'Hurry!' We all jumped up from the table and ran outside—Mom, Dad, my sister Betty, Jim, and I. The president of the United States was headed in our direction—right past 3828 Pake Avenue, the home of the Melville family. As he passed us in his shiny black open convertible—which would never be done now—less than fifteen feet away, he waved enthusiastically. 'Hi, President Roosevelt,' we shouted. He smiled, waved back, and returned our greetings. That moment was ours to share and remember always. The president of the United States had interacted with us alone. I had seen him when he made previous visits to Hawaii, but we were always in a crowd. When he waved then, it was to scores of people. This day no one else was around."

As they walked back to the house, Virginia's mother began laughing. "Look at Jim!" she cried. They all turned and saw that Jim still had his napkin tucked into the pants of his khaki uniform. "I'll bet that no one has ever greeted the president of the United States with a uniform like this," Jim chortled, looking down at himself.

Jim was sent to sea soon thereafter and missed his new wife terribly. He was comforted not only by her picture, which he kept in his locker aboard the U.S.S. *Pennsylvania,* but by several other vivid reminders of her that kept cropping up. As communications officer, he went over any coded publications, which were constantly being updated back at Pearl Harbor. Virginia, of course, was one of the people doing that job, and whenever she made a change, she had to initial it. Jim wrote to her, "I was surprised to discover that the general Signal Book I was using had been corrected by none other than 'VEM.' I told some of my shipmates about it and they were impressed. Since then I've come across your initials numerous times in various publications. Other than your beautiful picture, it's the next best thing to having you right here with me."

Virginia recalls, "I was extremely proud of the fact that publications I had corrected were being distributed throughout ships and shore bases in the Pacific. *My* publications were being referred to by U.S. and British

Right: Ensign James Cowart in November 1942. Below: Virginia Melville Cowart at age nineteen. Jim kept this photograph of her in his locker aboard ship.

TERRITORY OF HAWAII
CITY AND COUNTY
OF HONOLULU

NON-RESIDENT OPERATOR'S

PERMIT NO. **43079**

This is to certify that the person named and described below was issued a permit by the Examiner of Chauffeurs of the City and County of Honolulu, as a **AUTO GAS** Operator only under the provisions of Act 234, Session Laws of Hawaii 1937, for a period of 90-days from **8-23-43**

NAME **COWART Jas. Wm. Jr. LT. (jg)**
RESIDENCE ADDRESS **USNR**
LICENSE NO. **M 17073** STATE **Cal**

NON-RENEWABLE

Licensee must sign here in ink

Sgt J Ornellas
Examiner of Chauffeurs
City and County of Honolulu

LEFT Sec. E Row 9 Seat
WAIKIKI THEATER
Good Only
6:30 P. M.
SATURDAY SEPT. 18
AFTERNOON
WELDON, WILLIAMS & LICK, FT. SMITH, ARK.

Above: The driver's permit that Jim received just before his first date with Virginia, which allowed him to take her out in style instead of taking the bus. Right: The ticket stub from Hello, Frisco, Hello, *the movie Jim and Virginia saw on their first date.*

Jim and Virginia on their wedding day, July 19, 1944, in front of the Melville home in Honolulu, and their bridesmaids: Virginia's sister, Betty Ann (far right), Marian Kleinschmidt (next to Jim), and Barbara Donnell (next to Virginia).

V-Mail Christmas "card" from Jim and Virginia to his mother, sent December 9, 1944.

THIS CERTIFIES THAT

Virginia E. Melville
(VOID IF NOT SIGNED)

IS HEREBY AUTHORIZED TO WEAR THE NAVY "E" LAPEL BUTTON IN RECOGNITION OF MERITORIOUS WORK PERFORMED AS AN EMPLOYEE OF THE

U.S. Navy, Pearl Harbor COMPANY. PART OF
(FILL IN NAME)

THE BATTLE OF PRODUCTION IS BEING WON THROUGH YOUR EFFORTS AND THIS "E" BUTTON IS VISIBLE PROOF OF THE NAVY'S RECOGNITION OF YOUR ACCOMPLISHMENT. WEAR IT ALWAYS.

DATE *11/2/42* (SIGNED) *Frank Knox*
SECRETARY OF THE NAVY

The certificate Virginia received for her work during the war.

Jim and Virginia with their first child, daughter Shirley Ann, born on October 2, 1945, in the Chelsea Naval Hospital in Chelsea, Massachusetts.

Jim and Virginia on a trip to one of their favorite places, Honolulu, Hawaii, in 1988.

officers. The man I had married was using them on the U.S.S. *Pennsylvania* and wherever his duties took him."

James and Virginia Cowart have been married for fifty-six years and have two children and one granddaughter. (Unfortunately, they lost a grandson when he was twenty-four). "Jim kept his promise," Virginia says, "and showed me not only the States but the world. We settled in California, but Hawaii will always be home to me, and we return often for reunions, anniversaries, and vacations. We have Pearl Harbor and World War II to thank for bringing us together."

THE NONFRATERNIZATION RULES *designed to prevent officers and enlisted personnel from romantic involvement were applied very strictly on some bases, while on others, the senior officers looked the other way. There were also certain anomalies at work. While in training to become an officer, a young man could usually get away with dating an enlisted woman, particularly one in a different branch of the service. But once he was commissioned as an officer, the rules changed, and the resulting difficulties were sometimes comical, if not descending into outright farce.*

John Darr when he was an aviation cadet, in early 1944.
Angeline Brown Darr, yeoman second class, in 1943.

John and Angeline

DARR

In late 1943, John W. Darr was attending precadet training at the Army Aviation School of the Central Washington College of Education in Ellensburg, Washington. On Christmas, the students were given the day off. John and a friend were walking downtown that morning when they ran into a classmate and his girlfriend, who lived in town. She was having a party that night for friends who were home for the holidays, and because she was short of men, she asked John and his friend to come. They happily agreed.

At the party, John made particular note of the arrival of two very attractive Waves: a local girl and her roommate from Colorado. He found out later that they were both yeomen, stationed in Seattle at the Thirteenth Naval District Headquarters.

After some lively socializing, the entire party repaired to the local American Legion hall, where they spent the rest of the evening dancing and swapping life stories. John, by "great good fortune," selected Angeline Brown, the Wave from Greeley, Colorado, as his "date" for the evening. He had spent much of his youth on an Iowa farm and was fascinated by Angeline's very different background.

As their evening drew to a close, he asked his new friend for her address and promised to write to her. He knew another date anytime soon would be impossible; his outfit was just about to ship out to Santa Ana, California, for preflight training.

Over the next few months, John recalls, "a vigorous courtship evolved

155

via the mails, during which—contrary to all logic—we agreed to marry just as soon as I graduated from aviation cadet training. Summertime found me at Victorville Army Air Field, training to become a bombardier. As luck would have it, I became hospitalized. Upon learning of this, Angeline was granted leave to come to visit me."

John was released from the hospital while Angeline was there, and they were sorely tempted to get married right away. But they decided to be sensible and wait for his graduation.

"Graduation took place on Victorville's hot desert sands on Saturday morning, October 28, 1944," John recalls. Their wedding was scheduled for seven-thirty the following evening in Seattle's Prospect Congregational Church. "Both our mothers were in attendance," John relates, "plus a large contingent of U.S. Navy personnel. First among them was Captain Howard Berry, the fine old gentleman for whom Angeline served as yeoman and personal secretary. Because Angeline's father owned a large and very successful restaurant back in Greeley, and there was such a shortage of help during the war, it was impossible for him to take the time off to attend the wedding. So Captain Berry brought her down the aisle and 'gave her away.' Unfortunately, the navy could afford to do without Angeline's services for only a single day. Our honeymoon, therefore, took place at the famous and luxurious Olympic Hotel, today's Four Seasons, in downtown Seattle. The next morning's paper carried a small story about the wedding that appeared under the pithy headline 'Army-Navy Merger.'"

Then it was back to duty for them both. Angeline continued as secretary to the director of personnel, Captain Berry, until the war's end. John's duties took him first to Tonopah, Nevada, and then to Langley Field, Virginia, where he was trained in the B-24 Liberator bomber.

While John was at Tonopah, Angeline arrived for a week's visit. The base commander had instituted a strict nonfraternization policy between officers and enlisted personnel. There was also a regulation against military personnel wearing civilian clothing at any time, since material was difficult to procure. "These factors," John recalls, "combined to provide a few rather exciting moments as Angeline and I shared drinks with another couple at the Tonopah Club one evening.

"As might be expected, she was attired in her navy yeoman first class uniform, while I was obviously an army officer. A clear violation of the rules! Two military policemen discovered us together and promptly placed me under arrest. I explained (or was it complained?) that this young lady beside me was—'Believe me, Sergeant'—my wife. They were not convinced and took me into custody. Finally someone back at the air field was rousted out of bed to check my personnel records, where they found that, *indeed,* my wife was, *in fact,* an enlisted member of the U.S. Navy, and I was released from custody. Until proven otherwise, I claim to be the only person ever arrested for having been seen in public with his wife."

At the war's end, Angeline and John rejoined in Colorado, where he enrolled at the University of Colorado. Their first son, George, was born there in the summer of 1947. A second son, Steven, was born in 1952. John and Angeline now have four grandchildren and one great-grandchild.

"Angeline and I often reflect on our happenstance meeting, realizing that the odds against our having a satisfactory marriage were tremendous. But we've met and beaten those odds! We've done so, we believe, for a number of reasons: We take our obligations seriously, we try to be honest with ourselves and others, and we have both been endowed with a damning conscience. We love and respect each other greatly as we face the future from the perspective of these 'golden years.'"

Angeline and John on the day of their wedding in 1944.

Two "broken heart" pins, which John and Angeline bought before their wedding. Each of them wore one, out of sight under a lapel, until they were back together for good after the war.

Left: The army air force shoulder patch, in bullion as opposed to the more common plain cloth design. Right: The navy Waves collar insignia pin.

Angeline and John on their fiftieth wedding anniversary in 1994.

FOR MEMBERS OF THE ARMED services who left sweethearts or wives at home, or who had fallen in love in one part of the world only to be yanked suddenly to another, one of the primary obstacles was wartime transportation. No matter the mode—car, bus, train, or plane—all you could really count on was a problem. With cars, you had to scrape together enough ration coupons to buy gas. Buses always ran late. Trains were jammed. And your seat on an airplane could be commandeered by someone of higher rank. But young lovers found ways to get together, even if their trip required an unscheduled stop in the middle of nowhere.

Louis and Judy Funderburg while waiting for
Sunday dinner, which cost $1.60 for two, at
Mrs. Ketchem's Boarding House in Americus, Georgia.
They saved all week.

Louis and Judy
FUNDERBURG

Judy Underwood and Louis Funderburg had their first date in 1942, when she was still a high school student in Nashville, Arkansas. Louis had graduated from the same school the year before and was working at a defense plant in Texarkana, Texas. They dated for a while before Louis joined the navy, and they kept in touch by letter after he left. But their relationship was not exclusive. Judy dated other young men, and one day she wrote him a Dear John letter to say that she thought she would be marrying another man. As she recalls, "When I wrote him that letter, he came unglued. He wrote back and told me I had better forget that guy because *he* was the one I was going to marry." After several more persuasive letters, he won Judy over, and they became engaged by letter. Louis wrote to her that he would give her a ring when he could put it on her finger.

By early December 1944, Louis had been in the navy for two years. For the past year he had been serving on an oil tanker, shuttling oil from Aruba and Curacao in the Gulf of Mexico, through the Panama Canal to New Guinea and Darwin, Australia. He had served enough time to be eligible for a thirty-day leave, and while his ship was anchored at the canal, his commanding officer managed to find a replacement for him and get him the leave. Louis hoped he could get home to spend the Christmas holiday with his family. He and two other shipmates with leave left the ship, which was docked on the Pacific side of the canal. Their navy unit had a base in New Orleans, and they expected they would be transported there to get their leave papers. But they had no such luck.

Instead, they were sent on the Panama railway to a small naval base on the Caribbean side of the canal. There they waited for three days, checking constantly about their transportation to the States. Finally, a soldier found them and told them to follow him. They thought they'd be getting on a plane to New Orleans but were shocked to find they were being led to an LST [landing ship, tank] ship, a transportation ship for tanks that was heading for San Pedro, California. The first thing the ship did was pass through the canal, back to the side Louis and his friends had just come from, which took another whole day.

Once through the canal, Louis and the others had to help load supplies and fuel, and then they were finally on their way to the States. As luck—or their lack of it—would have it, a terrible storm hit the ship off the coast of Central America. An LST was not made for riding out such storms, and some of the crew even joked, "Let's open the doors [doors at the front of the vessel that swung open to unload tanks on beaches] and sink so we can get survivor's leave." To make matters even worse, one of the crew suffered an attack of appendicitis, and the LST had to steam to a port in Guatemala to get him medical care.

Finally, after twenty-one days on the LST, they reached San Pedro. Louis quickly looked into transportation from there and realized he would not quite be able to make it home for Christmas. He sent a telegram to Judy, asking her to meet him the day after Christmas in Texarkana. Because Texarkana bordered four states and hosted a large military base, it was a busy crossroads for thousands of men in all branches of the service. Louis decided to hitchhike to Texarkana, which was usually faster than taking buses during the war years, and almost any traveler would give a lift to a man in uniform.

He made such good time that he arrived way ahead of schedule, and rather than just wait around for Judy to arrive, he decided to take a bus to Arkansas. According to the schedule, he would arrive well before Judy left.

But the bus fell further and further behind schedule as the trip wore on, and by the time Louis got to Arkansas, he realized he had a problem. Judy had surely left for Texas—they would end up passing each other somewhere along the highway! He went up front and explained his plight to the driver. They were traveling along Highway 71 near Ashtown, Arkansas, and Louis calculated that if they could stop in Ashtown, the timing should be right to catch Judy's bus stopping there on its way west. Though this sounded like a good plan, the driver said that the stop for Ashtown was outside of town, on the highway, and he didn't think Judy's westbound bus would necessarily be stopping there. But he agreed to stop and try to flag down Judy's bus as it went by.

Sure enough, the bus from Nashville soon pulled into sight, and the driver put his arm out the window to hail it. The bus came to a stop, and Louis's driver called across to ask if there was a Judy Underwood on board. Sitting halfway back, Judy was startled when her driver called out her name, and cried out, "Yes, I'm here!" She rushed to the front of the bus, while Louis hopped off of his, and they bolted toward each other, meeting in the middle of Highway 71, where they embraced passionately to the loud cheers and whistles of the passengers aboard both buses.

Louis and Judy had decided that they would put off their wedding until he was out of the service, but their ardent reunion in the middle of Highway 71 prompted them to tie the knot right away. They climbed aboard the bus Louis had been traveling on, returned to Nashville, and were married at the home of a friend on New Year's Day, 1945.

Louis returned to his ship when his thirty-day leave ended. Judy had no idea how long it would be before she would see him again. Then, in early August of 1945, Louis's ship came into port briefly at Oakland, California, just north of San Francisco, and he cabled for Judy to come and visit. His ship was scheduled to return to sea on August 15, so after a wonderful but all too short visit, Judy returned to Arkansas on August 14, which turned out to be Victory in Japan Day. That afternoon, Louis heard the report that Emperor Hirohito had announced Japan's surrender in a radio broadcast. All aboard ship had been granted liberty until nine the next morning, and Louis decided to head to downtown San Francisco to take part in the huge celebration he was sure would be going on.

Louis wrote Judy a letter describing the celebration vividly:

Well, I couldn't resist going to Frisco. I know Frisco would celebrate in an all-out fashion. At first I wondered if I had done the right thing

Louis and his friend Glen Broomfield before they left Panama in November 1944.

Louis aboard the LST that took him on his circuitous journey from Panama to San Pedro.

*The cover of a coupon
book issued to Louis for
commissary meals at the
Panama Canal.*

*Louis and Judy having fun in Juarez,
Mexico, in 1943.*

*Louis and Judy at home,
Christmas 2000.*

or not, because from what I saw in Oakland, it was getting pretty rough. I could hardly believe my eyes. Most of the service men were kissing any woman they could get their hands on. Everyone was exchanging hats and clothes, and you might think it was a panic. . . . I wish you could have been with me, but still it wouldn't have been safe for you, because I know I wouldn't have stood for all those guys kissing you. . . . Some was the fault of the women, because I saw lots of them go up and kiss service men who weren't even drinking. . . . I walked to First and Market and the people had completely taken over Market Street. . . . The streetcar rail-guards had been broken off and every few feet I was stumbling over them or boxes and signs. . . . fire crackers were going off—some sounded like bombs. I was afraid one might land too close for comfort and later a few did come pretty close. . . . I walked down close to Fifth and there was a big bonfire in the middle of the street. They were burning everything they could find—War Bond booths, paper stands and flower stands. Almost everyone had a bottle, most of them partially gone. I saw one sailor drop a bottle almost full. He and his buddy were standing there weeping over it as if it were his dead mother. . . . People were climbing the tallest buildings—to the tenth and fifteenth stories. The statue of Franklin, close to Market and Stockton streets, was climbed, too. A Marine stood on top, holding a flag. . . . I took refuge in a USO to have a cup of coffee. There were plenty of drunks there—the celebration was in full session in the USO. There was a room for enlisted men and one for officers who had passed out, and they were stacking them up—loaded to the gills. . . . I was on the street slightly over two hours and I can say I've never seen such entertainment anywhere. . . . I know I'll never forget what I've seen, and there are millions like me.

Louis and Judy Funderburg celebrated their fifty-fifth wedding anniversary on New Year's Day, 2000, which Louis describes with a chuckle as "a good start" to a next century.

BEFORE WORLD WAR II, PARENTAL approval was widely regarded as necessary for a respectable marriage. Of course, some couples eloped in order to circumvent disapproving parents, but that usually led to a trail of gossip. The war changed these rules. Every day, all across America, young people who had known each other only a few months, weeks, or even days rushed off to get married, and in many instances, parents didn't even know about the relationship. But then there were quite different cases in which a parent—or grandparent—was actually the first to know that a wedding was about to happen, even before the bride and groom did.

Hugh and Maudie Owens on their wedding day,
December 19, 1945, in San Francisco.

Hugh and Maudie

OWENS

Maudie Matthews was attending Utah State University in 1942, away from her hometown, and living with her grandmother. A women's group on campus organized many social events to make soldiers in the area feel more at home, and one day Maudie was talked into attending one of these events. She found it terribly boring and vowed never to go to another. But when the quarter ended, most of the young women on campus headed home for the break, and with such a shortage of women left on campus for social functions, she was persuaded to do her duty and make one more appearance.

This time things were more lively, particularly after Hugh Owens, a marine who was attending radio material school at the college, struck up an engaging conversation with her. They had a wonderful time dancing, even though, as Maudie found out later, Hugh didn't really like to dance and had made a special effort because he was so taken with her. Despite restrictive rules for young women on campus regarding how to behave with young military men, when Hugh asked Maudie for her telephone number, she decided to give it to him.

Hugh called her the very next day and asked her to dinner that evening. She was pleased to hear from him, especially so quickly, and she suggested that they go to a nice restaurant in town called the Bluebird. They had such a good time that she started seeing Hugh regularly.

Maudie's grandmother, a tiny woman with a strong personality, was generally dismissive of young men who tried to court Maudie, but she liked Hugh immediately. He came to dinner on Sundays, and almost every week, Maudie's grandmother baked her special chocolate pie for him. "Grandmother also made beautiful quilts," Maudie remembers, "and one day I noticed that she was working on a new one." When Maudie asked her who the quilt was for, "she looked up at me and said, 'Why, you and Hugh, eventually.'" Maudie remembers thinking that her grandmother was getting a little ahead of things, but perhaps not all that much.

After Hugh finished radio material school, he was assigned to Treasure Island, off the coast of San Francisco, for another five months of training. While he was still in the U.S., Hugh wrote regularly, but when he shipped out to the South Pacific, his letters dwindled. She understood that: There was a war on, after all, and mail from the South Pacific took even longer to reach the States than mail from the European theater.

Back in Utah, Maudie grew restless and decided to join one of the services. She chose the navy—in large part, she now admits, because she thought the Waves had the prettiest uniforms. Maudie's mother wasn't exactly enthusiastic about the idea, but she finally agreed it would be all right as long as Maudie wasn't sent overseas; at that point in the war, Waves were not being sent for overseas postings.

Before making her final decision, Maudie also wrote Hugh a letter to ask him what he thought. Weeks went by without reply, so she decided to go ahead and sign up.

Like many other Waves, Maudie was sent east to New York's Hunter College for boot camp, then was assigned to San Francisco for training as a recruiter. After several months in San Francisco, she was assigned to a recruiting post in Salt Lake City, Utah. Ironically, she finally heard back from Hugh, who gave her the "go-ahead," and she was pleased to know he approved of the decision she'd long since made.

By this time, Hugh was assigned to the Twelfth Anti-Aircraft Battalion at Pearl Harbor. From there, his battalion was shipped out to Townsville, Australia, a major staging point for the war in the South Pacific. Subsequently, the battalion was stationed at Woodlark Island to protect the construction crew building an airstrip there. After that, they moved on to New Guinea, where a major front was opened against the Japanese in April 1944. Luckily for Hugh, he missed most of the difficult fighting in New Guinea because he had applied for officer training and was shipped back to the U.S.

Two openings for officer's positions in his battalion had come up, one as a warrant officer and the other as a second lieutenant. Both Hugh and a friend applied, and because the friend was too old to be commissioned as a second lieutenant, he ended up with the warrant officer's position and stayed with the battalion, while Hugh got the second lieutenant spot and was sent to Quantico, Virginia, for "ninety-day-wonder" officer's training.

After Hugh received his officer's commission, he was given three weeks' leave, and he went to visit his family in Topeka, Kansas. Maudie was delighted to receive a letter from him asking if she could come see him there, which meant that their relationship was becoming more serious. Maybe her grandmother had been right after all.

Because Maudie hadn't taken any leave yet, she had no trouble getting the time; but her trip to Topeka and back was a roundabout journey, to say the least. First she took the train from Salt Lake City to San Francisco to collect her leave papers. Then she headed back across the country to Topeka, where she stayed with Hugh's sister, who treated her wonderfully. On her return, she traveled all the way back to San Francisco before finally heading to Utah. Understandably, she was thoroughly sick of train travel by the time her leave was over.

But the trip was well worth the effort. Sure enough, during her stay, Hugh proposed, and Maudie immediately accepted. Hugh was being stationed in Hawaii right after his leave, and he busily set about buying Maudie an engagement ring, which he promised he'd send before he left.

When she returned to Utah, Maudie was reassigned to a new town, Ogden, where, as was typical for recruiters, she worked out of the main post office. Of course she shared her good news with her recruitment colleagues and the postal workers, and told them she was expecting her engagement ring in the mail. But then she waited day after day for the package from Hugh with no sign. To her chagrin, one of the male recruiters took to kidding her about whether or not the package would ever show up. Finally, after he apparently felt the joke had gone on long enough—maybe too long, Maudie thought—he handed her the package, which he had spotted when it arrived and had been hiding from her.

Back on Hawaii, Hugh had been assigned to administrative duties, but in mid-1945, he suddenly got the word that he was on draft to be sent to China. Luck prevailed for him once again, however, when his doctor recommended that he go in for a minor surgical procedure before heading overseas. For some reason that Hugh still can't comprehend, he was kept in the hospital for forty days after the procedure. By the time he was released, not only was his tour of duty up, but the war was over. Instead of heading to China, he was sent back to the mainland to be mustered out in Great Lakes, Michigan.

Hugh and Maudie were married on December 19, 1945, in San Francisco, where Maudie had been sent after her assignment in Ogden. Their most prized wedding gift was from Maudie's grandmother: the double-ring quilt she had started making early in Maudie and Hugh's relationship. They used the quilt for so many years that their two sons, Parker and David, were grown men by the time the quilt was in its final decline.

Hugh in his Marine Corps uniform, before he received his officer's commission.

Hugh, now a second lieutenant, in his new officer's uniform, with Maudie in her Waves uniform and his parents, Evelyn and Park, at their home in Topeka.

Hugh and Maudie on a cruise through the Panama Canal in March 1996.

ONE OF THE STRIKING FEATURES *of the World War II experience is the role that chance played, both in the fates of those soldiers fortunate enough to survive the bullets and bombs, and in so many of the brief encounters that sparked lifelong romances. For the soldiers, they could never know when they might find themselves under fire; but on the other hand, they might be lucky enough to find themselves mysteriously selected for special attention by a young woman making the most of her opportunities for finding Mr. Right.*

Harold and Adelle Jensen on their wedding day,
November 6, 1943.

Harold and Adelle

JENSEN

Harold Jensen joined the army in 1939 because, as he says, "the Depression was on and we couldn't get jobs. We were also too poor to go to school other than high school, and the military was advertising with posters saying 'We Want You,' so I joined." A year later, on January 9, 1940, he joined the army air corps and a month after that was assigned to Hickam Field at Pearl Harbor, as a mechanic and crew chief on a B-18 bomber. Hawaii was a great posting because of the beautiful weather, but Harold recalls that the trip to the islands, which now is a relatively easy flight, took him a full month, including passage through the Panama Canal. Harold had always dreamed of being a pilot, and after a year and a half, in July 1941, he applied and was accepted for pilot training. He was still awaiting transportation back to the States for training when, on December 7, at 7:53 in the morning of yet another gorgeous Hawaiian day, the first wave of squadron after squadron of Japanese bombers—353 in all—swooped down on Pearl Harbor, taking the forces there and at the nearby airfields by surprise. Harold recalls that "they just blew the devil out of us."

Although the greatest loss of life in the attack took place in the harbor itself, especially on the battleships *Arizona* and *Oklahoma*, Hickam Field was also hard hit. One bomb landed directly on the mess hall at the field, where thirty-five pilots were eating breakfast, and killed them all. The planes at the field, parked wingtip to wingtip, were sitting ducks for the Japanese bombers, and eighteen were destroyed before they could get off the ground.

Harold was awakened by the attack when a bomb hit the building next to his barracks. He remembers thinking that "it was the navy goofing off," running fire drills. But when a bomb crashed through the roof of his barracks just minutes later, he realized the attack was for real. As the crew chief of his bomber, his primary responsibility was for the safety of the plane, and he rushed to the hangar to find that a bomb had exploded right next to his plane. "You know, it was full of holes," he recalls, "but we took it out and patched it up later on." He also remembers that the Japanese planes were trying to shoot down an American flag atop a flag-pole, swooping down low over the barracks in repeated attempts. "They were strafing, too," he recounts, "and there were lots of guys laying around. Most of them dead." Harold started helping move men from the hangar to the medical facility on the base, and while he was assisting one man, a close friend of his, a bomb hit only about forty feet away, throwing Harold against the wall of the hangar. Shrapnel from the bomb tore into his arm, but Harold kept moving men. Many men lost most of their hearing temporarily from of the incredibly loud noise of the bombs.

Because Harold was one of the few soldiers on base who had access to a truck, he was sent to a nearby army post, Fort Kamehameha, to bring back stretchers. On his way back, he saw a Japanese plane fixing its sights on him, and he rushed out of his truck. "He was zeroing in on me, I'll guarantee you, because anything that moved, they'd strafe." Harold was shot in the shin. Not only was he worried that he would no longer be able to go to flight school, he was even more anxious about the (unfounded) rumors that the Japanese coated their bullets with poison. He was laid up in the hospital for several weeks after the attack.

Despite his worries, he was not prohibited from flight school, though he had to wait many more months before he could start. Finally, in July he left for the States for his training, after which he was assigned as a flight instructor in cargo gliders at an airbase in Lubbock, Texas. A few weeks after he arrived, an epidemic of trench mouth hit the flight line. A number of soldiers, including Harold, went to the base dental clinic for treatment. When Harold showed up for his first treatment, he was quite taken with the receptionist, a very pretty blonde. He'd been told there were a lot of pretty young women in Texas, and this receptionist "certainly fit the bill." But he also noticed that she was wearing an engagement ring, so he kept his interest to himself.

A few days after his first treatment, Harold had to report back to the dental clinic for additional care. The same receptionist greeted him warmly. He made note, with surprise, that she was no longer wearing the engagement ring, and wondered what the story was. After a few more days, he received notice of yet another appointment, and this time he managed to find out that the receptionist's name was Adelle Taylor.

When he had been called back several more times for clinic appointments, Harold began to wonder just what was going on. As far as he could tell, his trench mouth was fully cured. But he didn't much mind, because every time he went to the clinic, he had the chance to chat with the beautiful Adelle Taylor, and he was finally emboldened to ask her for a date. She quickly accepted. They got along wonderfully, and before long, Adelle confessed that she had been attracted to him from the start and had set him up. Turns out that the dental hygienist at the clinic was a good friend of hers and had agreed to keep Harold coming back for treatments that weren't really necessary. Adelle had also taken the precaution of checking Harold's medical file to see if he was married; in the past, she explained, a couple of soldiers had lied to her about their marital status.

Harold and Adelle dated very happily for several months, but then he got word that a search-and-rescue squadron was being formed in Denver, and he felt the call to volunteer. He thought this work was truly important and didn't want to pass up such an opportunity. His transfer might have spelled the end of their time together, but just before he left, Harold asked Adelle if she would wait for him—for who knew how long—until they could be married. She accepted, and when he gave her an engagement ring, she promised to keep this one on.

Their wait, as things turned out, wasn't long at all. Immediately upon arriving in Denver, Harold was informed that the new squadron had been canceled, and he was happily reassigned to Lubbock. He and Adelle were married there in November 1943. "We've been on our honeymoon ever since," Harold now quips. While many servicemen during World War II met their wives while recuperating in hospital wards, Harold figures there

Harold while in pilot school in 1942.

Harold living it up on Waikiki Beach in Honolulu in 1941.

Harold and Adelle as proud parents in Lubbock, Texas, in 1944.

The envelope carrying a letter from Adelle to Harold while he was serving combat duty in the Korean War, which apparently went through quite a few hands and took two months to reach him.

Harold and Adelle on their fifty-sixth wedding anniversary.

aren't many who can say there were brought together by a suspiciously lingering case of trench mouth.

After the war, he stayed in the service and retired as a career officer in the United States Air Force after twenty-two years of active duty, a good part of that overseas. He completed one combat tour during the Korean War, as well as two other overseas tours, including one in Taiwan, for which Adelle and their two sons joined him. After retiring from the air force, Harold worked at the White Sands Missile Range as a civil service range controller engineer for an additional seventeen years, retiring for good in 1978. Married for fifty-seven years, the couple still lives in New Mexico.

WOMEN CERTAINLY WEREN'T *the only ones who knew how to make the most out of a chance encounter.* *So many men and women met during the war purely by accident, spent a pleasant enough hour or so together, and then, despite the attraction they might feel, never saw each other again. But for some lucky couples, the hand of fate brought them together again. The question whether such a second meeting was really the work of fate, or was cleverly orchestrated, was an issue they were happy to leave a mystery.*

*Marjorie and Jack Vaira shortly after they became
engaged, while vacationing at the seafront resort
town of Torquay in April 1944.*

Jack and Marjorie

VAIRA

Marjorie Vaira was born in Plymouth, England, on the coast of Devon, in May 1924. She grew up in this most southerly of England's important channel ports, from which the Pilgrims sailed to America in 1620.

The Battle of Britain raged from July to October 1940, but Plymouth escaped the worst of the damage. In the spring of 1941, though, Hitler ordered two direct bombing attacks on Plymouth, each of which lasting for three days. These attacks were partly in retaliation for a recent rash of deadly bombings of German U-boats; three of the submarines sunk by the Brits had been captained by personal favorites of Hitler. During the second assault, Marjorie's home was destroyed, forcing the seventeen-year-old and her mother to take shelter with relatives for several months. In September, Marjorie's mother managed to buy a house in South Brent, an inland village of about two thousand people.

Then eighteen, Marjorie found a job with the British War Department Land Agency, which had also moved inland from the virtually destroyed Plymouth. The agency's function was to requisition land to house the American and British troops who were gradually being assembled for the coming invasion of Europe. Marjorie was accustomed to a rather exciting city life and quickly realized she would have to make a special effort to entertain herself in this inland village. So she was happy enough to volunteer some evenings at the canteen established by the British counterpart of America's USO.

On the night of January 11, 1944, Marjorie was walking the half mile from her home to the canteen in a heavy downpour when she saw two murky "shapes" in the night. Slightly worried, Marjorie called out a good evening. Two voices, which seemed friendly enough, replied.

Shortly after Marjorie got to the canteen, she saw two American officers enter, and soon recognized their voices as those of the shapes in the darkness. The officers, whose unit had arrived only that morning, asked what entertainment was available in South Brent. Then the officer who did most of the talking offered Marjorie a challenge. "I hear you English can't make coffee," he said. Marjorie couldn't let his comment pass and coyly replied, "You can come home with me, and my mother and I will make you some." Both of the officers accepted and walked her home. When they left, after coffee and pleasantries, it occurred to Marjorie that she might never see either of them again.

Fate would not allow that. The next morning, Marjorie found a leather glove on the outside doormat. At work, she managed to get the telephone number of the camp where the officers were stationed. She told the soldier who answered the phone about the found glove, but she couldn't remember the name of the lieutenant who had left it. She knew simply that his last name began with a "V." That's all she needed to know. The soldier knew it had to be Lieutenant Vaira—the only man in the place with a last name starting with "V." Marjorie asked the soldier to tell Lieutenant Vaira that he could collect his glove at her house if he wanted it back. That evening, Jack Vaira returned to her house to claim his glove and laid claim to her heart as well.

Jack's battalion, the 149th Engineer Combat, was stationed at South Brent for just ten days, after which they were transferred to Paignton, about twenty-five miles away. Jack and Marjorie saw each other only on weekends and had to travel by train to do so. Marjorie remembers that the last train left Paignton at nine P.M. "Not very romantic," she comments dryly.

Early in April, after just four months of dating, Jack asked Marjorie's father for permission to marry her. Her father agreed, and Jack and Marjorie considered themselves engaged, even though Jack had not yet been able to secure a ring. Later in April 1944, all troops were sequestered in preparation for D-Day. Marjorie did not see Jack again for nearly a year.

Jack was in the first wave of troops to land on Omaha Beach, where the greatest number of casualties occurred. The troops had great difficulty getting tanks and artillery onshore; once they were ashore, the best defending German division lay in wait for them, aided considerably by the surrounding cliffs and steep dunes. Marjorie would not know how terrible D-Day had been until much later, but luckily, Jack survived it.

Once Omaha Beach was secured, the American forces, somewhat miraculously, received a mail delivery. Jack had been waiting for a small package, which he finally got. He met with the captain of a ship that carried supplies to Omaha Beach from Plymouth, and asked him if he could take the package back to England and see that it was delivered.

In early August, Marjorie arrived home for lunch to find two American sailors waiting for her. Their captain had dispatched them from Plymouth during a layover to deliver Jack's package: In it were Marjorie's engagement and wedding rings.

In a letter, Jack told Marjorie that he had been promised the first leave after the war ended. His colonel kept his word, and Jack finally returned to England on Saturday, May 12, 1945. He and Marjorie wanted to be married at once, but first they had to get a license. Also, Marjorie had agreed to take the female lead in a local drama-society production of *Poison Pen*. How could she have known the war would end when it did? Her acting group was too small to have understudies, so Marjorie had to go on.

On May 17, the show's last night, Marjorie and Jack were married at three-forty-five P.M. that afternoon (the latest hour a wedding could be performed). Jack sat in the audience for Marjorie's final performance. "I believe he was as much 'on show' as I was," Marjorie says with a laugh, since everyone in town knew about the wedding. After wildly applauding his brand-new wife at the last curtain, Jack set off with Marjorie on their honeymoon.

Jack served for a year in the army of occupation in Germany, where Marjorie joined him. In 1947 they returned to America together on the troop ship *Willard A. Holbrook*.

They lived with great happiness until Jack's death in 1988. But Marjorie never did figure out the answer to one important question: She never found out whether Jack left that glove on her doorstep on purpose.

Jack and fellow officers on the seafront after their arrival at Paignton. Left to right: Captain Shumaker; Lieutenant Brown; Jack; and Lieutenant Romanek, the "coffee taster."

Jack with a "four-footed French friend" on Omaha Beach, after the army had secured it.

Jack and Marjorie just after their wedding ceremony in front of the South Brent Methodist Church, on May 17, 1945.

Jack and Marjorie aboard the Willard A. Holbrook on their way to the United States in July 1947.

Jack and Marjorie, at left, during a reunion of the 149th Engineer Combat Brigade in Kansas City with Beryl Newell and his wife, Laura, the only other bride from South Brent of a 149ther.

ROMANCE BROKE AS MANY HEARTS *as it sent soaring during World War II. Men fighting battles around the world saw so many friends wounded or killed that they became fatalistic about their own physical well-being. They came to see the fighting itself as a kind of lottery. You did your best and you either ended up lucky or you didn't. But while they may have become inured to the possibility of physical danger, many could not so easily escape the profound dread of a Dear John letter arriving from a sweetheart or a wife back home, announcing that a new love had entered their lives. And of course, the women back home often worried their man might find someone else to love in a busy port or bombed-out city halfway around the globe. But more often, it came to pass that romance, even that of fairy-tale proportions, was undone not by the fickleness of love but by one unlucky shell on the battlefield.*

*Eddie Swauger and Catherine Roberts leaving the Church
of St. Mary the Virgin on the Tidworth House grounds
after their wedding ceremony on February 19, 1943.*

Catherine M.

ROBERTS-SWAUGER

When Catherine Roberts first tried to join the women's auxiliary air force of England's Royal Air Force in the summer of 1941, her recruiting officer, a gray-haired flight sergeant with a pencil mustache, threw up his hands in bewilderment. Her papers said she was an American, and Americans were not allowed to join the WAAF. The young woman in the smart gray suit protested vehemently. Although she had been born in America to an American couple, she had been adopted by a Welsh couple and raised in Wales, and she thought of herself as Welsh. Besides, she pointed out, everyone knew there were lots of Americans in the RAF—which was true. Many young Americans who had wanted to join the war against Hitler before the United States officially entered had traveled to Canada in hopes of circumventing the rules. The recruiter explained to Catherine that those Americans were now considered Canadians, so Catherine's protests went unheeded.

Catherine had been born in Boston, Massachusetts, on March 4, 1920, to a German-American paperhanger named Barnard Abbot and his bride, Amanda, a Penobscot Indian. Six months later, the couple gave her up for adoption to Griffith and Dora Roberts. Griffith born in Wales, had run away to sea at thirteen, seen much of the world, joined the U.S. Navy in 1890, and fought in the Spanish-American War. He returned to Wales to see his family and stole the beautiful Dora from all the local Lotharios. He returned to America in 1910 with Dora as his bride. He served in the

U.S. Navy during World War I, then retired from the navy after twenty-eight years' service.

Dora had five miscarriages, and Catherine's adoption in 1920 brought the couple great happiness at last. In 1926, Griffith felt the pull of home once more, and he and Dora returned for good to the coastal town of Penryhyndeudraeth, Wales, with their adopted American daughter.

As a grown woman, Catherine became determined to play a real part in the war, even if her complicated origins made things difficult. She harassed both the British Air Ministry and the American embassy until she was finally told to write to General Dwight D. Eisenhower, who was visiting England in an advisory capacity. Her letter actually generated a response, and at last she gained permission to apply for enrollment in the WAAF. She reported to the RAF at Bridgnorth, Gloucestershire, on December 12, 1941—five days after Pearl Harbor brought the United States into the war.

Catherine found the next eight months quite intense. She had to withstand the rigors of training, including a daunting solo introduction to the use of a gas mask in a claustrophobic chamber. And she had adventures that she would remember for a lifetime. Late one drizzly afternoon, she stepped into a warm upscale pub. An American officer noticed the U.S.A. insignia on her British uniform and asked about it. She was surprised that he did not introduce himself—she'd noticed that Americans usually did the moment you met them. He did look awfully familiar, though she couldn't think quite why. When another American officer strolled up to join them, the answer hit her with quite a jolt: The strolling army air force colonel was unmistakably the lanky Jimmy Stewart, who'd starred in so many of her favorite movies; and the man with the big grin she had been talking to, she suddenly realized, was none other than Clark Gable.

Amid all the excitement of training and meeting soldiers from all over the world, Catherine was having some romantic difficulties. Two old flames, Jamie and William, had a hold on her heart, and both were in love with her. Yet her feelings toward them seemed to depend on which one she happened to be with at a particular moment, or whose letter she held in her hand.

In August 1942 she had an experience that made the decision for her—and changed her life forever. One morning, she saw an invitation to a dance posted on the notice board: "All ranks of the WAAF at RAF Old Sarum are invited to a dance to be held at Tidworth House, the ancestral home of the Duchess of Marlborough, this coming Saturday evening. Transport there and back will be provided by the U.S. Army. All who wish to avail themselves of this invitation are to assemble at the Guardroom at 1900 hours." Catherine decided to go. Tidworth House, she knew, had been lent to the American Red Cross as its headquarters, with Mrs. Teddy Roosevelt (the president's cousin by marriage) running things. She thought it would be grand to at least get a look at the famous mansion.

The band that night played "Don't Fence Me In" and "Little Brown Jug" and "Chattanooga Choo-Choo" for jiving to, and "I'll Remember You," "Stardust," and "As Time Goes By" for partners to draw a little closer. During a lull, as she was chatting with two friends, "a tall, blond Nordic type approached." He addressed her in a manner that she was certain came straight from the *U.S. Soldier's Guidebook to Britain:* "May I have the pleasure of the next dance, please?"

She nodded, the band struck up again, and she stepped forward to join him.

The soldier introduced himself as Eddie Swauger from Beaver, Pennsylvania. "I see that you have the U.S.A. badge on the shoulder of your British uniform," he said to Catherine. "How come?"

Lots of American men had asked that question of Catherine, even Clark Gable. But, Catherine clearly recalls, as the words fell from Eddie's lips, something came over her, taking her completely by surprise. For the first time in her life, she found herself head over heels in love at first sight. Thoughts of William and Jamie, about whom she'd been worrying and moping for days, suddenly vanished.

When the band stopped, Catherine remembers, "Eddie winked mischievously and said, 'Let's stay on the floor. I just can't risk anyone else taking you away now.'" For the rest of the evening, Eddie and Catherine danced rapturously and talked endlessly. Eddie told her about his small hometown, his trips into Pittsburgh with pals, and his weekend sailing excursions to Danesville on Lake Erie. He told her of being the youngest of three children, of his mother's death when he was only three years old, and of his father's remarriage to a woman with two sons. He told her how he dreamed of becoming a veterinary surgeon specializing in horses in the Blue Grass country of Kentucky. In turn, Catherine told him the story of her own unique past. When the evening ended, they eagerly agreed to meet again.

They saw each other again in Salisbury. Eddie had the evening all planned. "Come on," he urged her, "we're just in time to see one of the funniest films for years. It's Jack Benny and Kay Francis in *Charlie's Aunt*. We can go to the first show at the new picture house and still have time for something to eat and a drink afterwards." Catherine was utterly delighted. She told him how her family used to gather around the wireless to listen to the *Jack Benny Show* each week, and how hard she had laughed at the cinema in Barmouth, Wales, when she saw him in *Buck Benny Rides Again*. Suddenly she remembered that Jamie had been right at her side laughing along with her that day; but she pushed that thought out of her mind.

Catherine and Eddie saw each other frequently at Tidworth House dances, which were held five nights a week, with different combinations of servicemen and -women invited each time. They always got along wonderfully, until one day Eddie did something that shocked and very much disappointed Catherine. Catherine had been looking forward to the annual Charity Ball at the Salisbury Guild Hall for weeks. She had gone out of her way to make special arrangements to be off duty the evening of the ball. She had even borrowed a beautiful evening gown for the occasion. But Eddie clean forgot the date. Oblivious to Catherine's excitement and planning, he had agreed to attend the town's Welfare Committee meeting that night. When Catherine found out, she reacted with a "short but sharp explosion." Remaining calm, Eddie promised to work something out. "Don't worry, Cinderella must go to the ball," he said, and pulled her close to kiss her nose.

After pulling a few strings, Eddie found a friend to take his place at the meeting. He and Catherine attended the ball together, and both found it a thrilling occasion that more than justified its reputation as the "social event of the year."

As they strolled toward the RAF trucks waiting to transport people home, Catherine inquired about his interest in the welfare meeting, and asked whether he'd always been involved with other people's problems. Eddie, a bit sheepishly, said he guessed he had. He'd started his involvement in a choir at school that had raised money for elderly people's homes. He told her that while his family had been far from rich, his parents had always taken care of him. But he knew that thousands of kids had to manage on next to nothing. He didn't think of himself as a do-gooder and said he was merely trying to assuage his own guilt at the unfairness of things.

Hearing his quiet, eloquent words, Catherine stopped walking and kissed him, "lovingly at first, and then passionately," she remembers. She could hardly speak as they walked on. She felt like crying, she was so in love with this man from Beaver, Pennsylvania.

Eddie's involvement with the Welfare Committee wasn't his only act of service. Although only a private, Eddie had been enormously helpful to Mrs. Teddy Roosevelt. Whenever a special problem developed at Tidworth House, she always suggested calling on Eddie to fix it.

Catherine came to marvel at Eddie's remarkable ability to take charge and get things done, even those that seemed impossible. One day early in their relationship, she missed the bus back to her billet and had to accept a ride from an officer on a motorcycle. There was no real place to put her feet, so she just let them dangle. Just before they reached her billet, she let out a shriek, and the officer pulled the motorcycle to an abrupt halt. Catherine instantly tumbled off onto the ground in terror. Her shoe had caught fire—she'd been holding it over the searing exhaust pipe.

When she told Eddie what had happened, he took her shoes back to base with him and returned them with new soles—hardly an easy task in wartime Britain, where all materials were strictly rationed. So she wasn't all that surprised that Mrs. Roosevelt thought Eddie a treasure, too, even though she did tease him about it.

One day, Eddie teased her back. "You'll never guess what Mrs. Roosevelt said to me this morning," he said.

"That you were the handsomest GI in Britain?" Catherine suggested.

"No," said Eddie, and paused. "I don't think I should tell you."

"Don't be a tease." As Catherine looks back at their conversation, she remembers having a powerful sense at that moment that she was about to hear something related to her dearest wish in the world.

Eddie laughed and said, "Well, she said that if we ever thought about getting engaged to be married, we just had to let her know and she would give us a party to mark the occasion of the first American in the WAAF to marry a GI."

Before Catherine could say a word, Eddie jumped up and ran off, calling over his shoulder, "And now you can report me to your CC for careless talk."

Soon enough, the promised engagement party took place. Catherine was absolutely thrilled by the event. But when Mrs. Roosevelt "and her equally imperious friend, the Duchess of Marlborough," to whom Tidworth House belonged, began eagerly planning a wedding reception there, Catherine found herself a bit taken aback. Secretly, she had always hoped for a quiet wedding in Wales.

It soon became clear to her that the zealous enthusiasm of Mrs. Roosevelt and the Duchess stemmed not merely from their good wishes for the couple, but also from their desire to play off of the avid interest *Life* magazine had shown in the engagement party. A wedding reception would cap Catherine and Eddie's fairy-tale story—surely bolstering Anglo-American relations.

February 19, 1943, the wedding day, was cloudless and bright, quite unusual in England at that time of year. Catherine's parents had arrived in Salisbury earlier in the week, enjoying frequent and relaxing excursions into the countryside after weeks of scurrying around to collect clothing coupons from friends and relatives who could spare a few for Catherine to have a lovely traditional wedding gown. Flowers, thanks to careful planning by Eddie and Mrs. Roosevelt, were plentiful and beautiful. The wedding party, clothed in their fine attire, gathered excitedly to wait in the foyer of the hotel. Catherine's matron of honor wore a lovely pink gown, and the three bridesmaids turned out in their "best blue" uniforms with burnished brass buttons glistening brightly. Catherine's father waited with them, too, while her mother, the groom, and best man went ahead to the ancient Gothic Episcopalian Church of St. Mary the Virgin on the Tidworth House grounds.

After several minutes, Catherine made a stunning appearance at the top of the hotel stairs. "Stop right there!" a voice called out. Photographers from *Life* and the Associated Press rushed forward. Flashbulbs popped everywhere. Mrs. Roosevelt and the Duchess of Marlborough certainly would succeed in getting their full measure of symbolism and publicity out of the event.

But Catherine's father, knew from his own navy experience that the officers at the church should not be kept waiting. This ceremony needed to begin on time. He stepped forward to take charge, keeping overzealous photographers at bay so the wedding party could push past the crowd.

Eddie's commanding officer, Colonel McNeary, had given the whole of his unit the afternoon off to attend the ceremony. Mrs. Roosevelt greeted hundreds of guests as they arrived at the church in military limousines, staff cars, jeeps, trucks, even a half-track or two. The three hundred guests were seated, rows of U.S. Army khaki on the left, Royal Air Force blue on the right.

An organ prelude began the ceremony, followed by the first chords of Handel's "Arrival of the Queen of Sheba." As the majestic chords resonated through the church, Catherine began the walk down the aisle on the arm of her father. As Eddie and Catherine performed their vows and the ceremony continued, Private Marty McKenna, importing an American tradition, raised his dulcet tenor voice in renditions of "O Promise Me" and "I Love You Truly."

After the very successful ceremony, the Duchess of Marlborough and Mrs. Teddy Roosevelt led the way out of the church and across the oak-lined driveway back to Tidworth House. As the guests arrived, they gasped when they saw the lavish spread: platefuls of sliced honey-baked ham, salmon, roast pork, Cornish pasties, and sausage rolls of many kinds. Bowls of pineapple chunks, apricots, and peach slices stood between huge dishes of cream-topped trifle. There were American doughnuts, too. Mrs. Roosevelt flew much of the food in from the United States. "I didn't think there was that much food left in the world," one of Catherine's bridesmaids whispered.

On a table to one side stood the centerpiece of the reception: a three-tiered wedding cake that Eddie's unit ordered from the States. Press photographers scrambled everywhere to record the event. Even when

Catherine and Eddie left the reception and went to the Salisbury railway station for their trip to the Strand Hotel in London, where they would spend their brief honeymoon, the photographers followed. The American novelist and journalist Faith Baldwin awaited the couple at the station, where she interviewed them and took photographs for her own magazine. She informed them that President Roosevelt had specially requested a set of her photos.

Catherine and Eddie spent a luxurious but all too short honeymoon at the Strand Hotel. Then, right away, they each had to return to the demands of wartime duties. Eddie's division was about to begin a series of rigorous training exercises for amphibious assault landings. Meetings between the newlyweds became increasingly rare. As they parted at the end of one of their fleeting reunions, Eddie whispered in her ear, "Maybe when I come back from this exercise, I'll be a prospective father!"

Indeed, when Catherine went home on leave to visit her parents at the end of April, she felt queasy on two successive mornings. She said nothing to her parents but reported to the infirmary as soon as she got back to RAF Old Sarum. The doctor confirmed her suspicion: She was pregnant. Her days with the women's auxiliary air force would soon be over. On May 17, 1943, she was given an allowance of twelve pounds and ten shillings for civilian clothing and dismissed from the ranks of leading aircraftwomen.

Catherine returned home to her parents in Wales, where Eddie was able to see her only once, during a seven-day leave in October. On November 24, Catherine gave birth to a baby daughter whom they named Catherine and called Babsie for short. Eddie was thankfully given an unexpected "compassionate" leave to visit his wife and child. When he saw Babsie's blue eyes and curly golden hair, he said to Catherine, "Now I've got everything I ever wanted."

But the war still raged on. While Catherine tried to cope alone with her new baby and the rationing that stood in such stark contrast to the lavishness of their wedding feast, Eddie continued training for the invasion of Europe that everyone knew would come eventually.

On April 26, 1944, Eddie had the misfortune to be part of the disastrous large-scale exercise at Slapton Sands, between Dartmouth and Plymouth on the channel coast. Everything that could go wrong did. After all the mishaps, in a dramatic climax, German torpedo boats attacked the soldiers, killing more than seven hundred. Ten officers missing after the attack possessed confidential information regarding the United States' plans for D-Day. Had they been captured, all the plans would have had to be changed, for fear the captured might succumb to German torture tactics and spill crucial details. But, one by one, their dead bodies were recovered—a horrific sort of mixed blessing. Miraculously, Eddie came through this debacle unscathed. But like all the other soldiers who had taken part, he had gained a new and vivid sense of what they would face in a real invasion. Due to military censorship, he could communicate none of this to Catherine, so she remained unaware of the magnitude of danger her husband regularly faced.

Eddie would survive the D-Day invasion. He would survive the Battle of Hurtgen Forest in the autumn, in which thirty thousand Americans were killed or wounded. But his luck ran out, all too soon, during the infamous Battle of the Bulge.

A horrific counteroffensive by the Germans that began on December 16, 1944, the Battle of the Bulge left eighty thousand Americans and twenty-five hundred British soldiers dead, wounded, or in German captivity. Eddie was shot in the head, which left shrapnel lodged in his skull. Catherine received word in Wales that he was being sent to a hospital in the United States.

Catherine had to wait an entire year for Eddie's release from the hospital, whereupon she could finally join him in America. Finally, Eddie healed well enough to leave hospital grounds, and in April 1946, Catherine boarded a GI-bride transport ship, the *Bridgeport,* with Babsie, now two and a half years old.

After the long voyage across the Atlantic, Catherine finally saw the love of her life waiting for her on the dock in New York. But when she got to him, she realized that the man on that dock was no longer the Eddie she had known. "He was a stranger in civilian clothes," Catherine wrote in her journal. "The tall, blond, Nordic-looking man who courted me at Tidworth and Salisbury had gone. Now there was a man who seemed to have shrunk. He stooped and had a patch of sparse hair covering an ugly red cicatrix of a wound rising from his temple." Eddie still had shrapnel in his brain.

He took Catherine and their daughter to his hometown in Pennsylvania, but from the start, he and Catherine faced problems. Although his wounds appeared to have healed, the war had scarred Eddie's mind. In those days, post-traumatic stress disorder was not the common phrase it is today. Little was understood about the ravaging effect war could have on the psyche. Eddie never got the psychological help he needed to recover his lost self.

Just as Catherine was learning to cope with the changes in her relationship with Eddie, fate dealt her another blow. Her parents had preceded her to the United States by two months, moving back to Medford, Massachusetts, where Catherine had lived as a child. Suddenly, after an illness of just a few months, Catherine's father died. Another bulwark was gone from her life.

One afternoon Catherine returned home after taking Babsie for a walk to find Eddie packing. He had decided to rejoin the army. In the spring of 1947, they divorced, and Catherine moved east to be near her mother.

Now on her own with Babs, she enrolled at aviation training school. After graduation, she took a job with Trans Canada Airlines, which led to positions at Pan American, British Overseas Airways, and American Airlines. A hardworking employee, she worked her way up the corporate ladder from ground hostess to reservations agent to air freight administration.

Catherine, who had always loved to play the piano, also continued her studies at the Boston Conservatory of Music and gave a number of concerts. But mostly, she concentrated on raising her beautiful daughter, a living reminder of the joy she once had with Eddie. She never married again.

After thirty years with American Airlines, Catherine retired in 1980. A feisty soul, she couldn't endure sitting around the house, so she took a part-time job with a new branch of the USO welfare and entertainment organization that opened at Boston's Logan Airport. In 1984 she became full-time director of the Logan Airport center, and today, at eighty years old, she still works there as an assistant to the subsequent director.

Eddie Swauger, whom Catherine had loved so much, died in 1952. A fragment of the shrapnel in his brain moved suddenly, and in a few days he was gone. Looking back, Catherine has no regrets about marrying Eddie. She loved him deeply and still cherishes a thousand memories. Their daughter, who never knew the Eddie her mother had fallen in love with, blossomed into an exceptional woman.

Catherine fully accepts the life she has led. World War II blessed her with a great love, but then, as it did for so many others, it took that love away.

Catherine Roberts in her WAAF uniform in 1941.

News photograph of the wedding reception at Tidworth House, with the standard Red Cross refreshments—doughnuts—on the table. From left: Mrs. Teddy Roosevelt; Catherine's father, Griffith Roberts; Catherine and Eddie; Catherine's mother, Dora Roberts.

Catherine Roberts-Swauger in 1999, then director of the Logan Airport USO in Boston, Massachusetts, with photo of USO hero Bob Hope.

WHILE MRS. TEDDY ROOSEVELT and a duchess lavishly celebrated the marriage of one lucky English bride to an American officer, many other romances between English girls and American GIs bloomed with less fanfare in the pubs and tight little houses in working-class districts. America had made its name as the land of opportunity, where anyone could dream of becoming president. The working-class girls involved with Americans heard a great deal about the modern wonders so common in the United States. Yet on occasion, an English girl who crossed the ocean after the war with her new American husband could find herself in for quite a shock.

Floyd and Betty Bachman in Kansas City,
Missouri, in 1947.

Betty Law
BACHMAN

Betty Law grew up in Burton-on-Trent, Staffordshire, England. On September 1, 1939, when she was nearly thirteen, fifty-three German divisions invaded Poland, leading the British and French to declare war on Germany on September 3. By June 4, 1940, the British retreat from Dunkirk was over, and Paris fell to Hitler's forces on June 14. Less than a month later, on July 10, the Battle of Britain began, and German bombs rained down on England.

Betty's mother and stepfather both worked in a munitions factory, and Betty took a job at fourteen. "We were needed," she later recalled, because so many men had gone away to war.

She has never forgotten the first bomb that affected her personally. Betty lived with her widowed grandmother at the time, and they were sitting in the living room when Betty heard a whistling bomb fly overhead. "I screamed and dropped my hot chocolate on the rug. Granny sat calmly drinking her nightly hot toddy and got angry with me for spilling my chocolate. 'It's miles away,' she said." In fact, the bomb dropped only about fifteen minutes away, blowing out her uncle Fred's windows and chimney stack and demolishing the houses across the street from him. After work, Betty ran to join everyone else in the neighborhood looking at the disaster scene. "I was standing on a mattress that had been blown from a bed. Under it they [later] found the [body of the] woman who had lived in that house."

A few months later, Betty's grandmother died. Betty returned to live with her mother, stepfather, three younger sisters, and two younger brothers. After one night spent in a cold concrete shelter, with all of them huddled together for hours, awaiting the all-clear, her mother—Betty called her Mam—declared, "No more. If we're going to die, we will do it in our own beds." And that was the last time the family ever went to a group shelter. As the war continued, people built smaller shelters on every street, but nobody ever used the one put up in Betty's family's backyard. In fact, her mother bought some chickens and used the shelter as a henhouse. They ate the chickens for Christmas and New Year's dinner.

Betty had been working for some time at Pirelli, a company that manufactured tires for military vehicles, until she began feeling ill. It turned out that she was allergic to rubber, so she took a new job with the Cooperative Society, delivering bread and cakes from a horse-drawn wagon. "On my job I had two routes, one Tuesday, Thursday, and Saturday, and the other Monday, Wednesday, and Friday. Each route had two hundred customers. I enjoyed it after I got used to working in all weather."

In addition to holding a job, all fifteen-year-olds were encouraged to join an auxiliary service of some kind. "I had to be different and joined the fire service. I tried to get in as a dispatcher, with a motorbike, but I was too young to do that, so I became a telephonist. We went on duty every other night from nine P.M. to eight A.M. We wore a uniform and carried a gas mask and a steel helmet. We were trained to identify different gases by smell. On duty we stayed in an air-raid shelter with two bunk beds and four phones. Two of us were on duty each night. My mate was named Joan. We took turns sleeping. Our job was to be prepared if an incendiary bomb dropped somewhere. When we got the call, we would find out what size fire engine and other equipment should go out. After I got off duty at eight A.M., I would go home, change, and go to work."

Betty does remember having some fun in the fire service. "Even though food was rationed, one of the firemen was a butcher, and he would bring liver. Someone else had an allotment plot for growing vegetables, and he'd bring potatoes and onions. There was usually someone to get hold of some black-market lard. So I would cook liver, onions, and chips while Joan took care of the phones. It really wasn't allowed, so Joan was supposed to buzz me if an officer came in. One day she couldn't buzz, so they caught me with my hands in the liver, all bloody. All I could do was brazen it out. I just invited them to eat with us. They didn't, but I got away with it."

When Betty turned eighteen in 1944, she was allowed to go with her mother to pubs, which were like working-class clubs in those days, for a drink on the nights she wasn't doing her fire service duty. Betty enjoyed those evenings, as they gave her a chance to really talk to her mother. "We were like sisters. I would tell her everything. As I grew up, she was the only one I could talk to. She always worked; we never had her at home during the day. I never got to be a kid, as I was the eldest and always had to help get dinner and take care of the other kids."

Yanks often hung around the pub. The Americans had been stationed in England from the time Betty was fifteen, so they were a familiar sight. "The Yanks used to think we were sisters. I didn't like that, but Mam did, as she felt younger. As I got older, though, I began to think it was funny and got to like it myself. Who would want people to know you were out with your mother?"

One night at the pub, an American named Larry Turner, whom Betty had talked to many times, as he was quite homesick, brought in a Yank sergeant and introduced him to Betty. His name was Floyd Bachman. Floyd asked if he could walk Betty home. "I said, 'Yes, if you can behave yourself.' Anyway, he took me home and didn't behave, and I slapped his face. I figured sure, just like all men, out for one thing, so when I saw him again, I wouldn't speak to him. Then one day Larry said, 'Come on, you kids' put Floyd's hand in mine, and said, 'Go.' Floyd took me home again." Floyd apologized for his earlier behavior, then asked Betty, "'Will you marry me?' I said, 'Don't be daft! I'm not marrying a Yank!' I went in the house and told my mother some bloody fool Yank asked me to marry him."

Nevertheless, Betty continued to go out with Floyd, who always acted as a gentleman after that first night. "At one point we had a major falling-out. For the next few weeks, it went like this: I would get home from work, and Larry would be there. He would say, 'Hi, kiddo, how are you?' I would say, 'fine.' He would say, 'That's great, but I know someone who isn't.' I would say, 'Too bad.' This went on night after night. I would have a date or go out with my mother for a drink, and in would walk some Yank, spot me, and go back out. Next Floyd would come in. If I had a date and he left for the bathroom, Floyd would sit in [his] spot. So I would leave. The same thing happened everywhere I went.

"Finally, one night when I was having a drink with Mam, I told Floyd he could walk me home if we all went together. We left, and when we got outside, Mam went one way and pushed us the other way. So we walked home, never spoke one word all the way—it was at least a half-hour walk. When we got there, he asked me out [for] the next night. I said yes to get rid of him. We went to see an Errol Flynn picture. When we got home, he said, 'I will ask you once more. Will you marry me?' All of a sudden, I said yes. He didn't believe what he heard, so he said, 'What?' I repeated it, and he just took off without a good night."

Floyd came back the next night with "papers galore" for Betty's mother to sign. Soon Betty got a request to appear at U.S. Army head-quarters in the area. "The questions they asked were really something. The main one I got mad at was 'What are you getting married for? Are you pregnant, or what?' Then they asked Floyd the same question, and where he planned on living, England or the U.S.A. He said the U.S.A. We got permission but had to wait six months. Then they shipped him out to Germany in hopes he would change his mind."

They set their wedding date for April 25, 1945. All the invitations went out, the cake was made—and Floyd couldn't get leave. So they had to change the date to May 5. The night of May 4, Betty didn't sleep a wink, worried Floyd wouldn't make it again. He'd been out on maneuvers for forty-eight hours with no sleep, but he arrived for the wedding promptly at six A.M. "We had to fetch the flowers, they wouldn't deliver. We stopped and had a drink. Floyd went to Uncle Fred's house, since we figured it wouldn't look good with us both coming from Mother's, so he and Larry went to the church from there. We arrived at the church a half hour late." A truckload of Italian prisoners, whom the American soldiers were supposed to be guarding, sat outside the church. "The men we'd invited from Floyd's company just left the truck and went into the church. My mother gave me away, and instead of walking slow as we had practiced, we were at the altar before they'd finished playing 'Here Comes the Bride.' We had a high-church wedding in Latin. The only hymn I remember was 'Courage, brother, do not stumble, though thy path be dark as night: There's a star to guide the humble, trust in God.'

"After the wedding, we went into the vestibule and signed the license. When we came out, all the Yanks had rice to throw. Everyone was disgusted, as we hadn't seen rice to *eat* in ages. Then we took pictures outside the church. 'Bloody' is swearing in England, and there was Floyd trying to get everybody lined up, yelling, 'Come on, you bloody Yanks!' From there we went to the Smithfield Hotel for our wedding meal, which was sit-down. Our wedding cake had three tiers, with stars and stripes all over the sides. It was gorgeous and made like prewar, as my boss at work had arranged to get the ingredients to have it made. We had the fifth to get married and the sixth together, and he had to go back on duty on the seventh. He got as far as Southampton, and then the eighth turned out to be VE Day, so he got to come back for a couple of more days."

Once Floyd returned to the army, Betty returned to her usual pattern, working at the co-op during the day and also continuing with the National Fire Service for a while. She saw Floyd for a week in October 1945, but then not again until mid-1946 and her arrival in the United States, where Floyd had settled in New Mexico after his discharge in March of that year.

Betty's journey to America was a taxing one. When she embarked in June, she had to stay at the U.S. Army camp at Tidworth, England, for three days before her ship departed. Her suitcase broke along the way, and she had to borrow a belt to tie around it. "Talk about a poor immigrant," Betty recalls. Along with two hundred other women and some children, Betty crossed the Atlantic on the U.S.S. *Holbrook*, a seven-day voyage with another two days in dock at both ends of the crossing. "It was a miserable trip," she remembers vividly. "First they took us to a room where the captain talked to us. He told us to take seasick pills two or three times a day, but that had us all walking around like zombies, so most of us quit taking them. The ocean was rough, and I was on E Deck, which was below water level with no porthole. Four of us slept on bunk beds in a small cabin—one girl was going to New York, another to Minnesota, and a third to Utah. We stuck together all the time. The shower used salt water, but no one told us, and even though they gave us a special soap, it did nothing for the hair. The Red Cross and other officials had regular showers, but we weren't allowed to use them. We weren't allowed to talk to the crew, and to stop us from going up on A Deck after a certain hour, MPs were posted.

"We would sit on deck all day, with numbers pinned to our clothes. They would call the numbers when it was your turn to eat. Most of the time it was lamb stew for dinner. Whoever got down to the galley first would yell back up what there was to eat, and we'd all groan. Breakfast consisted of eggs with green yolks, bacon that seemed to have a box of salt on every strip, cereal if you wanted it, and coffee. We begged for tea but didn't get it. We were able to buy boxes of candy, though, and we'd share those. I would make sandwiches out of celery."

In addition to not having any decent food to eat, the girls endured some nasty comments from others on the ship. "One day the Red Cross had a style show for us. They told us all their clothes came from New York. They also said our in-laws probably wouldn't be happy to see us, so we all had a chip on our shoulder by the time we reached New York," Betty remembers.

Once the boat docked in New York, those met by their husbands were allowed off right away. Betty and her new friends, though, had another twenty-four hours to wait on board. They couldn't wait to get hold of something they could eat, so they quickly worked out a barter system with dockworkers. "They threw us doughnuts, we threw them cigarettes. The crew tried to stop us, but we did it anyway. Two of us even managed to sneak upstairs to the Red Cross cabins and take a real shower.

"Finally they put us on buses to Hoboken, New Jersey. There we got on a train. We were in the last coach and were shuttled from train to train as we crossed the country. People in the cars in front knew we were there, so they'd come back to peek at us. We finally got to say, 'Come on in and look at the monkeys.' One girl on her way to Seattle had twins. She was supposed to have the one compartment on the train. But they made her stay in a regular berth and the Red Cross women took the compartment, so we all took turns watching her kids so she could get some rest. We ate in the dining coach and were given corn on the cob. We tried cutting it, but that didn't work. So we picked it up and bit into it, and it was awful. No one told us we were supposed to put salt and butter on it."

The car with Betty and the other war brides was switched from train to train during the night, a noisy process that of course woke everyone up. After four long days and interrupted nights, an exhausted Betty finally reached Albuquerque, New Mexico. As the train neared its destination, Betty looked out and saw slums and dilapidated mud huts. "I thought, 'My God, what have I done!' I was the only one getting off. Floyd came running up, all 250 pounds of him. He'd weighed 195 when I'd last seen him. His mother was there, too. On the platform, there were many Indians, the women with papooses on their backs, selling baskets and pots. Talk about culture shock. The local Red Cross officials came over to interview me. I told the truth, that we were treated like prisoners and that the food had been horrible. They got angry, and my arrival wasn't written up in the paper after all; it was supposed to be, since I was the first GI bride to arrive in New Mexico."

Like quite a number of other war brides, Betty felt shell-shocked by her new situation. When she met her new mother-in-law, the first thing she said to Betty was "You're skinny and need fattening up." Floyd's brother George seemed a little weird but friendly. But Betty took an instant liking to her father-in-law when he came home from work at a grocery store. "He called me Betsy and gave me a big hug and a kiss, and I thought he was wonderful.

"Floyd had told me there were certain words I shouldn't say, but he didn't tell me I shouldn't have a drink." So when her father-in-law, who asked her to call him Dad, offered a beer, Betty accepted. No other woman in the group that evening had one. "My first mistake."

To make matters more uncomfortable, the meal her mother-in-law served didn't make Betty think she was going to get "fattened up" any time soon. She had to eat corn on the cob again, although at least Floyd showed her how to eat it properly this time. The mashed potatoes had lumps in them, just like her own mother's, so at least that seemed familiar. But she couldn't quite stomach the white gravy that went with the steak—a southwestern tradition she realized would definitely take some getting used to. When she caught sight of the cottage cheese, which she'd never encountered, she couldn't help but think it "looked like someone had already eaten it." After declining everything except the corn with a polite "no thank you," Betty resigned herself to the fact that "my first meal was a flop. I didn't make a good impression."

After supper, she and Floyd drove twenty-five miles to the house he had rented in Bernalillo. The three-room house contained a living room with a linoleum floor and a hide-a-bed, a second room with a table and some chairs, and a kitchen with an icebox, a two-burner hot plate, and "a kind of oven that fit over a burner." There was no running water, and that was the least of the hardships. "I asked to go to the toilet, and Floyd grabbed a shotgun and took me outside. He had whitewashed the hut and Purexed the seat, but I had never seen an outdoor toilet before. By then I was really shocked. All I heard from the Yanks in England was how backward we were and how modern America was. But at home I had an electric stove and running water in the house, plus a fireplace in every room."

It didn't help to learn that Floyd had brought out the shotgun to keep away the rattlesnakes. He also warned Betty not to leave her shoes on the floor, and to shake them and her clothes before putting them on to make sure no scorpions or black-widow spiders had attached themselves. When she woke up in the middle of the night and turned on the light, she saw bugs scurry all over the ceiling for cover.

Fortunately, Betty and Floyd did not stay long in Bernalillo, a town that consisted of three blocks of wooden sidewalks, a bus depot, a small department store, a tavern with spittoons and sawdust on the floor, a do-it-yourself laundry, and one doctor—"the drunken kind you see in old cowboy movies." Betty still hasn't forgotten how out of place she felt. "I was pure white, like a sheet, and everyone else—even the whites—were brown, so I stood out like a sore thumb."

In midsummer, Floyd's parents decided to move to Washington State, where they hoped to find better jobs. They expected Floyd and Betty to follow, but instead the newlyweds went to Kansas City, Missouri, where Larry Turner, the friend who had introduced them in England and been best man at their wedding, lived. Floyd got a job at the A&P for $35 a week, and Betty was hired at $40 a week by Wolferman's, an elite grocery and wine store run by Englishmen.

Neither of them liked Kansas City all that much, so after six months, they decided to join Floyd's folks in Washington after all. They blew the rods on their 1937 Packard on the way and had to stop to add oil every few miles. "When we came to Chinook Pass, it had just opened, and it was icy. I remember us stopping at the top, me with my foot on the brake, crying, and Floyd adding more oil."

They finally made it to Auburn, Washington, where Betty soon had more new adventures with nature, American-style. At least the house they rented was a step up from their abode in Bernalillo, with two bedrooms, a bathroom, and an eat-in kitchen. But one day they heard splashing coming from the bathroom and rushed in to discover a large rat swimming around in the toilet. Floyd ran next door to ask what to do, and his neighbor instructed him to just flush it back down—which, surprisingly, worked. For years after, Betty checked any new toilet she encountered to make sure it wasn't harboring a rat.

Shortly after they moved to Kent, Washington, Betty experienced her first earthquake. Pregnant at the time with their daughter, Juanita, she had walked across the street to the A&P where Floyd worked. She'd just gotten inside when the whole store began to shake. "Everything was falling off the shelves. The store rolled, and I stood there laughing. 'Run, you damned limey,' Floyd yelled." He broke the lock on the back door so they could get out of the store, but it wasn't much better outside, where cars rolled back and forth across the parking lot.

They survived the ordeal, though, and after a little while in Washington, Floyd heard of some job openings with the border patrol in Albuquerque. He got into shape, dieting back down to 195 pounds, and he and Betty returned to New Mexico. When they got there, they found to their dismay that federal jobs had been abruptly frozen. So he got a position instead as a traveling salesman for Campbell's soup. After seven months, they decided to head northwest to Washington again.

In 1953, Floyd got a sales job with Rainier Brewery. At long last, he and Betty and Juanita settled down for good. Floyd worked for Rainier for thirty-five years, until his retirement.

Betty Law Bachman wrote this account of the war years and her early experiences in America before her death in a car accident in 1998. Her daughter, Juanita, now adds that Betty lived a rewarding and happy life. "She put in over forty thousand hours of volunteer work at the VA hospital, working mostly with the blind in later years. She served the VFW auxiliary on the local, state, and national level. She also joined and became active in the local chapter of the Daughters of the British Empire. My parents vastly improved their standard of living from the early outhouse days. Mother went 'home' many times to visit family, although she said it was never the same after her mother died. She always referred to England as home and never lost her British accent and traditions, yet she was as American and patriotic as they come. She was very proud to be a naturalized citizen."

So, despite the shock of finding out that America wasn't quite the dreamy landscape she'd imagined, Betty ended up embracing life with her American husband in her new country with open arms.

The wallet photographs that Betty and Floyd exchanged to remember each other before she came to the United States.

Betty, Floyd, and their wedding party.

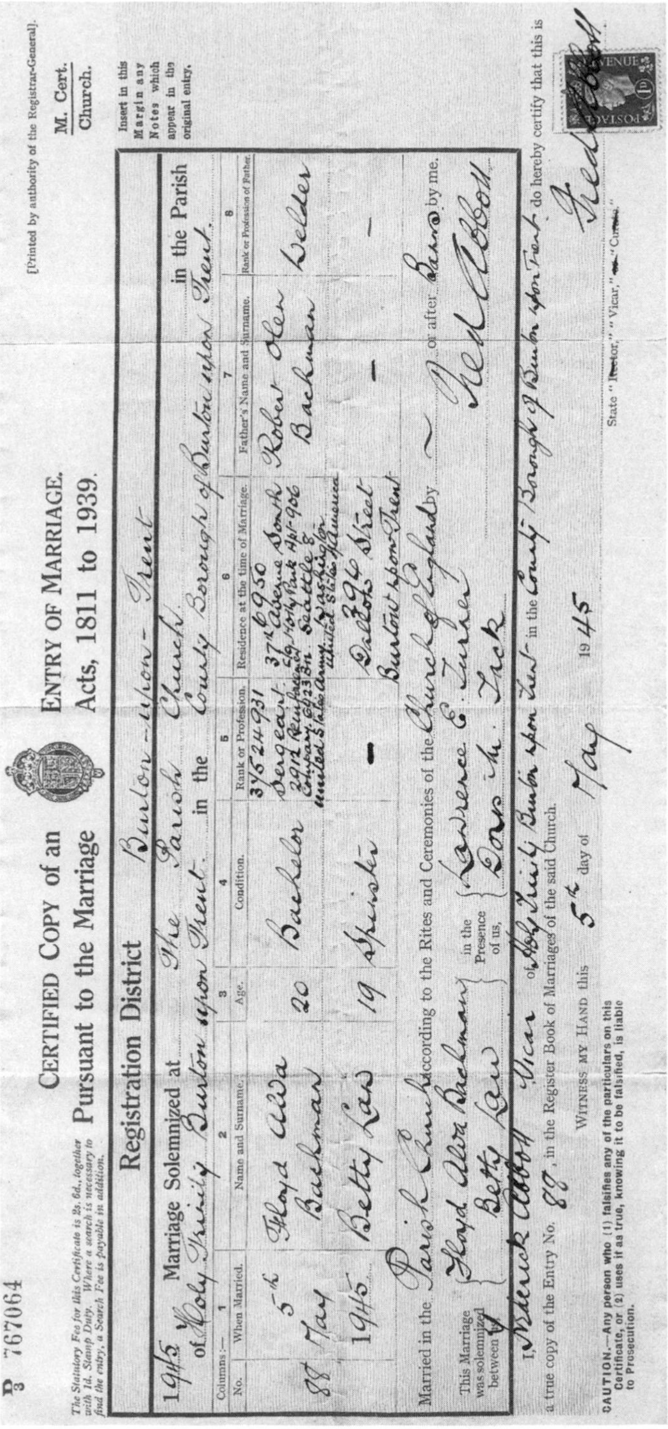

B3 767064

The Statutory Fee for this Certificate is 3s. 9d., together with 1d. Stamp Duty. Where a search is necessary to find the entry, a Search Fee is payable in addition.

CERTIFIED COPY of an ENTRY OF MARRIAGE.
Pursuant to the Marriage Acts, 1811 to 1939.

[Printed by authority of the Registrar-General].

M. Cert.
Church.

Insert in this Margin any Notes which appear in the original entry.

Registration District Burton-upon-Trent

1945 Marriage Solemnized at The Parish Church in the Parish of Holy Trinity Burton upon Trent in the County Borough of Burton upon Trent.

No.	When Married.	Name and Surname.	Age.	Condition.	Rank or Profession.	Residence at the time of Marriage.	Father's Name and Surname.	Rank or Profession of Father.
88	5th May 1945	Floyd Alva Bachman	20	Bachelor	37524931 Sergeant 2912 Reinforcement Company 6923 Bn. United States Army	3714 Avenue South 2009 North Park Apt 906 Seattle 8 Washington United States of America	Robert Olen Bachman	Welder
		Betty Law	19	Spinster	—	29a Dallow Street Burton upon Trent	—	

Married in the Parish Church according to the Rites and Ceremonies of the Church of England by ~ or after Banns by me.

This Marriage was solemnized between us, Floyd Alva Bachman, Betty Law; in the Presence of us, Lawrence E. Turner, Doris M. Tuck. Fred Abbott

I, Frederick Abbott Vicar of Holy Trinity Burton upon Trent in the County Borough of Burton upon Trent do hereby certify that this is a true copy of the Entry No. 88, in the Register Book of Marriages of the said Church.

WITNESS MY HAND this 5th day of May 1945. Fred Abbott

State "~~Rector,~~" "Vicar," ~~or "Curate."~~

CAUTION.—Any person who (1) falsifies any of the particulars on this Certificate, or (2) uses it as true, knowing it to be falsified, is liable to Prosecution.

Betty and Floyd's English wedding license.

Betty on board the
U.S.S. Holbrook, *making
her way to the U.S.*

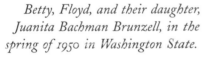

*Betty, Floyd, and their daughter,
Juanita Bachman Brunzell, in the
spring of 1950 in Washington State.*

*Betty Law Bachman
in 1997, the year
before her death.*

WHEN AN AMERICAN SERVICEMAN *fell in love with a young woman he met in a foreign country, the reactions of the girl's family varied greatly. In a recently liberated country, such an alliance was often considered a godsend, offering the daughter a much better life in America. Marriage under such circumstances might be actively facilitated by the family. In other cases, however, the overtures of an American serviceman were deeply resented and resisted by the family. Such reactions were particularly common in England, where feelings against "crass" upstart Americans still lingered from World War I days. A young woman had to be quite courageous to go through with a wedding that might well lead to a permanent breach with a parent.*

Max McClure in the cockpit of his P-47 fighter plane.
Ena McClure in 1945.

Max and Ena

McCLURE

In the last week of May 1943, Ena King's good friend Rosemary telephoned her in London and asked her to go on a blind date. Her American pilot friend was coming into town on an R&R leave, and another pilot, a buddy of his, was coming with him. Ena declined. She wasn't interested in going on a blind date, and she had heard some unpleasant things about American servicemen. The British generally had mixed feelings about the Americans living among them. They certainly recognized that the participation of the American forces was crucial to winning the war. But while the good-humored brashness of so many American GIs appealed to some Brits, especially young women, it rankled others. That was especially true for the young men who were losing so many dates to their American counterparts. Many British soldiers warned their sisters about the dangers of what they saw as "love 'em and leave 'em" affairs.

But when Ena turned down the date, her friend Rosemary leaned on her, telling her what a spoilsport she was. She also promised Ena that she wouldn't be left alone with the mystery man. Not wanting to disappoint her friend, Ena finally gave in when Rosemary asked a fourth time.

The date proved to be pleasant enough but nothing special, just dinner at a place that also had a dance floor. The day before had been Ena's birthday, and her brother had bought her a stunning red suit that she wore that night, setting off her black hair beautifully. Ena's date, Max McClure from Texas, was very handsome, but he wasn't much of a dancer, which was a real drawback during those dance-crazed times.

Even though she felt no special sparks during the date, when Max dropped her off at home, he asked her for her phone number. She didn't expect to hear from him again, but just in case—rather than give him her home number and risk her family discovering she'd dated an American—she gave him her work number at Mogashel Linens, the high-quality store where she was a receptionist.

The very next week, Max called to say he was coming to London again and asked her to dinner and the theater. She started warming to him on that second date, possibly because they were both more relaxed. She began to perceive the intelligence behind his Texan drawl. Over the next few weeks, Max traveled up to London to see Ena as often as possible. He was a P-47 fighter pilot in the 358th Fighter Group, and he escorted the bombers on their missions to France and Germany. Because he had volunteered to stay on for a second tour, after having flown the fifty missions that made a full tour, he was allowed to leave his base when he was not scheduled to fly.

On their dates, he and Ena would have a nice meal and go either to the theater or, more often, the movies. She particularly remembers going to see Irene Dunne in the tearjerker *The White Cliffs of Dover,* and how moved they both were. That afternoon, she remembers, while they were walking through Leicester Square, a young woman suddenly called out, "Hello, Max, how are you?" Max looked around hurriedly, didn't answer, and pulled Ena along so quickly that she didn't even get a look at the woman. Taken aback by his abruptness, Ena asked Max who the woman was and why he was so rude to her. He replied simply, "You don't want to know her." Suddenly she thought that Max might have another life she knew nothing about. Ena says that Max never again brought up the encounter, and she never pressed him about it. Sometimes things were better left unexplored, and, after all, Max had chosen to be with her. During the war years, it was almost a rule not to question soldiers too closely about their romantic past. There were almost always old girlfriends, and life had become very present-tense. Everyone was uprooted in some way, and the future was always uncertain.

One night when Max came up to London, they went to see the movie *A Yank in the RAF,* a piece of wartime froth starring Tyrone Power, Betty Grable, and the English actor John Sutton, who was a particular favorite of Ena's. Originally released three years earlier, in 1941, the picture seemed to be playing at one or another theater almost continually, like many popular films of the period. After the movie, Max took Ena home on the bus, which was their usual means of transportation. At eighteen, Ena was the baby of her family, with two older brothers and an older sister, and she lived with her parents. Just after Max and Ena got off the bus, air-raid sirens began blaring, followed by the "ack-ack" of anti-aircraft artillery. They began to hurry, and then Max abruptly stopped walking, turned to Ena, and asked her to marry him. In the midst of all those ominous sounds of war, she looked into Max's face, full of anticipation, and realized that she had fallen in love with him. She said yes immediately. When she is asked today what it was about Max that particularly attracted her, she says, "Everything. He was the one for me. I knew it."

As soon as Max left her at her door that night, she burst into the house and rushed excitedly to her parents' bedroom, announcing, "Mommy, Max has asked me to marry him!" Ena's father was an extremely sound sleeper; even air-raid sirens usually didn't wake him. But the moment Ena's momentous news was out of her mouth, her father sat bolt upright in bed and said, "Go to your room, turn off the light, and I don't want that American in this house ever again!" Nobody in the family ever disagreed with Ena's father. He was a tough disciplinarian, and she had rarely seen him so intense. She was stunned and crushed by his reaction, and she went to her room in despair.

But Ena was a determined young woman. She continued to see Max surreptitiously, despite her father's continuing opposition. Her mother approved but was not about to try to change her husband's mind. He was not the kind of man to enter into debate with either his wife or his children.

Sometime later, the weekend after D-Day, Ena went down to see Max in High Halden, Kent, where he was stationed. The land on which the airbase had been constructed was owned by Lady Morris, who had been allowed to remain in her beautiful home on the base. Max was friendly with her, often buying eggs from her, which were a precious commodity. He asked Lady Morris if Ena could stay with her for the weekend, and she agreed. Not the least snobbish or aloof, Lady Morris was very kind to Ena, welcoming her to the base for Max because he was out flying a mission. When he returned later that day, Ena and he went off on a picnic.

The base was in what was known as "buzzbomb country," a repeated target of German V1 rockets. Ena was used to falling bombs in London, the major target of the Battle of Britain, which still continued to be bombed sporadically. Like most Britons, she had learned to be fatalistic about bombs. You never knew when they might come, and if you thought about it much, you would be too afraid ever to leave your home. Even so, the countryside was so peaceful as they enjoyed their picnic that Ena was shocked to hear anti-aircraft guns fired nearby. "I nearly climbed a tree," Ena recalls.

Early the next morning, Max came to Lady Morris's house to tell Ena that his fighter group was leaving for France. He asked her to come to the end of the runway to watch them leave. As she stood there, surrounded by menacing barbed wire, she watched Max and the rest of his group take off one by one. She wondered how many of them would come back, and if she would ever see Max again, and her eyes filled with tears.

She did see Max again, but not for several weeks. In late August she went to see him at his new base in Atchem, near Shrewsbury, almost all the way to the Welsh border. He was approaching a hundred missions and the end of his second tour of duty. Not only was Max farther away now, but they knew they had to face some difficult decisions because he would soon be rotated back to the U.S. They decided to marry.

Though Ena's father was still strongly opposed to the relationship, Ena's mother felt differently. Her own marriage had been arranged, and she was determined that Ena should marry for love, so she signed the papers that allowed Ena to marry. Ena King and Max Whitely McClure were married at Shrewsbury on November 3, 1944.

Ena knew her father wouldn't attend, but he also forbade her mother to go. Since her mother had enraged her father by signing the marriage papers, Ena knew her mother was in no position to defy him further, but she was deeply hurt that her mother couldn't be there. The choice she had been forced to make between Max and her father was agonizing.

Ena and Max spent their honeymoon at a hotel called the Mytton & Mermaid. Then, just three days later, Max returned to the U.S. Ena's father was so angry about the marriage that he told her she was no longer his daughter. She had to move out of the house and live with her older sister. She would not see Max again for ten months.

Max had not described his hometown of Spur, Texas, in much detail. His father had founded the town newspaper in 1909 and the McClures had stayed happily rooted in Spur ever since. The town was tiny, he had warned her, even smaller than the smallest English village Max had seen. Ena's sister, on hearing this, said, "I give you three weeks there." But Ena was not worried. Receiving the word from Max that he was back home and ready for her to come over, she booked herself onto a Norwegian cargo ship that left England on August 31, 1945, paying her own way. Max wired her that he would be waiting for her in New York at the dock.

Max had bought chocolates and flowers for their hotel room and couldn't wait until she stepped off that ship. But when he called the shipping line on the day she was to arrive, to confirm the time of arrival, he discovered that the ship had been diverted to Baltimore. During the war, such diversions were common due to the war-related sea traffic. Now Max had to drive frantically down to Maryland, and he sent Ena a telegram to assure her he was on the way.

The ship docked in the shadow of Fort McHenry, celebrated in "The Star-Spangled Banner." The day was September 13, 1945, the 131st anniversary of the British naval bombardment of Fort McHenry in the War of 1812, and the harbor was bursting with fireworks as the ship came into port. Once she'd disembarked, Ena asked a nearby policeman what the fireworks were all about, and he answered, "This is the day we celebrate our liberation from the British." Such was her welcome to the United States.

When Ena arrived in Spur, she discovered the town was just as tiny as Max had warned, but also that it was a wonderfully friendly place. The whole town welcomed her like a long-lost relative. After all, she had married Max McClure, the returning war hero. After a period of adjustment to the American way of life, Ena settled down into a very happy routine in Spur. She wrote to her family often and received many letters back, but the rift between her and her father remained painful.

Then, in 1948, Ena's mother came to visit. Although she fully acknowledged how contented Ena and Max were together, and was pleased to find Ena as happy as she'd led them to believe, she nonetheless conveyed a distressing message from Ena's father: Unless Ena returned to England, he would consider her dead. After all this time, he still couldn't bring himself to accept that she'd "run off" with an American. There was no question about Ena's response: She told her mother to let her father know that she was deeply in love with Max and was very happy where she was.

Over the next two years, Ena's family worked on convincing her father that he had to accept Ena's marriage and make his peace with her. Finally, he consented to invite Ena to England for a visit, and he promised that he would join the rest of the family in meeting her at the train station in London. Ena made the crossing on the luxurious *Queen Mary* and took the train from Southampton to London. All the way over, she had felt more and more anxiety, mixed with anticipation, about the reunion with her father. After all of that, when she looked out on the platform, bursting with the excitement of seeing her family for the first time in years, she was stunned to discover that her father was not there. How could he have failed to come?

Deeply disappointed, she walked up to her family. "Where's your father?" her mother asked. "Not with me!" Ena replied in surprise. Her father, it turned out, had decided that he would meet Ena as she got off the ship in Southampton, then take the train with her up to London to meet the rest of them. Somehow, he had missed her there, and they learned what had happened only when he showed up in London three hours later.

After Ena had been home for several days, her father asked her to come into his study one afternoon. She went in and closed the door, not knowing what to expect. Her father asked her if she loved Max, and she replied that she did, very much. He asked her if she was happy with her life with Max, and she told him she was, very. "Very well, then," he said, "we won't talk about this again." Many years later, Max and Ena spent three years in London, during which time Ena's father got to know Max well and discovered that he quite liked his American son-in-law.

Despite the separation from her family, Ena McClure says in reflecting on her life with Max, "I was very lucky." She recalls that one day, during their fifty-first year of marriage, Max looked across the room at her and suddenly said, "Once I was this dashing fighter pilot, and I went to England and met a beautiful girl with black hair. She was wearing a red suit with white cuffs. And I fell in love." She had never known that he had remembered so vividly what she had been wearing on that fateful day.

Ena enjoyed fifty-one years and seven months of a wonderful marriage and love affair with a dashing P-47 fighter pilot from Spur, Texas. Major Max McClure passed away June 7, 1996, and is buried at Fort Sam Houston National Cemetery in San Antonio.

"THE MYTTON & MERMAID"
Atcham, Shrewsbury
Telephone : CROSS HOUSES 220
HALFWAY HOUSE TO PORTMEIRION

View of Hotel through the gateway to Attingham Park

A brochure for the Mytton & Mermaid, where Ena and Max spent their honeymoon.

Ena and Max on the front steps of his mother's house shortly after Ena arrived in Spur.

Ena and Max attending a formal at Web Air Force Base in 1953.

Ena and Max on one of many trips to England, in 1962.

B EGINNING IN ITALY IN LATE 1943, *then continuing across northern Europe through 1944 and 1945, American soldiers came as liberators. People who had suffered a great deal and lost much met them with joy and gratitude. The Americans brought a promise of eventual peace, of normal lives resumed, of days no longer consumed by fear. Sometimes they also brought the promise of love. Fulfilling that promise could bring about even more profound change for those who had already suffered so much. Was the love strong enough to make the separation from family, friends, and country worthwhile? These were difficult decisions to make, even in a world restored to peace.*

Harold and Jeanne Conn as newlyweds.

Harold and Jeanne

CONN

Jeanne Cuvelier was born in her maternal grandmother's house on February 23, 1927, in Adinkerke–De Panne, Belgium. She grew up in Brussels, where, she remembers, she had a very happy childhood. During school vacations, she and her brother Jean, who was eighteen months older, would visit their grandparents. "Grandmom would take all eight of her grandchildren and her dog to the dunes, where we would play all afternoon long," Jeanne remembers.

On May 10, 1940, the Germans invaded Belgium, and thirteen-year old Jeanne's dreamy, peaceful childhood came to an end.

"Lots of bridges and train stations were destroyed early on," Jeanne recalls. "We were not allowed to travel by train any farther than Ghent, so we did not see our grandparents. My parents bought a tandem bicycle to ride out and see their folks every few months. It was during that awful time that my grandfather died of a heart attack on the street, carrying a heavy bag of coal bought on the black market. My brother and I weren't allowed to go to his funeral. My parents rode their bike."

The strict rules set down by the Germans put a considerable strain on people trying to push their fear aside and get on with their daily lives. "There was a curfew, and adults needed special passes to be outdoors late at night. There was a complete blackout ordered, and we could be arrested if any light was seen through windows or doors. In the beginning there was no music allowed, and dancing was forbidden in the cafés. We were heavily rationed, and there was little food available, anyway. We would have to stand in line for hours in front of a fish store to be able to buy a couple of smoked herrings for a family of four. Toward the end of the month, we would just throw away our food stamps because the stores didn't have enough merchandise to supply everyone. Clothes and shoes were unavailable. People knitted sweaters and skirts when they were able to find some yarn somewhere."

Jeanne had elected to go to a French-speaking high school instead of a Flemish one (both languages are spoken in Belgium). Since her family spoke Flemish at home, she hoped to perfect her lesser command of French.

Soon, however, the Gestapo arrived to check the school records. Any student with Flemish roots was told they must go to a Flemish school. Luckily, the school administrators found a way around the rule. They hired a couple of young Flemish teachers and turned a large supply room into a classroom. "The Flemish department was formed, and the 'L'Ecole Professionelle Marius Renard' became bilingual. Since there were only five girls in my class, it was almost like private tutoring, and we received a fabulous high school education."

With the invasion of Normandy in June 1944, a new struggle for the control of Belgium developed. Jeanne remains deeply grateful to this day for the bravery of the American soldiers during the bloody Battle of the Bulge in eastern Belgium and Luxembourg, when "so many offered up their lives to liberate the Allied countries."

After the Americans and British finally pushed the German troops back out of Belgium, only the British troops were commonly seen in Brussels. "It wasn't until October or November that we started seeing a few American soldiers in Brussels for R&R. There were now large dance halls and clubs for the Allied military. We Belgian girls could get a membership card to participate in entertaining the troops. There were two bands, a continental British orchestra and a great American band. It took us no time to learn to do the boogie-woogie with GIs. After more than four years of restriction, we could dance again!

"On February 18, 1945, I accompanied a friend of mine whose mother ran a café. That's where I met a very nice and polite GI whose name was Harold Conn, but he was called 'H' for short. I had never heard of such a name. As I was about to leave, he insisted on walking me home. At the time, I was working for the Kredietbank downtown, and we made plans to meet again the next day in front of the Metropole Hotel."

After a few more encounters with "H," Jeanne took him in to meet her family after he walked her home one evening. It wasn't at all unusual for people to welcome soldiers into their homes in those days.

Jeanne celebrated her eighteenth birthday five days after she met Harold; he had his twenty-fifth three days after that. He was transferred to Antwerp in April to work on the docks, operating a crane to unload the big ships bringing in supplies for the Allied forces. Even so, he became Jeanne's steady date. "My father had already told me that it was 'out of the question' for me to become 'one of those war brides,' so anything serious seemed just a pipe dream. H [as she came to call him] was discharged at the end of November 1945. He made his way to France and then home to Pennsylvania just in time for Christmas."

Jeanne got a telegram from Hal that Christmas. She hadn't expected to hear from him again, but they corresponded for nineteen months. During that time, Hal proceeded to get the necessary papers for her to come to America. Jeanne very much wanted to go, and finally her father relented. After all, she was a young woman now, and she'd had nearly two years to decide it was what she wanted.

Unlike the war brides, who were brought to America at government expense, Jeanne had to pay for her own transportation. Women in her position were given only ninety-day visas to the United States. If they had not gotten married by the end of that period, they had to leave the country.

"On June 27, 1947, I left Brussels by Sabena Airlines to La Guardia Airport in New York City," Jeanne recalls. "It took sixteen hours with three refueling stops. When Hal picked me up at the airport, there were problems with immigration. Hal was supposed to have posted a $500 bond to cover my return expenses should we fail to marry in ninety days. This forced a twenty-four-hour stay at Ellis Island until Hal could get to the bank and post the bond. Luckily, his grandfather lived in New York and was able to help. After that adventure, we boarded a train for Philadelphia. Hal's mom welcomed me with open arms, and we became friends right away. I was very fortunate. Hal and I were married on July 10, 1947, and our first and only child, James, was born on July 2, 1948."

James gave Jeanne her own taste of what it can be like to lose a child to a foreign place. When Jim was a teenager, he decided to enter the priesthood. Jeanne had as hard a time with his decision as her own father had with her choice to go to America. Not only did Jim's choice mean she would never have grandchildren, but she feared that he would end up far away from home. "For the first time," she recollects, "I felt homesick, thinking about my parents and how hard it must have been for them to let me go to live so very far away."

But Father James J. Conn, SJ, has made her very proud. "He's a canon lawyer with a doctorate from the Pontifical Gregorian University in Rome, a civil law degree from Fordham University in New York, and is a member of the Maryland bar. He is currently a professor of canon law at the Gregorian University." Jeanne and Hal Conn celebrated their fifty-third wedding anniversary in Philadelphia, Pennsylvania, in July 2000.

Harold and Jeanne in front of her parents' house in Brussels in 1945.

Studio portraits of Harold and Jeanne, both taken in 1945.

Harold and Jeanne on their fiftieth wedding anniversary with their son, Reverend James J. Conn, SJ.

AMID THE RUBBLE AND DEPRIVATION
*of countries devastated by the war, first in
Italy, and later France, Belgium, Holland,
and ultimately Germany itself, American soldiers
offered vital assistance. Sometimes a kind response to
a request for help was all it took to make sparks fly
across cultures. Most of the European women whom
the soldiers met didn't speak English, but in such
circumstances, especially, a look or a touch of the hand
can speak volumes.*

Anna Della Casa Gonzales in 1944.

Anna Della Casa

GONZALES

Born in Naples, Italy, in 1926, Anna Della Casa survived a number of hair-raising adventures before coming to America as a war bride. Now living in San Bruno, California, near San Francisco, she tells her remarkable story with great verve and good humor, taking understandable pride in the fact that she did not meet her GI husband at a Red Cross or USO tea party or dance, but in the midst of a dangerous war-torn city. Only pluck and pure luck kept her alive until the day that Private John Gonzales entered her young life.

Anna was born a middle child in a Neapolitan family of sixteen girls and two boys. She says she wasn't scared when she heard people talking about the impending war, but once it started, she was scared all the time.

Anna experienced plenty of deprivation during the first three years of the war, but things got much worse when the Americans invaded Italy. The coming of the Americans didn't frighten the Italians very much—by that time, Americans were widely welcomed, as they provided hope that the Germans might one day be defeated. The Italians worried instead about the remaining presence of the German military on the mainland, ruthless troops whose job it was to thwart the American advance for as long as possible, and who regarded Italians with cruel contempt. The Pact of Steel alliance that Italy's fascist dictator Benito Mussolini had signed with Adolf Hitler in May 1939 brought little to the country but grief, and as time wore on, the German high command's increasing disdain for Mussolini funneled into a hatred of the ordinary Italian soldier. In turn, the Italian people came to hate the Germans, and as their dictator became increasingly unhinged, they understood that their salvation depended almost wholly on the success of the Allied invasion.

Many Italians also had relatives who had emigrated to the United States, so they felt a far greater sense of connection to America than to Germany. Berlin and Munich certainly had no "Little Italy" neighborhoods, as so many American cities did and still do.

The American, British, and Canadian forces began their invasion of Italy in Sicily on July 10, 1943. By the sixteenth, they had made sufficient headway for Prime Minister Winston Churchill and President Franklin D. Roosevelt to issue a joint statement calling for the surrender of Italy. They backed up that call with bombing raids on Rome and subsequently Naples. The bombardment of Naples was devastating, and Anna vividly remembers the terror of three days she spent in an air raid shelter during an intense period of bombing. The shelter was in an ancient tunnel under the city, built by the Romans during the days when Pompeii was a flourishing city on the Bay of Naples. Anna huddled in the shelter with some three hundred others and heard the crash of the building above them collapsing from what must have been a direct hit.

On July 25, the Grand Council of the Fascist party arrested Mussolini and replaced him with Marshal Pietro Badoglio. The replacement paved the way for the Italian surrender, signed in Sicily on September 3. Five days later, the surrender was officially announced to the world, after the Allies had already begun to invade the Italian mainland.

The Nazi forces continued to fight the Allies in Italy. During the fighting on Sicily, forty thousand German troops escaped to the mainland, augmenting their considerable presence there. The Nazi forces fought with such ferocity during the ensuing months that it took almost a year for the Allies to penetrate as far north as Florence.

While the American and British forces invaded mainland Italy in three places—Reggio at the toe of Italy's boot, Taranto on the inner heel, and Salerno, south of Naples—the Germans took control of Rome. They did not fully control Naples, but Anna Della Casa Gonzales remembers all too well that it felt like "they were everywhere." During this period, when she was eighteen, she had two frightening encounters with German troops.

American bombs had disrupted the water supply in the part of the city where she lived, so one day her mother dispatched her with a pail to get some water at the waterfront. "I complained, of course," Anna recalls. "But Mama said, 'Go.'" On the way, Anna heard a commotion and saw a crowd gathered in front of a delicatessen. Voices called out, "Free food! Free food!" Some German soldiers had broken in the door of the shop and were shouting at people, telling them to take whatever they wanted. Food was difficult to find in Naples, so a number of people rushed in, including Anna, who filled her pail with flour instead of water and grabbed a salami.

Just as she was about to run out, she saw the men shot dead right in front of her as they left the shop, by the same German soldiers who had broken down the door. Anna quickly realized she was caught in a cruel trap. As fast as she could, she made her way back through the shop and found a rear window big enough to crawl through. She then moved cautiously through the back streets of Naples, taking the most roundabout route home, so as not to be seen or followed.

Word of the shooting incident spread instantly all across town. Someone had seen Anna go into the shop with her pail, and told her horrified mother that Anna had never come out. When Anna rushed to her mother's side, having safely navigated a route home, calling, "Mama, I got some flour," her mother took one look and keeled over in a faint.

Shortly after her first face-to-face encounter with the cruelty of the German soldiers, she faced another situation that put her survival skills and bravery to an even greater test. One afternoon, a group of German soldiers rounded up and carted away her teenage brother and a couple of other boys. Everyone wrote them off for dead. The Italians knew that the Germans, now their official enemies, often shot teenage Italian boys who might otherwise grow to take up arms against them. They liked to make a vicious sport of it, taking the boys to the edge of the city, tying them to trees, and using them for target practice.

Anna had an older male cousin who owned a small truck. She and a couple of family friends piled into it and drove out to an area they knew the Germans favored for their deadly games. Sure enough, there were her brother and the two other boys tied to trees. The German soldiers were out of sight, although Anna and her friends could hear them a little way off in a wooded area.

To create a distraction, Anna ran down the road a few hundred yards, stood by some bushes where she couldn't be seen, and started screaming at the top of her lungs. After a couple of minutes, she heard the voices of the soldiers quickly coming toward her. As the soldiers searched for the source of her screams, her friends quickly freed the three boys. All except Anna clambered into the back of the truck and roared down the road just in time to grab her, now running for her life, as the Germans hit the road where she had stood. "We all got away safe!" Anna exclaims. "No one hurt!" She laughs, but even now there is a hint of breathlessness in her voice.

Anna and her family were immensely relieved when American soldiers took up temporary residence at the University of Naples, across the street from their house. Anna's new American neighbors proved very friendly. One day in September, Anna stood outside her house holding her niece, the daughter of an older sister who had been killed when an American bomb hit her house. The child and Anna's brother-in-law lived with Anna's family now. The family next door to Anna's house had arranged to do laundry for the soldiers, and this day, when a group came to pick up their laundry, one of the soldiers, John Gonzales, struck up a friendly conversation with Anna and her brother-in-law. A few days later, when some of the soldiers in John's company came by, they told Anna that John was interested in marrying her, and she told them to stop teasing her, adding, with her innate Neapolitan cheekiness, "If he likes me so much, tell him to get some food for this baby."

John promptly came to her house the next day with an armful of food for the baby. This was no easy task. Anna's family had the money to pay for food; there just wasn't any to buy. John's gift had a significance far greater than the monetary value of the goods he provided. After this, John came to visit often.

The large age gap between Anna and John, nearly twenty years her senior, was not out of the ordinary in Europe at the time. Still, Anna was cautious when John first suggested marriage, and told him she thought they ought to wait a while. John, hoping to encourage her not to put it off for too long, pointed out that he could be posted elsewhere at any time. He also added that his captain had his eye on Anna and might pull rank, which made Anna laugh.

Perhaps it helped that Anna's mother liked John and thought he would make a good husband. Not only would it be nice to have an American soldier in the family, but John also promised to take Anna to America as soon as the war was over. There she would have opportunities unavailable to her in Italy.

So Anna and John were married by a justice of the peace at the end of September 1943. Anna's family tried to persuade their parish priest to conduct a religious service to make the marriage legal in the eyes of the Catholic Church. Fortunately, John was also Catholic, which made things easier, and after weeks of inveigling, the priest agreed to marry them again at the beginning of January.

As it turned out, the religious ceremony took place just in the nick of time. Right after, they found John's captain waiting to deliver the news that the groom must report for duty immediately. His company had been ordered to leave Naples that very afternoon. John and Anna begged the captain to let them attend their wedding reception, at least for a little while, and of course to come join them himself. He agreed but, after just one hour, insisted that he and John leave. A tearful Anna kissed her husband good-bye, with no idea when or if she would ever see him again.

John was among the thirty-four thousand men to land at Anzio on January 22, 1944. Only thirteen soldiers died that day, a relatively small number compared to most days of battle, but John stepped on a mine and was very seriously injured. He barely survived and had to be hospitalized for a year and a half, first in Italy, then back in America. He delayed contacting Anna for a long time. For many months he was in no condition to write anyone, and nobody knew if he would ever recover—and if he did, to what extent. He feared that he would end up an unemployable invalid, hardly the sort of man he could expect a young girl like Anna, who had her whole life ahead of her, to cherish.

Anna, still in Italy, kept trying to obtain information about his whereabouts and condition from the Red Cross in Naples, to little avail. Wives everywhere, even back in America, often hit a brick wall when searching for their wounded husbands. In part, these difficulties arose due to continued security concerns as the war in Europe dragged on. They also occurred because the military bureaucracy was utterly overwhelmed.

Though they couldn't offer her much help, the Red Cross workers were always very nice to Anna and tried to lift her spirits by telling her stories about what it would be like for her to live in America after the war was over. Anna handled the lack of information about her husband with a patience and calm that belied her years. She found the taunts of young Italian men one of the hardest things to deal with. They'd tease her constantly, saying, "I see your wedding ring, but where's your husband?" Anna had no problem talking back to them, and her feisty wit may have saved her the indignity of having her hair cut off, a fate that befell a number of Italian girls who had married American servicemen.

In November 1945, over a year after she received word of his injury, Anna finally heard from John. He wrote to her from a veteran's hospital in Texas, where he was about to be released after nearly twenty months of surgery and recuperation. He told Anna that he was going to San Francisco to live with a sister and her husband, so he could save up some money once he found a job. And he sent her the necessary papers to bring her to the United States to join him.

Anna had never totally lost hope, but it seemed a miracle that, after so long, John should turn out to be still alive. She promptly wrote back to the San Francisco address but heard nothing back. Though she wondered what might be wrong, there were no problems regarding the validity of her papers, so she simply kept writing and preparing for her trip.

Her name headed the list of Italian war brides making the transatlantic crossing in May 1946 on the *Algonquin*. Rough weather at that time of year and very crowded conditions on an old, unrefurbished ship made the crossing quite difficult. Anna gives a kind of verbal shudder as she sums up her memories of the crossing. The storm-battered ship at last arrived, safe and sound, in New York on May 17, which was her birthday.

Anna was supposed to take a train across the country to San Francisco, but as there was a rail strike going on, she and the other war brides had to wait several days on the ship until a special train was commissioned to take them. She managed to send a telegram to John about her change in plans, but since she still hadn't gotten any reply to her earlier letters, she wasn't sure what to expect when she finally made it to San Francisco.

As she'd feared, when she arrived, she saw no sign of John at the station. Another war bride traveling with her kindly insisted that she come and stay with her for the time being. A helpful policewoman then located John at work. She said to him, "Your wife is here."

He replied, "No, my wife is in Italy."

"No, she's here in San Francisco," the officer repeated.

John refused to believe it. By the time he finally showed up to greet Anna, she'd just about given up and was ready to go home to Mama. She was quite angry, but John carefully explained to her that he had not received any of her letters, or her telegram. In fact, he had begun to worry that she had stopped loving him and wasn't going to come to America at all. When he looked at her with earnest tenderness and said, "Anna, I love you," all of her anger and frustration melted.

When Anna and John investigated the matter of the missing letters, they discovered that John's sister had thrown them all away. She thought John's marriage to Anna had been a terrible mistake. She got away with her attempt to sabotage their union for a long period of time, because John worked nights and was always asleep when the mail came.

Despite the sister's animosity, Anna and John had no choice but to stay with her and her husband. They simply didn't have enough money to get a place of their own yet. Anna's brother-in-law always treated her well, which made life bearable. Whenever the two men were absent, though, John's sister continued to give Anna a very hard time. Anna's almost immediate pregnancy put another strain on her relationship with John's sister, as the sister and her husband had been unable to have children. Anna felt uncomfortable during the days, but she made every effort to brighten up when John came home. She tried not to complain too much, since she was so happy being with him.

One day while the men were working, John's sister came into Anna and John's bedroom and told Anna to bring a particular chair downstairs. It was a favorite, she insisted, and she wanted it back. Anna, nine months pregnant, refused. Sitting in that chair was the only way she could be comfortable in her condition. In a fury, Anna's sister-in-law threatened to hit her. Anna wasn't about to let such a threat pass lightly. She had gotten through the war by learning how to deal with a crisis, and for the first time she stood up to her sister-in-law and made it clear she would fight back if necessary. Once she showed her grit, her sister-in-law left her alone.

Soon after the baby was born, Anna and John finally were able to get a place of their own. Anna had four more children over the next years, a total of three girls and two boys. After that, she told herself,

*Anna in Italy in 1944,
with an American army
truck in the background.*

*Photographs of Anna and
John taken after she had
arrived in the U.S.*

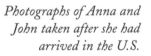

*A copy of Anna's Red Cross
membership card, listing
activities organized for the
wives of American servicemen.*

Anna and John celebrating their fortieth wedding anniversary in January 1984, just months before he passed away in June.

Anna (second from left, front row) with a group of war brides at a reunion party in San Mateo, California, on July 31, 1999. The cake is adorned with flags representing all of the countries the brides came from.

"I'd better stop, I don't want to become like my mama!" One of her sons, tragically, was killed by a drunk driver when he was nineteen. The other four have grown up and given her twenty-five grandchildren and seven great-grandchildren.

John Gonzales lived to be eighty-five, despite his extensive war injuries. "He still looked so young," Anna recalls. One of her granddaughters once said, "I want to have skin like yours," to which Anna replied, "No, you want skin like your grandpa's."

Anna still takes pride in having obtained her American citizenship all by herself in 1949. True, war brides didn't have to wait as long as other immigrants, but Anna worked hard on her English and studied for the test all on her own. After all, she was officially the first Italian war bride to come to the United States, and she felt she had a responsibility to live up to.

WAR BRIDES WERE NOT THE
only ones to experience difficulties due
to their romances with American
soldiers; sometimes the soldiers experienced problems
of their own. Some had to endure the agony of doubt
as they waited for their brides to show up on the
special cruises arranged by the government. Others
might encounter bureaucratic hassles in making
arrangements for the couple to be together again.

Erwin (Hal) and Eleonora (Nori)
Hayes in Milan, Italy, in 1946.

Erwin and Eleonora

HAYES

Erwin H. Hayes, known as Hal, met his future wife, Eleonora, in Milan, Italy, at the end of World War II. He had joined the army as a private in 1941 and was subsequently promoted to technical sergeant of the 751st GHQ tank battalion. His regiment began fighting in Tunisia and went on to take part in the campaigns of Naples to Foggia; Anzio, Rome, to the Arno, the North Appenines, and the Po Valley. In June 1944, Hal was commissioned a second lieutenant.

In recognition of the highly effective actions of Hal's battalion during the lengthy Italian campaign, they were given the honor of overseeing the beautiful city of Milan as it returned to normalcy. The battalion commander became, in effect, the mayor of Milan. A leader of the OSS gave a party for the officers of the 751st, which Eleonora Pozzi was invited to attend.

"I had recently received a battlefield promotion to first lieutenant," Hal says. "I spotted this lovely lady the minute she stepped off the elevator and onto the patio where the party was being held. I said to a friend, 'That I have to meet.' He laughed and said, 'Forget it. She's been escorting the colonel around town ever since we arrived.' I told him, 'The colonel's married. I'm going to dance with her.'"

And so he did. Nori, as her friends called her, turned out to be not only beautiful but also an exceptionally brave and accomplished young woman. She came from a prominent Milan family; her parents had built a prosperous construction and engineering firm, and her father was a colonel in the

Italian army. When her father refused to cooperate after Italy joined forces with Hitler, the Germans sent him to a concentration camp, where he was treated somewhat better as a senior officer than the other prisoners but witnessed brutal punishments. With Nori's father gone, the full responsibility of running the family business had fallen to her and her mother.

Hal and Nori fell in love almost at first sight. But the same battlefield valor and courage that had made it possible for Hal to approach the beautiful Nori and ask her to dance proved an obstacle to their marriage. He had served a total of 581 days in combat, a long time for a soldier. The army, presuming they were doing him a favor, decided it was time to ship the good soldier home to America. Hal, who considered this terrible news, requested reassignment in an attempt to stay in Italy long enough to get married—but to no avail.

It would take Hal a year to the day to return to Italy. First he had to fight with the State Department to get a passport. They told him, with no trace of irony, "There has been a war over there, and passports are not being issued for tourists." Hal finally convinced the State Department that, given his own part in freeing Italy, the least they could do was permit him to go back and marry the woman he loved.

But many hurdles still lay in his path. To get back into Italy, Hal had to have an Italian visa. The nearest Italian consulate to Spokane, Washington, where his family lived, was all the way in San Francisco, and Hal had no way to get there. He embarked on another battle by correspondence before he was finally granted a visa.

At last, Hal had his papers but no means of transportation to Italy. Only one line, the American Export Line headquartered in New York, was shipping into Italy at the time. Hal contacted the same friend he had been with in Milan the day he met Nori. That friend happened to live on Long Island, and he sent Hal the shipping company's address. American Export Line wrote Hal a vague letter telling him that they did "periodic sailings," but either there was no specific schedule or they were unwilling to provide it.

So Hal "took the bull by the horns." He packed a bag and hopped on the next train to New York. Arriving there on a Saturday morning, he went directly to the shipping line's offices. A sign on the door said they were closed on Saturday, but the door was open, so he walked right in.

Two clerks sat in a room containing about thirty empty desks. Hal approached the nearest clerk and quickly explained his situation. "The clerk reluctantly checked in a filing cabinet and, after a brief search, informed me that my file apparently had been shipped to the Seattle office. I told him that I had never been told there was a Seattle office, which was why I was not in Seattle but in New York, and that I was going to be on the next ship sailing for Italy no matter what."

The clerk asked Hal to wait a few minutes while he made a telephone call. "While talking on the phone, he placed his hand over the mouthpiece and asked if I could be ready to sail on the coming Thursday. I said I was ready to sail right then. The clerk talked to the party on the phone for another couple of minutes and hung up. He asked to see my passport and visa, and then he crossed out a name on the list he was working on and entered my name in its place. He told me I was lucky, because he was typing the manifest for the Thursday departure, and once it was finished, it couldn't be changed." Finally, a small stroke of fate had intervened on behalf of Hal and Nori.

When Hal's ship arrived in Genoa, Nori and her family were there to greet him. After a joyous reunion, the couple began the difficult process of obtaining a marriage license and getting permission to be married in a Catholic church. Hal converted to Catholicism, and at long last, they were married on September 28, 1946, in Milan.

They had decided to live in the United States but could not return without encountering a whole new set of bureaucratic difficulties. Nori needed a new passport, and a shipping and air strike had begun. When shipping at last resumed, Nori was a high-priority passenger as the wife of an American serviceman. But Hal himself now had no priority whatsoever. He was considered a mere tourist. Only after many frustrating visits to the American consulate was Hal finally able to return home to the United States with his new wife.

Hal Hayes fought two very different kinds of Italian campaigns. One he fought on the battlefield as a member of the 751st Tank Battalion; the other he fought on paper with bureaucrats on two continents. It was all worth it in the end, though, and Hal considers both campaigns victorious. "After fifty-four wonderful years," Hal says, "Nori and I are still having fun."

Hal in June 1944, just after being promoted to second lieutenant.

Hal being awarded the Silver Star medal by Lieutenant General Mark Clark in August 1944.

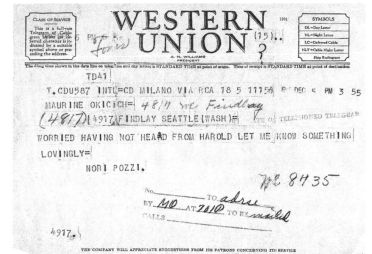

Telegram sent by Nori to Hal's sister in Seattle, asking for word of Hal because she hadn't heard from him for so long.

Hal and Nori after their wedding in September 1946.

Hal and Nori in 1999.

B ACK ON THE HOME FRONT, *American women who married or fell in love with men who immigrated from overseas and were not U.S. citizens could find their lives utterly disrupted. Some women married men before the war who were now regarded as threats because they retained their German or Italian citizenship. Those countries were among our enemies, and the American government had to be convinced that men who retained their citizenship were not spies or even saboteurs. While their backgrounds were checked, these men were often separated from their wives, held in detention camps in several states. Their experiences characterize a different kind of World War II love story.*

*Henry and Jane Schlosser in January 1941, before they
were married on a ski trip to the Bear Mountain resort
in upstate New York, with the Bear Mountain Inn
in the background.*

Henry and Jane
SCHLOSSER

In 1939, Jane Keller graduated from the Pratt Institute, the well-known art and design college in Brooklyn. Soon after, she found a job at an advertising firm on Fifty-third Street in Manhattan.

One morning in 1940, between Christmas and New Year's Day, she spotted a man in the lobby of her office building. He was dressed jauntily, sporting a hat with a large brim and a European-style double-breasted overcoat. Just as she looked at him, he put a handkerchief to his nose and blew with a loud honk. Jane turned away.

She soon discovered the man was a freelance artist, hired by her agency to work for a few days on a special project. His name was Henry Schlosser. It turned out that he had noticed her in the lobby that day, too. They exchanged pleasantries over the next few days, and on January 3, when they happened to lunch at the same restaurant, he suggested she sit with him.

That lunch launched a lifetime together.

They turned out to have a great deal in common, and conversation flowed with an ease and verve that is usually the hallmark of people who have known each other a very long time.

Henry was German by birth. He first came to the United States in 1928 when he was twenty-three. He loved America and everything about it, from baseball to apple pie. He had brought his German bride to Rochester, New York, where they had two daughters, Marion and Sylvia.

In 1937 the advertising company McCann-Erikson, for which Henry worked for a long time, sent him to Germany to head their offices there. But he disliked Hitler's Germany and wanted to return to America. His wife, however, did not, and they soon divorced. Henry had a very difficult time persuading the German authorities to permit him to leave the country in 1938, but he finally convinced them that with an American salary, he would be in a better position to support his two children. Once he got back to America, he decided to freelance rather than work for a single company, and he settled in New York City.

Jane Keller was born and raised in the Midwest, and her parents were quite conservative. "Henry was not exactly what they had in mind for me," Jane says. "A divorced foreigner with two children who was thirteen years older than I was, an artist—and a freelancer on top of that." But Jane was deeply smitten with Henry and, despite all objections, said yes when he asked her to marry him.

They got a license, but she kept putting off their wedding date, in part because of her parents' disapproval and in part because, as Jane admits, she is given to second thoughts. They eventually had to get another license. The day before the second one expired, September 21, 1941, they finally got married. Despite their hesitations, Jane's parents did attend. Her mother had worked all night to finish Jane's dress.

Henry lived in a sublet at the time, and they decided to find a new place immediately, ending up in the heart of Greenwich Village in an apartment on Bank Street, across from the New School for Social Research. Jane kept her job in advertising and Henry did quite well as a freelancer, often called on by major corporations like RCA and DuPont.

The days went by, and they were very happy. But on March 31, 1942, their doorbell rang. When they answered, two FBI agents confronted them. Henry had never officially become an American citizen. Back in the 1930s, he had started the application process but was interrupted when McCann-Erikson sent him back to Germany. Because of the difficulties he encountered in getting out of Germany, he spent so long abroad that he was required to start the naturalization process all over again, and he just hadn't quite got around to it.

With America at war with Germany and Italy, as well as Japan, the government professed concern regarding the loyalty of people from those countries who were living in America. Today, most know the stories of the internment camps for Japanese-Americans. Fewer know that there were also detention camps for Germans and Italians. Like many artists, Henry had a habit of saving photos and clippings of all sorts that interested him, so his apartment was full of "evidence" that could easily be taken the wrong way by a suspicious officer.

To Jane's horror, Henry was put into detention on Ellis Island in New York Harbor. He had some very distinguished company, including the great Metropolitan Opera star Ezio Pinza, who would later captivate all of America singing "Some Enchanted Evening" when he costarred with Mary Martin in *South Pacific* on Broadway. Pinza was still an Italian citizen, although he had lived in America for many years.

Henry, Pinza, and their fellow detainees were not treated badly. In between writing letters trying to regain his freedom, Henry entertained himself by making water color paintings of the camp. Soon the guards and other Ellis Island officials were offering him what amounted to cigarette money in exchange for a sketch. In the weeks leading up to Christmas, Henry hand-painted wooden toys for family and friends. No matter how well he was treated, though, the fact remained that he was incarcerated, separated from Jane and his livelihood as a commercial artist.

Thanks to his international fame and connections, Pinza was released fairly soon. But things got worse for Henry. He was transferred to Fort Meade in Maryland, and Jane moved to Baltimore and took a job there so that she could see him—for only twenty minutes every two weeks. After three months at Fort Meade, Henry was sent to yet another detention camp in Tennessee. Jane couldn't very well pull up stakes again, so she remained in Baltimore.

She planned to go home to her parents for Christmas of 1942. (Jane does give her parents great credit for never once saying "I told you so" when Henry was taken into custody.) Two days before she was to leave for Roslyn, she got a call from Henry. The letters he wrote from jail to friends and employers who could vouch for him had finally paid off. After a thorough investigation, the government had cleared his name. He didn't know exactly when he would be released, but he assured Jane that everything was all right and he would certainly see her soon. It was the best Christmas present Jane could have asked for.

*Henry on their
ski trip to Bear
Mountain.*

*Henry and Jane on
their wedding day,
September 21, 1941.*

A marriage certificate Henry painted and lettered for their first anniversary, while he was interned at Fort Meade.

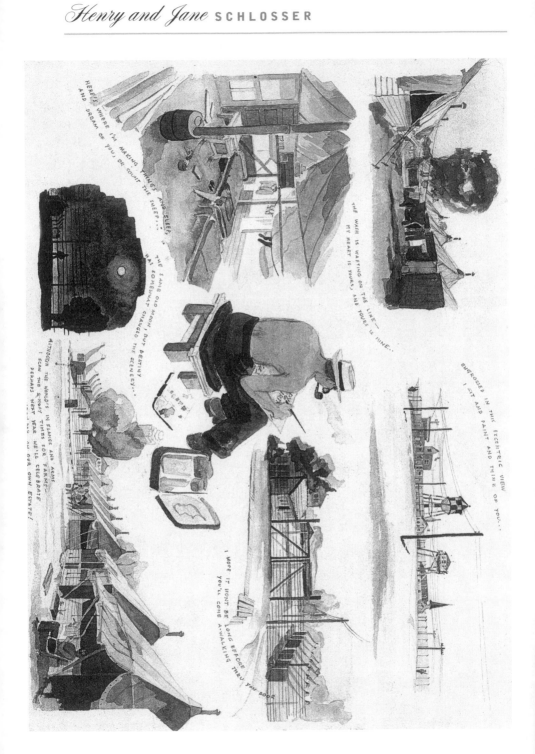

*A painting Henry did for Jane's birthday
while at Fort Meade.*

The Philadelphia Inquirer

a d   FRIDAY, FEBRUARY 14, 1947   22

A newspaper article about an exhibition of toys sent by German children to America in thanks for donations to a school feeding program.

GIFTS FROM GERMAN CHILDREN

School children of Darmstadt, Germany, grateful for gifts that made possible a school feeding program, made 1000 toys for American children, and sent them to the American Friends Service Committee. Henry Schlosser, Mrs. Jane Schlosser (left) and Miss Miriam Beck arrange the toys for exhibitions in schools.

They were finally reunited on January 6, 1943, and settled down again in New York. When their daughter, Heidi, was born in November of 1943, they decided to give up their work in advertising and moved to a farm near Roslyn, New York. Henry applied again for citizenship as soon as his detention was over, and in 1945 he at last became an American citizen. There, sparked by the enjoyment Henry had found making toys as Christmas presents, they started a business designing and making wooden toys. Since materials were still scarce due to the war, they used scrap material from bomb cases. The toys were sold nationwide as "Bonnie Barn" toys. Later in 1945, their son, Jon, was born, and the farm they were renting was sold, so they had to move again.

This time they moved to Chester County, near Jane's parents' new home. Henry and Jane ran a toy-importing business in the 1950s and '60s for shops called Christmas Stocking and Bonnie Barn, which they opened in various towns in Pennsylvania and in Ocean City, New Jersey. By 1973 they decided to sell the last shop they kept open, in King of Prussia, Pennsylvania, and started collecting and selling antique toys, establishing themselves as premier American dealers.

"We had fifty lovely years together," Jane remembers. "Henry died before we reached our actual fiftieth anniversary, but we made it to the anniversary of our first lunch together." Jane herself now runs a shop in the "antique country" around Adamstown, Pennsylvania. It is overflowing with exquisite treasures originally made for children but now coveted by adult collectors. Seeing the fanciful antiques every day reminds her of the wonderful life she and Henry shared.

WHILE THE UNRULY AMERICAN *west might have come as a shock to war brides from overseas, the rustic setting sometimes offered unexpected amenities to new brides and officers during the war—if you knew where to look. Many young couples did everything they could to be together for as long as possible before the husband was shipped overseas. Army air force pilots had to train over a longer period of time than those serving in the ground forces. Many of their wives, through pure ingenuity and tenacity, found ways to be with them during these long months of training. In makeshift and money-short accommodations, wives remained determined to make the best of their situation. Occasionally, a young couple even got lucky and stumbled into unusual circumstances that they would remember with great fondness for the rest of their lives.*

Wharton and Miriam
SCHNEIDER

When Morton Schneider got his first driver's license at the age of sixteen, someone at the DMV made a mistake and issued the license in the name of Wharton. Mr. Schneider liked his dignified new name well enough, so he decided not to fight city hall.

A few years later, when he sought a commission in the army air force during World War II, he realized problems might arise from the inconsistency. The army would want a transcript of his high school records, which carried his birth name of Morton. Surprisingly, the army took his situation right in stride; they told him they would add the name Morton to his file as an alias and request his high school records accordingly. He served as an army air force pilot officially named Wharton Schneider, and he's carried the name ever since.

Wharton met his Brooklyn-born wife, Miriam, while stationed in California in 1943. She was visiting an aunt in Hollywood when they happened to run into each other. They quickly realized they were meant for each other and got married in Hollywood that very December.

Shortly after the wedding, Wharton was transferred to Fort Sumner in New Mexico. The army informed him they had no available accommodations for spouses, but he and Miriam decided to give it a try anyway. Surely they could find someplace for her to live. The base turned out to be in the middle of nowhere, and Miriam ended up in a rundown hotel in Clovis, New Mexico, sixty miles east of her husband—hardly the best situation for a young woman.

A few weeks after their move to New Mexico, Wharton went out to dinner in the small town of Santa Rosa, New Mexico, fifty miles west of the base, with a couple of fellow pilots. When they finished eating, he went into a back room to telephone Miriam. They spoke on the phone for a long time, and when Wharton returned to the front of the bar, he realized that not a soul was left in the place. What was more, he was locked in.

Wharton immediately ran back to the phone, called the local operator, and apprised her of his situation. She asked his location, but he wasn't even sure where he was. The operator instructed him to go to the window, look out, and then come back and tell her what he saw. So Wharton walked over to the window, peered outside, and described it to the operator, who assured him that she'd call the owner, who would hopefully let him out. She soon called back to tell Wharton that the owner, Mr. Medley, was in the shower and wouldn't be able to get there for another fifteen minutes; in the meantime, Wharton should feel free to help himself to a cigar or some cream pie. More concerned with getting out than having cream pie, Wharton decided not to take advantage of the owner's kind offer. Luckily, he didn't have to wait too long.

When the owner showed up, he and Wharton hit it off immediately. Wharton learned during their friendly banter that Mr. Medley and his brother owned half the businesses in Santa Rosa: the restaurant, the movie theater and the drugstore. He also knew of a small motor inn with cooking facilities—perfect for Miriam.

Miriam moved there in the blink of an eye. It was nothing fancy, but at least she could cook for herself and for Wharton when he was off duty. Mr. Medley even drove the 110 miles to Clovis to help Miriam move to Santa Rosa. According to Wharton, the Medley brothers couldn't have been nicer to a young pilot and his wife—now pregnant—if they'd all been friends since childhood. One brother headed the local rationing board, so Wharton and Miriam got all the gas they needed. And one night, due to the distance Wharton still had to travel from Fort Sumner, he and Miriam arrived at the movie theater ten minutes after the feature had begun. The Medley brother in charge stopped the film, rewound it, and started it again from the beginning, just for them.

All over the country, the wives of young servicemen made do under difficult circumstances, having a hard time making ends meet. But one young couple in Santa Rosa, New Mexico, had a very nice time of it, thanks to two brothers named Medley.

Miriam was due to give birth about a week before Wharton was scheduled to go overseas. Suddenly, though, Wharton was asked to fly a special mission a few days earlier than originally planned. He asked if he could please stick around, since his first child was coming any day. The army relented and granted Wharton special permission to stay, transferring him to Kingman Army Air Force Base, outside of Kingman, Arizona.

According to a lot of soldiers, the army was usually pretty good about that sort of thing, although a lot depended on the attitude of one's superior officers. Wharton turned out to be luckier than he could have imagined. The plane he had been asked to fly on the special mission crashed, killing both pilots. That kind of eerie luck befell many soldiers during the war. But rather than feeling like they'd been saved by a miracle, those who survived just quietly accepted their good fortune. They knew all too well that next time around, things might not work out so much in their favor.

Miriam soon gave birth to a daughter at the base hospital. Shortly after the birth, Wharton had to say good-bye when Miriam's mother arrived to accompany Miriam and the baby back east for the duration of the war.

The air force sent Wharton to India to fly supplies over the Hump—the name pilots gave to the treacherous route over the Himalayas—and deliver them to General Chiang Kai-shek's forces in China: "the forgotten war," Wharton calls it, as his role in World War II doesn't get much press. But while the public may have forgotten, military historians know that the air force sent only the very best pilots to India to fly the Hump. The Himalayas rose dauntingly high, the weather was subject to wild fluctuations, and if your plane went down, you had virtually no chance of rescue. In order to survive the treacherous flight conditions, you not only had to possess an extraordinary instinct for flying, you had to have nerves of steel. Wharton is too modest a fellow to admit any of this, but to those who know, the mere mention of having flown the Hump speaks volumes.

After the hostilities in India diminished somewhat, Wharton was assigned for a few months as a flying safety officer in Calcutta. He received one last assignment to fly General Stone from Shanghai back to

WAR DEPARTMENT
HEADQUARTERS OF THE ARMY AIR FORCES
WASHINGTON

March 6, 1943

PERSONNEL ORDERS)
NO.   56   )

EXTRACT

4. Pursuant to authority contained in paragraph 2, sub-paragraph 2, Army Regulations 35-1480, dated October 10, 1942, the following-named officers, Air Corps (AUS), each of whom holds an aeronautical rating, are hereby required to participate in regular and frequent aerial flights, at such times as they are called to active duty with the Army Air Forces, U. S. Army, under competent authority, and are authorized to participate in regular and frequent aerial flights while on an inactive status, in accordance with the provisions of paragraph 52, A.R. 95-15, dated April 21, 1930.

      1st Lt. William Whitney Ward, (0-514738)
      2nd Lt. Marshall Charles Benedict, (0-514641)
      2nd Lt. Charles Castleman Bulger, (0-514746)
      2nd Lt. Manford Milton Owen, Jr., (0-514625)
      2nd Lt. Wharton Leo Schneider, (0-514626)

All orders in conflict with this order are revoked.

By command of Lieutenant General Arnold:

J. M. Bevans,
Colonel, Air Corps,
Director of Personnel.

OFFICIAL:

John H. Walls,
Captain, Air Corps,
Assistant Chief,
Military Personnel Division.

Note: When attached to pay voucher for purpose of collecting flying pay this order or true copies thereof, should be in duplicate and accompanied by duplicate –
      (a) Copies of order calling the officer to active duty.
      (b) Flight certificate of officer, duly signed by the Commanding Officer as called for by existing regulations.

3-7208-2, AF

Wharton Schneider's commission as a second lieutenant.

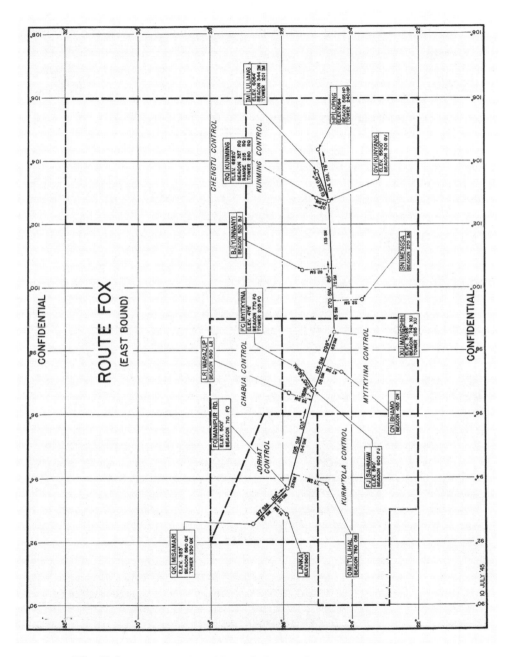

The flight route over "the Hump," the treacherous Himalayas.

the United States. The day before Christmas, 1945, he arrived home to be with his wife and daughter.

At the reunions of pilots who flew the Hump, Wharton and his fellow Hump veterans no doubt regale one another with tales and memories of those harrowing days trying to judge what the crazy winds of the Himalayas might do next. But in his day-to-day life, he prefers to talk about the happy days he spent with his young wife in Santa Rosa, New Mexico, under the ever helpful gaze of the Medley brothers.

SIXTEEN MILLION AMERICAN MEN *and women served in uniform in one branch of the service or another during World War II. Almost two-thirds of them were in the army, including the army air force. Four million served in the navy. Only a few more than five hundred thousand served in the marines who fought some of the toughest battles of the war in the South Pacific. Then there was the even smaller cadre of men who served in the merchant marine, who got supplies from the United States to Allied ports around the world. They faced grave danger throughout the war, even though the men didn't serve in any branch of the service. No supply was more important than the oil transported by the Esso fleet.*

*Harry and Mary Lou Heffelfinger aboard
one of Harry's ships.*

Harry E. and Mary Lou
HEFFELFINGER

While the stories of the men and women who served in the armed forces during World War II are featured most prominently in this book, there were other individuals who faced the dangers of military service even though they were not in the army, the navy, or the marines. One such man was Harry E. Heffelfinger, a captain in the fleet of Standard Oil tankers that delivered vital fuel to the Allied countries throughout the war, despite grave danger.

The crews on oil tankers were accustomed to being away from their loved ones for considerable periods of time, but the war required even longer tours of duty, as well as the constant threat of attack. These crews were every bit as crucial in the battle for freedom as military personnel. Most of their time was spent doing the same hard work they'd always done, but the everyday perils of sailing the high seas with an inflammable cargo were considerably intensified by the knowledge that they could fall under fire at any time from any direction by enemy ships or subs.

Harry Heffelfinger was born in landlocked Indiana in the first year of the twentieth century. Although he spent much of his youth wishing he could own a small farm, instead he went to sea. He shipped out for the first time in 1918, working on U.S. Shipping Board vessels. In December 1921, he joined the Esso fleet, aboard the *W. J. Hannah*. He worked his way up to master by July of 1933, and he served as the captain of many ships over the next two decades in the marine division of Humble Oil & Refining Company, a major Standard Oil constituent.

In 1940 he began dating Mary Lou Harris, a registered pediatric nurse in Newark, New Jersey, whom he had met through a mutual friend. They soon became engaged. Writing from aboard the *Peter Hurll* in September 1940, en route to Rio de Janeiro, Harry declared, "I'm having a terrible time snapping out of this tropical lethargy, what with a full moon, millions of stars, and you to dream of. Can you wonder I'm in a trance? . . . You have me right up in the clouds and I love it, and you, and life, and that makes the sun shine night and day for me."

In an even more ardent letter, Harry told Mary Lou that he knew it was raining in Newark, where she was, but added, "If we were there together it would be in full bloom, rain or shine. It's always that way with you, darling Mary Lou, your radiant beauty, and I want to come home to bask in it, naked too, must have the full benefit of your radiance. Baby, can I swing on the ice-box door?"

Harry sent Mary Lou bottles of perfume that he bought in his travels around the Caribbean and South America, when the ship put in at ports from Aruba to Venezuela to Brazil, scents like Shocking, Belladagia, and Scandal. Mary Lou always dabbed some on her letters back to Harry.

Though the war was already raging in Europe, the U.S. had not entered, and American shipping was not yet at danger from the German U-boat threat. Harry's letters from this period describe the usual daily life aboard ship, remarking on the few passengers, or lamenting the fact that stores of fresh food picked up along the way had been ruined by the ship's terrible new cook. Matters certainly improved in the food department on a subsequent voyage. With the kind of flourish usually reserved for luxury liners, a typed menu "tendered to" six named passengers with "The Compliments of Captain H. E. Heffelfinger" on December 18, 1940, included hearts of celery and salted almonds, cream of tomato soup, both roast turkey and Virginia ham, four vegetables, fresh salad, ice cream, fruit, and "Surprise Cake." Indeed, on board an American commercial ship in 1940, the war in Europe might well seem not to be happening at all. But as the captain of an oil tanker, Harry knew a good deal about what German subs were doing to British shipping, and the day would soon come when his letters would ominously portray the coming threat.

The day before the sumptuous feast Harry invited his passengers to, President Roosevelt discussed for the first time with members of his cabinet his idea for the Lend-Lease program, which would allow the beleaguered British to purchase food and raw materials, weapons, vehicles and other products from the United States without payment. The bill proposing the program was put before the still-isolationist Congress in January 1941 and passed with the crucial support of the Republican secretary of war, Henry L. Stimson, in March of that year. The Lend-Lease program was one of the most generous acts of assistance ever undertaken by one country on behalf of another.

The same month the Lend-Lease bill went to Congress, Harry and Mary Lou were married in Newark, New Jersey. After Harry returned to his ship, his letters from those subsequent trips are filled with testament to the fact that American commercial ships were no long safe in international waters. Harry wrote from Aruba: "Just got the lowdown on what happened to Capt. Bloomquist, it's rather a long story. Those dirty Germans, they torpedoed him without warning, put three torpedoes into the ship. Lucky everyone on board wasn't killed."

In another letter he told Mary Lou that one of the *Peter Hurll*'s sister tankers, returning from the Azores, had encountered a lifeboat adrift in the Atlantic. There were twelve men in it, all dead, apparently from starvation and thirst. The heavy clothes the dead sailors were wearing indicated that their ship must have been attacked somewhere in the North Atlantic and that they had drifted south, possibly for weeks.

By the end of that year, America had plunged into the war, and Mary Lou worried that her husband would be drafted. Harry wrote to her, "Don't worry about the draft board. Hell, the Army would be easy in comparison to this job." Besides, Harry was far too valuable where he was, transporting critical oil supplies.

Oil for the war effort was in such tight supply that strict gas rationing was instituted on the home front. By the fall of 1942, only three gallons of gas were allowed per week for American family cars, although doctors were allowed more, especially in rural areas with few hospitals where house calls were essential.

After the United States entered the war, the Atlantic routes plied by the tankers in the Standard Oil fleet became highly treacherous. By the end of January 1942, eleven German U-boats began stealthy operations along the East Coast of the United States, and their number quickly increased into the twenties. Their targets were usually merchant ships, and the bodies of sailors began washing up on the beaches of Florida.

The greatest danger to American ships came in the first few months after the U.S. entered the war. The British navy was furious with the U.S. Navy high command during this time; British merchant ships were being sunk, too, and the American navy refused to listen to British advice, despite the fact that the British had been dealing with U-boats for eighteen months. After the war, Winston Churchill declared that the only thing that truly frightened him during the war was the U-boat situation. He was greatly relieved when the U.S. Navy came to understand the peril involved and how to deal with it.

The public was not informed in any detail about these developments. Military censorship controlled not only what was published in newspapers and broadcast over the radio but also what could be written home to loved ones.

The crews aboard Esso ships technically came under the same censorship rules as members of the armed services, but the enforcement was not as strict, and in a letter sent from Aruba on May 2, 1942, Harry told Mary Lou a story that horrified her:

> Since you are curious to know if I had any excitement coming down, yes, we did. Don't know how much the censor will pass, but if you are anxious, we encountered the Nazis hand-to-hand, so to speak. He had me in a tight spot for a while, but we drove him off with the machine guns, nobody hurt on this side but I hope we gave him a belly full. It happened at night when we couldn't see the results. Two nights previous to that a sub opened up on two ships just ahead of me, close, yet far enough for me to see all the action but not be involved. Things were plenty hot up that way. We sailors are going to have a score to settle with those crazy Nazis even after this war is over. Gallant men they are, they sneak alongside of a ship at night and let go with everything they have.

Harry later told the story in more detail for a book published in 1946 by Standard Oil about the 135 vessels of the Esso fleet that transported 665 million barrels of oil during the war. Noting that armament had just been installed on the *Peter Hurll,* Harry relates how his ship and two others moved out of Hampton Roads, Virginia. The lead ship was the *Mercury Sun,* with the *Gulf of Mexico* second, followed by the *Peter Hurll.* On the first night out of Hampton Roads, Harry saw tracer bullets in the darkness ahead—the *Gulf of Mexico* was under machine-gun fire from a U-boat. Harry changed course immediately, and his ship escaped in the darkness. The other two vessels also survived that encounter, but the *Mercury Sun* was sunk six weeks later in the Caribbean.

More serious problems for the *Peter Hurll* developed the following night. "About 10 o'clock," Harry recalled in 1946,

> Chief Engineer Elliot C. Daniels called the bridge and said he would have to stop the port engine to make repairs. We were able to make only about seven knots on one engine. I called out the gun crew. It was a fine clear night and we were only about a mile and a half off shore. A submarine surfaced about 300 to 400 yards away and began firing machine guns at us, the tracer bullets coming close over the wheelhouse. We fired back with our 50 calibers on the bridge. I decided to try to ram the U-boat. When we headed for her she crash-dived. I phoned the engine room and called for all the revolutions we could get. We ran full speed on our starboard engine for about two and half hours and never saw the submarine again.

Harry speculated that the U-boat must have been running low on torpedoes and did not want to waste one on a ship headed south and loaded with ballast, not oil.

A letter Harry wrote to Mary Lou about this encounter was mailed from Curacao in June 1942. It was marked as having been read by a censor. Words were not blacked out, as usual, but actually cut out of the letter with a razor blade. Missing, for example, was a reference to how long the voyage down had taken, as well as a reference to another ship. But the censor did not remove these two frightening sentences: "The damn Nazis broadcast from Berlin that they had sunk us. So I guess they have us on their list." The U-boat portrayed its run-in with the *Peter Hurll* as a triumph. Distortions of casualty figures, and false accounts of planes downed and ships sunk, occurred on both sides during World War II, in part because hard numbers were sometimes difficult to ascertain. The Germans, however, were particularly prone to inflate their damage and casualty estimates.

While the U-boat threat along the East Coast and down into the Caribbean periodically abated, Harry and the other captains in the oil fleet never knew when the Nazis would increase the pressure again. Hitler often seemed to value the element of surprise over other military consid-erations, which had the desired effect of keeping the Allies continually on edge, although his orders sometimes went against the advice of his own officers and, in the end, undermined the German military.

Years later, Mary Lou told her children that she spent the war years dreading an overseas call to tell her that Harry's ship had been attacked and that he had been wounded or killed. As for Harry, he spent a good deal of his free time writing letters to her that continually asked for news of home. Harry and Mary Lou's first child, their son, Phil (who was nick-named Skipper), was born November 1, 1942, and Harry constantly inquired about how his son was coming along and whether the family's rambunctious dog, Smokey, was behaving himself. One such query was answered by Mary Lou in a brief Western Union cablegram sent to Harry at the Royal British Hotel, Glasgow, Scotland. It read,

FAMILY UNDER CONTROL BUT LONELY STAY WELL LOVE

Only a few of Mary Lou's letters to Harry have survived, but they are lively and full of amusing stories. On December 22, 1943, she wrote a letter that began, "I'm very lonesome for you but that is an old story— yes, no? Nonetheless, what you'd have on your hands if you were home!!!" After telling him about the muddled marriage plans of a rela-tive, she turned to her efforts to decorate the house. "Got down last year's ornaments & such—even the stand & it begins to feel Xmasy— hung bells & pine cones on the front door—they tinkle & Smokey is quite overcome—when he breaks down the door getting in he has a joy-ous time barking at 'em—all I do is just go & pick up the pieces. Four times I've pinned 'em back on the door (so far)." Her report on baby Phil reflected the vicissitudes of new motherhood: "Phil continues to be the Tarzan of 10 Jerome Street—now it's temper, so much so that Mrs. K. rushed upstairs to see if he was hurt. . . . Told her I was letting him cool off—so she proceeded to pick him up & love him back to sweetness. Hmm, did I ever feel the fool."

In another letter, Mary Lou commented on the public's failure to fully appreciate the importance and danger of the work that civilians like Harry and his crew members were doing, and that they made just as valuable a contribution as those in navy uniform. "If only they'd . . . realize how wonderful you people are. You go out in this weather and take a physical beating plus the horror that is constantly lurking in the sea—then you come ashore and are quiet about your discomforts—but some of these punks dash around in a uniform and have people kissing their feet. 'Taint fair, dear & you know it."

But there was one compensating advantage to Harry's civilian status: He did get home to see Mary Lou more often than most members of the armed services. These respites might have been short, occurring only once every several months, but they meant a great deal to both Harry and Mary Lou. One such visit home resulted in Mary Lou becoming pregnant again, and she gave birth to their daughter, Mary Jane, nicknamed Missi, on April 8, 1944.

Two months after Missi was born, the D-Day invasion took place, and from then on, Mary Lou worried less about her husband. The German military concentrated on efforts to stave off the Allied forces fighting their way toward Berlin, and the U-boats, having lost the French ports they used as bases, ceased to be a threat.

After the war, Harry continued to serve as the captain of numerous ships in the Standard Oil fleet. In 1952 he became group captain, and in November 1959 he was made assistant port captain, a position he held until his retirement in 1963, after more than forty-one years with the company. He died a year later, a much honored man who had traded in his early dreams of owning a small farm in Indiana to spend his life at sea.

Mary Lou Heffelfinger suffered a stroke in 1965, a year after her husband's death, and subsequently moved into a nursing home. She was allowed to bring only one suitcase of personal belongings aside from clothes. After her death in 1973, a good friend took charge of the suitcase for safekeeping. In the winter of 2000, the friend rediscovered the suitcase stored away in the attic, and asked Harry and Mary Lou's daughter, Missi, if she wanted it. Missi recalls that her heart leaped when she heard the suitcase existed. There was just one thing she hoped would be in it. When Missi was about sixteen, she came across something fascinating in the hall linen closet at the top of the stairs. It was a pink tin box that had once contained three pounds of Louis Sherry chocolates. In the box were several packets of old letters, tissue-thin and handwritten, tied with purple ribbons. Quickly realizing that they were written by her father to her mother during the war, she started to read them. But before long, her mother came upstairs, saw what she was up to, told her sternly that those letters were private, and took them away.

Sure enough, there was that same pink tin in the suitcase, just as Missi had hoped. Just a few days after recovering the letters, Missi's brother told her that he had seen a notice in the newspaper requesting World War II love stories for this book. The timing struck Missi as more than mere coincidence, and even though her mother had considered the letters too private for Missi to read when she was a teenager, Missi and her brother both felt that the letters honored their parents and that their story of the war should be shared with others. After all, those letters had been carefully preserved a very long time because they were so special.

FORM NO. 6.

WESTERN UNION

(THE WESTERN UNION TELEGRAPH COMPANY)

(INCORPORATED IN THE STATE OF NEW YORK, U.S.A., WITH LIMITED LIABILITY.)

CABLEGRAM

ANGLO-AMERICAN TELEGRAPH CO., LD. CANADIAN NATIONAL TELEGRAPHS.

RECEIVED AT 8, WATERLOO STREET, GLASGOW, C.2. (Tel. No. Central. 6363.)

Kirkintilloch, 1782. (After office hours.)

2 NEWARKNJ 19 12 1207P   1943 MAR 13   AM 7   15

CAPT HARRY HEFFELFINGER CARE MARSH

ROYAL BRITISH HOTEL GLASGOW

FAMILY UNDER CONTROL BUT LONELY STAY WELL LOVE

MARY HEFFLEFINGER +

The Western Union cablegram Mary Lou sent to Harry when he was in Glasglow, Scotland.

Harry and Mary Lou at a black-tie dance.

EVEN IN THE MIDST OF WAR, *humor somehow survives. In fact, humor may be one of the key things that got the soldiers through the fear and pain of being at the front during World War II. The humorous banter in which the soldiers sometimes engaged was often rough, cynical, even dark, a fragile moment of laughter in the horror. As they look back on their experience, many of those who fought in World War II—and the women they loved—can muster a wry comment here and there about it. But genuinely funny stories, the kind that engender cozy, happy, warm laughter, emerge only rarely during wartime.*

Al Goldis at flight school in 1943.

Alfred and Shirley

GOLDIS

Al Goldis was a twenty-year-old sophomore at the prestigious Massachusetts Institute of Technology in the spring of 1940. On the last day of
March of that year, he showed up at a "sweet sixteen" party in Newton, a
dozen miles away. He hadn't officially been invited, but the brother of the
birthday girl, who also attended MIT, had invited a classmate, who in
turn had suggested that Al tag along. Little did he know what that suggestion might lead to.

Shirley Shapiro, in whose honor the party was being given, was perfectly happy to have her big brother's college friends there. Al spent a few
moments talking with her, but he, along with most of the other young
men at the party, was mesmerized by one of Shirley's friends, a tall, leggy
blonde. She was a drum majorette, which every girl wanted to be, and
boys were attracted to her, Al recalls, "like bees to the honeypot."

Some weeks later, Al was invited to a big Intra-Fraternity Council
(IFC) dance weekend. He didn't belong to a fraternity, but these bashes
were usually open to anyone who had friends in any of the fraternities
involved. Al invited his sister to come up from Brooklyn, where the family lived, for the occasion. He hoped to show her a good time. But she
didn't go out much, as she was painfully shy, and at the last minute, she
decided not to join him.

Al wasn't having any luck finding another date until the same classmate who had invited him to the party where they'd met Shirley Shapiro
suggested that he give her a call. The dance was that very night, April 26,

so he called her at school. Students weren't supposed to take personal calls, but Al convinced a woman in the principal's office that it was a real emergency. When Shirley came to the phone, he implored her, "Don't say no right away," then told her about the big party in glowing detail. She said yes.

They had a great time that evening and started to see each other quite regularly after that. In fact, Al recalls that he almost flunked out of school because he spent more time on the phone with Shirley than he did studying.

By June of that year, the two began to talk seriously about marriage, but Al wanted to graduate first and get established, so they agreed to postpone engagement and marriage for about four years. But when Pearl Harbor was bombed in December 1941, they realized they might have to postpone their wedding even longer. Al enlisted in January and went off to learn to fly for the U.S. Army Air Corps.

Al graduated from flying school in February 1943. Corps tradition required that his wings be pinned on by someone "near and dear," so he invited Shirley to come to Blytheville, Arkansas, to do the honors. While she was visiting, they became engaged. Shirley returned to Newton, Massachusetts, and Al headed off first to Tucson, Arizona, to learn to fly B-24s and then to Herrington, Kansas, to pick up a plane and a crew. After a month of further flight training, he shipped out to Benghazi, Cyrenaica (Libya), where he was to report to the Ninth Bomber Command for combat duty.

Al and his crew arrived in Cyrenaica on Sunday, August 1, 1943, just as many crews were returning from a notorious treetop-level bombing mission over the Ploesti oil fields in Romania, held by the Germans. The scene was horrific. Badly damaged B-24s streamed in for precarious landings, and bloodied airmen were being loaded into ambulances.

Al's was the first replacement crew to arrive after the Ninth Bomber Command had been organized. Because the crews who had been there for months already were exhausted, he flew missions every day. At this time in the war, no crew was supposed to fly more than thirty missions, but the military soon increased that number to fifty out of necessity. When Al and his crew hit the fifty mark, the flight surgeon ordered them to go for some R&R.

There weren't many places for tired soldiers to go for R&R then. The surgeon explained to Al that Tel Aviv had been designated by the U.S. Army Air Force as its sole R&R station in the entire North African and Middle Eastern theater because it was the only place to get a clean room, a hot bath, and decent food. So Al and his crew flew to Tel Aviv.

After a couple of days in Tel Aviv, they found themselves on board a Red Cross tour bus, gallivanting around the Levant. One of the stops was Damascus, in Syria, and Al and his crew decided they had to sample a belly-dancing nightclub while they were there. The female Red Cross guides wanted to see some real belly dancing as well—Al hastens to add that belly dancing is not a burlesque attraction in the Middle East but a folk-dance art form—but according to Muslim law, women were not allowed outdoors except for an hour at noon with their children, and certainly not in nightclubs. Al and the other guys decided they'd try to get the women in anyway; Al protested to the manager of the club that American mores were different and should be respected. Surprisingly, the man agreed to let the women in.

The youngest and slimmest belly dancers came on first, but as the show continued, the real stars appeared, each one older and heavier than the last. The superstar was the fattest of all, but she made every inch of flesh ripple with expression, and the place went wild.

After the show, Al persuaded the youngest and slimmest of the dancers—in his eyes the prettiest, even if she was the least accomplished in the Syrian view—to go out with him. To his astonishment, he discovered that "going out" meant getting in a taxi and going to her home, where she rousted her parents from bed and the house so she and Al could take it over. Once their "involvement," as he refers to it, was over, Al decided the most sensible thing to do was head back to his hotel. Wandering through the dark streets that night, with mysterious shadows cast on the whitewashed walls, he says he felt in more danger than he had on any of his combat missions. Not till he got back to his hotel did he realize that he should have been on his guard even earlier; he had been "rolled" by the dancer and didn't have a dime left.

The next afternoon, the Red Cross guides took Al and his crew to a tea at the home of a wealthy British-educated merchant—what Americans would call a "merchant prince." The tea was strong and the crumpets were excellent. The host then showed his guests around his home, which was exquisite and decorated with many precious artifacts. He was clearly a man of great taste, and he charmed them all.

In a large atrium around which the house was built, rimmed by arches, Al noticed that under each arch lay a couch, and on each couch lolled a beautiful woman, "peeling a grape or gorging on a box of chocolates." Al thought to himself that this must be the man's harem, but as it turned out, all eight of them were his wives. In keeping with Muslim culture, they were not introduced to the men.

The merchant invited Al and the others to come to his shop the next day. It was a dazzling place. Particularly impressive was a set of inlaid living room furniture upholstered in royal blue plush velvet that the merchant said was about to be shipped to England. A British captain furnishing a new house for himself and his bride had stopped by and bought it for £8,000—in those days the equivalent of $40,000.

In another room lay bolts of cloth, the likes of which Al had never seen before. Silks and satins and brocades ravished the eye, particularly a silver brocade and a gold brocade, both shot through with threads of real gold and silver. Given the cost of the bedroom set, Al hardly dared to ask the price.

Miraculously, the merchant turned out to be selling the silver brocade for only about $12 a yard, which, the young women of the Red Cross quietly assured Al, was an extraordinary bargain. Such cloth would cost many times more in New York, probably $40 or $50 a yard. Al knew immediately that the silver brocade would make a perfect wedding gown for Shirley, whom he planned to marry as soon as he got home to America. But he had a problem. He sheepishly had to explain to the merchant that he had no money to pay for the brocade, since a belly dancer had picked his pocket the night before.

The merchant waved his hand airily. No problem, he assured Al, taking down a dusty old ledger from a shelf; Al could pay later. In the ledger, the merchant wrote down Al's name, rank, and serial number, and guaranteed him that the seven yards the Red Cross guides had decided would be enough for a dress with a full train would be shipped off to Shirley in Newton.

Al could not imagine by what channels that shipment would take place, but he decided not to inquire too closely. After all, he hadn't paid for it, so if it didn't arrive, well, so what?

Soon Al and his crew were back in the air over North Africa. Base operations had been relocated to Tunis by then, and they had to catch up with their unit. Al flew another twenty missions over North Africa and Italy, earning a Silver Star, a Distinguished Flying Cross, and several other medals. Finally, he was ordered back to America, but he got held up in Dakar in Senegal for two weeks, "a garden spot if ever there were one," as Al recalls, and during that time the D-Day invasion of Normandy took place. He got the word while "lollygagging" on the bean in Dakar.

When he returned to Newton at the end of June 1944, he was pleased to discover that Shirley had actually received the silver brocade and was thrilled with it. Her family persuaded her cousin Ida, who was the best seamstress in the Boston area, to make the wedding dress—she could not resist working with such exquisite fabric.

Al and Shirley were married on July 10, 1944. Shirley looked beautiful beyond words in her silver brocade from Damascus. It was the chief topic of conversation among the hundreds of family members and friends who gathered at the Belmont country club for the reception. Al wore his uniform, as required. He was, after all, still in the army air force, and the war was still on.

Over the next few months, accompanied by Shirley, Al worked as an air/sea rescue instructor first at Chanute Field in Champaign-Urbana, Illinois, and then at March Field in California. When the war in the Pacific ended, Al was the very first man at March Field to be demobilized. He won this distinction based on points accumulated through length of service, number of missions flown, and medals received. He and Shirley, already pregnant with their daughter, returned to Newton to live with her parents while he resumed and completed his studies at MIT.

One day, almost two years after their wedding, the doorbell rang while Al was at school. When Shirley answered the door, a gentleman with a pronounced British accent confronted her. Did a Mr. Alfred Collins live there? he inquired.

"No," Shirley replied. "My husband is Alfred Goldis."

The gentleman politely suggested that perhaps he had the name wrong, as the handwriting on the paper he had was unclear. Did she, by any chance, know anything about several yards of silver brocade?

"Why, yes," said Shirley, quite surprised. "That was used for my wedding dress."

The polite but firm British gentleman turned out to be a bill collector. Al had forgotten to send payment to the merchant prince for the brocade. Shirley went to the bank the next day and converted dollars to British pounds to take care of the debt.

Al maintains that Shirley has told the story of the bill collectors and brocade innumerable times. But being the wonderful wife she is, she has never in their fifty-five years of marriage asked him point-blank how he got rolled in the Damascan Casbah. Of course we know she knows, or this story would not be included here, as it is, with Shirley's full approval.

Shirley in her wedding dress made from the silver brocade Al sent her, and Al in full uniform.

Al and Shirley at home, Christmas 1998.

OF COURSE, MANY LOVE AFFAIRS
during the war ran into difficulties.
A couple often decided that, despite their
mutual affection, they weren't entirely ready to be man
and wife—they just got caught up in the excitement
of the moment. When the war ended and life returned
to normal, they simply chose to go their own ways.
Though some might stay in touch for a while, contact
was usually lost before long. But then circumstances,
sheer curiosity, or a sense of loss might engender a
reunion. What might happen if that passion from
the war reignited, this time under entirely different
circumstances?

Ron and Marilyn Smith in 1944.

Ron

SMITH

Ron Smith served as a torpedoman on the submarine U.S.S. *Seal,* one of only a handful of American subs to make it all the way through the war, from 1942 to 1945.

Ron met his first wife during a repair layover in San Francisco in 1944. The crew had divided into two groups, one of which remained with the sub while the other went on leave. When the latter group returned to the sub, those who had stayed went home to loved ones. Ron was in the second group, and since there was little to do aboard the *Seal* while it was being refitted, he had a good deal of time on his hands.

The crew lived in barracks onshore rather than on the sub. On Easter Sunday, he and a shipmate named Joe were the last to leave the barracks. They took the ferry over to the city, had breakfast, and decided to have a beer at a favorite bar on Georgia Street. The bar was closed, of course, on Easter Sunday morning, and Joe, somewhat out of the blue, suggested that maybe they should go to church. Ron agreed that wasn't such a bad idea—they could use a church service after what they'd been through in the Pacific.

They walked back a few blocks to a big church they'd passed earlier, but the service was just letting out. "Well, we had good intentions," Joe declared. Then they noticed two pretty girls coming out of the church, and the focus of their intentions changed instantly.

The two sailors fell into step on either side of the girls. When Ron said a cordial hello to the girl next to him, she retorted, "I don't talk to strangers, especially sailors." But she turned to look at him. He noticed she was even prettier up close, with long, dark brown hair and blue eyes, and a perfect figure. Ron didn't realize he was staring until she repeated that she didn't talk to strangers, but she smiled as she said it.

Ron and Joe introduced themselves and asked the girls' names. The one Ron was interested in said her name was Marilynn, "with two 'N's." Ron pointed out that now they weren't strangers anymore, and Marilynn replied that sailors were all alike.

Presently, the girls stopped at a movie theater, and Ron and Joe asked if they could join them. Marilynn said, "It's a free country."

They sat together in the balcony and ate popcorn and watched the movie. Ron leaned close to Marilynn and asked for some popcorn. Not realizing how close he was, she hit his face with the box when she moved her arm, and the popcorn flew everywhere. She laughed uproariously. He suddenly liked her even more. It wasn't just sexual attraction, although there was plenty of that. He felt something he'd never quite experienced.

They left the movie theater and stopped at a coffee shop, where Ron and Marilynn split a piece of Boston cream pie with their coffee. The girls had to move along, but Ron had managed to find out that Marilynn was a file clerk at the navy yard, in Building 101.

Ron found her there the next day, and he made a spectacle of himself until she agreed to meet him for lunch. After that he began to see her almost every day. Before too long, he told her he loved her, and to his joyful surprise, she declared she loved him, too.

Soon enough, he got invited to her home. Her father, Bruce Callaway, was an engineer on a navy yard train, and Mrs. Callaway and Marilynn's younger brothers made Ron feel most welcome. One night when they were going out to dinner and dancing, all dressed up, Marilynn's father offered to let them use his car. They made love for the first time at the end of that evening, in the car.

There was tension in Marilynn's family, especially between her and her mother, since the family was about to move back to Salida, Colorado, where Marilynn had grown up. Marilynn wanted to go ahead early and stay with her aunt Mary in Pueblo, Colorado, but her parents worried about her.

Since the time had come for Ron to take his leave, and he was going home to Indiana, he agreed to accompany Marilynn on the train as far as Pueblo. But they got off the train at Ogden, Utah, and spent the night there in a hotel. The next day, as they continued on to Pueblo, Marilynn decided she wanted to stay in a hotel for one more night before arriving at her aunt's. She called her aunt's house from the hotel to tell her that she was in town and would arrive shortly, but her uncle answered the phone. He soon showed up at the hotel acting strangely. For some reason he picked that moment to tell Marilynn that Bruce Callaway, the man she had always known as her father, was in fact her stepfather. Marilynn was so upset by the revelation that she couldn't face going to stay with her aunt and uncle.

Ron called his father and asked him to wire enough money to buy a ticket for Marilynn to come to Hammond, Indiana, with him. Ron's family welcomed Marilynn into their home. But a week later, Ron found her in her room crying. She told him she was pregnant. He didn't want to get married yet. He had to go back to sea all too soon, and he didn't want a wife back home to worry about, and certainly not a wife and child. But it never occurred to him not to marry Marilynn. If you got a girl pregnant, you married her, plain and simple. That was the code he'd been taught.

On a bright, breezy afternoon on the twenty-fourth of May, Ron Smith and Marilynn Callaway were married by a Methodist minister on his family's front lawn with his parents, younger brother and sister, and a few other relatives looking on. Marilynn's pregnancy later turned out to be a false alarm, but the marriage was for real.

One of Ron's uncles owned a used-car lot, and he gave them a good deal on a red 1940 Chevy. They got in touch with one of Ron's shipmates and his wife, who agreed to drive back to California with them, which gave them enough rationed gas to get there. On the way, they stopped off in Colorado to see Marilynn's parents, who had completed their move to Salida.

Then it was on to California, where the navy gave them a Quonset hut to live in for thirty days. After that, Marilynn found a room in Vallejo. They sold the Chevy. Ron said the payments were too much to keep up with, but he also didn't want Marilynn tooling around in that conspicuous flaming-red car while he was away. He seriously doubted that a girl who liked sex as much as Marilynn did was going to be faithful while he was at sea, and he didn't want her to attract too much attention from other men.

The *Seal* went to sea again soon after D-Day, without Ron. He had been transferred to a new submarine that was under construction. Then, during a routine physical, the medics decided that he was suffering from combat fatigue and no longer fit for submarine duty.

Three months later, Ron was transferred to fleet torpedo school in Great Lakes, Illinois, as an instructor. Marilynn went with him, and they found a one-room rental in Kenosha, Wisconsin, from which Ron commuted every day to Great Lakes, except when he was on duty and couldn't leave the base.

Meanwhile, Marilynn got pregnant for real, and the day after Christmas 1944, she returned home to stay with her mother for the duration of the pregnancy, as was customary then for military wives.

They wrote letters regularly, but Ron still felt out of touch with his young, pregnant bride. They couldn't afford long-distance phone calls except in emergencies, so they almost never spoke. Ron did get one happy call, though. On May 17, 1945, his mother-in-law phoned to tell him he had a son. The couple decided to name him Ronal Lynn, a combination of both their names.

In June, Ron was transferred to the naval ammunition depot at Crane, Indiana, where Marilynn was supposed to join him as soon as she and the baby were strong enough to travel. Instead, she sent him a "Dear John" letter.

Marilynn declared that their marriage had been a mistake. Ron was not entirely surprised. When he was discharged in August, shortly after the war ended, he was free to do what he wanted with his life, if only he knew what that was. Truthfully, he had expected to die in the war, as so many submariners had. His father reminded him that he had a son to think about, and he should earn some money and go try to patch things up with Marilynn. Ron knew his father was right.

So he went to work loading boxcars and set off for Colorado in November in a 1936 Pontiac he bought for $350. He ran into a blizzard but kept going, even persuading the state police to let him pass a barricade. He reached Salida at midday and got a motel room. He then went to the Callaways' house.

When Marilynn answered the door, she was stunned to see him standing there. When she starting crying and threw her arms around him, he figured things would turn out all right. After several days of steady persuading, she agreed to get back together with him. He sold the Pontiac for twice what it had cost him. He planned to go to Houston, where he had a few relatives and had heard there were lots of jobs available. Once he'd landed one, he would send for Marilynn and his son. He gave her half the money from the Pontiac to save for her journey.

He soon found a job, but Marilynn never came. He wrote, but she never answered. Her parents intercepted his phone calls. He finally gave up when the operator told him their phone had been disconnected.

Ron finished high school while working in a greasy spoon, then went back to see his family in Indiana for the summer. He had intended to attend Texas A&M in the fall, but he met a girl named Georgianna and fell in love. He got a divorce from Marilynn in absentia and married Georgianna. They soon moved to Houston, where he settled into a career as a factory representative for automobile manufacturers.

He and Georgianna had five children. Ron made many attempts over the years to find Marilynn and, particularly, his son. But it seemed like they had dropped off the face of the earth.

In 1963, Ron was traveling for Checker Motors when he wandered into a small restaurant in Albuquerque, New Mexico, for dinner. The guy next to him struck up a conversation. He told Ron he had worked for the railroads most of his life. Offhandedly, Ron asked if he had ever known a Bruce Callaway—Marilynn's stepfather—who had been an engineer at the navy yards in San Francisco all those years ago. "Sure!" the man exclaimed. "Hell, I've known Bruce for years. Just saw him the other day."

Ron couldn't believe his ears. It turned out Bruce lived in Colorado City and was working for the Denver & Rio Grande Railroad. Ron quickly finished his dinner and went back to his room at the Ramada Inn. He called information and got Bruce Callaway's number in Colorado City. A man answered the phone.

"Is this Bruce Callaway?" Ron asked.

"Yes, who's this?"

"This is Ron—Ronnie Smith."

After a long pause, Bruce finally realized to whom he was speaking.

He explained to Ron that he and Marilynn's mother had divorced long ago. Marilynn's mother had married a retired army guy and was living with him in Chandler, Arizona. Marilynn, in turn, had married someone else and was living somewhere in Nevada. Ron asked if his son was with Marilynn.

"No," replied Bruce, "he's with his grandmother in Chandler."

Ron thanked Bruce for the information. After an awkward silence, Bruce added, "Ronnie, I'm real sorry about what happened, but it wasn't my fault." Ron told him that he understood, thanked him again, and hung up.

Ron knew better than to try to reach his son through his former mother-in-law. But he knew the boy would have to be in high school, so he got the number of the Chandler school and called there directly the very next morning. When a clerk answered, Ron said, "This is an emergency, I need to talk to my son Ronal Lynn Smith."

The clerk said, "Let's see, oh, he's in math class, hold on, I'll get him."

In a few minutes, a young man's voice came on the line. "Hello?"

"Hello to you, this is your father."

Both too emotional to make much sense, they managed to stumble through an exchange of home addresses and phone numbers.

Just a few weeks later, Ron went to Chandler for a weekend visit with his son. He took a room in Scottsdale, picked up Ronal Lynn, and they spent the weekend together trying to get acquainted. It was an awkward time, but a few months later, his son made a reciprocal visit to Dallas, where Ron now lived with his family.

They began to correspond by mail. Over the years, the contacts became less frequent, until Ronal Lynn got married himself. His wife, Jeanne, made an effort to write to Ron more often, and the two men began to exchange phone calls on a regular basis. It was, Ron felt, as good an outcome as could be expected, considering that he hadn't seen his son since Ronal was an infant. They could never make up for the missing years, but they ultimately developed a very worthwhile friendship.

Meanwhile, Ron had other problems to deal with. He had two heart attacks a week apart in 1980 and had to undergo open-heart surgery in June, involving five bypasses. Ron quit smoking and recovered with few complications.

Then, in 1982, he was laid off from his job as a fleet administrator for a major oil-service company that was in a downsizing cycle. He got a similar job with another company, which only lasted nine months before he was downsized out of work again. He and Georgianna were forced into a "friendly foreclosure" on the house they had lived in for the past ten years.

Ron launched his own business making consoles for pickups, a device he had designed himself. The same oil slump that had cost Ron his jobs hit his younger brother Rex, who owned a furniture business in Texas. They joined forces to manufacture and sell the consoles Ron had created, and the business flourished.

In the meantime, under the strain of Ron's illnesses and their financial hardships, Ron and Georgianna had grown apart. They slept in separate bedrooms. All of their children were by then on their own. Their youngest boy was still in college at Rice University, but they'd furnished him with enough financial support to fend for himself.

Ron felt weary with his life and decided he needed a break to rejuvenate himself. Georgianna encouraged this and even arranged his flight plans and car rental through the travel agency where she had been working for the past four years. Ron started off his journey by flying to Sacramento and driving up to Willows, California, to visit Ronal Lynn and Jeanne for a couple of weeks.

Over the years, Ron had learned the benefits of forgiveness, coming to understand that grudges always hurt the person holding them the most. So he asked Ronal Lynn to arrange for his mother, who now lived 120 miles to the north in Yreka, to come down to Willows for a visit. Ronal did so, and soon it was settled that Marilynn would drive there, arriving early Friday evening. By eight o'clock on Friday night, she still hadn't arrived. Ron began to worry that she had changed her mind. About eight-thirty, though, she finally rolled into the driveway. Ron stood on the porch steps as Ronal Lynn and Jeanne went out to greet her and help her with her bags.

Ron looked at her as she walked toward him. She was older—the wrinkles around her mouth attested to that—and a little wider in the hips, but she was still quite a beautiful woman at sixty.

"Is that really you?" Marilynn asked as she walked toward him, squinting and then shading her eyes with her hand.

"Yes, it's me," Ron said and smiled at her.

She put out her hands, and Ron took them in his. They looked at each other for a long moment and then, as if it had been rehearsed, drew closer and kissed each other on the cheek, like old friends. They walked into the living room, where Ron stopped and took her hands again. He had gone over the words he wanted to say to her so many times in his head, and now he was able to say them out loud. "I just want to tell you that I forgive you anything you have done to me, and ask that you forgive me anything that I might have done to you."

She looked dumbfounded, and tears began rolling down her cheeks. The she threw her arms around him, crying out, "Oh God, it's always been you." They kissed fully and tenderly on the mouth. He pushed her away gently and looked into her ice-blue eyes and said, "My God, I'm still in love with you." It seemed to him that at that moment they were completely alone in the universe.

They spent the rest of the weekend driving into the mountains, going out to dinner, talking all the time. She laughed at all his jokes, funny or not. They talked most of the night. He invited her into his room, saying, "You don't have to worry. I'll stay under the covers and you can stay on top of them." And that's exactly what they did.

Marilynn called and arranged to take Monday off from work, too, giving them another day together. They agreed that Ron would return to Texas, conclude his involvements there, and come to live with Marilynn in Yreka.

Ron flew home and told Georgianna that he was moving to California permanently; he turned the business over to his brother Rex. Ronal Lynn flew down to help his dad drive to California, and they met Jeanne and Marilynn in Reno, spending the weekend there. Ron and Marilynn made love most of the night, as if it were their second honeymoon.

Monday morning, Ronal Lynn and Jeanne drove off to Willows, and Ron and Marilynn headed for Yreka. She was renting a cottage nestled at the foot of Mount Shasta.

Aggravated by the smallness of the space, and complicated by their ties to other people, including their children, from the past they had not shared, Ron and Marilyn's relationship was tempestuous. But in spite of all that, and despite a promise Marilynn had once made to herself never to marry again, she agreed to marry Ron.

Ron made several trips back to Texas to visit his children and help Rex with the business. In November 1985, Georgianna agreed to a divorce that was quickly settled. Ron was now free to marry Marilynn, but she kept hesitating. At one point, they went to Reno, with Ronal Lynn and Jeanne in tow, and got a marriage license. But the next day Marilynn backed out. It reminded Ron of the old times.

Finally, in June 1987, Ron decided that he'd had enough. He packed all his things and went back to Texas to stay with his brother. Not only did Marilynn refuse to marry him, she had also lost interest in sex. Marilynn had started feeling unwell in February 1987. Ron had taken her to several doctors, but they could find nothing wrong.

While Ron was in Texas, Marilynn called, crying, and begged him to come back. He never had been able to handle her crying, so he agreed, provided that she at last marry him for real. They were married in Las Vegas that August. Briefly, she seemed to feel better physically, but then her symptoms worsened. Ron was convinced they were psychosomatic, tied up somehow with their relationship. But in September, a new doctor diagnosed Marilynn with scleroderma, a rare progressive disease that gradually causes a hardening of the skin. The doctor ordered additional tests, but they had to be sent to Stanford Medical Center for confirmation, which could take as long as three weeks.

Marilynn urged Ron to visit Texas in the meantime, and he did, visiting his brother and two of his sons. He also saw Georgianna and was happy to find that they got along like old friends.

Ron flew back to California on Friday the thirteenth, deliberately pushing aside his superstition. There he found Marilynn suffering more than ever, sleeping fitfully and going to the bathroom nearly once an hour. In the morning he fixed her a big breakfast, but she ate very little. She said she needed a new nightgown and asked him to buy her one. Dutifully, he went out and purchased the kind of "shortie" she liked. Ron tried to watch television the rest of the day while Marilynn slept. He told her he would make some potato soup for supper, which she thought sounded good, but again she couldn't, or wouldn't, eat much.

At nine o'clock, Ron lay down beside her, very tired but almost too tense and fearful to sleep. At eleven-thirty, she woke him, asking him to help her to the bathroom. He went around to her side of the bed and knelt in front of her to help her stand. She put her hand on top of his head and cried out, "Oh, Ronnie, I love you so much." Ron smiled up at her, but she started coughing and grabbed her throat. "I can't breathe," she choked out, and fell back on her side of the bed. Her eyes were open but looked strange and vacant.

Ron felt for a heartbeat, but there was none. "Don't leave me!" he screamed.

He tried to give her CPR, stopping to call 911, then starting again. The paramedics arrived, and Ron followed the ambulance to the hospital. He waited more than an hour. Finally a doctor came out, shaking his head. "I'm sorry, we tried everything to revive her, she's gone." But Ron already knew.

The doctor asked Ron if he needed a prescription to help him sleep. He declined and went back to the house and lay down. That night he had an extremely vivid dream. He saw a vision of Marilynn walking up a beautiful green slope. A figure in white held her hand, and a brilliant light shimmered in the background. Marilynn turned back to him and smiled. "It's okay, honey. I'm fine now. I love you."

Ron went back to Texas. After a time, he and Georgianna remarried, and he knew that he was back where he belonged. But he feels that his reunion with Marilynn, and the late, last years with her, was something preordained. Fate insisted he return to her and finish the love they had begun so many years before.

Ron, torpedoman second class, home on leave in 1944.

Marilynn in front of the Vallejo, California, hotel where she and Ron lived, 1944.

ANY WAR BRINGS SUFFERING, BUT a global war creates truly unimaginable destruction. The death toll during World War II reached a staggering 50 million, an average of 192,307 dead for each week of the war. Yet some of those who survived don't see the war as an entirely destructive force. Many men and women who met and married in the course of World War II are acutely aware that if it had not been for the war, they never would have encountered each other. They mean no disrespect for the dead, nor do they make light in any way of the war's horrors; but there are those who feel that God was watching over them during the war, because the great conflict thrust them into each other's arms and lives. Because their lives together have meant so much, they cannot help but give thanks that the dire exigencies of war enabled them to find each other.

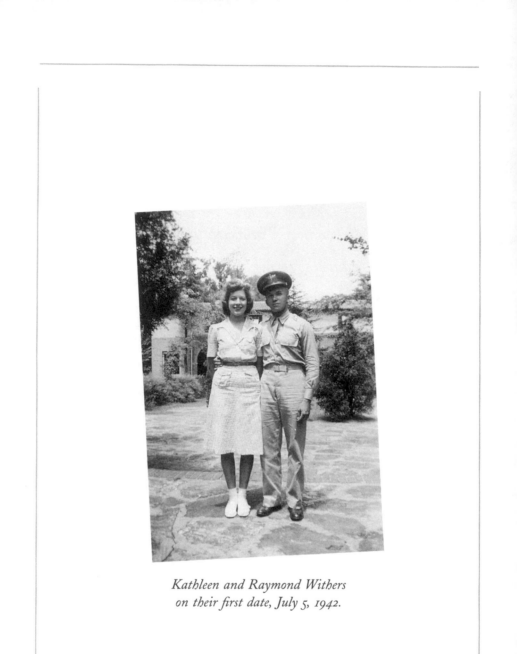

Kathleen and Raymond Withers
on their first date, July 5, 1942.

Raymond and Kathleen
WITHERS

On July 4, 1942, Clara Kathleen Mitchell, just eighteen, attended her first USO dance in her hometown of Birmingham, Alabama. She and a girl-friend danced with a number of soldiers that night, many of them from Maxwell Field in Montgomery. One of the soldiers was Raymond Withers, a Kentucky farm boy who had joined the FBI, then enlisted in the army air corps in 1941. Four years older than Kathleen (as she preferred to be called), he was training as an aviation cadet at Maxwell Field, in hopes of becoming a pilot.

Kathleen spent that night at her friend's house. The next day, another cadet, who was a friend of Ray's, had arranged a date with Kathleen's friend. When he called, he asked her to bring Kathleen along for Ray. The date started off by attending services at the Methodist church in downtown Birmingham, then they all had lunch together and went out to the Birmingham airport to watch the planes taking off and landing.

The group was having such a good time that they dawdled a little too long, and Ray and his friend missed the last bus back to Montgomery and Maxwell Field, where they were due at six P.M. The two cadets resorted to thumbing a ride. To their surprise, before long, a limousine stopped for them. The man riding in back turned out to be the state highway com-missioner, and he ordered his driver "to get these boys back to Maxwell Field" on time. So the limousine took off down the highway at high speed—with no worries about being stopped by the police—and Ray and his friend were delivered in plenty of time.

Kathleen had made quite an impression on Ray that day, and when he returned to Birmingham a while later, he called her for a date that night, but she was already booked. Ray would not be so easily thwarted, however, and he started a correspondence with her, writing letters and sending her flowers. As Ray recalls, "This was less than a year after Pearl Harbor, and members of the local communities around the bases were extremely hospitable, generous, and anxious to entertain soldiers. I met many young ladies in those days, but not one of them affected me like Kathleen had on only one weekend."

As his training continued, Ray was first transferred from Maxwell Field to Greenville, Mississippi, for basic flight school, and then to Dothan, Alabama, for advanced training. He continued to write to Kathleen during those many months and persuaded her to come to Dothan on February 16, 1943, to attend the ceremony at which he received his wings and his commission as a second lieutenant. A few days later, on his way to Westover Field, in Massachusetts, Ray stopped off to see Kathleen in Birmingham, spending three days. Those few days convinced Ray that Kathleen was the one for him, and shortly thereafter, he wrote to his mother to tell her he had met the girl he was going to marry. "But he didn't tell me that," Kathleen remembers with a laugh.

Ray says when he danced with Kathleen on that first night, "There was a mystical feeling and attraction about her. This attraction has grown continually and will never leave me." In addition to the obvious chemistry between them, Ray says she had a "physical pull on my heart."

Aside from their attraction, Ray believes other more practical factors also brought them together. "We were both from lower-middle-class rural areas—Kathleen's parents were from Alabama farm families, and my family was Kentucky farmers. We both knew about the sacrifices necessary to live a Christian life and to be proud of our heritage and country. Both of our families had hit bottom during the Depression, when we were children. Kathleen's father had lost his drugstore and had to start over doing various jobs. Until 1930 my father was a very successful tobacco farmer, but the Depression broke him both financially and physically. He lost his farm and had to start over on a small and less productive one. He never really recovered and died in 1938 at the age of sixty-four. We lived without electricity until 1936 and had never had indoor plumbing."

Both Ray and Kathleen worked all through high school, but despite their good grades, college proved too much of a financial hardship. Kathleen was granted a small scholarship, but it didn't cover enough of the expenses for college. Ray had saved enough money for three semesters at the University of Kentucky during 1938–39, but he eventually had to drop out to earn more money. He went from job to job, in addition to helping his mother and brother run the small family farm.

Ray took every possible civil service exam until he finally got a job as a fingerprint classifier at the FBI in Washington, D.C. He started there on February 23, 1941, and volunteered for the army air corps ten months later on December 9, two days after Pearl Harbor was bombed. That's when he was sent to Maxwell Field for training, where he arrived in March 1942. Kathleen, who had already had one post–high school job with Sears, Roebuck, was by then working for Tennessee Coal and Iron.

Through all the letter writing, and with all of this common experience, they developed a remarkable understanding, even though Ray's visit to Birmingham was just the third time they'd seen each other in six months. After Ray's visit to Birmingham, they didn't see each other again until Ray had flown a full tour of seventy-two missions as a P-47 pilot in the Eighth Air Force in England.

They continued to write letters back and forth. Kathleen sent Ray care packages, and he sent her flowers, gifts, and poems. Kathleen believes that these letters allowed them to get to know each other very deeply. "During the war," she says, "people had a tendency to know what was important and were able to express themselves more than we do today."

At the end of his first tour, Ray could either sign up for another tour, after a thirty-day leave back in the States, or he could choose assignment to noncombat duty in England with no leave. He felt he could not pass up a chance to see Kathleen, so he chose a second tour and arrived in New York for his leave on July 12, 1944. First he went to Kentucky to see his mother and brother, then hastened to Birmingham to visit Kathleen, arriving on July 24. This would be only the fourth time they had seen each other in the nearly two years since their dance at the USO.

That Monday night, Ray asked Kathleen to marry him. Although she considered herself quite mature for her twenty years, she wasn't sure she was ready to get married. Her first response was to suggest that it would be nice "just to be engaged" for a while. But Ray insisted that it was marriage or nothing. "I'm not going to go back overseas and get a Dear John letter," he told her.

On Wednesday, she still hadn't given him a definite answer. Then, walking in downtown Birmingham, they stopped at a corner to wait for the light to change. At that moment, something came together in Kathleen's head. "All right," she suddenly blurted out, "I will marry you." Ray looked at her in astonishment. "Well, this is a fine place to tell me, waiting for a light to change!"

They went across the street to a drugstore and sat down to talk over a Coke. First, they realized, they had to get blood tests. As they came out of the drugstore, Kathleen looked up and realized that the office of her father's doctor was in the building right in front of them. They went in and explained to the receptionist that they needed blood tests, and were told to sit in the waiting room, which was full of pregnant women. After just a few minutes, they were ushered into the office of a doctor, who turned out to be the brother of the doctor they were looking for, but he was happy to help them. He looked them over and told Kathleen that he knew she was a splendid young woman, and Ray was clearly a fine young man bravely serving his country. So they didn't have to bother with the blood test. He'd just sign the papers. With that taken care of, they went over to city hall to apply for the license and were told they could pick it up the very next day.

That night, Kathleen's father had plans to take them out to dinner. They needed his permission to marry, because Kathleen was under twenty-one. But Ray wouldn't bring up the subject while they were eating. Kathleen finally went to the ladies' room to leave the two men alone. When Ray asked her father's permission to take Kathleen's hand, her father readily granted it. But Ray has never forgotten the two things he said. First he looked keenly at Ray and said, "I'm losing a daughter, not gaining a son." He also offered his prospective son-in-law a piece of advice: "Never go to sleep angry at each other." In essence, Ray knows, he was "letting me know that I was now responsible for her."

On Thursday, Ray and Kathleen made the rest of their wedding arrangements. The ceremony took place at seven o'clock the Friday night after the Monday that Ray had proposed.

In a book of letters compiled for Ray by friends and family in honor of his eightieth birthday in August 1999, Kathleen wrote, "Our wedding day, with you, Daddy and Brother Astin the only men there—because everyone else was overseas—July 28, 1944, will always have such a special place among all my memories because that was the start of a wonderful life for me. Our honeymoon in Gatlinburg, Tennessee—swimming in the creek and then back to the room!!! Those wonderful meals in a place far removed from the worry of the war. The trip on the train to your hometown—meeting family and friends I had never met before, and that last night in Cincinnati, when we thought you were going overseas and we wouldn't see one another until after another tour of missions."

After their brief honeymoon, Kathleen returned to Birmingham and her job at Tennessee Coal and Iron, and Ray headed back east, expecting to ship out for England right away. But not long after, Ray called to tell Kathleen that he had been given the opportunity to spend a few days of R&R at a hotel in Atlantic City. She had to quit her job to go and meet him, but she didn't hesitate to catch the train north. This was only her second time on a train, and her first trip alone. "There was no air-conditioning in those days, of course," Kathleen notes, "and I was a sight when I got off the train in Atlantic City."

Ray had been staying since August 18 at the Ritz-Carlton Hotel, which the military had taken over as an R&R retreat. When Kathleen arrived on the twenty-first, they had no rooms for couples available, so in order to be together, she and Ray spent four nights at the Chelsea Hotel at $10 a night. For the following eight days, though, they were given a private room at the posh Ritz-Carlton, and they reveled in the luxury. Ray's total bill at the Ritz for seventeen days was $16.75. "That fantastic room for only pennies," Kathleen wrote in Ray's eightieth birthday letter, "and the walks on the boardwalk."

Kathleen endured a lonely trip back to Birmingham, where she soon got a new job with the government, operating calculating machines. Ray flew another full tour of missions, earning many medals, including a Silver Star, and finally returning to Birmingham on March 25, 1945.

Ray remained in the military even after the war. Their first child, their daughter Carol, was born December 20, 1945, in Fort Leavenworth, Kansas, where Ray was stationed at Sherman Field.

Ray and his crew with his P-47, with Kathleen's name painted on its nose.

The hut built by crew chief Tony Librandi, with Kathleen Ann flag flying.

Ray back in England for his second tour, sitting on the wing of his P-51.

Ray and Kathleen on their wedding day, July 28, 1944.

Ray and Kathleen at his retirement party in 1972.

Ray and Kathleen at home on their fifty-sixth wedding anniversary, July 28, 2000.

Over the years, Ray more than compensated for his initially truncated time at the University of Kentucky, earning a BEE from Ohio State University in 1949 and an MBA from the University of Chicago in 1953. He also studied Japanese for a year at Yale University before being posted to Japan from 1957 to 1960.

By that time, Kathleen decided that he'd had enough education, since every time he went back to school they had another child—four in all. They now have eleven grandchildren and three great-grandchildren and have been "having a ball" since Ray's retirement as a colonel in 1972.

Looking back on their fifty-seven happy years of marriage, Kathleen is gratified that she didn't listen to the people who were convinced that the two of them couldn't possibly have gotten to know each other well enough in the tiny amount of time they spent together before their wedding. For his part, Ray maintains, "I'm firmly convinced that God had a hand in my decision on July 4, 1942, to take a bus a hundred miles to Birmingham instead of going two miles into Montgomery after being confined to post for over two months."

ABOUT THE AUTHOR

LARRY KING is the Emmy-winning host of *Larry King Live* on CNN. He has received numerous broadcast and journalism awards, including the George Foster Peabody Award for Excellence in Broadcasting. He lives in Washington, D.C.

Helen and Lowell Baker on their wedding day,
March 24, 1945. Helen was a second lieutenant and
Lowell a staff sergeant at the time.

WHILE MANY WOMEN SERVED
as mechanics in the armed forces, or as recruiting officers, the greatest need was for nurses. Young women just out of nursing school, as well as many more experienced nurses, suddenly found themselves in military uniform, tending to millions of soldiers and sailors at training camps across the nation, or to the wounded who were shipped back home from the front. These women were given officer rank, which not only signified their importance but also discouraged them from dating enlisted men, due to the "no fraternization" rules between officers and enlisted soldiers. Some couples, however, weren't about to be thwarted.

PRISONERS OF SILENCE

Jonathan Kozol

PRISONERS OF SILENCE

Breaking the Bonds of Adult Illiteracy in the United States

CONTINUUM • NEW YORK

1980
The Continuum Publishing Corporation
815 Second Avenue
New York, N.Y. 10017

Portions of this book have appeared, in earlier versions, in *The Satur-day Review* and in *The New York Times*.

Printed in the United States of America

Library of Congress Cataloging in Publication Data
Kozol, Jonathan.   Prisoners of silence.
Bibliography.
1. Illiteracy—United States.   2. Reading (Adult
education)   I. Title.
LC151.K69   374'.012   79-25787
ISBN 0-8264-0005-1

Hungry man, reach for the book....

—BERTOLT BRECHT

ACKNOWLEDGMENTS

THE process of writing this book has involved me in long and thoughtful conversations with many men and women. Although I cannot possibly thank all of these people, I would like to thank especially David Seeley, Nancy Stimpfle, Anita Beaty, Alan Purves, Yvonne Golden, Charles Benton and Jack Wuest. In Ann Arbor, I was able to exchange ideas with Len and Val Suransky and, for two particularly valuable days, with Paulo Freire. In Boston, as the final draft approached completion, I relied especially upon the precise editorial judgment of Genise Schnitman.

Special thanks, finally, to Tisha Graham. This book is hers as much as mine. It would not have been written without her.

CONTENTS

	To the Reader	xi
	Preface: "An Indictment of Us All"	xiii
1	The Dimensions of the Problem	1
2	Beyond Statistics	8
3	Looking Abroad	15
4	Idea and Action	21
5	The Concept of the Active Words	27
6	Those Who Know Teach: A Plan for Calling Out Five Million Volunteers	34
7	Practical Details	44
8	Literacy: A Word in Search of Definition	52
9	How We Can Win	62
10	Logical Enemies/Unexpected Friends	72
11	Immediate Action: Organization, Leadership and the Fear of Victory	81
12	The Reinvention of Childhood	90
	Epilogue	99
	Appendix 1. Leads, Contacts, On-going Programs, Newsletters	103
	Appendix 2. The National Literacy Coalition	105
	Notes	107
	Bibliography	112

TO THE READER

THE first-person pronoun is given free rein in this book. I do not feel comfortable with books in which the author remains concealed behind third-person pronouns.

At times, in the text, the first-person pronoun changes from the singular to plural. At these times, I use the word *we* to refer to those students and teachers who have been associated with one another for two years as members of a broad, informal literacy coalition.

But the word is also intended to bear a slightly different meaning. There are many committed readers of my previous books who have written to our office. A large number have said that they would like to work beside us in the struggle to confront adult illiteracy in the United States. It is for this reason that I have listed some of our most active contacts in the final pages of the book. I hope that anyone who wishes to be in touch will write to us.

PREFACE

"An Indictment of Us All"

ON January 12, 1971, in his inaugural address as governor of Georgia, Jimmy Carter spoke of the problem of adult illiteracy:

> Our people are our most precious possession . . . We cannot afford to waste the talents and abilities given by God to one single Georgian. Every adult illiterate, every school drop-out, every untrained retarded child, is an indictment of us all. Our state pays a terrible price for those failures. . . . It is time to end this waste. If Switzerland and Israel and other people can end illiteracy, then so can we. The responsibility is our own and our government's. I will not shirk this responsibility.*

Today, nine years later, the problem of adult illiteracy is considerably worse than when the future president spoke those words.

If it was time for action in 1971, if it was "an indictment of us all" in 1971, if the price we paid was "a terrible price" in 1971, all of this is even more the case today. This book asks the people of this nation to address this problem now, before another year goes by, before another generation of illiterate men and women has grown one year older, before those men and women have been left to see their deepest dreams and most abiding hopes go down the drain of joblessness, of silence, of despair.

*For this quotation, and for all other matters of public record, see Notes, beginning on page 107.

1
THE DIMENSIONS OF
THE PROBLEM

THIS book is not intended to describe, from a detached and inert point of view, one further problem which the nation's leaders—responsible business people just as much as student organizers—already recognize to be of grave and growing danger. There will be only one brief chapter of statistical summation.

The purpose of this book is not to restate the complaint, but to begin the search for answers.

Estimates of the numbers of illiterate men and women in the nation differ so widely that only one thing seems beyond debate: Nobody knows how many adult illiterates there are today in the United States. Almost every estimate we have, however, is extremely high.

These estimates provide us with at least some ballpark figures:

In 1970 the percentage of adult illiterates in the United States was three times that in the Soviet Union. This figure, adjusted for the relative size of populations, was supplied by the United Nations.

In 1977, Oliver Patterson, in a study undertaken for the Office of Education, estimated the number of adult illiterates in the United States, using as criterion the comprehension of a daily paper: "If ability to read and understand the newspaper is used as the criterion of literacy, a conservative estimate [of adult illiterates] would be approximately twenty million."

In November 1978, *Newsweek* magazine estimated the figure for adult illiterates in the United States at twenty-three million.

In 1975, the "Adult Performance Level" study, under the direction of Dr. Norvell Northcutt, employed a more sophisticated instrument than had ever previously been used. The goal was *not* to find how many people lacked the skill to "write" or "read," but rather how many people lacked the skills with which to "manage" and "survive." Using a set of sixty-five "objectives"—areas of competence which were associated with Northcutt's definition of "adult success"—the study concluded that sixteen percent of whites, forty-four percent of blacks and fifty-six percent of Spanish-speaking adults were "functionally incompetent."

The Adult Performance Level report included a number of examples: Fourteen percent, when asked to fill out a check in a business transaction, made an error so serious that it was unlikely that the check would clear the bank. Thirteen percent did not address an envelope well enough to guarantee that it would reach its destination. Twenty-four percent did not place a return address on the same envelope. Twenty-eight percent of the sample population could not calculate the amount of change that they ought to get back after paying for a purchase with a twenty dollar bill.

On the basis of the Adult Performance Level, one government analyst in the Office of Education came to the conclusion that fifty-seven million Americans were unequipped to carry out most basic tasks. This figure is over thirty-five percent of the entire adult population.

The economic consequences of the present situation are difficult to determine. In part, this is because nobody knows exactly how many aspects of our economic life can be tied, directly or indirectly, to illiteracy. According to one source, the total cost to American tax-payers, solely in the funding of welfare programs and in loss of productivity, is at least six billion dollars yearly.

There are, however, several other direct or closely related costs, above and beyond those caused by the loss of productivity and increase in welfare. Almost seven billion more is spent each year to keep hundreds of thousands of illiterate prisoners in U.S. jails. No one knows how much is lost as a result of needless accidents which lead to the destruction of sophisticated technological equipment.

A simple example of the latter kind of cost is documented by Senator George McGovern, in a speech which he delivered before the U.S. Senate on September 8, 1978: "An astounding thirty percent of Navy recruits . . . are a danger to themselves and to costly naval equipment because they lack basic educational skills. One illiterate recruit recently caused two hundred fifty thousand dollars in damage because he could not read a repair manual." The tragedy of the situation of the worker is underscored in these words: "He tried [but] failed to follow the illustrations."

In speaking of illiterate men and women such as this young recruit, McGovern states: "We have closed the door of education behind poor students and the door of opportunity in front of them."

A few high school graduates, McGovern says, "refuse to forget what they did not learn in school. Recently a high school student of normal intelligence sued his school in San Francisco for educational malpractice—he had been awarded a diploma even though he could read only at a Fifth Grade level. Legal counsels of various state Offices of Education agree that the number of such suits will increase, and that increasingly they will succeed."

What of the many laws that Congress has enacted, and the many programs that have been initiated, to upgrade the teaching of reading in our public schools?

Title One of the Elementary and Secondary Education Act was passed into law in 1965, specifically to improve the teaching of basic skills to children from low-income backgrounds. Each year, the funds available under Title One grow less, while the problem we confront grows greater. In 1967, 7.6 million children were served by Title One, receiving an average of $378.00 each. Ten years later, only 5.2 million children were served at the same level.

Still more disturbing is the fact that Title One, according to available statistics, may very well hinder more children than it helps: Students in Title One spend less time in reading and in learning other basic skills than students who are *not* in Title One.

More to the point, whether they receive more instructional time or less, students in Title One too often tend to be the victims of those antiquated and lethargic programs that have never worked before. At best, even when Title One serves those who need it most, we end up with a situation of old error long-compounded. At worst, we end up with intensified injustice: inequality with a federal blessing.

If Title One were not a mere expanded version of the errors of the past, we would not have more illiterate adults today than in the year in which that legislation took effect.

Apart from all of the above, there is, of course, the obvious fact that Title One can be of no conceivable help to those who are already beyond school-age. Whether or not the public schools should find solutions to their reading problems in the years immediately ahead, millions of adults will nevertheless continue to lead marginal lives and to suffer social and economic isolation, solely because they cannot read or write.

What of those forms of legislation which were devised specifically to meet the needs of the illiterate adult?

The federal government first addressed the challenge of adult illiteracy in the Economic Opportunity Act of 1964—and again in the Adult Education Act of 1966. In spite of these two major pieces of legislation, the current federal allocation amounts to only one dollar for each illiterate adult. The funds available reach only two to four percent of those in need.

"In 1972," according to McGovern, "Congress reaffirmed its commitment to end illiteracy with the Right to Read program. That program was downgraded this past year [1978] after being labeled a failure by its own director."

The Senator's statement is based upon the words of Gilbert

Schiffman, former director of Right to Read. It is perhaps more harsh than Right to Read deserves. There seems no question but that Right to Read (like its predecessor, Adult Basic Education) achieved a great deal with those categories of adult illiterates who tend to respond best to this kind of program. It is the much larger number of those whom Right to Read did *not* reach that concerns us here. Who are they? Why is it that none of the various federal programs appears to be of any use to such large numbers of adults? Why is it that only two to four percent of those in need are being served?

There is a partial answer to this question in a recently completed study of the problem sponsored by the Ford Foundation. The report, written by David Harman and Carman St. John Hunter, seems to pull together many of the loose strands which have been left hanging here.

Harman and Hunter, first of all, have been able to clarify some of the reasons for the many contradictory estimates of numbers and varieties of adult illiterates in the United States. Their most useful contribution is to break up the over-all figure of fifty-seven million illiterate adults into categories that can be of use to those who hope to launch effective programs to reduce these figures.

In order to address this problem, Harman and Hunter attempt to divide the total number of adult illiterates into four groups according to the nature of their needs. Those in the first two groups are people who still possess a high degree of confidence that they themselves can make a difference in their own lives. (They also tend to live in communities which seem to share this confidence.) These people, according to Harman and Hunter, are appropriate clients for existing programs: "The fact that they can and do make progress in the programs confirms and strengthens their resolve."

A large number of those who do not prove responsive to these programs belong to the other two groups designated by Harman and Hunter. These are people whose experience has been filled with failure. Their few successful peers have moved away to other communities. "Those who remain are oppressed by multiple problems over which they appear to have little control. . . ." The distinctions between groups three and four are less significant than the problems which members of both groups share: "They live in the inner city or in rural poverty areas. The lack of credentials and the inability to perform tasks associated with literacy are only a small part of their lives. The majority . . . left school because they were failing. They could see little immediate pay-off. . . .

Group three, they write, "merges on the spectrum with another group, similar . . . yet different in one important aspect: the level of hope that can be kindled in them." People in this (fourth) group "have largely given up believing that anything they can do will make a difference . . ."

Groups three and four, according to this study, number between eighteen and twenty-eight million people. Another thirty to thirty-nine million fall somewhere in the area of groups one and two. The total, according to Harman and Hunter, is somewhere between fifty-four and sixty-four million people.

This breakdown roughly corresponds to the figures suggested by the Adult Performance Level. According to that study, as we saw, fifty-seven million Americans lacked skills that would be needed to perform most basic tasks. Of that number, twenty-three million lacked the skills to function at all within the context of the nation at the time the test was given. Thirty-four million could function, but only with great difficulty.

It is the former group—by my own estimate, approximately twenty-five million people—of whom we will be speaking and to whose dilemma I will address most of this book.

One rather unattractive argument has come up repeatedly during the public discussion of this issue throughout the past two years. It is often maintained that if it were not for the recent influx of so many people who do not speak English—predominantly Mexican and Puerto Rican—the nation would have no serious problem of illiteracy today.

The kinds of people who would use this type of argument are not likely to be satisfied or subdued by reason or persuasion. Nonetheless, it seems important to address this argument briefly, if for no other reason than to place our answer on the record. Perhaps there are some people who may only half-believe such lies and will, therefore, be open to a reasonable rebuttal.

The truth is that our nation has known such waves of foreign influx in a number of prior generations. In each generation, the new arrivals learned rapidly the English they needed, both in spoken and in written form. The explanations, heard now and then, that the most recent immigrants (i.e., Mexican-Americans and Puerto Ricans) "do not have a cultural background," "were illiterate in their own language as well," or "seem to lack the motivation of the immigrants of two generations back," are all—one way or other—racist arguments. They are facile and simplistic examples of shifting attention from an unjust situation to its most vulnerable target, blaming the victim for a social system which perceives him as expendable, socially and economically—an attitude never accepted in the United States when we were dealing with predominantly European immigrants.

In any event, the figures for adult illiterates in the United States exceed all possible estimates of the numbers of newly arrived legal (or illegal) "aliens." Moreover, "illegal aliens," of which there may be as many as eight million, would not appear in any official statistics anyway, since they would not willingly participate in any government survey which might end up by identification of their status, their location—or their mere existence.

2
BEYOND STATISTICS

STATISTICS such as those presented here cannot conceivably reveal the true dimensions of the problem in its human impact. Nor can the personal suffering involved be adequately conveyed by adding up bloodless statistics.

Interviews by some sensitive journalists, a few exceptional documentary films and many private conversations with young adults I have known, all help to create a somber portrait of the feeling of entrapment which so often overwhelms the man or woman who reaches the age of twenty-one or twenty-two and cannot read or write.

Early in the evolution of a situation of this kind, there is, in the classic case, the appearance of a whole line of defensive strategies against discovery by others. A terror of that moment when, much like an animal surrounded, the man or woman finds himself/herself exposed to general humiliation—this terror often leads adult illiterates to a complicated series of deceptions, obviations and evasions. An entire style of "lying low" and "watching out for traps" comes to be a way of life.

I once knew a young man, nineteen years of age, who lived with absolute outward confidence and self-possession for a number of years before I discovered that he could not read or write. His various methods of deception, which were also instruments of self-protection, were so skillful and so desperate that neither I nor any of his other adult friends were aware of his entire helplessness in face of written words until we went to dinner one night at a local restaurant—and suddenly discovered that he could not read.

Even here, it was not the first time we went out to eat, but something like the second or third, that Peter's desperation hit me full force. The first time, he was clever enough to study the menu for a moment, then look up to the waitress and ask her if he could have "just a coke and a hamburger." He told me later that he had been through the same thing many times before and that he had learned to act as if he were examining the menu: "Then I ask for coke and a hamburger. . . . Sometimes they give me hamburg on a plate with salad and potatoes. . . . Then I ask them for a roll and make my own hamburger."

As we began to go out to eat more frequently, Peter would ask to go to Howard Johnson's. I soon discovered the reason for his choice: The photographs, attached in cellophane containers to each of the standard items on the menu, spared him the necessity of struggling with the shape of words at all. Howard Johnson's, whether knowingly or not, had provided the perfect escape hatch for the endangered pride of an adult nonreader.

I say "escape hatch" purposely, because the whole mood of the moment, whenever we were out in the ordinary world together, was permeated by Peter's feeling of entrapment. It was as if he were afraid of being "caught." His hands would tremble slightly and his forehead would break out in perspiration. Once, during a long ride to New Hampshire, I remember that we stopped to eat at a good seafood restaurant. Peter said that he was tired and that he preferred to wait in the car. Only much later did he tell me that he had been stricken with a sense of terror. Even though he had already shared with me the "secret" of his inability to read and knew that he could count on me to help to cover for him, there would still be times like this when the sense of anxiety would overwhelm his sense of confidence altogether.

There came a point when Peter's anxiety began to be obsessive.

He did not dare to leave his father's two-room flat for days on end. When he did go out, it would be only to the corner store and back. (He lived, during most of the years I knew him, almost exclusively on precooked frozen foods and soups that came in cans. He memorized the labels, so that he could pick out what he wanted without asking.) His isolation from the daily patterns of the outside world came, after a while, to be virtually complete. Night turned into day for Peter. Stereo music and an average daily diet of twelve hours of television became his sole reliable companions. His mother was dead. His father, nearly illiterate himself, was seldom home. His father's girlfriend was illiterate as well. Four or five friends from grade-school days would come by now and then to say hello. They were, for the most part, illiterate too. Those who could read and write had long since disappeared into that world of hope, employment, aspiration which Peter regarded no longer with longing so much as with alarm.

If I were ever to ask him what he wanted most, Peter would give me ten or fifteen other answers before he would mention "learning how to read and write." It was my first experience in the risk and the romanticism of cheating somebody like Peter by naive, noncritical acceptance of his spoken wishes. If I did not know him very well, if we were not neighbors and if he did not view me as a friend, I doubt that I would have felt the right to press him to the point at which he would have dared to tell me, in response, that— more than anything else in the world—he wanted to have the chance to learn to read. But how much energy had already been squandered in those many months and years of desperate evasion? If only that energy could have been channeled, from the start, into a program of self-liberation.

This situation—fear, anxiety, at length a growing arsenal of self-protecting mechanisms—repeats itself in numerous anecdotes and stories told by those who have worked with illiterate adults.

In an excellent documentary produced by Dorothy Tod, a filmmaker from Montpelier, Vermont, a formerly illiterate cattle farmer speaks, in retrospect, of the anxiety he used to feel as a nonreader and describes the deceptive mechanisms he contrived to obviate the constant danger of humiliation: "You just feel so backward, so out of place a lot of times. You have to be careful not to . . . get into situations where it would leak out—or be with people that would make it show."

The man describes some of the strategies he used: "You always try to act intelligent, act like you knew about everything even if you did not. . . . If somebody give you something to read, you make believe you read it. . . . You must make out like you knew everything."

The patterns of deception, for this man as for so many other illiterate adults, seem to have begun when he was in the early years of school.

"I asked for help several times in school," he says. "The first year in school I learned to read like I was learning to memorize a poem. I could 'go through' the book. . . . I could look at the pictures and tell you everything that was said underneath. She thought I was reading. . . . I could repeat what was on the page without making a mistake. . . . So I never did . . . learn anything."

Another example of the same syndrome—fear, deception, barely submerged alarm—is reported in an interview published by *Philadelphia Magazine*. An illiterate young man, given the pseudonymn of Tommy, explains to a reporter the devices he would use to get himself a job. He would take with him a friend who knew of his problem and who would fill out the job application for him. If this was not convenient, or not possible, he would "tell the personnel people" that he "had to go to a wake" and would return the application form a little later. That would provide him with the time to bring it home and ask his wife to fill it in.

As a result of devices of this kind, many adult illiterates (very much like Peter) are able to put off for very long periods of time an ultimate confrontation with the problem of their own peculiar form of bondage.

In Tommy's case, there was the familiar sequence of postponement, sudden panic—and abject surrender. He was able to hold a job in a dairy laboratory testing milk, butter and bottles for impurities. He was very thorough and managed to do well by memorizing the crystals, the acids and their various reactions.

His boss, in fact, told him that his work was superior to that of two college graduates who had preceded him in the same job. A decision was made, therefore, to give him a promotion. First, however, an exam was necessary. He took home with him the books that had been given to him by his boss for preparation—and, of course, he never went back.

This story, one of hundreds that journalists, teachers and political organizers have begun to compile in the past few years, suggests at least one additional form of servitude suffered by the functional illiterate. This is the secret reliance of a wife upon husband, of a husband upon wife, or even of both (as is frequently the case) upon their children.

Many stories reiterate the painful syndrome of humiliation, of loss of individual autonomy, sometimes even of a pathological dependence that has power to destroy a family. In the cinematic portrait I described above, the Vermont farmer speaks of his former dependence in these words:

I was alone without her guidance [i.e., that of his wife] . . . when it come to readin'. . . . In order to find out what's goin' on . . . you've got to read. . . . And if you're handling money all the time, you've got to know how to . . . figure good . . . and fast. It's embarrassing to make mistakes in money. . . .

When you're on the farm with the cows they don't ask you no questions. They're happy the way you are. But when you're out in the public . . . you got to know it all.

In this situation, what began as a warm and supportive liaison between husband and wife ended by growing into a gnawing sense, on his part, that his wife enjoyed the situation.

"I don't know if she'll admit it or not," he says, "but she's done this so long for me that she hates to see me do things for myself.

. . . Now that I'm doing things for myself, she regrets it a little bit, I think."

He adds these words: "You know when you depend on another person . . . how they use it. . . . You don't feel that you accomplish anything. . . ."

Another, even more explicit version of this pathology is the total emotional breakdown of a man or woman. A tragic example is that of the illiterate adult who works a lifetime, somehow manages to sidestep every sort of obstacle that possibly could hold him back in his employment, then goes to pieces upon retirement, regresses to that period of his childhood in which he suffered most acutely from his inability to read—and, in this period of crisis, ends up as an alcoholic.

Alcoholism, however, is only one of several forms of personal breakdown and defeat which often can be directly traced to the peculiarly humiliating servitude of an illiterate adult.

After all else is said and done, the heart of the issue remains an economic argument. In the long run, for all the statistics of declining S.A.T. scores among children of the upper middle class, the deepest form of suffering is that which afflicts poor people and, above all, the minorities. Although a literate man or woman is by no means certain of a decent and rewarding job in our society, it is probably true that an illiterate man or woman has almost no chance at all.

Still worse, the illiterate adult loses almost all opportunity for articulate denunciation of an unjust allocation of the privileges, the pleasures and rewards that are available in our society. Those who are not merely excluded from the marketplace of decent, dignified employment, but also denied the voice with which to protest their denial and exclusion are twice oppressed.

A leader in the Third World effort to eradicate adult illiteracy once spoke of this compounded anguish in the following words: "Those who oppressed us, those who denied us, those who took away our voice of protest—when they were finished, they had married us to the lie. . . . So long as we were not free men, we were compelled to live in company with that lie. The world crumbles when a people chooses to live no longer with a lie."

The words are those of Raúl Ferrer, leader of the Cuban literacy struggle of 1961. It is time, perhaps, to stop one moment in examination of our own dilemmas, in order to take a look beyond our shores.

3

LOOKING ABROAD

OTHER nations have carried out wholly or partially successful adult literacy efforts. China, Israel, Cuba and, for a time, Brazil are four of the nations that have, reportedly, been able to show some measurable success.

I will refer here solely to the campaign that took place in Cuba. The Cuban struggle was, by all odds, the most comprehensive of all recent literacy efforts. The campaign in Cuba has been designated by UNESCO, as well as by other outside observers, as an almost unqualified success. The Cuban literacy venture, moreover, was carefully documented and may therefore be examined in great detail.

It is for these reasons that I made my own visits to Cuba—first in 1976, again in 1977—my initial curiosity having been sparked by the impressive report that had been published by UNESCO.

The Cuban literacy struggle is one which cannot easily be described in conventional academic language—not, at least, without denying to that struggle a large part of its emotional appeal. "The literacy campaign was not a dry event," the campaign director, Raúl Ferrer, once said to me during an interview. "It must not be talked about as if it were."

Ferrer's admonition is appropriate to the passion and enthusiasm that were identified with the Cuban effort. The main outline of the

Cuban venture, nonetheless, can be summarized in few words. In April and May of 1961, in response to the government's appeal, one hundred thousand Cuban children—forty percent of them younger than fifteen—joined in a massive battle against adult illiteracy among the rural poor. One hundred fifty thousand adults later joined their ranks, to form a total teaching force of two hundred fifty thousand people. The older volunteers, generally urban and often middle-class in origin, tended to work with those, among the illiterate population, who were closer to their homes. The younger literacy workers, "brigadistas," as the student volunteers were called, remained throughout that year the actual and symbolic spearhead of the struggle. It was they who ventured into the least accessible, most backward and poverty-stricken regions of the island, in order to live and work in the homes of the campesinos (peasants)—who represented, by far, the largest portion of those million Cuban adults who could neither read nor write.

The volunteers received ten days' instruction. Most instruction took place at a former tourist resort situated at Varadero Beach. The orientation given to the brigadistas was divided into three parts. The first part instructed them in the use of a literacy primer, developed especially for this purpose by the campaign's leaders after conducting a series of pilot programs to determine what would later be defined as "active" words and "generative" themes.

The second part prepared them in the use of a sophisticated multipurpose adaptation of a Coleman lantern. The lantern was essential, not only to offer a light by which to travel on the country roads but also to provide the means by which to carry on lessons in the evening or in the early mornings, prior to the dawn. (In most of the Cuban countryside in 1961, there was no electric power.)

The third part of the brigadistas' orientation consisted in the lesson of egalitarian behavior. This was the part, according to many of the former brigadistas, that mattered most of all. Volunteers were told that they would be asked to eat the same food, work in the same fields, sleep in the same house and sling their hammock above the same dirt floor as those whom they had been assigned to teach.

Progress with each pupil was measured by a series of three tests. After the last had been completed, the pupil would write a letter to inform Fidel of his or her success. When the last member of a family was able to pass the final test, a flag was flown from the doorway of the house: "This house is declared territory free from illiteracy." When the last house in a municipality had flown the flag, then the municipal capital could do so also.

A friendly competition soon evolved among the provinces of Cuba to see which one would be the first to win the right to fly the flag from the provincial capital.

The campaign was brought to an end at a massive rally in Havana on December 22. Cuba itself, a nation dotted by now with several hundred thousand paper flags of literate men and women, was declared by Fidel Castro to be "Territory Free from Illiteracy." In reality, the figure for adult illiterates had been reduced from twenty percent to less than five percent within less than one year. Today, after nearly two decades of follow-up work, the figure is reported to be two percent. UNESCO calls the Cuban undertaking "a success story that has no end."*

In looking back upon the Cuban struggle, perhaps the most useful observation we can make is one that underlines the many differences between the challenge faced by Cuba and that which is faced here in the U.S.A. Cuba's situation, at the start of 1961, was

---

*According to the latest census taken prior to the revolution, 23.6 percent of Cuban adults were illiterate. The number diminished slightly during the advance of the revolutionary army through the villages of Oriente during 1956, 1957 and 1958. A more substantial decrease in the number of illiterates is attributed to a period of experimental programs during 1959 and 1960. Simultaneously, the vast improvement and redoubled enrollment of the public schools served to reduce still more the number of illiterate adults. Estimates suggest that, by early 1961, the illiteracy rate had already been reduced to twenty percent.

not comparable, in any tactical respect, to the situation that we face today in the United States.

In Cuba, the population was, to an unusual degree, homogeneous. In the United States, of course, this is the very opposite of the case. We are dealing here with a vast number of different ethnic groups and socioeconomic levels. In addition, there are dozens of totally different geographic regions, comprising almost as many separate areas of moral concern, of economic need, of popular vocabulary and of divergent motivation.

In Cuba, again, the literacy workers were predominantly urban, but the prospective pupils were, for the most part, rural. In the United States, although with some significant exceptions, we are faced with precisely the reverse. In the North at least, prospective learners are, in large part, ghetto residents. They are the blacks, the foreign-born, the poor, the unemployed. They live on the fringe—or in the long-forsaken centers—of the cities. Those who teach—again in contrast to the Cuban situation—are likely to come from outside of the cities. The "line of march," therefore, of those who volunteer to teach adult illiterates, in at least the northern part of the United States, will be in somewhat the reverse direction from that of those who led the Cuban struggle during 1961.

A third important distinction is that which is inevitably caused by the differences between our governments and social systems and, possibly still more important, by the different historical moments in which we find ourselves. The mood in Cuba, during 1961, for all the conflicts of opinion, all the exiles, all the dissidents and expropriated members of the former ruling class, was nonetheless one of cheerful optimism. Several highly visible and charismatic leaders set the pace for energetic and self-sacrificing youth. The memory of the overthrow of Batista was still fresh; young people in the literacy campaign often wore the beads, berets and tattered ribbons of the revolutionary army as they headed out into the hills.

There is at least one other serious difference. In Cuba, there was, in 1961, considerable unanimity on the part of the illiterate campesinos in regard to their new leaders. Most of the illiterate poor, for instance, tended to accept the revolutionary government and its stated goals. In the United States, by way of contrast, the major breakdowns and distinctions within our target population seem to fall between those who do and those who do not believe in the "good life" that our social system claims to offer to those men and women who possess the appropriate skills.

Clearly, then, the Cuban literacy struggle must not be perceived, in a naive sense, as a model for imitation by a nation which is so much more heterogeneous in its demographic make-up and in the needs and character of its illiterate population. If it is to be of use to us at all, the Cuban struggle might logically serve not as a model, but as a kind of spur and challenge to our own imagination.

In what areas does that challenge lie?

It lies, certainly, in the Cubans' emphasis, both during and after the one-year campaign, upon a flexible and constantly readjusted definition of the term *illiterate*. Here, as in Cuba, it is essential that we not allow ourselves to settle for an arbitrary, unchanging, and school-oriented definition (e.g., "sixth-grade level"). The definition changes with the shifting needs and wishes of the individual, as well as with the rising levels of sophistication needed to participate in the full life of society. In both nations, this is changing constantly.

The challenge lies also in the whole idea of "teaching with," not "to" or "for," the people. Stated otherwise, it lies in an egalitarian approach which rests upon a dialogical relationship between teacher and learner, even for the most repetitive and didactic lessons.

Finally, the challenge lies in the very boldness of the project, in the sense of risk, adventure and bravado—all in contrast to the mechanistic, managerial approach suggested so frequently in the writings of American authors on this subject. It is this—the "all-out" character of the literacy campaign in Cuba—which seems to me to pose the most important challenge to the people of our nation.

As we begin, then, to attempt to map out certain possible approaches to our own literacy crisis here in the United States, I hope that we can keep in mind the Cuban challenge. I think it may sharpen our own dedication to the task at hand and may heighten our own sense of momentum. It may also help to rescue us from some of the laborious and arid jargon which seems to pervade so many of the discussions of this issue. There are all kinds of illiteracy. One of the worst is that of the expert who cannot speak in a language comprehensible except to other experts on illiteracy. We *can* speak of these issues in voices that are not only intelligent and precise but are, at the same time, within the realm of understanding of almost every citizen in the nation.

The language we select in our discussion of an issue, as George Dennison has observed, is never neutral. The words we use either restrict our dialogue to those who are already conversant with our private language, or else they open up our dialogue to the largest possible number of concerned and undefeated men and women.

I view this book as the beginning of that dialogue.

4
IDEA AND ACTION

SCHOLARS remind us, with irritating persistence, that literacy cannot "create" a job and that the lack of literacy is seldom the sole cause of a person's failure to obtain one. These points seem obvious. So long as there *are* jobs, however, it is clear that the lack of literacy skills is one sure way to guarantee that one will never have access to whatever opportunities exist. If acquisition of such skills still fails to lead to satisfactory employment, it will at very least lead to a heightened recognition—on the part of a poor person—of the unjust nature of an economic system which can, with so little hesitation, label an entire class of people as "expendable."

One other preliminary point seems important to repeat and clarify. There already *are* good programs in the United States. As we have seen, however, they do not reach more than two to four percent of those in need. There is no doubt that these are good and adequate programs for those people whom they reach. It may also be true that a generous expansion of these programs may reach a more substantial number of those who are not now being reached at all. For the great majority, however, something else is needed.

That "something else" is far more sweeping than anything that is being done today—more closely associated with parallel issues of

survival, with actions that emerge from education, with community participation on a massive scale, with an on-going dialogue between the teachers and the learners and with the recognition, on
the part of all concerned, that heightened political-economic consciousness will be one probable result.

The plan of action that will be presented in this chapter, and in
the two succeeding chapters, is in no respect intended as "the sole
solution." It is, at best, *one possible solution*. What will be outlined in
these pages is not THE ONE PLAN, but one of a number of suggested
plans. I offer it solely as a prototype and, in no instance, as some
sort of arbitrary and unalterable blueprint.

If this is the case, if it is to be so tentative, the question comes to
mind: Why do I feel it is important to present a plan which is so
detailed and specific?

All of my doubts and hesitations notwithstanding, it seems to me
it is my obligation to render concrete all that is abstract in general
discussions of this issue—and to do so through the vehicle of one
specific, therefore vulnerable, but vivid, imaginable and realistic
plan.

I am going to begin by spelling out a number of steps which
seem to constitute the necessary preconditions for a vigorous and
successful literacy struggle.

The first step, in my belief, is to deal with the inevitable obstacles that will be posed by vested interests of all kinds: government agencies, local organizations, church-based agencies, teacher
organizations, library groups, university scholars, individual
writers (like myself)—and "the private sector." In this book, there
will be many passages of disputation and of controversial personal
opinion. It seems important, wherever possible, however, to attempt to speak and work in a conciliatory manner—one which is
most likely to assist in forging an effective coalition of all interested
parties. In an enterprise so broad and sweeping as the one that we
propose, every participant has one special vested interest over all

the rest. It is a vested interest in avoiding small sectarian disputes, petty hostilities and needless confrontations.

A second form of reexamination which appears to be essential is a careful scrutiny of the multiple varieties of adult illiterates in the United States—a point discussed at length in Chapter 1. By virtue of this form of careful reexamination, we are able to recognize, and can comfortably concede, the genuine worth of on-going programs for a certain stratum of illiterate adults, but we are simultaneously released from the familiar trap of feeling that we have no viable alternatives to the mere expansion and re-funding of these programs. We are allowed, thereby, without denunciation of those people doing good work in the present, to free ourselves to work in far more ambitious and more comprehensive efforts for the future.

There is another form of reexamination which appears to be of value: If (as we believe) there is an urgent need for radical departures in our entire approach to the illiterate adult, why is it then that the United States has never yet embarked upon a venture either so radical or so broad in scope? It is not enough for us to set forth in an innocent fashion and announce to all the world what we are now about to do. It is important, as well, to take into consideration the ideological bias, and the economic and political interests, which have guaranteed that nothing *would* be done up to this time.

Seen from this point of view, the challenge inevitably becomes a great deal more demanding than most of us have previously believed. That challenge, to be blunt, is *not* that we do not know how to teach illiterate adults, but rather—in terms of public policy at least—that we don't *want* to. I do not like to render the challenge overwhelming, or intimidating, by exaggeration. When seeking change, however, it seems essential to find out why this particular kind of change has not been sought before. If we do not find an answer to this question, then we are bound to rerun all the errors of the past.

One final form of clarification, or of "reexamination," appears to me to be essential from the start. This is a point which has to do with the familiar view that literacy itself and, more important, its "delivery" as a skill are infinitely mysterious and complex. This is a myth. It isn't difficult to teach a person how to read. What *is* difficult is to create the context in which dialogue can take place between the would-be teacher and potential learner. In the case of those who have, for many years, been cheated and oppressed, that dialogue can be established only when there is a genuine sense of teaching *with*, not teaching *for* or teaching *to*.

In other words, the process must involve a high degree of shared endeavor in all aspects, from the setting up of classes and the choice of methods and materials to the selection of an optimal location. Once these preconditions have been met, the actual teaching may prove to go extremely fast. In Brazil, substantial literacy skills have been developed in considerably less than two months. In Cuba, as I was told by former literacy workers, the average requirement was two months' work per family—and a total of nine months for the entire nation.

In the United States, I have been able to bring a group of eighteen virtually illiterate teen-age students to a solid competence in reading and writing in approximately sixty days. Knowing almost nothing about reading at the time, I was relying solely on the training I received during a two-week crash course offered to a group of volunteers. One clue to our rapid success, however, may be the fact that we were operating in a dialogical context, one we did not need to create because it was created *for* us in our neighborhood of Boston by the strong, enthusiastic sense of camaraderie in the fight for civil rights. (We had our charismatic leaders too. So, in that sense, our situation was not wholly different from that of the Cuban brigadistas.)

Our sixty days of literacy work were interrupted only twice— both of them days on which I was obliged to share the leadership in a tenant-landlord battle, one which proved to be the first successful rent-strike in our city. Here, too, the connection was made (though certainly without intention in this case) between our work in class and things that happened out in the real world. I felt this was a fortunate circumstance.

Our students in Boston, like the peasants in Brazil and Cuba, knew that there would be a concrete and specific pay-off for the work that they put in. They wanted to be able to get jobs, to purchase cars, to pass the test to get a driver's license. In most cases, they were able to achieve their goals; in many cases, we were able to select materials for use in class which would lead directly to the test (or qualification or prerequisite) our students would be forced to pass or undertake. We felt no hesitation in raising the expectations of our students. We wanted them to feel that they would realize some direct results.

There are those who argue that we must be careful not to "offer too much." They seem to be uneasy that illiterate adults may be led to expect too much in terms of other social gains (health care, better housing, jobs) as a direct or indirect result of literacy instruction. My own belief is that we should not be reluctant to bestir such expectations.

Scholars urge us to clarify the goals of literacy programs "so that they do not promise more than they can deliver." (This is a theme consistent with the whole idea of taking care not to awaken nor injudiciously to elevate expectations.) I tend to favor the opposite position and will emphasize often in this book the positive results of *raising* expectations. Such "expectations," being the kind of basic human longings, human aspirations, human needs that seem both sound and proper, *ought* to be raised and, if they should subsequently meet with disappointment and frustration, then the formerly illiterate person will at least have power for the first time to articulate a history of grief and to break free from the silence of an age-old bondage.

I agree that we should not be reckless in the tone of our suggestions. But if we are not speaking of literacy as an instrument of possible access to a lot of other important things in life, then I do not see why we should take the time to speak of it at all.

There is another point which may be worth brief mention here. I believe it renders our efforts futile and foredoomed if, after looking at Cuba, we begin by taking the position that literacy work of any kind at all demands a total and prior transformation of the economic system. I do not believe that this is so and I think that adventurist language of this kind only postpones realistic action.

Success does not demand an economic or political revolution. It does, however, require an arduous, all-out, unrelenting struggle. It requires a sense of high priorities similar to those which would exist if we were faced with flood, with pestilence or with invasion. It also requires a readiness to accept a series of concomitant or resultant challenges to the accepted social order.

Success, in short, depends upon our willingness to make use of words, ideas and concepts, in the course of adult education, that represent a direct link-up with the paychecks of poor people, with the food in their refrigerators (or, more often, food which is not present in their homes because of its high price), with their often nonexistent health care, with their too often nonexistent jobs.

To state this in more specific pedagogic terms, success lies in our willingness to make use of a text, a series of texts or teaching materials of whatever kind, that do not seek to shy away from words that have the power to make people angry—words that have the power, therefore, to give poor people leverage to transform their lives. I recognize that this idea will have a negative effect on many readers; I do not believe, however, that there is any honest way to get around it.

In the long run, it is not only a case of action emerging from new learning; it is also a case of learning that emerges from new kinds of action. The tension between ideas and applications—the word and the world—will be at the heart of everything that follows.

5

THE CONCEPT OF THE
ACTIVE WORDS

IN the struggle to eradicate illiteracy, as in all other fields of national endeavor, nothing is gotten for nothing and nothing important ever comes for free. The necessary price tag for a serious attempt to end adult illiteracy in the United States is the willingness to open up our nation to the risk of living in the presence of indignant people—people who have been cheated long, and treated ill and who, therefore, upon the acquisition of the power of the written word, may very likely feel the inclination to make vocal their long-muted sense of rage at the unjust state of silent servitude in which they have, for so long, been allowed to live.

What are the kinds of words that might most vividly awaken the suppressed desires and the muted aspirations of the unempowered poor? A great many adult literacy programs have foundered on this question. If my own observations are correct, the reason that a notable success was possible in Cuba had much to do with the government's willingness to use those kinds of words which were designed to give the people power, if they so decided, to defy those who had *given* them the power—and, in the long run, to defy the government which had created the whole program in the first place. In Cuba, the methods used and words selected were unquestionably political in nature and unmistakably provocative in bias.

They were not, however, of a dulling and oppressive nature. (The bias was "anti-C.I.A." but it was also "anti-status quo.") The government was prepared to run the risk of a totally empowered population. So must we also if we hope to see a literacy struggle win success.

What are examples of the kinds of words that we in the United States might logically attempt to use? I do not mean to prescribe a list of generative or active words. I would, however, like to make suggestions in order to answer those who often ask me to be "more specific" or to offer five or ten conceivable examples.

I would *not* start with any list of facile and dispassionate words but, rather, with words like "grief" and "pain" and "love" and "lust" and "longing," "lease" and "license," "fever," "fear," "infection," "nation," "doctor," "danger," "fire" and "desire," "prison," "power," "protest," "progress" or "police."

These are a few examples of what I have in mind when I refer to active words, or what some of my colleagues label "dangerous" words, strong and volatile syllables of passion and of elucidation—the clarification, for example, of a complex system of oppressions that may or may not, before that moment, have been visible or vivid in the learner's mind. The words would differ surely from region to region, city to city, year to year. These are the kinds of words, however, which, in one particular Eastern (urban) context, would be most likely to develop in the process of dialogue, as learners and teachers begin to join in common efforts to create the parameters, choose the materials, determine the setting and establish the specific goals.

My purpose, in suggestion of a certain type of generative word, is not to encourage a radical's version of cultural invasion by arrogant prescription. The goal is not to try to "plant" these words and concepts in the minds of those who wish to learn to read and write. The purpose, rather, is—first through the process of prior dialogue, later in the day-to-day relationship of teacher and learner—to dig down into the deep soil of those incipient concepts, dreams, longings and ideals, and of those rich oral vocabularies as well, which exist already in the consciousness of even the most broken and seemingly silent of the poor.

In reminding ourselves of those oral vocabularies which exist already, we may thereby be able to obviate the condescending point of view of those who ask the age-old question: "How can we motivate these kinds of people? How can we somehow lead them to desire to learn?"

There would not be so much discussion of "the motivation process" if we were willing to give up, or were able at last to transcend, the tendency to search out and to "discover" a contrived and mechanistic motivation, especially one that satisfies our prior and often fatalistic expectations. I mean the expectations of those who are already addicts of surrender and who, no matter how earnest their intentions, do not in fact expect to see a program such as this achieve success.

The motivation which teachers often try in vain to "find" is already present, I am certain, in the people whom we hope to teach. It would be the course of least resistance not to "search out" but to *release* that motivation from the prison cell of silence and despair. Often, in dealing with illiterate adults of the most desperate kind— those who do not adhere to any conventional tenets of our social system and do not even feel the sense of privilege or power to articulate their longing for another set of social circumstances—teachers will comment that "they do not seem to have much motivation," or "their motivation-level is extremely low." In terms of conventional motivation, they are probably correct. I am thinking of something, however, very different from conventional motivation. There exists, submerged beneath the silence, a *potential* motivation, a motivation "about-to-be," ready to surface, to evolve and to find voice, but only if the right switch should be turned—or the right valve finally released.

One natural assumption, in light of this discussion, is that *whatever* words we choose will make their appearance in the context of some type of reader, primer or the like. Many educators, however, do not approve of the use of primers with adults. There are, certainly, a number of sensible objections and they come up regularly at many of the seminars and conferences that have to do with adult literacy work. The major objection is the juvenile tone of most familiar primers, although another frequent objection is the risk that a primer may represent an unwholesome outside imposition upon the individual learner—another vehicle, in short, of cultural invasion.

A primer, however, does not *need* to be juvenile in tone or in association; nor is there any reason why there ought to be, or has to be, a *single* primer. There might well be a large variety of primers, regionally selected or prepared, and the substance of such regional primers might well absorb a good deal of the input of the various communities in which they will be used. In this manner, conceived and created out of prior pilot programs, the regional primers might better reflect the needs, the longings and, most important by far, the active language of those men and women who will shortly read them.

In this way, although "standardized" in one sense to meet the purposes of a large and urgent national endeavor, and to meet the special needs of teachers who will not have had much preparation for their work (see Chapter 6), the primers need not necessarily represent any form of outside imposition. On the contrary, they might well be so skillfully designed as to hold a mirror up to every man or woman in the land.

I do not wish, however, to make this book prescriptive. It is entirely possible to do away with primers altogether; so this need not be an issue of contention.

There is a second question that has come up often in discussion of the issue of "the dangerous words." Is there, perhaps, some possible *danger* in the use of dangerous words? At times, it has seemed to me a comical question; but, in plain fact, it is a sensible concern—at least on the part of those who have a lot to lose from any transformation or disruption of the status quo.

Might poor black people who do not have doctors, to take one obvious example, become less docile, or more "dangerous," once they learn to read and write enough to recognize the grim statistics for black infant-death and black maternal-death rates in the United States? Will they be "dangerous" once they possess the skills to understand the lease they sign in order to inhabit an apartment they cannot abide for payment of a rent which they cannot afford? Will they be "dangerous" if they possess a license to drive mediocre cars out of a despairing slum into a neighborhood in which they still are not permitted to obtain a home by mortgage, or to send their kids to school?

Doctor. License. Lease. Three dangerous words . . .

These are the kinds of words that any literacy effort of the scale and energy which we propose would have to use if we should hope to reach some of our logical goals. If the goal of an all-out literacy struggle is something more than reading a few words, but full human competence and strength, awareness of rights, breadth of inquiry, ethical perseverance and persistence, if teachers hope to serve a truly liberating role, if they are striving to inspire poor people to emancipate themselves and one another from the crowded prisons of their souls, then I do not see how we can escape this danger.

To awaken people to intelligent and articulate dissent, to give voice to their longings, to give both lease and license to their rage, to empower the powerless, to give voice to those who are enslaved by their own silence—certainly this represents a certain kind of danger. It is, indeed, the type of danger which a just society, or one that aspires to justice, ought to be eager to foster, search out and encourage. If this is a danger which our social system cannot plausibly afford, then we may be obliged to ask ourselves if we can possibly afford this social system.

POSTSCRIPT: ON THE IDEA OF A REGIONAL PRIMER

I spoke above of the viewpoint of a number of education writers in regard to "literacy primers." I also pointed out that there is no reason to argue at great length about this issue, since it is entirely possible to do away with standard primers altogether.

If, however, texts or primers are going to be used at all, I think that we should give particular attention to the idea of "the regional primer." Local grass-roots organizations might well be the logical groups to oversee the preparation of a series of such primers: small, specific and provocative books, printed in papercover, developed along lines which have been explored in earlier sections of this book, making maximum use of local place names, radio/TV call letters, controversial figures in the local press, momentary items of news urgency, if they appear to hold high interest. All of this becomes realistic and conceivable in the publication of these little books because the purpose of these "regional readers," unlike almost any other primers ever published in the history of the United States, is to fulfill a one-year, one-place, one-time, catalytic function.

The purpose, this time, unlike the established and eternal goal of the entire educational book industry, is not to write a book to last forever, but rather to write a book that will become expendable ("a throw away," in every sense) once it has done its job. The primer for a follow-up program one year later should be a wholly new creation, likewise intended to become expendable, similarly to be thrown away once it has done its job.

The very success of one-time, one-place and (in situations where they are useful) one-issue readers can be directly tested by the speed with which they have outlived their purpose. The book that does the job in 1980 ought to be archaic and of little or no use by 1981. By that year, there should be new active words, provocative names and controversial themes.

After a month (or a season) has gone by, local communities —with the help of their teachers—might well choose to throw away even the best and newest of the regional primers and write others of their own. It is the early weeks I have in mind. During those early weeks, I am convinced that regional primers will be of enormous help—and perhaps most helpful where the literacy workers are the youngest and have therefore the least reason for initial confidence in their own strength and ingenuity.

6

THOSE WHO KNOW TEACH...
A PLAN FOR CALLING OUT FIVE
MILLION VOLUNTEERS

T HE concept of active words, of generative themes—the collaboration of the learners with their teachers both during and preceding the campaign—leads to an obvious question: Where will these teachers come from? What sort of man or woman will be able to participate in a program so demanding?

My own conviction is that young people, ranging in age from fifteen years to twenty-five or thirty, represent the ideal (if undiscovered) teaching force we need. I say that it is "undiscovered"—but it is a force which will remain so only as long as we accept the myth that literacy is a mystery and that teaching someone how to read requires the credential or the discipline of a special sort of priesthood. With the demolition of that myth, it suddenly comes to be entirely plausible that hundreds of thousands of very young people and several million in their late teens and early and mid-twenties might participate in the forefront of this struggle and are, furthermore, the ideal ones to do so.

To many readers, it may easily appear that there is an unattractive bias against older people here. I am aware of this possible misconception and would like to deal with it now. Adults

—particularly those who are either near or past retirement—seem to me the ideal partners for young people in this struggle. In certain situations, they might well serve either as the pedagogic mentors or team leaders of the young.

It always seems a dreadful waste of energy and imagination when people who are striving to make possible a major social transformation begin with the assumption that all people over forty are going to sit back and watch while history moves on. If this ever was true, it is by no means true today—an era in which many millions of people well into middle age and older are feeling the freedom to venture into new careers, returning often to college or graduate school in order to begin again to take an active role within in the world around them.

There is a reason, however, why young people seem to me to be the necessary *vanguard* in this literacy struggle. The combination of physical hardship and psychological stress calls for literacy workers with enormous personal resilience. In all candor, I also think that younger people are more likely to possess the energy and zeal to *join* a campaign of this nature in the first place.

There is nothing new, of course, about the idea of an "army" of young volunteers. In the United States, the Southern Christian Leadership Conference, SNCC, CORE, the Peace Corps and other groups have for many years issued their appeal predominantly to those who were of college age or scarcely older. In the field of literacy itself, there have been several groups that worked primarily with youthful volunteers, and there are several of such groups conducting active programs in most sections of the United States today.

The problem, however, as I have stated earlier, is not only that those programs now in existence are too few, and too meagerly funded, for those sections of the population which they have the competence to reach, but also that, even with substantial increase in their funding, these programs are, with rare exceptions, unprepared to reach the largest numbers of those whom I have described here as the "twice oppressed"—the so-called "underclass"—poor people, most of them black or foreign-born, locked into the urban ghettos or the rural slums. For these people, as we have seen, a new approach is needed—one conducted "on war footing." The kind of army needed for this type of struggle must be not only energetic and impassioned beyond any precedent we know in the United States, but also massive in sheer numbers. *It will require a total of at least five million volunteers.*

Most writers and speakers on this subject tend to keep their recommendations in the realm of generalities. How, then, are we able to pinpoint a concrete number?

We look, first, at a ballpark figure of twenty to thirty million adults who are not now being reached—nor likely to be reached—by programs which exist today. We settle on a round figure (hardly reckless, probably conservative) of twenty-five million. We listen to those who tell us that a teacher-learner ratio, in a situation where the need is for equality and dialogue between the teacher and the taught, ought to be as close as possible to one-to-one. Granting that each potential literacy worker can work on an individual basis with as many as five learners, it then makes sense to establish a total teacher-learner ratio of one-to-five. Hence the estimate of five million volunteers.

Not all of the learners will necessarily live in distant areas where access would be difficult and physical conditions hard to handle. Some may well live close enough to so-called "grey" or "border" areas (marginal neighborhoods of cities, for example) to make it perfectly plausible and simple for older people to participate in the teaching process. It may be, therefore, that as many as two out of five million estimated literacy workers might come from the ranks of people well above the age of twenty-five or thirty. For the rest of the five million, nonetheless, I am convinced that students constitute the single feasible *and available* source of activist and egalitarian volunteers.

If this scenario of an all-out struggle is to take effect, it will require that the high schools and the colleges and universities release from all their classroom obligations those of their pupils who wish to participate and who demonstrate the level of maturity to do so.

I have drawn the parallel already to some previous efforts at mass-mobilization such as the voter-registration work of S.C.L.C., led by Martin Luther King. Some journalistic summaries of this proposal have suggested the VISTA program—Volunteers in Service to America, the domestic version of the Peace Corps—as another precedent. There is at least one important difference, however, between our own suggestion and the characteristic emphasis of VISTA. Most of the VISTA programs did not allow the introduction of political consciousness in any form at all—nor anything similar to what I call "idea and action"—or what Harman and Hunter have described as "the curriculum of action."

Many of the VISTA volunteers who did make efforts to engage those of the so-called underclass with whom they worked in anything like "a dialogue of equals" were promptly suspended, transferred or dismissed. These programs, being basically reformist in approach, could seldom escape the style and tone of "bringing a gift to help the poor," with all of the misguided zeal which this implies. VISTA has drawn good people and has managed, despite the odds, to run some highly effective programs in the past ten years. For all the best intentions, nonetheless, the missionary flavor has remained.

The literacy army that we have proposed will not be working in the tradition either of missionaries or of benefactors. We will be joining in a shared struggle to raise not just the reading levels of poor people, but also their sense of personal autonomy and leverage.

There are many possible objections to the idea of a youthful mobilization of this kind; but the final argument, in my own view, is that there is no other task force of sufficient numbers and mobility to do the job. Certainly we cannot hope to find three to five million volunteers among the teachers in the public schools. Those teachers who are already there, in largest numbers, will be obliged to stay. Many, moreover, will not be prepared to join a grass-roots struggle of this kind. Others will not be suited to attack a problem that the schools in which they work have, in some instances, helped to create. Still others may *wish* to join and help, but only in a supervisory role, held back by permanent family obligations from anything like a total personal commitment to a struggle so consuming and so vast.

It is not extravagant to suggest, then, that we might look to students who are now in universities and high schools. In view of the extended childhood to which we are accustomed here in the United States and most of Europe, it would not be realistic to appeal for help to boys and girls as young as ten or twelve, as was the case in Cuba. It is for this reason that my own suggestion is to appeal primarily to those who fall into the age range of fifteen to twenty-five.

Again in the interest of concreteness—not as an arbitrary plan, but as one *possible* plan—perhaps it will help to specify the duration of the commitment we intend to ask for, as well as to outline the schedule of study sessions that might actually take place. All of these ideas, as I have said before, ought to be open to drastic alteration not only at the hands of other teachers, but also (and above all) in the course of dialogue as it evolves between the literacy workers and those individuals, families and communities with which they will eventually join in common struggle.

In Cuba, students gave up most of one full year of school. Schools officially closed in April of 1961 and opened again in January of 1962. A modified version of this approach, in the context of the United States, might be a plan that asks young people to give up only one summer and one fall semester, a total of six months from June until December—losing thereby no more than one full term of academic work. A program of such short duration would, however, call for an entire immersion, all-out involvement, during the period in question. It would also call for several summers (or subsequent semesters) of follow-up work, either by the same young people or by others who are carefully prepared to carry on the work that has begun, in order not to lose the gains which have been made in the initial period.

It is also possible that I am wrong, that this suggestion is too complicated, and that a larger commitment should be asked of the initial group of literacy workers: one full year perhaps, with one or two summers of follow-up work by the same volunteers with the same learners. I have made the suggestion of a shorter time span solely in order to be realistic about the competing pressures on a person's time in the United States today, especially in a period of economic stress. I also believe that the initial effort, if it is well planned and well prepared by many months of prior dialogue and adaptation and adjustment of materials and goals, need not consume more than six months of full-time concentration on the part of either the teachers or the learners.

If literacy sessions with each family, unit, individual, were to take place for two hours daily, and if they were to take place also for five days each week, if instruction took place (as I have suggested above) by ratios of one-to-five—but, whenever possible, in teaching situations of only one-to-one—there would be plenty of time to hold one hundred sessions and two hundred hours of instruction in the course of only five months. The extra time involved allows for preparation of the teacher in specifics of instruction, as well as for the more important preparation of a prior dialogue that begins to search out and discover common ground.

Is this estimate of a six-month program, with five months of actual teaching, a romantic daydream, or is it justified by precedent, by actual examples? I have taught adolescents to read and write, in nonschool settings, as I have stated above, in considerably shorter periods of time: approximately sixty days. My pupils ranged from twelve to seventeen. Other teachers I know have managed to do this in even shorter periods of time. In Brazil, literacy was taught in less than sixty days to hundreds of thousands of poor people in the early 1960s under Paulo Freire's guidance. Freire's approach was similar, in many ways, to that which was employed in Cuba, with the significant difference that the Cuban government wholly backed the Cuban program and made certain of an energetic follow-up. (There is also the important difference that Freire's program, for a multitude of reasons, could not call upon large numbers of young people, as was the case in Cuba.) In Brazil, in any event, the program was cut short as soon as it began to show results. Freire was sent to prison and soon left Brazil to live in exile. A rightwing coup brought into power a conservative regime that promptly called a halt to any literacy effort that gave evidence of either ethical or political contamination.

It was only in 1979, after sixteen years of exile, that Freire was finally invited to return.

One problem we will encounter in using Freire's work (or that of Cuba) as a precedent for our own is the phonetic difference between English and both Portuguese and Spanish. So long as we base our optimism on the Cuban and Brazilian ventures, there will be scholars appearing on all sides to tell us that the more erratic, often inexplicable phonetic patterns of the English language render *all* comparisons, *all* precedents from Latin nations, totally irrelevant.

This is inaccurate.

English makes less sense phonetically than Spanish; but this does not mean that it makes *no* sense. The basic approach of learning active words, breaking them into syllables, then using those syllables as building blocks for five or ten new words, remains the same, no matter how many exceptions to the phonetic patterns English may present. One reasonable solution for the teacher, in view of the large number of phonetically irregular words within our language, is to select, out of the learner's active words, those which will offer the linguistic units—recurring syllables, word-parts, portions of words which (re-combined) form numerous other words—that we can best exploit for our own intentions.

To state this more simply: Out of all the active (generative) words that may emerge in course of dialogue with the learner, it is

a simple matter for ingenious teachers to select, with logical anticipation, those active words which *also* are composed of predictable
linguistic units—units from which we know that we can easily con-
struct a number of new words.

What about words, however, that do *not* so easily fit into neat
patterns of syllabication—words that do not make phonetic sense of
any kind—what textbooks call "exceptions"? My own inclination is
to bypass words like these entirely, to work around them for as
long as we can (and we *can* work around them for a long time if we
wish). Once the learner has developed a strong grasp of several
hundred words—words of a more predictable and logical sound
structure—in short, once the pupil feels the self-assurance to set
down on paper or to recognize in print words and sentences that
resonate with passion and importance, once the learner has
achieved this temporary plateau of success, then (but not before) I
think a teacher can confidently explore and explicate the full range
of sound peculiarities, phonetic aberrations, which, of course, do
constitute essential aspects of a thorough and far-reaching competence.

What might be a reasonable training period for literacy workers?
Volunteers could probably learn all they would need during a
training session of no longer than two weeks: one that might begin
by the third week of June in order that the actual work could start
during the first week of July.

Where should these training sessions be conducted? It would
probably pose impossible logistic problems to hold them in the
neighborhoods themselves. The latter location is attractive, as one
which would be most consistent with the tone and guidelines of the
plan, but it would probably prove impractical. Certainly, however,
if the training and orientation of the volunteers can be conducted at
any level of decentralized control, it will encourage regional input
and will help to guarantee that preparations for the period of teaching will be more realistic and more relevant to each community's
racial, ethnic and economic needs.

There is another practical matter to consider in planning the tactics of recruitment and of preparation. What if we were to ask the high schools, colleges and universities to grant their pupils academic credit for the time they spend in doing literacy work? In talking with college students, high school students and their teachers, I have heard a number of reasons why this seems to make good sense.

There are, first of all, large numbers of politically committed students who go to college on a tight and careful budget and who, therefore, could not afford to join a literacy campaign if they did not, at the very least, receive course credit for the time involved.

Second, this kind of work can hardly be construed as pedagogic "free time" or a whimsical escape from serious education. The work involved would be constructive, challenging and, above all, educative. It seems at least within the realm of reason, therefore, that schools and universities might willingly give their pupils academic credit for the time that they commit.

Illiterate adults will be learning from young people; but young people, simultaneously, will learn from those they teach. The first will gradually achieve the power of the written word; the second will gain unprecedented knowledge of the world in which they live. It is the sort of knowledge that can seldom be attained within that air tent of "inert ideas" that was described by Alfred North Whitehead as one constant characteristic of the public schools.*

Apart from all else, it seems to me that there is a high degree of practical and political logic in any plan that can liberate young people for one full semester from such courses as "The Problems of Democracy," in order to enable them to go into the real world and begin to *solve* one of those problems. Very few programs could be more apt, more earnest or more decent than one which asks for a year or half-year of a student's life in an all-out struggle to em-

---

*See Chapter 12, p. 90.

power poor people to obtain a sense of repossession of their own existence.

"The people themselves," as Harman and Hunter have written, "would have the major voice in the determination of what they and their communities want to work on. . . ." This remains undisputed and unquestioned in the plan that we propose. What seems essential, however, is that there be the necessary source of skills available to *answer* the needs which the communities define. It is a basic presupposition of this book that literacy to meet the demands of basic communication and survival in the U.S.A. will be one of those needs, and probably will be among those which are first perceived as preconditions to attainment of all others.

I have tried to be specific, therefore, in suggestion of one means by which those literacy needs can find responsive answers among those who have the time and energy to act upon their own convictions. It is my belief that we should start by looking to young people. At the same time, we should spell out a specific structure to enable these young people to move from mere conviction into action with the greatest possible facility—and with the least delay.

7

PRACTICAL DETAILS

ONCE there are sufficient volunteers, once they are organized in regional units or divisions of whatever kind, once they are assigned to neighborhoods, to specific communities and specific goals, who will arrange for them to get the money that they need? Who will assume responsibility—and through what funding channels? How much money will young volunteers require?

A small stipend, sufficient to enable volunteers to live at roughly the same level as the men and women whom they teach, seems to me one very good way by which to heighten the likelihood that volunteers will not be entering upon this period of work with condescending views—or, more to the point, in situations where they *do*, to guarantee that views like these will not prevail beyond the first few days.

Young people who choose to live at the same economic level as those men and women who are soon to be co-workers in a shared endeavor will be obliged to learn—if they do not already know— the taste of inexpensive food, the sense of weariness of those who work long hours for little pay or else (more frequently) of those who have no work at all but who exhaust their energies day after day in fruitless efforts to obtain a worthwhile job. Volunteers will learn also to keep up with the unending pressures of the hour-to-hour struggle for survival in an urban tenement or in a rural shack, where children of all ages pose the constant problems of unsatisfied appetite, untreated sickness, congenital illness, personal anguish and confusion in an overcrowded space, too many needs, too little sleep, too little peace to stop and even repossess one's thoughts.

Thus, through the real experience of shared disorder, the noise of the streets, anxiety about excesses (or absences) of police, the devastation of narcotics and whatever other problems tend to prosper in a neighborhood of grief, there will be a powerful antidote to the familiar, if unconscious, condescension of so many previous participants in this type of undertaking. This, of course, is at the heart of the whole plan. The campaign that we are proposing here is different in kind from any struggle that I know in the United States; and any likelihood of its success in touching the lives of those who never have been served by even the best of efforts in the past depends upon reiteration of that difference. The people who are to benefit the most must be empowered, from the very start, to join in the planning and in the analysis of problems that lead at length to any or all of the specific goals that have been stated here.

"We recommend," write Harman and Hunter, "the establishment of new, pluralistic, community-based initiatives whose specific objective will be to serve the *most* disadvantaged hard-core poor, the bulk of whom never enroll in any existing programs. . . ." These initiatives "would focus on persons in the communities where they live. The initiatives would require the adults themselves to contribute to developing programs based on concrete learning needs growing out of specific issues affecting their lives in their communities."

While I agree with this approach entirely, it would be naive to imagine that all—or even very many—of these "community-based initiatives" are likely to come into being if there is no prior spark of catalytic fire from an outside force. The people themselves, according to Harman and Hunter, ought to have a dominant voice in the process of deciding what it is they want to learn to do. But, if the community is one whose voice has been forever silent, if the community is one which never has felt the right and power to "initiate its own initiatives," then none of this will happen by spontaneous generation. Nothing comes out of nothing; and people cannot possibly initiate an action they have never heard of, nor voice a longing for a form of self-realization to which they do not yet believe they have a right.

My own inclination, therefore, is to try to overcome that awkward sense of hesitation—hesitation which often proves to be immobilizing in its impact—the hesitation of those outside volunteers who feel that, in order to be wary of all hint of condescension, they must be willing to tie one hand behind their back, offer less than they can and bring forth less than what they really know.

It is important to speak of community initiatives as one of the two essential factors in a venture of this kind; but, if that venture is to be coequal, then the literacy workers must feel free to offer what *they* think to be of value too. It seems to me that volunteers can earn the right to join with the community in a dialogue of equals, so long as they are willing to share the hardships and commit themselves to a steadfast and consistent period of work.

Volunteers will not be driving into the community at two o'clock on a summer afternoon, only to take off for the beaches with their "real" friends at a quarter after four. Volunteers will share, as much as possible, the total life experience of those who are to be their allies, pupils and co-workers.

This is not to say that we must copy mindlessly the Cuban model, especially that part which stipulated that each literacy worker ought to live within the learner's home. In striving to make progress with an illiterate pupil, whether within a crowded tenement or in a two-room country shack, many organizers I have met suggest that literacy workers would probably do best to establish a collective "Literacy House" in an independent building, situated on the block or in the neighborhood in which they plan to work and live.

A Literacy House might very well be nothing more spectacular than a vacant apartment, for example, in the urban setting, or possibly an entire building (a deserted corner grocery might be ideal) with a storefront on the street floor and two or more apartments just above. The building would provide both living quarters for the literacy workers and a quiet and reflective learning center for their pupils.

If old, deteriorated buildings of this kind are not in condition for the use of volunteers and learners, this then might suggest a first—and uncontrived—experience in what I call "a shared endeavor." It might suggest to volunteers a chance to work with community parents and teen-agers in doing a rapid job of renovation. (It doesn't take long to do this kind of work, so long as the job is done in common with two dozen energetic friends: teachers-in-training, learners-to-be.) More often than not, the previously unrecognized or, at any rate, unvalued skills of men and women in the neighborhood will prove to be superior to those of younger people coming from outside.

Is it probable that community people would really wish to work so hard to help a group of strangers rehabilitate an empty house? It *is* entirely probable, so long as community people share in the decision to establish such a program in the first place. This factor—prior dialogue and participation in selection of specifics—lies at the heart of everything that we suggest.

What is a sensible starting date for the program that I have described?

According to one scenario that I can easily imagine, it might be during April, May and June that discussion groups of various kinds would have been set in motion in the neighborhood organizations, churches, living rooms, kitchens and local community centers of all kinds, in order to create a climate both receptive and intelligently demanding of the "summer soldiers." In using this term—in speaking of the "summer soldiers"—I am thinking of some of those good-natured but fast-moving summer volunteers in various struggles of the past fifteen or twenty years, young people who would come with a good heart but who would disappear as soon as times got rough.

The volunteers we need for an effective and sophisticated struggle will differ from their random predecessors of a decade past in one important sense: They will not be free, without the payment of the price of great humiliation and enormous disappointment on the part of both their pupils and their peers, to slip away once autumn comes and leaves begin to fall in late September. Those who do will not be able to escape the recognition of their dual betrayal both of their pupils and themselves.

In order to be certain that the Literacy House, renovated with and for the literacy workers, will later return to the control of the community, a political and economic organization such as a Tenants' Council ought to be created in each neighborhood. The creation of the legal vehicles by which to guarantee the acquisition of this house by the community, and to determine governance of a Tenants' Council, might well be one energetic and energizing theme for use of learners and of teachers during the process of their literacy work.

In the two summers that follow the initial year of the campaign, I have suggested that an intensive follow-up program ought to be developed. During those summers, the Literacy House might logically serve as a center for this work. In subsequent years, it should be up to community decision to decide on the most useful function of this house: whether it can best be used as an on-going center serving pedagogic goals, as the organizational center of a Tenants' Council, as a daycare center, health clinic, center for legal defense or childrens' rights—or simply as a decent apartment building for the use of people in the neighborhood.

The teaching plan includes one final and important aspect. It would be helpful to organize the reading volunteers into a number of small cohesive "teams," containing perhaps fifteen or twenty people each, trained to work within a neighborhood together, grouped intentionally in such a way as to achieve a class and racial mix. There are two reasons for this idea of a class and ethnic mix. First, the mix of kids from multiple backgrounds is a useful instrument for mutual education in the group itself. It also serves as an additional defense against the risks of class or racial condescension.

The team, depending on the area in which it is to work, might be composed of white, black, Native American and Hispanic volunteers, including young people from a wide variety of backgrounds, ranging from the children of privileged people to those whose families have very little in the way of privilege at all. Wherever possible, the inclusion on each team of people who grew up within the neighborhoods in question would be a most effective way to minimize condescension and facilitate a true and comfortable sense of dialogue.

One argument is frequently brought forward at this stage. The press has reported a number of stories about nonreading graduates of high school in the past few years. If these reports are accurate, the question will be asked: Where will the competent and energetic volunteers that I describe be found? Who will be qualified to teach the very poor if nobody is learning to read and write correctly any more?

For all the complaints by university instructors concerning the inadequacy of composition skills among the freshman pupils they must teach, we are in another world entirely when we speak of the pedagogic problems of the poor. Whatever the percentile drop in college S.A.T. scores and the like, the fact remains that several million white, black and Spanish-surname pupils have been able to achieve a competence in use of words which is entirely equal to the challenges of an adult literacy struggle. Anyone who tries to argue that the problems of those pupils now in college and in public high school are so severe that they cannot conceivably spare the time or energy to help somebody else is using the implausible to justify the indefensible. It is cruel logic—and one that simply helps perpetuate the gulf between the very rich and very poor.

In the face of a myth so broad and so pervasive in the media today, it may prove to be of help to restate certain easily tested truths: (1) There are millions of literate and highly confident university and secondary-level pupils in the United States. (2) Many of these pupils can afford the time and energy to share their skills with others. (3) Wherever marginal deficiencies exist, pupils will generally advance their own skills by the exercise of sharing what they know with others. In areas like basic math and literacy skills, it seems almost impossible to help somebody else without the simultaneous enhancement of one's own effectiveness.

POSTSCRIPT: THE ENDLESS CIRCLE

There are an endless number of ways by which we can discourage earnest activists from working with confidence and energy at any concrete task they undertake. One means, as we have seen, is by the tendency not just to emphasize the factor of community participation, but to do so in a manner which appears to tie the hands of any one who hopes to enter into active solidarity. There is such a thing as "a dialogue of equals" in which nobody who comes in from outside is ever allowed to feel he is the equal of community participants. A tyranny by those least able to conceive of "a way out" begins to take effect. The end result becomes a caricature of anything that resembles a real dialogue.

There is another way of undercutting confidence and energy. It is by the introduction of the concept of an "Endless Circle" of potential causes for whatever problem we confront. Instead of stirring us to find sequential items of specific action that will lead, at length, to *other* items of potential change, the idea of an "Endless Circle" seems to suggest that no one difference has the power to bring about a major change. According to this myth, we learn to pose all problems in such terms as tend to dwarf whatever specific expertise or leverage we possess.

In any serious struggle to confront the problem of adult illiteracy in the United States, it is important to encourage literacy workers to believe that what they do *can* make a difference in and of itself, even if this difference only leads us and our pupils to recognize a number of other challenges which will immediately appear to be essential too. It is a logical assumption, from the start, that nothing done in any one area will prevail for long without a subsequent transformation in a dozen other areas as well. Nonetheless, it seems important (in order to overcome the sense of impotence that media and academia will otherwise impose) that we develop the will, and sometimes the bravado, to take a stand and fight the battle at whatever spot along the total spectrum we may be.

If we were doctors, we might begin by speaking about health care. If we were lawyers, we might begin our struggles in the state and federal courts. If we were social workers, we might begin by working to dismantle the entire welfare system. We are not doctors, however. We are not lawyers. We are not social workers. We are either teachers or else those who would, for a particular period of their lives, filfill the role of teachers in a very specific, limited and concrete way.

Whoever we are, wherever we stand, it is our obligation to engage in struggle to guarantee that we are not defrauded of our sense of leverage and our sense of power—the power it takes to start the work of transformation in an unjust and imperfect world.

8

LITERACY: A WORD IN SEARCH OF DEFINITION

In a schooled society, it is difficult to overcome the tendency to define all types of competence, whether literacy or any other, by the longitude and latitude of school-delineated numbers.

Hence, the inclination to assign "school numbers" to a nonschool situation in order to achieve some means of measurement of the skills to be attained in adult literacy programs. In Cuba, the initial goal was pegged at "third grade level." Soon it was raised to "sixth grade level," and today the goal is to achieve "a minimal ninth grade level" for all people. In the United States, too, scholars have, at various times since 1968, established a number of different grade equivalents for adult progress. Some, estimating that most newspapers are written with a "seventh grade" vocabulary, decided to set the minimal adult standard at that level. Others looked at military needs and decided, on the basis of these, that the definition of a literate person should be someone who can read and write at "eighth grade level." (On the other hand, during World War II, the U.S. Army settled on "the fifth grade level" as acceptable.) The Adult Basic Education Act of 1968 also established eighth grade as the appropriate goal.

There are some obvious problems, however, in attempting to establish absolute grade levels as the measure of a literate adult. First of all, we do not say very much when we speak of "sixth," "seventh" or "eighth grade" levels. Nobody really knows for sure what any of them are. Grade level equivalents only become meaningful in some way when they are derived from certain tests which are accepted by particular cities, states or local systems. In such a case, however, we are obliged to ask: which tests? what cities, states, school systems? chosen by whom? and testing what?

There is another reason why grade levels are not very helpful: Whichever grade level we select is, by necessity, an arbitrary choice. Since "school designations" have always had a great deal more to do with the needs of society than with those of the individual, these definitions cannot conceivably be useful to those whom public school has failed and then consigned to an illiterate oblivion. Grade level equivalents, then, are not a useful way for us to designate whatever we mean by competence or literacy among adults.

The United Nations has approached the question with a series of more practical, but nonetheless highly arbitrary, definitions. In 1948, the U.N.'s definition of literacy was "the ability to read and write a simple message." In 1951, UNESCO's definition was still rather arbitrary: "A person is literate who can with understanding both read and write a short, simple statement on his everyday life." By 1962, UNESCO had settled on a slightly more sophisticated definition: "A person is literate when he has acquired the essential knowledge and skills which enable him to engage in all those activities in which literacy is required for effective functioning in his group and community and whose attainments in reading and writing and arithmetic make it possible for him to continue to use these skills toward his own and the community's development." (It is only in these final words that we begin to see the stirrings of a definition that might be compatible with one that serves our present needs.)

In the United States, one definition that appears to come closer to being workable and useful than most others is the one that was developed in Texas in the study known as "A.P.L." (Adult Performance Level).* The virtue of the A.P.L. was its refusal to assign grade levels any longer. Instead, as we have seen, the A.P.L. defined a literate person as one who met a certain number of objectives "derived from predetermined adult living requisites." The levels were identified with various levels of "adult success." The criteria, in general, were directly related to tasks that were considered "real" in the society.

One serious problem with the A.P.L., however, is the fact that all "objectives" which were measured were items selected in advance by those (academics, bureaucrats, etc.) who had their own idea of what is meant by "adult living requisites," as well as by "adult success." While the ability to read instructions and follow orders necessary to hold down a certain type of job might well be included in these "requisites," it is not likely that the personal (or community) capability to change or question the nature of that job would be included. The A.P.L. might well measure a person's success in fitting into "real" (and preestablished) slots within society; but it does not seem likely to include the "objective" of thinking critically about society and knowing how to change it.

The consequence of relying on criteria like those adopted by the A.P.L. is the use, in many conventional adult literacy efforts, of reading materials which will effectively indoctrinate the previously illiterate adult, rather than awaken consciousness (or empower action based upon the consciousness) of the unjust social order which has found it acceptable—and sometimes useful—to maintain so many people in a powerless position for so long. It is self-evident that dangerous, active or generative words would not have much appeal for those who have established these criteria and requisites.

If one point seems to emerge from all of the above, it is the fact that no one, either in the United States or elsewhere in the world, has yet been able to agree upon a standard definition of a literate man or woman.

*See Chapter 1, pp. 2ff.

In order to avoid potentially immobilizing periods of hesitation and of indecision, it may be of help to us if we can establish, first, the difference between "raw literacy" and "functional literacy"— and then make clear that it is only the second which we view as a legitimate and serious objective. The former tends to coincide with earlier UNESCO definitions, as well as with those of standard Western economic interests: the ability, essentially, to read, write and comprehend signs, instructions, labels, orders given to us by others—and, most frequently, as a result, to serve the interests of those "others." The latter ("functional literacy") implies, for me, all—or almost all—of the above, but also includes at least two new ingredients: (1) the ability to question the legitimacy of all such instructions, orders and directions; (2) the capacity, furthermore, to participate in the operation and, if necessary, in the transformation of a system, corporation or society, whenever it appears that individual and community interests have been sacrificed to national or corporate objectives.

Another way of making the same point is to say that our efforts ought to be directed at a type (and level) of literacy which is determined in the process of dialogue with the people whom we seek to teach, and that all "requisites" beyond the most obvious facets of initial literacy ought to be developed not by outside experts but, at least in significant part, by those who are the poor themselves. I do *not* believe in the abdication of an equal and effective role by literacy workers; but I do think that the final definition of a "functionally literate" adult ought to have a lot to do with goals which that adult has chosen and articulated, rather than with goals selected by a government, an army or a major corporation.

The role of the literacy worker, as I have discussed above, should be neither passive on the one hand nor prescriptive on the other. Our approach, however, should be sufficiently provocative to serve to open up more options and more possibilities in the choice of literacy goals than most persons, long oppressed, are likely to be able to imagine on their own.

The final goal is a competence to read and write and comprehend at a level which conforms to the real needs of men and women in American society. Those real needs cannot conceivably be met by a domesticating form of education, by literacy aimed at "adaptation" to the way things are. They must be met by literacy which serves the goal of human liberation. Only the latter can fulfill the true spirit of "functional" as opposed to "mechanistic" competence.

This is why it will not serve the interests of the poor to begin with our own preestablished set of adult requisites. Instead, I think we should begin with "minimal requisites," to be expanded, deepened and developed in the process of our literacy work. If this makes testing and evaluation that much harder, even conceivably impossible, I do not think that this is too great a price for us to pay.

What are some of the variant definitions that this flexible concept of functional literacy might logically assume?

In certain communities, a literate adult would surely want to possess some knowledge of law (of street law, in particular), of loan interest (and of the math required to calculate how much one can or cannot pay), of tenants' rights and landlord-tenant relations, of access to health care and some basic comprehension of the medical vocabulary, especially the type of words that tend to mystify the patient while intimidating those who wish to question why a certain procedure or particular medication has been recommended.

In various areas of the United States, there are, I am sure, entire realms of useful or essential competence which I cannot conceivably imagine from my vantage point in the Northeast. I have already spoken of this briefly in my discussion of "the active words." This time, however, I am thinking not only of the reading and spelling of the words themselves, but also of entire realms of comprehension and of information access: not only how to read the facts, but also how to *get* them. (This might well mean some competence in research skills, to give just one example.)

I am thinking, also, not only of the competence to read a magazine or newspaper, but also of the sense of leverage, the critical analysis—"the lever of skepticism"—which will give a person power to see through the bias (or the pretense of "no bias") in the national and local press. This latter item (the lever of skepticism in the face of a non-neutral press) is perhaps one aspect of full literacy which would be of use to people almost anywhere; but I am convinced that there is a great deal more variety than uniformity of need among the hundreds of thousands of illiterate communities in the United States. I hesitate, therefore, to speculate any further on the possible needs of each community, leaving it to others to acquire the information which will render possible a series of useful and widely divergent pilot programs.

One very different aspect of literacy, seldom discussed by literacy experts—just as it is scarcely discussed in governmental agencies or universities—is the role of moral values in the teaching-learning process. It is the question of the possible beneficial or cataclysmic uses to which a skill, a competence, may be applied. So long as we think of our pupils as eternal victims, eternally oppressed, then this issue does not tend to force itself upon our minds. Once we begin to perceive the future possibilities of a man or woman, newly empowered to alter his or her entire role within the world, all at once the question of the *uses of power* comes right to the fore.

Education, of whatever kind, is never neutral. Nor are those skills which are derived from education. The former victim, in almost any social order, can too easily become the victimizer. The formerly illiterate tenant can rapidly become the ally, "front man," "straw," for a dishonest landlord, manipulative broker, bondsman, lawyer or the like. That same former illiterate might also *become* a lawyer in his or her own right; and, with a new-found power, there will be a new-found choice. How is an attorney to use his or her expertise—to serve primarily the corporations and those others who can manage a high fee? to serve those who have very little money? or to work to change a legal system which *depends* upon the power of purchased competence to start with?

The former victim, newly empowered to enter college, engineering school or university, may end up as a technician, physicist or program planner in a war-related industry—in nuclear weapons research, for example, working with other physicists to dream up ever greater weapons of destruction. The same person also has the means to *stop* those dangerous wheels from turning: the power to help prevent that research from proceeding to its goals. This very point—the matter of ethical determinants in the uses of a skill—seems to me to be a necessary part of any literacy campaign.

Those who have been silent, those who have been crippled, those who have forever been oppressed, may seem to be so far from any possible malignant exercise of power as to rule out ethical considerations of this kind. My own concern is based somewhat on memories of certain very poor people I have known who, freed from bondage, rose quite rapidly into positions of remorseless, if sometimes unconscious, cruelty.

If is for this reason that I think these questions should be part of any literacy struggle we may hope to undertake: literate for *what?* competent to go *where?* skillful to achieve what decent or destructive goals? Values like these have seldom been part of public school curricula in the United States or any other nation that I know: All the more reason why an adult literacy struggle must not be modeled upon the workings or curricula of the public schools.

There is one totally different point which frequently is raised in speaking about literacy work. It is a point that seems to come up increasingly nowadays as "future-thinkers" tend to dominate discussion of these issues, bringing with them an entirely new vocabulary of "futurist," media-oriented language. I have tried above to broaden the definition of the term *literate* beyond the initial implication of a simple competence to read signs, orders and instructions. It is possible, however, to expand the definition to a range so large, and scope so broad, that it begins to mean *everything*—or *nothing*. In spite of my own determination to open up the definition to include participation of the learner in delineation of his or her own actual goal, there is a point at which we render an objective meaningless by limitless expansion of its definition.

It is at this point that the literacy worker and the illiterate alike begin to feel a sense of impotence, and of global futility, because the task ahead begins to loom so large. If the definition of a literate adult expands to the dimensions often argued by some of those whom I have called "the future-thinkers," the battle seems too long and hard for any normal person even to attempt it.

There are those, for example, who instantly transcend such matters as street law, medical terminology, reading, writing and demystifying print—and throw us instead into a realm that most of us have never dreamed of. They point to the recent expansion of the modes of information access and dissemination and tell us, therefore, that a person, to be viewed as literate, must be able to do more than read and write words or be able to do basic mathematical computation. They point to what they call a "higher level of literacy"—namely, competence in understanding (or "decoding") media, in working with computers, in handling quantifications of all kinds. The futurists often point to authors like Marshall McLuhan to underscore their point. Contemporary literacy, they say, if we are speaking of a nation such as the United States rather than a nation such as Cuba, implies a level of sophistication in the use and comprehension of words, numbers and symbols that cannot be achieved by the mere competence to read and write and do arithmetic.

The point is, in part, a realistic one and it is, of course, a very appealing and sophisticated approach to a complicated issue. It is also, however, an excellent way of obviating issues of injustice. Once we begin to redefine a literate person in such lofty terms, not just the poor, the black, the economically deprived, but even the rich may call themselves "illiterate."

No matter that they can write, read words, advance themselves (if they so wish) in their careers. The fact is that they cannot understand computer science or decode the nonstop media-messages "impinging" on their brains. Therfore, they are "illiterate"—just like the folks in Harlem, Appalachia and the Bronx. Well, not *exactly* the same, but not entirely different either. It is a cruel, self-serving game.

In spite of the vogue that "future-thinkers" are enjoying nowadays, their argument, in reference to adult illiteracy, is both diversionary and, at length, immobilizing. They may be absolutely right that soon we will enter an age when many new forms of information storage will compete effectively with printed words. The printed word, however, remains the "access route" to almost every other form of necessary information. How can people possibly find out what they do not know if they cannot read enough to understand the very books that underscore these points? *Who will read McLuhan's writing to them?*

"What you don't know yourself," wrote Bertolt Brecht, "you don't know!" This is the point that is repeatedly ignored when those who already have had a privileged education and are well prepared and fully competent in the use of print communication, begin to speak of the futility of bringing poor black, white, Chicano men and women to the level of a functional effectiveness based chiefly upon the use of written words.

According to such critics, literacy takes on, not merely a more challenging meaning, but a totally different meaning in a nation like our own. In the decade of the 1980s, they say, electronics and computer science have created a wholly new definition of a literate man or woman. That definition is so vast and sweeping as to dwarf all efforts we may ever undertake to win some piecemeal victories in specific and familiar areas—like the use of words.

The idea of "a higher level of literacy" makes excellent sense for those who have the opportunity to entertain such interesting speculations, but any chance of reaching such a level depends upon a prior competence of a relatively conventional form: mastery of the written and printed word and basic computation skills.

Until illiterate people have achieved this prior competence, who is it who will explain to them that there is another, still more challenging area of information even farther from their reach?

The answer is that people must have the power to inform themselves. Very little else is possible without a basic and initial comprehension of the written word.

There are, no doubt, a limitless number of "higher levels" which a newly literate person (or one who has been literate for forty years) might well desire to attain. If we are not to despair of the struggle, however, even before we have the opportunity to begin, I believe that we should start without apologies at the beginning.

9

HOW WE CAN WIN

APART from all the other goals established in preceding chapters, it goes without saying that we also have one fairly obvious and straightforward goal: We want to win concrete results.

In order to do so, we are going to have to work out certain ways of joining up our efforts with the efforts of those men and women who command financial and political power, as well as with those of men and women who have some managerial experience. A number of questions will be raised as a result:

(1) How can we possibly work beside, or in coordination with, large groups of people who do not share any of our deepest views?

(2) How can we seriously expect that men and women from the private sector will choose to collaborate in a campaign that either has, or else proposes, goals which pose a number of dangers for the people who now hold the largest share of wealth and power in our nation?

(3) Is it realistic to believe that large numbers of people would be willing to work against their ultimate economic interests, motivated solely by a sense of ethics or compassion?

(4) Are there perhaps some *other* motivations (having to do with unperceived, unrecognized areas of personal self-interest on the part of corporate leaders, for example) which may induce such people to work at our sides?

(5) To what degree do we incur the risk of going through a ritual of impotence, co-option and predictable defeat in asking those who have such totally divergent interests to attempt to work together?

It is, to start with, a foolish assumption and a glib mistake to attribute absolute unmitigated cynicism to an entire category of men and women, whether they are in corporate positions, major foundations or seats of political power. The only way these categorical assumptions ever seem to work is if we refuse to let ourselves become acquainted with such people. For whatever reasons (and there obviously are many possibilities), a number of people in any social system seem able to break all pessimistic expectations by their willingness to work for decent goals against their own apparent selfish economic interests. It is also true that there are certain forms of short-term economic interest which, for many people in the private sector, operate as much stronger motivations than the long-term factors.

In speaking of the ever-present dangers of co-option, there is another point that may be of some use: There is such a thing as keeping so clear of any possible contamination that we end up doing nothing. Some people prefer an eloquent failure to an even slightly tarnished victory; I don't think that many of the poorest people in this land would share that preference.

In this situation, it appears that a highly unusual coalition is politically conceivable. Our wisest strategy, I believe, is to take our allies where we find them—neither with self-immobilizing guilt nor with abusive condescension. We should accept them with full recognition of the ironies at stake and with a willingness to live in company with some bewildering contradictions as one of the inevitable preconditions of attempting any form of widespread social change.

Those who refuse to work for social change *within* the present context—which does, perhaps, mean the soiling of hands and living with some temporary contradictions—have no choice but to engage exclusively in projects that are minor (and, moreover, doomed to failure) or else to postpone all significant actions until a future socioeconomic transformation has already taken place. Either path would mean surrender for the present generation. This is why we have no choice but to prepare ourselves right now to live and work in company with contradictions.

I am suggesting, then, a practical marriage between a number of different sectors of the population that have, by tradition, been at odds with one another for a long, long time. At the farthest extremes, I have in mind the business sector, the student population and those who constitute the permanent underclass of the United States: i.e., the black, the Spanish-speaking and the rural poor.

What are some examples of specific—and essential—functions that might be accepted by a group of people from the business sector?

If a number of business leaders—to give only one example—who possess some understanding of the operations of the federal government, can help to make available the funds we need, whether for preparation of materials, for medical back-up of the literacy workers or for the weekly stipends of those volunteers, then it will obviously spare the rest of us the loss of many hours which might otherwise be devoted to the tasks of dialogue and education: It would be a self-destructive act to turn down any possible assistance of this kind.

Men and women with managerial and financial backgrounds might be the ideal people to work out the funding channels in order to facilitate an effective operation of the program. They might, for instance, help in the creation of a smooth-running fiscal "pipeline" in order to be sure that literacy workers receive their living stipends on the days when they are due. Slowness or delay in funding is a seemingly small matter, but it is just the sort of issue on which many thousands of programs, set up under local control but with a distant funding source, have repeatedly foundered in the struggles of the past.

Some of the same people might also be in a position to use *major* governmental clout to bypass *minor* government obstructions, to nail down workable arrangements, for example, with such local bodies as the trustee boards of universities, municipal school committees and state boards of education, handling negotiations also for release of pupils from their classes, arranging course credit for their efforts and income-as-usual for those of their teachers who have chosen to support them in this work.

Beyond these varieties of financial and logistical support, it seems to me that it would be ideal if little by way of power were assigned to managers and other representatives of the business sector: no meddlesome supervision, for example, in the daily operations of the literacy workers, no feasibility studies, no tedious statistical analyses—above all, no conventional evaluations.

It would be a blessing above all others if, just for once, we could escape the prior step—so often an excuse for dilatory measures and delays—of feasibility studies. These types of heavily financed research programs (as opposed to certain small and genuinely helpful pilot projects) summon up, for most experienced activists, too many associations of postponement and obstruction. It is difficult for anyone familiar with certain of the major civil rights upheavals of the 1960s to look upon that phrase—"feasibility study"—without frustration and despair.

The research process, as symbolized by the feasibility study at the present period in the United States, is too often the weapon of choice by which a certain portion of the academic world is able to postpone almost all solemn, honorable and risk-taking actions with the stated intention of gathering "further information," accumulating greater quantities of "more conclusive data," precisely in those areas within which there already exists a high degree of certitude but little will to pay the price that transformation calls for. It often appears to be a great deal easier to obtain two hundred thousand dollars to do a research study on "the Feasibility of the Establishment of a National Campaign to Eradicate Adult Illiteracy" than it would be to find the same amount of money to set up an excellent, tangible and visible pilot program which might demonstrate that the idea can *work*.

It is not hard to gain from this the powerful impression that the true purpose of much academic research is not to determine the proper steps that must be taken in order to go about a realistic plan of action, but rather to keep a number of intelligent people occupied for a reasonable period of time with a plausible sense of honorable intention and, at the same time, to maintain them with an adequate income. (One of the most familiar "final recommendations" of the heavily financed research programs I have seen is that "we need a lot of further research" in order to be sure of "where we stand"—or "which priorities we should establish.")

Despite these ironies, this is the nation that we live in. Hundreds of thousands of dollars are available for looking into "feasibilities," "aspects," "implications," but often not a dime for payroll or survival. It seems essential, therefore, that any group of people from the world of business, working to help to finance—and to act as "power broker" for—a national literacy effort, must work very hard to turn around these strange priorities and to reverse the sequence by which so many dollars go first for research studies, then for concrete applications.

There will surely be persistent skepticism among many people in regard to this: what will be viewed by some as an open and trusting invitation to those in the private sector who seem well-disposed and willing to participate in a program of this kind.

My memories go back twelve years and more, into the racial struggles of the middle and late sixties. I have many remarkable memories, drawn from that period of work, both of action and of collaboration with a number of business people at the grass-roots level in my own community of Boston. Throughout the last years of the 1960s right up to 1973 or 1974, various parent groups in the black neighborhoods of Boston founded a number of small and independent Free Schools for their children. They would issue appeals to several of the larger corporations in the area, asking for badly needed help in organizing a nonprofit corporation, raising funds, creating an administrative structure—then locating volunteers.

At certain times, and for particular reasons, it was not possible to locate those whom we believed we needed. More often than not, however, businesses and large corporations have responded energetically—and very fast. I have asked a local corporation to "lend" to us a group of people who could help us in fund raising, in administration and in legal matters. Within a week, a group of very effective men and women from that corporation, from a half-dozen others and from M.I.T. appeared in our offices and asked us what it was, exactly, they could do. They were eager to go to work, but not impatient with us for the fact that we were not prepared to start the same day they arrived.

They came again, without complaints about the last time, and brought with them several more people than they had had the time before. We had, by now, settled on several chores of various kinds that we could not do on our own, so we were finally in a position to present detailed requests. The group—perhaps ten or eleven people—split into two committees and began to work at various facets of fund raising, as well as in the administrative set-up of our school.

Not long after they had started, one member of the group—a tall and rather aristocratic man—asked why they could not participate in the pedagogic aspect of our work as well. We felt embarrassed to have slotted them so carelessly. It had been our first assumption that they would not feel at ease outside their area of expertise. Having completed the initial work we had requested of them, they now were eager to do more.

They became part of a one-to-one tutoring program we had organized in the afternoons and evenings. According to the director of that program, they were more reliable, persistent and successful than any other group that had signed up to volunteer. Their motivation was not consciously political. None of them seemed to come into our program with an explicit ideological approach. On the other hand, they did not question, or attempt to undercut, our own political ideas. They tried their best to do exactly what we asked. They did it well and seemed to improve the atmosphere a lot by their good-natured, noncombative attitudes.

In this instance, a remorseless ideological blood test as a requirement of entrance would have killed off something very, very good. Today, the people I have described above still work for major corporations and, no doubt, still have their quiet differences of viewpoint with some of the young teachers whom they met, and with most of those neighborhood people whom they taught, when they first worked with us almost eleven years ago. It occurs to me, though, that people of this kind would be the ideal adult volunteers for the literacy program which we have proposed. They are, in large part, somewhat past middle age and tied by certain family obligations. I doubt, therefore, that they would wish to go a very great distance from their homes. I could see them easily, however, helping in the homes of people in the cities not far from their own. I do not see them as ideological partisans. I do not see them as political co-workers. I do not see them as activist allies.

I *do* see them as hard-working people who might very well do a better job than some of those who are more ideological but less patient. I see them, too, as people who, for reasons of their own, are not afraid of freedom—not in themselves, not in the people whom they teach. If there are certain forms of freedom which they might not find to their own taste, or which they might at length find frightening, I do not think that they would have this in their minds at the beginning. If they should think of it later on, I suspect that it won't matter a great deal by then, because they will have known a long-sustained experience of satisfaction in the concrete process of the job. I do not think that ideology alone will matter a lot to anyone by then.

POSTSCRIPT: TEACHERS WHO ARE NOT AFRAID TO TEACH

I wrote, in Chapter 7, of the risk that literacy workers, over-whelmed by the repetitive emphasis upon "participation" of those whom they will teach, may end up with a sense of having one hand tied behind their back. This is especially the case if local dem-agogues should find themselves in a position to exploit an easy opportunity to build their power on the broken bones of timid—and intimidated—volunteers. I have argued that there ought to be an authentic dialogue; but, in a dialogue, both sides must have the right to speak—and both with equal earnestness, intensity and force. Since this issue has come up so many times before, in strug-gles of all kinds, it seems important to anticipate the problem in ad-vance.

The sense of inhibition is particularly alarming at the point where it begins to minimize the real effectiveness of literacy work-ers. This point seems to me of special importance nowadays in view of the nondirective fashions ("open classroom," "British infant method") of the past ten years—above all, in view of the noncritical acceptance of these fashions by so many people. It is especially in-appropriate in the present case because we are dealing here not with young children, but with adults. Even with youngsters, how-ever, the fashions I describe have ended up by demonstrating some preposterous results.

Many teachers, wishing to avoid a top-down attitude in working with a pupil, and having in mind the dictatorial approach of old-time teachers whose methods and materials they find distasteful, often make the error of believing that their only possible role is "to be present" as some sort of household spirit of encouragement and cheer, rather than as an energetic and persistent guide.

The risk is especially great among those teachers (or teachers-to-be) who may have had an overdose of the romantic school-re-formist writings of the 1960s and the early 1970s—writings in which the viewpoint often was purveyed that none of us really knows much more than anybody else, that people should learn spontaneously, organically, at their own pace and whim, but that no one ought to set out with the will to *teach* them.

"Teach," in effect, became a dirty word for those who had been overwhelmed by books like these. From the old days of the classroom tyrant, who had frequently been the only person in the class who was permitted to wield power, suddenly the teacher came to be the only person in the room with *none*.

I have observed a number of teachers who have arrived at length at the impossible position of being unwilling even to be described as such. I will often walk into a third grade classroom and approach the tallest person in the room, taller perhaps by three or four feet than all twenty-seven others.

"Are you the teacher?" I will ask.

The answers, too often, are all of a kind: "Well . . . we don't like to speak of 'teachers' in this school. We'd rather speak of 'resource persons,' or 'facilitators' . . ." Or else: "We're all just learning and teaching together at the same time."

The fact is that, in these foolish but too frequent situations, the teacher has effectively agreed to abdicate adulthood, creating a vacuum of intelligent persistence or direction, yet living with the fanciful idea that this is "innovation."

It is very important, in a campaign where the life-and-death stakes are so high and where so many people will not likely have a second chance, that literacy workers take great care that they do not rerun the errors of those well-intending but self-abdicating teachers who have read too many books about "spontaneous" and "organic" education. We need teachers who are open, earnest, undogmatic, humble, humorous, relaxed and ethically egalitarian; but we *do* need teachers.

We do *not* need simply "good souls" strolling through the neighborhoods of desperation. We do *not* need simply amiable—and now and then hard-working—"resource persons." We need nonstop, inventive, hard-driving and determined literacy teachers. No one, no matter how young, if taking up this banner, ought to be ashamed to be identified as one who TEACHES SKILLS.

The same point applies to the preparatory sessions: the period, for example, during which materials are to be selected or at least suggested. Some of the advocates of "maximum participation" of communities will go so far as to assert that *only* the community itself is in a position to define its wishes, needs and aspirations. It is always bewildering to confront this argument. To disagree appears to place one on the side of those who lack respect for "the community." To accede, however, is to agree to reenact the least productive and most futile scenarios of the 1960s.

As soon as we limit all significant input to "the community" itself, we run into a problem that Paul Goodman once described. Goodman said that people live in "a closed room of the imagination." Once they are locked within that room, it is seldom possible to dream of the resources and realities that may exist on the outside.

It seems naive, and hopeless, to limit not only the definition of a problem, but also every possible solution, to definitions and solutions "as perceived by those who are the victims." The fact is, once locked within a closed room, people can sense some obvious needs but cannot possibly discover the full range of answers. People can only think of things they've heard of. To defer everything "to the community" is to imprison that community in its own small cell of diminished possibilities. In the guise of service, it is to defraud, to delimit, to deny.

The literacy workers, therefore, should set out with certain specific pedagogic goals and then develop others of a more profound and more responsive nature as the dialogue proceeds. If the literacy workers do not feel the right to set out with at least a minimal definition of their goals there will be very little literacy work at all, but only a dialogue of silence and the participatory fervor of the uninformed.

10

LOGICAL ENEMIES/
UNEXPECTED FRIENDS

NOT all the partisans of a national campaign are either poor or even advocates of social change. Some are the leading executives of large corporations. Others come from the middle levels of management, as well as from other strata of the corporate world.

It would be foolish to exaggerate the numbers of potential partisans and allies in the corporate world. It is inevitable that certain segments of the private sector will not look with equanimity upon the program we propose. There are those, for example—possibly a quite substantial number—who honestly believe what they would probably never wish to say: namely, that corporate prosperity *depends* upon perpetuation of a voiceless, disenfranchised pool of powerless men and women. Others are uneasy with all programs that appear to offer services "for free" to people they regard as undeserving. Some may possibly feel alarm, as well, that certain conventional sources of cheap labor may be lost forever by a pedagogic drive that liberates those who, up to now, have been obliged to earn their livelihood by various forms of servile and unattractive work.

One might well ask the logical, if disturbing, question: Who will there be, after a truly successful and far-reaching literacy campaign, to serve the drinks and scrub the kitchen floors of those who live out in the suburbs—or, more to the point, of people living in remote and elegant estates who are accustomed, no matter with how much sense of benefaction, to the presence of domestic servants in their homes? Domestic servants may, in fact, become, at long last, an extinct and well-forgotten species.

Our allies, fortunately, appear to come in larger numbers. They come out of the ranks of those who *do* think hard and whose thought processes have led them to a steadfast and consistent backing of the whole idea of this campaign, or else of one that is a great deal like it.

There are, first of all, those men and women who are cognizant of welfare costs and who see, in any serious adult literacy struggle, one means at least (though, clearly, not the sole means) by which to reduce the rate of unemployment. It is argued persuasively, as we have seen, that literacy by no means guarantees a man or woman will be able to obtain a good job. (If a certain degree of unemployment is endemic in our economic system, then of course there will never be sufficient jobs.) On the other hand, while it is true that it cannot guarantee a job, literacy increasingly has come to be a precondition for employment. Even entry-level work in many modern corporations appears to call for minimal skills in reading, writing and the use of numbers. Shortsighted business firms, in search of inexpensive labor, might sometimes employ illiterate men and women for this work, but only at great risk and at great cost when errors or accidents occur.

Mass literacy, Harman and Hunter have observed, does not cure the corporate ills of a society: "unemployment, poverty, discrimination, or the marginal status of certain sub-groups." This is a point with which we can agree without dispute or qualification. On the other hand, many large corporations today are insistent in stating that they could employ considerably larger numbers of those who are jobless if these men and women possessed some more substantial literacy skills.

An article in *The Wall Street Journal* of October 16, 1978, reports that, in the opinion of labor experts, a large proportion of the job-less are precisely those who lack the elementary skills for jobs which are already "there"—jobs, however, which remain unfilled for lack of competent applicants. They also note that unskilled and illiterate young people, "stuck in unappealing jobs that often pay little more than welfare benefits, tend to move frequently from job to job . . . [becoming] periodically unemployed during the transi-tions."

The Wall Street Journal documents, across the nation, "localized difficulties in finding clerical workers, bank tellers, nurses, para-legals. . . ." One of the largest employment agencies in the United States, Snelling and Snelling, tells *The Journal* that, in each of these categories, it is proving impossible to locate sufficient men and women to "keep up with orders."

It is not a case of shifting blame, or burden of responsibility, to those (the poor) who are the victims of an unfair economic struc-ture and an inefficient and unequal pedagogic system. Nor is it a case of assigning idealistic motives to corporate leaders who have been given the power which they hold solely in order to maximize the profits of shareholders. It *is* a case of seeing what a certain number of corporate leaders now believe to be their real self-in-terest. To dismiss the value of such allies, simply because they may take action on the problem of illiteracy out of motives of self-in-terest, is to penalize no one else except the ones who stand to suffer most: namely, the poor.

Another category of unexpected allies is that very large segment of the population which is troubled by the increase in the rate of crime—and by its end result in massive prison intake and recidi-vism. The cost, on both sides of the issue, is directly or indirectly tied to literacy problems: The highest single locus of illiterate men and women is in prison.

Any effort to translate this catastrophe into dollars is demeaning, since it seems to view the personal tragedies at stake as secondary matters. The financial cost, however, *is* significant to those who are obsessed at all times with the possible waste of government funds.

The reports of experts indicate that the cost to government merely to feed and house a prison inmate ranges between fifteen and thirty thousand dollars yearly.

The expense involved to pay for those in prison is only one small index of the breadth and the complexity of the problem. For every man and woman who has been arrested and convicted, there might be another fifty or one hundred who commit the same offence but still are on the streets. Thus we discover, as our unexpected allies, many of those people who are identified with "law and order." The classic response to street crime is for voters to elect to office people who promise to invest large sums of money in sophisticated technological devices, more expensive methods of surveillance and redoubled foot patrols. It would seem to make more sense to place our funds in programs that can build up solid literacy skills, enabling people to live and work with personal control over their lives.

A fourth constituency—one which seems most likely to be ready to provide its backing for a massive literacy effort—is that portion of the insurance industry that deals with liability for industrial accidents. It is not only a matter of basic inhumanity and recklessness to allow a man or woman to be working in an area of corrosive vapors, or of carcinogenic dangers, with no capacity to read and comprehend the warning signs, but situations of this kind also prove to be very expensive for those corporations which must pay the compensation for the worker, as well as the replacement cost of damaged or demolished instruments. In the long run, those who pay insurance premiums of every kind, whether those of the home owner or those of the automobile driver, end up by subsidizing the expenses of insurance companies.

"When green light blinks twice, depress right arm of fire-prevention apparatus. If light continues to blink, sound warning signal and immediately leave room. . . ."

Men and women cannot realistically be expected to survive within this social system if they cannot read and understand those forms of admonition that relate directly to their health and safety. The warning sign printed above is only the most blatant and mechanical reminder of one definition of survival. It is also a definition that would not go unnoticed by a corporation leader with an eye to profits.

A fifth constituency of unexpected friends is the print media: the publishers of daily papers and of weekly magazines, as well as the publishers of books. It is to the direct advantage of all who market printed words to multiply the numbers of those men and women who can read them. The president of McGraw-Hill, Alexander Burke, made this point during a White House conference in September 1978. After conceding that the cost of coping with the problem might be very high, Burke stated: "The cost of *not* solving this problem may in the long run be even greater." If the problem is taken seriously, he said, "it will require nothing less than a reassessment of national priorities."

Burke pinpointed certain obvious reasons for the urgent concern of people in the publishing domain: "Over the past ten years there has been a steady decline in the number of hardcover books sold. Newspaper readership is declining. Libraries are experiencing declining usage and low acquisitions. . . . The United States ranks twenty-fourth in the world in terms of books produced per capita."

The concerns of a corporation like McGraw-Hill are not, in all likelihood, the same as the concerns of most of those people who would be likely to join the type of literacy campaign that we propose, whether as prospective pupils or as literacy workers. The sale of books by major U.S. corporations is surely among the last objectives that would motivate most of the youthful volunteers. What matters, however, is not whether an argument appeals to me or to my friends. What matters is whether it appeals to somebody—to *anyone*—who holds in his/her hands the power to enhance the sweep and the momentum of this struggle.

The search for broader markets of competent and literate people is a strong and obvious motive for a corporation that produces books. It would be self-destructive for the advocates of a literacy campaign to view potential allies of this nature, motivated by intelligent self-interest, with uneasiness or with contempt.

POSTSCRIPT: THE PERSISTENCE OF THE MYTH

A number of people, as we have seen, argue that most of the social and economic problems which have been discussed above (street crime and unemployment, for example) cannot be seriously confronted or relieved by anything so specific, and so restricted in immediate impact, as a national literacy struggle. Most of the problems that afflict poor people will remain as logical and unavoidable consequences of our present economic system, no matter how many people learn to read and write.

One of the points which has been made by those who share this view is that it is "credentials," rather than the skills it takes to nail down those credentials, which constitute the real prerequisites for attractive jobs. Harman and Hunter have stated this general idea in the following words:

The ability to read and write and to use mathematical symbols is so much a part of the lives of literate persons that they find it almost impossible to imagine themselves without those skills. Literacy skills open the way to information, to the enjoyment of literature, and to certain kinds of communication and self-expression. In a literate society, they also confer independence in managing ones own affairs. They qualify persons for certain credentials. As we noted earlier, however, these formal credentials themselves may weigh more heavily in the competition for jobs than they do as a part of the actual skills required to perform the jobs.

Literate persons often believe that it is their literacy *per se* that has been responsible for opening doors for them in the society, conferring social status or economic success. . . . They are inclined, therefore, to endorse literacy campaigns under the illusion that illiteracy is the cause of the poverty, ill-health, and the crime-infested neighborhoods in which they see others living.

The solution to the serious problems that afflict the majority of illiterates is not so simple.

I do not disagree with any part of this. Moreover, I think it represents a healthy turnaround of Paul Goodman's concept of "the closed room" of one's imagination to recognize that literate persons also live in their own closed room of false assumptions and that they also find it very difficult to imagine what it's like "on the outside."

It is not the substance, but the psychological impact of the quoted statement that seems troubling. It is, of course, true that a schooled society tends to assign rewards, in both prestige and income, not by measurable skills, but by the "numbers printed on our forehead." It is also true that competence alone can never win for us the jobs and self-esteem which, in reality, are granted only by the school's credentials.

The practical fact, however—as Harman and Hunter seem to recognize themselves but somehow present here as "a lesser truth"—is the one which they touch on lightly, as in passing, when they state that literacy skills do "qualify persons for certain credentials." Whether or not the credentials "weigh more heavily" than the skills themselves in winning people jobs, the fact remains that, without the second, one cannot win the first. This will be true so long as we remain a schooled and school-credentialized society.

It is interesting, therefore—but it may not really help us a great deal—to dwell on the difference between the credential itself and the competence which enables us to acquire that credential. In ultimate effect, this emphasis tends to foster the same sense of futility and hopelessness as the notion of the "Endless Circle." By reminding us of all the things we cannot change (the schools, credentials, "credit hours," "prerequisites," et al.), it simply tends to dull the sharp edge of our passion, drive, determination, to achieve some concrete progress in an area in which we *do* have power to make a difference here and now.

Illiteracy is not, of course, the sole, or even major, cause of poverty, of crime-infested neighborhoods, etc. It is, however, *one* cause and one symptom at the same time. It is, moreover, a cause which leads to several others. It is also one of the few important causes which ordinary people, with only minimal preparation, can address directly without waiting for larger or more earthshaking forms of transformation of the social order.

To return to the specific issue of the interests of the corporations: Illiteracy is one identifiable cause of poverty, welfare, accidents and other social ills which is accepted, *and believed to be important,* by very large numbers of those kinds of people without whose backing our endeavor cannot hope to be successful—not in this nation, not at the time in which we live. If this is the case, then it can only be subversive of our goals to insist on telling one another what we know already to be true: The solution to the problem is, indeed, "not so simple. . . ." But a massive literacy effort might very well be one of the few realistic and practicable ways by which to make that problem far *more* simple. It is also a realistic way by which to start a chain reaction that might lead rapidly to many other necessary changes.

This will never be the case, of course, if literacy work is carried out by unprovocative and conventional approaches. A neutral and mechanistic method of approaching the illiterate population might be useful to those who still believe in the familiar myths of self-improvement and "reward for merit." It will *not* be useful to those very large numbers of illiterate adults who no longer share such faith. Only an approach which begins in dialogue, and proceeds by methods partly dictated by the outcome of that dialogue, an approach which does not tend to steer away from dangerous ideas and active words, can simultaneously both reach those who are in the greatest need and also serve a catalytic function in leading to other forms of social change.

The question is asked: What if it does not work? What if it only raises expectations and then disappoints those who have been led to believe that a major effort to achieve effective mastery of words and numbers will make a visible difference in their lives? (I have referred to this in Chapter 4.) The point is made that such an outcome can serve only to debilitate poor people while reinforcing liberal deceptions. It is possible, for instance, that we might well see a partial (or disguised) resurgence of the tendency to "blame the victim"—to attribute the responsibility for failure to those among the poor who try, lose heart and at length give up in the pursuit of a desired skill.

The probable gains seem to me to far outweigh such risks. If, as many scholars now expect, those "available jobs" fail to materialize after poor people have engaged in arduous efforts to achieve the competence which is said to be required for employment, then at very least the massive reduction of adult illiteracy will call the bluff of those in management positions who adamantly insist that the economy has room for all with genuine skills for sale. It will also bring, among its first results, a sudden increase in the ranks of those who may conceive the need to change an economic system that does not have room for them—people, too, who will possess, for the first time, what they did not possess before: *the tools to do so.*

Much of the above has the inevitable effect of placing me in the role of one who is prepared to settle for incremental gains, as opposed to one who asks for "everything—or nothing." This is no different from the role in which I also find myself in working for such piecemeal gains as school desegregation and a nationalized health program. Neither constitutes a socioeconomic revolution. Both, however, immeasurably diminish the real and immediate suffering of many millions of poor people, and both are also likely to empower a large segment of the population to make deeper and more far-reaching demands as they begin to feel more confident and strong. Both, too—like the drive for adult literacy itself—require a degree of sensible collaboration with a certain number of people whose long-range objectives may be considerably less sweeping than our own: people, indeed, who might, in other situations, view themselves as adversaries of our goals.

11

IMMEDIATE ACTION: ORGANIZATION, LEADERSHIP AND THE FEAR OF VICTORY

A national literacy struggle of the kind we propose can start out from any number of concrete and specific local actions. It can begin at the grass roots. It can begin by the initiative of presently existing groups in the diverse communities that stand to profit from a new, expanded literacy drive. It can also begin, however, by the initiative of progressive public figures, whether political or in the academic world or in the private sector.

It seems to me dogmatic and self-crippling for any of us to establish in advance an arbitrary set of rules, dictated (as these things so often are) by recent or accepted fashion, and then to exclude all other initiatives which do not begin in the manner we prescribe.

The worst inheritance of the last lost causes of the 1960s is a mindless and noncritical application of the code expression "maximum possible community participation." By now, I hope it will be clear that a national struggle such as we propose, if we are seriously committed to reaching those who are the most in need, must be firmly rooted in honest community participation and must evolve through a process of authentic dialogue between the teachers and the taught. I have been close enough, however, to dozens of community ventures of the past ten or twelve years, to sense the weary futility of those programs that romanticize community initiative to a degree that cripples the best efforts even of those teachers and organizers chosen by the community itself.

Thus, for example, it has become painfully familiar to see social planners with even the most humane intentions setting out to undermine and to obstruct any and all suggested plans if they do not begin with an abject act of deference to "the will of the community." The word *community* is frequently used in an unreflective and sentimental manner that suggests too little concrete knowledge of any actual community, but rather a sense of acquiescence and intimidation in the face of the writings of those who carry on the cult of "the infallible community."

More often than not, these writers themselves have very little first-hand knowledge of poor people and of the oppressed communities in which they live. They are, for this reason, all the more subject to the myth that "the community" of which they speak must constitute a pre-liberated social entity that can transcend, right from the start, all of those errors of limited vision, political manipulation or internal decimation which they consistently attribute only to "outsiders."

This degree of romanticism does very little good for "the community," since it attributes far too much to one of several vulnerable participants and meanwhile tends to intimidate all of those others who may wish to play a role, and may well have a lot to offer.

It is a curious and disheartening situation: defrauding the poor, inhibiting the skilled, profiting no one but denying to all of us the full use of our own real gifts. I have known people—whether outside volunteers or organizers chosen from within—who have ended up functioning, *by intention*, at one-half their normal zest and energy, only in order to be certain that they would not appear, by any mistake, to be overly effective, articulate or, indeed, successful in the very task to which they were assigned.

I have seen a cogent and wonderfully inventive organizer end up by developing a mild stammer in the midst of community meetings—a stammer he had never had before—solely from the bizarre phenomenon of fearing that he might offend the sensibilities of the neighborhood by speaking too clearly, or with too much passion and determination, of the very tactics, goals, ideas they wanted most to hear. At length, it required a kindly and inspired neighborhood leader to tell him, in so many words—right in the presence of everybody else—that he did nobody a service by denying his real skills. Nor did he do the community an honor by presenting a front of false ineptitude out of the fear of doing "too well" in the eyes of his co-workers.

Emphasis on, and reiteration of, this point may perhaps enable us to feel more comfortable and less dogmatic in regard to the question of *where* an idea happens to take root. If there could be a spontaneous outcropping of a multitude of grass-roots community demands, then this would be a good place to begin. In the absence of such demands, it makes sense to look for a catalyst, a stimulus, a starting point, wherever we believe that one exists. One such potential starting point is the creation of a National Literacy Commission.

A commission can come into being for all of the wrong reasons: to advance research and, at the same time, to postpone all realistic action. It can also come into being for some of the right reasons: to draw conclusions from research already carried out, to gather together people of like minds and promptly to launch forth into a set of useful actions. What, specifically, are some of the "useful actions" that a National Literacy Commission might begin to undertake?

One starting point might be to gather and summarize as many examples as possible of local programs that appear, for whatever reasons, to be more successful than others in reaching those people who seldom have been reached by conventional literacy programs. The commission would need to have the means to assemble, publish and disseminate this kind of information, sharing it with scholars, community organizers, as well as with the population as a whole. The commission might also look abroad at programs that have taken place in other North Atlantic nations—nations such as Great Britain, for example, where the BBC effectively conducted a literacy drive by television. In the same vein, the commission might also publicize, for the use of those who have no way to know, a summary of all of those presently existing programs in this nation which, although they may not be able to reach the poorest and most alienated people, *do* serve the needs of a great many people at the present time and probably could serve much larger numbers of those who are susceptible to their approach if they were given larger budgets. I am thinking of the two major national initiatives—"Adult Basic Education" and "Right to Read"—as well as several volunteer groups that have been working with adult illiterates for years.

Another function of a national commission might be the sponsorship of a number of small pilot programs—prototypes for the specific kind of program that is outlined here, but carried out on a basis sufficiently modest, and with goals sufficiently cautious, to allow these programs to be set into motion with minimal delay. These pilot programs would offer needed feedback, concerning danger areas as well as areas of strength, for the major national thrust which might still be a year, or several years, ahead.

A third function of a literacy commission might be the difficult task of estimation and projection of costs. Although the final cost of a literacy struggle could not very easily be established in advance (inasmuch as the precise numbers of functional illiterates cannot be known until the literacy work has actually begun) there has to be some way to calculate certain preliminary costs—or else the nation will not be prepared even to take the first step.

In the search for preliminary figures, the commission should solicit the widest possible range of data from all people informed, whether by experience or else by scholarship. Hearings, if they are to be held, should probably be regional. As other writers have argued already, they should take place, as often as possible, in the rural neighborhoods and on the city blocks.

The commission should also be charged with the task of helping to create a climate of opinion that will be open to the challenge and dimensions of this kind of national campaign. This does not imply the manufacture of some sort of artificial propaganda to awaken backing for the plan. All it should take is honest dissemination of the facts: national persuasion by the unfamiliar vehicle of public access to the truth.

A final function, among a number of others that a literacy commission might plausibly assume, is that of propagation of dozens of regional committees, as well as thousands of neighborhood committees and local study groups (see Chapter 9). In other words, a national commission ought to begin the process of awakening as many as possible of those varied grass-roots efforts that will ultimately constitute the literacy campaign itself and, at length, transcend the need for a national commission altogether.

One plan that has been presented to the nation in the past few years incorporates the germ of the idea of "a national commission," although it is not presented in a form so specific as the one that I have recommended here. The proposal came from Senator George McGovern. It was first presented to the Ninety-fifth Senate in September 1978, and introduced as a bill on the floor of the Senate eight months later.

McGovern's suggestions seem important to mention in the context of this chapter because of his willingness to approach the issue from outside the conventional structures of education.

"The current educational establishment," McGovern said, "faces an inherent conflict of interest in attempting to address the problems of illiteracy." A national commission, he proposed, "should consider alternative solutions outside traditional school settings." It has been empirically demonstrated, he observed, that people make "tremendous gains in reading" when they are not taught in isolation from all possible chance for concrete applications of the new skills they have gained, or hope to gain.

McGovern argued for a national commission that would begin by close examination of on-going programs but would not be restricted, in its recommendations, to mere expansion or elaboration of those programs. Moreover, he insisted that the process of examination and evaluation must be conducted by a group that has no vested interest in the outcome of its own investigation.

He referred, in his speech, to a recent study carried out by the National Institute of Education. The study, he said, was "an excuse [for,] rather than an examination of, illiteracy." Too often, he went on, studies of this kind "absolve the industry" they have been asked to judge and to evaluate. "The N.I.E. study," McGovern said, "proves one point above all others." That point, he said, is that we need an independent group to look into the problem.

McGovern's proposed commission is intended to *be* that "independent group."

If there is one aspect of Senator McGovern's plan that may leave people uneasy, it is the emphasis on information-gathering as opposed to concrete actions. Many of my friends and colleagues have shared with me their own concern that McGovern's commission might, in the end, prove to be another one of those familiar research programs that serve the same old function of postponement of effective action based upon the things that we already know.

My own inclination is to believe in the basic usefulness of this proposal, but to be wary about the risks of long postponement and to establish, therefore, some realistic deadlines. One such deadline, for example, might be a requirement that the literacy commission must propose certain kinds of pilot programs by the end of six months, and a fullscale national program by the end of twelve. These numbers—six months, twelve months—are purely hypothetical. The point is to establish certain outer limits on delay.

Whatever the plan—whether this one or another—the ultimate goal is not to create a commission that will last forever, but to inspire a number of regional groups (and, on a more local level, neighborhood groups and study groups) first to come together into workable coalitions, then to appoint *themselves* as hosts or sponsors of a series of grass-roots "events"—conferences, hearings or whatever.

While it would seem preferable for these grass-roots groups to come together on their own, it is more realistic once again to recognize that this is not likely to happen by spontaneous combustion. Something or someone has to strike the spark. A national commission would be in an excellent position from which to do this: to strike the spark, to fan the fire, at length to provoke the illiterate themselves to come up with ideas and options of their own.

For the present, I think we would do well to encourage, not to scorn, the idea of a national commission, pushing always for the special goals we have described—and working, meanwhile, with effective, decent allies when we find them. If it is not to be McGovern's commission, then there ought to be suggestions for another. If it is not one which is to be fostered by the U.S. Senate, then it should be suggested and created by somebody else. If it is not begun by "someone else," then it should be done at length by us.

Things that matter do not need to be begun forever by "somebody else." Every so often, we ought to seize the right and power to be the catalysts ourselves.

POSTSCRIPT: DECENTRALIZED CONTROL

The type of national commission that has been described above might, if successful, represent a strong supportive link between the powerless and agencies of power.

At the next level of national coordination, it seems to me that there might be the highest likelihood of mass participation if the administrative structure can be broken up into a number of regional divisions: twelve at least, possibly as many as twenty-five or thirty. Each might be organized in such a way as to govern itself by its own democratic guidelines, in keeping with the general theme of "dialogue between coequals."

One final admonition may be useful: Outsiders—as we have emphasized before—are not the only possible forces of oppression and of manipulation of the poor. Men and women who come out of the community itself are also capable of manipulating their own neighbors under the very banner of "community participation." There is no way to neutralize the risk of such manipulation from within —any more than one can ward off overzealous or self-serving volunteers. It can only be emphasized, stated and restated that the purpose of participation in this program must not be "in order to participate." *It is to make sure that people learn to read and write.*

Dialogue need not imply what, far too frequently, sectarian participants seem to believe: chaos, malice, anarchy or misdirected rage. There is no reason why it has to mean these things; but vigilance of a certain kind is needed if we are to be quite sure that we avoid these risks.

A regional committee would function in the role of mediator between the federal level and those many thousands of small neighborhood and teacher groups: not only those local groups that represent the population of the various communities but also the tens of thousands of teams of literacy workers. The regional councils might also be given the job of recommendation and dissemination of materials for possible use or adaptation by the local groups.

At one level beneath the regional committees, there ought to be a vast proliferation of much smaller groups, each of which would operate as close as possible to the grass roots: "block councils" (in the cities) or, in rural sections, "neighborhood committees." Whether in a rural or in an urban context, the function of a small accessible council of this kind is to involve as many neighbors as possible in the planning stages, to review, amend or reject whatever materials may be offered by the regional committees, to attempt to locate uninhabited buildings suitable for use as Literacy Houses, to begin a cooperative and mutually supportive effort at recruitment of potential learners (basically, a grass-roots "prior literacy census"), to create the mechanisms of initial governance and organization of all details of the program to take place in each community.

At approximately the same time that the neighborhood committees are in process of formation, thousands of small study groups of literacy workers might begin to form. These groups might stem from organizations which exist already (as, for example, literacy groups that now exist in certain academic circles) or else they might be groups that do not yet exist but would come into being precisely for this purpose. A study group might logically contain a number of students who are prospective volunteers, concerned teachers who hope to be team leaders and other competent adults of various ages and professions. Members of these informal study groups might come together, centered about a school or university, in order to discuss specific questions about teaching methods, in order to assess and probe the various possibilities among available (and unavailable) materials, in order to explore something of the risks or challenges they face or fear. They also might discuss some of the ways by which an outside person, coming into a community with a specific goal in mind, can overcome some of the tendencies toward missionary attitudes in entering a struggle of this kind. They would, in short, be working to prepare one portion of that dialogue of equals that would commence once literacy workers and the neighborhood committees finally meet.

It would be an ideal climax to all of these localized and preparatory efforts if both groups, in every neighborhood and city block, could coalesce into a single unit (volunteer teachers, prospective learners) several weeks before the first days of the actual campaign. In this manner, literacy workers and their pupils would be able to begin the summer on a note of genuine friendship and collaboration, not prior to an active dialogue, but in the midst of one.

12

THE REINVENTION
OF CHILDHOOD

To speak of a campaign, plan or struggle which is built primarily upon the activism of the young is to awaken immediately a sense of doubt and hesitation as to whether young people ever could undertake a venture so far-reaching and so vast.

Thus, the questions of "the definition of childhood," "the definition of youth," become almost as important to this book as the definition of literacy itself. If young men and women are, indeed, as docile, as lacking in commitment and as distant and divorced from history as we have been encouraged to believe, then nothing that I have stated here can make much sense. It will appear to most observers not as a realistic plan of action, but as a wistful and romantic dream.

I am convinced that it is *not* a dream. I am also aware, however, of the reason why so many adults are likely to regard it in this light. People tend to look upon children, adolescents and those still in universities and schools as representing an inactive, nonparticipant, self-concerned and even narcissistic entity. We look upon children in this light, however, only to the degree that we still pay obeisance to an old, archaic and no-longer-accurate definition of "youth, childhood and adolescence." So long as we accept this definition, we will not be able to look upon the literacy campaign as something which is plausible or realistic.

The familiar definition of childhood, which I have briefly summarized above, did not really exist as such until about four centuries ago. There was a long period, up until the last part of the sixteenth century, when childhood as "a discrete episode," "a postponement," "a holding pattern on real life," did not exist at all. Young people, once beyond the years of infancy, dressed, acted, and were treated much like adults, with proper allowance made for their frail bodies and small size.

(I am using the term *childhood* in order to avoid the complication and confusion of a multitude of slightly variant phrases. What I mean by this, however, is a much longer age span than the term *childhood* would ordinarily suggest. I am thinking of the total period of years in which young people remain "in school"—a period which includes the years of university as well as high school.)

With the invention of childhood as a "unique condition," lasting often into and sometimes beyond the years of adolescence, the role of youth began to undergo dramatic change. Little by little, children came to be regarded as they would be viewed for most of the next four centuries. Children (including adolescents) were regarded as "preparatory people," "humans-in-training," small problems patiently waiting to be big ones. These, clearly, were not the kinds of ethical, autonomous and inquiring people who would view themselves, or who would someday be regarded, as the possible vanguard of a national campaign.

For centuries, childhood was given a consistently demeaning definition: passive, transitional and noncontributive. The possibility that children might have something worth donation, benefaction, contribution was not even in the adult frame of reference. This is the definition of childhood with which most people today grew into their own adulthood, and it is with this definition—and a consequent skepticism—that they tend to look upon the kind of youth campaign we are proposing here.

That hardened and archaic view of childhood has only recently begun to change. Signs of a partial tremor beneath the surface of age-old beliefs began to be detected some years back with the first stirrings of the whole idea of children as "moral beings" or as "moral thinkers." More recently, they have begun to be regarded, in a still more interesting and invigorating way, as those who might not only function as "ethical thinkers" but—in special situations and with certain sensible restraints—as the ethical spearhead of society itself.

It is interesting to ask ourselves what it is that has provoked this recent shake-up in our views. What has awakened our recent recognition of the wasted possibilities of those whom we had previously consigned to the back attic of ineptitude and uselessness?

In part, I think it was the impact of a number of intelligent and influential authors such as Ivan Illich and Paul Goodman. In part, too, it was the model set for us by the revitalized role of youth in several other nations—Cuba and Israel probably the most important and most memorable. In part, possibly in largest part, it was the vivid example given to us by young men and women here at home, whether in their courageous activism in the voter-registration projects of the early 1960s or in their moral and symbolic stance in opposition to the war in Vietnam.

In any event, and for whatever reasons, the age-old definition of the possibilities of youth has finally started to collapse—and, with it, that debilitating role which has, for a century at least, been forced upon our public schools. The school, as Whitehead long ago perceived, is built upon inert ideas, ideas which lead to nothing—not to action, not to passion, not to transformation, but (at most) to good term papers and examinations. Childhood thereby becomes a moratorium on life, a time in which young people spend about one-quarter of their projected biological existence in rote drill and readiness for those three-quarters they may never live to know. Youth is thus defined as preparation *for* life, not a portion *of* it.

"It doesn't seem real," one student in Schenectedy said to me while I was visiting his class. "Everything we do in school is like a simulation of some other thing that would be real if it weren't taking place in school."

The ultimate irony at which our schools too frequently arrive is the introduction of that perfect vehicle of school-delineated alienation: "the simulation game." We close up the windows, pull down the blinds, ventilate the air, deflect the light, absorb the sound, etherize the heart and neutralize the soul. Then we bring in simulation games to try to imitate the world we have, with such great effort and at such enormous costs, excluded.

One consequence of situations such as these is the way that children come to view their own role in the face of history. School, university, moral struggle—and, indeed, all social transformation—come to be things (from the children's point of view) "not that we do, but that are done to us." The student's relationship to history becomes that of the object to the verb, or that of the viewer to the screen, but never that of the actor to the stage.

Asking students in a suburban U.S. high school how they conceived of history, I got back the same answers that my own peers (and those of my parents, I suspect) would offer:

"History is everything that happened in the past and now is over."

"History is what is done by serious and important people."

Few people, it appears, will bother to dispute that this is how we feel—our children and their parents too—in the United States. It is no longer true, however, in all other nations. Visiting a junior high school in the Cuban countryside not long ago, I presented the same question I had asked so many times before: "What do you think of when you think of history?"

"History," said one student in the ninth grade, "is what we do in the morning about the things we thought about the night before."

Something is changing, and it is a very deep and sweeping change, when children, in whatever nation, dare to speak this way at last about the world in which they live.

In a grade school near Havana, in the fall of 1976, I stood and watched a class of third grade children taking small amounts of a black, powderlike substance from large wooden barrels in one corner of the room, pouring it carefully onto small square pieces of thin cloth or paper, then slowly stitching it together with needle and thread. It was a few minutes before I recognized what it was, precisely, they had done. The little labels which they stitched by string to every little bag at last revealed the purpose of their toil. They were making tea bags.

I asked—and learned—that they (along with their co-workers in the other third grades of the Cuban nation) were, in fact, producing all the tea bags that would be required by the population in the next twelve months.

A modest event: forty-five minutes out of the full day. The children did not work unduly hard; nor did they injure their backs or strain their arms. They simply took a small and seemingly enjoyable role in helping to provide one of the basic needs of their society.

Once we begin to view young people in this way—as potentially effective actors on the stage of history—suddenly the active participation of young people in a literacy campaign ceases to appear implausible. Already, in the public schools of the United States, students have begun to break out of the mold that first was cast for them four centuries ago.

In one secondary school I know in Boston, a number of pupils study "Early Childhood Development" in the mornings, then work with troubled youngsters in community day-care centers in the afternoons. In other high schools, students learn to tutor elementary-level pupils in basic math and reading skills. They deepen their own competence while helping those who are ten years their junior to make rapid progress through intensive one-to-one attention.

Still closer to the plan which is presented in the pages of this book: A team of college pupils and professors in Miami in the early 1970s developed a program to do literacy work on an intensive basis in the prisons, in the ghetto neighborhoods and in the residential treatment centers for disturbed or for disruptive youngsters. The program enabled students to receive course credit from their college for the work they did. (Three separate departments of the University of Miami were recruited as sponsors and participants.) In all, over the course of four years, more than one thousand students and sixty college professors joined the project. Instruction took place not on the college campus, but in the prisons, in the residential centers or else in community buildings in the target neighborhoods. The Florida project appears to have been a good, dynamic and successful program. The project director is convinced that the same idea and applications will work at other colleges, and in other sections, of the United States.

One enterprising and creative English teacher in the Midwest, meanwhile, has recently announced that he was going to "release" his pupils to engage in adult literacy projects and, moreover, that he would join those projects *with* his pupils in order to offer practical assistance and direction.

These efforts, programs, operations—small and scattered as they are—seem to suggest some interesting clues to major changes in the air. A time may be coming when schools no longer will feel the need to use their scarce resources to prescribe and purchase simulation games. Childhood, as we have seen, is a relatively new invention: all of four centuries old. As we struggle to outgrow this "new invention," perhaps we can also outgrow our own conception of the very purpose of the schools and colleges in which our children are immobilized and rendered powerless.

Young people need not remain, in the words of Ivan Illich, "a consumer definition for a commodity known as school." They can also be forces to transform their schools and, with them, their societies. Students can be conditioned to cringe and duck low as history flies over. Or they can become a force to make less the pain within this world: their own world, and the older one their parents must inhabit. The literacy campaign we have proposed is one important, ethical and realistic way that they can do this.

POSTSCRIPT: THE TEMPER OF THE TIMES

Even if young people can at length achieve the right to fill a useful and a liberating role in our society, the question must be asked: How do we know that they would want to? What evidence is there to support the view that students will wish to rally in response to such a call? Doesn't the evidence suggest the opposite?

There is, certainly, a great deal in the press these days to lead us to believe that the conscience of the student population has gone dead during the past ten years. There is also a good deal on radio and television to foster such a view; academic commentators tend to reinforce and bolster these opinions.

There is more, however, within the quiet words and earnest actions of the students and the teachers in the schools and in the universities of the nation to tell us that the ethical fervor of young people remains vigorous and strong. Students are not gathering in massive crowds today in front of television cameras but, quietly and persistently in almost every section of the land, they are still involved in many thousands of effective, decent and important actions. They work in storefront clinics for the poor, child advocacy centers, tenants' councils, public interest research groups, women's centers, prisoners' aid and education groups. They work in small projects. They work in big ones too. They struggle against the dangers of the radiation given off by nuclear reactors. They struggle on behalf of captive nations. They struggle against the use of funds for military goals. They struggle, in every way they can, for peace.

There are those who believe that very few young people would respond to an appeal based on such plain and simple motivation as the will to take a role in shaping history. My own experience leads me to disagree. The energy and idealism of the students that I meet are lucid and inspiring. Their will to enter, shape and alter history is steadfast and unbroken. For almost a decade, however, students have lacked a single and dramatic focus for their energies. The struggle which we are now proposing offers just that focus.

On several occasions during the time I spent in Cuba, I spoke with the man who had been leader of the "Great Campaign" of 1961. I asked him, in one of our interviews, whether he would place a price tag on the work that had been done during the course of the campaign. Raúl Ferrer is so much a symbol of poetic passion and of political exhiliration that a question of "numbers"—of statistical enumeration—seemed incongruous. I told him, though, that I had been asked to get the answer to this question by an editor in New York.

Dr. Ferrer tried to run down some of the costs in a few sentences. Soon, however, he came to a halt as he began to recognize the hopelessness of summing up all of the direct and indirect expenses and, then, the still greater hopelessness of calculating the real pay-off for his people in terms of technological progress, heightened productivity, as well as heightened national esteem.

He threw up his hands at last, looked at me in eloquent frustration, then put one hand across my arm. "We must disappoint your editor," he said, "but we will send that man an answer all the same. It is precisely this: If you must always count up everything in numbers, and must forever calculate the cost in dollars, you do not succeed, and never will succeed, in struggles of this kind. . . ." In the struggle against illiteracy, he said, there can be "no balance sheet for justice." The treasure of a nation is "the treasure of the people, not their cash. We do not deny the necessity of money; but, in these kinds of struggles, the real price is something that cannot be put in numbers."

In our nation, too, the real treasure—the only scarce resource—is the energy and ethics of the people. The virtue of the literacy campaign that we propose is that it will release that treasure not only in the students who leave school and university, but in the poor and the illiterate as well. Both those who teach and those who learn will have the opportunity to know, to "name"—and to transform—the world. Both will earn the power, thereby, to enter—and to alter—history. The poor will discover "the word," the young will discover "the world." Together, they will discover their own potency and leverage as the subjects of historic change.

The process of dialogue, upon which the entire campaign must depend, begins as a dialogue between the victims and (in part, at least) the rebel children of the victimizers. As the latter learn to share, more and more deeply, in the total consciousness of those with whom they work, and as the former gain the skills by which to take control of the direction of their learning, their dialogue begins to be the dialogue of equals.

Both learner and teacher undergo change. The change is irreversible and profound. The world will never be the same again—not for the one, not for the other. The silence is broken. The slave begins to learn how to be free.

EPILOGUE

IN various sections of this book, I have spoken of certain
motives that might prompt a number of different segments of the
population to recognize a common interest in the struggle against
adult illiteracy. There is one form of common interest which I did
not yet discuss. It is the matter of international esteem.

The United States spends a vast amount of money to win loyalty
or purchase friendship in the Third World nations. Too often, we
have been persuaded to invest our money in the least productive
and least ethical devices for achieving little pockets of hegemony.
Slipping funds covertly to those elements in Chile who were plotting to destroy the government of Salvador Allende, selling
weapons of war to people like General Somoza or to the government of South Korea—these are the unfortunate tactics that may
win us short-term victories, but only at enormous long-term cost in
loss of any possible allegiance from the poorest people and the most
progressive elements in these nations.

Our stated objective is to win "the hearts and minds" of the poor
people of the earth; but we never will win their hearts or minds
(nor, least of all, their love) with antiquated and dehumanizing tactics of this kind. We just may win some genuine esteem and some
unpurchased admiration if we can give an example to the world of
pedagogic progress on a sweeping and breathtaking scale: the sort

of thing that catches the imagination of all nations by surprise and something which will not be subject to those sudden shifts of power that have recently been common in the Third World.

An additional point, in terms of the real pay-off, concerns not so much the possibilities of winning international esteem as the realistic likelihood of winning the invaluable role of "ally and educator" to those nations which are now (or soon will be) attempting major literacy efforts of their own. It is worth noting, in this respect, that the Cuban government is very much alert to this consideration.

In recent years, chiefly since 1976, a number of African nations have solicited the advice of Cuban teachers in establishing effective literacy plans. A group of two thousand literacy teachers, working under the dramatic designation "Ernesto Che Guevara International Pedagogical Detachment," is teaching at present in Africa, often in collaboration with progressive teams from Western Europe.

The consequence for Cuba may well prove to be of far more lasting impact than any gains that might be won by military aid. Ironically, it is Cuba's military ventures, rather than her pedagogic efforts, which the U.S. government views with most alarm. The military impact is ephemeral and, in certain instances, counterproductive. The impact of a "a teaching batallion," on the other hand, especially of a group that is already well versed in precisely that endeavor which is most important—and most often a prerequisite—to any further socioeconomic progress in a newly liberated land, is obviously an impact that will last for years to come.

The United States cannot hope to offer other nations what we cannot yet provide for our own people. We will be able to share with others only a competence that we have first tested and found viable in our own nation: in rural Appalachia, in the hills of South Dakota, in the northern city slums.

This is the sort of payoff which is not at first apparent when a citizen asks what it will cost and what we hope to gain. It is, however, a most important payoff—above all, as we gradually awaken to the recognition of our isolation as an Anglo-Saxon, white and wealthy nation in a world of poor and nonwhite people who have little reason to respect or trust us.

An all-out literacy struggle on our own home soil, wholly apart from the esteem it stands to win us and the good it stands to *do* us, is also one of the few responsible starting points for any further efforts to be "teachers to the teachers" of the Third World. Until we demonstrate that we can come to terms with the catastrophe in our own urban ghettos and our rural slums, there does not seem much reason to expect that other nations will, or ought to, seek out our advice.

It is within our power to transform the situation; but the price will be a large one and the task will not be easy.

Appendix 1

LEADS, CONTACTS, ON-GOING PROGRAMS, NEWSLETTERS

Office of Senator George
  McGovern
United States Senate
4239 Dirksen Building
Washington, D.C. 20510

Adult Performance Level Project
University of Texas at Austin
Education Annex S-21
Austin, Texas 78712

Adult Basic Education
Regional Office Building #3
Room 5636
7th and D Streets, S.W.
Washington, D.C. 20202

Literacy Volunteers of America
700 East Water Street
Midtown Plaza, Room 623
Syracuse, New York 13210

Literacy Action, Inc.
201 Washington Street, S.W.
Atlanta, Georgia 30303

Laubach Literacy International,
  Inc.
1320 Jamesville Avenue
Box 131
Syracuse, New York 13210

National Institute of Education
Brown Building
19th and M Streets, N.W.
Washington, D.C. 20208

American Library Association
50 East Huron Street
Chicago, Illinois 60611
(Publishers of the Directory of
  Literacy and Adult Learning
  Programs)

National Commission on Libraries
  and Information Science
1717 K Street, N.W.
Washington, D.C. 20036

World Education
1414 Sixth Avenue
New York, New York 10019

Ms. Dorothy Tod
Producer and Distributor of the
  film *What if you couldn't read?*
20 Bailey Avenue
Montpelier, Vermont 05602

The Center for Cuban Studies
220 East 23rd Street
New York, New York 10010

National Center for Voluntary
  Action
1785 Massachusetts Avenue, N.W.
Washington, D.C. 20036

National Affiliation for Literacy
  Advance
101 Ostrom Street
Syracuse, New York 13210

4 A's Literacy Project
P.O. Box 81826
Lincoln, Nebraska 68501

Reading Reform Foundation
7054 East Indian School Road
Scottsdale, Arizona 85251

Reading is Fundamental (RIF)
475 L'Enfant Plaza, Suite 4800
Smithsonian Institute
Washington, D.C. 20560

Council for Basic Education
725 15th Street, N.W.
Washington, D.C. 20005

International Reading Association
Indiana University
Education Department, Room 227
Bloomington, Indiana 47401

Center for Understanding Media
69 Horatio Street
New York, New York 10014

International Visual Literacy
  Association
35 Olive Court
Iowa City, Iowa 52240

Unifon Alphabet Association
13 Plaza, Suite 13
Park Forest, Illinois 60466

THE NATIONAL LITERACY COALITION (Regional Breakdown)

Education Action Fund
Jonathan Kozol/Tisha Graham
P.O. Box 84
Boston, Massachusetts 02112

St. Charles Kids School
Dean Schneider
85 Custer Avenue
Newark, New Jersey 07112

National Literacy Coalition
  Coordinator
Marcy Fink
1704 Kilbourne Place, N.W.
Washington, D.C. 20010

The Alternative Schools Network
Jack Wuest
1105 West Lawrence Avenue,
  Room 211
Chicago, Illinois 60604

North Carolina Task Force on
  Community Based Education
Tim and Lana Brannan
P.O. Box 18134
Charlotte, North Carolina
  28212

RAP/LIFE
Anita Beaty
Waccamaw, E.O.C., Inc.
P.O. Box 1467
Conway, South Carolina 29526

Basic Choices, Inc.
1121 University Avenue
Madison, Wisconsin 53715

Education Exploration Center
Linda Hutchinson
P.O. Box 7339
Powderhorn Station
Minneapolis, Minnesota 55407

Education Project
Eleanor Burchill
2203 Princeton
Lawrence, Kansas 66044

University for Man
Jim Kallacky
1221 Thurston
Manhattan, Kansas 66502

National Literacy Coalition
  Coordinator
Martha Spoor
The Project for Alternate
  Learning
17½ So. Last Chance Gulch Mall
Helena, Montana 59601

Rio Grande Education Association
Ed Nagel
P.O. Box 2241
Santa Fe, New Mexico 87501

Pacific Region Alternative Schools
  Association
Fernando Gonzalez
1119 Geary Street
San Francisco, California 94109

Community Education
Michael James
275 19th Avenue
San Francisco, California 94121

National Literacy Coalition
  Coordinator
Yvonne Golden
742 37th Avenue
San Francisco, California 94121

NOTES

xiii The quotation from Jimmy Carter is taken from his inaugural speech as the governor of Georgia, delivered on January 12, 1971. See *Addresses of Jimmy Carter* (James Earl Carter), Frank Daniel, compiler. Distributed by the Department of Archives and History, Atlanta, Georgia, 1975.

1 Comparative figures supplied by the United Nations are available in *Statistical Yearbook* (New York and Paris: United Nations Educational, Scientific and Cultural Organization, 1977), pp. 46–50.

1 Oliver Patterson's study undertaken for the Office of Education is entitled "Functional Adult Illiteracy." See *Projections for Reading: Preschool Through Adulthood* (Washington, D.C.: U.S. Office of Education, 1978), pp. 71–81.

2 *Newsweek's* coverage of the problems and programs related to adult illiteracy appears in the October 6, 1978 issue. See pp. 106–112.

2 The Final Report of the Adult Performance Level Project, conducted by Norvell Northcutt, was published in August 1977, and is available through the Adult Performance Level Project. (See Appendix 1.) For further data on results listed here, see pp. 21–28 of the report.

2 The figure of fifty-seven million adult illiterates in the United States is derived from a U.S.O.E. study of the A.P.L. The figure is quoted in a study for the Ford Foundation entitled *Adult Illiteracy in the United States* by Carman St. John Hunter and David Harman, (New York: McGraw-Hill Book Company, 1979), pp. 27–28.

2 The figure of six billion dollars spent yearly in welfare costs and

loss of productivity is drawn from a speech delivered by Senator George McGovern on International Literacy Day, September 8, 1978. See the *Congressional Record*, Proceedings and Debates of the Ninety-fifth Congress, Second Session, Volume 124, Number 139, Washington, D.C.

3   The figure for upkeep of illiterate prisoners in U.S. jails is supplied by Laubach Literacy International. (See Appendix 1.) For additional figures and discussion of this issue, see note for p. 75.

3   For discussion of damage to U.S. Naval equipment, see "Illiteracy Among Recruits Threatens to Sink U.S. Navy," in *Palo Alto Times*, June 23, 1977.

3   Senator George McGovern is quoted from his speech of September 8, 1978.

3   For charges and statistics in regard to Title I, see Hearings before the Subcommittee on Elementary, Secondary, and Vocational Education of the Committee on Education and Labor, House of Representatives, Ninety-fifth Congress, H.R. 15, part 16, October 6, 18, 19 and 20, 1977, p. 8.

4   Title I's purpose is to provide supplementary basic skills instruction for individuals under the age of twenty-one in the United States who are reading or performing two grade levels below expected standards. There is a poverty requirement as well, although it is applied to the school district, rather than to the individual. A certain percentage of Title I funding is available for the use of individuals in various types of institutions (e.g., prisons) who are under the age of twenty-one and who do not have either a high school diploma or a G.E.D. certificate. This information was provided by Laura Mersky, Title I Director of the Massachusetts Department of Corrections.

4   The percentage of illiterate adults actually being reached through federal programs is drawn from Harman and Hunter. See pp. 103 and 115. Senator George McGovern is quoted from his speech of September 8, 1978.

5   For further descriptive data on groups one through four, as well as total figures for adult illiterates, see Harman and Hunter, pp. 112–17.

7   Figures on illegal aliens are provided by Harman and Hunter, pp. 24n–25n.

10   Information on Dorothy Tod's film *What if you couldn't read?* is available by writing to Ms. Tod, Producer and Distributor, 20 Bailey Avenue, Montpelier, Vermont 05602.

11 The material on "Tommy" is drawn from Carol Saline's article, "Abirt ca folner sett Lindexh: To one Philadelphian in six, this is the way everything reads," in *Philadelphia Magazine* (May 1979).

13 Raúl Ferrer is quoted here in conversation with the author. See *Children of the Revolution* (New York: Delacorte Press, 1978), p. 88.

15 For references to literacy rates in China, Israel, Cuba and Brazil, see Harman and Hunter, p. 108.

For the complete interview with Raúl Ferrer, see *Children of the Revolution,* pp. 82–95.

17 For UNESCO's comment on the Cuban literacy struggle, see Arthur Gillette's *Youth and Literacy* (New York and Paris: UNESCO, 1972), pp. 53–55.

17n Statistics and assertions discussed here are drawn from *Children of the Revolution,* p. 53.

42 Alfred North Whitehead is quoted from *The Aims of Education* (New York: The Free Press, 1929), pp. 1–2.

43 Harman and Hunter, p. 118.

45 Harman and Hunter, pp. 104–5.

52 Various grade level equivalents used in efforts to define adult literacy are further discussed in Oliver Patterson's study. See *Projections for Reading: Preschool Through Adulthood,* pp. 71–72. See also Harman and Hunter's study, pp. 16–17.

53 The UNESCO definitions of illiteracy for the years 1948, 1951 and 1962 are drawn from "Literacy as a Factor in Development" (Paris: UNESCO, 1965).

For further discussion of the objective behind the Adult Performance Level Project, see *Final Report: The Adult Performance Level Study,* pp. 2–5. For further descriptions of adult living requisites, see pp. 12–14.

60 Bertolt Brecht is quoted from "In Praise of Learning," included in a collection entitled *The Politics of Literacy,* edited by Martin Hoyles (London: Writers and Readers Publishing Cooperative, 1977), p. 78.

71 Paul Goodman is quoted from *Growing Up Absurd* (New York: Vintage Books, 1970), p. 72 and chapter entitled "An Apparently Closed Room."

73 Harman and Hunter, pp. 107–8.

74 The statement that the prison system represents the highest single locus of illiterate men and women is validated by Jonathan McKallip, Assistant Director of Field Services, Literacy Volunteers of America, Syracuse, New York.

75 According to Joseph Landolfi, Program Development Specialist

of the Research Division at the Massachusetts Department of Corrections, it costs an average of $15,000 yearly to house and feed one prison inmate (in Massachusetts). In an unpublished private paper for the Georgia Right to Read Program titled "The Social and Economic Impact of Illiteracy in Georgia," the Center for Educational Research at Georgia State University reports $21,410 as the per person yearly cost for incarceration in 1970. With inflation, this figure should rise close to $30,000 in 1980.

76   Alexander Burke's statement at the White House conference in September 1978 is quoted from *Publishers Weekly*, September 25, 1978, p. 47.

77   Harman and Hunter, pp. 107–8.

78   Harman and Hunter, p. 108.

84   Large numbers of "Reading Academies" have organized and found funding under the umbrella of Right to Read. Many of these academies come closer to the grass roots than any other literacy efforts we have seen. One outstanding example of a literacy program close to the poor people it serves is RAP/LIFE, directed by Anita Beaty in Conway, South Carolina. (See the National Literacy Coalition, listed in Appendix 2). There are also two nongovernmental groups which have taken an active role in literacy work. One is Laubach Literacy International, Inc. and the other is Literacy Volunteers of America. Both groups often contract with Right to Read or Adult Basic Education to carry out their literacy programs.

Of the two major federal programs mentioned in the text, one— Right to Read—comes to the end of its grant period and will no longer exist after June of 1980. Many projects, previously sustained by Right to Read, will continue to receive Federal support under Title II: a recent amendment (1978) to the Elementary and Secondary Education Act of 1965.

85   Senator McGovern is quoted from his speech of September 8, 1978.

87   Harman and Hunter have suggested something similar to our own proposal for the sponsorship of conferences and hearings by the poor themselves. In their study, they have compiled a list of "Specific Recommendations" which outlines what the authors wish to see done, by whom and how. Their Specific Recommendation #2 suggests that "a series of well-publicized regional conferences should be held to gather data and to create a climate for implementing the central proposal for new community-based approaches. The conferences would include a large group of 'clients,' representing the young unemployed, older persons, racial and ethnic minorities,

aliens, prisoners, and others from specific communities and sub-groups of the most educationally disadvantaged who are not in any existing programs. These persons would be the *speakers* at the conference. The *hearers* or *learners* would be persons professionally engaged in community services . . . as well as persons from the business community, legislators, representatives of government and private-sector funding agencies, and labor leaders." See Harman and Hunter, p. 106.

91   For a comprehensive history of modern childhood and its evolution, see *Centuries of Childhood* by Phillipe Ariès (New York: Vintage Books, 1962).

93   For quoted conversation between the author and students in a suburban U.S. high school, see *The Night Is Dark And I Am Far From Home* (Boston: Houghton Mifflin Company, 1975), p. 82.

94   Information on the literacy project conducted at the University of Miami during 1969 and 1973 is taken from correspondence between the project director, Norman Manasa, and the author.

95   Statement of Ivan Illich is from a lecture delivered in September, 1969, Centro International de Documentacion (CIDOC), Cuernavaca, Mexico.

97   Dr. Raúl Ferrer's words are quoted from *Children of the Revolution*, pp. 93–94.

100 For a report on the African presence of the "Ernesto Che Guevara International Pedagogical Detachment," see the Center for Cuban Studies publication, *Cuba Update*, Number 4, Summer 1979, p. 3.

BIBLIOGRAPHY

This is a selected bibliography. Many books and government publications on the subject of adult illiteracy are not mentioned; nor are all sources mentioned here directly quoted in this book.

Ariès, Phillipe. *Centuries of Childhood.* New York: Vintage Books, 1962.

Childers, Thomas, assisted by Post, Joyce A. *The Information Poor in America.* New Jersey: The Scarecrow Press, 1975.

Copperman, Paul. *The Literacy Hoax: The Decline of Reading, Writing and Learning in the Public Schools and What We Can Do About It.* New York: William Morrow and Company, Inc., 1978.

Final Report: The Adult Performance Level Study. Division of Extension of the University of Texas at Austin, 1977.

Gillette, Arthur. *Youth and Literacy.* New York and Paris: UNESCO, 1972.

Goodman, Paul. *Growing Up Absurd.* New York: Vintage Books, 1970.

Hoyles, Martin, ed. *The Politics of Literacy.* London: Writers and Readers Publishing Cooperative, 1977.

Hunter, Carman St. John, and Harman, David. *Adult Illiteracy in the United States.* New York: McGraw-Hill Book Company, 1979.

Kozol, Jonathan. *Children of the Revolution.* New York: Delacorte Press, 1978.

Laubach Literacy International. *Programs and Projects.* Syracuse, New York, 1978.

Literacy as a Factor in Development. Paris, UNESCO, Minedlit/3, 1965.

Literacy Volunteers of America, Inc. *Policies and Procedures Manual.* Syracuse, New York, 1979.

Mezirow, Jack; Darkenwald, Gordon G.; and Knox, Alan B. *Last Gam-*

ble On Education. Washington, D.C., Adult Education Association of the U.S.A., 1975.

Projections for Reading: Preschool Through Adulthood. Washington, D.C., U.S. Department of Health, Education, and Welfare, 1978.

Judy, Stephen. *The ABC's of Literacy.* New York: Oxford University Press, 1980.

Whitehead, Alfred North, *The Aims of Education.* New York: The Free Press, 1929.